HUMAN RESOURCES IN
SPORTS
A Managerial Approach

Bonnie Tiell, DSM

Professor of Management
School of Business
Tiffin University
Tiffin, Ohio

with

Kelley Walton, JD, SPHR

Instructor
Department of Sports Administration
Ohio University
Athens, Ohio

JONES & BARTLETT
LEARNING

W0006619

World Headquarters
Jones & Bartlett Learning
5 Wall Street
Burlington, MA 01803
978-443-5000
info@jblearning.com
www.jblearning.com

Jones & Bartlett Learning books and products are available through most bookstores and online booksellers. To contact Jones & Bartlett Learning directly, call 800-832-0034, fax 978-443-8000, or visit our website, www.jblearning.com.

10272-7

Production Credits

VP, Executive Publisher: David D. Cella
Publisher: Cathy L. Esperti
Acquisitions Editor: Sean Fabery
Editorial Assistant: Hannah Dziezanowski
Director of Vendor Management: Amy Rose
Vendor Manager: Juna Abrams
Director of Marketing: Andrea DeFronzo
VP, Manufacturing and Inventory Control:
    Therese Connell
Composition: S4Carlisle Publishing Services

Project Management: S4Carlisle Publishing Services
Cover Design: Timothy Dziewit
Director of Rights & Media: Joanna Gallant
Rights & Media Specialist: Robert Boder
Media Development Editor: Shannon Sheehan
Cover Image (Title Page, Part Opener, Chapter Opener):
    © Dusit/Shutterstock.
Printing and Binding: LSC Communications
Cover Printing: LSC Communications

To order this product, use ISBN: 9781284102659

Library of Congress Cataloging-in-Publication Data
Name: Tiell, Bonnie, author.
Title: Human resources in sports : a managerial approach / Bonnie Tiell.
Description: First edition. | Burlington, Massachusetts : Jones & Bartlett
    Learning, 2017. | Includes bibliographical references and index.
Identifiers: LCCN 2017011801 | ISBN 9781284102659 (pbk. : alk. paper)
Subjects: LCSH: Sports administration. | Personnel management.
Classification: LCC GV713 .T58 2017 | DDC 796.06/9--dc23 LC record available at https://lccn.loc.gov/2017011801

6048

Printed in the United States of America
21 20 19 18 17   10 9 8 7 6 5 4 3 2 1

DEDICATION

This textbook is dedicated to my brother, Dr. West Hamryka. No words can express the depth of my gratitude for your selfless and unconditional support that positively transformed the life of a young adult . . . maybe this dedication will scratch the surface.

BT

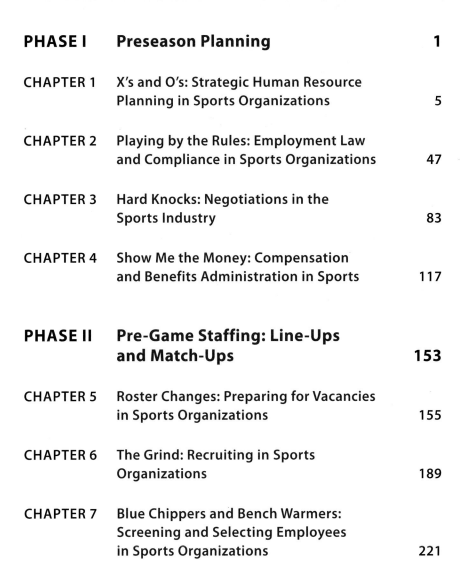

CONTENTS

My contributions to this text in an advisory capacity are based on more than a decade of experience in the sport industry. Seven of those years were spent working as the director of human resources for the Columbus Blue Jackets, a member club of the National Hockey League (NHL). It has been a phenomenal journey to lend my practitioner-based expertise to an accomplished scholar and former athletic administrator.

When I joined the Blue Jackets organization in 2000 as a law clerk, the team was beginning its first season as an expansion franchise. After passing the Ohio Bar Exam, I served as the Legal/Immigration Associate until 2003 when I made the move from the legal department to creating and overseeing the human resources department. My duties early on included overseeing immigration efforts and workers' compensation administration, in addition to assisting the general counsel, chief financial officer, and controller with sponsor contracts, lease agreements, insurance plans, 401(k) arrangements, and various legal issues. With more than 150 full-time and 300 part-time employees between the Blue Jackets and the arena management company, it was apparent the NHL team was in need of a centralized place to manage human resource–related functions. In 2003, the team president, general counsel, and executive staff agreed to establish a human resources department, and I was appointed as the director.

Over the next 7 years, the department hired a staff; developed, reviewed, and updated policies; and provided a centralized unit that supported the operations of both its leaders and employees. The newly established department offered direct guidance to administrators to assist with recruiting efforts, annual performance appraisals, and occasional disciplinary action. The department also engaged in activities supporting the Blue Jackets' general employees, such as benefits administration, retirement-planning assistance, and programming for career development. This textbook addresses many of the routine and non-routine responsibilities and tasks that I supervised or performed during my time as director of human resources for the NHL Blue Jackets.

I did not meet the author of this text until a number of years after I left the Blue Jackets organization. Her oldest daughter, who was enrolled in one of my courses at a small, private university in Columbus, Ohio, expressed that the two of us were very like-minded in our approach to teaching, working with students, and discussing the business side of sports. Before long, the three of us met at a coffee shop, and almost immediately, Dr. Tiell and I were commiserating about the fact that every textbook related to sports and human resources was either outdated or from a publisher outside the United States. In less than a half hour, we decided we could "build a better mousetrap" and began to outline the chapters of a text that could be an industry market leader for sports educators in higher education. The rest of the story, as they say, is history! Over the 4½ years since that initial meeting, Dr. Tiell has devoted an enormous amount of time and energy to research and writing this textbook, while my role morphed into primarily being a supportive colleague and sounding board. My main writing contribution can be found in the chapters related to employment law in sports and compensation and benefits.

Dr. Tiell masterfully presents a logical and practical overview of human resource processes, responsibilities, and trends applied to a diverse sports industry and a diverse workforce. The scope of this text is beneficial both for workers in a large, professional sports franchise employing an autonomous, fully functioning human resource department, such as the Columbus Blue Jackets, and for a manager of a small public golf course or fitness facility tasked with hiring workers and administering weekly paychecks. Dr. Tiell writes a well-documented, managerial-focused, and applied textbook that should engage future and current practitioners in all sectors of sports while facilitating a greater appreciation of human resources as the most valuable asset of an organization.

It is no secret that many sports organizations today are similar to the early days of the Columbus Blue Jackets in that they can operate without a separate human resource department or, like many organizations, with a very small human resources department. The focus of *Human Resources in Sports: A Managerial Approach* is thus to provide general human resource–related foundational material for managers and supervisors in organizations operating without any dedicated human resource personnel. Although some individuals who use this text might someday have a career focus in human resources, most will not. Instead, they will go on to work in sports organizations in sales, marketing, or operations and will use foundational human resource knowledge as a supervisor and not as a human resource professional.

The information in *Human Resources in Sports: A Managerial Approach* is well-organized and well-documented, but—most importantly—it accurately reflects the nuances of human resource activities apparent in a majority of sports organizations operating in the United States. Students and practitioners will enjoy the examples of human resource activities in action while appreciating the availability of templates and sample documents used in sports organizations such as the Columbus Blue Jackets. Finally, readers will appreciate the information in each chapter's Global Spotlight, which portrays the human resource functions and roles of leaders and personnel working in sports organizations around the world.

I am proud and privileged to lend my expertise to the lead author, a well-respected colleague who shares a passion for embracing best practices for human resources in all sports businesses. Dr. Tiell has written an extraordinary textbook that truly addresses a managerial approach to human resources in the sports industry. The journey to this point has forged an incredible friendship and appreciation for perseverance, value-added relationships, and like-mindedness in the vocation of teaching.

Kelly Walton

Human Resources in Sports: A Managerial Approach uses a practitioner approach to address human resource practices and trends in an industry that includes a dissimilar workforce composed of full-time, part-time, seasonal, and volunteer labor. This text presents practical applications to assist industry professionals and future practitioners to navigate through the field of sports supervision while remaining cognizant of the antecedents and consequences of policies and procedures guiding business decisions and employment practices.

Section I of the text is designed to emphasize foundational knowledge for human resource practices, setting the stage for presenting a practitioner approach to staffing (Section II), supervision (Section III), and addressing selected workplace issues as well as industry trends (Section IV). No previous text has included the depth of practical applications of human resource tools and activities originating from real professionals with real experience in the field. The infusion of information from sports organizations around the world adds a global perspective while building on the universal theme of a managerial approach to human resource practices.

The field of human resources is very strategic. The diverse nature of the sports industry doesn't allow for standard processes and procedures in human resource functions. This text is written from the perspective of knowing that most sports organizations do not have the luxury of a fully functioning human resource department. The intent is to equip managers and supervisors in sports organizations with practical tools when having to assume roles involving human resource activities, such as hiring personnel, designing a compensation system, or negotiating a third-party vendor contract for payroll services. It addresses foundational knowledge for staffing and supervision while examining current trends and issues impacting human resources in sports organizations and preparation activities for practitioners.

Organized in 14 chapters spanning four sections, the textbook takes the reader on a journey of human resource preparatory activities, operational functions, and issues and trends that apply specifically to the sports industry in the United States and around the world. Audiences will appreciate the best practices and real-life sports applications that span the pages of each chapter, all of which culminate with a Case Study and a Global Spotlight. In addition to the samples of documents and forms used for human resource activities in sports organizations, the following features are included in every chapter:

- The **Industry Voice** feature opens each chapter with a quote from a professional working in the field.
- **Learning Outcomes** help readers guide and focus their study.
- **Key Terms** are listed at the beginning of the chapter and are presented in boldface type the first time they are used. Definitions can be found in the end-of-text Glossary.
- The **Lead-Off** section at the beginning of each chapter offers a preview of the material that will be presented.
- **Action Shot** boxed features provide applied scenarios and information.
- The **Global Spotlight** boxed feature highlights human resource issues in sports organizations around the world.
- The **Recap** section at the end of each chapter summarizes its contents.
- **Discussion Questions** encourage readers to debate topics relevant to the chapter with their peers.
- **Applied Activities** suggest exercises that allow readers to apply what has been learned in the chapter.
- The **Case Study** at the end of each chapter encourages readers to immerse themselves in a true-to-life scenario highlighting concepts presented in the text.

In addition to serving as a resource for practitioners in the field who engage in human resource activities, this book is written for upper-level undergraduate and graduate students pursuing a degree in sports and recreation management, sports administration, coaching, physical education, sports business, recreation and leisure, and other, similar areas. The presented information aligns with several domains of recommended sports management curriculum, including management principles, leadership, governance, sports ethics, and legal aspects.

The advantage of working with Kelley Walton, J.D., a former human resource practitioner in the NHL, is that it lends credibility to the applied nature of this textbook. It has been an incredible experience to author a textbook with a scholar, advisor, legal counsel, and friend who shares a passion for teaching and impacting lives of future sport management professionals. The primary advice for any and every one preparing to or already working in the industry is to make "productivity" a habit and simply strive to be productive—every day.

Bonnie Tiell

Dr. Bonnie Tiell, Professor of Management at Tiffin University and a national faculty member of the U.S. Sports Academy, has been recognized for her contributions to intercollegiate athletics administration and global sports. She coordinates the Olympic Academic Experience (2004 Athens, 2008 Beijing, 2012 London, 2016 Rio, and 2020 Tokyo) and works with members of the World Olympians Association to supervise educational programs and a humanitarian project in conjunction with the Olympic Games. She has presented research, taught, or collaborated on sports projects on five continents and has authored dozens of manuscripts. She is a co-founder of the Women's Leadership Symposium (WLS), an educational program sponsored by the National Collegiate Athletic Association (NCAA) and Women Leaders in College Sports to attract, retain, and advance females in intercollegiate athletics.

At Tiffin University, Tiell has served as dean of graduate education, NCAA faculty athletic representative, MBA chairperson, senior woman administrator, assistant athletic director, and head coach for volleyball, softball (national qualifier 1993), and tennis (national qualifier 2003). She earned a Bachelor of Education from Troy University, a Masters in Sport Administration from the University of North Carolina–Chapel Hill, and a Doctorate in Sport Management and Human Resources from the U.S. Sports Academy, where she was recognized as the 2014 Alumnus of Year. Recognized twice for the Region 4 Excellence in Teaching Award through the Accreditation Council for Business Schools and Programs (2008 and 2016), Tiell is also a member of the Tiffin University Athletic Hall of Fame and recipient of the 2013 NCAA II Great Lakes Intercollegiate Athletics Conference (GLIAC) Donahue Service Award. In 2016, she was named Woman of the Year in Sports on behalf of the Cleveland Chapter of Women in Sports and Events (WISE). She has taught for the Tiffin University executive MBA program in Bucharest, Romania, and on behalf of the U.S. Sports Academy, she was the lead faculty for the 2017 International Sport Management Certification Program in Bangkok, Thailand.

Tiell and her husband (Greg) reside in Tiffin, Ohio, where she operates Tiell Total Sports, LLC, and contributes a monthly sports column for *The Advertiser-Tribune* newspaper. Their two daughters, Kim and Katie, currently reside in Atlanta, Georgia, and Boca Raton, Florida.

Kelley Walton, JD, SPHR, is a part-time instructor in the Department of Sports Administration at Ohio University. She is also an attorney and consultant specializing in career counseling and human resources in the sports industry. Walton also teaches as an adjunct instructor/lecturer at the Fisher College of Business at The Ohio State University, Capital University, and Ohio Dominican University. Prior to working in academics, she was the director of human resources for the Columbus Blue Jackets (NHL). She has a bachelor's degree from Eastern Michigan University and a Juris Doctor from Capital University Law School. She is certified as a Senior Professional in Human Resources. Primarily serving in an advisory role, Walton is considered a contributing author to *Human Resources in Sports: A Managerial Approach.*

To my exceptional daughters and supportive husband: First, thank you to my oldest daughter, Kimberly Elise, for connecting me to one of her college professors and being part of the first conversation that led to this textbook. Thank you to my youngest daughter, Katie Michelle, whose determination and spunk remind me that every day is an opportunity to shine like the sun. Thank you to my husband, Greg, for being my ground force and home base, no matter where my professional aspirations take me across the United States or around the world.

To Kelley Walton, JD: Your credibility and connections in the industry and belief in the value of this project cannot be overstated.

To the sports industry experts contributing to the contents of this text: Thank you to everyone who was interviewed and featured in an Industry Voice, Action Shot, Global Spotlight, or Case Study feature. Thank you also to the sports experts not mentioned in this text who were part of a focus group or an individual interview, namely Janet Kuieter, Kyle Chones, Laurie Massa, Miechelle Willis, Rhonda Curry, Mark Galuska, Ryan Leitenberger, and Amitoj Garg. Finally, I wish to acknowledge my professional colleagues and friends throughout the sports industry who work hard every day to make the industry great for others.

To the production and editing team: Thank you to everyone who played a role in editing and producing this textbook, including the staff at Jones & Bartlett Learning and S4Carlisle Production Services. Thank you to my personal team of editorial assistants: Kelley Walton, JD; Dr. John Millar; Matt Procopio; and Matthew Baker.

To my Tiffin University family and personal friends: My list of green and gold allies runs deep, and I am blessed to work at a supportive, entre-preneurial institution. I am especially grateful to my jogging colleagues, walking pal, golf partner, tennis adversary, and all who listened, learned, and appreciated the process. Thank you to anyone not mentioned who supported my efforts or shaped the contents of this text.

May all who read this textbook be challenged to make productivity a daily habit!

BE PRODUCTIVE! — Every Day!

Corinne Farneti, PhD
Assistant Professor
Mount St. Mary's University
Emmitsburg, MD

Michael A. Odio, PhD
Assistant Professor
University of Cincinnati
Cincinnati, OH

Sungick Min, PhD
Assistant Professor
State University of New York at Fredonia
Fredonia, NY

Anthony F. Patterson, PhD
Assistant Professor
North Carolina Central University
Durham, NC

Preseason Planning

Preface

The Key to Success Is Planning, and the Key to Planning Is Anticipation

Before embarking on Phase I exploring the foundational components of human resource activities in organizations, managers, supervisors, and future practitioners should understand the general size and scope of the sports industry to stay abreast of factors that may affect labor conditions and employment practices.

An industry analytics report estimated the size of the U.S. sports industry to be $498 billion and the global sports industry to be $1.5 trillion (Plunkett Research, 2015). The sports marketplace in the United States alone is predicted to reach $76.67 billion by 2020, according to an economic forecast that considers gate receipts, media rights, sports sponsorship, and merchandising (PricewaterhouseCoopers, 2016). The U.S. marketplace represents only a portion of the much larger and diverse sports industry landscape that is defined and segmented by multiple classification systems (see **Table 1**). Contributions to the economic impact, for example, include the revenue derived from the valuation of professional franchises, construction of sports facilities, recreation and leisure services, amateur sports (intercollegiate, scholastic, general public), national governing bodies (NGBs), and sports retail business.

1

TABLE 1: Segments of the Sports Industry

Milano and Chelladurai (2011)	Parks, Zanger, and Quarterman (1998)	Meek (1997)	Pitts, Fielding, Miller (1994)
1. Sport consumption (Entertainment and Recreation; Products and Service; Advertising)	1. Intercollegiate sport	1. Sporting goods, footwear, and apparel	1. Sport performance
2. Sport-related government expenditures	2. Professional sport	2. Sponsorship, endorsements, radio, TV, newspapers	2. Sport production
3. Sport imports and exports (equipment)	3. Participant sport	3. Trading cards, video games, books tapes, magazines	3. Sport promotion
4. Sport investments	4. Campus recreation	4. Construction	
	5. Sport communication	5. Participant sports	
	6. Sport marketing	6. Sports medicine	
	7. Sport event and facility management	7. Admissions	
	8. Sports medicine and health promotion	8. Concessions and souvenirs	
	9. Sport tourism	9. Betting	
	10. Sport management and marketing agencies		
	11. International sport		
	12. Sport management education		

The material in Phase I addressing strategic human resource planning, employment law, compensation/benefits administration, and negotiations provides the foundation for managers and supervisors in sports organizations to advertise for vacancies, select and screen candidates, evaluate performance, design orientation and training programs, discipline employees, and renew a coaching contract. This information is relevant to understanding the human resource implications for mega-retail giants such as Under Armour and Nike as they grow their workforces. Under Armour, for example, announced a $5.5 billion project to build a 50-acre waterfront campus in 2017 expected to assist the company in expanding its workforce fivefold to 10,000 people (Sherman, 2016). Nike's workforce of 62,600 reported in 2015 represents a 60% increase in 5 years (Manning, 2016).

The magnitude of Nike's and Under Armour's workforce expansion exemplifies the need for effective planning and preparation, which is the basis for the first phase of a textbook devoted to a managerial approach to human resources in sports. After all, how could Under Armour and Nike grow their workforces in a relatively short period without professionals who have amassed the foundational knowledge and competencies to effectively plan for vacancies and follow through with hiring, training, compensating, and evaluating employees?

Phase I begins with Chapter 1 addressing strategic human resource planning for establishing goals and action-oriented activities that directly align with the mission of the organization. Strategic human resource planning guides decision making and budget activities in areas such as recruitment, training, retention, performance management, and employee development. Whether involved in launching a business from the ground floor or in connection with one that is growing or downsizing, strategic human resource planning is beneficial for defining organizational capacity and personnel needs.

Chapter 2 addresses employment law. It is imperative that managers and supervisors involved in human resource activities are knowledgeable of the basic federal and state laws governing employment relationships and protecting the rights of employees. In addition to a general knowledge of laws, statutes, and regulations, it is important to have familiarity with the governing agencies overseeing certain employment areas and the entities most commonly associated with labor relations in the sports industry. An overview of employment law presents the opportunity to address fairly unique areas in sports, such as immigration practices and the unionization attempt of intercollegiate football players at Northwestern University. Although these legal issues may have little impact on the decisions and activities of managers and supervisors in recreational sports organizations, the information fits within the scope of employment and labor law while adding to the breadth of knowledge applied to human resource practices in the industry.

Chapter 3 addresses negotiation skills important to human resource functions in sports organizations. Managers and supervisors must have a basic understanding of the negotiation process for employment agreements and third-party vendor contracts, which are common in many sectors of the sports field. The information also addresses negotiations tied to the collective bargaining process in professional sports, components of standard employment agreements, and the role of mediation and arbitration for dispute resolution.

Chapter 4 addresses compensation and benefits administration in sports organizations. The information includes a comprehensive overview of wages and benefits to effectively design compensation packages and develop processes for administering benefits and payroll. Sports organization supervisors and managers with staffing responsibilities often have some degree of involvement in determining the rate of pay for new hires, the annual wage increases for current employees, and the structure for allocating legal and voluntary benefits, such as bonuses, incentive pay, or vacation time. The smaller the organization (e.g., a private fitness facility), the greater the discretion and authority managers typically have in determining wage and benefit packages and the processes for administering these areas. In larger organizations, such as a giant global retail sports manufacturing firm, managers responsible for staffing still have some, albeit a smaller degree, of input into determining wages and benefits for employees.

The foundational components of human resources addressed in Phase I affirm the logical insight that the key to success is planning, and the key to planning is anticipation. In reviewing the four areas important in appropriately preparing for executing the human resource functions of staffing and supervision in sports organizations, it is evident that the planning stage is essential.

REFERENCES

Manning, J. (2016, May 2). Booming sports companies look to fill hundreds of jobs. *The Oregonian*. Retrieved from http://www.oregonlive.com/business/index.ssf/2016/05/booming_sports_companies_look.html

Plunkett Research. (2015). *Sports industry statistics and market size overview.* Retrieved from https://www.plunkettresearch.com/statistics/sports-industry/

PricewaterhouseCoopers. (2016). *PwC sports outlook: At the game and beyond—outlook for the sports market in North America through 2020.* Retrieved from http://www.pwc.com/us/en/industry/entertainment-media/publications/sports-outlook-north-america.html

Sherman, S. (2016, August 28). Under Armour's value to city colors TIF talks. *Baltimore Sun*, A-20.

CHAPTER 1

X'S and O'S

STRATEGIC HUMAN RESOURCE
PLANNING IN SPORTS ORGANIZATIONS

Strategic human resource planning is important in my job to ensure organizational, financial, and operational efficiency. It is critical to outline your plan to figure out the overall roles and positions required to staff appropriately, then to budget for these positions in coordination with your overall cash-flow plan.

I've always said, 'You can teach skills, but you can't teach passion.' This quote has been the foundation of my hiring process for some time. Needless to say, candidates must have the right credentials; however, the real key to finding the right people can be summed up in these three questions:

1. *Do they possess passion and drive?*
2. *Do they fit within your culture?*
3. *Do they have the skill set to succeed in this area?*

Being able to hire the right personnel is one of the outcomes of preplanning. Strategic human resource plans help to ensure staffing and labor needs will be met, which is critical for events with massive, global implications. To run a successful world championship event, a lot of planning in the area of human resources must be done ahead of time.

Meredith Scerba
Director, 2017 World Rowing Championships

LEARNING OUTCOMES

1. Identify the steps in the strategic planning process.
2. Distinguish between strategic organizational planning and strategic human resource planning.
3. Identify the applicability of internal and external assessment to analyze human resources in sports organizations.
4. Describe techniques for setting goals and objectives and for connecting key performance indicators in sports organizations.
5. Describe how strategic implementation charts can be used to drive performance measures in sports organizations.
6. Identify the role of evaluation in human resource planning for sports organizations.

KEY TERMS

Affinity chart	Human resource generalist	Nominal group technique
Assessment	Human resource specialist	PEST analysis
Balanced scorecard	Key performance indicators (KPIs)	SMART goal-setting
Benchmarking	Market analysis	Strategic plan
Brainstorming	Mission statement	Strategies
Dashboard	Monitoring	Strategy map
Delphi technique		SWOT analysis

Lead-Off

Most business professionals will concur that the most valuable asset of any company is its employees, which certainly resonates in the sports industry. A certified aerobics instructor with high energy will have a positive impact on member retention just as much as an innovative, entrepreneurial, business-minded health club manager or the director of a world championship event will likely have a positive impact on profitability. To achieve organizational success, it is imperative that managers in sports clubs, businesses, and organizations take a strategic approach to selecting, training, and managing their employees, regardless of whether they have the luxury of a separate and fully functioning human resource department.

A strategic approach to human resources and personnel management considers the mix, number, and performance of employees in relation to achieving organizational goals. It also considers how the functional areas of human resources are structured and managed to maximize organizational efficiency and effectiveness.

As a sports business grows with new members, new profits, an expanded facility, or greater responsibilities, it may become necessary to hire additional staff. On the contrary, as strategies change or business declines, it may become necessary to reduce the size of the workforce. It is necessary for sports organizations to develop a basic human resource plan for how to functionally operate, and it is equally important to use the planning process in all facets of human re-

The Sporting News magazine laid off 12 writers and editors in 2012.

source activities to determine the right number and right mix of employees. The ultimate goal is to find the most efficient and effective means to achieve strategic objectives.

Consider the processes involved in the decision to lay off 12 writers and editors for *Sporting News* when the news company dropped its print magazine to provide strictly digital content after 126 consecutive years of publication. Exactly how the chief executive officer (CEO) and editor in chief arrived at the specific number and mix of reductions involved a careful analysis of labor-cost factors and an assessment of the resources needed to effectively and efficiently carry out the evolving mission as the world's leading digital sports media news source (Beaujon, 2012).

Linking human resource decisions to strategic thinking is an integral component of managing sports organizations. Strategic thinking allows for sports managers to implement decisions and processes that align with the basic business goals of maximizing the organization's efficiency and effectiveness. Human resource planning, for example, can assist managers to anticipate the impact improved technology may have on jobs, employees, and budgets or to determine the level of recruitment and training needed to derive the maximum benefits.

This chapter describes the relationship between human resource planning and organizational planning. The chapter additionally identifies the stages of the strategic planning process and provides information on common tools and practices used in the sports industry for addressing human resource planning. Initially, however, this chapter provides foundational information relating to occupations and primary roles in the field of human resources.

The Field of Human Resources

The field of human resources is one that crosses the spectrum of all businesses and industries. The functions related to human resources generally include recruiting, training and development, compensation administration, benefits administration, employee relations, workers' compensation administration, recordkeeping, budgeting, compliance, and strategic planning (see **Exhibit 1-1**). Depending on the size and nature of the organization, some of these functions may be assumed by a team of personnel, or they may be assigned to one specific individual.

Activities in human resources may involve placing advertisements with an online search engine company, tracking applications, and/or interviewing candidates. Individuals responsible for human resources may provide training to staff, or they may coordinate training efforts for certain departments. The varied responsibilities in the field encompass payroll processing, salary changes, wage ranges for employees, and administration of medical and dental plans. Responsibilities also include disciplining behavior violations, planning the annual company picnic, soliciting bids for health providers, and answering questions about benefit coverage and deductibles.

It is apparent in many sectors of the sports industry that a separate human resource department doesn't exist; therefore, managers and executives for minor league sport teams, recreation facilities, golf courses, and municipal recreation or aquatic departments perform the functions necessary to effectively staff, supervise, and administer payroll and benefits for the organization. The field of human resources is very broad, and the diverse nature of the different sectors of the sports industry is one where all types of structures exist to carry out human resource functions and roles.

Regardless of whether organizations support a stand-alone department, a strategic approach to human resources creates a strategic partner for management in aligning organizational priorities that affect employee needs and interests. As a strategic business partner, human resource professionals or individuals tasked with the roles of staffing and supervision are viewed as internal consultants who help managers build professional relationships with employees and help develop coaching, leadership, and delegation skills. When human resource roles and responsibilities are assumed by management, there is typically a natural alignment with organizational priorities. Understanding the primary occupations and roles in human resource management assists organizations in appreciating the all-encompassing nature of the field that is vitally important to operational effectiveness.

EXHIBIT 1-1: HUMAN RESOURCE DEPARTMENT FUNCTIONS

Employment and Recruiting

- Recruiting
- Background checks
- New employee orientation
- Employment verification
- Internship program
- Termination
- Turnover analysis

Training and Development

- Orientation of new employees
- Employee evaluations
- Tuition assistance
- Training
- Career development

Compensation

- Wage/salary administration
- Job descriptions
- Payroll administration
- Compensation structure management
- Reference inquiries

Benefits

- Vacation/sick-leave policies and administration
- Insurance benefits administration
  - Medical/dental/vision
  - Long-term disability
  - Short-term disability
  - Life
  - Supplemental life
  - Consolidated Omnibus Budget Reconciliation Act (COBRA)
- Unemployment compensation

(continues)

EXHIBIT 1-1: HUMAN RESOURCE DEPARTMENT FUNCTIONS (*CONTINUED*)

- Health Center memberships
- Pension/retirement plan administration
- 401(k) enrollment
- 401(k) funding
- Withdrawals
- Loans

Employee Relations

- Recreation/social programs
- Relocation
- Disciplinary procedures/corrective action
- Complaint procedures
- Exit interviews
- Award/recognition programs
- Policy administration

Personnel Records

- Personnel recordkeeping
- Promotion/transfer/separation processing
- Medical records

Workers' Compensation Administration

Strategic Planning

- Human resource forecasting/planning
- Organization development

Departmental Budget

Compliance/Reports

- Federal Labor Standards Act (FLSA)
- Family Medical Leave Act (FMLA)
- Equal Employment Opportunity Commission (EEOC)
- Occupational Safety and Health and Administration (OSHA)
- Health Insurance Portability and Accountability Act (HIPAA)
- Minimum wage

Immigration

HUMAN RESOURCE OCCUPATIONS

The Bureau of National Affairs (2015, p. iv) indicates that it is common for organizations to have at least one human resource professional for every 80–100 employees. From 2013 to 2015, however, budget constraints caused a slight decline from 1.3 to 1.1 human resource professionals per 100 full-time employees.

Determining the level of optimal human resources support goes well beyond the number of employees. If an organization has a high level of turnover that requires a high level of support along with recruiting, more human resource staff members are needed to support those recruiting functions. If the organization has relatively stable employees, resulting in little need for recruiting support, then there is less need for human resources support in the area of recruiting and likely less need for human resources support in general.

Individuals employed in human resource occupations are typically titled generalists, specialists, or administrative support assistants. An organization such as the Columbus Blue Jackets with a fully functioning separate human resource department may employ all three positions, whereas other sports businesses are fortunate if one individual assumes responsibilities for human resources.

Figure 1-1 depicts a portion of an organizational chart that focuses on the human resource department. The chart illustrates an organization with a vice president who reports directly to the president and three employees who report directly to the vice president of human resources. The vice president and human resource manager are considered generalists, whereas the payroll manager and benefits manager are considered specialists.

A **human resource generalist** has responsibilities and knowledge in more than one area of human resources. Generalists typically have a broad knowledge of human resource activities and provide work in a variety of functional areas. Generalists may be seasoned executives assuming a title such as vice president of human resources, or they may occupy a mid- to entry-level position, such as human resource manager. The organization with only one individual responsible for human resource activities will likely employ a generalist.

A **human resource specialist** is an individual who has an in-depth knowledge or degree of expertise in one specific area of human resources, such as compensation, benefits, or safety. These positions, apparent in larger sports organizations such as retail chains and professional leagues, are

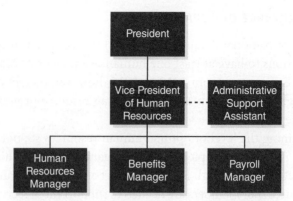

Figure 1-1 Sample organizational chart for a Human Resource department

very specific to one area of human resources, such as a benefits manager or payroll specialist. These individuals likely have some familiarity with other areas of human resources, but they typically do not possess the broad knowledge of a generalist because their focus is on a specific functional competency.

The third type of occupational position held by human resources professionals is that of an administrative and support role. Individuals in these heavily task-oriented positions are often involved with coordinating human resources processes and procedures, such as recording time-card or vacation hours. Examples of titles for individuals in an administrative support position include Human resource assistant, employee benefit clerk, and payroll clerk.

HUMAN RESOURCE ROLES AND FUNCTIONS

The three general roles of human resource personnel or individuals who perform human resource activities are advisory, service, and control. In general, human resources should be considered a horizontal solution for supporting management while operating the administrative functions to keep the organization compliant with employment laws and associated regulations.

Advisory

In an advisory role to management and leadership, human resource personnel, or individuals tasked with these functions, act as a strategic business partner. They gather information, analyze problems, and offer solutions. They provide ideas on strategies for staffing or redesigning a performance management system. They provide guidance on job descriptions or on processes to handle employee complaints. They provide guidance and leadership when an organization is dealing with change, such as the 2016 merger of two giant sports conglomerates International Management Group (IMG) and William Morris Endeavor (WME) or the 2012 acquisition of Adams Golf by TaylorMade. When morale needs a boost, they work with senior leadership to create incentives and/or experiences to increase employee satisfaction. When the company is feeling a pinch financially, the human resource arm provides guidance on cost savings if changing benefit service providers.

TaylorMade Golf is the official sponsor of Dustin Johnson, ranked number 1 in the PGA in 2017. Additional human resource services were necessary when TaylorMade acquired Adams Golf in 2011.

Service

The service role in human resources is provided when activities and functions support the leadership team and/or the employees. Posting a job on the National Collegiate Athletic Association (NCAA) Marketplace (online search engine) and reviewing job applications are examples of service roles, as are providing orientation for new employees and communicating changes in healthcare benefits.

Control

The control role in human resources is exemplified by establishing policies and rules for the organization, monitoring compliance with these policies and rules, and monitoring compliance with employment laws, such as the Family Medical Leave Act (FMLA), the Fair Labor Standards Act (FLSA), and the Consolidated Omnibus Budget Reconciliation Act (COBRA). A YMCA manager who meets with an employee about FMLA questions and ensures that the proper COBRA paperwork is sent to a terminated employee demonstrate how the role of control is carried out in human resources. Another example of demonstrating the control function is revising summer vacation policies for university athletic coaches.

Linking Human Resource Planning to Organizational Planning

Many of the functions in human resources require effective planning. Individuals tasked with responsibilities and roles in human resources add tremendous value to both strategic and operational planning for an organization. A **strategic plan** is a document spanning several years that outlines an organization's strategies and directions in addition to the means to achieve specific goals. The plan addresses the relatively long-term needs of a business in a multitude of areas, whereas a strategic human resource plan specifically addresses the relatively long-term needs of a business in the area of personnel. A strategic human resource plan for a collegiate athletic office, for example, may address its organizational structure, workplace policies, leadership, additional personnel needs if adding a new sport, legal compliance, or the return on investment for instituting a wellness program. Linking the two (strategic human resource plans and strategic plans) provides the foundation for the alignment of personnel and policies to effectively carry out the goals and priorities of the business or association.

Human resource planning may be embedded in a strategic organizational plan, or it may be a distinct, stand-alone plan. Rarely will a strategic organizational plan not have a section devoted specifically to addressing personnel factors that can enhance the mission, goals, and values of the entire organization.

The NCAA requires member colleges and universities to access the strategic plan for their respective division (I, II, or III) prior to completing an institutional self-study guide (ISSG). Sections of the ISSG require information that forms the foundational components of a strategic plan, including the athletic department's mission statement and an analysis of the organizational structure and personnel. Many universities have required their athletic departments to create a strategic plan. For example, the strategic plan for the Purdue University Athletic Department, titled "Plan 2020," includes goals and the expectation that Purdue will "employ a diverse and qualified group of coaches, administrators and support staff in the athletics department and create an environment that provides opportunities and training for all staff equally" (Purdue University, 2014, p. 10). The plan also outlines a common set of values addressing "a commitment to inclusiveness—and the courage to lead" (Purdue University, 2014, p. 13).

Although the strategic organizational plan for most university and college athletics departments (e.g., the University of Carolina, Purdue University, and Ohio University) will incorporate a section on human resource activities, the University of Tennessee has a complete and separate strategic human resource planning document for the institution specifically focusing on personnel issues. The strategic resource plan forms the basis for implementing actions to achieve goals, strategies, and accountability measures in relation to recruitment, training, retention, performance management, and employee development. The University of Tennessee's plan includes priorities, implementation strategies, and a monitoring system for the categories of compensation, human resource technology and metrics, performance management, professional development, recruitment, workforce strategic planning, and work culture enhancement (University of Tennessee, 2015).

Strategic Planning Process

Strategic planning involves a long-term commitment in resources and requires major decisions. It is ideal for a strategic plan to extend for a period of several years (3–5) and to include a fairly large number of employees from different areas of the business in the process. A strong planning process provides a sense of ownership at all levels of an organization, allows for scrutiny of ideas, and provides a roadmap to keep employees focused on objectives. The process increases communication flow within the organization, and the end result establishes milestones for meeting long-term goals.

The general purpose of a human resource strategic plan is to identify the extent to which programs and policies are aligned with the objectives of the organization and to provide direction for decisions to initiate, retain, decrease, or outsource human resource activities.

The basic steps in the strategic planning process for human resources are to (1) develop a mission statement, (2) conduct an analysis, (3) establish goals and objectives, (4) formulate a strategy, (5) implement that strategy, and (6) evaluate the process and results (see **Figure 1-2**).

STEP 1: MISSION STATEMENT

The first step in the strategic planning process is to develop or review the organization's **mission statement**. A mission statement should be one to

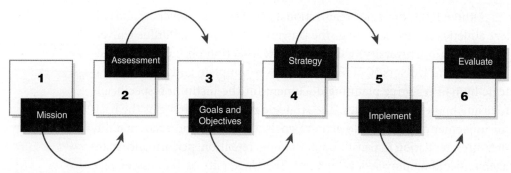

Figure 1-2 Steps in the strategic planning process

two sentences that describe the reason the organization exists and its main goal or goals to help guide executives, managers, and employees in making decisions. For example, the mission statement of the U.S. Olympic Committee (USOC) is "to support U.S. Olympic and Paralympic athletes in achieving sustained competitive excellence while demonstrating the values of the Olympic Movement, thereby inspiring all Americans" (Team USA, 2017).

For an organization looking to complete a human resources strategic plan, the mission statement is typically related directly to human resources—for example: "to serve as a strategic business partner and provide excellent human resource functional support to the employees, managers, and executives of Sports Incorporated."

Action Shot 1-1 is a brief representation of the link between the mission statement and human resource planning for the Chicago Bulls of the National Basketball Association (NBA).

STEP 2: ASSESSMENT—CONDUCT AN ANALYSIS

The second step in the strategic planning process is **assessment**, which incorporates available data to consider internal and external variables related to people and processes. Assessment can be completed by conducting an analysis of the situation and all relevant data. There may be a need for a full departmental or organizational analysis, or it may be more specific, such as the New York Knicks conducting an analysis of its human resources department structure or the structure of its newly revamped department for ticket sales, service, retention, and operations.

▶ ACTION SHOT 1-1

NBA Chicago Bulls Mission Statement and Link to Human Resource Planning

The mission of the NBA Chicago Bulls organization is, "a sports entertainment company dedicated to winning NBA Championships, growing new basketball fans, and providing superior entertainment, value and service" (NBA.com, 2017).

The premise of strategic planning, regardless of whether it is for an organizational plan or a human resource plan, is to develop goals and action-oriented activities that support the mission. The Bulls' management team could easily develop personnel-related goals and strategies to assist in fulfilling the organization's mission. As such, a strategic human resource plan for the Bulls would ideally begin by focusing on the following concepts:

1. Ensure employees are trained and committed to enhancing the core product (win NBA Championships).
2. Increase the number of individuals who identify with the Bulls brand (grow new basketball fans).
3. Operate with a focused business acumen (provide superior entertainment, value, and service).

Each of these variables in the Bulls' mission statement affects decisions regarding strategies for hiring, training, and compensating everyone from players, coaches, and trainers to the executives and front-office staff.

Analysis can be completed through the application of one or more common assessment tools used by managers, such a SWOT analysis, a PEST analysis, a market analysis, and/or benchmarking. A combination of several analyses allows for greater research-driven decisions for identifying appropriate outcomes, key performance indicators (KPIs), and strategies to implement.

SWOT Analysis

A **SWOT analysis** is a common planning tool providing an environmental check of an organization's internal factors, identified as **s**trengths and **w**eaknesses, and external factors, identified as **o**pportunities and **t**hreats. Strengths and weaknesses specifically apply to the internal aspects of an organization, whereas opportunities and threats apply externally to any organization operating in the same industry or sector. In other words, a strength or weakness for Dick's Sporting Goods stores may or may not apply to other sporting goods stores;

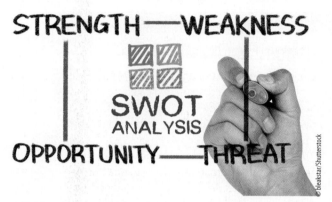

A SWOT analysis for Dick's Sporting Goods store differentiates between internal strengths and weaknesses and external opportunities and threats.

Dick's Sporting Goods, a leading industry retailer after the closing of MC Sports and Sports Authority chains in 2016 and 2017, is not impervious to economic threats.

however, an opportunity or threat for Dick's Sporting Goods should also be an opportunity or threat for any retail sporting goods chain, such as Dunham's Sports or Hibbett Sports.

From a human resource perspective, the strengths and weaknesses of an organization address what a business does and doesn't do well. An analysis of strengths and weaknesses includes such factors as the company culture, core competencies, key staff, organizational structure, experience, financial resources, training programs, employee satisfaction levels, employee performance measures, turnover, morale, benefits, policies, procedures, development programs, compensation, and reward systems. Questions to ask when determining the internal strengths and weaknesses of an organization include the following:

- What is the strength of the organization's brand?
- Does the organization have strong community support?
- Is the facility a strength or a weakness (e.g., location, age)?
- Is history/tradition relevant to the organization's success?
- Is the organization financially secure?

The opportunities and threats of an organization answer the questions, *What are the possibilities for the business?* and *What are the challenges?* Examples of threats and opportunities in human resources include legal compliance with a collective bargaining agreement (CBA), available labor pools, outcomes of a draft, the economic environment, partnerships and alliances, technology, changes in market conditions, and occupational outlooks based on U.S. Census data. When looking at external factors or the environmental opportunities and/or threats, a manager will want to review developing or new markets, the potential for economic growth, political/legal issues, industry trends, and economic conditions.

A SWOT analysis can be completed on a larger-scale, organization-wide basis or on a more specific basis to address one issue, such as recruiting practices (see sample SWOT in **Table 1-1**). For example, strategic planning in human resources permits a business to analyze whether it has sufficient staffing for the size, type, and location(s) of an organization. After review of the mission statement, a SWOT analysis for analyzing the human resource function of an organization would include the following questions:

1. What are the staffing needs of the organization at the present time, and are those needs being met?
2. What are the human resources staffing needs of the organization at the present time, and are those needs being met?
3. Are employees loyal and committed to the company?
4. Is employee satisfaction high?
5. Does the market provide high-level job candidates for open positions?
6. Is the company up to date with technology advances?
7. Is there a talent surplus/shortage?
8. Does the company have a succession plan in place for filling vacancies?

PEST Analysis

PEST analysis is another tool commonly used for assessment purposes in a strategic plan. PEST analyses evaluate external factors that affect the organization relative to the **p**olitical, **e**conomic, **s**ocial, and **t**echnological environment.

TABLE 1-1: Sample Human Resources SWOT Analysis

SWOT	Strengths	Weaknesses
Organizational	• Highly skilled employees • Loyal, satisfied employees • Innovative, creative employees	• Lack of succession planning • Outdated training practices
	Opportunities	**Threats**
Environmental	• Unexplored and expanding job markets • Technology advances	• Economic uncertainty • Uncertain political environment surrounding arena/stadium

A PEST analysis can be extremely useful for human resources in assisting an organization to adapt proactively to changes in a dynamic environment.

Political factors include an assessment of changes in legislation, compliance, and regulations. For example, Major League Baseball (MLB) employs hundreds of immigrants every year. A total of 238 foreign-born players from 18 countries out of the 864 roster spots in the MLB were listed on the opening day of the 2016 season, with the Seattle Mariners leading the league (MLB, 2015). Foreign-born players and staff affect the training necessary for human resource personnel, who are tasked with ensuring that work permits and visas are up to date. Political factors, therefore, may delay or prevent a team from signing a foreign-born player.

The MLB Seattle Mariners led the MLB in 2016 for the number of foreign-born players on the opening day roster.

An economic analysis considers financial data from employee overtime pay to monthly commissions to the organization's annual revenue-to-profit ratio. Even if two professional sports teams were to report identical revenues from tickets sales, media contracts, and ancillary areas, the vast fluctuations in payroll from franchise to franchise would affect profitability. Economic factors, therefore, may affect the ability to hire personnel or offer equitable compensation.

Social factors that may affect human resources within an organization center on cultural, lifestyle, and demographic issues. Within the intercollegiate athletics industry, for instance, there is a huge disparity in the percentage of women serving as head coaches of female teams and as directors of athletics, touted as the top administrator position (Acosta & Carpenter, 2014). One of the primary reasons identified for the shortage of female coaches is the inability of intercollegiate athletics employees to achieve work–life integration (Dixon et al., 2008). Therefore, by considering the social factors that affect human resources, professionals in higher education can review and/or create flexible policies, such as child-care provisions in a coaching contract or policies that permit families and caregivers to travel with a team.

Technology is the final factor in a PEST analysis. Technology has revolutionized the way sports tickets are sold and team travel is arranged. Automation in the manufacturing of sporting equipment and apparel has shifted human resource priorities in terms of workforce needs; for example, employees may need training programs to understand and effectively apply new technology. Technology such as data analytics software and cloud-based platforms, which facilitate easy sharing of files, has also had a tremendous impact on the efficiency of human resource functions. There is a smorgasbord of customizable human resource software programs available for everything from succession planning to benefits administration. In 2013, the Chicago Cubs used UltiPro software to streamline payroll processes, Taleo talent-management solutions as a recruiting aid, and Halogen for performance management reports (Rush, 2013).

The MLB Chicago Cubs, 2016 World Champions, are one of many professional organizations using software solutions to streamline human resource functions.

Market Analysis

A **market analysis** answers questions about where and how the organization competes in terms of acquiring, developing, and deploying resources. Survey research is the most common tool used in a market analysis. Survey research may include data from published records, focus-group interviews, individual interviews, associations, league offices, or actual questionnaires targeting employees, executives, or human resource professionals across a spectrum of the identified industry sector. Survey research can be used to create a competitive pay analysis for head coaches within the relatively new National Women's Soccer League (NWSL) or to examine labor market trends for staffing a world championship event.

Benchmarking

Benchmarking involves identifying aspiration or high-performing organizations in the same industry (e.g., the sports industry) and making comparisons. Benchmarking allows organizations to retrieve data and measurable information about different aspects of the business to compare with a standard. There are two basic forms of benchmarking, internal and external, yielding either an internal or an external comparison of performance or information.

Internal benchmarking makes comparisons with similar operations within an organization. Employee satisfaction ratings across the NBA Celtics, National Hockey League (NHL) Bruins, and affiliates working in Boston's TD Gardens, for example, can be benchmarked or compared with the 3-year average or with the one best-rated year for the facility. An external benchmark, on the other hand, makes comparisons with direct competitors or peer organizations with similar profiles. A municipal parks and recreation department, for example, may wish to benchmark competitive wages for the senior management team by using industry averages or by using data on the salaries of a parks and recreation department in a different community with similar attributes.

Benchmarking permits a gap analysis to determine deficiencies in a particular area. For instance, benchmarking is widely practiced to assess forecasting needs in terms of the number of people and skills required for a particular job. A golf course preparing for a tournament with 96 players may use information from a competitor club to research optimal staffing levels. Benchmarking can be used to assess the demographic characteristics, occupational qualifications, eligibility, and skill availability of the potential workforce. **Box 1-1** presents a six-step model of benchmarking adapted from Camp (1989).

Published reports are excellent sources of baseline data for benchmark comparisons that can assist human resource planning. An industry report useful for benchmarking and comparing workforce diversity and compensation is the Racial and Gender Equity Report Card, which provides data on diversity among coaches, players, front-office staff, athletic department personnel, presidents, CEOs, majority owners, and trainers in the Women's National Basketball Association (WNBA), Major League Soccer (MLS), the

---

BOX 1-1

Six-Step Benchmarking Model

1. Identify essential functions, processes, or outputs to benchmark (e.g., front-desk customer service).
2. Identify external organizations or functions within the organization with superior work practices for comparison (e.g., customer-service attributes at Walt Disney Properties).
3. Determine what data sources are to be used (e.g., observations of body language and customer-service satisfaction surveys).
4. Determine the aspiration standards of performance from the identified source.
5. Determine the current level of baseline performance.
6. Determine the gap between the aspiration and current performance level.

NBA, the National Football League (NFL), MLB, and intercollegiate athletics (Lapchick, 2017). Similarly, Acosta and Carpenter's (2014) national longitudinal study on women in intercollegiate sports is a benchmark tool that can be used to measure gender diversity for administrators, coaches, and support staff across the three divisions of the NCAA. The Equity in Athletics Data Analysis (EADA) Cutting Tool published by the U.S. Department of Education (2017) provides benchmark

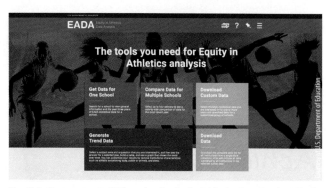

The U.S. Department of Education Equity in Athletics Data Analysis Tool provides benchmark data on salaries for head and assistant coaches at member NCAA institutions.

data for average base compensation of coaches and assistant coaches in intercollegiate athletics.

STEP 3: SETTING GOALS AND OBJECTIVES

The third step in the strategic human resource planning process involves setting goals and objectives. Setting goals and objectives in the strategic planning process for human resources is an activity that culminates with defining the outcomes the organization will strive to achieve in areas related to personnel management, operations, and support.

Outcomes may be articulated as goals, objectives, initiatives, or priorities, depending on the privy of the strategic planning team. In the previously mentioned Purdue University (2014) Athletic Department Strategic Plan, goal-setting led to the creation of objectives, such as the one to attract the very best student-athletes, coaches, and staff. The example from the University of Tennessee (2015), the Strategic Plan for Human Resources, however, uses the term *priorities*.

SMART Acronym

Regardless of the term used, it is important that the outcomes established can be evaluated to determine if the strategic plan is on track. **SMART goal-setting** is a common technique applied to articulate the necessary conditions for the evaluation of an outcome. SMART represents the following concepts:

- **S**pecific
- **M**easurable

GOAL SETTING

Specific
Measurable
Achievable
Realistic
Timely

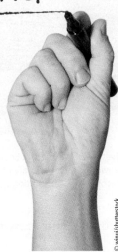

© winui/shutterstock

- **A**chievable
- **R**ealistic
- **T**imely

Consider the example of a fictitious ski resort that discovered through the assessment stage that payroll expenses were extremely high during the peak season from December through February. To apply the SMART principle, the strategic planning team needs to identify the *specific* outcome, such as "reduce payroll expenses." A *measurable* component needs to be added, such as identifying a "15% payroll reduction." That measurement needs to be evaluated to determine if the outcome is *achievable*. Suggesting an 80%–90% payroll reduction, for instance, would be seemingly unachievable and unrealistic. *Realistic* is the fourth element, referring the subjective appraisal of whether a goal is attainable. Finally, the outcome needs to have a *time-oriented* element to assist in the evaluation. The assessment noted a specific period of extremely high payroll expenses; therefore, the time orientation for the outcome should include a comparison for the identical 3 months (quarter) from the previous year. The SMART goal or outcome for the fictitious ski resort would state the following:

- **Goal or Outcome:** Reduce payroll by 15% for the quarter ending February 28, 2017, from the previous identical period ending February 15, 2016.

Key Performance Indicators

KPIs are another means by which a goal or objective can be quantified. For example, a goal may be simplified (e.g., "reduce payroll"), but attaching a KPI provides a framework for evaluation. Consider the KPI identified for the following general goal:

- **Goal or Outcome**: Lower payroll
- **KPI**: 15% for the quarter ending February 28, 2017, from the previous identical period ending February 15, 2015.

Generally, outcomes or goals are established through a **brainstorming** session after thoroughly reviewing information and data from the assessment stage. Brainstorming allows the strategic planning team to spontaneously generate ideas about a topic or issue without interpretation or evaluation.

KPIs are established after brainstorming. Benchmarking is an excellent tool to assist in the creation of appropriate KPIs to identify a threshold to reach by a deadline based on an assessment of "like" or "aspirational" organizations or to determine appropriate percentages or data points for measurement.

Sport Management Resources, a team of consultants focusing on athletics in educational institutions, lists diversity KPIs that can align with a number of human resource goals. For example, three diversity-related KPIs for a general goal related to staff recruitment that would ensure an adequate pool of candidates from underrepresented groups are as follows:

1. Number (#) and percentage (%) of members of search committee for each open position who themselves are from underrepresented groups (gender, race/ethnicity, disability, etc.)
2. Number (#) and percentage (%) of open position advertisements in electronic or print media outlets specifically targeting underrepresented populations
3. Number (#) of visits or phone calls made by open position to individuals from underrepresented groups to advise them of the position opening and urge their candidacy and number (#) that applied as a result of such contact (Lopiano & Zotos, 2013)

Similarly, appropriate diversity KPIs for assessing a general human resource goal related to optimal organizational climate would measure the following:

1. Number (#) and percentage (%) by gender and by white and non-white who, on an annual survey, characterize the athletics department climate as (a) welcoming, (b) sensitive to diversity issues, (c) committed to diversity, and (d) respectful of individual differences
2. Number (#) and percentage (%) by gender and by white and non-white who, on an annual survey, characterize the athletic department climate as treating all staff and student-athletes fairly (Lopiano & Zotos, 2013)

Minor League Baseball teams may use affinity charts and other planning tools to design game promotions such as kids running bases.

Group Decision-Making Techniques

Because the strategic planning process typically incorporates a relatively large number of individuals from different functional areas of an organization, and because brainstorming doesn't allow for scrutiny of an idea, challenges may occur in narrowing options, garnering consensus, or making final decisions on goals. Affinity charting, the nominal group process, and the Delhi technique are methods to aid in decision-making processes.

Affinity Charts

Affinity charts provide a tool to organize a large number of ideas into groups based on their natural relationships. To develop an affinity chart, a facilitator will initially write down ideas from a brainstorming session. Next, the group discusses emerging themes or characteristics from the list of ideas. For example, the director of game entertainment for a Minor League Baseball franchise may use affinity charting with his or her staff to develop ideas for promotions targeting specific demographic and psychographic markets. The facilitator/director would first create headings representing emerging themes (in this case, target markets), and group members would then place the suggestions under the appropriate category.

In terms of strategic human resource planning, a brainstorming session with a retail sporting goods chain may produce a list of 15 outcomes that seem to fit into three emerging themes related to employee morale, training, and communication. After scrutinizing the ideas and categorizing each under one of the three themes, the team may be able to establish priorities and outcomes representative of the composite list.

Nominal Group Technique

Nominal group technique is a method of brainstorming involving a facilitator who directs a small or medium-sized group of people to write down suggestions for a particular issue or topic, such as leave policies, diversity initiatives, or professional development. Each person shares his or her idea, which is then recorded on a device such as a flipchart or whiteboard. Contributors next openly discuss each suggestion to gain clarity and justifications for potential adoption. Group members then rank each idea, usually from high (10) to low (1), and the tally of responses yields the basis for prioritizing suggestions.

The nominal group technique may be applied when a municipal recreation department is considering restructuring or reorganizing personnel to better serve the community. The individuals in key positions in the department would express their ideas and provide a rationale for each strategy that explains how it would achieve the desired outcome, and the strategies would then be ranked and prioritized.

Delphi Technique

The **Delphi technique** is similar to the nominal group technique in that the initial step involves a facilitator guiding participants to write down suggestions about a particular issue or topic. The difference is that the participants are considered knowledgeable professionals and are directed to provide expert justification and reasoning for their responses. This step is followed by the facilitator evaluating the collection of results and preparing an analysis report. Participants next review the report and openly discuss their rationalizations for what should be the one best answer among the collection of responses. The rounds of moderated discussion continue until a consensus is reached.

The Delphi technique could be used by a sports organization to collect input about potential hires from search-committee members who have knowledge of the candidates. The chair of the search committee would prepare an initial report of committee preferences for the candidates interviewed for a head coaching position within an intercollegiate athletic department. Committee members then discuss the report and continue discussions until a definitive selection is made or until an alternate course of action is purported (e.g., reopen the search). Of course, this strategy is contingent on the search committee having the authority to decide on the best-suited candidate.

In strategic human resource planning, the Delphi technique is popular with key constituents for narrowing the list of final goals to ones that will become part of the actual plan. For example, in a strategic human resource planning session for a sporting goods manufacturer, the management team may use the Delhi technique to narrow down the goals that were previously selected by a larger group.

STEP 4: FORMULATE STRATEGY

The fourth step in the strategic planning process is to formulate a strategy. Once a manager has determined the mission, assessed the organization's situation, and developed the goals and objectives, the manager or leadership team can then formulate a strategy to meet the goals and objectives that have been set.

Strategies are the action-oriented items that tell how the organization can meet or surpass KPIs by providing a roadmap, of sorts. Consider the example of the fictitious ski resort with the stated outcome of reducing payroll and a KPI of 15% for the quarter ending February 28, 2017. The assessment phase of the strategic planning process may have indicated that a significant amount of overtime accumulated during the previous quarter ending in February (the "peak" season) and that there was a shortage of staff members available to maintain the industry-standard threshold ratio for staff to skiers of 1:20. Applying the knowledge learned from the assessment to answer the question of how to lower payroll by the stated amount over the given time period leads to the formulation of one or more strategies to achieve the outcome as measured by the KPI. For example, a strategy of eliminating overtime would potentially decrease quarterly payroll by 15%, which would serve to achieve the goal to reduce payroll:

- **Goal**: Reduce payroll
- **KPI**: Decrease quarterly payroll during peak season by 15%
- **Strategy**: Eliminate overtime

STEP 5: IMPLEMENT STRATEGY

The fifth step in the strategic planning process is to implement the strategy. The implementation step simply explains how to apply the strategy and which persons will be responsible for implementing the strategy. It is often referred to as the operational planning that follows the strategic planning process. Basically, it is a tool enabling accountability for the actions aligning with the plan.

In the example of the fictitious ski resort with the general goal to lower payroll, each step in the implementation chart (see **Table 1-2**) represents

TABLE 1-2: Sample Implementation Chart for a Fictitious Ski Resort's Strategic Human Resource Plan

GOAL 1: Reduce Payroll

KPI: Decrease quarterly payroll during peak season by 15%

STRATEGY 1: Eliminate Overtime

No.	Implementation Step	Resources	Responsible	Deadline
1.1.1	Purchase and use RevPASS or similar software to calculate daily total of lift-ticket revenue for the peak season.	$499—new technology	Director of Ski Operations	May 1, 2017
1.1.2	Use software to calculate metrics to determine the maximum number of staff needed to meet 1:20 ratio on a full-capacity day in addition to the average staff needed on weekdays, weekends, and holidays.	$0	Director of Ski Operations	June 1, 2017
1.1.3	Assess the pool of returning staff and calculate the gap in the maximum needed to meet the 1:20 ratio on full-capacity days.	$0	Director of Ski Operations/ Human Resource Director	June 1, 2017
1.1.4	Recruit, hire, and train additional staff.	$500— advertising, training pay	Human Resource Director	October 1, 2017
1.1.5	Emphasize elimination of overtime hours to employees through meetings and notices.	$25—print/ postage	CEO	October 1, 2017
1.1.6	Train scheduling supervisor to monitor daily staffing needs and to communicate needs to recruit additional staff.	$0	Human Resource Director	October 1, 2017
1.1.7	Create a checks-and-balance system to note if a staffer is close to overtime.	$0	Supervisor/ Human Resource Director	November 1, 2017

actions to execute the first strategy (eliminate overtime) to meet the KPI of decreasing the quarterly payroll during peak season by 15%. The implementation steps identify specific activities in addition to the resources needed (typically monetary), the person responsible for carrying out the action (accountability), and any deadline imposed.

The numbering system is important because more than one strategy is typically identified under a goal. More than one strategy would be instituted to ensure the ski resort could reduce payroll by 15% as indicated in the KPI. A second strategy, for example, could be to reduce operation hours, which would incorporate new implementation steps. When a strategy is added to Goal 1, the numbering system begins again with the second strategy and a list of accompanying implementation steps:

- 1.2.1 Goal 1/Strategy 2/Implementation Step 1
- 1.2.2 Goal 1/Strategy 2/Implementation Step 2
- 1.2.3 Goal 1/Strategy 2/Implementation Step 3
- 1.2.4 Goal 1/Strategy 2/Implementation Step 4

The numbering system changes as a new goal is identified, along with each new strategy and the accompanying implementation steps:

- 2.1.1 Goal 2/Strategy 1/Implementation Step 1
- 2.1.2 Goal 2/Strategy 1/Implementation Step 2
- 2.1.3 Goal 2/Strategy 1/Implementation Step 3
- 2.1.4 Goal 2/Strategy 1/Implementation Step 4

The number classification is important in systematically charting the progress of KPIs and outcomes during interval stages because the strategic plan may cover a 3- to 5-year period.

STEP 6: EVALUATE

The final step in the strategic planning process is to evaluate the plan. Evaluation is a process that assesses whether the strategies are providing the outcomes the strategic planning team identifies. If a soccer sports training facility identifies the goal to improve the safety awareness of head coaches and a KPI of 100% receiving first-aid and cardiopulmonary resuscitation (CPR) certification within 1 month of their hire date, a progress-reporting mechanism for the KPI needs to be established. Progress reporting allows for readjustment of activities or resources to stay on course. If, for instance, it was determined after the first 6 months that most coaches at the soccer sports training facility were not being certified within the initial month, the initial requirement could be adjusted to reflect a more realistic time period for the remainder of the strategic plan.

Although strategic plans are evaluated at the end of the planning cycle (3–5 years) to determine which outcomes were achieved according to the KPIs, typically, some type of review also occurs on an interval basis, such as annually, biannually, quarterly, or monthly. It is common to create and use a system to periodically monitor each and every implementation step in addition to the outcome and KPI.

A simple system to monitor progress is to design a scale to indicate the level of achievement. One means to apply the scale is by adding a column next to the KPI and next to each implementation step to record results and summary statements. A shortcut approach is to simply record progress next to a list of the identification numbers matching the implementation chart, as in the example corresponding to the fictitious ski resort in the progress report depicted in **Box 1-2**.

Although this type of reporting system is useful, the evaluation is subjective and may result in inaccurate assessments as a result of single-rater bias. Similar to the increase in reliability from a 360-degree performance evaluation that uses more than one rater, objectivity is enhanced by having multiple individuals participate in the monitoring phase. Monitoring tools commonly used in strategic planning include balanced scorecards, dashboards, and strategy maps.

Balanced Scorecards

The **balanced scorecard,** an approach developed in the early 1990s, provides the most comprehensive measurement tool for evaluating a business's performance (Kaplan & Norton, 1992). A balanced scorecard aligns the activities of the business with the organization's mission and vision to measure whether management is achieving the desired outcomes or goals. The four categories in a balanced scorecard are (1) financial perspectives, (2) internal business perspectives, (3) innovation and learning, and (4) customer perspective.

BOX 1-2

Sample Progress Report Scale for Strategic Planning Document

+ (Plus Sign)	Accomplished or ongoing with excellent or above average results
✓ (Check Mark)	Accomplished or ongoing with average results
− (Minus Sign)	Below pace for satisfactory achievement
Ø (Circle with a Slash)	Not accomplished

In a human resource strategic plan, the financial perspective for a sports organization would consider areas such as return on capital employed and turnover costs. It is extremely important to control turnover in the seasonal labor conditions characteristic of many sports sectors. Examples of internal business perspectives for a sports organization include the functionality of the organizational chart and policy implementation. Strategic human resource planning benefits from including the organizational structure (or re-structure) and defining policy reviews. Innovation and learning perspectives for a sports organization such as an outdoor adventure camp would include employee (counselor) learning opportunities for an adapted ropes course or for leadership training. Finally, the customer perspective may focus on client retention and satisfaction with the stadium staff or the cleanliness of the restroom facilities. The affinity chart is an excellent tool to categorize outcomes according to the four areas of evaluation.

A template for a balance scorecard charts four categories with a place to list each goal and the accompanying measurement (**Figure 1-3**). The diagram allows the strategic planning team to use a symbol, number, or graded system to measure the progress of each goal according to the KPI.

Dashboard

Dashboard is a term describing a visual diagram that is used to measure performance. Dashboards are designed around KPIs and have the element of "real-time" metrics that allows for the progress of a goal or outcome to be measured at any moment in time. The primary function of a dashboard is to quickly and clearly communicate progress in a compelling format

Abundant templates are available for dashboard creation. The growing market of strategic management software focuses on simple and sophisticated s dashboard designs that allow managers to accurately, predictively, and quickly measure performance, such as membership sales at a health club, reservations at a skating rink, or registrations for a new hip-hop aerobics class. In terms of dashboards for human resources in a sports organization, data can be graphically displayed for areas such as the percentage of intercollegiate athletic coaches who pass the NCAA Eligibility Certification test on the first attempt and attendance at mandatory education meetings. Dashboards organize goals, KPIs, data, and other information in a useful visual presentation that is easy to navigate.

Strategy Maps

A **strategy map** is a graphic representation of the entire strategic plan that demonstrates the integration, relationships, and interdependencies for

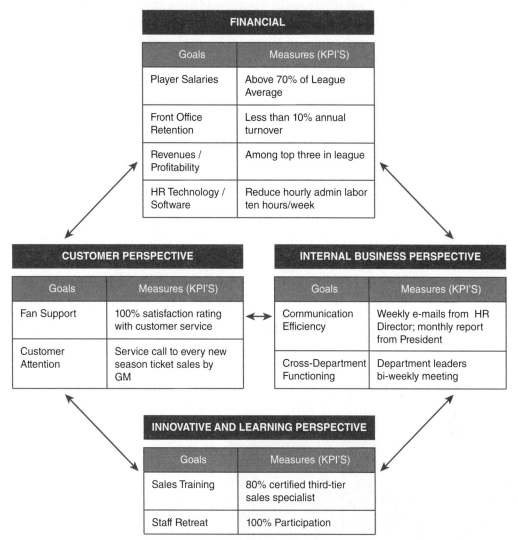

Balanced HR Scorecard - Team XYZ

FINANCIAL	
Goals	Measures (KPI'S)
Player Salaries	Above 70% of League Average
Front Office Retention	Less than 10% annual turnover
Revenues / Profitability	Among top three in league
HR Technology / Software	Reduce hourly admin labor ten hours/week

CUSTOMER PERSPECTIVE	
Goals	Measures (KPI'S)
Fan Support	100% satisfaction rating with customer service
Customer Attention	Service call to every new season ticket sales by GM

INTERNAL BUSINESS PERSPECTIVE	
Goals	Measures (KPI'S)
Communication Efficiency	Weekly e-mails from HR Director; monthly report from President
Cross-Department Functioning	Department leaders bi-weekly meeting

INNOVATIVE AND LEARNING PERSPECTIVE	
Goals	Measures (KPI'S)
Sales Training	80% certified third-tier sales specialist
Staff Retreat	100% Participation

Figure 1-3 Balanced scorecard example
Data from Kaplan, R. S., & Norton, D. P. (1992, January–February). The balanced scorecard: Measures that drive performance. *Harvard Business Review*, 71–79.

each element. Typically, a strategy map is part of the documentation of the balanced scorecard and includes the mission statement or vision statement at the top of the page with sectioned areas for each of the four categories below it. At the top of each section is the associated outcome(s) followed by the KPI. Arrows or lines are used to demonstrate connections and relationships between outcomes. In general, the strategy is a visual reproduction of the entire strategic plan. Although it is not necessary to use software to create a strategy map, various programs are available. Diagram applications in Microsoft Word also offer an effective means for creating strategy maps.

Recap

A foundation of human resource management is the application of strategic planning to help organizations realize their full potential and to operate under the general business conditions of efficiency and effectiveness. The stages of the strategic planning process are to (1) develop a mission statement, (2) conduct an analysis, (3) establish goals and objectives, (4) formulate a strategy, (5) implement that strategy, and (6) evaluate the process and results. These efforts can be arduous because of budgetary limitations and heavy scrutiny from administrators with ultimate decision-making power.

Before considering how to monitor the outcomes and implementation steps of a strategic plan, it is integral to address communication strategies to keep all employees informed of how the strategic plan ties in with the organization's overall strategic plan, what changes will be made in policies or activities to support the strategic plan, how staff will be supported during any changes, and the overall time frame.

In sports organizations, human resource strategic planning can assist supervisors in determining staffing needs for a competitive season

or training needs for new ticketing technology. The outcomes of strategic plans for human resources serve as blueprints for operations. Sports organizations in municipal settings, collegiate settings, and professional leagues are accustomed to strategic planning with a focus on human resource initiatives.

Common assessment tools used in strategic human resource planning activities include SWOT analysis, PEST analysis, market analysis, and benchmarking. The EADA website and the Gender Equity Report Card are two resources in the sports industry that can be utilized for benchmarking.

Assessment precedes the stage of developing goals and objectives that are "SMART," which represents the characteristics of being specific, measurable, attainable, relevant, and timely. Brainstorming, affinity charts, the nominal group technique, and the Delhi technique may be used to create consensus among participants in the strategic planning process.

The strategy implementation stage results in a sequential list of action-oriented activities intended to assist the organization in achieving the goals and outcomes. Accountability factors such as a target completion date, a responsible party, and necessary resources are aligned with each activity.

The final monitoring or evaluation stage requires a review of progress with KPIs. Human resource strategic planning typically occurs every 3–5 years, but a progress check is administered more frequently as part of the monitoring phase.

 GLOBAL SPOTLIGHT 1-1

Strategic Planning Process for Archery Canada Human Resources

The Executive Committee of Archery Canada created a strategic plan in 2012 to drive the National Sports Governing Body dedicated to the promotion of the sport of archery for all Canadians. The process began in Ottawa, Canada, with a planning meeting attended by the Executive Committee, which developed an initial draft of strategic directions and discussed the organization's vision and mission. Several months later, interviews were used to gather input from Canada's archery community (archers, coaches, and volunteers) and members of the World Archery Federation. A 2-day planning meeting several months later with 25 participants shaped the draft strategic plan. A consultant worked with Archery Canada's executive director and president to develop measurable objectives and deadlines. Additional working sessions on governance finalized the plan, which was eventually adopted by the Executive Committee.

Key focus area 3.1 of the plan is devoted to the human resource functions of the organization. The focus addresses human resources, communication, and leadership. Following is the outline of actions, implementation time periods, objectives, and completion target dates from the strategic plan.

Example of Part of a Strategic Planning Document Pertaining to Key Focus 3.1 on Human Resources

Action	Initiation/ Implementation	Objective and Completion Target
Key Focus Area 3.1—Strong Organization		
3.1.1.1. *Human Resources*: Hire a high-performance director or tournament director	Initiate 2012 Implement 2013	Executive director to propose potential job description, revenue sources, and hiring plans to executive director by January 2013. Hiring process initiated by April 2013.
3.1.1.2. Form a recruiting and hiring committee.	Initiate 2012 Implement 2013	Recruiting and Hiring Working Group (RHWG) formed by October 2012.
3.1.1.3. Create a Human Resources Plan, including succession planning and incentives and recognition planning, a performance appraisal system, and review and revision of volunteer and staff position descriptions.	Initiate 2012 Implement 2013	RHWG develops Human Resources Plan, including revised job descriptions (see 3.1.3), for board approval by August 2013.
3.1.1.4. Hire/contract additional volunteers and paid staff.	Initiate 2012 Implement 2013	Hiring/recruitment per approved RHWG Human Resources Plan implemented in August 2013.
3.1.2.1 *Communications*: Initiate regular conference calls with Provincial Sport Organizations (PSOs) and other internal groups to improve coordination.	Initiate 2012 Implement 2012	(See 2.2.1.) Executive director and president initiate monthly PSO calls by November 2012. Identification of additional groups for regular calls by December 2012.
3.1.2.2. Review website requirements and create specifications for revised web-based communication (e.g., website, social media, etc.)	Initiate 2012 Implement 2013	Communications Working Group (CWG) formed by August 2012. CWG develops media plan, including website specifications, for board approval by February 2013. CWG develops and recommends social media policy to Executive Committee by January 2013. Social media policy to board for approval by August 2013.

Action	Initiation/ Implementation	Objective and Completion Target
3.1.3.1. *Leadership*: Adopt new governance model consistent with the pillars of this strategic plan.	Initiate 2012 Implement 2013	Consultant develops governance model proposal by November 2012. Member input and executive approval by April 13. Board approval by August 2013.
3.1.3.2. Recruit additional board and/or committee volunteers with specific targeted skills that complement strategic plan and governance needs.	Initiate 2012 Implement 2013	In conjunction with governance model development (3.1.3.2) and Human Resources Plan (3.1.1.3), RHWG and executive director identify volunteer requirements by August 2013.
3.1.3.3. Review and update or augment committee terms of reference, bylaws, policies, procedures, and business plans consistent with new governance model to improve management. Review and revise at least once a quadrennial.	Initiate 2012 Implement 2013	Development by RHWG 2013–2014.

Reproduced from Archery Canada (2012, pp. 14–15).

DISCUSSION QUESTIONS

1. How are strategic planning and strategic planning for human resources, alike and how do they differ?
2. Identify assessment tools that might be useful for planning the staffing needs of a sports facility.
3. Compare and contrast the three reports that can be used in the sports industry for benchmarking the diversity of employees.
4. Would the Delphi or the nominal group technique be more appropriate for facilitating a brainstorming session as part of a human resource strategic planning team at a private golf and tennis facility? Why?
5. Why is it important to identify a numbering system when creating an implementation chart?
6. How would a balanced scorecard be useful in evaluating the human resource functions for a minor league hockey franchise?

APPLIED ACTIVITIES

1. Use the Internet to search for and download a strategic plan for several intercollegiate athletics departments. Create an inventory of outcomes, strategies, KPIs, and implementation steps that apply to human resources in each.

2. Select a sports organization you are familiar with or conduct an Internet search for a sports business. Conduct a SWOT analysis and a PEST analysis. In response to the PEST and/or SWOT analysis, suggest general strategies related to personnel management for the next 3 years. Outline at least two outcomes related to staffing or employment issues.

3. Review the following goals and strategies related to personnel as published in the Ohio University 2015–2020 Athletic Department Strategic Plan (2015). For each strategy, list a KPI and at least three implementation steps in a chart form. Remember to assign a target completion date, responsible party, and budget line if applicable.

GOAL: Attract, hire, and retain staff members who are committed to the integrity, excellence, and development of the student-athlete.

Strategies:

- Plan at least two all-staff, family social events (picnic, etc.) to enhance relationships within the department.
- Produce and annually update a "Why Ohio?" presentation for all searches that promotes Ohio athletics, Ohio University, attributes of the unit/sport, and the Athens community.
- Review the current employee performance evaluation format and make necessary adjustments to include adherence to respective annual plans.
- Develop a staff recruiting/hiring manual that details the recommended steps in hiring new staff, emphasizing the active recruiting of candidates.
- Maximize efficiency within the department through regular review of the administrative organizational chart and job responsibilities to ensure that they are consistent with the future direction and plans of the athletic department.
- Include a commitment to adherence to university and department policies and NCAA compliance as a part of the annual performance evaluation for all department staff.
- Evaluate current staffing needs and address as appropriate.

CASE STUDY

Strategic Human Resource Planning for World Rowing Championships

Staffing the operational side of the 2017 World Rowing Championships and 2018 World Rowing Masters Regatta falls under the responsibility of Director Meredith Scerba, hired by Suncoast Aquatic Nature Center Associates, Inc. (SANCA) to a fixed 2-year term that commenced in October 2015. This marks the first time the International Federation of Rowing Associations (FISA) has selected the United States to host the championships in more than two decades; the competition will be held in Sarasota, Florida, from September 23–October 1, 2017. The Championships is a qualifier for the 2020 Tokyo Olympics. Scerba is responsible for assembling a staff of approximately 100 volunteers and paid employees in addition to necessary contract services.

Profile of Meredith Scerba

An All-American swimmer at the University of Findlay (Ohio), Meredith (Allen) Scerba earned a Bachelor of Science in Marketing and Business Management. Her summers were spent in North Carolina, where she was a lifeguard and kid's club director at Pinehurst Country Club. Her husband, Matt Scerba, was also a collegiate swimmer at the University of Findlay.

Scerba's professional career began with the NBA Cleveland Cavaliers, where she worked as a group event coordinator. In 2005 she was hired by the Cleveland Sports Commission as director of operations and rose through the ranks to become the senior vice president of marketing and operations. The Commission is responsible for attracting and managing sports events in the city of Cleveland, and its economic impact has exceeded $450 million. Scerba was mentored by David Gilbert, president and CEO of the Greater Cleveland Sports Commission,

Positively Cleveland, and the Host Committee for the 2015 National Republican Convention. Remarking on her capabilities, Gilbert (2017) expressed,

> I have worked with Meredith Scerba for the past 8 years and have always been impressed by her organizational skills and ability to see both the big picture and the details necessary to make a project work, no matter how complex.

In 2007, Scerba recruited and managed a staff of over 1000 volunteers for the NCAA Women's Final Four. In 2008, she was recognized by Crain's *Business Cleveland Magazine* as a "Top Twenty in Their 20s," and in 2010, she was named Chapter President of Cleveland's Women in Sports and Events. She served as executive director of the 2013 National Senior Games, which included over 23,000 spectators and 11,000 athletes participating in 26 sports. Scerba's responsibilities included the overall planning, fundraising ($4.1 million), staffing, and operations for the event, which had an impact of $36 million for the city. The same year, she was named as one of the Distinguished Sales and Marketing Association's Top Executives.

When hired to direct the 2017 World Rowing Championships for the city of Sarasota, Scerba was in the planning stages as director for the 2016 Transplant Games of America.

Job Description for World Rowing Championships Event Director

Following is a brief description and a list of job qualifications and responsibilities published by Prodigy Sports (2015), the sports executive recruiting firm selected to assist with hiring the event director for the 2017 World Rowing Championships.

General Description

With a guaranteed annual salary of $150,000 over each year, the event director for the 2017 World Rowing Championships is responsible for organizing an operations staff and coordinating volunteers for the 9 days of international competition. The director is expected to maximize and strategically develop sustainable revenue streams through an aggressive ticket package campaign, regional sponsor sales and activation, merchandising, and other creative funding sources while building community support and working collaboratively with FISA and all state and regional government officials to stage a world-class event.

Qualifications and Skills

The ideal candidate will possess 10–15 years of experience in managing public, corporate, and/or sports-related events. This experience will include a successful track record in managing the entirety of large- and medium-sized events, with particular expertise in successfully leading high-performing staff focused on project management, operational logistics, sponsor development, and event marketing and promotion. The ideal candidate will offer a proven track record of exceeding expectations while working in a high-pressure, time-sensitive, and team-oriented environment. The ability to manage multiple work streams requires an exemplary detail orientation and outstanding organizational and time-management skills.

Responsibilities

- Oversee all elements of project management and bid compliance, including the development and communication of key dates and deadlines, master schedules, site plans, and contract fulfillment.

- Lead a select team of experienced event staff responsible for delivering a world-class experience for athletes, teams, media, guests, and corporate partners of the Organizing Committee and FISA, as manifest in seamless logistics, including accommodations, transportation, parking, catering, security, and on- and off-site experiences.

- Coordinate expert planning, preparation, and temporary construction of all athlete and guest requirements.

- Oversee staff, committee, and partner resources responsible for the successful marketing and promotion of the 2017 World Rowing Championships and the sport of rowing.

- Maintain meticulous management and control over the event budget, and ensure that all legal, financial, human resources, and risk management requirements are flawlessly executed. Oversee postevent wrap-up, evaluation, and reporting.

2017 World Rowing Championship Information

The 2017 World Rowing Championships anticipates being broadcast to a worldwide television audience of 130 million people. The event expects to attract 40,000 spectators and 1000 Olympic-caliber athletes from over 70 countries. There are 14 boat classes for the men's and women's regular and lightweight divisions. There is also a demonstration para-rowing event showcasing rowers with disabilities. The race distance for each regatta is 2 kilometers, which can be completed in 5–7 minutes at the elite level. Day 1 is reserved for training and meetings for umpires, technical and rescue crews, and the Fairness

Committee. Finals and the Closing Ceremony are on day 9. Training runs from 7:00–9:45 A.M. daily, and events (or additional training times) are scheduled from 10:00–7:30.

Strategic Planning Activities to Staff Championships

To effectively accomplish the responsibility for staffing the 2017 World Rowing Championships, Scerba engaged in the human resource strategic planning activities summarized in the following subsections.

Step 1: Mission Statement Review

Scerba carefully reviewed relevant mission statements that would impact her goals and objectives relative to human resource planning for the event. The mission of the Suncoast Aquatic Nature Center Associates (2017) is to "improve the quality of life for our community and be an economic generator for our region." The mission statement for FISA, which governs world rowing, is "to make rowing a universally practiced and globally relevant sport" (World Rowing, 2017).

Step 2: Conduct an Analysis

To conduct an analysis of factors that would affect staffing for the 2017 event, Scerba attended the 2015 World Championships staged in Aiguebelette, France. She conducted PEST and SWOT analyses based on observations, discussions, meetings, records, and research (e.g., Sarasota census data, job descriptions, etc.) acquired from local government officials, SANCA, FISA, and additional sources.

Step 3: Establish Goals and Objectives

Goals and objectives along with KPIs were established to address the type and number of positions necessary to effectively operate each functional staffing area for the World Championships event. The goals were generally focused on hiring a primary coordinator or director for each functional area. The associated KPI addressed the level of staffing needed in each functional area and the time period for employment.

Step 4: Formulate a Strategy

Next, Scerba developed a list of action steps for each staffing goal. She prepared job descriptions and job announcements highlighting credentials required. She created an organizational chart of the local organizing committee structure and developed strategies for sourcing the best candidates to join her team. The analysis phase helped her determine the appropriate distribution outlets to advertise vacancies. She established plausible timelines and the processes to track applications, screen candidates, make selections, and train the personnel she would hire to effectively perform the assigned duties for their functional area.

Step 5: Implement Strategies

To implement the strategies designed to meet her human resource goals, Scerba developed a staff planning chart that included periods of employment in quarters, staff titles, priority hiring status, a brief job description, dates corresponding to length of employment, and salary information. The chart was color-coded to designate the months of temporary employment status (24, 21–22, 17, 13, and 3).

Partial Contents of 2017 World Rowing Staffing Plan

Period	Staff	Length of Employment	Job Description
Q1-16	Director 2017 World Rowing Championships		Oversee and manage the everyday business of every aspect 2017 WRC; Host Committee, FISA, Finance, Operations, Competition, Marketing/Communications, Programming, Fan Services, Broadcast, etc.
Q1-16	Office Manager/Administrative	24 months (January 15, 2016–December 15, 2017)	Responsible for office administration: HR components, Office Management, Finance, Meeting Coordination, Insurance
Q1-16	Director of Partnerships	24 months (January 1, 2016–December 15, 2017)	Responsible for the research, package development and raising of the required funds to run the 2017 WRC as well as the activation of the partnerships made
Q1-16	Director of Marketing and Communications	24 months (December 1, 2015–December 1, 2017)	Responsible for the development of the Overall Marketing/Communications Plan to promote, advertise, and brand the 2017 WRC, inclusive of all grassroots, multimedia, social media elements, press, and décor
Q1-16	Director of Operations	24 months (December 1, 2015–December 1, 2017)	Manage and oversee all operational aspects, including all event logistics, build-outs/breakdowns, equipment, transportation, hospitality, event staffing, volunteer programs
Q1-16	Broadcast Contractor	21 months (sporadic) (January 1, 2016–October 15, 2017)	Contracted to assist with the broadcast negotiations and execution of production contract; on-site liaison from LOC to manage all broadcast elements
Q2-16	Marketing Coordinator	22 months (January 1, 2016–November 2, 2017	All social media, website, collateral, graphics, branding standards
Q2-16	Ticketing Manager	21 months (February 1, 2016–November 2, 2017)	Management of the ticketing system, Reunion Row, and corporate space
Q3-16	Operations Manager	17 months (June 2016–November 2017)	Assist with the planning and execution of all operational aspects, including all event logistics, build-outs/breakdowns, equipment, transportation, hospitality, event staffing, volunteer programs

Period	Staff	Length of Employment	Job Description
Q3-16	Communications/PR/Media Relations Manager	17 months (June 2016–November 2017)	Must work directly with Marketing/PR Director and the media, publicize WRC in a positive manner by creating and publishing press releases, web pages, and other event collateral
Q3-16	Volunteers and Programming Manager	17 months (June 2016–November 2017)	Create volunteer job descriptions, recruit and assign volunteers, provide all necessary communication and information to volunteers, ensuring all areas are adequately fulfilled; develop and implement community programming, administer fundraising for WRC
Q3-16	Special Events and Fan Services Manager	17 months (June 2016–November 2017)	Oversee all WRC ancillary events (Opening Ceremonies, Closing Ceremonies, Award Ceremony, VIP Events, Congress, Coaches and Managers Meetings); this position will also manage an Athlete & Fan Services Coordinator responsible for working with the Visitors Bureau to provide excursion packages and "Things to Do in the Community" communication
Q3-17	Volunteer Fellowship	13 months (October 2016–November 2017)	Oversee the execution of the volunteer program
Q1-17	Activation Coordinator	13 months (October 2016–November 2017)	Assist with the fulfillment of sponsorship contracts for WRC, create contracts, and manage value-in-kind donations
	Temporary Staff	3 months (August–October)	
	Event Contractors	3 months (August–October)	
	Interns and Event Crew	3 months (August–October)	

© World Rowing Championships.

Step 6: Evaluate the Process and Results

The staff planning chart was the dashboard to assess progress for hiring the appropriate personnel according to the anticipated start dates.

CASE QUESTIONS AND ACTIVITIES

1. What experiences in Scerba's professional profile matched the job description for the event director of the 2017 World Rowing Championships?

2. Based on the mission statements of FISA and SANCA, what would be an appropriate mission statement related to human resources for the 2017 World Rowing Championships?

3. Using information from the case and data available on the Internet, conduct a PEST analysis for staffing the 2017 World Championships.

4. What are several KPIs that Scerba could identify for her staffing goal?

5. What additional data would be beneficial to include in the implementation of a World Championships staffing plan?

6. Are there additional tools to assist Scerba in evaluating the effectiveness of her strategic planning activities for human resources at the 2017 World Championships?

7. How would strategic planning for human resources differ if Scerba were hired by a sports organization that did not have a temporary workforce?

REFERENCES

Acosta, V., & Carpenter, L. (2014). *Women in intercollegiate sport. A longitudinal, national study thirty-seven-year update.* West Brookfield, MA: Smith's College's Project on Women and Social Change and Brooklyn College of the City University of New York.

Archery Canada. (2012, August 10). *Strategic plan.* Retrieved from http://www .archerycanada.ca/images/stories/FCA/Administraion/12StratPlan/Approved _ArC_Strategic_Plan_10Aug2012.pdf

Beaujon, A. (2012, May 11). *Sporting News ships its last print edition.* Retrieved from http://www.poynter.org/latest-news/mediawire/197771/sporting-news-ships -its-last-print-edition/

Brennan, C. (2012, October 2). Tigers should dump Peralta for postseason. *USA Today.* Retrieved from http://www.usatoday.com/story/sports/mlb/tigers/2013/10/02 /christine-brennan-column-peralta-returns/2911791/

Bureau of National Affairs. (2015). *Bloomberg BNA human resource departments benchmarks and analysis.* Retrieved from https://www.bna.com/bloomberg -bna-releases-pr57982062516/

Camp, R. C. (1989). *Benchmarking. The search for industry best practices that lead to superior performance.* Milwaukee, WI: ASQC Quality Press.

Dixon, M. A., Tiell, B., Lough, N., Sweeney, K., Osbourne, B., & Bruening, J. (2008). The work/life interface in intercollegiate athletics: An examination of policies, programs, and institutional climate. *Journal for the Study of Sports and Athletes in Education, 2,* 137–160.

Gilbert, D. (2017). Recommendation for Meredith Scerba. *LinkedIn.* Retrieved from https://www.linkedin.com/in/meredith-scerba

Kaplan, R. S., & Norton, D. P. (1992, January–February). The balanced scorecard: Measures that drive performance. *Harvard Business Review,* 71–79.

Lapchick, R. (2017). *Racial and gender equity report card.* Orlando, FL: Institute for Diversity and Ethics in Sports and DeVos Sports Management Program, University of Central Florida.

Lopiano, D., & Zotos, C. (2013). Diversity key performance indicators. *The athletics director's handbook: A comprehensive practical guide to the management of scholastic and intercollegiate athletics programs.* Champaign, IL: Human Kinetics.

Major League Baseball. (2015, April 6). *Opening day rosters feature 230 players born outside the U.S.* Retrieved from http://m.mlb.com/news/article/116591920/opening-day-rosters-feature-230-players-born-outside-the-us

Meek, A. (1997). An estimate of the size and supported economic impact of the sports industry in the United States. *Sports Marketing Quarterly, 6,* 4, 15–21.

Milano, M. & Chelladuria, P. (2011). Gross domestic sport product: The size of the sports industry in the United States. *Journal of Sport Management, 25.* 24–35.

NBA.com. (2017). *Chicago Bulls mission statement.* Retrieved from http://www.nba.com/bulls/news/mission_statement.html

Ohio University Athletic Department. (2015). Goals for personnel. *Ohio University Athletic Department 2015–2020 Strategic Plan.* Retrieved from http://grfx.cstv.com/photos/schools/ohio/genrel/auto_pdf/2014-15/misc_non_event/strategic_plan.pdf

Parks J., Zanger B., & Quarterman, J. (1998). Contemporary Sport Management. Human Kinetics

Pitts, B., Fielding, L., & Miller, L. (1994). Industry segmentation theory and the sports industry: Developing a sports industry segment model. *Sports Marketing Quarterly, 3,* 1. 15-24.

Prodigy Sports. (2015). *Event director—World rowing championships.* Retrieved from http://prodigysports.net/job-board/2015/08/13/event-director-world-rowing-championships/

Purdue University. (2014). *Purdue University Division of Intercollegiate Athletics strategic plan.* Retrieved from http://grfx.cstv.com/photos/schools/pur/genrel/auto_pdf/2008-2014StrategicPlan.pdf

Rush, R. (2013). Technology resources identified for human resource manager for program development for the Chicago Cubs, as cited in Mehta, A. (2013). Human resources in professional sports: Chicago Cubs. *HR Certification Institute.* Retrieved from http://www.hrci.org/certified-community/certified-publication/featured-stories/human-resources-in-professional-sports-chicago-cubs

Suncoast Aquatic Nature Center Associates. (2017). *SANCA mission and priorities.* Retrieved from http://nathanbendersonpark.org/about-us/sanca-mission.html

Team USA. (2017). *Mission and culture.* Retrieved from http://www.teamusa.org /careers/mission-and-culture

University of Tennessee. (2015, August). *Human resources five-year strategic plan.* Retrieved from http://hr.tennessee.edu/wp-content/uploads/2016/03/HR-Strategic -Plan-2015.pdf

U.S. Department of Education. (2017). *Equity in athletics data analysis cutting tool.* Retrieved from http://ope.ed.gov/athletics/

World Rowing. (2017). *About FISA. FISA's goals and objectives.* Retrieved from http:// www.worldrowing.com/fisa/

CHAPTER 2

Playing by the Rules

EMPLOYMENT LAW AND COMPLIANCE
IN SPORTS ORGANIZATIONS

A hot legal topic for sports organizations is the Fair Labor Standards Act (FLSA), which establishes the minimum wage and overtime rules in the United States. New FLSA regulations may have a dramatic impact on the sports industry as low-salaried employees who work more than 40 hours will also need to be paid overtime. Understanding the FLSA is important in creating job descriptions, establishing salaries, and tracking hours worked.

Barbara Osborne, J.D.
Professor, Exercise and Sport Science, and Adjunct Professor of Law
University of North Carolina, Chapel Hill

Our office spent countless hours this past year in meetings and on conference calls with numerous constituents to determine how we would comply with the new FLSA regulations. Everything in our department is vetted through the institution's general human resource office and through the central human resource office regulating all 16 campuses in the University of North Carolina (UNC) system. The director of athletics was consulted, and legal counsel was involved, especially in conversations with the central office and human resource reps from all the UNC branch campuses. The strategy in athletics to ensure we would be legal was to increase salaries for certain staff employees by the December 1, 2016, deadline. No athletic employees would have changed from salaried to hourly status. The injunction put a halt, or at least delayed, having to comply with the new regulations. In the end, fewer than 10 employees in the athletic department at UNC Chapel Hill would have been impacted.

Joyce Dalgleish
Director of Athletic Human Resource Services
University of North Carolina, Chapel Hill

LEARNING OUTCOMES

1. Identify relevant employment laws that affect sports organizations.
2. Determine whether an employment relationship exists.
3. Explain the Fair Labor Standards Act minimum wage and overtime provisions.
4. Determine whether an employee should be classified as exempt or nonexempt.
5. Define types of discrimination claims.
6. Distinguish between disparate impact and disparate treatment claims.

KEY TERMS

Constitution	Failure to reasonably accommodate	Retaliation
Discriminate		*Stare decisis*
Disparate treatment	Law	Statute
Disparate impact	Legislative body	Union
Employee	Plaintiff	U.S. Department of Labor
Employment law	*Prima facie*	
Executive order	Protected class	

Lead-Off

In addition to strategic planning, employment law is yet another vitally important foundational area for sports managers and supervisors, especially for those responsible for staffing and supervision. Sports organizations are no different from non-sports organizations when it comes to the requirements of complying with laws and regulations. Individuals must presumably know the laws pertaining to their organizations and comply accordingly.

The information in the industry voice pertains to the important federal regulations governing overtime and wages as defined by the United States Department of Labor's (DOL) Fair Labor Standards Act (FLSA). Institutions such as the University of North Carolina exhausted countless hours and manpower to determine how to comply with new FLSA policies that did not go into effect December 1, 2016 as originally planned by the DOL. There is still a possibility that some type of change to the FLSA policy will occur, however, a high level of uncertainty is cast over any timeline or determination of an actual change taking place. It is important that sport managers remain diligent in their awareness of the possibility that labor policies and regulations may occur that will have an impact on their business.

With the wide variety of types of sports organizations in existence, it's difficult to provide a complete guide of employment policies that applies to all sports businesses. Some organizations are a part of a much larger corporation (e.g., ESPN is a subsidiary of Disney Enterprises, Inc.) and therefore have the availability of an autonomous human resource department or even a specialist to execute many back-end regulatory functions. Regardless of the operational setup of support assistance, supervisors and managers in both large and small sports organizations are obligated to remain compliant with the laws and regulations governing employment.

The scope of employment law is challenging in any industry. Laws resonate from different sources and apply to varying conditions. The landscape of federal, state, and local laws may intersect or even trump one other. The numerous laws applicable to hiring, firing, and general work conditions make it imperative that supervisors and managers have a basic understanding of employment legislation and have access to legal sources.

Understanding the basics of employment law and the human resource implications assists in ensuring that sports managers are capable of creating appropriate policies and procedures to minimize legal risk while also being mindful of situations in which it is best to refer to legal counsel. This chapter provides information on the foundations of employment law and the basics of discrimination claims. It also addresses common employment laws applying to sports organizations; however, it is not meant to be a comprehensive listing of all laws governing employment.

Foundations of Employment Law

Employment law governs employer and **employee** relationships as they pertain to a broad spectrum of conditions, such as workplace rights, responsibilities, safety and well-being, and equity, to name a few. Sports managers and supervisors must ensure the organization operates within the scope of employment laws by having knowledgeable personnel and creating and communicating policies or procedures that comply with the

© ayzek/shutterstock

various requirements. Sports organizations are just as susceptible as any other business to violations of rules and regulations. A general knowledge of the basic nuances of employment law provides a minimal foundation for understanding; however, knowledge of legislation and legal statutes is not enough to warrant compliance.

An initial step in broadly understanding employment law is to know whether a particular law applies to an organization. The organization must know (1) whether the business operates as a public (e.g., a municipal recreation center) or a private (e.g., a commercial sports facility) entity, and (2) the specific number of full-time and part-time employees. For example, certain laws apply only to government entities, other laws apply only to private organizations, and some laws apply to both the public (government) and the private sector. Some laws apply to organizations with over 15 employees (e.g., Title VII of Civil Rights Act), and some only apply to companies with over 50 employees (e.g., Family and Medical Leave Act [FMLA]).

Further understanding of the basics of employment law is enhanced by addressing the nature of employment relationships, the general sources of law creation, and the federal agencies governing employment legislation.

EMPLOYMENT RELATIONSHIPS

Employment law is predicated on the relationship between an employee and an employer; therefore, one of the most important considerations in most employment law situations is to determine whether there is a true employment relationship. The nature of an employment relationship is critical in determining the applicability of laws governing areas such as overtime wage requirements or Social Security contributions. The distinction is important in determining how to pay an individual (e.g., through the Internal Revenue Service) and whether certain laws will apply.

Many sectors of the sports industry rely on volunteers (i.e., youth coaches in recreation and operations workers for the Olympics), who generally are not considered employees of an organization. Independent contractors

Volunteer labor, such as those who worked at the 2016 Olympics in Rio de Janeiro, are not considered "employees."

and third-party vendors, too, have a limited relationship with the employer. Organizations may mistakenly believe they have sole authorization to decide who is and who is not technically an employee; however, there are federal guidelines for determining employment status. The Internal Revenue Service (2015), for example, considers three main controlling factors to determine the type of employment relationship:

1. Does the company control what the worker's job is and how he or she does it?
2. Are the business aspects of the worker's job controlled by the payer?
3. Are there written contracts or employee benefits, will the relationship continue, and is the work performed a key aspect of the business?

The **U.S.** DOL also applies a set of standards to determine employment relationships. For example, the DOL distinguishes between blue-collar and white-collar workers. The DOL also sets guidelines to distinguish independent contractors by virtue of their economic independence as opposed to a reliance on the employer (DOL, Wage and Hour Division, 2014).

SOURCES OF LAW

Laws, including those that govern employment, are established at the federal, state, and local municipal level. Legislation is created through a variety of measures. The basic sources of law creation addressed in this chapter include constitutions, statutes, executive orders, and court rulings.

Constitutions serve as the source of laws governing individuals or citizens under the regime of a supreme authority. For example, the well-recognized Constitution of the United States of America guarantees all of its citizens certain inalienable rights (life, liberty, and pursuit of happiness), and the constitution of the U.S. Amateur Athletic Union (2016, p. 2) addresses conditions of membership and committee representation. Constitutions rely on a supreme body that governs over a group of individuals (citizens or members) for interpretation and enforcement. Every state in America has its own constitution to protect individual liberties and define jurisdiction.

Similar to constitutional laws are **statutes**, which can be created at the municipal, state, and/or federal levels. Statutes, however, typically do not supersede a constitutional law. A statute is a written law passed by a **legislative body** that has the authority to make, amend, or repeal a law. The 2004 Adventurous Activity Licensing Authority Regulations by order of the United Kingdom Health and Safety Executive (2017) represents an example of legal

In the United Kingdom, an Adventure Activities License is mandated for operators and supervisors of high risk sports such as rock-climbing, mountain biking, and hang-gliding.

statutes applying to operators and supervisors of high-risk sports such as rock-climbing or hang-gliding. An example of a legislative body is the U.S. Congress which has passed several employment-related laws, including Title VII of the Civil Rights Act of 1964, the FLSA, and the FMLA.

Executive orders are another source of law. An executive order is a rule issued by the president of the United States to the executive branch of the government. State governors also have the power to create executive orders for the executive branch of their state.

This rule carries the effect of a law; however, it is only applicable to the executive branch. For example, Executive Order 11246 created by President Lyndon B. Johnson in 1965 required government contractors to take "affirmative action" to ensure that applicants are employed without regard to race, color, religion, sex, or national origin, thereby creating a requirement for affirmative action programs for federal contractors. Affirmative action is practiced by numerous university athletic departments employing coaches, administrators, and support staffs. Job announcements often include a statement noting the organization is an equal opportunity/equal access/affirmative action employer.

The headquarters for Fédération Internationale de Football Association (FIFA) in Zurich, Switzerland, is an example of an international sport organization subject to the ruling of the Court of Arbitration in Sports in cases of labor disputes.

Court decisions also serve as a source of law. The process by which a court relies on a previous court's decision (case precedent) is called *stare decisis*, meaning "to stand by that which is decided." When faced with a legal issue that has already been decided, courts will often rely on previous interpretations of that rule of law to make and justify their decisions. For example, in deciding the outcomes of employment disputes in sports, references have been made to decisions rendered by the Court of Arbitration in Sports (CAS), considered one of the supreme entities of global sports. The CAS has ruled on numerous employment and other judicial arguments associated with the Olympic Games and International Sport Federations such as the Fédération Internationale de Football Association (FIFA). It is surmised that frequent citations given to CAS awards for legal remedies (i.e., arbitration outcomes) suggests a de facto doctrine of *stare decisis*, especially in demonstrating general equitable principles (Bersegal, 2012, p. 203).

FEDERAL AGENCIES GOVERNING EMPLOYMENT LAW

The primary federal agencies governing employment law include the National Labor Relations Board (NLRB), the U.S. DOL, and the Equal Employment Opportunity Commission (EEOC). The U.S. Department of Education's Office for Civil Rights (OCR) is another federal agency governing employment law; however, regulatory actions are specific to educational institutions (i.e., intercollegiate athletics and scholastic sports). All sports organizations must comply with employment laws and regulations under the authority of the respective federal agencies. In addition to governing and enforcing employment laws, each agency serves as a repository for educating employers and assisting them in understanding their rights and responsibilities.

National Labor Relations Board

The NLRB is the independent federal agency in the United States charged with enforcing the rules of the National Labor Relations Act (NLRA) enacted by Congress in 1935 to protect the rights of employees. The NLRA governs the rules of good-faith bargaining (collective bargaining) for both management and employees. A collective bargaining agreement (CBA) is the document representing the agreed-upon labor conditions collectively approved by both the general laborers (employees) and the management or ownership of an organization. In general, the NLRA provides the framework governing labor relations between management and employees.

The NLRB primarily oversees labor activities applying to the private sector, such as nonprofits, employee-owned businesses, large retailers, and labor organizations. A **union** is a labor organization comprising employees of the same trade formed for the purpose of advancing member interests related to working conditions. Federal, state, and local government employees; agricultural laborers; and independent contractors are not generally governed by the NLRB.

BOX 2-1

Selected Program Areas Administered by the Department of Labor

- Occupational Safety and Health Administration
- Bureau of Labor Statistics
- Bureau of International Labor Affairs
- Pension Benefit Guaranty Corporation

- Office of Disability Employment Policy
- Wage and Hour Division
- Office of Workers' Compensation Programs
- Employee Benefits Security Administration

U.S. Department of Labor

The U.S. DOL is an organization of interconnected agencies and offices overseeing a majority of federal employment laws and regulations. Although the scope of programs, policies, and laws is vast, the DOL is generally responsible for regulations and standards for wages, workplace safety and health, workers' compensation, and retirement securities (refer to **Box 2-1**). The DOL also addresses the issues of and administers programs for niche groups, such as migrant workers and veterans.

The mission of the DOL is "to foster, promote, and develop the welfare of the wage earners, job seekers, and retirees of the United States; improve working conditions; advance opportunities for profitable employment; and assure work-related benefits and rights" (DOL, 2016b). The DOL, for example, is the authority for FLSA legislation, which is challenging intercollegiate athletic departments and many other organizations as a result of the recent increase in minimum-wage standards governing exemptions from overtime pay.

Equal Employment Opportunity Commission

The EEOC was created by the Civil Rights Act of 1964 and is the entity responsible for enforcing federal laws that protect against employment discrimination. The EEOC has the authority to investigate charges of discrimination and settle claims on behalf of job applicants or employees facing discrimination. Although the agency doesn't create laws, it is charged with enforcement and is responsible for oversight and coordination of all federal equal opportunity regulations, practices, and policies. The EEOC also provides education and assistance programs to help prevent workplace discrimination.

In 2016, five members of the U.S. women's national soccer team filed a complaint with the EEOC for wage discrimination. The claim attests that female players are paid less than their male counterparts. Upon completing its investigation of the claims, the EEOC has the authority to dismiss the complaint or require the U.S. Soccer Federation to remedy the disparity.

Office for Civil Rights

The Department of Education's OCR is a federal agency with roles and duties similar to those of the EEOC. The OCR enforces federal regulations pertaining to employment discrimination in school systems (e.g., athletic departments and physical education classrooms). A caveat to OCR regulations is that the institution must receive federal financial assistance. In addition to the 50 state education agencies in America, the OCR applies to approximately 16,000 local education institutions and 3200 colleges (U.S. Department of Education, OCR, 1991).

One of the most recognizable employment complaints received by the OCR involves Title IX issues, which are generally understood as the regulations governing equal opportunities for men and women. Although Title IX is generally misunderstood as exclusively pertaining to sports programs, the scope of the law does address employment issues for athletic coaches and personnel related to equity in recruitment, advertising, hiring, promotions, tenure, firing, rates of pay, fringe benefits, and administrative leave for pregnancy and childbirth.

Employment Discrimination and the Law

As indicated in the overview of federal agencies enforcing employment laws, the EEOC and the OCR both have responsibilities with respect to employment discrimination laws, but the OCR exclusively serves school systems. **Discrimination** can occur when posting a job, during the pre-employment screening of a prospective employee, during the job-offer process, in promotion considerations, during termination of an employee, in regard to shift scheduling, and in many other employment situations. An employer can be held responsible for intentional or unintentional discrimination.

Supervisors and administrators in sports who practice a managerial approach to human resources have adopted a mindset to refrain from actions and behaviors in all facets of employment areas (e.g., hiring, promotions, raises, or dismissals) that may be perceived as discriminatory. In addition to Title VII, Title IX, and the Americans with Disabilities Act (ADA) covered in this chapter, examples of federal laws providing various classes of individuals with protections against employment-related discrimination include the (1) Age Discrimination in Employment Act (age 40 and over), (2) the Pregnancy Discrimination Act, and (3) the Uniformed Services Employment and Reemployment Rights Act (military service).

Sports managers must be aware that in addition to federal legislation, state laws also address employment discrimination, especially in applying

Almost all states have adopted discrimination laws to protect employees beyond the scope of Title VII and ADA. State laws protect employees from discrimination based on a variety of factors such as HIV-AIDS, weight, and gender-identification.

to **protected classes** not recognized by U.S. statutes. For example, the National Collegiate Athletic Association (NCAA) acknowledges that there are no federal guidelines protecting for gender identity or expression, meaning individuals have to rely on state anti-discrimination legislation for protection (Guyan & Clifton, 2015). Although clarification on gender identity and expression by the NCAA is in the context of athletics participation, state legislation is necessary to provide protection for transgender individuals applying for a job as a coach or sports administrator. Recognizing the need to extend protection against employment discrimination, various states have passed legislation to designate a protected class based on sexual orientation, tobacco/alcohol use, HIV/AIDS, arrest/criminal conviction, weight, and personal appearance. It is important that individuals in sports businesses charged with hiring, promoting, disciplining, and/or firing employees are familiar with both federal and state protection laws and any protections provided.

Following a general overview of employment discrimination claims, selected laws that apply to sports are addressed, including Title VII, Title IX, and the ADA.

EMPLOYMENT DISCRIMINATION CLAIMS

Managers and supervisors in the sports industry must be prudent and judicious in their treatment of applicants for a position or in matters involving staff to avoid perceptions of discrimination or unfair practices. There are countless examples of legal cases in all sectors of sports where an individual claimed he or she was overlooked for a promotion, paid on a different wage scale than an employee with similar skills and experience, or reassigned/terminated shortly after bringing attention to improprieties within the organization.

One of the most disgraceful legal cases in college sports is the 2011 Penn State University scandal involving a conspiracy to cover up the actions of a coach (Jerry Sandusky) who had been sexually abusing young men (children) for over a decade. The former Penn State assistant football coach identified as the "whistleblower" in the case (Mike McQueary) was awarded $7.3 million in damages resulting from being retaliated against for assisting with the original sexual abuse case trial (Sports Business News, 2016). A judge supported the retaliation claim, noting that after testifying in the Sandusky trial, the university suspended McQueary from his coaching duties, placed him on administrative leave, barred him from team facilities, and denied a contract renewal.

Former Penn State University assistant football coach Mike McQueary was awarded over $7 million after claims of retaliation for his role as a whistle-blower in a widely-publicized sex abuse scandal.

The judgment in favor of McQueary echoes the need for prudent managerial practices and ethical decision making by athletic directors and other individuals with oversight responsibilities in sports. Coaches, trainers, and any employee who perceives he or she is not treated fairly may have cause to file legal action through the court system or a federal agency governing employment legislation.

There are generally four types of employment discrimination claims that can be brought against an employer: (1) failure to reasonably accommodate, (2) disparate treatment, (3) disparate impact, and (4) retaliation.

Failure to Reasonably Accommodate

Failure to reasonably accommodate is a claim addressing employment discrimination based on religion or disability. Legislation requires an employer to reasonably accommodate an employee's religious needs or his or her disabilities. A common accommodation for religion is flexible scheduling. Similarly, a common accommodation for a prospective employee with disabilities would be the provision of a sign language interpreter for a job interview or the accessible technology for the application process.

In 2015, three guest services representatives filed a discrimination lawsuit in the U.S. district courts against the Major League Baseball (MLB) Washington Nationals team, citing a failure to reasonably accommodate religious beliefs. The workers were Seventh-Day Adventists whose religion forbade them from working from sun-up to sundown on the Sabbath. The circumstances limited their availability to work during games held on Friday evenings and Saturdays, meaning the employees failed to meet the

The MLB Washington Nationals were accused of failing to provide accommodations for a trio of stadium workers in 2015 due to their religious beliefs.

Nationals' 80% attendance requirement. When the workers were not rehired for the 2016 season, the lawsuit was filed. The claim, settled out of court, demanded reinstatement and $300,000 in damages as a result of the failure of the Washington Nationals to accommodate their religious beliefs (Altman, 2015; Grow, 2015).

Disparate Treatment

Disparate treatment is a claim involving intentional unequal treatment of an employee (or prospective employee). It is important to note that disparate treatment applies to the unequal treatment of an *individual*, not a class of individuals. When a disparate treatment claim is filed, courts typically use the framework set forth in *McDonnell-Douglas v. Green* (411 U.S. 792 (1973)), which is a burden-shifting analysis in which the **plaintiff** (the party who brings a claim against another party) must first establish a *prima facie* case of discrimination. *Prima facie* is a legal term purporting that sufficient facts of a case are true until or unless proven otherwise.

Depending on the type of claim filed, the proof necessary for *prima facie* case will change, but in general, plaintiffs or employees must prove that they are a member of a protected class, that they were qualified for the position in question, and that there was some adverse employment action (not hired, denied promotion, terminated, transferred, etc.). **Action Shot 2-1** describes a legal dispute within the University of Iowa athletic department citing disparate treatment.

Disparate Impact

Disparate impact is similar to disparate treatment with the distinction that a protected class (e.g., women, ethnic minorities) is the target of the discrimination, and the discrimination is not intentional. Disparate impact is the unintentional unequal treatment of a class of persons whereby an employer's neutral employment practice has a discriminatory effect on a protected class of which the plaintiff is a member. To prove a claim of disparate impact, a plaintiff must prove that (1) an employer uses a particular employment practice that causes a disparate impact on a protected group, (2) the practice is not related to the job or position in question, and (3) the employment practice is not consistent with a legitimate business necessity.

For example, a multipurpose sports facility that posts a job description for janitorial staff requiring all applicants to be at least 6 feet tall is an example of disparate impact. If it is proven that the average woman is 5 feet 5 inches tall, then this policy, although neutral on its face, would have a discriminatory effect on women, who are considered a protected class under the category of sex/gender.

In 2015, a former equipment manager for the Los Angeles Rams dropped an age discrimination lawsuit.

A former equipment manager who began working for the Los Angeles Rams when he was 11 years old dropped a 4-year age discrimination suit in 2015. The employee was dismissed 10 months prior to being eligible for extended health benefits for himself and his family and early retirement (Mann, 2012). The claim of disparate impact cited numerous employees over the age of 50 who were terminated when a new coach was hired. The age discrimination dispute, an example of disparate impact, was initially abdicated to binding arbitration by the National Football League (NFL) commissioner (Mullineaux, 2016).

Retaliation

Retaliation purports that an employee was treated unjustly as a result of engaging in a protected activity in the workplace. Protected activities include assisting in a workplace investigation or filing a claim with the EEOC or OCR.

In a retaliation claim, a plaintiff must prove that (1) he or she engaged in some type of protected conduct, (2) the decision maker knew of the protected conduct, (3) the plaintiff suffered an adverse employment action (termination, transfer, demotion, etc.), and (4) a causal link existed between the protected conduct and the adverse action.

Retaliation was cited by Penn State University's former assistant coach Mike McQueary, who won a judgment for actions against him following his testimony in the Jerry Sandusky trial. Retaliation was also cited in the University of Iowa athletic case described in **Action Shot 2-1**.

▶ ACTION SHOT 2-1

Retaliation and Disparate Treatment: University of Iowa Athletics Case

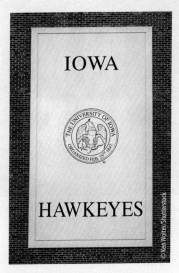

IOWA

HAWKEYES

© Ken Wolter/Shutterstock

The lawyer representing Tracey Griesbaum, the University of Iowa's (IU) head field hockey coach fired for allegedly mistreating players, used the term "retaliation" in describing the potentially illegal reassignment of IU's Senior Associate Athletic Director Jane Meyer (*Herald-Sun*, 2014). After Griesbaum's dismissal, Meyer, her long-term partner, addressed a letter to the director of athletics citing disparate treatment and concerns over failing to reinstate the fired female field hockey coach.

IU claimed the threat of a wrongful termination lawsuit by Griesbaum was the reason for Meyer's temporary transfer to the facilities department (Clayworth, 2014). Meyer was eventually reassigned to the College of Liberal Arts and Sciences before being dismissed by the university in September 2016 (Charis-Carlson, 2016). The former administrator claimed the reassignment was a violation of her rights (Associated Press, 2014, 2015; *Herald-Sun*, 2014; O'Leary, 2015).

Griesbaum originally filed a complaint with the Iowa Civil Rights Commission in addition to a civil lawsuit citing discrimination within the athletic department. Four field hockey players under Griesbaum also filed a Title IX complaint against IU in January 2015 alleging that the university holds different standards for male and female coaches (Cooney, 2015).

Several years following the initial allegations, an independent judge ruled that the university reserved the right to dismiss Meyer for unspecified reasons (Jordan, 2016). After her dismissal in September 2016, Meyer filed a federal complaint citing a violation of her first amendment rights and Title IX. Meyer's previous allegations against IU and IU Board of Regents claiming discriminatory and retaliatory treatment was scheduled for trial in April 2017 (Charis-Carlson, 2016).

TITLE VII OF THE CIVIL RIGHTS ACT OF 1964

Many cases involving disparate impact or disparate treatment are predicated upon Title VII of the Civil Rights Act of 1964, which is the broadest federal law specifically addressing discriminatory practices in employment. Managers and supervisors in sports organizations must be aware of the potential for legal action by employees if they perceive they have been discriminated against (e.g., not hired or promoted or paid fairly) because of their race, color, religion, sex (gender), or national origin (see **Action Shot 2-2**).

Title VII applies to all educational institutions (public or private) and to state and local governments. The act applies to employers with 15 or more

▶ ACTION SHOT 2-2

Morris v. Wallace Community College–Selma

In *Morris v. Wallace Community College-Selma* (125 F.Supp. 2d 1315 (S.D. Ala. 2001)), Morris was a white female coach employed part time in the athletics department in 1989 and employed full time since 1992. When the athletic director for the department retired in 1996, Morris had expressed interest in the position. Instead, the college named Todd Alford, a white male, as athletic director. When Alford resigned in 1997, the college named Raji Gourdine, a black male, as athletic director.

In determining whether Morris had a valid claim of discrimination for not being considered for either vacancy, the court used the *McDonnell-Douglas* burden-shifting analysis. First, the plaintiff was required to demonstrate (1) that she belongs to a protected class; (2) that she applied for and was qualified for the job for which the employer was seeking applicants; (3) that she was rejected for the promotion; and (4) after the rejection, the position remained open or was filled by a person outside the protected class.

The first part of the *prima facie* claim was met because Morris is a white female and thus belongs to the protected classes of race and sex/gender. The second part of the *prima facie* case was more difficult to prove because the employer did not accept applications but simply promoted two people into the athletic director role. The court found that an employer has a duty to consider all persons who might reasonably be interested, and the fact that the employer did not accept applications does not mean that the applicant did not express interest. The process of not accepting applications does not allow an employer to defeat liability. The college argued that it was seeking to hire an administrator instead of a coach and that Morris was not qualified; however, the choice of a chemistry teacher over a coach led to sufficient questions as to whether the college truly considered the qualifications.

The third and fourth parts of the *prima facie* case were established because it was clear that Morris was rejected for the promotion and that the position was filled by a black male, a person not a member of the plaintiff's protected class.

The burden then shifted to the college to provide a legitimate nondiscriminatory reason for not promoting Morris. The college argued that Morris did not follow rules, was a troublemaker, and was not an administrator.

The burden then shifted back to Morris to show that the college's assertion that she was a troublemaker and not an administrator were, in fact, a pretext to discrimination. Morris provided annual reviews that were positive in addition to an employee file that included zero reprimands. Although it was true that she was not an administrator, the college hired a chemistry teacher who also was not an administrator. Therefore, the court found in favor of Morris and that there was indeed discrimination in her failure-to-promote claim (*Morris v. Wallace Community College–Selma*, 125 F.Supp. 2d 1315 (S.D. Ala. 2001)).

The *Morris* case reinforces the components of Title VII legislation while also demonstrating a need for administrators of sports programs and all others responsible for hiring to make employment decisions based on merit. It also demonstrates a need to document employee problems. In the aforementioned case, if Morris was truly a troublemaker (not following rules, complaints about her coaching, etc.), there should have been some type of documentation in an annual review or some type of evidence of disciplinary action. Finally, the case represents a need for best practices in posting jobs in conspicuous places and reviewing applicants based on qualifications, not race or gender.

employees who work at least 20 calendar weeks in a given year. Title VII specifically claims it is an unlawful for an employer to

1. fail or refuse to hire or to discharge any individual, or otherwise to discriminate against any individual with respect to his compensation, terms, conditions, or privileges or employment, because of such individual's race, color, religion, sex or national origin; or
2. limit, segregate, or classify his employees or applicants for employment in any way which would deprive or tend to deprive any individual of employment opportunities or otherwise adversely affect his status as an employee, because of such individual's race, color, religion, sex or national origin (Title VII of the Civil Rights Act of 1964, Section 2000e-2)

TITLE IX

Most managers and supervisors (e.g., athletic directors) in intercollegiate and scholastic sports are generally aware of the premise of Title IX as legislation prohibiting discrimination based on gender. Title IX of the Educational Amendments of 1972 applies to employers that are educational institutions and receive federal funds. Title IX most often is used in legal claims to support an athlete's right to equal or proportionate opportunities in athletic participation, scholarship allocations, and a litany of other areas, such as coaching expertise, training and practice facilities, and equipment.

Title IX: No person in the United States shall, on the basis of sex, be excluded from participation in, be denied the benefits of, or be subjected to discrimination under any education program or activity receiving Federal financial assistance.

There are, however, examples, of settlements and lawsuits citing Title IX especially referencing disparities in pay and equal treatment or in retaliation for advocating for gender rights. For example, in 2015, federal lawsuits were filed against Rider College and Louisiana State University by the respective former head coaches for a softball and women's tennis program released by their institutions. In separate lawsuits, each alleged the dismissal was a result of retaliation for expressing Title IX complaints to the administration (Guilbeau, 2015; Toutant, 2015).

AMERICAN WITH DISABILITIES ACT (ADA)

The ADA prohibits private employers, state and local governments, employment agencies, and labor unions from discriminating against qualified individuals with disabilities in job application procedures, hiring, firing, advancement, compensation, job training, and other terms, conditions, and privileges of employment. The ADA applies to employers with 15 or more employees, including state and local governments. Although it is prudent to provide a work environment that is conducive to accommodate employees with disabilities, an employer is not required to provide an accommodation unless an individual has made a request.

In addition to the American Disability Act mandating sport facilities provide reasonable accommodations for fans with disabilities, organizations must also accommodate the special needs of an employee with a disability.

According to the U.S. Department of Justice Civil Rights Division (2015), in reference to the ADA of 1990, an individual with a disability is a person who has a physical or mental impairment that substantially limits one or more major life activities; has a record of such an impairment; or is regarded as having such an impairment. Sports organizations are among all employers required to make a reasonable accommodation of a qualified applicant or employee if it would not impose an undue hardship on the operations of the business. For example, because of ADA requirements, the Houston Rockets of the National Basketball Association (NBA) had to provide a top draft pick (Royce White) the opportunity to be escorted to games via ground transportation because of the player's anxiety disorder related to a fear of flying (Claybault, 2012). On the other end of spectrum, the St. Louis Rams of the NFL were fined $134,000 by the EEOC for failing to comply with ADA regulations after dismissing a long-time trainer diagnosed with trauma-induced epilepsy (Walter, 2009).

Although accommodations vary based on the situation, examples of those that are typically found to be reasonable accommodations include the provision of a sign language interpreter for a deaf applicant applying for a job as a ticket taker for a sports arena, the provision of scheduled breaks for the testing of blood glucose levels for a sports franchise equipment manager with diabetes, and the provision of assistance in reading information posted to all employees for a visually impaired telemarketer for a sports agency.

Additionally, ensuring that sports facilities are readily accessible, restructuring job duties, or modifying equipment are just a few strategies sports managers and supervisors can employ to provide reasonable accommodations for employees with disabilities.

Selected Laws of the U.S. Department of Labor

The U.S. DOL (2016c) enforces over 180 federal laws that apply to over 10 million employers. In addition to being responsible for governing laws and regulations, the agency also serves as a repository of information for employers and employees. Sports managers and supervisors may have a general understanding of DOL legislative areas as they relate to employment, but because of the sheer volume of laws, it is more important to be able to locate applicable resources when recognizing a need for expert advice or legal assistance.

Three common laws administered by the DOL include the FLSA, the FMLA, and the Immigration Nationalities Act.

FAIR LABOR STANDARDS ACT (FLSA)

The FLSA establishes standards for wages, overtime, and exemptions. For the FLSA to apply, an organization must have at least 15 employees, and an employee must actually be deemed an "employee" under the law. For instance, FLSA guidelines would not apply to the owner of a batting cage with only three workers or to students volunteering as unpaid interns.

The FLSA requires organizations to pay the state's minimum wage when it is higher than the national minimum. For example, minimum-wage workers at the Staples Center in Los Angeles, California (home of the NBA Clippers, NBA Lakers, Women's National Basketball Association [WNBA] Sparks, and National Hockey League [NHL] Kings) earned the state minimum of $9.00 per hour in 2017 as opposed to the federal minimum of $7.25. Similarly, Florida employees paid minimum wages at the Orlando Citrus Bowl Stadium and George M. Steinbrenner Field in Tampa earn $8.05 per hour (effective January 1, 2015) as opposed to $7.25.

The FLSA also requires employers to provide overtime pay to nonexempt

Minimum wage workers at the Staples Center in Los Angeles earn almost $2.00 more per hour than the national minimum wage due to FLSA regulations.

employees at a rate equivalent to at least one and one-half times his or her regular wages for each hour worked in excess of 40 hours in a workweek. An important, complex, and somewhat controversial component of the FLSA (Section 13 (a)(1)) is the exemption standards from overtime pay for salaried workers qualifying as a professional or executive. To be exempt from overtime pay, FLSA regulations stipulate that salaried workers must earn more than $455 per week ($23,660 annually).

When the DOL (2016a) proposed nearly doubling the wage exemption standard in 2016 to $913 per week ($47,476 annually), many organizations responded by shifting salaried employees to hourly labor or awarded pay increases to low-wage salaried workers who were close to the threshold. However, within days of the new wage-earning standards taking effect, a federal judge filed an injunction, and the mandate was put on hold. Twenty-one states and countless business agencies had claimed that the DOL was overstepping its authority and that the mandate would cause "irreparable harm" (DeSantis, 2016). Despite the financial ramifications for numerous businesses and intercollegiate athletic departments (see **Action Shot 2-3**), the overtime exemption threshold in January 2017 remained at a rate of $455 per week.

The FLSA has also been challenged in the courts with respect to its application to seasonal labor, which is the crux of many sectors of the sports industry. A section in the FSLA provides overtime exemptions for organizations in the business of recreation or entertainment that operate seasonally (less than 7 months per year) (FLSA 13(a)(3)). This exemption has been used both successfully and unsuccessfully by professional sports organizations. For instance, the Sixth Circuit Court concluded that a sports franchise (Cincinnati Reds) was a year-round business and therefore required to pay overtime to maintenance staff workers (*Bridewell v. Cincinnati Reds*, 68 F.3d 136 (6th Cir. 1995)), whereas the Eleventh Circuit Court determined that another baseball sports franchise (Sarasota White Sox) was a seasonal operation and therefore not required to pay employees overtime (*Jeffery v. Sarasota White Sox*, 64 F.3d 590 (11th Cir. 1995)). Under the same FLSA interpretation in the Sarasota White Sox case, the U.S. District Court in New York dismissed a

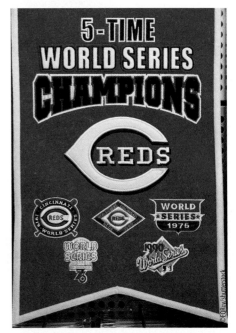

A legal challenge against the MLB Cincinnati Reds affirmed the organization was not exempt from overtime requirements mandated by the Fair Labor Standards Act (FLSA) after trying to convince the court that it was an amusement establishment that operated less than seven months of the year.

▶ ACTION SHOT 2-3

Impact of FLSA Exemption Standards in Intercollegiate Athletics

Only a fraction of college assistant coaches and athletic trainers earn annual salaries greater than $47,476, the new proposed federal minimum standard for exemption from overtime pay announced by U.S. Department of Labor (DOL) in May 2016 (DOL, Wage and Hour Division, 2016a). Athletic directors and presidents feared the financial burden of either increasing salaries or paying overtime or facing the consequences of restricting employee hours to under 40 per week. Within several days of the Fair Labor Standards Act (FLSA) changes taking place, a federal judge filed an injunction, and the new mandate was put on hold.

The detriment to an institution's budget was expected to be in the millions considering the modest salaries provided to administrative and low-end supervisors throughout a college. For example, the revenue estimate for bringing salary lines in compliance with the new federal regulations was reportedly in excess of $60 million for the state university systems in Florida and at least $15 million for Indiana University (Anderson, 2016). The other option for compliance with FLSA salary standards is to ensure that nonexempt employees do not work more than 40 hours per week, which could potentially cause organizations to suffer the consequences of diminished service.

One of the relief points to raising salaries, paying overtime to low-wage earners, or restricting overtime hours is in the interpretation of the FLSA's definition of "exempt" status. Accordingly, an employee's primary, major, or most important duty as a bona fide professional (i.e., teaching or academic administrative roles in higher education) impacts his or her exemption status (DOL, Wage and Hour Division, 2016b, p. 2). The same exemption status is granted to individuals working in a white-collar or professional occupation, such as a doctor or lawyer. On the other hand, professional positions in blue-collar occupations, such as police, security, fire, and emergency personnel, that would be subcontracted or assigned to a sports venue would not qualify for exemption status and therefore would be required to receive overtime pay if working over 40 hours in a week.

Experts in higher education and the National Collegiate Athletic Association (NCAA) have asserted that the "teaching" and "academic advising" status of coaches permits their exemption from overtime pay regardless of whether their salary meets the minimum threshold. Similarly, it has been asserted that intercollegiate athletic trainers may fall under an exemption for "learned professionals." A challenge for enrollment-driven institutions is to assert that the "recruitment" role of coaches in maintaining a minimum squad size is secondary to the role as a teacher.

Although the stipulation for the new minimum did not go into effect in December of 2016, the FLSA regulations remain a controversial area that is being highly monitored by universities and conference offices. Individuals tasked with human resource duties for athletics personnel must understand the legislation and remain ethical when determining exemptions and salary implications to ensure compliance with all federal mandates. In the interim, while states continue to lobby against the new legislation, universities will continue to closely monitor hours and responsibilities.

BOX 2-2

FLSA Policy Impact in Sports Organizations

The following two cases includes an analysis of whether a particular position within the sports industry would be exempt from Fair Labor Standards Act (FLSA) overtime eligibility.

Case A

Position: A retail sales associate at a sports team's merchandise store located in the team's arena

Facts: The retail sales associate is hired at a rate of $9.50 per hour. That employee will generally work 36–40 hours per week, earning on average $360 per week.

Analysis: For an individual to be exempt under any of the exemption tests, the first part of each test states that an individual must be compensated on a salary basis at a rate not less than $455 per week. The retail sales associate makes $9.50 per hour, which is not a salary basis, so this easily does not meet the criteria for exempt status. In addition, the individual earnings total of $360 per week is less than the $455 per week minimum requirement. Therefore, the employee is not exempt, and the employer must pay overtime.

Case B

Position: A vice president of ticket sales for a professional sports franchise

Facts: A vice president (VP) of ticket sales is hired by a professional sports team at a salary of $100,000 per year. The VP will oversee all ticket sales and ticket operation functions for the team. This position will be responsible for all employment decisions (hiring, firing, promotions, performance evaluations) for 25 ticket sales and operations staff members.

Analysis: For a VP of ticket sales, the executive exemption test will be used to determine whether this position is exempt from FLSA.

1. For an employee to be exempt, that employee must be compensated on a salary basis at a rate not less than $455 per week. The VP of ticket sales is paid on a salary basis and is paid at a rate of $100,000 per year, which is over $1923 per week ($100,000 divided by 52 weeks). Therefore, the VP meets the minimum salary standard criterion.

2. The employee's primary duty must be managing the enterprise or a customarily recognized department or subdivision. Ticket sales is a customarily recognized department in sports organizations, and the VP will oversee all efforts of this department. Therefore, because the VP manages a customarily recognized department, the second criterion has been met.

3. The employee must customarily and regularly direct the work of at least two or more full-time employees or their equivalent. In this case, the VP oversees 25 employees of the ticket sales department and therefore meets the third criterion for the exemption.

4. The employee must have the authority to hire or fire other employees, or the employee's suggestions are given particular weight in hiring/firing decisions. In this case, the VP hires and fires all staff and therefore meets the fourth requirement.

The VP of ticket sales meets all four criteria and therefore qualifies as an exempt employee. The employer is not required to pay overtime for time worked over 40 hours per week.

class-action case against the MLB on behalf of 2000 Fan Fest volunteers during the annual All Star weekend at the Jacob K. Javits Center because the Fan Fest met the conditions as an amusement establishment operating for less than 7 months per year (Calder, 2014; Cho & Smith, 2015). **Box 2-2** provides two examples of the application of FLSA policies in sports organizations.

FAMILY AND MEDICAL LEAVE ACT

A second important law under the U.S. DOL is the FMLA. The law provides eligible employees with the ability to take an *unpaid, job-protected* leave for certain family and medical reasons. **Box 2-3** identifies the general coverage areas for applying FMLA policies in addition to eligibility requirements for taking up to 26 weeks of unpaid job-protected leave in a 12-month period. Similarly, **Box 2-4** elaborates on the eligibility for taking up to 12 weeks of unpaid job-protected leave.

Sports managers and supervisors must work within the scope of FMLA policies to provide eligible employees time off. In 2009, a high school teacher and football coach who was fired from his coaching duties after taking FMLA time was granted over $200,000 by the school district (*Gary Community School Corporation v. Tom Powell*, 2008-45S03-0809-CV-482 (2008)). Although the case focused on the school's retaliation for exercising the right to use FMLA and rather than denial of the benefit, it highlights the availability of the federal law for both male and female employees. Additional information on the application of FMLA law within the sports industry is provided in chapter 4 addressing compensation and benefits administration.

BOX 2-3

Family and Medical Leave Act

Time off for a coach, trainer, or any employee to care for a newborn baby or for a sick family member is guaranteed by the Family and Medical Leave Act (FMLA) of the U.S. Department of Labor (DOL). An eligible employee is entitled to 26 workweeks of unpaid, job-protected leave during a single 12-month period to care for a covered individual with a serious injury or illness if the eligible employee is the individual's spouse, son, daughter, parent, or next of kin. The policy is inclusive of spouses in same-sex marriages (DOL, Wage and Hour Division, 2015).

Employees are eligible for FMLA if they (a) work for a covered employer, (b) have worked for the employer for at least 12 months, (c) have had at least 1250 hours of service to the employer during the 12-month period immediately preceding the leave, and (d) work at a location where the employer has at least 50 employees in 20 or more hours of workweeks within 75 miles (DOL, Wage and Hour Division, 2012).

BOX 2-4

Family Medical Leave: Conditions for Using up to 12 Weeks of Unpaid Leave

Under the Family and Medical Leave Act (FMLA), eligible employees can take up to 12 weeks of unpaid leave in the following situations:

- The birth of a child and to care for the newborn child within 1 year of birth

- The placement with the employee of a child for adoption or foster care and to care for the newly placed child within 1 year of placement

- To care for the employee's spouse, child, or parent who has a serious health condition

- A serious health condition that makes the employee unable to perform the essential functions of his or her job

- Any qualifying emergency arising out of the fact that the employee's spouse, son, daughter, or parent is a covered military member on "covered active duty."

Although FMLA is a federal regulation, states have opted to provide paid coverage. In December of 2016, the District of Columbia passed a bill permitting up to 11 weeks of paid leave for the birth or adoption of a child (Associated Press, 2016). New York is expected to follow suit in 2018, and California, New Jersey, and Rhode Island already provide paid leave for family issues as an extension of the FMLA. The programs are funded either through payroll taxes on businesses (District of Columbia) or through employee contribution programs.

IMMIGRATION AND NATIONALITY ACT

The DOL works with the U.S. Department of Homeland Security to govern laws and provide advisement on employing immigrants. Obviously, professional sports are inundated with foreign-born players, which challenges managers and human resource personnel to continually work with federal agencies to ensure compliance. Non-U.S. citizens are also employed in university athletic departments and sports club systems as coaches, trainers, and administrators. One of the unique aspects of sports is the global connectivity of individuals through competition, media productions, and sale of apparel/equipment. It is an industry that attracts foreign-born talent.

The United States Department of Homeland Security works in conjunction with the Department of Labor to regulate employment of foreign-born citizens.

Sports managers and supervisors charged with overseeing immigration compliance must be aware of such issues as knowing that J visas have certain limitations (time and scope of training) and H-1B visas are subject to a maximum number of approvals each year. Attorneys, paralegals, and immigration specialists assist with determining the appropriate status and paperwork required for non-U.S. citizens.

The Immigration and Nationality Act administered by the DOL quantifies the number (and type) of foreign immigrants who may work in the United States from a given country. Regardless of citizenship, upon being hired in the United States, all individuals must verify their identity with their employers and the U.S. government. The most common document serving as proof or verification of identity is an unexpired foreign passport with an I-94 card attached indicating employment authorization. Other acceptable identity-verification documents for a non-U.S. citizen include the following:

1. Alien Registration Receipt Card (I-151 or I-551)
2. Unexpired Temporary Card (I-688)
3. Unexpired Reentry Permit (I-327)
4. Unexpired Refugee Travel Document (I-571)

In addition to verification of identification, federal law requires non-U.S. citizens to obtain a visa to work in the United States. There are generally two types of working visas granted to non-U.S. citizens: those issued to individuals who wish to permanently live in the United States and those granted to individuals who wish to work in the United States only temporarily. **Table 2-1** lists the categories of employment visas that may be relevant to sports organizations.

TABLE 2-1: Employment Visa Categories

B-1	Business visitor (not paid by U.S. company)
F	Student
H-1B	Specialty occupations in fields requiring highly specialized knowledge
J	Trainee
P	Performing athlete, artist, entertainer
I	Media, journalist
O	Foreign national with extraordinary ability in sciences, arts, education, business, or athletics
TN/TD	North American Free Trade Agreement (NAFTA) professional worker

Knowledge of visa processes and immigration laws is important in sports organizations such as teams in the NHL, where over half of its professional players are foreigners. MLB and the NBA are both steadily filling roster spots with professional athletes from countries in Latin and South America. Prudent managerial practices require organizations to understand and comply with DOL federal laws for hiring a foreign-born player, coach, trainer, or support staff.

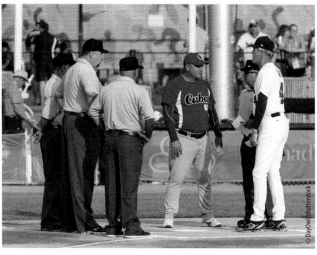

The MLB Tampa Rays faced immigration and visa issues during the team's historic 2016 exhibition tour to compete against Cuba's national team.

Sports managers and human resource specialists in the United States must also comply with immigration policies in other countries when their employees are on work-related trips outside of America. For example, personnel in the MLB Tampa Rays office had to handle immigration issues when the 2016 squad traveled to Havana, Cuba, for the historic exhibition game against Cuba's national team. There are always risks for immigrants to be refused new visas or reentry into the United States or their home countries.

In addition to professional franchises, national governing sports entities, such as U.S.A. Track and Field (USATF), also deal with federal immigration laws. On an annual basis, the USATF receives several hundred requests from international athletes seeking P (1) or O (1) visas to provide written statements detailing how the athletes are internationally recognized. The USATF headquarters office in Indianapolis, Indiana, receives an abundance of requests from athletes native to Kenya and Ethiopia but also writes letters for athletes native to Morocco, Jamaica, Canada, Great Britain, the Netherlands, Turkey, Russia, Djibouti, and Trinidad and Tobago. The USATF has also provided letters of support for U.S. athletes who wish to compete in other countries that require permission for entry, such as Italy, Japan, Costa Rica, and Spain (S. Austin, personal communication, April 21, 2016).

Recap

"Managers need to know about employment law not to 'play lawyer,' but rather to institute policies that prevent violations, recognize situations that raise legal concerns, and know when to seek legal advice" (Walsh, 2016). Because of the complex nature of employment law at the federal, state, and local levels, it is imperative for sports supervisors and managers to have access to experts in the field. The first step in broadly understanding employment law is to know whether a particular law applies to an organization. To determine the applicability of many employment laws, the organization must know whether the business operates as a public (e.g., a municipal recreation center) or a private (e.g., a commercial sports facility) entity, and the organization must know the specific number of full-time and part-time employees.

The NLRB, the U.S. DOL, and the Equal Employment Opportunities Commission (EEOC) are three federal agencies that govern employment law in the United States. The NLRB and DOL govern general labor employment laws. The NLRB oversees the NLRA, which has protected employees' rights to form unions and to bargain with employers over working conditions since 1935. The NLRB governs the collective bargaining process in professional sports.

The EEOC governs laws related to discrimination, such as Title VII, the FMLA, and the ADA. The OCR, through the U.S. Department of Education, is another federal agency governing employment discrimination cases; however, its authority applies only to entities receiving federal education funding. Cases of employment discrimination cite claims of disparate treatment, disparate impact, retaliation, or a failure to reasonably accommodate a disability or religious belief.

The DOL oversees some 180 employment laws. Several of these laws especially common in the sports industry include the FLSA, the FMLA, and the Immigration and Nationality Act. The unique nature of the sports industry as a global commodity through competition, media exposure, and the sale of apparel and shoes has created the need for sports managers and supervisors to be aware of applicable immigration issues and laws.

The underlying notion of employment law in the sports industry is to understand the obligation to remain compliant even in the absence of large human resource departments or in-house legal counsel to oversee rules and regulations for hiring, discipline, and other employment functions. The key for most sports supervisors and managers is to have access to legal experts to receive advisement and consultation on employment matters.

Nike: Discrimination Case in the Netherlands

In 2008, NEON, a wholly owned subsidiary of Nike Inc., a European operation in Hilversum, the Netherlands, allegedly engaged in age and sex discrimination in its termination of Loredana Ranza. A former product-line sales manager for NEON working for the Nike subsidiary since 1998, Ranza received a severance package equivalent to over $200,000 USD. She initially filed complaints with the Netherlands' Dutch Equal Treatment Commission and with the Equal Opportunity Employment Commission (EEOC) in the United States. Both commissions independently concluded that the plaintiff's claims "lacked merit."

© Rose Carson/shutterstock

Following the decisions, Ranza filed a lawsuit in the U.S. District Court of Oregon, which was referred to a magistrate judge. The judge articulated that because the alleged discrimination occurred in the Netherlands, and the relevant documents and witnesses were also located in Europe, it would be a hardship for Nike to defend itself in the district court of Oregon, despite the fact that Nike, a global brand of sports footwear and apparel, is based in Oregon. In statements publicizing the decision on July 16, 2015, the Ninth Circuit upheld the dismissal of the lawsuit, citing that it was "inefficient" and "inadvisable" to relitigate claims that had already been considered by a lower court and that had been determined to lack merit according to the Dutch Equal Treatment Commission and the EEOC (U.S. Court of Appeals Ninth Circuit, No. 13-3251 (2015)).

This case demonstrates the need to consider the adequate and convenient court to litigate a plaintiff's claims, whether in a different state or a different country. The case also provides an example of entities in other countries that are responsible for adjudicating violations of equal protection laws and matters of employment discrimination. Finally, the case demonstrates to employers that a well-drafted employment agreement may avoid the cost and time of bringing a jurisdictional motion in the first place.

DISCUSSION QUESTIONS

1. What can a sports manager do to minimize legal risk in relation to hiring an employee?
2. Explain the difference between disparate treatment and disparate impact.
3. Explain why an organization with only five employees is not required to comply with Title VII of the Civil Rights Act of 1964.
4. Speculate on how the enhanced diplomatic relationship between Cuba and the U.S. government present in 2016 might impact the future of immigration in professional sports.

APPLIED ACTIVITIES

1. SPORT Incorporated is a private professional sports team with 75 employees. The president of SPORT Incorporated has recently hired three new employees. Determine the FLSA status of each new employee. Include your analysis for each determination.

   a. Employee A has been hired as a director of group sales at a salary of $75,000 per year. Employee A will oversee group ticket sales but will not oversee any employees.

   b. Employee B has been hired as a box office associate at a rate of $8.00 per hour. Employee B expects to work between 15 and 20 hours per week and will not oversee any employees.

   c. Employee C has been hired as the vice president of sales at a salary of $100,000 per year. Employee C will oversee all operations of the club, including revenue generation and facility operation.

2. Assume the role of a manager of an indoor–outdoor watersports action resort that operates 12 months per year. The role includes designing a training session on employment laws for new employees, of which one is female, one is disabled, one is African, and one is Muslim. Select the laws you believe are most applicable to the employees to protect them from discrimination. Provide a brief description of each law and the potential impact on each employee.

CASE STUDY

Legal Implication of Northwestern Football Team's Union Attempt

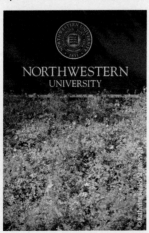

When intercollegiate athletic departments consider legal issues related to human resource planning, the focus is on complying with state and federal laws in the recruitment, hiring, and administration of services for coaches and staff members, not student-athletes. Student-athletes have historically not been considered "employees." The highlights from the landmark case of Northwestern University's football players who attempted to form a union are the consideration of who qualifies as an "employee," the rights and privileges of employees, and how jurisdiction plays a role in the adjudication of a decision.

Case Facts

In a revolutionary decision made on March 26, 2014, Peter Ohr, the director of a regional branch of the National Labor Relations Board (NLRB), ruled that scholarship members of the football team at Northwestern University qualified as statutory employees under the National Labor Relations Act and could therefore legally form the first union for college players (NLRB, 2015). The university filed an appeal, and almost 2 years later, the five members of the federal NLRB (2015) unanimously agreed to dismiss the players' petition to qualify as a union (Cancino, 2015; Kelderman, 2015; Tracy, 2015).

Northwestern is one of over 120 institutions competing in the Division I National Collegiate Athletic Association's (NCAA) Football Bowl Subdivision. A member of the Big Ten Conference, the football program is one of 19 varsity sports programs at the university (Northwestern, 2017). The bid to form a union was championed by Ramogi Huma, president of the National College Players Association (NCPA), which is a nonprofit organization with over 17,000 members supported by the United Steelworkers Union (NCPA, 2017). According to a profile on the NCPA (2017) website, Huma's motivation behind forming a players' association came after witnessing the NCAA suspend his UCLA teammate for accepting groceries when his monthly scholarship money ran out. Among the points of contention noted by the athletes at Northwestern petitioning for a union were the following three items:

1. Financial coverage of sport-related medical expenses for current and former players,
2. An educational trust fund to assist former players in finishing graduation requirements, and
3. The right to receive royalties or fees for commercial sponsorship deals from video games, memorabilia, and so forth. (Cancino, 2015)

Ballots were cast by members of the football team in April 2014 but were immediately impounded and not counted due to the NLRB's consideration of the appeal. Briefs were filed in May 2014, and 17 months after officials at Northwestern University appealed the regional ruling declaring that scholarship football players had the right to form a union, a reverse decision was rendered by the NLRB. On August 17, 2015, the Office of Congressional Public Affairs issued a press release on the Northwestern case decision stating that the NRLB (2015) was declining to assert jurisdiction, and therefore the petition for union representation by Northwestern players was officially dismissed.

Rationale for Considering Scholarship Athletes as Employees

Peter Sung Ohr's determination that scholarship football players are employees stems from an interpretation of the common or broad definition of an employee within the scope of the National Labor Relations Act. Generally, an employee is "a person in the service of another under any contract of hire, express or implied, oral or written, where the employer has the power or right to control and direct the employee in the material details of how the work is to be performed" (Garner, 2014).

The legal team for the players' association argued that college football is a commercial enterprise relying on labor to generate billions of dollars in revenue, which therefore creates an employee–employer relationship between scholarship athletes and the school (Bennett, 2014). Ohr's brief indicated that Northwestern's football program produced over $230 million in revenue between 2003 and 2012, and players worked 50 to 60 hours per season (Culhane, 2015). The regional director concluded in a 24-page opinion that scholarships were the form of compensation, and the coaches were the supervisors or managers directing how work was to be performed (Farry, 2015). Basically, Ohr suggested that players were hired, paid, and controlled by Northwestern and that scholarships were payment for their athletic services on the field, not in a classroom.

Case precedent indicates that some private institutions have permitted graduate teaching assistants and research assistants to form a union despite a 2004 NLRB decision stating that graduate assistants at private institutions were primarily students with an educational, not economic, relationship with their institutions (Wolverton, 2014). In Ohr's view, there are striking similarities between graduate assistants and student-athletes, which strengthens the rationale to argue for the right to unionize and be classified as institutional/statutory employees under Ohr's interpretation of the common definition of an employee.

Rationale for the NLRB Decision

The rationale for the NLRB (2015) to dismiss the petition for the Northwestern football players' bid to unionize was a lack of jurisdiction. The board asserted lack of jurisdiction primarily because as a single entity in the NCAA Football Bowl Subdivision, Northwestern University is not representative of the entire league, which comprises over 125 teams, of which a majority are state run. The NLRB concluded that it does not have jurisdiction over public, state-run institutions.

Northwestern is a private institution, and the only private institution in the Big Ten Conference (Kelderman, 2015). If certified as a union, the players at Northwestern would be bargaining labor issues with a single employer over policies that have ramifications for all schools in their division. Therefore, the NLRB concluded that it does not have jurisdiction, and Northwestern's football players would not be permitted to form a union.

Issues to Consider

- The NLRB did not rule on whether or not scholarship athletes are considered employees. The board basically said "no comment" by asserting a lack of jurisdiction over a single institution that competes in a large subdivision. Between the time of the regional ruling and the federal decision in August 2015, Ohio enacted a state law stating that student-athletes at public universities are not employees.

- A position statement by the president of the American Council on Education (2015) indicated that under federal labor laws, students cannot be classified as employees and "to do so would be an unprecedented intrusion into the educational missions of universities that would impinge on academic freedom and only serve to exacerbate many of the problems critics find with intercollegiate athletics." In response to the initial union proposal, the chief legal officer for the NCAA (2016) stated that athletes are not employees because they volunteer to participate in sports.

- Since the decision, the Big Ten Conference has made a commitment to guarantee multi-year scholarships and improve medical coverage. Additionally, many other conferences and universities have pledged greater scholarship protection and better health care (Tracy, 2015). Food restrictions for student-athletes have been lifted, and a U.S. federal judge ruled that players can receive compensation for the use of their images and that universities should create trust funds for athletes after they leave college (Farry, 2015).

CASE STUDY QUESTIONS

1. What are the legal and factual arguments that can be made to support the ruling of Peter Sung Ohr that scholarship football players at Northwestern University are employees and have the right to form a union?

2. What were the weaknesses of the argument that made the NLRB overturn the ruling, and what arguments could be made to make the ruling stand in a future similar situation?

3. What are the legal and factual arguments that can be made to support the decision of the federal NLRB? What would need to change for the NLRB to determine that it would indeed have jurisdiction in a similar situation?

4. What are the legal implications related to human resource planning for sports organizations that are apparent in the case of the Northwestern University football players' attempt to form a union?

5. What are the arguments for and against scholarship student-athletes being considered statutory employees under the National Labor Relations Act?

6. If permitted to form a union, what rights and privileges under the Fair Labor Standards Act could scholarship student-athletes address in collective bargaining? What other labor issues could be addressed in collective bargaining?

7. Predict the status of student-athletes at NCAA institutions in 25 years from a human resource perspective. Consider issues related to working (practice and playing) conditions, compensation, and fair treatment.

Laws:

Civil Rights Act of 1964 § 7, 42 U.S.C. §2000e et seq. (1964).

Executive Order 11246, Part II, Subpart B, Sect. 202 (1).

Title IX of the Education Amendments of 1972, 20 U.S.C. §§ 1681–1688.

Cases:

Bridewell v. Cincinnati Reds, 68 F.3d 136 (6th Cir. 1995)

Gary Community School Corporation v. Tom Powell (State of Indiana 45S03-0809-CV-482 (2008))

Green et al. v. Washington Nationals Baseball Club LLC, case number 1:15-cv-00505 (U.S. District Court for the District of Columbia, April 7, 2015)

Jeffery v. Sarasota White Sox, 64 F.3d 590 (11th Cir. 1995)

Loredana Ranza v. Nike, Inc., 13-3251 (9th Cir. 2015)

McDonnell-Douglas v. Green, 411 U.S. 792 (1973)

Morris v. Wallace Community College-Selma, 125 F.Supp. 2d 1315 (S.D. Ala. 2001)

REFERENCES

Altman, B. (2015, April 9). Washington Nationals lawsuit: "Reckless disregard of the rights of the plaintiffs." *CBS Sports*. Retrieved from http://washington.cbslocal.com/2015/04/09/washington-nationals-lawsuit-reckless-disregard-of-the-rights-of-the-plaintiffs/

American Council on Education. (2015, August 17). *Statement by ACE President Molly Corbett on the National Labor Relation Board's decision in the Northwestern student-athlete case.* Retrieved from http://www.acenet.edu/news-room/Pages/Statement-by-ACE-President-Molly-Corbett-Broad-on-the-National-Labor-Relations-Boards-decision-in-the-Northwestern-Student.aspx

Anderson, D. (2016, March 29). Potentially dire impacts. *Inside Higher Ed*. Retrieved from https://www.insidehighered.com/views/2016/03/29/proposed-new-overtime-pay-regulations-could-negatively-impact-colleges-and-their

Associated Press. (2014, December 11). Iowa reassigns associate AD Jane Meyer. *ESPN*. Retrieved from http://espn.go.com/college-sports/story/_/id/12017480/iowa-hawkeyes-reassign-associate-ad-jane-meyer-facilities-management-office-amid-threat-wrongful-termination-lawsuit-partner

Associated Press. (2015, March 17). 5 ways that an Iowa open records law exemption shields info. *Newton Daily News*. Retrieved from http://www.newtondailynews.com/2015/03/16/5-ways-that-an-iowa-open-records-law-exemption-shields-info/auxusrz/

Associated Press. (2016, November 29). DC lawmakers to vote next week on generous family leave benefits. *Advertiser Tribune* (Tiffin, Ohio), 5A.

Bennett, B. (2014, March 27). Northwestern players get union vote. *ESPN*. Retrieved from http://espn.go.com/college-football/story/_/id/10677763/northwestern-wildcats-football-players-win-bid-unionize

Bersegal, A. (2012, April 15). Is there a *stare decisis* doctrine in the Court of Arbitration for sport? An analysis of published awards for anti-doping disputes in Track and Field. *Pepperdine Dispute Resolution Law Journal, 12*(2), 188–213.

Calder, R. (2014, March 267). Judge tosses FanFest volunteer suit against MLB. *New York Post*. Retrieved from http://nypost.com/?s=rich+calder+mlb+volunteers

Cancino, A. (2015, August 18). Labor board dismisses Northwestern union petition; whether players are school employees is left undecided. *Baltimore Sun*, 3D.

Charis-Carlson, J. (2016, November 23). Jane Meyer files new claim against IU in federal court. *The DesMoines Register*. Retrieved from http://www .desmoinesregister.com/story/news/education/university-of-iowa/2016/11/23 /jane-meyer-files-new-claim-against-ui-federal-court/94349684/

Cho, S., & Smith, J. (2015). *Chen v. Major League Baseball*: Hybrid collective action under rule 23 and the Fair Labor Standards Act 216(b). *Journal of Legal Aspects of Sport, 25,* 154–175.

Claybault, D. (2012, December 30). Fear of flying offers workplace lessons. A*tlanta Journal Constitution*, 2D.

Clayworth, J. (2014, December 17). Second woman makes retaliation claim against UI. *Des Moines Register*. Retrieved from http://www.desmoinesregister .com/story/news/crime-and-courts/2014/12/17/university-iowa-retaliation -claim-teresa-wagner-jane-meyer/20548017/

Cooney, B. (2015, July 29). Former field hockey coach intends to file lawsuit against UI. *Daily Iowan*. Retrieved from http://www.dailyiowan.com/2015/07/29 /Metro/42656.html

Culhane, J. (2015, August 19). *College football players deserve the right to unionize.* Retrieved from http://www.slate.com/articles/sports/sports_nut/2015/08 /northwestern_unionization_how_the_national_labor_relations_board_failed .html

DeSantis, N. (2016, November 22). Federal judge blocks Obama's overtime rule. *Chronicle of Higher Education*. Retrieved from http://www.chronicle.com/blogs /ticker/federal-judge-blocks-obamas-overtime-pay-rule/115716

Farry, T. (2015, August 17). Northwestern players denied request to form first union for athletes. *ESPN*. Retrieved from http://espn.go.com/college-football/story /_/id/13455477/nlrb-says-northwestern-players-cannot-unionize

Garner, B. (Ed.). (2014). *Black's law dictionary* (10th ed.). Eagan, MN: West Group Publishing.

Grow, N. (2015, April 8). *Washington National sued for religious discrimination.* Retrieved from http://www.fangraphs.com/blogs/instagraphs/washington -nationals-sued-for-religious-discrimination/

Guilbeau, G. (2015, July 5). No love in tennis coach lawsuit against LSU. *USA Today*. Retrieved from http://www.usatoday.com/story/sports/college/2014/07/05 /lsu-tennis-coach-lawsuit-joe-alleva/12254483/

Guyan, A., & Clifton, G. (2015, June 11). The NCAA and transgender student-athlete participation. *Collegiate and Professional Sport Law Blog*. Retrieved from http://www.collegeandprosportslaw.com/uncategorized /the-ncaa-and-transgender-student-athlete-participation/

Herald-Sun. (2014, December 10). Iowa reassigns administrator, citing partner's case, B2.

Internal Revenue Service. (2015). *IRS independent contractor or employee.* Retrieved from http://www.irs.gov/Businesses/Small-Businesses-&-Self-Employed /Independent-Contractor-Self-Employed-or-Employee

Jordan, E. (2016, August 29). University of Iowa may dismiss Jane Meyer, judge rules. *The Gazette.* Retrieved from http://www.thegazette.com/subject/news/education /higher-education/university-of-iowa-may-dismiss-jane-meyer-judge-rules-20160829

Kelderman, E. (2015, September 9). Labor bar sets high bar for college athlete unions. *Chronicle of Higher Education, 62*(1), A22.

Mann, J. (2012, June 1). Former Rams employee claims bias in firing equipment manager says he was let go because of his age. *St. Louis Post Dispatch* (Missouri), News, A3.

Mullineaux, J. (2016). The latest NFL fumble. Using its commissioner as the sole arbitrator. *University of Missouri Journal of Dispute Resolution*, No. 229.

National College Players Association. (2017). *About.* Retrieved from http://www .ncpanow.org/about

National Collegiate Athletic Association. (2016). *NCAA responds to union proposal.* Retrieved from http://www.ncaa.org/about/resources/media-center /press-releases/ncaa-responds-union-proposal

National Labor Relations Board. (2015, August 17). *Board unanimously decides to decline jurisdiction in Northwestern Case.* Retrieved from https://www.nlrb.gov/news-outreach /news-story/board-unanimously-decides-decline-jurisdiction-northwestern-case

Northwestern. (2017). *Facts and figures. Northwestern University.* Retrieved from http://www.northwestern.edu/about/

O'Leary, J. (2015, February 14). Griesbaum: Numbers speak on UI gender bias. *Iowa City Press Citizen.* Retrieved from http://www.press-citizen.com/story/news /local/2015/02/13/griesbaum-ui-athletics-gender-bias-numbers/23388271/

Sports Business News. (2016, October 28). Ex-assistant Mike McQueary awarded over $7 million in Penn State defamation case. *Sports Business News.* Retrieved from http://sportsbusinessnews.com/content/ex-assistant-mike-mcqueary -awarded-over-7m-penn-state-defamation-case

Toutant, C. (2015, June 29). Rider faces Title IX suit over softball coaches' dismissal. New Jersey Law Journal. Retrieved from http://www.njlawjournal.com /id=1202730868155/Rider-Faces-TX-IX-Suit-Over-Softball-Coachs-Dismissal

Tracy, M. (2015, August 18). Union ruling underlines NCAA evolution. *New York Times,* B7.

United Kingdom Health and Safety Executive. (2017). *Information about adventure activities licensing.* Retrieved from http://www.hse.gov.uk/aala/about -activities-licensing.htm

U.S. Amateur Athletic Union, Inc. (2016). *Constitution of the United States Amateur Athletic Union, Inc. Article I.* Lake Buena Vista, FL: Author.

U.S. Department of Education, Office for Civil Rights. (1991, August). *Nondiscrimination in employment practices in education.* Retrieved from http://www2 .ed.gov/about/offices/list/ocr/docs/hq53e8.html

U.S. Department of Justice, Civil Rights Division. (2015). *Introduction to ADA. Information and assistance on the American Disabilities Act.* Retrieved from http://www.ada.gov/ada_intro.htm

U.S. Department of Labor. (2016a). *Exemptions—Fair Labor Standards Act.* Retrieved from http://www.dol.gov/elaws/esa/flsa/screen75.asp

U.S. Department of Labor. (2016b). *Our mission.* Retrieved from https://www.dol
.gov/general/aboutdol/mission

U.S. Department of Labor. (2016c). *Summary of the major laws of the Department of Labor.* Retrieved from https://www.dol.gov/general/aboutdol/majorlaws

U.S. Department of Labor, Wage and Hour Division. (2012). *Fact sheet 28: The Family and Medical Leave Act.* Retrieved from https://www.dol.gov/whd/regs /compliance/whdfs28.pdf.

U.S. Department of Labor, Wage and Hour Division. (2014, May). *Fact sheet 13: Am I an employee? Employment relationship under the Fair Labor Standards Act.* Retrieved from https://www.dol.gov/whd/regs/compliance/whdfs13.pdf

U.S. Department of Labor, Wage and Hour Division. (2015, March 27). *Family and Medical Leave Act. Final rule to revise the definition of "spouse" under the FMLA.* Retrieved from https://www.dol.gov/whd/fmla/spouse/index.htm

U.S. Department of Labor, Wage and Hour Division. (2016a, May 16). *Fact sheet: Final rule to update the regulations defining and delimiting the exemption for executive, administrative, and professional employees.* Retrieved from https:// www.dol.gov/whd/overtime/final2016/overtime-factsheet.htm

U.S. Department of Labor, Wage and Hour Division. (2016b, May 18). *Guidance for higher education institutions on paying overtime under the Fair Labor Standards Act.* Retrieved from https://www.dol.gov/whd/overtime/final2016/highered -guidance.pdf

Walsh, David J. (2016). *Employment law for human resource practice* (5th ed.). Mason, OH: Cengage Learning.

Walter, D. (2009, August 19). St. Louis Rams settle discrimination case. *Missouri Lawyers Media.* Retrieved from http://molawyersmedia.com/2009/10/12 /st-louis-rams-settle-discrimination-case/

Wolverton, B. (2014, January 29). College football athletes seek to form a labor union. *Chronicle of Higher Education.*

CHAPTER 3

Hard Knocks

NEGOTIATIONS IN THE SPORTS INDUSTRY

Courtesy of Darryl Greene

Before the Windsor Express of the National Basketball League of Canada won the 2014 championship, their star player and the Finals MVP had the opportunity to sign a contract in Europe. The offer of $5000 of tax-free money for 9 months to play in France was twice what he was earning in Canada for only 4 months, but he turned it down to stay with the Express. After the season, I was able to arrange a spot for him to tour China and play exhibition games against teams in the Chinese Basketball Association, which is known for signing a lot of former National Basketball Association (NBA) players such as Tracy McGrady and Ron Artest. When one of the teams offered him a 10- to 11-day contract for $30,000 to replace an injured regular, he jumped at the chance without contacting his agent. The player he replaced was earning $1.7 million, which, when broken down, meant our guy should have negotiated a deal for over $100,000. The guy also didn't read the fine print in his standard league contract, which explained that if a player is released midseason, he is ineligible to play for any other team in China for the remainder of the year. His next move was to play for $2500 a month in Iceland, where he became the leading scorer on the continent. The kid lost a lot of money because he didn't think he needed to negotiate through an agent. The moral of the story is don't bite off the hand that feeds you. Loyalty means a lot in this business.

Darryl Greene

President, National Basketball League of America
Certified Player Agent, NBA
Former Director of Player Personnel, Windsor Express
President and General Manager, Omaha Chargers and Dakota Magic

83

LEARNING OUTCOMES

1. Distinguish between integrative and distributive negotiations, and provide an example of each strategy as it is applicable in the sports industry.
2. Identify the five stages of negotiations.
3. Identify components of employment agreements and collective bargaining agreements that may be negotiated.
4. Explain the correlation between styles of negotiations and conflict resolution techniques.
5. Describe how mediation and arbitration may be used to settle labor disputes in sports.

KEY TERMS

Agreement	Dispute	Noncompete clause
Alternative dispute resolution	Distributive negotiations	Outsourcing
	Integrative negotiations	Reassignment clause
Arbitration	Labor relations	Reservation point
At-will employee	Lockout	Rollover clause
Bargaining range	Mediation	Severance pay
Breach of contract	Memorandum of understanding	Strike
Buyout clause		Tactical vendor
Collective bargaining	Moral turpitude	Termination
Collective bargaining agreement	Negotiations	Union
	Negotiation strategy	Vendor management
Contract	Negotiation style	

Lead-Off

Sports agents and league presidents are just a couple positions in the industry where negotiation skills are important. All types of sports managers, supervisors, athletic directors, and even human resource personnel benefit from being able to effectively negotiate deals. Knowledge and practice with strategic planning and employment law are the building blocks for negotiating employment agreements, but the scope of negotiations for labor management and human resources includes other territories.

Negotiations are actions or discussions between two or more parties for the purpose of arranging an agreement or transaction. There are numerous types of agreements and contracts managers in the sports industry may be accustomed to negotiating, including those pertaining to employment, benefits and insurance, third-party vendor services, sponsorships, dispute resolution, and collective bargaining.

An **agreement** is a less formal means of designating an obligation between two entities, whether it is one party accepting an offer from another or an actual two-way exchange of promises. A **contract**, on the other hand, is a legally binding agreement between and accepted by two entities enforceable by a judicial court system. The essential difference is that an agreement doesn't place an obligation on either side to provide consideration or a value assigned for the exchange of a service or promise by the other party. It is a matter of discretion for most sports organizations as to whether a contract or an agreement is used for employing personnel; however, contracts are the norm in professional leagues (i.e., standard player contracts) and when procuring outsourced services such as accounting and legal counsel.

The value of effective negotiation skills spans far beyond the ability to effectively engage in the collective bargaining process or agree to the bonus pay structure for postseason play or targeted graduation rates. Negotiations are important in everyday business operations. The ability to negotiate is simply an important skill for sports managers and supervisors.

Negotiations are a large part of dispute or conflict resolution, whether applied to two employees, departments, or vendors or to a larger labor relations issue between management and workers. Intercollegiate athletic directors, for example, are accustomed to negotiating typical **disputes** with or between their coaches over items such as extra job duties, compensatory time for weekend work, overlapping practice times in a single facility, squad sizes or travel parties, locker-room space, per diems, and transportation preferences. Negotiating terms for the myriad of insurance and healthcare benefits for an organization in addition to simply securing third-party services (e.g., accounting, legal representation, security, payroll, etc.) are other areas where sports managers need to acquire skills to effectively leverage relationships and close a deal.

Effective negotiations for sports managers and supervisors potentially lead to substantial economic benefits for the organization and build mutually favorable relationships with employees and/or supply vendors. Negotiation is an essential skill that affects profitability and organizational performance. Generally, managers and supervisors in sports organizations are responsible for negotiating a variety of matters and activities related to human resources (see **Box 3-1**).

Negotiations may involve a third party (sports agent) or legal representative, such as Darryl Greene. The sports agency representation business is

BOX 3-1

Selected Human Resource Issues and Items Negotiated in Sports Organizations

- Employee salaries, raises, and promotions
- Employee disputes
- Prices and terms for retaining or outsourcing third-party services (e.g., legal counsel, accounting, security, technology, marketing, cleaning, hospitality, concessions, merchandising, printing, ticket sales, etc.)
- Prices, availability, and terms of employee insurance policies and benefits (retirement, disability, etc.)
- Equitable systems for determining company policies, such as vacation approval, suspension terms, or break periods

- Provisions of a merger or acquisition (e.g., Dick's Sporting Goods' acquisition of Sports Authority stores after the latter declared bankruptcy in 2016)
- Prices and terms for purchasing apparel, equipment, uniforms, or merchandise
- Prices and terms for team licensing deals
- Prices and terms for sponsorship, advertising, and media deals
- Prices and terms for lease and rental agreements

The naming rights for the American Airlines Center in Texas, home of the NBA Dallas Mavericks and NHL Dallas Stars, runs through 2031 and nets over $6 billion per year (ESPN, 2015).

a viable industry, especially since the advent of free agency in professional sports. Contract terms for professional athletes and high-profile coaches are often negotiated by an agent working independently or representing a sports management or marketing firm, such as Creative Artist Agency (CAA), Octagon, Wasserman Media Group (WMG), Rosenhaus Sports, or Steinberg Sports and Entertainment. Additionally, sports marketing firms are often hired to negotiate sponsorships, advertising, and media rights deals on behalf of leagues, teams, tournaments, or events.

This chapter addresses negotiations, labor relations, collective bargaining, various agreements and contracts (employment, sponsorships, and third party), and vendor management.

Negotiations

Negotiations can be simple or complex. The captains from two pickup basketball teams discussing how to determine who gets possession of the ball to start a game (e.g., a coin flip, rock–scissors–paper challenge, odd–even guess, or a jump ball) is an example of simple negotiations. Agreeing to terms on a 5-year labor agreement in a professional sports league is an example of complex negotiations. Sports managers and supervisors seem to engage in both extremes and everything between. One of the keys to effective negotiations is the ability to leverage both strategy and style to strike an agreement or finalize the terms of a contract.

A coin flip to determine who gains initial possession is an example of simple negotiations.

Agreements and transactions in everyday business include discussions and dialogue as part of negotiating or finalizing timelines, costs, and assets. Negotiations are especially integral when resources are scarce or tension is apparent in an organization. Understanding the stages of negotiations and applying the strategies and styles appropriate for the situation facilitates effective outcomes when agreements need to be reached.

STEPS TO NEGOTIATIONS

Molly Fletcher is a former sports agent who signed iconic athletes and coaches such as Joe Theismann, John Smoltz, Matt Kuchar, Doc Rivers, Erin Andrews, Bobby Cox, and Tom Izzo. One of her business books (*A Winner's Guide to Negotiating: How Conversation Gets Deals Done*) provides a strategic framework of five steps to improve negotiation skills, as follows:

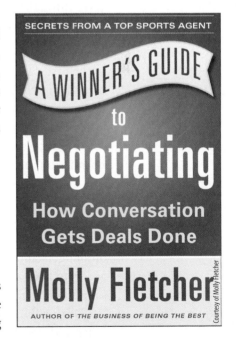

1. Set the stage
2. Find common ground
3. Ask with confidence
4. Embrace the pause
5. Know when to leave

Fletcher suggests that in salary negotiations, it is important to embrace all five of the areas, but perhaps the most important is to "embrace the pause." Why? Embracing

Figure 3-1 Five stages of negotiations

the pause is perhaps the least comfortable for people but is the one area that can yield the greatest results if someone is confident enough to hold his or her space (M. Fletcher, personal communication, April 26, 2016). In the end, however, negotiations must be considered as a dialogue, and every step is deemed important.

Negotiations are process driven. Similar to the steps advocated by Fletcher, the process behind negotiations can be generalized into stages that researchers often derive from adaptations to the steps defined in conflict resolution or problem solving. Investigators have segmented negotiations into a basic three-stage model involving (1) information exploration, (2) problem solving, and (3) resolution (Holmes, 1992). Other models have added preparation and planning as a separate phase (Littlefield, Love, Peck, & Wertheim, 1993). Global research has identified the "elicit win condition" as the initial stage to essentially predetermine the anticipated outcome (Sofian, Salwah, & Shahamiri, 2014).

Sports managers and supervisors may take shortcuts or add steps to the process, but essentially, negotiations between two or more parties traverse through the five stages (see **Figure 3-1**).

Preparation and Planning

In the first stage (preparation and planning), both parties gather and organize the necessary information to guide their activities. Fletcher refers to these activities as "setting the stage." It may also be prudent to consult with legal counsel or accountants to gather data during this stage of negotiations.

During planning and preparation, the history and context of why the negotiations are taking place are examined and the involved parties assess the importance of what is included in negotiations while developing perceptions of the expected consequences. Some degree of preparation and planning is advised for all negotiations; however, the necessity of preliminary homework may be greatest for topics that have a direct impact on budgets and employee morale. To preparing for salary negotiations, access to first- and third-party data reports assists in gathering compensation figures for market comparisons.

During the stage of preparation and planning, the parties establish the framework and logistics for conducting the negotiation activities. The ground rules define the processes and procedures, typically beginning with outlining the location, time, duration, and parties involved in negotiations. There may be mandated exclusions to discussion topics or requirements regarding the public or private nature of the negotiations, such as when representatives from a professional players' association and the league office agree to nondisclosure while in the midst of bargaining sessions. Ground rules may include an agenda and an explanation of what occurs if negotiations are not successful. The role of third parties (i.e., mediators, agents, and arbitrators) may also be identified in the ground rules.

Initial Offers

In the second stage (initial offers), at least one party of the negotiations identifies its initial offer, proposal, demand, or position. In salary negotiations when filling a coaching vacancy in an intercollegiate athletic department, for example, the athletic director typically presents an initial offer on behalf of the institution and the prospective employee counters with his or her suggested pay scale. Professional teams also make initial offers to sign players, and agents present a counteroffer.

Justification

The third stage (justification) involves educating and informing the opposite party of the reason, motivation, or rationalization behind the initial offer. The importance of the expected outcome is typically expressed, and supplement information is provided to justify the position. A cost–benefit analysis may be presented, for example, if negotiating an agreement for a search firm to execute staffing functions for a new stadium manager.

Bargaining

The fourth stage (bargaining) includes problem solving and describes the activities for the parties to establish an actual agreement or plan that will essentially end negotiations. Often referred to as option generation or problem solving, this phase typically includes bartering or haggling over issues, prices, or the terms and conditions of the item(s) or service(s) being negotiated. Concessions may be necessary to settle disagreements or disputes among staff. For example, an athletic director negotiating limited gym space for sports coaches may ask each to concede 15 minutes of their practice time to accommodate another team during prime time.

Implementation (Agreement)

The final fifth stage (implementation) includes formalizing the outcomes of the negotiations in an agreement or contract, be it written or verbal. Important to the negotiation process is a method for monitoring the implementation and effects of negotiations. Simple negotiations (e.g., negotiating gym time) may not always require a formal contract or agreement. Recording the outcome of negotiations, even informally, serves to build a repository of decisions and information in the event that case precedent is necessary to resolve future disputes.

NEGOTIATION STRATEGIES

Although negotiations are very process oriented, a **reservation point** or other conditions can cause a stall or breakdown in one of the stages, which may necessitate a different strategy to obtain the desired outcome. The ability to apply different strategies to increase the likelihood of successful negotiations draws on a combination of experience, individual traits, and the ability to leverage external resources. The carrot and the stick is a common metaphor to describe strategies for eliciting a desired response from an opposing party through leveraging benefits and rewards (a carrot) or penalties (a stick).

Sports managers and supervisors should be mindful of the best alternative to a negotiated agreement (BATNA), which is the most ideal alternative acceptable when agreement can't be reached. Similarly, supervisors and managers should know the **bargaining range** of negotiations, which is represented by the distance between the two reservation points. When negotiations stall or reach the point of an impasse, a change in strategy may assist efforts to bring two sides to an agreement.

Negotiation strategy simply refers to the methods or tactics to achieve an objective. The two strategies in negotiations are classified as integrative and distributive.

Distributive negotiations focus on dividing or allocating a fixed sum and are described metaphorically as "splitting a pie." For example, distributive negotiations may be used by an independent sports marketing agency and a college athletic department that must agree on how to split $10,000 in a signing bonus from the premier sponsor of an annual tip-off classic. The two parties (the marketing firm rep and the athletic director) essentially compete to gain the largest share of available funds in a negotiations structure that is typically described as a win–lose, zero-sum scenario. This type of negotiation is also referred to as a position-based strategy because one party's gain is the other party's loss.

Integrative negotiations, on the other hand, seek to mutually satisfy the needs and interests of both parties. This type of collaborative negotiation process ideally results in a win–win scenario and joint gains of both parties. Commonly referred to as interest-based negotiations, this strategy facilitates both parties achieving their primary interests in a mutually beneficial agreement. For example, integrative negotiations may be used by management and employees of a chain of Planet Fitness Health Clubs to determine incentives for membership retention or customer-service satisfaction. Similarly, it can be used by university athletic departments to develop strategic alliances and partnerships with profit-generating businesses for marketing, promotions, concessions, or other services.

Integrative negotiations may occur between management and employees at a Planet Fitness Center to determine new incentives to offer members.

NEGOTIATION STYLES

The choice of style selected by an individual during negotiations is dependent on numerous factors, such as personality, the assertiveness necessary to achieve agreement, the importance or significance of the outcome, time, and the emotional context of the situation. **Negotiation style** refers to the behavioral approach used to arrange an agreement or transaction. Styles used to negotiate outcomes are typically drawn from the 1971 research of Kenneth Thomas and Ralph Kilmann, who defined five modes of conflict resolution techniques (Schneider & Brown, 2013, p. 560): compromise, avoidance, collaboration, competition, and accommodation.

The *competitive* style is the most aggressive style and is used for negotiating outcomes of great importance or significance or ones that are unpopular. Individuals use this style by being firm and taking control of a conversation while competing for the most favorable distribution of a limited resource or a decision whereby any advantage for one party is a disadvantage for the other. When one side wins, the other side loses. For example, in personnel relations, a competitive style may be instituted when negotiating raises for a coaching staff considering a limited pool of available money to distribute. Similarly, a competitive style may be necessary in distributing additional job duties for client representatives at a sports marketing agency as a result of downsizing.

*Accommodation i*s a negotiations style whereby one party agrees to concede to the other, which typically includes a sacrifice or demonstration

A group ticket sales rep for a hockey franchise may accommodate a client's price point to meet a monthly quota.

of selflessness. Accommodating the other party may be the result of a decision regarding time preservation or an acceptance of what is presumably the best solution. An accommodating style is also used as a strategy to gain favor for a future negotiation of greater importance. For example, the facilities director at a sports facility may concede working a Saturday shift but expects to gain favor in negotiating a future weekend date. Similarly, a group sales associate for a professional hockey franchise may accommodate a client's price point to reach his or her monthly quota.

Avoidance is similar to the accommodation style because both are considered passive behaviors. Refusing to enter negotiations by avoiding the issues signifies blatant neutrality and a lack of concern for the outcome. Trivial items such as the date of the staff picnic for a health club may spark avoidance in parties requested to provide an alternative.

Compromise is a style that suggests agreement on a resolution that is minimally acceptable to all parties, typically at the halfway point, and presents relatively fair and equitable outcomes. Occasionally, compromise suggests creating acceptable solutions in the face of time constraints or to protect relationships. In negotiating health benefits for workers at a sporting goods store, a compromise may lower out-of-pocket and copay expenses but raise deductibles or vice versa. Compromise is ideal in collective bargaining negotiations for sharing revenue between players and the league and to avoid a lockout or strike.

A *collaborative* style uses innovative solutions to add value while satisfying both parties' interests. Beyond negotiating together in a fair and relatively transparent and trusting environment, collaboration is expected to provide additional benefits to each party that may not have been realized in a simple compromise. The example of the negotiations for health benefits at a sporting goods store may move from compromise to collaborative if discussions begin focusing on servicing employees, providing free health screenings, or devising a better system to pay premiums.

The style of negotiations will differ depending on the numerous variables that may impede or enhance the actions and dialogue for reaching an agreement or making a transaction. Individuals working in the sports industry should note personal strengths and challenges in using the different styles to achieve optimum results.

Negotiating Employment Agreements

Employment contracts are generally not provided to part-time, seasonal, or entry-level employees in the sports industry. Sports managers and supervisors generally define employment terms to these groups, although employees may barter for days off.

Before fully deploying the staffing function for full-time employees, sports managers should have the skill set to effectively negotiate compensation packages and define the terms of employment that will be represented in an agreement or contract. Most employment agreements in the industry are in the form of a standard letter of appointment or a **memorandum of understanding** (MOU), which is nonlegal document establishing a formal arrangement between two parties. Agreements may also be in the form of a contract, which is a legally binding document that is enforceable by a court system.

Letters of appointment and MOUs provide little protection for workers who are considered **at-will employees** because they can be terminated without warning or without the organization providing just cause. Contracts are designed to protect employees from termination without cause; however, there are no foolproof protectionist guarantees in light of the intricacies of legal systems, market and economic conditions, and general unforeseen circumstances. The difference between an employment agreement, MOU, and a contract is that the latter has the backing of legal precedence.

Negotiating employment conditions, such as base salaries and performance pay incentives, is the predecessor of executing a contract. Sports managers and human resource professionals typically employ the services of legal professionals when drafting or modifying employment contracts. Templates for creating basic employment agreements are

Most employment agreements are in the form of an appointment letter which details terms such as length of service, wages, and other items.

plentiful and easily found through Internet searches and by means of talent software. If no legal representation is available within a company or business, outsourcing services to design or modify employment contracts is a prudent practice to protect the organization's interests.

NEGOTIATIONS IN EMPLOYMENT CONTRACTS

Compared with contracts for chief executive officers (CEOs), contracts of high-profile coaches typically tie compensation more closely to performance, are shorter in duration, and contain bigger severance payouts (Thomas & VanHorn, 2016, p. 191). The front matter of standard employment contracts typically defines the involved parties and specifies the primary position and accompanying responsibilities of each. In addition, the agreement defines the enforceability of the contract under applicable law and geographical jurisdiction. Areas of negotiations in standard employment contracts typically include (1) length and general terms of employment, (2) compensation and benefits, (3) other provisions, and (4) termination and severance.

Length and General Terms of Employment

The length or duration of employment is considered a contentious issue, especially for professional players and coaches categorically considered in an industry marked by a relatively short career span. Primarily as a result of the pressure to produce winning records, the average length of appointment of a collegiate head coach in the Football Bowl Subdivision (FBS) before being replaced is approximately 3 years (Greenberg, 2001). Thomas and VanHorn (2016, p. 215) noted an average career length of 4.6 years for football coaches at National Collegiate Athletic Association (NCAA) Division I institutions between 1995 and 2013. An examination of professional players drafted between 1980 and 1989 in the four major American sports leagues (National Football League [NFL], National Basketball Association [NBA], Major League Baseball [MLB], National Hockey League [NHL]) indicated an average career length ranging from 5.4 to 8.1 years (Baker, Koza, Kunglb, Fraser-Thomasa, & Schorerc, 2013).

Negotiating the length or duration of initial appointment provides employees with minimal security for a specified period, unless foreseen or unforeseen conditions prevail to otherwise end the relationship. Options and clauses may be negotiated to reflect conditions affecting duration of a contract. For example, contracts may include **rollover clauses** specifying automatic reappointment or renewal of terms. Rollovers simply extend the life of a contract until either party intervenes.

Compensation and Benefits

For full-time employees who are under contract, the most negotiated areas are typically compensation and benefits. Considering the explosion of media revenue in the sports realm, negotiating compensation packages for athletes, coaches, and executives has become increasingly competitive. Adding to the complexity is the influence of third-party agents or financial advisors in negotiations.

Sports managers may negotiate base wages and bonus or incentive wages, but they typically do not have a great deal of leverage to limit outside wage earnings. Base wages represent standard pay based on time worked. Bonus or incentive clauses tie wages to a goal or outcome standard. Outside wages represent income derived from a third party that is self-disclosed by the employee. It has been suggested that 50%–80% of a high-profile coaches' pay in intercollegiate athletics is derived from outside sources such as television shows and camps, endorsement deals, and appearances (Greenberg, 1992).

Negotiating incentive clauses in employment contracts for coaches, professional players, and sports employees in sales or sponsorship roles is fairly common. A university president may negotiate the bonus payout for a coach winning a national championship, or a franchise owner may negotiate a bonus provision for the general manager if the organization performs well financially over a certain period of time. Employees may negotiate an annuity or "balloon payment" whereby a bonus is tied to the actual length of a contract. For example, the contract for Denny Crum, a former coach at the University of Louisville Division I (NCAA) before Rick Pitino took the helm, included a $1 million bonus for remaining with the institution for a minimum of 10 years (Greenberg, 1992, p. 107).

Sports managers may or may not negotiate the extent of discretionary benefits available to an employee, but certainly perquisites or fringe benefits are negotiable. Perquisites (perks) or fringe benefits are afforded to one or several employees but not to everyone in the organization. For example, The Ohio State University's (2015) employment agreement with head football coach Urban Meyer includes

Prior to Rick Pitino (pictured) taking over at the University of Louisville, former head men's basketball coach Denny Crum negotiated a $1 million "balloon payment" in his contract by agreeing to remain at the institution for ten years.

© Christopher Halloran/Shutterstock

language for ensuring a private charter plane for recruiting trips (p. 12) and a paid membership to a private golf club (p. 13). Because of their economic value, certain perquisites (e.g., golf memberships) are treated as taxable income and are therefore subject to applicable to withholdings of payroll taxes.

Other Contract Provisions

Employment negotiations revolving around other provisions in a contract may include any topic important to either the organization or the employee that is not specifically addressed in the general agreement terms or area of compensation and benefits. Other provisions may include terms for attendance at specific organizational events (e.g., charity golf outing or a university convocation) or conditions of a **moral turpitude** clause governing behavior or conduct expectations. Negotiating terms for moral turpitude clauses are challenging because of the ambiguity in identifying the conditions that may constitute action and behavior considered detrimental to the best interest of the organization.

Parties may negotiate the stipulation for a noncompete clause, reassignment provisions, or nonrecruit requirements in an employment agreement or contract. A **reassignment clause** removes an employee from his or her current position and reassigns the employee's duties to another role within the organization (see **Action Shot 3-1**). **Noncompete clauses** specify a time period precluding an employee from accepting a position with a program or business that competes with the original organization. Additionally, noncompete clauses include provisions not to use or retain software and records from the original organization. Similar to the premise of noncompete stipulations in a contract, nonrecruit clauses preclude a coach who has been hired at a new organization or institution from recruiting athletes identified as a prospect of the coaches' original organization. Each of these areas includes terms that may be negotiated.

Termination and Severance

The fourth negotiated area of employment agreements is the terms for **termination** and **severance pay.** Termination and severance both reflect an end in the employment relationship regardless of who initiated the departure. This section typically includes language specifying that either party may terminate the agreement, for any reason, provided that a certain and reasonable amount of notice is given.

Areas that can be negotiated related to termination and severance clauses include (1) the length of prior notice necessary to terminate the contract, (2) the right to end the relationship if predefined conditions surface, and (3) provisions

▶ ACTION SHOT 3-1

Reassignment Clauses in Intercollegiate Athletic Contracts

In the wake of a new head football coach appointed at Kent State University in 2011, an assistant defensive coach in the middle of a 28-month contract failed to be hired on the new staff. Therefore, the institution honored the contract by reassigning the coach to a position as the assistant to the athletic director, whereby he would assume identical salary and benefits. After being terminated for refusal to assume the new position, the assistant coach filed litigation alleging that the university breached its contract and that the reassignment to a noncoaching position was a "constructive discharge," which asserts that a reasonable person in an identical circumstance would be compelled to resign as a result of intolerable working conditions. The university was found liable for breach of contract but not for constructive discharge (Ohio Court of Appeals, 2014).

The reassignment of a coach to a noncoaching position is fairly common in intercollegiate athletics, often as a means of avoiding wrongful termination under the provisions of a contract. In 2016, the University of Texas reassigned Augie Garrido, the college's winningest baseball coach (five national championships), as special assistant to the athletic director (Autullo, 2016). He had 1 year remaining on his contract. Similarly, a North Carolina State University (2016) assistant basketball coach was reassigned to the role of special assistant to the deputy athletic director for external operations. Examples of coaches reassigned to another position in the institution, whether voluntarily or mandated, are plentiful. Negotiations occur between parties to define the terms of reassignment, or the terms may be dictated without an opportunity to alter any conditions.

A lesson from the Kent State University case is to address reassignment in employment negotiations to allow for the removal of a staff member from a coaching position to a noncoaching position. A reassignment clause permits an institution to legally terminate a contract if a coach refuses a new assignment.

for financial remuneration in the event that specific conditions arise. When addressing one of his biggest mistakes as a team owner during a sports business conference, Dan Gilbert (2016), majority owner of the NBA Cleveland Cavaliers, joked that the organization had six or seven head coaches on staff even though only one was actually on the job. Gilbert was alluding to honoring contract provisions for several coaches who were terminated. Similarly, due to buyout clauses, NFL former coach Chip Kelly was earning millions from two different franchises after being fired from the Philadelphia Eagles in 2015 and from the San Francisco 49ers in 2016 (Breech, 2017).

There are assumptions as to whether every part of an employment agreement can be negotiated. Agreements may simply include language and clauses that must be agreed upon. For example, employers may simply provide a

TABLE 3-1: For-Cause Termination Provisions in Division I College Football Coaches' Contracts, 1995–2013

Provision	Percentage of Contracts with Provision
Violation of NCAA rules	93.1
Gross misconduct	85.0
Unprofessional conduct	65.4
Neglect of duties	82.3
Breach of contract	60.8
Moral turpitude	50.5
Fraud or dishonesty	30.5
Felony	31.1
Substance abuse	15.1
Gambling	11.7
Drug test program failure	7.7
Conflict of interest	4.6

Data from Thomas, Randall and Van Horn, Lawrence (2016) "College Football Coaches' Pay and Contracts: Are They Overpaid and Unfairly Treated??," Indiana Law Journal: Vol. 91: Iss. 2, Article 1. Available at: http://www.repository.law.indiana.edu/ilj/vol91/iss2/.

clause specifying a legal right to terminate an employee if he or she can no longer perform his or her job as a result of becoming permanently disabled by a physical or mental illness. Specific grounds for termination of an employee agreement "with cause" usually specify actions or behaviors related to gross ethical and judicial (felony) violations.

A **breach of contract**, whereby one party does not fulfil or honor part of an agreement, serves as a legal condition for termination of the relationship and possibly for the award of liquidated damages. The term *liquidated damages* refers to the amount of money that would satisfactorily and equitably compensate the opposing party for breach-of-a-contract provision. Either party may declare a breach if conditions warrant and be awarded liquidated damages as a means to be equitably compensated for a violation.

Violation of NCAA rules is one of the most frequently noted termination grounds reported in the contracts for intercollegiate coaches. **Table 3-1** identifies the percentage of contracts between 1995 and 2013 for 106 NCAA Division I college football coaches that included clauses pertaining to termination "for cause" (Thomas & Van Horn, 2016, p. 232).

Negotiated areas in a termination clause may include severance pay or voluntary compensation afforded to the employee in the event of a specific type of layoff. Severance pay serves to protect the goodwill of an organization while also serving as a potential release of liability from a lawsuit. Severance pay is not mandated in employment contracts; however, many businesses choose to include the provision.

Negotiating **buyout clause** options is also a contentious area because employers must agree to pay a specific amount for terminating a contract before the agreed-upon end date. Buyout clauses are typically included in the termination provisions for professional athletes and high-profile coaches. The Urban Meyer contract at The Ohio State University (2016, p. 22), for example, stipulates a $2 million payment to the institution if the head coach accepts a

The Ohio State Buckeyes are coached by Urban Meyers who has a $2 million dollar penalty provision in his contract for accepting future employment within 12-months of terminating the agreement.

new job coaching a professional or Division I collegiate football team or a position as a media commentator for a national television or cable station within 12 months of tendering a resignation.

Negotiating Vendor Agreements

Negotiating and managing vendor agreements with organizations or individuals is another important role of sports managers and supervisors. **Vendor management** includes all the activities for researching, procuring, monitoring, and evaluating all aspects of a third-party arrangement. Whether securing an outside source to assist with legal compliance representation, payroll services, benefits administration, recruiting, or training, vendor management is a crucial component of ensuring satisfaction in terms of pricing, service delivery, and anticipated outcomes.

OUTSOURCING

Outsourcing is a form of a vendor arrangement in which an outside supplier assists with an organization's noncore business functions. Outsourcing has the potential to yield tremendous cost savings, time savings, and risk management benefits for organizations. For example, many large sports facilities outsource concessions, catering, and general suite services to reputable providers such as Sodexho Marriott, Delaware North, or Aramark.

Additionally, teams or organizations lease space to private or chain restaurants for game-day services. A section of Progressive Field in Cleveland, for instance, provides spectators with food options ranging from the Melt to Sweet Moses. Similarly, a growing trend in Division I intercollegiate athletics is to outsource marketing, media, and ticket operations to outside organizations that specialize in those operations, such as IMG College, Learfield Sports, International Sport Properties, and Host Communications (Zullo, Burden, & Lee, 2014).

When considering outsourcing opportunities with or without profit potential, the key is to initially solicit bids from possible suitors. Interested vendors in areas that derive a profit typically research market demographics and the history of an organization before submitting a bid proposal that includes an initial capital investment to secure a deal and an offer of a percentage of derived revenue. The vendor with the most attractive bid is either accepted or invited to engage in negotiations for what is potentially an ideal integrative win-win outcome.

When securing a vendor that doesn't expect to derive profits from its services (e.g., maintenance, information technology, legal representation, insurance provider, or software installation), cost is only one factor in a bid comparison. The organization must consider intangible benefits of the vendor supplier such as client satisfaction ratings, customer support, or response time. In the event of similar bids, successful negotiations on items such as price or delivery time help to ensure that the right vendor is selected.

MANAGING VENDOR RELATIONSHIPS

Action Shot 3-2 illustrates how exploring opportunities when negotiating the terms of vendor agreements ideally leverages potential benefits for both parties. An agreement between a stadium and a concessionaire company, for example, may require that newly installed equipment is depreciated annually until the facility assumes ownership when the contract expires.

When negotiating for mutual satisfaction, organizations may seek to create a strategic alliance that adds value to each party as a result of the relationship. In creating strategic alliances, it is likely that a vendor will become a partner that is managed as opposed to being viewed only as a bill of sales. Although the negotiations for securing a vendor include the same processes as those for negotiating an employment agreement, there is a definitive point where vendor relations are as important as labor relations for a business. In addition to securing negotiated terms in a legally binding contract specifying the obligations of both parties, it is important to assess the value of the arrangement over time.

▶ ACTION SHOT 3-2

Lessons from Negotiating Insurance for Professional Athletes and Entertainers

Jim Convertino is Director of professional athletes and entertainers for The McGowan Companies, a relatively small, private firm headquartered in Cleveland, Ohio, offering risk management and insurance solutions. With location in Austin, Dallas, Atlanta, Miami, and Baltimore, McGowan employs more than 300 agents and offers a menu of services ranging from umbrella liability insurance to a wide assortment of property and casualty coverage.

Convertino formerly worked in the same capacity for Britton Gallagher's Athlete and Entertainer (A&E) division in Cleveland which listed among its expertise areas were coverage plans for amusement parks, extortion and kidnapping, commercial markets, pharmaceutical companies, and pyrotechnics. He estimated an $11 million valuation for Britton Gallagher's niche market including over $4 million in revenues from 2013 to 2015 for just the A&E division (J. Convertino, personal communication, April 1, 2016).

After a failed pitching tryout with the MLB Cleveland Indians, Convertino remained in Ohio to pursue a career as a paralegal and eventually in the insurance industry. He is a member of the Sport Lawyers Association and Sport Financial Advisor Association. Among his clients are professional players, coaches, and front-office personnel in the NFL, MLB, and NBA, television and movie producers, screen writers, and ball-club owners. His specialty is "gap" coverage, which basically describes anything and everything not covered in a standard insurance policy for an individual or organization. For example, a fresh draft pick by the NFL Chicago Bears, whose sudden acclaimed wealth triggers a spending spree, is a prime candidate for additional gap coverage for newly acquired cars, jewelry, or vacation home purchases.

Convertino's recommendation for acquiring success in any sales-driven industry is to be an asset for clients as opposed to a service provider for customers. Agents or anyone "selling" or "negotiating" insurance services, for example, should strive to educate their clients on the value and benefits of a purchase, whether in the form of a wealth management portfolio or family protection plan. Service, according to the director, is the distinguishing factor among competition. Being willing to go places where others can't and being accessible when others aren't are key ingredients to a service mentality that can make a difference in who is ultimately selected as a business partner.

One idea for procuring and successfully managing vendor relationships is for sports facilities or organizations to hold on-site vendor events to solicit and exchange ideas. There is also added value in creating a tiered structure of vendor relationships. For example, a **tactical vendor** or tier 1 vendor is one that may offer the best service for the lowest price, whereas a partner or tier 2 vendor is classified according to its ability to navigate challenges and solve problems. A shared risk model in vendor contracts ideally builds on the idea of a strategic partner relationship (Blythe, 2016, p. 22).

Sports managers and supervisors who negotiate the terms of a vendor agreement follow a similar process as that used in negotiating employment agreements. It is important to prepare and plan for negotiations, set ground rules, provide justification and clarification for bargaining points, engage in problem solving, and, finally, implement an agreement through a contract. If receiving a draft of a contract from a service provider, it is beneficial to read through the document line by line to highlight statements needing further clarification or those that should be changed or eliminated. A managerial approach to contract negotiations ensures an advantage in managing outsource partners and other vendor relationships.

Negotiations and Labor Relations in Sports

Negotiations are an integral component of labor relations. **Labor relations** is a broad term representing the relationship and interactions between labor (employees) and management. The premise behind labor relations is that employees have a legal right to safe working conditions and that, collectively, a group of employees may address (negotiate or bargain) issues with management. Most sports managers and supervisors will be involved in negotiating disputes between departments or individuals to improve labor relations in an organization. Negotiating space allocation, responsibility for particular processes, or competing policies for leave requests requires an integrative approach to seek win–win relationships. The sports manager or supervisor serves as a counselor for the two sides.

ROLE OF THE COMMISSIONER

In the sports industry, labor relations commonly describe the relationship between a professional league and the players who are represented by a players' association union (i.e., National Football League Players Association, National Basketball Players Association, and Major League Baseball Players

Association). The neutral party in labor relations for professional sports is the commissioner.

Commissioners are the central authority figures governing professional leagues, community sports leagues (i.e., Pop Warner Football or a county baseball/softball league), state high school associations, and intercollegiate athletic conferences. They are empowered to act and make decisions considered to be in the best interest of the league or association. Governing authority for commissioners includes but is not limited to dispute resolution, disciplinary measures, negotiations of league-wide contracts, and general operational business oversight. The scope of authority for a commissioner is derived from the constitutional bylaws and rules outlined in the governing articles of a league or association, such as a collective bargaining agreement.

COLLECTIVE BARGAINING

Collective bargaining is a negotiations process to agree to terms over conditions governing the employment relationship. **Collective bargaining agreements** (CBAs) define the general terms of employment for the entire organization.

Roger Goodell, Commissioner of the NFL, is the central authority governing the league. Pictured with Cam Newton, one of the roles of the Commissioner is to oversee the annual draft.

Primarily, collective bargaining in professional sports refers to the multiyear agreements between franchise owners of a league (e.g., NFL, MLB, and NBA) and the players. In December 2016, both the MLB and NBA agreed to terms for new CBAs (**Action Shot 3-3**). However, collective bargaining is more widespread in the industry. Globally, labor organizations have bargained for the establishment of universal standards for working conditions (e.g., hours, age limits, and wages) to curtail the proliferation of sweatshop factories manufacturing sporting goods equipment, shoes, and apparel in international markets such as Asia and South America. Collective bargaining also occurs in municipal recreation settings where workers are considered public employees.

Most sports managers and supervisors will not be directly involved in the negotiating side of a CBA governing labor relations, especially in

▶ ACTION SHOT 3-3

2016 New Collective Bargaining Agreement for MLB

MLB Commissioner,
Rob Manfred

The collective bargaining agreement (CBA) for Major League Baseball (MLB) was renewed within 3 hours of the expiration deadline of December 1, 2016 (Sheinin & Svrluga, 2016). The new agreement incrementally raises the competitive balance (luxury) tax for teams exceeding payroll limits. The CBA also declares that the winner of the All-Star Game will no longer be afforded the home-field advantage for the World Series.

The CBA for the National Basketball Association (NBA) was renewed in December as well. The new 7-year deal, effective 2017–2024, retains the player-advantage 51%–49% split of basketball-related income (BRI) and provides leverage for teams to retain players prior to free agency (Zillgitt, 2016).

The first CBA in MLB was negotiated in 1968, the same year as the first CBA for the National Football League (NFL). During the 1994–1995 MLB player strike, which cancelled the World Series, owners hired replacement workers (scabs) who received a $5000 signing bonus, a minimum $80 daily per diem, and a quaranteed prorated salary of $115,000 for making it to the 1995 Opening

Day roster (Verducchi, 2015, p. 54.). A judicial order officially ended the strike several days before the start to the 1995 season, whereby the scabs were re leased and the existing CBA was ordered to take precedence until the two sides could ratify a new document. After surviving eight work stoppages in the 1970s, 1980s, and the latest in the 1990s, the MLB has endured over 20 years of relatively harmonious relations between owners and players, representing the longest tenure of labor peace among the major U.S. professional leagues.

Prior to the expiration of the CBA spanning 2012–2016, Rob Manfred was elected to replace Commissioner Bud Selig. In his former role as executive vice president of human resources and labor relations for MLB, Manfred was the leagues' lead negotiator for the 2002, 2006, and 2011 CBAs. Tony Clark, executive director of the Major League Baseball Players Association (MLBPA) and former TV analyst, is the first former player and first person of color to serve as chief liaison. Clark also has had an official role as a member of the player's negotiation team since the 2002 labor agreement.

One of the most contentious issues of any CBA is revenue sharing. Economic reports indicate that the percentage of league-wide revenue for professional baseball players has declined precipitously over the past decade, as much as 33% over a 12-year period (Brown, Link, & Rubin, 2015). Debating accounting measures, however, likely contributes to potential disagreements when bargaining for

Tony Clark, Executive Director of the MLB Players Association

a larger share of revenues for either side. Other common issues negotiated in the CBA include debt service thresholds and rules, competitive balance (i.e., luxury) tax, and free agency. The length of the schedule or the number of games in a season is a sensitive issue for the league and players, especially in regard to impact on salaries.

The CBA for MLB includes 25 articles. The revenue-sharing plan (Article 24) defines components of gross revenues, central revenues, and local revenues. The agreement indicates that clubs must pay 34% of local revenues to the league (MLB, 2011, p. 121). Local revenues include everything from gate receipts to a portion of television broadcast revenues as reported annually on a financial information questionnaire.

Examples of other articles in the CBA include salaries, termination pay, grievance procedures, discipline, spring training conditions, deferred compensation, reserve systems, rule changes, management rights, and the competitive balance tax. Although MLB does not use a salary cap system, due to the terms of the CBA, the league was able to assess clubs' additional fees payable to a central fund if they exceeded a tax threshold noted as $189 million from 2014 to 2016 (MLB, 2011, p. 98). The CBA that expired in 2016 was the first to identify the testing of players for human growth hormone.

professional sports. In professional sports, bargaining for the employees is done through a **union**, an independent agency within a particular trade, such as the players' association. Bargaining on behalf of management is done by the owners and team executives within the league.

Common components in CBAs for professional leagues include minimum salaries, team salary caps, eligibility for free agency, luxury tax rates, draft rules, and revenue-sharing plans, for example. The four most contentious labor issues in professional sports are free agency, luxury tax, salary caps, and team work rules. Additional labor issues unique to professional sports include revenue sharing, the draft process, and the prohibition of no-trade contracts.

LABOR DISPUTES

The National Labor Relations Act (NLRA) identifies a list of mandatory issues that are to be bargained between management and labor, but it does

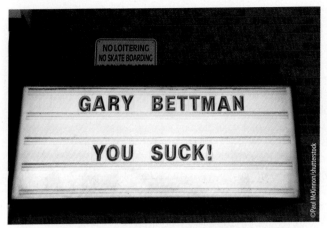

A sign at PJ Quigleys bar in Ottawa, Ontario, Canada expressed the frustration of fans with Commissioner Gary Bettman over the 2012 NHL lockout.

MLB baseball umpires have staged several work stoppages including a mass resignation in 1999. The current labor deal between the World Umpire's Association and the MLB will expire in 2019.

not stipulate that each of the two sides has to provide the other with concessions or agree to terms. In collective bargaining, a dispute between both sides of the labor force that cannot be settled in a reasonable manner is referred to as an impasse. When an impasse occurs, opposing sides may employ coercive tactics to force some type of accommodation or resolution.

Employees (players) may select to stage a **strike**, which is a collective, organized, and intentional refusal to work for an organization. The **lockout** is a tactic used by the employer to force accommodation or resolution of a labor dispute. A lockout is a temporary closure of a business as a means to prevent and deny employees (players) the opportunity to work and collect wages.

The NLRA collective bargaining rules (Sections 8(b)(3) and 8(d), 29 U.S.C. §§ 151–169 (1935)) stipulate provisions for notifying the other party of a decision to strike or stage a lockout. The NLRA also includes provisions ensuring job protection for employees engaging in a permissible strike (National Labor Relations Board [NLRB], 2016). Before, during, or after the threat of a strike or lockout, **alternative dispute resolution** (ADR) may suffice to resolve labor issues.

Strikes and lockouts have been a part of major professional sports leagues in the United States since the first NFL work stoppage in 1968 over pay disputes (Corapi, 2011, p. 806). Officials and umpires have staged several work stoppages as well. The NLRA recently stipulated that employers retain the right to hire replacement workers on a permanent basis as long as there are not discriminatory effects on the employees engaging in a permissible strike (Ballard Spahr, 2016).

ALTERNATIVE DISPUTE RESOLUTION

When two sides cannot agree to settle a dispute (e.g., the terms of a CBA or a disagreement between a supervisor and employee) or when attempting to resolve a dispute proves to be too arduous, alternate resolution techniques may be used as a means to negotiate a harmonious outcome. ADR refers to the methods and techniques used to settle a disagreement without jurisprudence in a legal court setting. The two forms of ADR are mediation and arbitration.

Mediation is a tool to facilitate an agreement whereby a third neutral party assists both sides in reaching a settlement that is amenable to and voluntarily accepted by both parties. Individuals appointed as mediators are impartial entities expected to assist opposing sides in resolving contentious disagreements through counseling, advisement, collaboration, or compromise. Mediation is nonbinding. A mediator has no authority to mandate a settlement or resolution. With mediation, both sides of a dispute remain actively involved in crafting their own resolution with the guidance of the neutral third-party mediator.

Unlike the amendable resolution efforts of a mediator, **arbitration**, on the other hand, results in a binding decision provided by a third party who is not a representative of the legal court system. Similar to a judge in the court system, an independent neutral party evaluates evidence from each side of a case and is empowered to make a final decision or award. Established in the early 1980s, the Court of Arbitration for Sport (CAS) in Lausanne, Switzerland, was initiated through the International Olympic Committee (IOC) but serves to settle disputes throughout many sectors of the sports industry (Blackshaw, 2013).

Salary disputes are common in professional sports. The respective leagues utilize arbitration to settle salary disputes in hockey and baseball (NHL and MLB). A salary grievance by the agent of a player eligible for arbitration (based on years of service) is presented to a club. If the club refuses to meet the salary demand, the dispute goes to arbitration. A representative of the club and the player's agent each provide supporting arguments to an appointed panel that decides the salary the player will receive

Lausanne, Switzerland is home to the Olympic Museum, the IOC Headquarters, and the Court of Arbitration for Sport.

In 2016, over 150 MLB players filed for salary arbitration resulting in a binding decision for payment rendered by the league.

©Garsya/Shutterstock

for the upcoming season. A total of 156 MLB players filed for salary arbitration in 2016, and three-fourths won, which is considered unusual because owners have the better record over the lifetime of the system (Associated Press, 2016).

Although ADR is common in professional sports, it is also used throughout all sectors of the industry. The American Arbitration Association, for example, includes attorneys, retired judges, and sports law professors who settle disputes when member institutions decide to terminate association with a conference or to settle commercial and business disputes involving labor issues. Whether the labor dispute involves a vendor arrangement or policy disagreement, the premise is that ADR can successfully settle a dispute as an alternate means to a judicial remedy in a legal setting.

Recap

Negotiations are an important skill for human resource professionals and managers in the sports industry. Generally, there are five stages of the negotiations process: (1) preparation and planning, (2) initial offer(s), (3) justification, (4) bargaining, and (5) implementation.

Sports managers and supervisors may be involved in contract negotiations. Standard employment contracts typically include the following basic components: (1) length and general terms of employment, (2) compensation and benefits, (3) other provisions, and (4) termination and severance. Employment contracts for coaches are somewhat similar to contracts developed for CEOs in terms of the inclusion of graduated compensation in addition to a base salary and accompanying perquisites; however, coaching contracts are typically shorter in duration and tied more closely to performance outcomes.

A large segment of the sports industry relies on vendor contracts for outsourced labor; therefore, negotiating the terms and prices of service units is common for sports managers and supervisors. In addition to negotiating deals with suppliers, it is important to approach outsourcing as a vendor management relationship instead of a bill of sales.

Labor relations refer to the relationships between employers (ownership/management) and their employees. CBAs govern labor relations in professional sports, in large retail sports businesses, and in sectors of recreation aligned with government agencies. Unions may negotiate the terms of a CBA for employees. The unions in professional sports are the respective players' associations. Lawyers may be involved in negotiating terms for employees in the absence of a union.

Labor disputes may be a result of an impasse in collective bargaining or a disagreement between individuals. In lieu of judicial measures in a court of law, ADR may be selected to resolve disagreements. Mediation and arbitration are two forms of ADR used in the sports industry.

 GLOBAL SPOTLIGHT 3-1

Selected Labor Facts for Professional European Football Coaches

Europe has numerous trade unions representing professional soccer coaches, such as the Alliance of European Football Coaches Association (AEDCA) and the European Association of Sport Employers. Europe's Premier League is considered the worldwide pinnacle of professional football. Premier League coaches are required to have a professional license awarded by the Union of European Football Associations (UEFA). Interesting facts concerning labor issues and professional football (soccer) coaches in different countries in Europe include the following:

Portugal: In Portugal, a collective bargaining agreement exists between the Portuguese Professional Football League and the National Association of Football Coaches from Portugal that stipulates a 70% fine for breach of contract by either party (Colantuoni, 2015, p. 400).

Netherlands: A Disciplinary or Arbitration Committee of the Dutch Football Association settles disputes between a coach and the Professional Football Prosecutor. The prosecutor has authority to mandate fines and suspensions for football-related issues, such as the €10 million penalty assigned to a club that failed to stop or prevent fans from inappropriate behavior during a match (Pieters, 2016).

Argentina: In Argentina, professional football coaches are considered technical directors. The Association of the Technical Director of Argentinean Football (ATFA) serves as the union organization representing coaches. A collective bargaining agreement exists between the Association of the Argentinean Football (AFA) and the ATFA covering terms of a standard coaching contract. Many coaches, however, enter into additional agreements with clubs for better salaries and tax benefits (Colantuoni, 2015, p. 403).

DISCUSSION QUESTIONS

1. After providing an example of integrative and distribute negotiations applicable in the sports industry, explain the basic premise of each type.
2. What is the basic recommended strategy to successfully negotiate a vendor agreement?
3. What is the correlation between styles of negotiations and conflict resolution techniques, and what determines the choice of style?
4. Which ADR method is preferred for negotiating a professional player's salary, and why?
5. Why are employment contracts for coaches similar to contracts for corporate executive officers?

APPLIED ACTIVITIES

1. Use the Internet to research the International Council of Arbitration for Sport (ICAS) and CAS. Prepare a paper addressing the relationship between the ICAS and CAS in respect to labor disputes.
2. Lost at Sea Rankings: Working with four or five group members, imagine you are lost at sea in a rubber lifeboat. First, individually rank the following 15 items in order of importance for survival.

Watch	Nylon rope	Compass	Mason jar	Fishing hook
Blanket	Shaving mirror	Shark repellent	Map of ocean	2 bananas
Liter of rum	Life preserver	Cell phone	1 gallon water	An oar

    Next, work with the group to form a consensus ranking of the items in order of importance. When the task has been completed, discuss the style of negotiations used by each member to complete the task.

3. Celebrity Sports Endorsement Negotiations: Work in pairs. See **Exhibit 3-1** for the accompanying worksheet.
   a. Step 1: Decide which individual will serve as the representative for ABC Sports and which will serve as the agent for Swift Stanley. Read the background information.
   b. Step 2: Independently, complete the corresponding column of the Celebrity Sports Star Negotiations worksheet (Exhibit 3-1), noting the ideal terms and conditions for an agreement (approximately 10 minutes).
   c. Step 3: Verbally discuss each item, then conduct negotiations to determine the agreed-upon results to appear in the "Negotiated" column

of the Celebrity Sports Star Negotiations worksheet (approximately 20 minutes).

d. Step 4: Calculate revenues to be collected and distributed based on terms of the negotiations associated with commercial and personal appearances (bottom of Exhibit 3-1).

e. Step 5: Share the calculations and terms of the agreement areas with other groups, and discuss the style and strategies used by each side to negotiate the outcomes.

Background Information: Swift "Swifty" Stanley has emerged as a bona fide table-tennis star. Only 21 years old, Swifty has won 8 of the last 11 major table-tennis tournaments over the past 3 years, breaking virtually every table-tennis record in the process. Swifty is poised, articulate, and good-looking, and he has a radiant smile, which (combined with his seeming invincibility) have prompted the inevitable comparisons to Tiger Woods. Because of his good looks, newfound wealth, instant success, and youthful indiscretions, the tabloid magazines (e.g., *US Magazine*, *People*) dish up stories about Swifty's fast cars, hard partying, and revolving door of girlfriends. Still, Swift Stanley has caught the attention of ABC Sports, Inc., a leading manufacturer of indoor sports equipment (billiards, darts, foosball, table tennis, etc.). The items in Exhibit 3-1 represent negotiation items for ABC and Swifty's agent to consider for a product endorsement agreement for a line of signature table-tennis paddles.

EXHIBIT 3-1: CELEBRITY SPORT STAR NEGOTIATIONS WORKSHEET

This form accompanies Applied Activity 3

	ABC Sports	Swift Stanley	Negotiated Terms
Length of Agreement			
General Compensation Amount			
Terms of General Compensation (Lump sum or per year)			
Official Name of Endorsed Paddle			
Territory			
Royalty Fee—Product Endorsement Compensation			
Labeling of Endorsed Product			

Quality Controls			
Commercials per Year			
Commercial Fees			
Personal Appearances per Year			
Personal Appearance Fees			
Expense Allocations for Personal Appearances			
Termination Conditions			
Moral Turpitude Clause			
Advancement			
Agent Fees Conditions and Amount			
Other			

_____ Gross revenue for Swifty based on minimum number of commercial and personal appearances, including advance

_____ Gross revenue for Swifty's agent

_____ Net revenue for Swifty

CASE STUDY

Cross-Cultural Negotiations in Japan Sports Turf Market

Three-time Olympian Willie Banks, founder of HSJ Incorporated and master-distributor for Fieldturf Tarkett Inc.

© Larry French/Getty Images Sport/Getty

Of the many human resource functions in larger sports organizations, one of the most arduous may be negotiating agreements with employees, unions, and outside vendors. Willie Banks, a three-time Olympian and former World Record holder in the triple jump, demonstrates the importance of remaining ethical while mitigating cultural, procedural, or other variances in a successful negotiation. Patience, precision, and practice are the three Ps behind the science and art of negotiating deals the "Willie Way."

Willie Banks transitioned from a world-class athlete to a successful international sports business tycoon after commandeering the Japanese market in the artificial sports turf industry. Banks is founder and CEO of Hop, Skip, Jump (HSJ) Incorporated, a global sports management consulting firm specializing in a range of services, from evaluating the strategic objectives for Midhar Sport Enterprise in the Middle East (Jordan) to assisting countries such as Stockholm, Sweden, in preparing an official bid to host an Olympic Games. HSJ also negotiates multinational distribution channels to sell specialty sports products to Asia, such as the Halo high-performance sports headband with a sweat-control silicone strip.

Banks and HSJ's most successful enterprise is negotiating deals for supplying stadiums in Japan and Taiwan with artificial grass manufactured by the American company Fieldturf Tarkett Incorporated. In the United States, Fieldturf is used at Lucas Oil Stadium, Ford Field, Giants Stadium, Tropicana Field, Gillette Stadium, and dozens of university sports facilities. In Japan, the synthetic material can be found in the Tokyo Dome, Yokohama Stadium (baseball), the Fukuoka Dome, and a number of collegiate stadiums, including Hosei University, which, through the assistance of Banks, purchased licensing rights from Boise State University to install artificial blue turf.

As the master distributor over two large Asian territories, Banks operates with precision as an independent contractor negotiating third-party vendor agreements for international manufacturers and buyers. Handling the contractual details for all sales, installation, and maintenance jobs, Banks worked in the Japanese market for over two decades before believing he had earned the trust and privilege to negotiate deals with Asian customers.

Initially, Banks was relegated to communicating only with the *Kaishain* workers, or entry-level employees, within a company. Because Japan is a collective society, most Japanese workers remain with the same company for their entire lifespan, and many of the *Kaishain* workers Banks knew were promoted to a *Buchou* position (a mid-level department chief with limited authority) and eventually to positions as a high-level president or vice president. By sustaining a relationship with these men over two decades, Banks has negotiated with the same individuals over time, and most of his colleagues are now the central authority figures and highest-ranking officials for their respective companies.

Banks was always sensitive to the language and structure of the Japanese concept known as 上下 *Jouge kanke* ("relationships above and below"), which dictates the chain of command of an organization (W. Banks, personal communication, March 7, 2017). Over time, Banks clearly secured a reputation in the Japanese business world as a trusted and reliable "senior" distributor of sports turf products. Any new sales representative or distributor entering the Japanese market would find it almost impossible to have the same relationship with buyers as Banks currently has.

Banks notes that infiltrating the higher-order decision-making ranks in the Japanese or Taiwanese business world is a highly complex and lengthy process whereby foreigners have almost a 0% chance of making a deal unless they have an inside connection. Similar to many Asian countries, the culture of Japan and Taiwan is highly institutionalized, with a hierarchical seniority system that Banks has been able to penetrate successfully.

To demonstrate an aspect of cross-cultural negotiations with Asian businessmen and politicians, Banks tells a story of a Hungarian colleague who once warned him of the near impossibility of engaging in a conversation at an International Olympic Committee (IOC) meeting with a highly respected member of the Korean delegation. As forewarned, the Korean automatically snubbed the Olympian's direct intrusion into his personal space. Several months later when Banks was formally introduced to the Korean by a "mutual" colleague, however, the cold shoulder suddenly warmed up to what has since become a long-lasting friendship. Banks uses the story as a reminder to his American associates that successfully dealing with Asian customers doesn't occur through impression management, flashy presentations, or promises of product or service superiority. Whether looking to enter a market or resolve a conflict in the Japanese market, intermediaries are almost always a necessity to open a door and establish an initial level of trust. Once the door is open, however, successful negotiations still require the three Ps—precision, practice, and plenty of patience—to have any chance of eventually closing a deal.

CASE STUDY QUESTIONS

1. What types of sports negotiations and businesses operations does HSJ deal with in addition to serving as a distributor of artificial turf for international markets?

2. What are the labels for entry-level and mid-level employees in a traditional Japanese company?

3. Does the concept of 上下 *Jouge-kanke* apply in American business negotiations?

4. To what degree does Willie Banks's reputation as a world-class Olympic athlete apply to his success in negotiating licensing agreements and other deals in Japan and Taiwan?

5. What are several keys to successful cross-cultural sports negotiations in Asian markets?

Laws:
National Labor Relations, 29 U.S.C. §§ 151–169 (1935)

Cases:
James M. Fleming v. Kent State University, 10th Appellate District, No. 13AP-942, Ohio Court of Appeals (2014, August 12).

REFERENCES

Associated Press. (2016, January 28). Player win arbitration season winning 3 out of 4 cases in 2016. *Fox Sports.* Retrieved from http://www.foxsports.com/mlb /story/arbitration-cases-players-beat-owners-3-1-021716

Autullo, R. (2016, May 31). Garrido out after 20 years. *Austin American Statesman,* C-1.

Baker, J., Koza, D., Kunglb, A., Fraser-Thomasa, J., & Schorerc, J. (2013). Staying at the top: Playing position and performance affect career length in professional sport. *High Abilities Studies, 24*(1), 63–76.

Ballard Spahr. (2016, June 6). *NLRB reverses precedent on permanent replacements for striking workers.* Retrieved from http://www.ballardspahr.com/alertspublica- tions/legalalerts/2016-06-06-nlrb-splits-on-permanent-replacements-rule.aspx

Blackshaw, I. (2013, September 1). ADT and sport: Settling disputes through the court of arbitration for sport, the FIFA dispute resolution chamber, and the WIPO arbitration and mediation center. *Marquette Sports Law Review,* 1–57.

Blythe, D. (2016, May 1). 7 ways to get the most from your vendors. *Vendor Man- agement. Computerworld Digital Magazine,* 19–22.

Breech, J. (2017, January 2). Here's how Chip Kelly could make millions from three different NFL teams in 2017. *CBSsports.com.* Retrieved from http://www.cbssports.com/nfl/news/ heres-how-chip-kelly-could-make-millions-from-three-different-nfl-teams-in-2017/

Britton Gallagher. (2016). *James Convertino. Director of professional athletes and entertainers and personal risk management.* Retrieved from http://www .brittongallagher.com/james-j.-convertino.

Brown, D., Link, C., & Rubin, S. (2015, October 21). Moneyball after 10 years: How have major League Baseball salaries adjusted? *Journal of Sport Economics.* doi:1527002515609665

Colantuoni, L. (2015). Coaches and managers contracts in football: Peculiarities and termination Int'l and comparative study. *International Sports Law Review, 11*(12), 391–403.

Corapi, J. (2011). Huddle up: Using mediation to help settle the National Football League labor dispute. *Fordham Intellectual Property, Media, and Entertainment Law Journal,* 789–838.

Gilbert, D. (2016, November 4). *Afternoon keynote with Dan Gilbert and Stephen Ross.* Presentation, Michigan Sport Business Conference at the Ross School of Business, University of Michigan, Ann Arbor, Michigan.

Greenberg, M. (1992). Representation of college coaches in contract negotiations. *Marquette Sports Law Journal, 3,* 101–109.

Greenberg, M. (2001). College coaching contracts revisited: A practical perspective. *Marquette Sports Law Journal, 12,* 153–156.

Holmes, M. E. (1992). Phase models in negotiation. In L. L. Putnam & M. E. Roloff (Eds.), *Communication and negotiation* (pp. 83–105). Newbury Park, CA: Sage.

Littlefield, L., Love, T., Peck, C., & Wertheim, E. (1993). A model for resolving conflict: Some theoretical, empirical and practical implications. *Australian Psychologist, 28,* 80–85.

Major League Baseball. (2011). *2012–2016 Basic agreement.* Retrieved from http:// mlb.mlb.com/pa/pdf/cba_english.pdf

National Labor Relations Board. (2016). *Right to strike and picket.* Retrieved from https:// www.nlrb.gov/rights-we-protect/whats-law/employees/i-am-represented-union /right-strike-and-picket

North Carolina State University. (2016). *Bobby Lutz named special assistant to deputy athletic director.* Retrieved from http://gopack.com/news/2016/4/12/lutz-named -special-assistant-deputy-athletic-director.aspx?path=mbball

Pieters, J. (2016, April 8). *Lynching black footballer in effigy could lead to Ajax hardcore fan match bans.* Retrieved from http://www.nltimes.nl/2016/04/08 /lynching-black-footballer-in-effigy-could-lead-to-ajax-hardcore-fan-match-bans/

Schneider, A., & Brown, J. (2013, September 1). Negotiation barometry: A dynamic measure of conflict management style. *Ohio State Journal on Conflict Resolution, 28*(3), 557–580.

Sheinin, D., & Svrluga, B. (2016, December 1). MLB's players' union agrees to deal. *Washington Post,* Sports, D01.

Sofian, H., Salwah, S., & Shahamiri, S. (2014). A requirements negotiation process model that integrates easy win-win with quality assurance and multi-criteria preference techniques. *Arabian Journal of Scientific Engineering, 39,* 4667–4681.

The Ohio State University. (2015). *Employment agreement* (File 00167943-1). Retrieved from http://grfx.cstv.com/photos/schools/osu/sports/m-footbl/auto_pdf /2012-13/misc_non_event/UrbanMeyerContract.pdf

Thomas, J., & VanHorn, L. (2016). College football coaches' pay and contracts: Are they overpaid and unduly privileged? *Indiana Law Journal, 91*(2), 189–242.

Verducchi, T. (2015). The sham spring. *Sports Illustrated,* 50–58.

Zillgitt, J. (2016, December 14). NBA players' union reach tentative deal for new CBA. *USA Today.* Retrieved from http://www.usatoday.com/story/sports /nba/2016/12/14/nba-nbpa-cba-adam-silver-michele-roberts/95449262/

Zullo, R., Burden, W., & Li, M. (2014, February 11). Outsourced marketing in NCAA Division I institutions: The companies' perspective. *The Sporting Journal.* Retrieved from http://thesportjournal.org/article/outsourced -marketing-in-ncaa-division-i-institutions-the-companies-perspective/

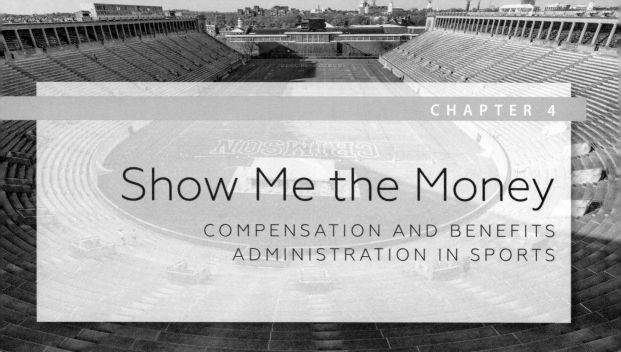

CHAPTER 4

Show Me the Money

COMPENSATION AND BENEFITS
ADMINISTRATION IN SPORTS

When defining terms to retain a top employee, it is important to consider financial and nonfinancial benefits. By understanding what motivates that employee and the reasons for that employee to possibly seek other employment, there will be a clear understanding of which negotiating points will be the most helpful to retain the employee's service. Keep in mind that money always talks. If trying to retain a key employee and the budget allows, offering a substantial salary increase is a great tool. Where the employee is in his or her personal life and where that employee is in current compensation will help determine the right level of salary increase. Just remember that although $10,000 may seem like a generous salary increase, it typically amounts to $200 or so per paycheck, which is not necessarily life changing.

It is essential to have a clear understanding of the marketplace for people in the top employee's role before giving a salary increase. Other negotiable benefits to retain a top employee include a title promotion, increase in vacation time, remote/work-from-home capability (if it is of interest to the employee), and a monthly expense stipend or a stipend increase (if applicable to employee's position).

Carolyne Savini
Senior Vice President and General Manager
Turnkey Sports & Entertainment Search Division

LEARNING OUTCOMES

1. Explain total rewards compensation.
2. Gain an awareness of the complexities of employee compensation.
3. List the different types of compensation and benefits used by companies to reward employees.
4. Determine a successful compensation strategy for a position within an organization.
5. Describe the legal issues that affect compensation decisions.
6. Explain full-time employment status.
7. Calculate full-time equivalents for an organization.

KEY TERMS

Benefit	Incentive pay	Salary
Bonus	Internal equity	Stock options
Compensation	Market rate	Total rewards
Disability insurance	Pay compression	Unemployment compensation
Full-time equivalent (FTE)	Pension	Wages

Lead-Off

Before staffing occurs, the organization must define total compensation and determine the procedures to pay employees in compliance with state and federal regulations. Sports managers and supervisors who understand the foundations of strategic planning, employment law, and negotiations are likely to be more effective in designing appropriate compensation packages to attract or retain talent and to streamline processes for administering payroll and benefits.

Compensation is much more complex than solely considering an individual's rate of pay; thus, there is a great need for sports managers and supervisors to acquire a thorough understanding of the various monetary and nonmonetary forms of compensation available to employees. Compensation is almost always the largest expenditure for organizations and must be closely monitored. Universally, it is one of the—if not *the*—most critical determinants of employee job satisfaction (Espinoza, Ukleja, & Rusch, 2010; Green & Heywood, 2008; Kellison, Kim, & Magnusen, 2013; Smucker & Kent, 2004). It can be the determining factor in whether a candidate accepts a job offer.

Compensation is manifested in the form of salaries, bonuses, health-care benefits, stock options, and a smorgasbord of other forms of tangible and intangible benefits such as incentives, paid time off, retirement plans, educational assistance, professional development, workers' compensation, unemployment compensation, Social Security, wellness plans, and perks. Echoing what Carolyne Savini advocates in the chapter-opening quote, research suggests that advancement opportunities and benefits are common tools for fueling satisfaction with low-paying jobs such as those in the sports industry (Kellison et al., 2013). Although compensation is one of the most complex areas to manage, it is an integral driver of performance.

An example of a sports organization demonstrating the value of compensation as a tool to satisfy employees is The Ohio State University Athletics Department, which includes approximately 400 staff among more than 44,000 total employees at the institution. In 2015, the Athletics Department was the only college institution named one of the "10 Best Organizations to Work for in Sports" by *Forbes* magazine (Murray, 2015). Other recognized sports organizations included the Arizona Diamondbacks, the Cleveland Cavaliers, the National Football League (NFL), the Aspire Group, and Turnkey Sports and Entertainment. One of the reasons for Ohio State's recognition is its competitive **total rewards** package, which is administered equitably and consistently across the university. According to the Ohio State Human Resource Department, there is a goal to provide competitive salaries and a competitive total rewards framework that is "clearly communicated to staff and easily administered by managers" (The Ohio State University, 2016, p. 3).

Not all sports organizations have a fully functioning human resource department comparable to that of the Ohio State University Athletic Department. Because the sports industry includes an abundance of smaller organizations (under 50 employees), many managers and supervisors without access to any type of human resource department must solely design compensation packages and determine the systems to administer payroll and benefits. Other sports managers choose to outsource the responsibilities to a third-party vendor

In 2015, The Ohio State University athletics department was the only college institution named one of the "10 Best Organizations to Work For in Sports" by *Forbes Magazine*.

A small fitness facility operates much differently than a large stadium or retail sports conglomerate when administering compensation and benefits for employees.

or use some type of mixed approach by completing selected tasks in-house and contracting outside services for other tasks. These decisions are largely dependent on the size of the organization (number of employees), the type of business (i.e., profit vs. nonprofit), and the available resources (e.g., intellectual capital and technology). A collegiate athletic department housed within a large public university operates differently than one housed at a small, private institution. A small fitness center operates and compensates employees differently than a major league professional sports team. Similarly, a Minor League Baseball team in a small market operates differently from an international arena management company.

This chapter addresses the components of compensation and benefits in addition to processes for administering benefits and payroll. It also provides guidance on general principles for determining an effective compensation strategy.

Wages

Wages strictly include monetary forms of compensation as opposed to benefits that range from health insurance to cell-phone reimbursements. These payments are calculated from the amount of time worked by an employee and represent the monetary amount received.

Between 2007 and 2011, the average rate of pay for 947 National Collegiate Athletic Association Division I (NCAA) head coaches in the Football Bowl Subdivision (FBS) increased by 44% compared with a 23% average pay increase for chief executive officers (CEOs) at public corporations (Thomas & VanHorn, 2016, p. 192). Salaries for directors, managers, and executives in professional sports (see **Table 4-1**) are fairly appealing and supported by the fact that compensation generally increases when factoring in age, seniority, and experience (King, 2012). Despite examples of enticing salaries for many positions, the sports industry is saturated with a heavy supply-versus-demand model (large number of applicants

TABLE 4-1: 2012 Mean Average Total Compensation Package for Directors, Managers, and Executives in Professional Sports (Annual)

Average Annual Compensation	Position/Category
$ 58,476	Individuals age 18–29
$ 111,959	Individuals age 30–39
$ 139,852	Individuals in current role for 3–5 years
$ 175,769	Individuals in current role for 9 or more years
$ 69,821	Senior or associate managers
$ 110,524	Ticket/suite/club sales directors
$ 115,250	Senior or associate directors
$ 325,000	Executive or senior vice president
$ 409,000	President/chief executive officer/chief operations officer

Highlights of a salary report administered to 500 executives representing over 120 professional sports teams by Street and Smith Sports Business Daily and Turnkey Sports and Entertainment (King, 2012).
Data from King, Bill. "What's the payoff in sports?" Sports Business Daily. American City Business Journals. 13 Aug. 2012.

for small number of jobs), which partially explains why pay, especially for entry-level positions, is often relatively low or even declining compared with other fields. For example, an annual fitness industry compensation report indicated that the average wages for a program director in 2015 ($43,317) totaled approximately $7000 less than the 2010 annual salary (Schroeder, 2015).

TYPES OF WAGES

Sports managers and supervisors must understand the type of wages provided in their organization from the hourly to the salaried employees. The nature of a position may lend itself to include bonus opportunities for employees, whether it is an act of generosity (i.e., Christmas bonus pay) or based on an incentive such as a sales quota. Included in an individual's wage calculations are regular pay and bonus pay for work performed.

Regular Wages

Regular wage is considered the standard compensation or base pay for work performed either in the form of a salary or hourly pay. An employee hired at an hourly rate will be compensated based on the amount of time worked multiplied by the hourly rate. The wage would consider the number of hours work during the specified pay period (day, week, month, etc.) multiplied by the hourly rate. A part-time stadium usher hired at the rate of $8.00 who worked 15 hours in a pay period would receive wages of $120. (Note that there will be deductions from this wage payment, such as federal taxes.)

A **salary** is a fixed payment rate for work, typically calculated on an annual basis. A salary is paid at the same rate for a given pay period regardless of the number of hours worked. An athletic trainer earning an annual salary of $50,000, for example, would receive $2083.33 per pay period if the organization paid its employees twice a month. (Note that there will be deductions from this salary payment, such as federal taxes.) This payment amount will remain the same regardless of whether the employee works 35 hours per week or 45 hours per week.

Bonus Wages

Bonus wages are a type of compensation that is not considered as part of an employee's base pay or regular wages. The seven NCAA head football coaches who earned in excess of $5 million for the 2015 season, for example, had maximum bonuses in their employment contracts ranging between $750,000 and $1,475,000 (Berkowitz, Upton, Schnaars, Dourgherty, & Neuharth-Keusch, 2016).

The most common type of bonus is **incentive pay** or commission dependent upon the employee meeting or exceeding certain benchmark criteria. Incentive pay is tied to performance goals, whether defined in terms of sales units, market share, profit margins, victories, graduation rates, or another standard. For example, an inside sales representative for a National Hockey League (NHL) franchise may receive a $1000 bonus for exceeding a goal of $100,000 in ticket sales for the month, and a head basketball coach for a university may receive a $5000 bonus for his or her team qualifying for postseason (i.e., March Madness NCAA Tournament).

DESIGNING A WAGE COMPENSATION STRATEGY

In determining a salary (or salary increase), sports managers must consider a variety of factors and employ a systematic approach to ensure equitable and consistent procedures for assigning a rate of compensation. Payment

Bonus pay is often provided to NCAA Coaches who advance in the March Madness Final Four Tournament.

to employees is the largest operational expense of an organization and one that must be administered and monitored closely. Before staffing occurs, it is crucial that budget parameters are established for wages (and benefits) and for actual recruitment expenditures. Determining compensation packages is a deliberate process that rivals strategic human resource planning in terms of the extent of preparation and critical analyses necessary for effectiveness.

There are several compensation strategies available to employers, the choice of which is predicated on the company's overall business strategy, especially the financial picture. Best practices suggest that human resource policies, including compensation strategies, should align with the company's overall mission and strategy. Generally, developing a compensation strategy involves a four-step process: (1) reviewing external compensation strategies, (2) assessing the internal alignment, (3) conducting a financial and legal assessment, and (4) formulating the wage compensation (see **Figure 4-1**).

Step 1: Review External Compensation Strategies

The initial step in designing a wage compensation strategy is reviewing external compensation strategies for comparable positions. To make an external compensation comparison, an organization must determine the market rates for certain positions and then decide how the organization will respond. The **market rate** is the amount of compensation employers pay employees for a job. The three basic strategies used to respond to the market rate are (1) meet the market, (2) above market, and (3) below market.

Meet the market is the compensation strategy whereby employers position themselves in the middle of the pay range (i.e., market) for the position.

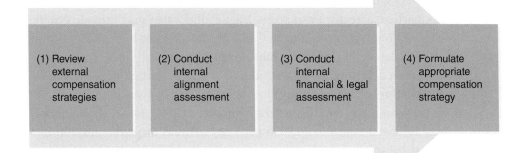

Figure 4-1 Steps to designing a compensation strategy

In this strategy, approximately 50% of companies provide a higher level of compensation, and approximately 50% provide a lower level of compensation. An *above-market* strategy provides compensation at a rate higher than 75% of companies. Employers use this strategy when hiring high-quality candidates and retention are important or as a means to diversify staffs. Finally, the *below-market* strategy provides compensation at a level lower than 75% of companies. A company might choose this strategy for a number of reasons—for example, it does not have the capital or revenue to compete at a higher compensation rate, there is an abundance of quality workers available, or the company is performing poorly financially and cannot afford to pay above the market.

In the end, organizations may decide that it is in their best interest to use multiple strategies for different positions in consideration of the scope of responsibilities, geographic location, or number of qualified applicants. A football stadium may use a meet-the-market approach if hiring is fairly easy for entry-level positions (e.g., concession workers or ushers) but determine that an above-the-market strategy is necessary to compensate analytics and media acquisition personnel, which are jobs more difficult to fill with high-quality applicants.

As part of the process for determining which market strategy to use, resources are available, such as the U.S. Department of Education's Equity in Athletics Data Analysis (EADA) website, which publishes aggregate salary information of head and assistant coaches for all institutions receiving federal financial aid. Nonprofit organizations are also required to report the salaries of their top executives; however, there is no mandate to publish wage information for other employees, which makes it difficult to conduct a market analysis when salary information is not readily available. One means to collect salary data is to conduct survey research on sports professionals in a particular sector or to access league offices that may provide general information that may not be tied specifically to teams but can be of assistance in determining market value for particular positions.

When determining market value, it is also important to consider how the location of the organization may affect market value. A marketing manager in a large market with a high cost of living (a.k.a., Los Angeles) may receive a salary of $65,000 per year, whereas the same position in a city with a small to medium market, such as Raleigh, North Carolina, may earn only $50,000 per year. It is important to understand the relationship between market value and location because it will affect the organization's ability to attract talent nationally, regionally, or locally.

Step 2: Internal Alignment Assessment

The second step in determining an appropriate wage compensation strategy is to conduct an assessment of internal alignment for pay structures. *Internal alignment* refers to the comparison of pay within an organization for different levels of positions. **Internal equity** involves the perceived fairness within an organization for factors such as pay differentials among different jobs or comparable workload.

At its very core, **compensation** is predicated on the practice of paying different rates for different jobs based on the value to the organization. It is well known that a CEO will have a higher compensation than an entry-level marketing coordinator; however, that doesn't mean that the marketing coordinator isn't valuable. The value of the marketing coordinator for the organization is simply different from that of a CEO, and in an internal market comparison, the coordinator ranks lower than the executive. The following three questions can be asked to assist in determining the right level of internal alignment:

1. What positions have the highest value?
2. What positions require a high level of skill?
3. What positions require a high level of experience?

Equity is important to internal assessment. Employees have an expectation for being compensated fairly compared with other employees with similar experience in the organization. An entry-level sales representative generally understands that his or her value to the company cannot be compared to that of a CEO; however, the sales associate will still expect to be paid equitably for his or her contribution to the company in line with other employees of comparable experience and worth.

When conducting the internal assessment to determine salary alignment, consideration must be given to the susceptibility of **pay compression**, which may skew perceptions of internal equity. Pay compression occurs when a long-term employee is making equal to or less than newly hired employees, despite the fact that the long-term employee has a higher level of education, skill, and/or experience. For example, consider the professional sports franchise that decides to use a meet-the-market strategy to offer a social media manager a comparable market value of $60,000 while three social media managers currently on staff each earn between $50,000 and $55,000 annually. If a new social media manager is hired at $60,000, pay compression will have occurred unless the candidate has a higher level of education, experience, and/or skill. The prudent business practice to minimize the legal risk of discrimination is to either lower the salary offer for the new hire or increase the salary of the internal employees.

One strategy to minimize issues involving pay equity is to devise a classification system for a pay-grade scale such as the one purportedly used for executives at ESPN (see **Action Shot 4-1**). Many public universities are required to use pay-grade scales, and athletic department staff members are therefore subject to a particular compensation rate. To devise a pay scale, jobs requiring similar effort, ability, responsibility, and experience are group together, ranked, and assigned a comparable wage amount reflective of differences in categories above and below. The advantage of these scales is that they facilitate the perception of pay equity; however, there are challenges to incentivize a prospective employee who may be lost to a competitor that is not restricted by a pay-grade system.

▶ ACTION SHOT 4-1

Pay-Grade System at ESPN

Based in Bristol, Connecticut, ESPN, Inc. (2016) includes approximately 8000 employees worldwide and 4000 in the United States. The media giant is owned primarily by ABC, Inc., which is an indirect subsidiary of the Walt Disney Company, and by the Hearst Corporation, which holds a 20% interest in ESPN (ESPN, Inc., 2016). Since its inception in 1979, the company has acquired numerous corporations (e.g., Classic Sports Network and Creative Sports) and launched countless spin-offs (e.g., espn-U, espn-W, ESPN Sports Zone theme restaurants, and *ESPN the Magazine*). Its global extension, overall growth, and ever-changing landscape have altered the organizational structure on countless occasions.

An unauthorized copy of ESPN's pay-scale system includes at least 25 ranks, with the bottom ranks (21–25) designated for entry-level staff, 18–20 reserved for mid-level managers, and 11 beginning the ranking for vice presidents and senior positions. The salary for each level includes a minimum and maximum contingent upon eligibility for basic bonus pay in each quarter. The pay-grade change is based on geographic location. For example, an E18 level employee in Bristol, Connecticut, may have a maximum salary of $67,200, whereas the maximum for an employee at the same level and with similar responsibilities in Montgomery, Alabama, would only be $54,521 (Koblin, 2013).

Step 3: Financial and Legal Assessment

A financial and legal assessment is the third step in designing an effective wage compensation strategy after reviewing external market information and evaluating internal equity. Anti-discrimination and Fair Labor Standards Act (FSLA) policies, especially new legislation for overtime exemption status, should be reviewed to ensure compliance. Additionally, sports managers and supervisors must either have control over the organizational budget or work closely with a company's chief financial officer (CFO) to ensure that all employee costs have been considered when developing a compensation strategy. Limited funds may be available for compensation increases regardless of the intention to employ a particular market strategy or to achieve internal equity. For example, an external market analysis by a newly formed Minor League Baseball team may have determined that an average salary of $45,000 is appropriate for a manager of community outreach, but in reality, the budget for this position is $40,000.

Step 4: Formulate Compensation Strategy

In the final step of designing a wage compensation strategy, there must be an integration of the results from the external market analysis, the internal alignment, and the financial and legal assessment. At this final stage, it is important to review whether the proposed strategy supports the organization's mission. If the strategy supports the organization's mission, provides the organization with quality employees, and motivate employees to perform at high levels, then the compensation strategy is complete.

Benefits

A **benefit** is an indirect reward given to an employee as part of his or her employment and as part of the employee's overall compensation package. There are three basic categories of benefits: legal, discretionary, and perquisites (see **Table 4-2**).

The NFL (2017) offers full-time employees a personalized benefits package comprised of a mixture of mandatory and discretionary benefits. Automatic coverage is provided for long-term disability insurance, basic life insurance, and accidental death/dismemberment insurance. Medical, dental, and vision coverage is provided in addition to flexible spending accounts, a 401(k) plan, and retirement pension. The NFL (2017) also provides work/life assistance programs, gym reimbursements, adoption assistance, paid holidays, vacation and personal days, and employee discounts in the team shop.

TABLE 4-2: Components of Employment Benefits	
Legal Benefits	Benefits required by the state or federal government whereby the employer contributes a portion to pay toward Social Security, Medicare, unemployment fund, health care under the Affordable Care Act, family medical leave, and workers' compensation.
Discretionary (Voluntary) Benefits	Nonmandated benefits afforded to all employees in the organization covering areas such as medical, vision, dental, tuition reimbursement, discounted services, retirement, leave, lending agencies, etc.
Perquisites or Fringe Benefits	Voluntary benefits afforded to one or several employees but not everyone in the organization, such as automobile lease, luxury suites, use of private aircraft, country club or golf membership, fitness club membership, clothing allowance, moving expenses, cell phone, family travel provisions, child-care arrangements, or use of vacation homes.

MANDATORY (LEGAL) BENEFITS

Mandatory benefits represent a form of indirect financial compensation for employees. Managers and supervisors in sports organizations must know what benefits they are required by law to provide employees. They must know the parameters of the law (generally, a stipulation dependent on the number of full-time employees) that may cause the organization to be exempt from having to comply with a legal mandate. Indeed, the unique nature of the sports industry accommodates a large number of smaller businesses (under 50 employees) that are generally exempt from having to provide certain mandatory benefits.

The typical mandatory benefits provided to full-time employees in organizations over 50 employees include Social Security (and Medicare), workers' compensation, unemployment insurance, family medical leave, and minimal health insurance.

Social Security

Social Security is a system of retirement whereby the government provides monetary assistance (public funding) to individuals who are unable to work. The system includes Supplemental Security Income (SSI), Social Security Disability Insurance (SSDI), and Medicare, which provides healthcare benefits for the elderly. Contributions to the Social Security Administration are mandated by federal law for both employers and employees. Through payroll taxes to the Internal Revenue Service (IRS), employers pay half of the cost of Social Security insurance. In 2017, the total Social Security tax rate was 12.4%, or 6.2% for the employer and the employee up to $127,200 (Social Security Administration, 2017).

Workers' Compensation

The Federal Employee Compensation Act (FECA) requires employers to provide workers' compensation in the form of replacement wages if someone is injured or disabled while on the job. For example, a clerk at a Foot Locker franchise who falls and sustains an injury while climbing a ladder to stock a shelf will be entitled to receive a paycheck if the employee is unable to work for a period of time (or indefinitely). Coverage for workers' compensation may be offered through a private insurance company, a state insurance fund, or self-insurance, depending on the state and the type of employer. The insurance benefits may extend to pay for medical treatment and vocational training.

In general, workers' compensation can be fairly complex. Each state has different requirements for how workers' injuries are to be handled. including exclusions, limits on the amount of compensation that can be awarded, and the statute of limitations for filing a claim. **Action Shot 4-2** explores the variances in state legislation when processing workers' compensation claims for the rash of NFL concussion cases over the years.

▶ ACTION SHOT 4-2

Workers' Compensation and Concussions in the NFL

The nature of professional sports has been an impetus for several states, such as Virginia and Kentucky, to exclude professional athletes from workers' compensation and for other states, such as Pennsylvania, Iowa, and Michigan, to limit the amount of an award (Modery, 2011, p. 258). These state differences are apparent in analyzing the rash of NFL players and ex-players filing claims related to concussions.

Research on 2552 retired NFL players indicated that over 60% had sustained a concussion during their career, and 24% had sustained three or more concussions (Guskiewicz et al., 2005). Because of the variances in state legislation for administering workers' compensation, California has seen the most cases of NFL concussion-related suits because the state supposedly has more "worker-friendly" compensation laws compared with a state such as Tennessee, which recently ruled that severity and longevity cannot be considered (Roche, 2014). California is the only state that permits awards for "cumulative trauma," which provides the foundation for the onset of concussion-related dementia in retired players (Rovell, 2012).

It is important that individuals responsible for wage administration are familiar with state laws and requirements and to have someone well versed in workers' compensation costs and processes to provide guidance in administering the program should a claim arise.

Unemployment Compensation

Unemployment compensation is a legal benefit administered at the state level for full-time employees who are out of work through no fault of their own. Eligibility for the program requires individuals to be available for suitable work (actively job prospecting) if a position were to become available.

A regular full-time employee of a sports team or sports facility who is out of work and actively looking for employment will likely qualify for unemployment compensation; however, individuals who are fired for misconduct or are not actively seeking employment are generally denied unemployment benefits.

Unemployment compensation is paid for by employers who pay a tax based on an experience rating, which is based on the number of claims filed by workers who have left the company. The more claims filed against an employer for unemployment, the higher that employer's experience rating will be. The higher the experience rating, the higher the tax rate.

Family Medical Leave

Employers with at least 50 employees are required to provide up to 26 un-paid weeks of time off per year for family medical leave under provisions of the Family and Medical Leave Act (FMLA). The birth of a child, care for a newly adopted or foster child, an emergency involving a family member on active military duty, or time off to care for a sick family member are all provisions covered under the FMLA (U.S. Department of Labor, Wage and Hour Division, 2012). **Action Shot 4-3** addresses the availability and actual usage of family medical leave coverage by employees working in intercollegiate college athletic departments.

Health Insurance

In 2010, the first ever mandatory federal law was passed requiring health insurance benefits for all full-time employees. The Patient Protection and Affordable Care Act (ACA) (42 U.S.C. § 18001 et seq. (2010)) requires all businesses with 50 or more **full-time equivalent (FTE)** employees to provide coverage to 95% of those employees and their dependents, up to age 26. The ACA mandates that employers must pay at least half of the health insurance premium, limit out-of-pocket costs for employees, and ensure

ACTION SHOT 4-3

Family Medical Leave Usage in Intercollegiate Athletics

The late Pat Summitt, former head women's basketball coach of the University of Tennessee, is pictured with son Tyler.

Intercollegiate athletics operates in a pressurized environment that isn't always conducive to extra time for raising children or caring for a sick parent. Although the Family and Medical Leave Act (FMLA) is available to employees, it often is not used or is not used to the full extent in intercollegiate athletics for a variety of reasons, with the primary one being concern about leaving the job for an extended period.

A female working up through pregnancy is fairly common in the coaching profession. The late Pat Summitt, for example, was on a basketball recruiting trip in Pennsylvania when she went into labor. The late legendary coach demanded that her private jet return to her home state of Tennessee instead of making an emergency stop in Virginia to deliver her first child (Parks, 2016). Similarly, a high school basketball coach gave birth at 10:18 p.m. following a playoff game and elected to return and coach a game at 2:00 p.m., less than 24 hours after her delivery (Miller, 2011).

Employers have the option to develop policies that are more generous than the minimum standards set forth under FMLA federal guidelines, such as permitting this leave to coincide with part or all of an individual's paid time-off benefits, such as short-term disability, vacation time, or sick leave. The head women's volleyball coach at the University of San Diego, for example, twice handed the reins to her assistant to take advantage of an institutional benefit providing an extension of the FMLA policy that permitted her to take a leave of absence for the entire season because of pregnancy (Farnum, 2011).

One university recognizing the unique nature of sports in its impact on leave usage for athletic coaches compared with administrative staff is Bowdoin College. The institution's leave policies provide athletic staff with 5 days of paid leave in addition to FMLA because "coaching positions require irregular hours, including nights and weekends, and extensive travel for matches and recruiting" (Bowdoin College, 2015).

that costs will not exceed more than 9.5% of an employee's only income (ObamaCareFacts.com, 2016).

Although a portion of the expense for an organization carrying the minimal healthcare coverage is passed down to the employee through payroll deductions and out-of-pocket expenses, the cost for a business is substantial. To ensure compliance, penalties amount to $695 per year or 2.5% of

AFFORDABLE CARE ACT

© Atstock Productions/Shutterstock

annual wages for eligible employees who refuse coverage, and employees are subject to daily fines through tax returns (IRS, 2016a).

The ACA has guidelines for specific services to be rendered only through preferred provider organizations (PPOs). Qualifying organizations must provide employees with either a bronze, silver, or gold healthcare plan, which varies according to the percentage of employer contribution. Employers pay 60% of health insurance expenses for the bronze plan, 70% for the silver plan, and a minimum of 80% for the gold plan (ObamaCareFacts.com, 2016).

The seasonal nature of sectors of the sports industry impacts ACA requirements. If an employer's workforce exceeds 50 full-time employees for 120 days or fewer in a calendar year and the employees exceeding the 50 full-time-employee threshold are considered seasonal labor, then the employer is not required to comply with the ACA requirements. One of the challenges for organizations is simply having to spend time on calculations of hours. Hourly employees who will add to their FTE minimum include those who consistently meet a threshold of 30 hours per week (see **Box 4-1**).

DISCRETIONARY BENEFITS

Discretionary employee benefits are provided voluntarily by the employer (i.e., not mandated through law). For example, the 30+ faculty and other full-time employees at the Chandigarh Lawn Tennis Association in India

---

BOX 4-1

Calculating FTE for the Affordable Care Act

A full-time equivalent (FTE) is the addition of the number of full-time employees who work over 30 hours a week plus the number of hours worked by part-time employees in a given month divided by 120 (120 is used as a representation of 4 weeks multiplied by 30 hours).

- FTEs = (Number of hours worked by part-time employees/120)

- Total full-time employees = Full-time employees + FTEs

receive the Diwali Bonanza in the form of either a 1-month salary bonus or a relatively expensive gift coinciding with the Diwali Festival (A. Garf, personal communication, August 12, 2015).

Discretionary benefits are becoming increasingly important in sectors of the sports industry to attract and retain workers, especially when wages aren't high for many positions. Cafeteria plans for controlling costs of discretionary benefits have increased in popularity. In these plans, employers contribute a fixed sum of money into an individual account for each employee, and the employee can select options from a menu of discretionary benefits based on needs and interests. Items on a cafeteria plan, for example, may include healthcare reimbursement, dependent-care assistance, group term life insurance, and contributions to health savings accounts.

There is an almost endless number of discretionary benefits that may be offered in an organization; hence, it is only feasible to provide an overview of those that are common in sports businesses.

Additional Health Care

Supplemental healthcare benefits are those offered to employees beyond the bronze plan that meets the minimum qualifications for federal compliance with the ACA. Healthcare benefits are a significant cost for an organization, and prices for insurance vary greatly because of the variances in premiums, copays, and deductibles. The National Basketball Association (NBA) and NHL pay an estimated equivalency of 4% of player salaries for a basic league-wide health insurance plan through BWD Sports and Entertainment, LLC (*The Economist,* 2013). In 2016, the cost of health benefits for the entire United States was reported at 7.6% for employees in the private sector, 8.3% for public/civilian workers, and 11.8% for government personnel (U.S. Department of Labor, Bureau of Labor Statistics, 2016 p. 3).

Among the numerous strategies to supplement basic health insurance include such employer actions as assuming a greater cost for premiums, providing affordable vision and dental plans, contributing to a pretax flexible spending or health savings account, paying all or some of prescription medicine plans, extending coverage to spouses, and providing employees with term or indefinite insurance health plans upon retirement (see **Action Shot 4-4**).

Supplemental healthcare benefits may also extend to cover mental health, rehabilitation treatment, hospice, and wellness and a litany of other programs ranging from hospitalization coverage to reimbursements for mileage when traveling to medical appointments. A great deal of comparative analysis in

▶ ACTION SHOT 4-4

Supplemental Healthcare Benefits for Retired Pro Players

In the National Hockey League (NHL), a majority of current and former players are from Canada and Europe, where they already benefit from publicly funded universal healthcare policies. The United States has recently instituted the Affordable Care Act as its own socialized plan for health insurance; however, the burden of the cost is shared between employers and employees.

Healthcare benefits for retired professional players in professional leagues vary in terms of eligibility status and availability or service options. In Major League Baseball (MLB), players on a roster for over 4 years have an indefinite healthcare plan, and players whose length of service is under 4 years are limited to a 2-year plan (Fisher, 2016).

The National Football League (NFL) provides players who competed for 3 or more years only 5 years of limited health insurance (Fisher, 2016). Limited health benefits are coordinated by the NFL Alumni, an association of retired players. One of the programs (Plan 88) provides reimbursement of care costs for "vested" players diagnosed with dementia and other neurodegenerative diseases such as Parkinson disease and amyotrophic lateral sclerosis (ALS). Among other health benefits offered in the NFL for "eligible" retired players are joint replacement programs, Medicare supplement programs, and neurological care programs (NFL Alumni, 2016).

In 2016, the National Basketball Association's Players Union (NBAPA) became the first in North American professional sports to provide health insurance for all retired players. "Retired" refers to all players who are no longer active, whether disengagement was a personal decision or through a roster cut. The caveat is that the individual must have been a roster player in the league for at least 3 years. Healthcare coverage is also available for children and spouses of former NBA players with a minimum of 10 years of service (Fisher, 2016).

plan coverage and costs from multiple providers is prudent in coordinating benefits for an organization. Many businesses elect to establish a standing committee for periodic review of healthcare benefits and costs.

Employee Assistance Program

Individuals who have personal and/or work-related problems may have the option to seek assistance through an organization's employee assistance program (EAP), which typically offers free and confidential assessments, short-term counseling, referrals, and follow-up services. Often, EAPs have term limitations for usage (i.e., 5 or 10 appointments annually). The range of concerns may relate to smoking cessation, drug addiction, alcoholism, anger management, posttraumatic distress disorder, marriage difficulties, abuse, anxiety, gambling, eating disorders, grief counseling, or other types of psychological, behavioral, or emotional issues.

EAP programs are commonly accessible to professional athletes in the four major leagues, intercollegiate athletic department employees, and workers in recreational agencies operated through the local or state government. Most individual franchises in professional sports do not offer an EAP because it is available through the league. Initiated in 2001, the MLB San Francisco Giants was reportedly the only internal EAP in U.S. professional sports in 2010, servicing approximately 250 year-round employees and over 1000 seasonal game-day workers (Vesely, 2012). The NBA was the first professional league to provide a 24-hour hotline for players and family members for immediate connections to free counseling services provided by psychologists, social workers, lawyers, and financial and physical rehabilitation counselors (Goldaper, 1981).

Life Insurance

Life insurance is a type of insurance that pays a lump sum amount to a beneficiary or beneficiaries upon the death of the employee. An organization purchasing life insurance for numerous individuals provides employers leverage in securing low monthly rates for the insurance. Some employers opt to pay monthly premiums for their employees, which becomes an added reward and a part of a total compensation strategy. Dick's Sporting Goods (2016), for example, provides eligible employees up to 1.5 annual base earnings in a basic life insurance plan.

Disability Insurance

Disability insurance is insurance that provides a benefit when a person becomes mentally or physically disabled. This type of insurance is categorized as short term (typically less than 90 days) or long term (typically 90 or more days). Full-time workers employed by the NBA Memphis Grizzlies, for example, are provided basic life insurance at the rate of two times an individual's annual salary up to a predetermined maximum (NBA, 2016). Supplemental life insurance, spouse/child life insurance, and/or accidental death and dismemberment insurance is available through payroll deductions, and short-term disability insurance is a company-paid benefit covering 60% of an individual's salary at the organization (NBA, 2016).

Retirement Plans

There are a variety of retirement plans that organizations offer employees to supplement the federally mandated Social Security benefits. Employers that elect to institute a retirement plan beyond Social Security must adhere to

minimum standards according to the Employee Retirement Income Security Act (ERISA) of 1974, which was created to protect employee investments. ERISA establishes standards for participation (length of service and age), vesting, benefit accrual, and funding.

The most common "additional" retirement plans are defined plans, where the employer and sometimes the employee make a monetary contribution in order for the employee to receive a defined benefit amount upon his or her retirement. The predetermined benefits are based on a variety of factors, such as the age and longevity of the employee. When an employee retires, he or she receives a specific amount of money, often weekly or monthly, based on a predetermined benefit calculation.

Pensions are a type of a defined benefit plan where an individual receives regular payments through a company's investment fund to which that person or his or her employer has contributed during the employee's working life. Some professional sports offer pension plans for their retired athletes, but eligibility varies, such as 43 days in the MLB, one game in the NHL, and 3 years of service in the NFL and NBA that can be collected at the ages of 55 and 52, respectively (Lipovsky, 2016). Intercollegiate athletic department employees (especially those employed by a state university system) and municipal government employees (e.g., recreation directors) may be more likely to have access to a pension plan, but there are variances in the availability of these types of benefits with the changing landscape of support programs and escalating costs for all types of insurance.

A defined contribution plan is another similar type of retirement plan that depends largely on contributions and investment rates. There is no set defined benefit as with a pension plan because the payout depends on the specific investments, the market, and the total revenues contributed. Some plans allow for employee contributions, and other plans are employer-only contributions. Examples of defined contribution plans include 401(k) plans, employee stock ownership plans, and profit-sharing plans. The NFL, for example, provides a two-for-one employer-matching 401(k) plan to players after only two seasons and a player annuity program after four seasons (Lipovsky, 2016).

Defined contribution plans are fairly common for large retail sports merchants with a global appeal (e.g., Nike and Under Armour). According to the U.S. Securities and Exchange Commission (2015) form 11-K for Nike, Inc. employees with a minimum of 1 year or 1000 hours of service are eligible to receive benefits of a defined profit-sharing plan. Sport Direct, the largest sports retailer in the United Kingdom, created a highly successful profit-sharing plan in 2009 that doubled the salaries for approximately 2000 full-time employees the year prior to and the year following the successful London Olympics (*Liverpool Echo,* 2013; Poulter, 2011). The owner had been lauded for instituting the seemingly rewarding and innovative employee profit-sharing plan; however, criticism loomed because less than 10% of Sport Direct's workforce had been afforded the options, and staff members were compensated below minimum wage (Kelly, 2016).

© Rose Carson/Shutterstock

Stock Options

Stock options are a discretionary benefit available to employees working in only a niche-market segment of the sports industry if the ownership of the company or business is dispersed among public entities. Stock options are a type of incentivized bonus payment opportunity whereby employees of publicly traded companies are offered the option to purchase shares of the business at a discounted or fixed rate to be eligible to receive dividends.

As part of a stimulus package to usurp talent from the rival Women's National Basketball Association (WNBA), the now-defunct American Basketball League (ABL) offered stock options to its 100+ players, making them the first professional athletes to have the purchasing opportunity (Ruyter, 1998). Only a few professional sports franchises have public ownership models, such as the Atlanta Braves, with part ownership ties with the Liberty Media Corporation, and the New York Knicks and Rangers, which belong to Madison Square Garden (Hubman, 2011).

In the sports arena, publicly traded companies include retailers (e.g., Nike, Under Armour, Callaway Golf, Dick's Sporting Goods, and Hibbett Sports), certain facilities (e.g., Madison Square Garden and the International Speedway

A rival to the WNBA in the late nineties, the now-defunct American Basketball League offered players stock options making them the first professional athletes in America to have the opportunity to exercise shareholder opportunities.

Corporation), and entertainment or "content" providers (e.g., ESPN, and TBS). Most sports organizations in the United States, such as intercollegiate athletic departments, municipal recreation departments, private or government-owned businesses, are not publicly traded entities.

Time-Off Benefits

Because there is no legal requirement to offer time off except for unpaid leave to care for family medical issues through FMLA, the type and availability of discretionary time-off benefits vary. Time off is manifested in the form of holiday pay, vacation pay, sick pay, jury duty leave, bereavement leave, and/or any combination time off used by employees. Some employers break the type of paid time off into separate categories where employees will earn vacation and/or sick time based on the number of hours or months or years worked. Some employers combine all paid time off together and do not require employees to designate whether time is taken off for vacation, personal, or sick time. Employers may choose to lump sum time leave into "paid time off," commonly referred to as PTO, instead of a classification system. The PTO system combines all paid leave into a total number of days/hours that an employee can take off in a given period.

In the United States, typical employers offer 8–12 paid holidays off per year, which may include New Year's Day, Martin Luther King Day, President's Day, Memorial Day, Independence Day, Labor Day, Thanksgiving, and Christmas. Some employers offer more than one day at Thanksgiving and/ or Christmas, and some also include Columbus Day and Veterans Day. It is standard for employers to pay time-and-a-half for hourly employees who work on holidays, but there is no federal or state requirement for providing extra compensation. Without a federal or state mandate and because of the special nature of sectors of the sports industry that purposefully schedule games on holidays (e.g., intercollegiate athletics and professional sports), hourly and part-time employees may not receive holiday pay. New Year's Eve or New Year's Day college football bowl games, NFL games on Thanksgiving, NBA games on Christmas, and golf or auto racing on Memorial Day and Labor Day are just a few examples of sports contests on holidays.

Whether an NBA or NFL game played on Thanksgiving, an NCAA football bowl game scheduled on New Year's Day, or a holiday marathon, sport events on holidays require staffing and overtime pay for hourly wage workers.

There is no federal or state requirement to provide vacation pay and no regulation that states how much or little must be offered, so there is no industry standard for vacation plans. Some organizations allow employees to "roll over" vacation pay that has been earned into future calendar years, and some organizations have a use-it-or-lose-it policy whereby any vacation not used by the end of the calendar year (or date used for calculating vacation) will be lost. Because of the unique nature of the industry and its irregular hours, college athletic coaches and trainers may be restricted in the use of vacation benefits around seasons of competition. Athletic coaches on a 12-month contract at Young Harris College (2013), for example, are restricted to vacations only during summer dates; however, language in the employee manual designates the availability to work "customary office hours" during the period when vacation times are being taken.

Most employers who provide sick-time leave for full-time employees use an accrual-based method for allocations. For example, coaches, trainers, and athletics staff at the University of Texas at Austin (2015) appointed to work 40 hours per week are permitted 8 hours of sick leave each month, whereas leave for employees appointed to work between 20 and 39 hours per week is accrued based on the proportion of the hours worked (see **Table 4-3**).

© tanuha2001/shutterstock

Time-off benefits are often viewed as an easy, cost-effective way to provide employee benefits; however, these benefits can be costly, and managers should be mindful of the budget implications. Sports managers and supervisors should know that while time-off can be a useful tool to allow employees to take important time away from work for personal, family or medical reasons; the costs associated with time-off plans may impact productivity.

TABLE 4-3: Vacation Accrual at University of Texas at Austin (2017)

Total Years of State Service	Total Months of State Service	Hours Accrued Each Month
Less than 2 years	Less than 24 months	8
At least 2 years but less than 5	At least 24 months but less than 60	9
At least 5 years but less than 10	At least 60 months but less than 120	10
At least 10 years but less than 15	At least 120 months but less than 180	11
At least 15 years but less than 20	At least 180 months but less than 240	13
At least 20 years but less than 25	At least 240 months but less than 300	15
At least 25 years but less than 30	At least 300 months but less than 360	17
At least 30 years but less than 35	At least 360 months but less than 420	19
At least 35 years	At least 420 months	21

Courtesy of Texas State Auditor's Office

Dependent-Care Support

A dependent-care assistance program is a discretionary benefit regulated by the IRS in which the employer sponsors a program that provides reimbursement for dependent care. Dependent-care support includes child care (up to age 13), elder care, and sick care. Child care includes licensed day care, preschool or nursery programs, holiday or summer camps, private sitters, pickup late fees caused by work schedules, and general supervision. Employers may simply support employees by providing paid (on unpaid) time off for dependent care, or they may actually incur expenses, provide or contribute to a pretax payment option, or even provide an on-site facility for child care. On-site child-care facilities are common in YMCA facilities and community recreation centers. The benefits for employees include utilization of services for free or for a discounted rate.

If an organization participates in an actual dependent-care assistance program, reimbursement is capped at $2500 for singles and $5000 for married couples if certain conditions are met; however, employees enrolled in the program are not permitted to claim the child- or dependent-care credit on their tax returns, but employees are permitted to deduct related expenses from their paychecks on a pretax basis (IRS, 2016b).

Personal and/or Professional Development

Employers may provide time, resources, and financial support for workers to engage in personal or professional development endeavors. Personal development focuses primarily on wellness and health (fitness). Employees may receive access to workout areas in an athletic department or team facility or a partial to full reimbursement for the cost of a gym membership, country club membership, or spa day. Corporate wellness plans may even incentivize employees for meeting participation goals, participating in assessment activities (e.g., cholesterol check), or achieving specific health standards.

Professional development focuses on employees gaining knowledge, skills, and/or abilities relative to their careers. In addition to providing time, resources, and financial support for workers to participate in a workshop, conference, meeting, or educational seminar, tuition assistance may also be available as a discretionary benefit. Personnel in intercollegiate athletics, club and recreational sports departments, and intramural programs are in an ideal setting to take advantage of advanced education opportunities contingent on intuitional policies and eligibility. Educational assistance typically includes tuition payment, tuition reimbursement, and/or other educational resources (e.g., books and training materials).

Fox Sports, ESPN, Turner Broadcasting System (TBS), and Delaware North (a leader in food, beverage, and retail management systems for stadiums and arenas) are examples of sports organizations that provide tuition assistance programs. Often, employers will have a requirement that the recipient of the education assistance benefits is required to remain with the organization for a certain period of time after the completion of his or her program. This practice ensures the employer receives some type of derived benefit of the educational investment in its employee.

Educational assistance is commonly available to professional athletes through respective players' associations. Each year, there are examples of draft picks for professional sports organizations who "left early" before earning a degree. The unions for these organizations have funding and "plans" for players to essentially earn their degrees while they are active players or when they retire. The NFL Tuition Assistance Plan established in 2002, for example, specifies that players with at least 1 year of service or retired players with 5 or more years of credited seasons are eligible for reimbursement under specified conditions (Hewit, 2015).

Perquisites of Fringe Benefits

Perks or "fringe" benefits apply to opportunities afforded to specific employees, such as a clothing allowance or lease car. During the 2016 World Series, front-office staff at the Cleveland Indians were divided into two groups to designate which day they would receive a ticket and a seat aboard the team's charter plane for games at Wrigley Field in Chicago (A. Madison, personal communication, October 26, 2016). Selected perquisites for select employees may include the use of team exercise facilities, free meals in the cafeteria, cell-phone plans, iPads, complimentary parking, or other creative benefits.

One of the changes detailed in the 2016–2020 MLB Collective Bargaining Agreement decreased the daily game-day per diem for players from $100.50 to $30 (Associated Press, 2016). In return, clubhouses are providing food for both home games and road trips, which is estimated to save players approximately $6000 annually.

Administering Payroll and Benefits

Sports managers and supervisors have varying degrees of responsibilities aligned with payroll and benefits administration. At the very least, they must understand the processes.

Payroll administration takes into account any financial impact on an employee's wages as a result of benefits (i.e., payroll deduction or reimbursement). Benefits administration precedes payroll because the latter includes tax deductions and contributions to employees triggered by the types of benefits afforded to workers.

Software is abundant to assist in administering these areas, as is the availability of third-party vendor services. Still, sports managers and supervisors have a large role in payroll and benefits administration even if an accounting or human resource firm is retained.

BENEFITS ADMINISTRATION

The scope of benefits administration is laden with meticulous recordkeeping. The administrator is a conduit for the organization and external business affiliates and is tasked with an endless stream of interaction with employees, managers, insurance companies, accountants, and multiple plan providers. The supervisor is the direct line to approve and coordinate time-off benefits (e.g., vacations), and managers are primarily responsible for establishing the actual procedures and practices for awarding benefits.

Sports managers and supervisors involved in benefits administration must be knowledgeable in the intricacies of all insurance policies for a company, and they must be diligent in communicating important benefits information to employees, such as annual open-enrollment periods or changes in programs, deductibles, or exclusions. Internally tracking benefits usage and ensuring payroll deductions and reimbursements are accurate are primary responsibilities in benefits administration.

An employee manual is an excellent place to explain how specific benefits will be handled by the organization. For example, the manual dictates policies for cell-phone reimbursements in respect to eligibility, any restrictions, maximum remuneration, and the frequency of payment (monthly, bi-weekly, etc.).

Sports supervisors and managers may have sole responsibility for decisions regarding benefits, or they may be assigned to a committee that gathers and analyzes data from plan providers to make recommendations for new programs or changes in existing policies. Vendor contracts, invoices, and statements must also be reviewed on a regular basis for reconciliation of payments due or those owed to service providers.

In sum, benefits administration is more complex and cumbersome than payroll administration, especially because of changing legislation in healthcare policies and FMLA laws, but the two processes are closely linked,

which is why a managerial approach
should ensure that the right systems
and personnel are in place to handle
responsibilities.

PAYROLL ADMINISTRATION

In general, payroll administration con-
sists of ensuring accurate payment of
salaried and hourly employees. Payroll
includes the total amount of wages
and salaries paid to all employees.
The outcome of payroll administration should be a timely paycheck

for every employee and accurate documentation of tax information in
accordance with state and federal compliance regulations. Organizations
may process payroll internally by appointing a specific individual or
department to undertake responsibilities, or they may process payroll
externally by contracting with an outside agency to perform the required
activities.

Payroll administration begins with collecting and processing a series
of federal and state employment forms (I-9s and W-4s) when a candidate
is initially hired; however, form processing represents only a small portion
of the activities required to accurately produce paychecks or direct deposits
(see **Box 4-2**). The primary considerations in processing payroll are accountability and accuracy. Another consideration is whether an organization
processes payroll internally or externally through a third-party independent
contractor. Software such as Quick Books, Timelogix, Kronos, or UltiPro
is widely available to assist with many payroll functions.

Recap

Total compensation or a compensation package includes both wage earnings and benefits. Managers and supervisors must apply business acumen
when making compensation decisions, such as determining the appropriate
salary to offer a new hire that is both enticing and equitable. Compensation
strategies vary in organizations and are dependent on external and internal
factors. There is no one-size-fits-all advice for developing compensation
strategies, and although two similarly situated organizations may take

BOX 4-2

General Process for Payroll Administration

1. Ensure all federal and state employment forms are on file for all employees (including W4s, I-9s, and any required immigration forms for non-U.S. citizens).
2. Define a pay period based on the frequency of pay (i.e., weekly, bi-weekly, or monthly), and devise a payroll processing schedule that allows ample time to process paperwork, review reports, and correct errors before employees receive a paycheck.
3. Review and edit payroll records to account for any changes occurring during the payroll period (addition or deletion of voluntary deductions, changes in address, etc.).
4. Compute or review salary information, including data from time sheets reflecting regular, overtime, and vacation hours.
5. Allocate bonuses, commission, retroactive pay, or any nonstandard alterations in pay, including

due overpayment and/or underpayment from a prior pay period.
6. Adjust pay to allocate for other appropriations, such as bonuses, commissions, retroactive pay resulting from a pay raise, or garnered wage deductions resulting from overpayment in a prior pay period.
7. Review reports to verify payroll amounts for each employee prior to printing paychecks or generating direct deposit slips. Make adjustments accordingly.
8. Run payroll by providing data to an accounting firm, or print paychecks and direct deposit forms internally.
9. Share or send payroll information to specified managers.
10. Store payroll information in a secure, confidential location.

a comparable approach, the two likely will not have the same effect at each business.

Benefits are vitally important to attract and retain employees in the sports and recreation industry, especially for low-paying positions. Legal benefits are the mandatory benefits available for all employees in an organization, whether paid or partially paid by the employer (e.g., health, life, and disability insurance). There is also a wide range of discretionary benefits and perquisites (fringe benefits) in the sports industry. One of the relatively unique characteristics of the sports industry is the ability to offer creative or nontraditional benefits such as complimentary game tickets or opportunities to meet and mingle with professional athletes.

Determining the policies for administering benefits is important before designing the processes to administer payroll because deductibles and reimbursements must be accounted for in preparing accurate employee paychecks and direct-deposit notes. These functions may be administered internally or outsourced to a third party. The overall goal of payroll administration is timely and accurate payment.

🌐 GLOBAL SPOTLIGHT 4-1

Compensation Challenges for Fitness Clubs in Eastern Europe

Michelle Dietrich Skaggs

Michelle Dietrich Skaggs is an American citizen with over 15 years of management and consulting experience in the fitness and spa industry in Eastern Europe. She served as general manager and vice president of World Class in Romania prior to her appointment as the country manager for World Class Health Academy in Poland and, eventually, as manager for World Class International.

An ex-pat from the United States, Dietrich Skaggs originally moved to Warsaw, Poland, in 1995 with her husband, who was then a Polish citizen, in an era soon after the country's revolution. She moved to Bucharest, Romania, in 2001 when afforded the opportunity to manage the country's inaugural World Class Health Academy at the Grand J.W. Marriott Hotel.

A worldwide provider of fitness established in 1983, World Class exploded internationally with over 30 locations throughout 14 countries in Europe and the Middle East. The company's founder, former Swedish bodybuilding champion Ulf Bengtsson, had a mission to create a five-star luxury wellness experience for sports lovers. Consequently, many facilities were connected to high-end hotel properties offering spa treatments and personalized structured workouts for individuals and groups. In addition to providing services for hotel guests, World Class offered high-end priced memberships to the upscale market. In 2005, World Class expanded to its second Romanian location in the Bucharest Radisson Hotel, and soon, the company had seven properties throughout the capital city, Constanta, Timisoara, and Cluj-Napoca (Dietrich Skaggs, M., personal communication, September 13, 2016).

When Dietrich Skaggs was initially hired as the general manager for the first Romanian World Class facility at the Bucharest Marriott, she supervised approximately 10 salaried employees, each of whom was signed to a lifetime contract. The club's payroll included receptionists, trainers, massage therapists, managers, and kid-club supervisors who serviced approximately 2500 members and 80 daily hotel guests (Dietrich Skaggs, M., personal communication, September 13, 2016). Under the model of indefinite contracts, businesses operated with fewer employees who ideally could do more than what could be accomplished with a larger staff of specialized talent. As a "lifetime employee," each worker was expected to service clients and resolve any and every issue, no matter the employee's particular job title or scope of expertise.

In 2001, Romania and much of Eastern Europe was still transitioning to a market-based economy following decades of Communist rule and a socialist attitude that stifled free enterprise. The people of Romania, Poland, Slovakia, Hungary, Bulgaria, and neighboring countries were accustomed to a protectionist government structure that promoted lifetime labor agreements marked by low wage earnings. During that time, Dietrich Skaggs was faced with the challenge of facilitating economic liberalization by converting lifetime salaried employees into freelance, independent, third-party hourly wage earners. The idea of capitalism was almost nonexistent in the country, which meant the pretense of a new type of socialized injustice was thrust upon the current employees relegated to learning that all labor agreements were dissolved and no longer valid.

The "new" compensation arrangements included an hourly wage scale and zero employee benefits beyond personal use of facilities. Emphasizing the advantages of being able to work at multiple fitness locations as a freelance employee was the modus operandi to encourage trainers and other workers to refrain from legal action against World Class.

Dietrich Skaggs played a role in designing and implementing a graduated hourly wage system based on longevity, certification level, and educational attainment. Depending on these factors, exercise specialists were tiered as (1) Basic Fitness Instructors, (2) Intermediate Trainers, and (3) Master Trainers. Because the industry attracted relatively young workers (average age of 25–26), the lowest level of longevity was based on only 2 years of consecutive employment. A performance-based incentive plan was included to compensate employees on the basis of the number of training sessions taught in a given time period. Therefore, there were many pay structures to entice employees to continue working with World Class while also marketing their services to other businesses.

Dietrich Skaggs was lured back to Poland in 2011 to turn around one of World Class's unprofitable operations in Warsaw. While helping the club to almost break even, she left World Class in 2012 to obtain her doctorate degree in business administration and to refocus her personal and professional priorities. In 2017 she was still consulting for fitness enterprises in Poland, Romania, and Turkey.

The global spotlight was adapted from an original case featuring Michelle Dietrich Skaggs written by Dr. Perry Haan, Professor of Marketing, Tiffin University.

DISCUSSION QUESTIONS

1. What are the reasons a sports organization might use a below-the-market strategy when determining compensation for an open position?
2. What are the concerns with using a below-the-market strategy?
3. What can an employer do to attract high-quality candidates even though the compensation may be lower than market value?
4. What considerations do hiring managers consider when hiring for a company that publishes salary data?
5. What can organizations do to prevent pay compression?
6. Noting the perception that the sports industry commonly has lower entry-level pay compared with other industries, how can organizations attract and retain employees?
7. Why is it important to devise procedures for administering benefits before developing payroll processes?

APPLIED ACTIVITIES

1. Considering the role of a senior associate athletic director at the University of Oregon with an opening for an associate athletic director for compliance, formulate a compensation strategy for this position using the four steps outlined in the chapter.
2. Create a PTO plan for a sports organization. Determine whether to include sick time, vacation time, and other PTO benefits. Determine whether the organization will have one PTO plan or whether sick time and vacation time will be calculated separately. Determine how this will be applied to full-time, part-time, salaried, and hourly employees.

CASE STUDY

Compensation Strategy in Action

The following represents a fictitious scenario for a human resource specialist in a professional sports setting to demonstrate how to execute the steps and activities necessary to develop an appropriate compensation package for a management position.

The position of director of communications has become available on a member team of the National Basketball Association (NBA). The director will provide oversight for all sporting events and nonsporting events hosted at the arena. The position requires overseeing a staff of 10 individuals who are responsible for providing communications support related to media and business operations.

The Human Resource Specialist Reviews External Compensation Strategies

To review external strategies, the human resource (HR) specialist contacts the NBA League offices and four other NBA teams located in similar markets to obtain general salary data for this type of position. The HR specialist determines that the market value for this position is between $90,000 and $120,000 depending on education, experience, and skill. The HR specialist determines that paying at market value of this range is appropriate, as the hire will have several public initiatives within his or her scope of responsibility. The HR specialist would like to recommend that the organization should pay the communication director above market value to get the best person available, but with the understanding that the team has not had a winning season in 4 years and is in a difficult financial situation for the next one to two seasons, a meet-the-market strategy is determined to be the appropriate tactic.

An Internal Alignment Assessment Is Conducted

The HR specialist researches internal payroll information and learns that the employees who would be reporting to this position earn salaries between $45,000 and $75,000. It is also learned that other director-level positions within the organization earn salaries between $70,000 and $140,000. The director-level position with a salary of $140,000, however, is a long-term employee with over 20 years of experience that has an additional financial role that requires a specialized knowledge and skill set. It is determined that the meet-the-market strategy of compensating the new employee in the range of $90,000–$120,000 passes the internal alignment analysis.

A Legal and Financial Assessment Is Conducted

After meeting with several team executives and reviewing extensive budget reports, the HR specialist concludes that, financially, the company is stable but not overly profitable. Although reports indicate that the company does operate consistently with a slight profit, it is apparent that fiscal responsibility is necessary to maintain the slim margins. That assessment is valuable to assess the opportunity to hire someone on the high or low end of the suggested pay scale.

The HR specialist determines that if a candidate arises with a higher-than-expected level of education, experience, and/or skill (15 plus years), it might warrant paying at the higher end of the salary, or $120,000. If, however, a qualified candidate emerges who has less experience (6–10 years) but still has a high potential, a starting salary of closer to $100,000 would be appropriate and perhaps preferred given the financial implications. Furthermore, the HR specialist concludes that given the current landscape of employees in terms of gender, race, and ethnicity, there is no expectation of discrimination concerns regardless of which candidate is selected.

The Compensation Strategy Is Defined

Given the desire for a high-level, experienced candidate, the HR specialist recommends that the expectation for starting salary should be $100,000–$110,000.

CASE STUDY QUESTIONS

1. How is the external market value for the position of director of communications for an NBA franchise determined?

2. Why did a salary range of $90,000–$120,000 seem to pass the internal assessment or equity test?

3. How did the financial assessment of the organization factor into the final salary range ($100,000–$110,000) for the new position?

Laws

Patient Protection and Affordable Care Act, 42 U.S.C. § 18001 (2010)

REFERENCES

Associated Press. (2016, December 5). MLB meal money cut, but teams assume cost of clubhouse food. *USA Today*. Retrieved from http://www.usatoday.com/story/sports/mlb/2016/12/05/mlb-meal-money-cut-but-teams-assume-cost-of-clubhouse-food/95015932/

Berkowitz, S., Upton, J., Schnaars, C., Dourgherty, S., & Neuharth-Keusch, A. (2016). 2015 NCAA coaches' salaries. *USA Today*. Retrieved from http://sports.usatoday.com/ncaa/salaries/

Bowdoin College. (2015). *Athletic coaches. Bowdoin College: Medical absences and leave policies for athletic coaches and laboratory instructors*. Retrieved from https://www.bowdoin.edu/hr/pdf/benefits-absence-mgmt-coaches-lab-instructors.pdf

Dick's Sporting Goods. (2016). *Golfworks 2016 medical*. Retrieved from http://benefityourliferesources.com/index.php?option=com_content&view=article&id=61&Itemid=184

Espinoza, C, Ukleja, M., & Rusch, C. (2010). *Managing the millennials: Discover the core competencies for managing today's workforce*. New York: John Wiley & Sons.

ESPN, Inc. (2016). *Media zone. Fact sheet*. Retrieved from http://espnmediazone.com/us/espn-inc-fact-sheet/

Farnum, A. (2011, October 7). *A delicate balancing act: Petrie hands over coaching duties to trustworthy assistant.* Retrieved from http://www.ncaa.com/news /volleyball-women/article/2011-10-01/delicate-balancing-act

Fisher, N. (2016, July 28). NBA enters health insurance in unprecedented way. *Forbes.* Retrieved from http://www.nflalumni.org/healthcare-benefits

Goldaper, A. (1981, March 17). NBA adds counseling services. *New York Times,* B18.

Green, C., & Heywood, J. (2008). Does performance pay increase job satisfaction? *Económica, 75,* 710–728.

Guskiewicz, K., Marshall, S., Bailes, J., McCrea, M., Cantu, R., Randolph, C., & Jordan, B. (2005, October). Association between recurrent concussion and late-life cognitive impairment in retired professional football players. *Neurosurgery, 57*(4), 719–726.

Hewit, A. (2015, May). *NFL Player Tuition Assistance Plan. Tuition Playbook. Summary Plan Description.* Retrieved from https://nflpaweb.blob.core .windows.net/media/Default/PDFs/Player%20Development/2015TuitionSPD .pdf

Hubman, J. (2011). *A financial analysis of publicly traded professional sports teams.* Honors Thesis, the College at Brockport, State University of New York, Brockport, NY.

Internal Revenue Service. (2016a). *Affordable Care Act.* Retrieved from https:// www.irs.gov/affordable-care-act/employers/questions-and-answers-on -employer-shared-responsibility-provisions-under-the-affordable-care-act #Basics

Internal Revenue Service. (2016b). *Dependent care assistance.* Retrieved from https://www.irs.gov/publications/p15b/ar02.html#en_US_2016_publink100 0193662

Kellison, T., Kim, Y., & Magnusen, M. (2013). The work attitudes of millennials in collegiate recreation sports. *Journal of Park and Recreation Administration, 31*(1), 78–97.

Kelly, M. (2016, September 11). Is he, in fact, our savior? *Sunday Sun National Edition,* p. 32.

King, B. (2012, August 13). What is the salary pay-off in sports? Industry salary survey. *Street & Smith Sports Business Daily.* Retrieved from http://www.sports businessdaily.com/Journal/Issues/2012/08/13/In-Depth/Salary-survey.aspx

Koblin, J. (2013, June 27). *Curious how much ESPN executives make? We have pay grade charts.* Retrieved from http://deadspin.com/curious-how-much-espn -executives-make-we-have-pay-grad-594069649

Lipovsky, W. (2016, July 8). NFL pension plan: Retirement plan and retirement pay details. *First Quarter Finance.* Retrieved from http://firstquarterfinance .com/nfl-pension-plan-retirement-plan/

Liverpool Echo. (2013, July 22). Windfall for staff at Sports Direct, p. 15.

Miller, J. (2011, March 4). Texas coach gives birth, then gains semi-final berth. *USA Today,* Sports, 8C.

Modery, M. (2011). Justifying workers' compensation awards to retired athletes with concussion-caused dementia. *Temple Law Review, 84,* 247–282.

Murray, A. (2015, March 4). Forbes names Ohio State University Athletics Department one of the 10 best organizations to work for in sports. *The Ohio State University*. Retrieved from https://news.osu.edu/news/2015/03/04/forbes-ohio-state-athletics-top-organization-to-work-for/

National Basketball Association. (2016). *Benefits overview. Memphis Grizzlies. Life and disability insurance*. Retrieved from http://www.nba.com/grizzlies/about/careers/benefits-overview/

National Football League. (2017). *League employment benefits*. Retrieved from http://www.nfl.com/careers/benefits

National Football League Alumni. (2016). *Healthcare benefits*. Retrieved from http://www.nflalumni.org/healthcare-benefits

ObamaCareFacts.com. (2016). *Open enrollment 2016*. Retrieved from http://obamacarefacts.com/2015/10/28/open-enrollment-2016/

Parks, M. (2016, June 29). Legendary basketball coach advanced women's sports. *Washington Post*, A1.

Poulter, S. (2011, July 15). *A 643,000 windfall for 2000 Sports Direct staff. London Daily Mail Consumer Report*. Retrieved from http://www.dailymail.co.uk/news/article-2369797/2-000-Sports-Direct-staff-line-76-500-windfall-profits-leap-40.html

Roche, F. (2014, July 9). Former Tennessee Titans take hit under new workers' comp law. *The Tennessean*. Retrieved from http://www.tennessean.com/story/news/2014/07/08/former-tennessee-titans-take-hit-new-workers-comp-law/12322817/

Rovell, D. (2012, August 30). Teams face workers comp threat. *ESPN*. Retrieved from http://www.espn.com/espn/otl/story/_/id/8316657/nfl-teams-facing-large-bills-related-workers-compensation-claims-head-injuries

Ruyter, T. (1998, July). Employee stock options for professional sport players. *Plan Sponsor Magazine*. Retrieved from http://www.plansponsor.com/MagazineArticle.aspx?Id=6442461393

Schroeder, J. (2015, October). 2015 IDEA fitness industry compensation trend report. *IDEA Fitness Journal*, 42–53.

Smucker, M., & Kent, A. (2004, January 1). The influence of referent selection on pay, supervision, work, and co-worker satisfaction across three distinct sport industry segments. *International Journal of Sport Management, 8*(1), 27–43.

Social Security Administration. (2017). *Information for people working. Update 2017*. Retrieved from Social Security Administration.gov at https://www.ssa.gov/pubs/EN-05-10003.pdf

The Economist. (2013, January 26). *The economics of sport insurance: The claim game*. Retrieved from http://www.economist.com/news/finance-and-economics/21570723-calculations-behind-insurance-athletes-claim-game

The Ohio State University. (2016, May). *Human resources. Compensation overview*. Retrieved from https://hr.osu.edu/services/compensation/

Thomas, R., & VanHorn, L. (2016). College football coaches' pay and contracts: Are they overpaid and unfairly treated? *Indiana Law Journal, 91*(2), 189–242.

University of Texas at Austin. (2015). *Annual leave: Accruing your leave. Human resources.* Retrieved from http://hr.utexas.edu/current/leave/annual.html

U.S. Department of Labor, Wage and Hour Division. (2012). *Fact sheet 28: The Family Medical Leave Act.* Retrieved from https://www.dol.gov/whd/regs/compliance/whdfs28.pdf

U.S. Department of Labor, Bureau of Labor Statistics. (2016, September 8). *Employer cost for compensation, September 2016.* Retrieved from https://www.bls.gov/news.release/pdf/ecec.pdf

U.S. Securities and Exchange Commission. (2015). *Form 11-K. Nike, Inc.: 401(k) Savings and profit sharing plan for Employees of Nike, Inc.* Retrieved from https://www.sec.gov/Archives/edgar/data/320187/000119312512479172/d442874d11k.htm

Vesely, R. (2012, February 21). *EAP proves a giant step for ballplayers.* Retrieved from http://www.workforce.com/2012/02/21/eap-proves-a-giant-step-for-ballplayers/

Young Harris College. (2013, October 25). *Vacation benefits. Young Harris College employee handbook.* Retrieved from http://www.yhc.edu/employeehandbook/pol303.html

Pre-Game Staffing
LINE-UPS AND MATCH-UPS

Preface
Preparation Never Ceases

Shortly after the 2016 World Series ended for Major League Baseball's (MLB) Cleveland Indians and Chicago Cubs, the human resource departments in each organization were already busy addressing staffing for the 2017 season. While anticipating a spike in attendance as a result of the World Series euphoria the season prior, management knew it would remain a challenge to sell out stadiums in their franchise locations in the windy city (Chicago) and city on the lake (Cleveland) during the cold spring months.

Calculating the optimal staff levels for sports organizations, events, and facilities is both a science and an art that accounts for predictable and unpredictable variables that can affect employment needs. The return of LeBron James to the National Basketball Association's (NBA) Cleveland Cavaliers in 2010 and the franchise's World Championship in 2016 exemplify how staffing needs for an organization can change as a result of a marquee player or acclaimed success. The Cavaliers had actually downsized their sales force shortly after 2010 season and increased other types of workers on game days.

Phase II addresses staffing. "Staff" generally refers to the employees who work for an organization. In most sectors of the sports industry, the staff includes employees and "nonemployees" who work on behalf of an organization as volunteers, interns, or independent contractors (e.g., referees, accountants, security personnel, etc.).

Phase II begins with Chapter 5, which addresses activities associated with planning for vacancies in sports organizations. The chapter provides an overview of the emergence of analytics in sports organizations as one of the drivers of employment decisions. Analytics is a relatively novel area in sports and especially in conjunction with human resource activities, but it serves as a valuable tool in supporting managerial decisions and effectiveness. Chapter 5 addresses the means to predict vacancies and respond to planned and unplanned openings to maintain appropriate staffing levels. The chapter also addresses the requirements for developing the blueprints for recruitment plans, including flowcharts, job descriptions, and selected communication strategies.

Chapter 6 addresses the activities for recruiting in sports organizations, including procedures for developing effective marketing materials, decision factors for selecting appropriate distribution channels, steps to manage applicants, and considerations in reviewing candidate files. The chapter also explores the practice of recruiting volunteer labor, which is a common staffing approach in the sports industry as a means to control costs, provide experience for future practitioners, and satisfy the altruistic needs of individuals.

Chapter 7 addresses the screening and selection process involved in talent acquisition for sports organizations. Information is presented on strategies for conducting different types of interviews, the applicability of assessment tests in the sports industry, and the procedures for communicating with references and conducting background checks. The chapter concludes with an examination of the important considerations in notifying applicants of their selection and the information included in the onboarding process.

Phase II is a sequenced journey through the tasks of publicizing vacancies, sourcing qualified candidates, communicating with applicants, managing application materials, reviewing resumes and materials, checking references, conducting background checks, evaluating the results of any assessment tests, selecting a candidate, notifying candidates selected and *not* selected, and onboarding a new employee. Phase II is also infused with the foundational knowledge presented in Phase I by addressing strategic human resource planning, employment law, compensation and benefits administration, and negotiations as they apply to the function of staffing sports organizations.

When employees of the Cubs and Indians devote time and resources to seasonal staffing, a managerial approach provides the impetus for appreciating that preparation never ceases. In turn, the organizations can reap the benefit of the likelihood of making the right hiring decisions and adequately preparing their employees for success.

CHAPTER 5

Roster Changes

PREPARING FOR VACANCIES IN SPORTS ORGANIZATIONS

In terms of planning to fill vacancies, we partner closely with SAFE Management, ARAMARK, SP+, Chimes, and the Maryland Stadium Authority to staff our seasonal workers. Because we have only 10 to 15 events per year in the stadium, we rely heavily on these partners to help with determining staffing levels. Each company can keep the workforce more engaged (and employed longer) than the National Football League (NFL) team itself. The Baltimore Ravens partners with each vendor and then designs and delivers the necessary training to seasonal employees specific to M&T Bank Stadium and the Ravens organization. We are challenged with ensuring the workforce is solid and represents us well, and in 2016, we are continuing to examine ways to improve in order to provide optimal service to our fans and to our employees.

Elizabeth Jackson
Vice President of Human Resources
Baltimore Ravens (National Football League)

LEARNING OUTCOMES

1. Explain the role of analytics in the human resource functions of sports organizations.

2. Apply a formula to calculate annual employee turnover rates in an organization.

3. Identify tools and factors to consider when predicting vacancies in sports organizations.

4. Explain how labor demand and labor supply are calculated in a workforce analysis.

5. Identify components of a recruitment plan flowchart for sports employment positions.
6. Identify the functions of a search committee.
7. Explain the importance of planning communication strategies before recruiting employees.

KEY TERMS

Analytics	Labor supply	Skills inventory
Boiled frog phenomenon	Organizational flowchart	Stakeholder
Communication strategy chart	Organizational structure analysis	Succession planning
Essential functions	Planned vacancies	Trend analysis
Employee inventory	Recruitment flowchart	Turnover rate
Job analysis	Recruitment plan	Unplanned vacancies
Job description	Reengineering	Vacancies
Labor demand	Search firm	Workforce analysis

Lead-Off

Armed with knowledge of strategic planning, employment law, negotiations, employment agreements, and compensation administration processes, sports managers and supervisors can be effective in the role of staffing. Before the actual recruiting begins to fill vacancies, there is still the necessity of additional planning. Strategic planning in human resources identifies the over-reaching goals related to organizational capacity and personnel and the strategies for achieving the initiatives. Tactical planning, however, adds a layer of specificity requiring supervisors and managers to get in the trenches and actually execute short-term activities to achieve their objectives. Tactical plans and activities to fill vacancies assist managers in moving closer to acquiring talent through the processes of recruitment, screening, and selection.

Sports managers who anticipate increases or decreases in staffing needs and are prepared to fill vacancies with qualified candidates demonstrate the value of human capital as one of the most important assets of an organization. Elizabeth Jackson of the NFL Baltimore Ravens and other practitioners in the area of human resources are sensitive to the impact of staffing decisions on both operational effectiveness and the financial viability of the organization.

Labor cost is the biggest line item in a budget, but managing a facility or business below optimal staffing levels can adversely impact the efficiency and effectiveness of the organization. A fitness center may save money by staffing the front desk with one only employee, but if a single worker cannot adequately handle the demands of the position, dissatisfied members may choose to join another facility, therefore causing the organization to lose revenues from lost dues.

How many volunteers will be needed to effectively supply the hospitality booths at the venues for the 2020 Olympic Games in Tokyo, Japan? What specific tasks are needed? Who will be available and qualified to serve as volunteers from inside the home country or from abroad? What are the language competencies needed and available? Who will be tasked with training the volunteers, and who will directly supervise the workers? What are the needs for part-time workers, seasonal workers, commission-based workers, volunteers, interns, or full-time employees for the Olympic Games?

The Tokyo 2020 Olympics will continue the practice of using over 70,000 volunteers.

The answers to these types of questions assist in planning for staffing needs. The application of workforce analysis, research, and planning tools will provide the necessary information to facilitate data-driven decisions to address staffing.

Most sectors of the sports industry are considered service-oriented enterprises. Sports managers, supervisors, and owners of stadiums, arenas, gyms, bowling alleys, boat docks, recreation centers, and little league parks need to be knowledgeable about the number of staff and the requisite skills necessary to effectively and efficiently service the needs of their customers, members, or clients in given period. Although it may be a short-term cost-saving initiative, understaffing typically results in a negative impact on organizational performance and customer or client satisfaction. Overstaffing, on the other hand, typically results in high labor costs, stagnant workers, and lower profits. Sports managers must decide on the optimal staffing levels to meet the demands of the environmental and situational context, such as peak times, seasonal fluctuations, or growth initiatives.

This chapter explores the value of data analytics in human resource activities applied to sports organizations, especially for predicting vacancies. Additionally, this chapter describes the process of preparing for vacancies, including job descriptions, search committees, and the tasks involved in recruitment planning.

Analytics in Sports Organizations

The NFL Cleveland Browns hired Paul DePodesta, one of the most recognized sports analytics professionals in the business, just prior to the 2016 season. A Harvard graduate, DePodesta previously worked for the Major League Baseball (MLB) franchise and was the source for the depiction of the character featured in the movie *Moneyball* who helped Billy Beane and the 2002 Oakland A's to their acclaimed success. One of DePodesta's first assignments with the Browns was to serve on the search committee to hire a new head coach. Flanked with the insights from an analytics specialist skilled in the application of criterion charts and predictive measurement tools, the Browns capitalized on data-driven approaches to assess the skills and attributes of candidates and eventually hired Hue Jackson, former offensive coordinator for the Cincinnati Bengals. Cleveland finished 1–15 for the 2016–17 season but retained Jackson for the following season.

A fairly recent trend in the front offices of the major professional sport franchises has been to employ data analytics specialists to assist team executives in making informed business decisions on everything from dynamic ticket-pricing strategies to draft picks and player acquisitions (see **Action Shot 5-1**). Although colleges such as the University of Nebraska Athletic Department are adding new positions for data analytics specialists, and independent agencies such as Turnkey Intelligence and Front Row Marketing Services are renowned for providing customized data analysis services for a host of sports organizations, professional sports teams are seeing the most growth in the field of sports analytics.

The basic premise of **analytics** is to systematically examine data to determine patterns, trends, or relationships. Historical data, for instance, can determine the average time to source candidates or fill a vacancy. Relational data analytics evaluates multiple variables, such as the correlation between the length of an interview and the selection of a candidate for an entry-level lifeguard position. Predictive data are the most sophisticated type of analytics and are used in conjunction with models, formulas, and algorithms to forecast events or behaviors. Predictive data, for example, can isolate competencies or attributes in a job seeker that are best in predicting future performance for a specific organization. A predictive index is an analytical tool developed to evaluate candidates in the recruiting process. Similarly, a predictive index and other analytics tools are useful to learn what it is

© iQoncept/shutterstock

Sport Analytics was popularized by the movie *Moneyball*, depicting the mathematical expertise of a scout who provided the owner of the 2002 Oakland A's with sophisticated statistical data analysis on players.

▶ ACTION SHOT 5-1

Boston Analytics Specialists Provide Solutions to Team Presidents

Tim Zue—MLB Boston Red Sox

Josh Brinkman—NHL Boston Bruins and TD Gardens

As analytics rapidly evolves in the sports arena, so do the individuals tasked with making sense out of data and information to present to team presidents and owners. Two analytics specialists providing valuable insights for professional sports teams in Boston are Tim Zue of the MLB Red Sox and Josh Brickman of the NHL Bruins and TD Gardens.

Zue, Senior Vice President of Finance, Strategy, and Analytics, reports directly to the Red Sox team President. His staff is comprised of ten staff members in the finance area and three in the business strategy & analytics department. One of the responsibilities of his department is to synthesize customer data to build profile models for market segmentation based on "tiered" levels of fan engagement. Analysis of real-time and stored data assists in determining ticket-pricing strategies and provides justification for revenue-based decisions such as resource allocations for targeted marketing campaigns. According to Zue (personal communication, December 14, 2016), analytics is a five-step process whereby data are (1) gathered, (2) organized, (3) analyzed, (4) presented, and (5) used to guide decisions. The MIT graduate centralizes data silos, develops hypotheses, uses real-time data flow, and provides key insights that the organization relies on for business decisions.

Josh Brickman, vice president of business strategy, is a valued executive for the NHL Bruins and TD Gardens. His former roles with the NFL Philadelphia Eagles, Turnkey Sports, and Monumental Sports & Entertainment (the ownership group for the Washington Wizards [NBA], Capitals [NHL], Mystics [WNBA], and Verizon Center) focused on ticket analytics, research, and strategy. Currently, Brickman oversees sales and service, marketing, and the information technology/e-business department.

Brickman speculates that analytics can be applied to decisions within human resources. Feedback from satisfaction surveys and interviews, for example, may assist managers and supervisors to determine the factors most likely to increase retention of low-level employees, whether it is the opportunity to skate on the ice, complimentary tickets to bring family and friends to an event in the facility, or limited access to a player appearance (J. Brickman, personal communication, December 15, 2016). Brickman also speculates that the emerging field of partner-based analytics will grow in the professional sports sector as collaborative data-sharing initiatives build stronger ties between sponsors and teams.

Both Brickman and Zue stress the value of visual data analytics tools such as Tableau for creating customized reports that are easily digestible for business presentations. In Boston, these solution-based strategists are facilitating dynamic knowledge creation that drives big and small business decisions in sports.

about employees early in their career that can increase the propensity for leadership and management positions.

The sabermetric gurus employed as analytics specialists are generally skilled mathematicians, finance experts, or economists tasked with mining data on everything from player health statistics to stadium capacity to seasonal turnover rates. Their role in the organization is generally to provide information that ties data-driven decision making to revenue streams. Historical, relational, and predictive data assist sports organizations to operate efficiently and effectively. Analysts who can gather and make sense out of convoluted information are a valuable asset to organizations. **Action Shot 5-2** describes the qualifications and responsibilities for an entry-level position in the NBA for a sports analyst in a support role.

It is apparent that not all analytics specialists in professional sports report directly to the team president. Many are in support roles. A majority of sports organizations outside of the professional sector, in fact, operate without an analytics specialist because it is such a new and dynamic field. An analytics specialist won't be employed at a local recreation center or skating rink, but the field is opening up to industry sectors other than professional sports, including sporting goods and sports media conglomerates such as Nike and ESPN. Interpreting information provided by analysts is essential for senior management to appreciate the impact of human resources as an asset for an organization and to minimize bias and provide data-driven justification for decisions.

Because the sports industry includes a vast and diverse landscape and many small businesses, the appointment of an analytics team or specialist is impractical for most organizations. However, there is great value in having employees with analytical competencies or employing individuals skilled in using analytics for human resource purposes. It isn't necessary to hire a sabermetric guru to manage data and use basic statistics to improve decision making as long as similar skills exist within the workforce.

Managers generally use some form of analytics in making daily decisions tied to operational duties. A utility analysis, for example, is a common analytical tool to quantify or measure the return on investment for advertising, training, and other human resource activities. Analytics can predict vacancies or potentially high performers or even populations with high or low retention rates. Analytics can also determine which sourcing channels produce the most top-level talent and how changes in benefit options based on employee demographics would impact the bottom-line costs of the organization.

🎬 ACTION SHOT 5-2

NBA Sacramento Kings Advertisement for an Entry-Level Analytics Specialist

The following is a job advertisement for an entry-level analytics specialist for the NBA Sacramento Kings that appeared on the Teamwork Online (2015) website.

Summary:
Recognizing the power of technology, data, and computational science to transform the business, the Sacramento Kings have formed the Engagement Lab to drive transformational change through evidence-based decision making at the company. The Analytics Specialist position is an entry-level position as a member of the Engagement Lab and the decision science practice within the organization.

Key Responsibility Areas (KRAs):

- Support execution and reporting of marketing campaigns across multiple channels.
- Collaborate with others to answer challenging business questions that can assist us in gaining a competitive advantage by using data-mining techniques.
- Creates actionable insight and understanding through the analysis of both quantitative and qualitative data, building recommendations that directly address business objectives.
- Execute ongoing and ad-hoc reporting and analysis to support key business stakeholders, driving revenue and innovation.
- Create engaging visualizations of data analyzed in order to depict outcomes.
- Write and execute Structured Query Language (SQL) for standard and ad hoc data mining purposes.
- Assist in all customer relationship management (CRM) efforts including sales and marketing campaign setup and administration.

Qualifications:

- Bachelor's degree from 4-year college or university in information systems, statistics, computer science, or related field.
- One (1) to three (3) years' experience in the applied analytics space.
- Minimum of one (1) year of experience with notable business intelligence (BI) tools.
- Experience with Microsoft Office: Word, Excel, Access, and SQ.
- Strong communication, prioritization, and organization skills.
- Excellent problem-solving and logic skills.
- Service oriented; committed to teamwork and catering to customers.
- Results oriented; ability to manage multiple priorities and deadlines.
- Capable of working extended hours, such as nights, weekends, overtime, and on-call.

The advantage of analytics in workforce planning is that it validates decisions for succession planning, new hires, downsizing, or restructuring. Trend analyses, turnover rates, and other analytics facilitate a prudent approach to human resource management for sports practitioners and provide tools to make decisions based on data-driven information as opposed to intuition alone.

Predicting Vacancies

Data analytics can assist sports organizations to predict future vacancies. The term **vacancy** is interchangeable with the term *job opening*. The U.S. Bureau of Labor Statistics (2003) defines a vacancy or job opening as "a position that is not filled with the condition that work is available for that position."

Former NBA Commissioner David Stern

Planned vacancies are open positions resulting from a deliberate, calculated, and intentional action, such as the 2014 retirement of former NBA commissioner David Stern and former MLB commissioner Bud Selig or the expiration of a term limit for a board member at a private golf and country club. Planned vacancies also include any deliberate managerial decision to reassign, promote, terminate, or replace an employee. The intentional restructuring of organizational reporting lines or a reassessment of staff needs may result in planned vacancies as well.

Unplanned vacancies, on the other hand, are the unexpected openings resulting from an unforeseen situation, such as a resignation, death, or abrupt, on-the-spot termination. For example, a stadium usher who is observed using an illegal substance while on the job may be immediately dismissed.

Predicting vacancies is a function of knowing the answers to numerous inquiry areas that directly and indirectly affect employee departures (see **Box 5-1**).

Analytics will assist in answering the types of questions listed in Box 5-1 through an assessment of available information about a workforce resulting from surveys, interviews, employee records, company databases, and performance evaluations. The ability to predict when vacancies will occur in particular areas (departments or units) places less burden on managers responsible for recruiting. For instance, if all factors are the same, the operations manager for a professional or collegiate sports venue should know exactly how many vacancies need to be filled at the beginning of each season by having an understanding of how

Former MLB Commissioner Allan H. "Bud" Selig

BOX 5-1

Questions to Assist in Predicting Vacancies

- Which employees have the highest risk of voluntary departure from an organization?
- What are the reasons employees leave?
- Which reasons have the most statistical significance in explaining why employees leave?

- What is the profile of the employees who are most likely to leave?
- What is the tenure of the employees who voluntarily leave?

many employees are returning and how many positions need to be filled. Still, the manager must consider reasons that may alter whether the total number of staff from one year will increase or decrease, such as economic conditions, environmental factors, technology advancements, or a realignment in corporate objectives.

Supervisors or administrators who aren't responsive to subtle or obvious changes in their environment (e.g., increased or decreased ticket sales, marquee player acquisition, or technology advances) have a greater likelihood of falling into the managerial pitfall known as the **boiled frog phenomenon**. The phenomenon is based on the premise that if a frog is dropped into a pot of lukewarm water being slowly heated on a stove, it will boil to death if it remains unreceptive to the subtle changes in its environment (rising temperature). In business, the analogy of the boiled frog phenomenon is evidenced when managers fail to notice incremental changes in internal or external conditions until there is a detrimental impact on business operations. A manager who misses the signs for pending vacancies will be surprised by open positions with no plan or timeline for filling the roles. The result creates workload issues for employees and potentially affects sales and profits.

Perhaps the most dramatic outside influence creating additional job openings in sporting venues occurred in the aftermath of the terrorist attacks of September 11, 2001 (9/11) as the need for greatly improved security measures and larger security staffs infiltrated almost every industry. Stadiums, arenas, racetracks, and other large sporting venues swiftly had to increase their

Security concerns at mass gatherings in the aftermath of 9-11 necessitated the increase in game day workers at stadiums, arenas, and racetracks.

game-day staff to have enough employees to perform the necessary nuisance of spectator bag checks and infrared screenings, which were not as routinely administered prior to the worst terrorist attack in U.S. history. Policy and operational procedure changes resulting from 9/11 exemplify how extraneous variables can affect vacancies in the sports industry.

Analytics can predict future vacancies with greater accuracy than intuition alone, but managers who combine intuitive thinking with analytics such as turnover rates have the best advantage in predicting and preparing for vacancies. **Action Shot 5-3** goes a step further to demonstrate predictions in game-day staffing for the MLB Cleveland Indians based on new stadium renovations and an appraisal from the team's analytics specialist of variables affecting attendance for the season.

▶ ACTION SHOT 5-3

Ballpark Renovations Affect More Than Seasonal Vacancies for the Cleveland Indians

The redesign of Progressive Field in Ohio, home of the MLB Cleveland Indians, was partly responsible for the addition of a brand new full-time position to oversee the hiring of seasonal employees for the 2015 season. The renovation plans for the 20-year-old stadium eliminated over 7000 seats (including 16 suites) but created more open areas and standing-room space in social areas, which was predicted to increase overall game attendance. The senior vice president of strategy and business analytics and his staff were instrumental in the redesign, which added five new neighborhood-themed food stations, created new mezzanine-level gathering areas, and expanded the popular Kids Clubhouse to two tiers (Jarboe, 2014).

The year prior to the stadium renovations (2015), Cleveland's Progressive field averaged 17,806 fans per game and following the makeover (2016), attendance increased to an average of 19,650 per game (ESPN, 2017). Although construction renovations reduced the overall stadium seating capacity, the focus on improving the fan experience led the Indians to expect significantly increased average attendance. Proactively, the Indians added a full-time person in the human resource department to oversee the seasonal workers, and in 2017, the staff directory included six personnel in the department (Cleveland Indians, 2017). The Indians also hired more ushers, vendors, and concession workers than were required in any previous season.

Gabe Gershenfeld, an analytics specialist for the Indians in 2015, designed a formula to predict attendance using historical data, trend analyses for promotional activities, market-size demographics, weather forecasts, opponents, team performance, and the night of the week and time of year (Kleps, 2014). The ability to accurately predict future attendance assisted in determining the additional seasonal hires needed for the 2015 season. The following season (2016), the Indians won the American East Championship and lost to the Chicago Cubs in the World Series.

TURNOVER RATE

For the most part, predicting vacancies is a function of a **trend analysis** of **turnover rates** over specified time periods, such as annually, monthly, quarterly, or biannually. Assuming conditions in the organization are stable, predictions for the number of vacancies would be relatively unchanged from year to year.

The basic formula for determining turnover rate divides the number of workers who left an organization in a given time period by the overall number of employment positions during the same time period. For example, a full-service health, fitness, and tennis club with 80 full-time positions that lost 11 employees during the year as a result of retirement, attrition, resignation, or termination will have a 13.7% turnover rate. The formula divides the number of employees who are no longer with the club (11) by the total number of positions (80), then multiplies the result by 100 to convert it to a percentage (13.7%). The mathematical computation for the example is $11 \div 80 = .137 \times 100 = 13.7\%$.

The trend analysis simply averages the turnover rates over a particular time period. **Table 5-1** is an example of a turnover trend analysis for a fitness center over a 5-year period.

Turnover rates can be skewed by a dramatic increase or decrease in available positions that were not part of the organization in the previous season. A professional franchise that acquires a marquee player (e.g., the LeBron James effect in Miami and then Cleveland) provides justification for executives to predict an increased need for ushers, security, parking attendants, and concession workers while also mitigating a decreased need for ticket sales associates. Similarly, a reduction in vacancies may result from declining

TABLE 5-1: Average Turnover for Athletic Club Based on 5-Year Data Analysis

	Number of Employees Separated from Company	Total Number of Employees	Percentage of Turnover
2017	11	80	13.75
2016	15	80	18.75
2015	9	80	11.25
2014	10	75	13.33
2013	16	75	21.33
			Average = 15.68%

LeBron James' return to the NBA Cleveland Cavaliers prompted executives to consider impact on staffing.

membership at a health club or the elimination of a university football team (e.g., University of Alabama–Birmingham following the 2014 season [reinstated for 2017]).

Greater accuracy in predicting vacancies occurs when considering both turnover rates and additional contributory factors. For example, the number of employees who departed within the first year of their hire date may yield interesting information, as would an analysis of turnover rates for each separate department. Valid information could be derived from examining departures in each department attributed to retirement, termination, promotion, demotion, transfer, layoff, or another cause. A critical investigation of turnover data along with a keen sense for acknowledging how change may influence vacancies facilitates a better understanding of where and when openings will occur. The additional information typically stems from a type of predictive analytics known as workforce analysis.

WORKFORCE ANALYSIS

Workforce analysis is broadly defined as a data-driven approach to tracking employee information and organizational practices related to labor and staffing. It provides more information than the turnover rate in forecasting vacancies. Workforce analysis relies on historical data and allows managers and supervisors to assess both the supply and demand of labor in an organization. Combining workforce analysis with intuition provides the necessary information for making practical decisions related to developing strategies to address turnover, downsizing, or retention, for instance.

There are numerous methodologies, templates, and tools available for conducting a workforce analysis. Organizations must initially decide what information is necessary to best fit the intended purpose of an analysis. For example, a junior college athletics and intramural department might be interested in an organizational analysis of student-worker positions to determine how many would likely need to be replaced over the next 3 years.

A simple chart depicting each job, the current student employed, the likelihood of rehire, and the worker's classification (freshman, sophomore, junior, or senior) would provide the information needed to predict vacancies. In another case, executives of a chain of retail sporting goods stores tasked with determining how and where to reduce labor costs by a minimum of 10% would require a much more complex workforce analysis than the junior college example. An assessment of the organizational flowchart and a review of employee information relative to performance evaluations, status (part time or full time), hire dates, and retirement eligibility are necessary components for managers to consider in a more thorough analysis.

Employee Inventories, Skills Inventories, and Gap Analysis

Employee and skills inventories are data sets used in workforce planning. A gap analysis is an assessment procedure analyzing two pieces or sets of data. The **employee inventory** is a record of information on all personnel in an organization. The inventory includes pertinent information such as educational attainment, job title, length of employment, appointment status (temporary, part time, or full time), specific responsibilities, salary level, performance ratings, equipment issued, account passwords, and/or special skills or certifications.

A **job analysis**, also referred to as a **skills inventory**, focuses on work performed in a business and is based on the duties and responsibilities involved in each position in an organization. The analysis is usually organized in a spreadsheet or database format and includes information on job classifications, duties, responsibilities, and the requisite skills, knowledge, or competencies deemed integral to a position. The workforce investigation uses the job analysis to determine the number and types of employees needed to effectively perform the skills required for each position. The job analysis is also the tool used for developing job descriptions in the recruiting process to fill vacancies.

Integration of current employee information and the data from a job analysis provides information to conduct a gap analysis, which is an investigation of labor demands compared with **labor supply**. **Labor demand** is predicated on the types and number of workers necessary to accomplish the organization's goals in a specific time period (e.g., past, current, or future). Labor supply, on the other hand, can be determined by assessing the present workforce in terms of numbers and the skill sets or competencies available to meet demands. The gap analysis identifies who (if anyone) has the competencies deemed necessary for each position to determine if there is a surplus or shortage. For example, a professional sports team that has an opening for a marketing manager would be able to use a workforce analysis to review the competencies of current employees to determine who has the requisite experience, education, and skills to potentially fill the position.

Managers must implement strategies to overcome a shortage or deal with an excess of labor supply. If forecasted labor demands exceed workforce supply projections, management may need to create vacancy openings or train and promote internal employees to fill gaps. On the other hand, if the demand forecast falls short of the projected supply of workers, strategies may necessitate decisions to downsize the organization or shift work classifications.

Youth, college, and professional sports teams use a form of a workforce analysis to account for position depth. Coaches, general managers, and executives analyze information on their players to determine if there is an unmet need that should be filled or an overabundance of talent in a particular area. The analysis leads to data-driven decisions for adding to a roster, releasing individuals, or reassigning positions. Similarly, a gap analysis can target an overabundance of workers with a particular skill set, leading to reassignments or layoffs, or it can identify shortfalls necessitating training or recruiting to fill vacancies.

Labor supply and demand are influenced by such activities as budget cuts, restructuring, and outsourcing decisions, which is why a gap analysis requires intuitive thinking in addition to factual information. For example, age variables identify the number of employees eligible for retirement, which may skew projections based on current labor availability alone.

Human resource technology solution firms, such as Oracle, Kronos, SAP, and Halogen, advocate the benefits of programs that can easily merge inventory databases, automatically apply algorithms, and provide numerous analytic reports. Human capital software programs can aid retention by spotting patterns that indicate employees who are more likely to quit, followed by an automated notification sent to management, who can then decide if an intervention is warranted. When software systems are used over time, their analytical capabilities can be refined through manual entry of data identifying which predictions were right or wrong.

Oracle is a technology company offering database solutions for human resource needs. The company has naming rights to Oracle Arena in Oakland, California, home of the NBA Golden State Warriors.

Excel spreadsheets prove useful in categorizing and sorting human resource information; however, the complexity and customization of data integration are limited. Sports organizations are often smaller companies with limited resources to afford human capital software programs. All businesses, regardless of size or scope, should appreciate the value of technological tools to manage employee information even those as simple as an Excel spreadsheet

Organizational Structure Analysis

Organizational structure analysis provides an opportunity to evaluate the productivity of human capital and capacity based on status and relationships within the organization. An **organizational flowchart** is a pictorial diagram identifying the structure of the business, with an emphasis on the relationships and ranks of employees and departments. It is useful in a workforce analysis as a supplement to employee and skills inventories.

Most sports organizations create an organizational flowchart depicting work groups arranged by the function of the jobs performed (e.g., coaching, training, marketing, community relations, administration, compliance, ticket sales, etc.). The second most common structure for sports organizations is one using an overlapping matrix incorporating functional assignments and a second variable, such as geographic region or customer type. Global sports organizations such as the International Olympic Committee (IOC), Nike, and Adidas add geography to the organizational structure to create a matrix design. Fitness centers may design a structure that crosses functional areas, with a customer-focused approach to servicing toddlers, youths, teens, adults, and seniors.

The organizational chart identifies factors such as reporting lines, chains of command, communication flow, span of control, geographic dispersion, and the extent of centralization or decentralization in the business. An effective chart configuration facilitates the speed of information and decisions. An assessment considers the total number of layers from the lowest-level operational employee to the highest-level owner or executive and clarifies who is responsible for making decisions and what positions have overlapping responsibilities.

The analysis of an organizational flowchart may lead to **reengineering** a structure to best suit a business's ability to maximize efficiency and effectiveness. Reengineering departments and business functions into a leaner organizational structure can lead to pinpointing positions that are no longer viable, therefore providing justifications for layoffs. The restructuring

Six sport photographers for *Sports Illustrated* were laid off in 2014 after the parent company (Time, Inc.) restructured.

of organizations is typically a means for management to reduce payroll without compromising the level of service or quality in production areas. For example, Sports Illustrated laid off six photographers after a restructure of its parent company (Time Incorporated) provided pink slips (dismissals) to almost 500 employees in 2014 (Larimer, 2015). Similarly, a new president of the NBA Portland Trailblazers laid off nine employees on the business operations side after assessing the organizational structure of the franchise (Golliver, 2013). Finally, in 2015 ESPN eliminated 300 employees, primarily in the technology and production areas, which was the second layoff in 3 years for the company, which had 8000 employees worldwide and another 4200 based in Connecticut (Haar, 2015). Most of ESPN's broadcasters and on-air personalities are independent contractors and were not affected by the layoffs.

Conversely, reconfiguration can also pinpoint new structural needs that require specific talent acquisition that can be accomplished by shifting employee responsibilities, developing internal talent, or locating external talent. **Action-Shot 5-4** demonstrates the volatile nature of organizational restructuring that can affect staff levels, however, emerging trends in the sport industry such as increased specialization may also have an impact.

Throughout sports organizations, new roles have been developed to address the social and digital media revolution in communications and an emphasis on data analytics and fan engagement. The NBA Philadelphia 76ers (2017) employ a separate digital media department, which would have been unheard of a decade ago, and the Cleveland Indians (2017) have a separate Live Experience Department. Similarly, social media content specialists are listed on the staff directories of almost all professional league teams, as are staff devoted to analytics. Data analytics is also infiltrating the college ranks, as evidenced by the University of Nebraska, which developed a position for a director of sports analytics and data analysis (Husker, 2015). Adding positions as a result of restructuring and analyzing organizational structure can result in favorable outcomes for increasing a workforce.

▶ ACTION SHOT 5-4

Adidas Organizational Restructuring a Common Business Function

Adidas, the German-based brand owning TaylorMade Golf, Reebok, Rockport, and numerous other companies underwent a massive reorganization in 2009 resulting in layoffs for some locations and expansion for others. Between 2000 and 2009, Adidas grew from 95 companies to over 190 global businesses (Adidas Group, 2009). Acquisitions, mergers, and market conditions caused the brand to assess its organizational structure almost continuously.

At the North American headquarters, the company realigned its marketing and sales staff in 2008 into four geographic regions, resulting in layoffs for 40–80 workers in Portland, Oregon. Two years later, the Portland office reported a net increase of 60 jobs following additional restructuring (Siemers, 2010).

Restructuring created new positions that required different skill sets than what was currently available among the internal labor pool, prompting the company to replace some workers with external talent instead of training and developing internal employees. The 2008 restructuring initiatives created over 1500 jobs (130 brand new) in a new 1.9 million square foot distribution center in Spartanburg, South Carolina (Sports Business Journal, 2010).

The Adidas company exemplifies the volatile nature of organizational restructuring. In 2014, restructuring of the golf side of Adidas added three executive positions to TaylorMade despite consolidating its Adams affiliate headquarters and relocating it from Plano, Texas, to the company's global headquarters in Carlsbad, California, resulting in 138 layoffs (Carlisle, 2014). Two years later, Adidas announced an overhaul of its Reebok brand including moving the company headquarters to Boston, closing stores, and laying off 150 employees (Thomasson, 2016). Positions and reporting lines are likely to experience further changes in 2017.

SUCCESSION PLANNING

Succession planning not only predicts vacancies resulting from retirement or an unexpected departure of an employee, but it also identifies an internal pool of prospective replacements for impending openings. Succession plans assist management in estimating timelines for filling positions and determining if and when internal candidates have the requisite skills or can be trained or developed to assume new roles. Plans are typically crafted to represent vacancy replacement opportunities in light of impending retirements or to address needs to replace the most key constituents in the organization who may be lost to an unexpected death or departure. Succession plans are useful for proactively addressing critical personnel isolated in a particular geographic region (e.g., a director of global basketball operations in Asia) or for addressing positions with high turnover (e.g., an entry-level ticket sales accountant for an arena football team).

There are numerous means for managers and human resource personnel to address succession planning, such as through the development of talent identification charts, competency charts, or readiness assessment tables. A competency chart, for example, lists "critical" positions and ranks individuals on each competency area required of the position to determine whether the person is proficient, skilled, or would need development. Similarly, a readiness chart or table identifies position titles along with characteristics of potential candidates who could potentially fill role assignments (see **Table 5-2**).

Succession planning includes both critical data analysis and a degree of intuitive thinking to rank competencies or estimate the time period in which a candidate might be prepared to step into a new role. The example in Table 5-2 indicates a high need to develop one or more staff members

TABLE 5-2: Segment of a Sample Succession Template for an Intercollegiate Athletics Department

Position Title	Job Rank	Incumbent Name	Retirement Status	Number of Staff Ready Now	Number of Staff Ready in 1–2 Years
Director of Athletics	1		C	1	1
Deputy Director of Athletics—Internal Affairs	2		C	1	2
Assistant Director of Athletics—External Affairs	2		B	2	2
Director of Compliance	1		A	0	4

Job Rank:
(1) Critical—Replace ASAP.
(2) Very Important—Replace within 6 months.

Retirement Status:
(A): Retirement likely—1 year.
(B): Retirement likely—2 years.
(C): Retirement eligible—5 years.

for the position of director of compliance in an intercollegiate athletics department because the incumbent is in a critical position and likely to retire with 1 year. The example also indicates only a moderate or low need to develop a replacement for the director of athletics position because at least one staff member is ready to assume the position almost immediately, and the incumbent is not likely to retire in the next 5 years.

Recruitment Plans

Prior to engaging in recruitment activities to fill vacancies, especially with external candidates, a plan must address responsibilities, timelines, **stakeholders**, and processes to search, screen, and secure candidates. A **recruitment plan** essentially contains the blueprints and guidelines for the process of acquiring talent from start to finish. An example of a recruitment plan for youth coaches published by the Positive Coaching Alliance (2014) outlines activities beginning with identifying a recruiting manager to the final step of evaluating the entire process after the selection of a candidate.

Although companies and professional organizations may have a policy manual or staff handbook addressing general recruitment practices, such as who authorizes each hire or a commitment to equal opportunity employment, it is common to revisit the general practice and develop an individual plan for each job opening to address specifics such as the deadline to accept résumés or the names of individuals responsible for recommending a candidate.

Included in recruitment plans are job descriptions and information regarding individuals involved in the process (e.g., search committee). Two important components of the recruitment plan are the structural issues, which can be detailed in a recruitment flowchart, and the communication strategies for executing the plan.

JOB DESCRIPTIONS

Job descriptions are an essential component in recruitment planning and stem from the job analysis (see **Box 5-2** for best practices in preparing a job description). A **job description** is a profile of a particular position, including the knowledge, skills, and abilities necessary to perform the job, divided into requirements and preferences. The requirements listed in the job description must support the essential functions and serve as the primary criteria for selecting/rejecting candidates. **Essential functions** are those tasks or responsibilities of a particular position that are fundamental to the job. Knowing the essential functions aids in writing appropriate interview questions,

BOX 5-2

Best Practices for Preparing a Job Description

- Use examples/explanations for words that have varying interpretations.
- Use nontechnical language whenever possible.
- Explain objectives, duties, and responsibilities of a job so that they are understandable even to a layperson.
- Keep sentence structure as simple as possible.
- Begin each sentence with an active verb, always using the present tense.
- Whenever possible, describe the desired outcome of the work rather than the method for accomplishing that outcome.

- Avoid words that don't tell specifically what the employee does, such as *handles*. Others you may want to avoid include *checks, prepares, examines,* and *sends.* If these words are the most accurate and specific ones available, it may be acceptable to use them, but if a more specific term would describe the task more clearly, use it.
- Use generic terms instead of proprietary names (avoid *Microsoft, Xerox, Macintosh,* etc.).
- Avoid using gender-based language; for example, use *he or she* rather than *he.*

determining whether a person is qualified to perform the essential duties, and identifying reasonable accommodations to enable a disabled person to perform the essential functions.

In identifying essential functions, it is important to consider (1) whether employees in the position actually are required to perform the function and (2) whether removing that function would fundamentally change the job. A job description for a special projects manager for the Orlando City Soccer Club, the 2015 Major League Soccer (MLS) expansion team, listed responsibilities such as "assist with tracking budgets, strategic plans and other metrics for regular report to the Executive Office" (Teamwork Online, 2014). If, however, a candidate could be hired into the role as a special projects manager without being required to provide data-driven metrics, the job description should include alternate language because of its inclusion of a nonessential function. Similarly, if someone is hired to proofread player contracts and other documents, the ability to proofread accurately is an essential function to be noted in the job description because it is the primary reason the position exists. Therefore, proofreading is vital in the job description.

The job description notes the essential qualifications necessary for performing the responsibilities of the position but may be expanded to identify preferred qualifications, such as a certification or advanced education. Once a job description is crafted, it should be reviewed and approved by all appropriate parties, such as a vice president, supervisor, or director. The approving authority forwards the job description to the organization's human resource representative for archiving. Documents should be easily accessible when a vacancy becomes available. An example of a job description for an entry-level analytics specialist for the NBA Sacramento Kings was provided in Action Shot 5-2.

RECRUITMENT FLOWCHART

The structural components of a recruitment plan to fill a vacancy (or multiple vacancies) include the logistical information to execute the stages of searching, screening, and selecting a candidate. A **recruitment flowchart** is the detailed road map that streamlines processes and answers the following questions:

- What specific activities need to be accomplished?
- What is the logical order of activities to be accomplished?
- Who will accomplish each activity?
- When should each activity start and end?
- What resources are necessary to accomplish each activity?

The chart is a planning document that sequences processes and identifies necessary resources to execute activities such as job board announcements, representation at job fairs, consulting functions, referral programs, outsourcing functions, background checks, drug testing, and so forth. The four steps to create a recruitment flowchart (see partial example in **Table 5-3**) are as follows:

1. Chronologically list each recruitment activity under the headings "Search," "Screen," and "Select" (number activities accordingly).
2. Identify date parameters for starting and ending each activity.
3. Identify the individual responsible for the execution of each activity.
4. Allocate the type of resources necessary for each step (e.g., money or equipment) and assign a dollar amount.

TABLE 5-3: Sample Segment in the Search Phase of a Recruitment Flowchart

SEARCH PHASE				
Filter resumes by minimum education and work experience requirement	6-15-2017	6-20-2017	Director of Human Resources	None $0

Details in the recruitment flowchart facilitate the development of an operating budget, which is the sum of the expenses associated with each activity under the column for resources. Modifications may be made by eliminating, adding, or trimming line items, but it should be cautioned that aspects of the recruitment plan will be affected by any change in funding. For example, if a recruitment plan for the executive director of a regional district of YMCA branch locations has allocated mileage reimbursement for three in-person interviews, and two candidates are from locations from distances requiring airline travel, a decision will have to be made to exceed the budget, eliminate a candidate, or narrow the geographical search area.

Timelines are also essential to the recruitment plan. Individuals responsible for crafting the plan must consider the time necessary to advertise a position, screen applicants, select a final candidate, and receive an acceptance of an offer. Consideration needs to be given to account for a reasonable time period between a new hire's appointment and his or her first day on the job. In essence, the recruitment flowchart serves as a system to ensure an efficient and effective process.

COMMUNICATION STRATEGIES FOR RECRUITMENT PLANS

Planned communication is essential for the individuals involved in executing the recruitment plan because it facilitates accountability and confidentiality. Because even the best-laid plan is vulnerable to misinterpretation, conversing with and briefing involved parties must occur in the beginning stages of the process. Consider a clause in a recruitment plan to check that all qualified applicants for any new summer camp counselor position are certified in water safety instruction and have passed through a criminal background check. If the responsible parties filtering candidates overlook the requirement, delays may result, with applicants improperly believing they are viable candidates.

Communication at the beginning and throughout the recruitment stages keeps the hiring authority and all stakeholders informed. College admissions offices tailor messages to prospective students based on attributes, interests, and other criteria learned in the application process. Online advertisers and marketers tailor messages to consumers based on an assessment of Internet habits. The sports industry can benefit by emulating the ideas of planned, deliberate communications to strengthen recruitment activities.

A **communication strategy chart** can appropriately articulate communications strategies in a recruitment plan to indicate how and when information will be shared with each stakeholder group (see **Table 5-4**). Driving

TABLE 5-4: Sample Section from Communication Strategy Chart for Recruiting a Head Basketball Coach

Campus interviews scheduled—itineraries and candidate materials will be distributed to parties involved a minimum of 1 week prior to interview

Audience	Method	Time Period	Responsible
Search Committee including Human Resource Representative	E-mail	Within 24 hours of confirmation by each candidate	Search Committee Chair
Director of Athletics	E-mail	Within 24 hours of confirmation by each candidate	Search Committee Chair
Assistant Basketball Coach	E-mail	Within 48 hours of notification to Athletic Director	Director of Athletics
President and Cabinet	Face-to-face: Update at weekly cabinet meeting	First cabinet meeting following confirmation by each candidate	Director of Athletics
Board of Trustees	Electronic memo	A minimum of 2 weeks prior to first interview date	President's Executive Assistant
Athletic Department	Electronic memo	A minimum of 2 weeks prior to first interview date	Athletic Director's Office Manager
Team Members	Face-to-face meeting	A minimum of 2 weeks prior to first interview date	Assistant Basketball Coach
Faculty and Staff	N/A	N/A	N/A
Alumni	N/A	N/A	N/A
Boosters	N/A	N/A	N/A
Community	N/A	N/A	N/A
Other: *Faculty, staff, alumni, or personnel part of campus interview*	Electronic memo	A minimum of 2 weeks prior to first interview date	Search Committee Chair

the design of the chart is the message that needs to be shared with each audience type. For each message, the chart outlines the intended audience, the methods or tools to deliver information, the timing or frequency of planned communications, and the responsible entity to deliver the messages accurately and according to the established time frame. It should be noted that not every stakeholder group needs to be informed of every message, which is a deliberate technique to facilitate confidentiality.

The timing and mode for delivering the message are extremely important. For example, a face-to-face group or individual meeting may sometimes be necessary to filter questions and clarify objectives, whereas in other cases, an electronic message with very little explanation will suffice in expediting sharing of information. Determining the lead time for receiving information allows individuals involved with upcoming activities an opportunity to check calendars and clear schedules.

Ensuring that the appropriate messenger is delivering the communication is also an important consideration. Accountability is established, and deliberate designation of the messenger responsible for reporting to a stakeholder group allows for lines of authority to follow the appropriate channel. The "keeper" of the communication strategy chart, such as the chair of the selection committee, a department manager, or a human resource director, should routinely check with the designated messenger to determine successful completion by the date outlined. The communication feedback assists in creating an efficient and timely process for all recruitment activities.

Search Committees

The premise of appointing a search committee is predicated on the assumption that multiple individuals with a vested interest will strengthen the recruitment process and better ensure consistency, fairness, and transparency. Typically, the composition of search committees is reviewed and approved before individuals are authorized to perform respective duties. Ideally, a committee is diverse in ethnicity, age, and rank. The committee essentially carries out the functions to screen candidates before making a recommendation to a board or hiring authority.

A search committee charged with recommending an intercollegiate head coach or director of athletics may include representatives from the community, faculty, administration, staff, alumni, students, and board of trustees. The role of the search committee is to oversee and execute tasks involved in the recruitment of candidates.

In the *Best Hiring Practices* booklet published by the National Collegiate Athletic Association (2012, p. 4), Floyd Keith, former executive director of the Black Coaches Association, identified the following considerations for developing a search committee:

1. Who is involved with the search team?
2. What is the gender and ethnic diversity of the search team?
3. Does the search have a realistic time frame?
4. Is the search consistent with the institution's affirmative action principles?

Generally, once a search committee is appointed, a chair or spokesperson is identified to lead the candidate review process. The chairperson often has the greatest vested interest in the outcome of the selection; however, organizations may prefer to name a respected neutral party with a more dispassionate view in order to minimize the potential for bias. A chair must remain objective and avoid perpetuating the subculture of a team of which he or she is a part. The basic role of the chair is to keep participants on task and to manage all phases of recruitment activities to ensure an effective, efficient, and accountable process. The chair is also expected to communicate regularly to hiring officials and to cultivate consensus among members for a recommendation.

There are no standard procedures for the use of search committees; however, it is important for members to understand their respective roles and responsibilities. When a search committee is assembled, members are typically briefed on their specific charge (e.g., forward three names) and provided information and instructions to complete their tasks (see **Box 5-3**).

BOX 5-3

Information for Search Committee Initial Briefing

- The scope of responsibility of the chair
- Specific guidelines for the evaluation of candidates based on advertised skills and abilities
- The latitude members have regarding designing processes or executing phases of the search
- A list of recruiting policies
- Budget allocations and approval processes for requisitioning monies
- Clarification of individual role assignments
- Any and all timelines
- Explanations for avoiding breaches of confidentiality
- Explanations of illegal interview questions
- Consequences for breaching confidentiality or for any activities circumventing the process
- The contact point to clarify issues or concerns

SEARCH FIRMS AND ALTERNATIVES TO SEARCH COMMITTEES

Search firms are commonly used to assist or replace search committees, such as in the case of replacing former NFL commissioner Paul Tagliabue, as described in **Action Shot 5-5**. Search firms are acquired or contracted especially for procuring candidates for high-profile positions in intercollegiate sports, professional sports, and large corporations such as Nike or William Morris Endeavor/International Management Group (WME/IMG). In the collegiate ranks, search firms are used to hire football and basketball coaches in addition to athletics directors. In the professional sports ranks, firms are used to hire general managers, chief executive officers (CEOs), presidents, and a variety of other executives. Large sports corporations also use firms to hire high-ranking executives.

▶ ACTION SHOT 5-5

The Replacement of Former NFL Commissioner Pete Rozelle

It took three distinct search committees before a new NFL commissioner was voted in to replace Pete Rozelle in 1989. The NFL's initially appointed six-person high-profile search committee was dissolved and replaced by no less than two new groups to oversee the recommendation of final candidates to replace long-time Commissioner Rozelle. Reportedly, the election of Jim Finks to the commissioner role was blocked by 11 franchise owners who abstained from the vote (George, 1989; Oates, 1989). Finks was the general manager for the New Orleans Saints and a unanimous candidate of the original search committee. The abstention votes of the 11 disenchanted franchise representatives were orchestrated not as a symbol of disapproval of Fink but to send a message to the NFL headquarters that the owners should have a greater role in the selection process.

The first replacement committee recommended four candidates, which included Finks and Paul Tagliabue, who tied in the number of votes received by NFL owners. The NFL's third appointed search committee was thereafter charged with making a single recommendation for the role of commissioner among the four candidates. Tagliabue was the unanimous recommendation and was eventually voted in by a majority of NFL owners to replace Rozelle, who died of brain cancer in 1996. Fink was offered a position as the first president of NFL Operations, but he declined. The search firm of Heidrick and Struggles was contracted to assist each group.

The Green Bay Packers secured the services of the Spencer Stuart agency in 2007 when seeking a replacement for departing CEO John Jones, who suffered from the residual effects of multiple heart surgeries (NFL, 2012). As noted in Action Shot 5-5, the firm of Heidrick and Struggles assisted the NFL in its search for a new commissioner in 1989. The search firm Parker Executive Search (2017) was used by the U.S. Olympic Committee, the National Collegiate Athletic Association (NCAA), and the Atlanta Dream of the Women's National Basketball Association. Turnkey Sports and Entertainment (2017) serves the

The WNBA Atlanta Dream is one of the sports organizations using executive search firms.

PGA Tour and numerous major league franchises as a reputable search firm. Alden and Associates (2017) is a search firm under the umbrella of Spellman Johnson that specializes in higher education and intercollegiate athletics.

With fees ranging from four to six figures, search firms provide professional recruiting services that are typically test proven. A retainer representing a percentage of the total fees paid in advance is often required before rendering services. The advantage of using a search firm is that the firm should provide a broadened candidate pool that ideally yields higher quality applicants as opposed to a traditional search conducted solely by the organization. An intangible benefit is the valuable time a search firm saves an organization that outsources tedious tasks such as background checks.

An alternative to the traditional search committee is to abdicate hiring authority to the department or unit head, such as when a head basketball coach hires a student manager or part-time clock operator. Other alternatives include single-unit decisions to expedite the process or the use of an omnibus search committee that functions solely to recruit candidates for all departments.

Recap

Human resource decisions have a significant impact on an organization's financial performance and an impact on organizational efficiency. Preparing for vacancies in a sports organization is a routine function for managers, supervisors, and human resource specialists who are accustomed to making staffing decisions. Analytics, the systematic examination of data to determine patterns, trends, or relationships, is appropriate in the field of human resources to assist professionals in predicting vacancies and making staffing decisions validated on factual information as opposed to intuition. Analytic specialists are employed by most professional sports franchises in order to provide executives with information that ties data-driven decisions to revenue streams such as player personnel selections and trades.

A workforce analysis assesses an organization's structure and the gap between demand and supply forecasts obtained through employee and skills inventories. The workforce analysis facilitates strategy development to manage a surplus or shortfall of workers.

Succession planning to identify internal candidates prepared to assume vacancies in an organization relies on analytics and data management. Individuals using analytics need to be cognizant of internal conditions and/or external environmental, technological, or societal factors that may also impact staffing levels, such as 9/11's influence on the need for a greater number of security personnel in large sporting venues.

Plans to address an impending vacancy provide the blueprints and accountability indicators for recruiting activities. A recruitment flowchart identifying steps in the plan, responsible personnel, a timeline, and resource implications assists in preparing an operating budget and providing accountability. Search committees are often appointed when hiring for a relatively important position within an organization. Job descriptions are essential to the preparation plans. Most importantly, a recruiting plan needs to include the proper communication channels and messages for the intended audience type. Communication plans provide accountability and controls for confidentiality.

 GLOBAL SPOTLIGHT 5-1

Succession Plan for Germany's Adidas Executive, Herbert Hainer

Herbert Hainer, chief executive officer for Adidas, has the longest tenure as the head of any blue-chip corporation in Germany. Hainer's contract, due to expire in 2015, was extended to 2017 under the condition that he develop a succession plan for his replacement. In 2016, Adidas announced Kasper Rorsted from Denmark as his replacement effective October 1. Rorsted lived in Germany since 1991 and previously worked at Henkel, Oracle, Compaq and Hewlett Packard (Chatterly and Handley, 2017). Hainer remained on contract during a 2-month transition period. A graduate of Harvard with an extensive international orientation,

© Juergen Faelchle/shutterstock

© tanuha2001/shutterstock

The rationale for a 2-year extension was to avoid potential leadership changes during either of the two largest global sporting events in the world during his reign, the 2016 Summer Olympics in Brazil and the 2018 World Cup in in Russia. Igor Landau, chairman of the Adidas supervisory board in charge of the search, noted the company's commitment to pursue a generation change already initiated a year prior when the head of global brands, with 30 years of service, was replaced and 12 directors, all new to their positions, were appointed (Thomasson, 2014).

The executive search firm of Egon Zehnder International Inc. was secured to assist Adidas with identifying Hainer's successor. Egon Zehnder (2015) operates 69 offices in 41 countries throughout Europe, the Asia Pacific, the Americas, Africa, and the Middle East.

DISCUSSION QUESTIONS

1. Why are turnover rates alone not enough to accurately predict vacancies?
2. How does the boiled frog phenomenon apply to a sports manager who doesn't use intuition to account for environmental changes when predicting vacancies in a local gym?
3. What analytics are involved in a workforce analysis for a Planet Fitness Center that has just acquired a second location that will be managed by the same owner?
4. What are the important considerations involved in developing a communication plan for recruiting a high-profile coach in the NFL that are not typically part of a communication plan to recruit a high school basketball coach?

APPLIED ACTIVITIES

To complete the activities, review the case study for this chapter, "Increasing Staff at Forest Grove Parks and Recreation," and conduct additional research on the organization's website through an Internet search for Forest Grove Parks and Recreation in Oregon. After reviewing the information, complete the following activities:

1. Develop a job description for a new full-time position in the parks division.
2. Develop a recruitment flowchart for the position that spans 6 to 10 weeks.
3. Identify five sources of job candidates for the position.
4. Develop a communication strategy chart for interviewing the top three candidates.

CASE STUDY

Increasing Staff at Forest Grove Parks and Recreation

The Forest Grove Parks and Recreation Department for the state of Oregon includes an aquatic center and 14 parks encompassing over 350 acres within the city limits. In 2014, the population of the city of Forest Grove was 23,096, which included an increase of 2008 residents over a 4-year period (U.S. Census Bureau, 2015).

Governing the Forest Grove Parks and Recreation Department is a nine-member Commission representing five areas of the city, the school district, and two at-large positions. The Commission reports to the City Council and advises on such areas as recreation programming, planning, and facility development.

The aquatics center is home to the Forest Grove swim club, the Forest Grove High School water polo and swim teams, and the Pacific University swim teams. The center is staffed with one full-time employee, two half-time employees, and approximately 30 seasonal part-time workers (primarily lifeguards).

The Forest Grove Parks are staffed with the equivalent of four full-time employees year-round, with the addition of another full-time worker in the summer (Bray, 2013a). The department has implemented a successful volunteer program that provides opportunities for individuals or groups to commit to a single day of service, several days, or an ongoing assignment through the Adopt-a-Park program. Volunteers primarily maintain the parks by weeding, removing litter, and planting foliage. Facilities for 10 of the parks are highlighted in **Table 5-5** (Forest Grove, 2017).

In 2013, it was brought to the attention of the Commission that within the past year, the parks division experienced a 25% increase in pool usage and a 20% increase in acreage managed by the department over the past 10 years (Bray, 2013a). This information, as well as consideration for the increasing population growth for the city, triggered concern in the ability to maintain the expected standards of service to the community with the current staffing level.

The Commission decided to explore an increase in staffing. The first step was to form a subcommittee tasked with drafting a formal proposal to present to the Forest Grove city manager and finance director. The anticipated economic impact for a full-time employee was $50,000 for salaries and benefits (Bray, 2013a). The Committee discussed the merit of adding a minimum of at least one full-time parks employee, increasing a half-time aquatics position to full time, and adding one additional half-time employee.

Table 5-5: Parks and Facilities for Forest Grove, Oregon

Park	Facilities
Bard Park 2921 22nd Avenue 22nd & Kingwood	Basketball court, barbeques, picnic tables, playground equipment, shelter, walking path
Forest Glen Park—Lower 101 Gales Creek Road, south end of Lavina	Basketball court, trails
Forest Glen Park—Upper 3250 Forest Gale Drive, corner of Circle Crest	Barbeque, picnic tables, playground equipment
Hazel Sills Park 1627 Willamina Avenue	Barbeques, picnic tables, playground equipment
Joseph Gale Park 3014 18th Avenue 18th and Maple	Baseball fields, softball field, barbeques, picnic tables, playground equipment, restrooms
Knox Ridge Park 2422 Strasburg Drive, corner of Strasburg Drive and Kalex Lane	Playground including play structure, swings, picnic tables, benches and the best view of the coast range
Lincoln Park 2725 Main Street, between Main and Sunset Drive North of Aquatic Center	Baseball fields, softball field, barbeques, picnic shelters, picnic tables, playground equipment, restrooms, BMX course, skatepark, track, soccer field, walking path
Rogers Park 2421 17th Avenue, 18th and Elm	Barbeques, picnic shelter, picnic tables, playground equipment, tennis court, Porta-Potty, walking path
Talisman Park 1210 Willamina Avenue	Barbeques, picnic shelter, picnic tables, playground equipment, walking path
Thatcher Park 750 NW David Hill Road	Baseball fields, picnic shelter, picnic tables, playground equipment, restrooms, soccer field, softball fields, walking path, off-leash dog area

The actual proposal included a 10-year analysis of staffing for both the Aquatics Center and the Parks Division. Justifications for the recommended budget allocations were outlined, and a statement of needs and benefits was provided. Important in the process was the timeline to submit the proposal in consideration of the budgetary impact. The subcommittee submitted the formal request and accompanying documentation 1 month prior to the city's formal budget meetings and 2 months prior to the approval date. Aligning the proposal submission with the city's annual budget cycle for decision packages was a crucial component of the process.

The final result was an increase in the hours of one administrative employee in the aquatics department from half time to three-quarters time and the approval of an increase from half time to full time for an employee in the parks department (Bray, 2013b).

CASE STUDY QUESTIONS

1. Why did the Commission believe there was a need to increase staff levels for the Forest Grove Parks Division and at the Aquatics Center?

2. What types of analytics assisted the Forest Grove Parks and Recreation Commission subcommittee in forecasting staffing needs for the city?

3. Why was the timing of when the proposal was submitted to the city manager and finance director important?

4. What was the difference between the staff increases requested and the final outcome?

5. What strategies or additional analytical information in the proposal do you believe may have persuaded the City Council to permit the increase in staffing at the levels requested?

REFERENCES

Adidas Group. (2009, May 5). *Adidas group accelerates restructuring initiatives.* Retrieved from http://www.adidas-group.com/en/media/news-archive/press-releases/2009/adidas-group-accelerates-restructuring-initiatives/

Alden and Associates. (2017). *Executive search clients.* Retrieved from http://www.aldenandassoc.com/our-clients/executive-search-clients.html

Bray, K. (2013a, February 21). Forest Grove Parks & Recreation Commission calls for increased parks staffing. *Oregonian Live.* Retrieved from http://www.oregonlive.com/forest-grove/index.ssf/2013/02/forest_grove_parks_recreation.html

Bray, K. (2013b, May 21). Forest Grove budget breakdown allocates increased levy funds for city functions. *Oregonian Live.* Retrieved from http://www.oregonlive.com/forest-grove/index.ssf/2013/05/forest_grove_budget_breakdown.html

Carlisle, C. (2014, August 19). Adams golf to shutter Plano headquarters, lay off 138 employees after acquisition. *Dallas Business Journal.* Retrieved from http://www.bizjournals.com/dallas/news/2014/08/18/adams-golf-to-shutter-plano-headquarters-lay-off.html

Chatterly, J., & Handley, L. (2017, January 18). Adidas CEO Kasper Rorsted 'ready to fight' Under Armour, credits digital marketing for U.S. growth. *CNBC.* Retrieved from http://www.cnbc.com/2017/01/18/adidas-ceo-kasper-rorsted-ready-to-fight-under-armour.html

Cleveland Indians. (2017). *Front office.* Retrieved from http://cleveland.indians.mlb.com/team/front_office.jsp?c_id=cle

Egon Zehnder. (2015). *About us.* Company information. Retrieved from http://www.egonzehnder.com/us/about-us.html

ESPN. (2017). *MLB attendance report.* Retrieved from http://www.espn.com/mlb/attendance

Forest Grove. (2017). *Parks and recreation. City parks locations.* Retrieved from http://www.forestgrove-or.gov/city-hall/parks-recreation/parks-a-recreation-city-parks-locations.html

George, T. (1989, October 2). The quest for a commissioner. *New York Times,* Sports, C4.

Golliver, B. (2013. May 30). *Blazers execute third round of layoffs under President Chris McGowen.* Retrieved from http://www.blazersedge.com/2013/5/30/4381208/blazers-execute-another-round-of-lay-offs-under-president-chris

Haar, D. (2015, October 22). ESPN layoffs signals broader changes. *Hartford Courant,* A1.

Husker, M. (2015, July 8). *Nebraska hires director of sports analytics and data analysis. University of Nebraska.* Retrieved from http://www.cornnation.com/2015/7/8/8913787/nebraska-hires-director-of-sports-analytics-and-data-analysis

Jarboe, M. (2014, August 8). Cleveland Indians detail multimillion-dollar renovation plans, seat cuts at Progressive Field. *Cleveland Plain Dealer.* Retrieved from http://www.cleveland.com/business/index.ssf/2014/08/cleveland_indians_detail_multi.html

Kleps, K. (2014, July 28). Indians are forecasting, studying park attendance. *Crain's Cleveland Business.* Retrieved from http://www.crainscleveland.com/article/20140727/SUB1/307279990/indians-are-forecasting-studying-park-attendance

Larimer, S. (2015, January 23). Sports Illustrated lays off its staff photographers. *Washington Post.* Retrieved from http://www.washingtonpost.com/blogs/early-lead/wp/2015/01/23/sports-illustrated-lays-off-its-staff-photographers/

National Collegiate Athletic Association. (2012). Search committee makeup. *Best hiring practices: NCAA, NACWAA, BCA. Partnering for a better tomorrow.* Indianapolis, IN: Author.

National Football League. (2012, July 26). *Packers form search committee for new CEO.* Retrieved from http://www.nfl.com/news/story/09000d5d80026382/printable/packers-form-search-committee-for-new-ceo

Oates, Bob. (1989, July 20). NFL meetings: Rozelle appoints new search committee—Al Davis on it. *Los Angeles Times.* Retrieved from http://articles.latimes.com/1989-07-20/sports/sp-5056_1_search-committee

Parker Executive Search. (2017). *Our clients.* Retrieved from https://www.parkersearch.com/practices-areas/sports

Philadelphia 76ers. (2017). *Front office directory.* Retrieved from http://www.nba.com/sixers/front-office-directory

Positive Coaching Alliance. (2014). *Coach recruitment plan.* Retrieved from http://devzone.positivecoach.org/resource/article/coach-recruitment-plan

Siemers, E. (2010, February, 3). *After layoffs, Adidas to add 60 jobs in Portland.* Retrieved from http://www.bizjournals.com/portland/stories/2010/02/01/daily25.html

Sports Business Journal. (2010, May 19). Adidas set to open $150M distribution center in South Carolina. *Morning Buzz. Sport Business Journal.* Retrieved from http://www.sportsbusinessdaily.com/Daily/Morning-Buzz/2010/05/19/Morning-Buzz.aspx?hl=Spartanburg%2C%20South%20Carolina%20&sc=0

Teamwork Online. (2014). *Current available jobs that match Orlando. Facility operations/security: Event guest relations for Daytona International Speedway.* Retrieved from http://mls.teamworkonline.com/teamwork/jobs/jobskey.cfm?s=orlando#73490

Teamwork Online. (2015, February 28). *NBA team career opportunities.* Retrieved from http://nbateamjobs.teamworkonline.com/teamwork/r.cfm?i=77801

Thomasson, E. (2014). Adidas extends CEO contract as starts succession plan. *Yahoo Finance.* Retrieved from http://finance.yahoo.com/news/adidas-extends-ceo-contract-starts-142743961.html

Thomasson, E. (2016, November 3). New Adidas CEO acts to reshape Reebok, support growth. *Reuters Business News.* Retrieved from http://www.reuters.com/article/us-adidas-results-idUSKBN12Y0GD

Turnkey Sports and Entertainment. (2017). *Sports and entertainment recruiting experts.* Retrieved from http://recruiting.turnkeyse.com/team-turnkey/

U.S. Bureau of Labor Statistics. (2003, August 4). *Job openings and labor turnover survey: Data definitions.* Retrieved from http://www.bls.gov/jlt/jltdef.htm#2

U.S. Census Bureau. (2015, December 2). *Forest Grove, Oregon quick facts.* Retrieved from http://quickfacts.census.gov/qfd/states/41/4126200.html

CHAPTER 6

The Grind

RECRUITING IN SPORTS ORGANIZATIONS

Professional scouts are always searching for top talent to bring to their team. My role is to serve as the scout to find that same caliber of talent to bring to the business operations side of the Indians organization. Sports knowledge is helpful for entry-level employees to keep them motivated on the job, but it is unessential for executive and business positions. Transferable skills are more important to our business operations.

Mailynh Vu
Director of Talent Acquisition
Major League Baseball (MLB) Cleveland Indians
2016 World Series Runner-Up

LEARNING OUTCOMES

1. Distinguish the functions involved in talent acquisition and in recruiting.

2. Identify the primary and secondary elements included in a job announcement.

3. Explain the role of technology in facilitating the recruitment of employees specifically in the sports industry.

4. Identify the advantages and disadvantages of various distribution channels commonly used for publicizing job announcements for sports employment positions.

5. Identify the characteristics of an effective filing system for candidate materials and documents.

6. Distinguish the purpose of an initial and detailed review of application materials for an employment candidate.

KEY TERMS

Applicant

Applicant tracking
system (ATS)

Distribution channels

Document and material
collection

Electronic storage system

External candidate

Hard-copy storage system

Hegemonic masculinity

Internal candidate

Job announcement

Managing applicants

Portable document
format (PDF)

Recruitment

Signaling theory

Talent acquisition

Web-based application

Lead-Off

The value of the employee as the most important asset for an organization cannot be understated. Therefore, identifying and securing the best and the brightest talent suggests that **recruitment** is the most important function in human resources, regardless of the industry sector. Recruitment refers to the search for candidates to fill a vacancy or opening. **Talent acquisition** is the inclusive process of recruiting, screening, and selecting candidates.

Sports managers and supervisors who are effective recruiters understand the basics of employment law, are good negotiators, are knowledgeable of the intricacies of compensation and benefits, and can effectively plan strategically as well as tactically. Effective recruiting leads to effective talent acquisition, which is the essence of staffing.

Similar to the restaurant industry and other service sectors, it is no secret that many organizations in sports are characterized by high turnover, especially at the entry level. Ticket account executives for minor or major league professional offices, activity counselors at residential summer sports camps, and front-desk workers throughout the health club industry are just several examples of positions that characteristically experience high turnover. Because the sports industry is inundated with high turnover, recruiting can be an ongoing, never-ending, process-oriented activity.

Many service-related employment positions in sports are occupied by temporary, seasonal labor. Replacing a high percentage of temporary, entry-level workers each season is an expectation for recruiters working in ballparks and arenas. Therein is where recruiting becomes very process oriented. Throughout an organization, great attention must be given to the processes and procedures to attract qualified talent to fill every position, from entry to executive level.

Individuals in sports organizations tasked with recruiting must generate and implement carefully designed recruitment plans to search, screen, and secure the necessary talent for effective operations. This chapter overviews the recruiting function to attract applicants. It includes information on publicizing vacancies, preparing job announcements, selecting an appropriate mix of distribution channels, and the means to collect, store, and track application materials. This chapter also addresses initial communication with job applicants.

Vendors selling ice cold beer at the Cincinnati Reds stadium is an entry level position experiencing high seasonal turnover.

Recruitment

Recruitment refers to activities intended to entice qualified candidates to apply for a job opening. Many consider *recruiting* and *talent acquisition* interchangeable terms; however, the latter is more descriptive of the entire process to search, screen, and secure the overall best candidate for a position. Recruitment is more descriptive of the initial phase of talent acquisition, the search to publicize openings, entice qualified candidates to apply, and manage inquiries.

In a study of factors impacting the decision of sports management faculty to consider leaving their current institution for a new position, salary and location were noted as most important (Mahony, Mondello, Hums, & Judd, 2006). Subjective factors such as the quality of the faculty at the new institution and their potential fit in the organization were also noted as important, suggesting that information in recruiting materials can facilitate enticing a candidate to consider changing employment locations. In generalizing the findings to recruiting employees within the sports industry, recognizing the importance of compensation and creating marketing materials that feature location attributes, language for assessing job fit, and information that distinguishes the organization's reputation are important to increasing the likelihood of attracting applicants.

When the information included on an organization's website unquestionably impacts the intentions of individuals in the recruiting process, this is an example of **signaling theory**. This theory suggests a website serves as a tool to "signal" job seekers about cues important in deciding whether to apply for a particular position, especially when information is not available in a job advertisement. The abundance of information accessible on a website to build upon an organization's reputation is an important factor in decisions to apply

Company websites provide unsolicited information an organization that may influence a job seekers decision to apply for an opening.

for an opening (Mauer & Cook, 2011). Research on recruiting messages and the role of organizational reputation determined that a website describing such company values as a commitment to diversity and to work–life balance does increase job-pursuit intentions (Behrend, Baker, & Thomson, 2009). This finding coincides with research suggesting the general importance of the reputation of an organization in a decision to apply for a position (Lee, Hwang, & Yeh, 2013; Maurer & Cook, 2011; Phillip, Meade, & Kroustalis, 2008).

Recruiting may be abdicated to an individual within the organization, such as a collegiate head coach provided with the authority to personally recruit and hire his or her team manager. In other cases, recruitment is the function of a search committee or an auxiliary business entity, such as the human resource department, an administrative assistant, or an independent search firm. In most cases, recruitment takes place through coordinated efforts of multiple entities with support from the individual who authorizes final hiring approval.

Internal Versus External Candidates

An important factor impacting recruitment efforts is whether the organization is seeking an internal or external candidate. An **internal candidate** is employed by the business, and an **external candidate** has no affiliation with the organization. Although internal candidates can "hit the ground running," the value of an external candidate is the ability to provide an impartial, outside perspective to the organization. It is also common for an organization to conduct an external search but encourage internal employees to apply. Efforts to recruit qualified applicants to apply for an opening differ based on the goal of attracting internal or external candidates. When recruiting internal candidates, recruiting efforts are focused on informing and developing or grooming current employees to fill positions. The focus when recruiting external candidates is to cast a wide net to attract a large pool of qualified applicants.

Although there are advantages and disadvantages to hiring an internal or an external applicant, a practical policy is to consider both types of candidates and allow the recruiting process to function neutrally to determine the best overall person for the job, regardless of whether the individual previously worked for the organization (see **Action Shot 6-1**). Whether sourcing hires internally or externally, it is prudent to develop an efficient system to collect and store materials, track applicants, and communicate effectively with candidates.

When a decision is made to recruit only internal candidates, employees are typically notified in person, through the company e-mail system, or by an announcement posted on a bulletin board. Recruiting external candidates requires greater coordination of activities to define and publicize an opening.

PUBLICIZING VACANCIES

Sports managers and supervisors need to publicize job openings to advertise a vacancy. In the case of a decision to only conduct an internal search to reassign or promote an employee (i.e., succession planning), the candidate list is relatively small and may not require any advertising distribution channel for posting the job announcement. The external search, however, casts a wider net to attract qualified candidates and requires a more complex approach to advertising. Publicizing vacancies requires creating a document that includes elements from the job announcement and describes the process for expressing interest. Determining the appropriate distribution channels for advertising is the other important aspect.

Job Announcements

The **job announcement** provides an accurate yet concise description of the position being recruited and is usually the first point of contact for a new employee. It is also referred to as a realistic job preview. The importance of a job announcement cannot be understated in terms of its role in either encouraging or discouraging potential applicants. The announcement also serves as a tool to define a commitment to diversity and inclusion if crafted with the intention to express a nondiscrimination clause or that women and minorities are encouraged to apply.

The job description is the primary referral document for crafting the announcement. Much of the wording is identical to the job description to ensure applicants have the necessary qualifications for the position. It is important that any piece of information representing the organization, especially in a public domain, is proofread and approved.

▶ ACTION SHOT 6-1

Internal Versus External Candidates—Tiffin University's Search for a Head Women's Soccer Coach

Aston Villa CEO Paul Faulkner (Premier League) and Pacesetter Executive Director Coach Jimmy Walker at Villa Park in Birmingham, England. Ashton Villa Football is one of the oldest clubs in England and one of the top five teams in the history of the English Premier League.

In 1997, the committee assembled to conduct a national search for a new head women's soccer coach at Tiffin University, then a small National Association of Intercollegiate Athletics (NAIA) institution in northwest Ohio, unanimously agreed on a preference for an outside candidate. However, the assistant coach, who was also a former player for the university, was permitted to submit his application, which made enough of an overwhelmingly favorable impression that he was among the final candidates interviewed. James Walker, the assistant coach, was eventually hired as the head coach, with 100% support from the search committee.

The hire proved to be an impactful decision. Under Walker's leadership, Tiffin University's teams reached the Regional Final Four in each of his six seasons and twice appeared as a national quarterfinalist. Walker was named American Mideast Coach of the Year and Ohio Collegiate Soccer Association Coach of the Year three times while additionally honored as runner-up for the National Coach of the Year (Penn State Athletics, 2008).

Following his appointment at Tiffin University, Walker was hired as the head women's coach for Division I Duquesne University in the Atlantic 10 Conference. He was soon appointed as assistant men's coach for Penn State University in the Big Ten Conference. The native of Birmingham, England, left Penn State to become the executive director for the Pacesetters Soccer Club in Toledo, Ohio, which has produced numerous collegiate and national team players, including Adam Montague, who participated in the 2015 Major League Soccer (MLS) player combine (MLS Press Box, 2014) and Danilo Radjen drafted in 2017 by the Houston Dynamo (mlssoccer.com, 2017).

Members of the search committee with the preconceived attitude to favor only outside candidates were not initially aware of Walker's strong bloodline in soccer, including a father, also named James, who coached for 25 years and captured two championships in the English Premier League. The committee was also not aware that between finishing his playing career and returning as an assistant coach, Walker competed 3 years at the professional level with the Kalamazoo Kingdom and the Cleveland Caps of the U.S. Interregional Soccer League (Penn State Athletics, 2008). As executive director of coaching at Pacesetters Soccer Club, Walker forged a partnership with Ashton Villa Football Club, one of the oldest and most successful football clubs in England and a member of the Premier League. Ashton Villa Football has a rich history, including winning the European Cup, the English League Championship, and multiple League Cup titles.

The content of an announcement is clearly integral to driving interest in a position. In a study of 301 announcements for interscholastic athletic administrators over a 2-year period in Texas, 73% of the positions required the applicant to also coach a men's sport (Miller, Whisenant, & Persersen, 2007). Additionally, 94% of the job advertisements for an administrator/coach were aligned with the sport of football. The requirement for athletic administrators to also coach a boys' sport (e.g., football) is an example of **hegemonic masculinity** or

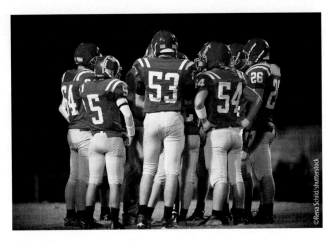

In interscholastic athletic programs, an advertisement for a position such as the Athletic Director has often included a requirement for the candidate to also serve as the Head Football coach.

systematic bias because such recruitment practices promote a social ideology that the position of a male is superior to that of a female. Although a female may apply for the athletic administrative positions, there is a presumption that a male candidate is preferred because the vacancy requires coaching a male team. This finding, which purports a culture of male hegemony, is consistent with additional research within interscholastic athletic departments and faculty positions in higher education in Australia (Kjeldal, Rindfleish, & Sheridan, 2005; Whisenant, 2005, 2008). Individuals crafting job announcements should remain cognizant of language and requirements in job announcements to ensure there is no correlation with any type of unintentional bias.

The primary items to include in a job announcement are the job title, the type of position (e.g., full time, part time, temporary), the qualifications, and the instructions to officially apply for the position, which indicates the means by which to submit a résumé or application materials (electronic or postal mail) and the address for where to send documents (see **Box 6-1**).

When crafting announcements, it is recommended to refrain from language suggesting absolute qualifiers that may deter candidates from applying. Stringent requirements may prevent an otherwise qualified applicant from applying for a position. A technique to ensure a broad candidate pool is to avoid being overly restrictive by using terminology such as *preferred* when describing educational attainment or qualifications. For example, job announcements may replace the term *earned* with *preferred* when suggesting a master's degree as an educational attainment satisfier.

BOX 6-1

Items in a Job Announcement

- A description of the organization
- The geographic location
- Reporting and supervisory relationships
- Responsibilities
- Skills important to perform the job
- Desirable or necessary credentials, certifications, or continuing education credits

- Additional qualifications, such as the requisite years of experience
- The minimally acceptable educational attainment
- Salary range or benefits information
- Closing date
- When the appointment begins
- A statement of affirmative action or nondiscrimination

Job announcements should also have a compliance statement identifying policies to ensure nondiscrimination. Many organizations identify themselves as an equal opportunity and/or affirmative action employer by citing the acronym AA/EOE somewhere on the announcement. Because the sports industry is categorically described as a male-dominated profession, statements on job announcements that encourage diversity are a proactive means to expand the candidate pool and specifically solicit female and minority candidates.

Addressing compensation in the job announcement allows job seekers to appreciate that the organization understands that money is an important consideration. Three generic phrases used to convey a general message about compensation include *salary negotiable*, *competitive pay*, and *salary commensurate with experience.*

Job announcements may be shortened to fit a particular space, such as a newspaper advertisement. The job title, necessary qualifications, and application instructions are the minimal pieces of information that must be included in an announcement. **Action Shot 6-2** shows a job announcement for a position at Daytona International Speedway posted on the search engine site operated by Teamwork Online LLC (2014).

The primary objective of job announcements and advertising is to attract the attention of qualified applicants. The general impressions or recruitment images are a critical factor influencing organizational attractiveness and, therefore, a strong predictor of job-choice decisions among individuals searching for positions (Lee et al., 2002). The job announcement in conventional recruitment practices influences initial attraction to a company before formal recruitment. The design and message should be inclusive of information that facilitates a positive impression to potential applicants.

Research has indicated that announcements emphasizing the need demands (duties and responsibilities) of a particular job more than the supply demands

▶ ACTION SHOT 6-2

Sample Job Announcement

Facility Operations/Security: Event Guest Relations

Seasonal Credential Assistant—Daytona International Speedway (Daytona Beach, FL)

Daytona International Speedway is the home of "The Great American Race"—the DAYTONA 500. The season-opening NASCAR Sprint Cup event garners the largest audience in motorsports. The enormous 480-acre motorsports complex is in the middle of a massive $400 million renovation called DAYTONA Rising. Once DAYTONA Rising is complete in January 2016, it will be host to the only stadium experience in racing. Daytona International Speedway is currently looking for motivated and outgoing crew that will deliver the best experience in motorsports!

Info Fan Crew:

The Info Fan Crew member will assist with guest information at info booths and assist with the assistant transportation via golf carts. The position contributes to the efficiency and effectiveness of activities at Daytona International Speedway and its ability to deliver consistently high-quality service to all guests.
Shift length: 8–12 hours depending on specific event needs

Qualifications/Requirements:

  Customer service experience preferred

  Strong communication skills

  Fast learner

  Ability to work in a fast-paced and high-stress environment

  Ability to be on feet in variable weather for extended periods of time

  Must be able to work nights, weekends, and holidays as assigned

  Friendly, outgoing, and personable

Fan Crew is a seasonal/temporary event-based position. However, this position will require non-event day shifts. Shifts and hours will vary depending on specific event needs.

To Apply: *Applicants must have an active account with Teamwork and must apply online. Please note that your application will not be considered unless you complete all four steps in this process and press "SUBMIT APPLICATION" and see the Thank You message at the end.*

(qualifications) may produce more applicants (Schmidt, Chapman, & Jones, 2015). Similarly, a study evaluating the attractiveness of job announcements noted that those specifying an in-person interview as the method of selection resulted in a greater number of applications than advertisements that specified only the evaluation of grade point average and relevant experience (Reeve & Shultz, 2004). Information in a job announcement can have a profound impact on the applicant pool, especially in emphasizing a specific type of "fit" to favorably influence an applicant's perceived suitability, attraction, and eventual behavior to submit a résumé. If advertisements fail to include the information that prospects can use to determine a potential fit, recruiting organizations risk losing high-quality applicants. An inaccurate fit perception can influence job seekers to opt out of the recruitment process before submitting a résumé.

Partially explaining the overabundance of résumés for entry-level jobs in professional sports leagues is the perception that the name or brand recognition of an organization attracts more applicants (Lee et al., 2002). Without any distinct brand recognition tied to a stadium, team, or other sports entity (e.g., Nike, U.S. Olympics, etc.), the job announcement has a purpose to drive the submission of résumés with information suggesting a favorable impression of the organization as a viable employment location. For Major League Soccer (MLS), the Women's National Basketball Association (WNBA), and the four primary sports leagues in America—the National Football League (NFL), National Basketball Association (NBA), Major League Baseball (MLB), and National Hockey League (NHL)—brand recognition means a public search can yield several hundred résumés within the first 24 hours of posting, regardless of the location of an advertisement.

Distribution Channels

Determining the location for placing a job announcement is contingent upon factors such as the desired geographical reach, the sector of the sports industry being targeted, and financial resources. Selecting the appropriate location(s) for placing a job announcement is partially determined by justifying the **distribution channels** expected to yield the largest pool of qualified candidates.

The rapid evolution of technology has influenced the landscape of distribution for job announcements with the onset of search engines, social media sites, and mobile platforms. Research indicates that a greater number of jobs can be found through an Internet search as opposed to what were once considered traditional search methods, such as classified ads and bulletin board postings, but a combination of methods has the greatest potential to yield the best results (Rooy, Alonso, & Fairchild, 2003). Although the World Wide Web and mobile technology have dramatically altered the way job seekers locate vacancies, a study of recruiting preferences indicated that offline application procedures were less biased than online procedures (Thielsch, Traumer, & Pytlik, 2012). Similarly, in a study examining relationships among five traditional recruiting sources and eventual hires, employee referrals and direct applications yielded a greater number of job offers than college placement offices, newspaper advertisements, and career fairs (Breaugh, Greising, Taggert, & Chen, 2003).

Free search engines common for posting or sourcing vacancies in the United States are Monster.com, Indeed.com, and CareerBuilder.com, but in the niche sports marketplace, there are numerous options to direct job seekers in a more concerted effort to target a specific audience (**Box 6-2**). Although many websites with searchable job announcements are free for job seekers, employers usually must pay for the privilege to post an opening on third-party accounts.

The sector of the sports industry or the nature of the employment position may dictate the most appropriate avenues for posting job announcements. A certified golf professional, for example, would customarily seek a job using a job board through the Professional Golf Association (PGA) or Ladies Professional Golf Association (LPGA). Similarly, individuals seeking employment in intercollegiate athletic departments are accustomed to accessing the free online National Collegiate Athletic Association (NCAA) and National Association of Intercollegiate Athletics (NAIA) Marketplace advertisements, which provide searchable openings by type or location along with specific job details and contact information. Similarly, individuals seeking employment with a facility or camp operated by the Young Men's Christian Association (YMCA) can access the free online career opportunity webpage for YMCAs to search for openings in all 50 states. Yet another free searchable database for positions specifically in the area of campus recreation is available through the National Intramural and Recreational Sports Association (NIRSA), which partners with a third-party agency to post job openings. With the rise in the percentage of individuals using smart phones to

The NCAA website provides a searchable database of intercollegiate athletic jobs, internships, and graduate assistantships.

access the Internet, search providers such as teamworkonline are making it a priority to invest financial resources in technology to ensure websites are mobile friendly (Buffy Filippell, personal communication, January 19, 2017).

Sports-specific electronic recruiting platforms are in the business of providing a broad list of available openings, occasionally with a targeted audience in mind, such as female candidates, individuals seeking entry-level positions, or those seeking international opportunities. Some search engines are free for job seekers, some simply require a registration process and uploaded résumé, and others require a subscription fee. A hybrid version requires a subscription fee only for upgrade services, such as the benefit of viewing how many applicants are seeking the same position at a particular sports organization. Electronic job boards are available for a wide range of sports sectors. Numerous leagues and governing bodies, such as the NFL Players Association, the LPGA, National Association of Stock Car Auto Racing (NASCAR), and the U.S. Olympic Committee (USOC), have a specific page on the main website to list available openings within the organization. Sports brands (e.g., Adidas, Under Armour, and Nike) and agencies (e.g., Octagon, IMG, and Wunderman) also use a mobile-friendly webpage to inform jobseekers of vacancies. Professional sports associations have tapped into the market of providing job postings, some of which are public and some of which are password protected to emphasize the value of a paid membership. Many sport-related associations have a job-search page that is publicly accessible without a password or fee (see **Box 6-3**).

BOX 6-3

Professional Associations in Sports with a Job-Search Webpage

- Women Leaders in College Sports
- National Parks and Recreation Association (NPRA)
- National Association of Directors of Athletics (NACDA)
- Women in Sports and Events (WISE)
- National Athletics Trainers Association (NATA)
- America Camp Association

TABLE 6-1: Advantages and Disadvantages of Distribution Channels

Distribution Channel	Advantage(s)	Disadvantage(s)
Bulletin boards	Location of boards can be advantageous for targeting specific groups	Potentially cumbersome to keep bulletin boards current
Job fairs	Focused market of candidates	Large crowds don't allow enough time for enough contact; primarily for entry-level jobs
Referrals (word of mouth)	Trusted recommendation; built-in reference; generates a higher yield ratio of hires per applicants	Obligation may be felt to provide an interview; not 100% trustworthy
Employment/staffing agencies	Experienced professionals facilitate process; saves time	Budget implications
Newsletters	Information tailored to audience	Circulation may be low
Newspaper	Flexibility for local, regional, or national distribution	Tabbed as a dying breed of employment sources with decreasing circulation nationwide; budget implications
Trade journals	Targeted audience	Budget implications
Media guides	Targeted audience; may also serve to demonstrate philanthropy for supporting a school or program	Often only seasonal and localized, with small market reach; budget implications
Conferences and seminars	Face-to-face impressions possible; structured opportunities	Limited time to interview candidates; typically a meat-market approach
Professional associations	Credibility enhanced and potential for locating third-party references	Typically only for higher-level positions
E-mail distribution lists	Mass approach to advertising at no or little cost	Faulty e-mails with no forwarding address; typically third-party access
Social media websites	Mass approach to advertising at little or no cost	Highly public; potential to generate high volumes of résumés for candidates with little or no experience
Generic job-search engines	Variety of platforms available that reach a wide market	Potential to be outdated quickly; potential to produce high volumes of candidates with little or no experience
Sports-specific job-search engines	Targeted audience; potential for screening services	Budget implications

Search engines and electronic job boards are only two distribution channels for posting job announcements. **Table 6-1** notes the advantages and disadvantages associated with a variety of distribution channels for publicizing vacancies.

Managing Applicants

Sports managers and supervisors leading recruiting efforts must design and implement the system or method to collect, store, and securely share documents; track candidate information; and communicate throughout the process while remaining compliant with state and federal statutes governing employment law. When a candidate fulfills the initial requirement of applying for a position, he or she becomes an **applicant**.

Information in the job announcements specifies the materials or documents applicants must submit for consideration of a position. Entry- and mid-level sports positions typically require an application, a résumé, a list of references, and/or a cover letter. Higher-level positions and employment in educational institutions (high school or collegiate) typically require a letter of application, a résumé, a list of references, and transcripts. Additional documents in the form of certifications, proof of licensure, and/or proof of continuing education units are necessary for specialized positions such as lifeguard, umpire, or personal fitness trainer. Position openings for sports communication or sports marketing professionals may require work samples either at the stage of application or in the screening phase once the candidate pool is narrowed.

On occasion, prospective employees may send unsolicited documents such as proof of certifications or letters of reference in addition to the required application materials. Whether sent electronically or through postal mail, organizations must maintain an efficient system for collecting and storing materials and for **managing applicants**.

DOCUMENT AND MATERIAL COLLECTION

Document and material collection refers to how materials are submitted to the hiring organization. Materials may be submitted through postal mail as hard copies, or they may be submitted electronically through a mobile application, e-mail, or **web-based application** system. Web-based or online systems such as Survey Monkey and Google.doc forms are free, user-friendly programs for creating custom applications. These programs, however, do not always have the capability for applicants to upload a résumé, and there are typically restrictions unless subscribers (i.e., vendors) pay a fee to upgrade to premium services.

Electronically submitting résumés, cover letters, and other material is possible through e-mail attachments or through web-based application systems with more sophisticated capabilities. For instance, the "To Apply" information at the bottom of the job announcement for the Daytona 500 Fan Crew position in Action Shot 6-2 indicates that candidates must have an active online account with Teamworkonline.com. To create an active online account, the job seeker must upload a résumé, which is a free service for applicants.

The content of an announcement is clearly integral to driving interest in a position. In a study of 301 announcements for interscholastic athletic administrators over a 2-year period in Texas, 73% of the positions required the applicant to also coach a men's sport (Miller, Whisenant, & Persersen, 2007). Additionally, 94% of the job advertisements for an administrator/coach were aligned with the sport of football. The requirement for athletic administrators to also coach a boys' sport (e.g., football) is an example of **hegemonic masculinity** or

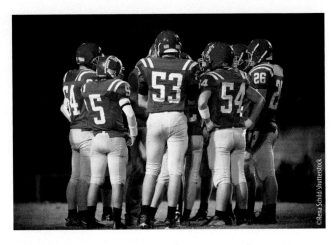

In interscholastic athletic programs, an advertisement for a position such as the Athletic Director has often included a requirement for the candidate to also serve as the Head Football coach.

systematic bias because such recruitment practices promote a social ideology that the position of a male is superior to that of a female. Although a female may apply for the athletic administrative positions, there is a presumption that a male candidate is preferred because the vacancy requires coaching a male team. This finding, which purports a culture of male hegemony, is consistent with additional research within interscholastic athletic departments and faculty positions in higher education in Australia (Kjeldal, Rindfleish, & Sheridan, 2005; Whisenant, 2005, 2008). Individuals crafting job announcements should remain cognizant of language and requirements in job announcements to ensure there is no correlation with any type of unintentional bias.

The primary items to include in a job announcement are the job title, the type of position (e.g., full time, part time, temporary), the qualifications, and the instructions to officially apply for the position, which indicates the means by which to submit a résumé or application materials (electronic or postal mail) and the address for where to send documents (see **Box 6-1**).

When crafting announcements, it is recommended to refrain from language suggesting absolute qualifiers that may deter candidates from applying. Stringent requirements may prevent an otherwise qualified applicant from applying for a position. A technique to ensure a broad candidate pool is to avoid being overly restrictive by using terminology such as *preferred* when describing educational attainment or qualifications. For example, job announcements may replace the term *earned* with *preferred* when suggesting a master's degree as an educational attainment satisfier.

BOX 6-1

Items in a Job Announcement

- A description of the organization
- The geographic location
- Reporting and supervisory relationships
- Responsibilities
- Skills important to perform the job
- Desirable or necessary credentials, certifications, or continuing education credits

- Additional qualifications, such as the requisite years of experience
- The minimally acceptable educational attainment
- Salary range or benefits information
- Closing date
- When the appointment begins
- A statement of affirmative action or nondiscrimination

Job announcements should also have a compliance statement identifying policies to ensure nondiscrimination. Many organizations identify themselves as an equal opportunity and/or affirmative action employer by citing the acronym AA/EOE somewhere on the announcement. Because the sports industry is categorically described as a male-dominated profession, statements on job announcements that encourage diversity are a proactive means to expand the candidate pool and specifically solicit female and minority candidates.

Addressing compensation in the job announcement allows job seekers to appreciate that the organization understands that money is an important consideration. Three generic phrases used to convey a general message about compensation include *salary negotiable*, *competitive pay*, and *salary commensurate with experience.*

Job announcements may be shortened to fit a particular space, such as a newspaper advertisement. The job title, necessary qualifications, and application instructions are the minimal pieces of information that must be included in an announcement. **Action Shot 6-2** shows a job announcement for a position at Daytona International Speedway posted on the search engine site operated by Teamwork Online LLC (2014).

The primary objective of job announcements and advertising is to attract the attention of qualified applicants. The general impressions or recruitment images are a critical factor influencing organizational attractiveness and, therefore, a strong predictor of job-choice decisions among individuals searching for positions (Lee et al., 2002). The job announcement in conventional recruitment practices influences initial attraction to a company before formal recruitment. The design and message should be inclusive of information that facilitates a positive impression to potential applicants.

Research has indicated that announcements emphasizing the need demands (duties and responsibilities) of a particular job more than the supply demands

DOCUMENT AND MATERIALS STORAGE

Sports managers and supervisors must consider space availability, the projected number of applicants, the types of documents to be collected, and the availability of resources (e.g., time, human capability, and funding) to determine the location and method to store materials. To maintain confidentiality, it is essential that the location for storing application materials is secure. For example, password-protected access should minimally be standard for any computer housing documents. Another characteristic of an effective document storage system is to maintain an organized system for easy retrieval of a candidate's file or remote filing locations such as a cloud system.

Hard-Copy Storage

When hard copies of a résumé are received, occasionally, a date is stamped or hand-written on the corner of the documents as an easy means to track when items are received by an organization, whether retained in their original format or converted to an electronic version, through a **hard-copy storage system**. Hard copies of materials are typically stored in folders placed or filed in a secure desk or cabinet for easy access and retrieval.

A local sports retail store advertising for a part-time sales associate to join the company's eight other employees may only need to use a traditional single-folder filing system for a relatively small number of applicants. Application materials from each candidate may be clipped together and the sets placed into a single folder. In slightly larger organizations, such as a mid-size municipal recreation department or an intercollegiate athletic department, materials for each candidate are typically stored in an individual folder with the applicant's name affixed or hand-written at the top.

Electronic Storage Systems

Electronic filing of applicant documents has become a preferred means to store information, whether materials are originally received in an electronic format or if hard copies are scanned or photographed and converted to a digital format. **Electronic storage** provides a

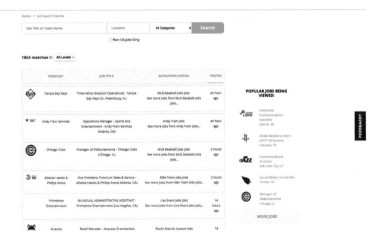

Teamworkonline is a search engine primarily for jobs and internships in professional sports.

convenient and economical means to index, retain, preserve, retrieve, and reproduce records.

Electronic filing without the aid of advanced software has become more common as the ease and access of technology have evolved. Screening a hard copy of a résumé and converting it to a word document or digital file such as a **portable document format (PDF)** or a joint photographic expert group (JPEG) file requires little training or added expense for organizations with a functioning scanner and computer. Adobe Acrobat, for example, is a relatively simple computer program allowing the user to continuously add PDF documents over time to one file. The same small local retail sports store using physical folders may alternatively scan hard documents and organize them into either one lengthy report of all candidates or into a separate report for each applicant. Similarly, an electronic folder can be created for each applicant, and documents can be added to the folder as they are received.

Electronic folders can be created and stored on one primary computer, or they can be stored in a cloud system or cyberspace location that permits shared access from multiple computers. To permit shared access, organizations can access free, cloud-based Web applications, such as Google Docs or Dropbox.

The key to using electronic filing systems, regardless of whether storing information on a single computer or in cyberspace, is to index documents appropriately for easy cross referencing and retrieval. For example, a primary folder may be created for the résumés of all candidates applying for a position as a varsity high school basketball coach Within the main résumé folder, however, may be subfolders for subdividing candidates based on those with previous head coaching experience and those without head coaching experience. Similarly, subfolders may be created to segment the pool of candidates according to years of experience, gender, educational attainment, geographical distance, or any other demographic classification for organizational purposes.

Using Web applications to develop storage systems is somewhat time-consuming, especially if the organization requires duplicate copies of files. Using integrated human resource management software systems or outsourcing document collection and storage is a consideration when dealing with especially high volumes of applicants.

TRACKING APPLICANTS AND MATERIALS

In tracking applicants and materials submitted for consideration of a job opening, the goal is to help hiring managers and recruiters conveniently

					Source of
Name	**Résumé**	**Reference List**	**Recommendation**	**Transcripts**	**Submission**
John Doe	2-15-17	2-15-17	2-17-17	Yes	Referral
Jane Doe	1-21-17	2-21-17	2-24-17	No	Teamwork Online

TABLE 6-2: Sample Spreadsheet to Track Applicants

Note: Dates correspond with submission of materials

identify candidates with the skills, education, and experience that are most desired of candidates. Tracking systems should easily distinguish candidates meeting the minimal qualifications for a vacancy (e.g., minimal education) and those who do not have the required qualifications. The recruiting plan for a position should specify the organization's system or means to collect documents and track application materials received.

A rudimentary electronic system for tracking applicants and materials is a Microsoft Excel or Access spreadsheet to input information for each individual who submits a résumé or other documents. The headings or labels at the top of the spreadsheet identify the desired information for the organization's tracking purposes. Typically, dates are recorded when a résumé or application is received. In the case where official transcripts are required for proof of educational attainment, the field is added to the chart headers. Tracking the source of submission provides valuable data to an organization, especially in determining the return on investment if using a paid advertising service. **Table 6-2** provides an example of a simple spreadsheet for tracking applicants.

Alternatively, technology-based **applicant tracking systems (ATSs)** have become more common in organizing information collected from candidates, especially in mid-size and large organizations. In recruiting prospective student-athletes, integrated human resource or talent management software offered by businesses such as JumpForward, Front Rush, Blue Chip, ACS, ARMS, CyperSports, and Scoutware provide technology applications for ease of database management, tracking correspondence, collecting application documents, and a variety of other services that are closely related to the functions of recruiting employees (Nichols, 2011, p. 12).

Many businesses offer services for human resource technology solutions with features such as mass e-mailing, data segmentation, and electronic-signature filing. UltiPro, for example, is a talent management software system that has been used by the MLB Arizona Diamondbacks and NBA Phoenix Suns (hrlab.com, 2015). SAP (2017) software solutions are another example of human resource

Teams in Major League Baseball are using technology solution tools such as Ultimate Software to assist with managing human resource information.

and talent management technology catering to the sports and entertainment industry. The MLB Cleveland Indians use UltiPro Ultimate Software to centralize recruiting into a one-stop shop that permits anyone who has access to the program to connect remotely to review résumés (M. Vu, personal communication, March 31, 2016). The ATS is also useful as a communications tool to generate letters to applicants and can provide valuable analytics, such as the number of applications received per week, cost of sales postings, and sourcing locations.

What TurboTax software offers for streamlining accounting solutions for individuals and small businesses is similar to what ATS or talent management software programs provide in functionality for the primary purpose of streamlining human resource activities, including the recruiting process. Software programs can simplify database management and electronic filing, but many organizations choose to manage hard-copy and electronic filing in-house. When an applicant's information is downloaded into a software tracking system or entered on some type of chart, hard copies are destroyed or filed and stored in some type of organized method that allows easy retrieval.

RESPONDING TO APPLICANTS

Regardless of when a search period ends, the recruiting plans should specify the time period and method to respond to applicants. It is a professional courtesy and a prudent managerial practice to respond to job seekers in a timely manner to acknowledge initial receipt of application materials, generally within a 48- to 72-hour period. A bulk mailing or mass e-mail to all candidates within a short period of the official closing date suffices to acknowledge receipt.

Organizations may also exercise their discretion to accept late candidate files, therefore possibly delaying official communication until after an initial screening of candidates. The decision to accept late candidate files is partially dependent on the urgency of filling an opening and whether the original search period has yielded a large enough pool of qualified candidates. One common technique for organizations to ensure a candidate pool includes minority candidates or both genders is to reopen a search or extend the application deadline. At some point after all applications have been reviewed, a majority of applicants will typically receive a standard letter indicating that they are no longer being considered by the organization.

When initially responding to applicants, a standard letter typically thanks the candidate for submitting an application and identifies the next stage of the process (i.e., reviewing materials and scheduling interviews). A standard letter also identifies the follow-up communication that may be expected, such as the time period for notification of unsuccessful candidates. Often an electronic signature from the hiring authority or search committee chair is affixed to the bottom of the letter, and a mail-merge process is used to personalize the document sent to each applicant either through e-mail or postal mail.

A less personal but efficient means to acknowledge receipt of documents is to have a preset automated response message when a job seeker clicks a submission button for an online application. The automated response provides a convenient means to caution that an application is not considered complete until all required documents have been submitted.

Box 6-4 shows a standard letter for responding to first-round applicants for a city recreational youth director position.

Although contacting all candidates who have initially applied for a position is ideal, not every organization adheres to the practice because it is not always feasible. There are occasions when a sports organization, such as an NFL or NBA team, that experiences a high volume of résumés for a position will state on a job announcement that "only candidates considered for an interview will be contacted." Similarly, job announcements may

BOX 6-4

Sample Letter to Applicants

Dear First Name/Last Name [mail merge],

Thank you for your interest in the position as Youth Director for the ANY CITY Municipal Recreation Department. This letter is to acknowledge receipt of your résumé, references, and application. The review of candidates will commence over the next 3 weeks. You will either receive a telephone call to schedule an interview or a follow-up letter noting that you have not advanced to the next stage of the review process.

Thank you again for your interest,
Sincerely,
Signature

clearly indicate a "do not call" message to articulate the expressed wishes of the organization to refrain from corresponding with applicants. A solution for businesses dealing with a high volume of inquiries and applications is to incorporate an ATS that permits applicants to view their accounts and the status of their submissions (e.g., application received, application under review, other qualified candidates being considered, position filled, etc.).

Materials Review

Sports managers and supervisors responsible for recruiting candidates must set aside time to review application materials after a closing deadline unless the responsibility has been assigned. One individual may be designated to begin the review process; in other cases, multiple individuals may be involved. The "Lake Wobegon" effect suggests a third-party "referee" can be assigned the arduous task of weeding out unqualified candidates in the initial review phase (Morgan, 2003).

INITIAL REVIEW

The initial review process is, by all means, a process to separate applications that require further inspection for a job fit. In many sectors of the sports industry, one position may yield thousands of résumés, especially for an entry-level job. To initially narrow a field of candidates, applications or résumés are skimmed and separated into two (or three) piles to weed out individuals who unmistakably don't have the qualifications required for the job. For instance, applications submitted for a position as a lifeguard are quickly discarded if there is no lifesaving or first-aid certification noted.

It typically takes only a few seconds to scan an application or résumé to determine if a candidate has the credentials to perform a job by noting relative experience, educational attainment, and possibly the academic discipline. For many entry-level sports positions, such as a ground crew worker, team-store cashier, or front-desk employee at a fitness center, the initial scan may focus more on the attention to details in the presentation of the résumé or cover letter (i.e., spelling, grammar, and formatting) because experience is not as critical in the requirements to effectively perform the duties of the job. The look and feel of a résumé from an aesthetic point of view are often the candidate's chance to make a first impression, especially when résumés are given less than 10 seconds of consideration.

The more important experience is relevant to a position, the more time is devoted in the initial scan of application materials in determining matching qualifications. Initial reviews of applications for a team-store manager in an NFL stadium or a head coach for a collegiate field hockey team, for instance, requires a bit more time to gain a sense of whether the applicant has the experience and qualifications specific to the requirements of the position.

The initial review stage may or may not include an appraisal of accompanying documents, such as a cover letter or any certifications. For instance, a cover letter assesses a candidate's written communication skills, and proof of certification can reaffirm an applicant's qualifications. Sometimes, these documents are not necessary if a résumé alone can qualify or disqualify a candidate. One reason for considering additional documents in an initial review is to determine of an individual can follow instructions, especially if a job announcement specifies items such as the inclusion of a professional reference list, transcripts, or recommendation letters.

When organizations invest in ATS software technology, such as Resumator, Recruiterbox, or BambooHR, to streamline the recruiting process, the initial review of applications is automated. The software works with a filtering system to scan for key words that match the job advertisement. The search optimization locates grammar and spelling errors as well as geographic locations and other details that provide valuable information. The automated system may yield a grade or ranking for each application, allowing a human eye to follow the processes with a more in-depth review of candidates selected for further consideration.

DETAILED REVIEW

Once a résumé or application passes the initial review phase, a detailed review is conducted to further narrow the field to a manageable number for interviewing. Depending on the specifications of a recruiting plan, the detailed review may be conducted by one individual or by multiple people, such as an entire search committee. The applicants requiring a further review have

©Constantine Pankin/Shutterstock

seemingly been deemed minimally qualified for the position. Separating the crop of average and outstanding job seekers requires time and diligence.

The hiring organization has an interest in evidence that the applicant is qualified and can meet the demands of the position. Detailed reviews include a more comprehensive examination of a candidate's résumé and accompanying documents. The most important factor in a more comprehensive review is whether the applicant demonstrates evidence specifically related to the qualifications and skills outlined in the job announcement. Résumés serve to answer questions such as whether a candidate has worked in a similar size organization, has industry experience, or whether he or she has had a history of advancing through more challenging or higher ranking positions.

Employers from selected sports organizations (e.g., ESPN, Bleacher Report, and the University of Texas Athletic Department) meeting during the NFL Washington Redskins Training Camp agreed that résumés formatted chronologically were preferred for reviewing a candidate's employment history, achievements, and job responsibilities (Bowser, 2014). These important work related items on a résumé are critical in many sports positions to further assess a candidate's ability to work in a high-pressure industry. Hiring personnel search for red flags such as gaps between jobs, decreased responsibilities, short-term employment dates, or multiple shifts in career paths.

Cover letters may be scrutinized during detailed reviews, and materials such as transcripts, recommendations letters, and certificates may be studied to assist in determining suitability for the job. Any and all materials are compared with materials from other candidates to continue the review process.

Recruiting Volunteers

The value of sports volunteerism in the United States alone has been estimated at over $50 billion (Chelladurai, 2006). The worldwide estimate would be challenging to calculate. Volunteers are a crucial necessity among the labor force for all types of sports segments, ranging from small recreational settings to large sports mega-events.

Six months prior to the 2016 Rio Games, 50,000 volunteers received their confirmation letter, 82% of whom were from Brazil, and 18% of whom hailed primarily from the United States, Great Britain, Russia, and China (Rio2016.com, 2015). Over 70,000 served as official volunteers at the 2016 Rio Olympics, 20,000 more than the 2014 World Cup in Rio de Janeiro. The Tokyo 2020 Olympics is expected to secure 80,000 volunteers (Blanc and Masami, 2016).

Over 5000 volunteers were recruited to work NFL Super Bowl 50 won by Peyton Manning and the Denver Broncos on February 7, 2016 in Levi Stadium in Santa Clara, California.

Mega-sport events other than the Olympics also rely on a large volunteer labor force. The 2018 Commonwealth Games in Australia began advertising a need for 15,000 volunteers 2 years prior to the event (Gold Coast 2018, 2017). The 2018 FIFA World Cup in Russia similarly advertised for 15,000 volunteers (FIFA.com, 2017).

Volunteer labor is also abundant in the community and municipal sports sector, especially in youth leagues and for fundraising events (e.g., road races). Intercollegiate and professional athletics utilize volunteers to work as stadium ushers, parking attendants, and a host of other service positions. Long gone is the nonprofit sector serving as the primary beneficiary of volunteer labor. The 2014 NFL Super Bowl at MetLife Stadium in Rutherford, New Jersey, provided 9000 volunteer opportunities and paid 1500 temporary staff (Pedulla, 2014). The 2017 Super Bowl Host Committee for Houston (2016)advertised for 10,000 volunteers.

The traditional recruitment practices oriented toward companies, businesses, and stadiums do not always apply when recruiting volunteers. Targeted marketing campaigns stressing the intangible psychological benefits of serving in a volunteer position are necessary to attract applicants (Karl, Peluchette, & Hall, 2008). It has also been suggested that managing volunteers in a sports club setting is similar to a democratic approach for handling mass disorder (Schlesinger, Klenk, & Nagle, 2015, p. 205). Sports managers and supervisors are routinely working through a trusted committee or task force for carrying out functions in recruiting, training, and managing volunteers.

For an event such as the Olympics or World Cup, simply the opportunity to be associated with the event is enough of a benefit to motivate an individual to serve a volunteer. Role assignments or the working conditions may also be a motivating factor, as suggested by volunteers at the British Women's Golf Open, who cited the an "autonomy-supportive work climate" as a primary motivator for their participation (Allen & Bartle, 2014). Other benefits such as language courses, training workshops, and the opportunity to build professional networks and expand a résumé serve to motivate individuals to volunteer for assignments. Therefore, recruiting materials must include information on the intangible benefits that will entice individuals to apply for volunteer positions.

Recap

Talent acquisition is represented by the stages of searching, screening, and selecting candidates. The goal of talent acquisition is to develop a large pool of qualified candidates that is narrowed down to one single candidate considered the most likely to succeed and fit in with the organization's culture. Recruiting refers primarily to the first phase of talent acquisition in the search for qualified candidates. These activities include defining a job opening and publicizing vacancies in a manner that will attract qualified candidates.

The objective of recruiting is to build an initial candidate list before screening activities narrow the pool. Ensuring recruiting activities are candidate-friendly through timely notifications and the maintenance of an organized collection system facilitates a managerial approach to the process.

Technology has enhanced the efficiency of recruitment practices in the sports industry, especially with the growth of sports-specific search engines, such as teamworkonline.com and workinsports.com, for posting job announcements and the availability of ATSs, especially in mid-size and large corporations, to collect, store, and organize materials and documents. When storing materials, consideration is given to the methods for indexing, retaining, preserving, retrieving, and reproducing records.

Reviewing applications is necessary to weed out candidates who are not qualified for a position. ATS systems have sophisticated technology to sort materials and rank or score candidates. An initial review of a résumé takes a relatively short time period to identify a candidate's minimal qualifications for a position.

Recruitment of volunteers is common in sports organizations, whether for a mega-event, a 5K road race, or a youth league. Of great importance in the recruiting materials advertised are the benefits associated with volunteering.

🌐 GLOBAL SPOTLIGHT 6-1

Recruiting for Global Sports Mega-Events

The organizing committee for the 2018 PyeongChang Olympics includes a temporary workforce with responsibilities to staff and manage volunteers.

The volunteer recruitment and management functions associated with the 2016 Olympics and Paralympics in Rio de Janeiro, Brazil provides a wealth of information to assist the local organizing committees preparing for the 2020 Games in Tokyo.

Sports mega-events for international competitors such as the World Cup, Olympics, Continental Cup, Pan-American Games, Boston Marathon, and Tour de France are faced with unique challenges in recruitment because a majority of employees are temporary and volunteer workers. The 119 members of the local organizing committee for the 2018 PyeongChang Winter Olympics Games in South Korea will disband following its final report to the International Olympic Committee. It was established in October of 2011 and includes a president, advisory committee, advisory group, executive committee, six vice chairmen, and a secretariat group of vice presidents, seven bureaus, three directors, one inspector, one spokesmen, 59 teams, and seven sports managers (PyeongChang2018.org, 2017). Many of the appointments occupy full-time salaried positions in the sports field or ranks of the government; however, the majority of the operational workforce will consist of volunteers.

One of the greatest challenges to identifying and securing tens of thousands of laborers necessary to staff a sports mega-event is the issue of reliability and dependability. No less than 70,000 volunteers were recruited for the 2016 Brazil Summer Olympics (Rio2016.com, 2015, p. 2), which is similar to the number of "Games Makers" who were authorized as volunteers at the 2012 Games in London (International Olympic Committee, 2013, p. 6) and is 10,000 less than what is speculated to work the 2020 Games in Tokyo, Japan.

On a smaller scale, the 2014 Winter Olympics in Sochi, Russia, utilized approximately 25,000 volunteers (Greene, 2014). The volunteer labor force for the Boston Marathon requires approximately 10,000 individuals; however, a slight increase of over 1500 additional workers were recruited for the year following a terrorist bombing that killed three spectators (Annear, 2013).

For the 2016 Rio de Janeiro Summer Olympic Games, over 240,000 volunteer applications from 192 countries were reportedly received during the registration period, which ended approximately 18 months prior to the Opening Ceremony. Among the advertised 500 roles for volunteer positions were assignments as assistants in the Olympic Village, press assistants for media personnel, photographers, flag bearers for medal ceremonies, seamstresses to sew country codes on athlete apparel, and Olympic Games agents to assist with drug testing. In addition to the 70,000 volunteers recruited, the Organizing Committee for the Rio Olympic Games used a third-party vendor to recruit 8000 paid temporary workers. The vendor, Manpower Group, is an online recruiting platform operated by a search firm in Brazil. The requirements for serving as an

official Olympic Volunteer for the 2016 Games included a minimum age requirement of 18 which is the same requirement for volunteers of the 2020 Tokyo Games. Volunteers are also required to have a basic understanding of the native language, and a commitment to several training dates within 4 months of the Opening Ceremony. Paid positions required a variety of specific skills and experience matching the employment opportunities.

For effectively recruiting volunteers to work a sports mega-event, the organizing committee utilized a centralized system and established both a local and a global connection to potential candidates. In addition, the process, limitations (e.g., visa requirements), and benefits (e.g., apparel) for volunteering were clearly identified to influence candidates to apply. One of the benefits for volunteers was a free 12-month culture and language immersion course. To reach the desired number of applicants for the 2016 Brazil Olympics, the registration deadline was extended by a month.

Table 6-3 provides a list of the formal activities and a brief description for each stage of the recruitment process that yielded approximately 70,000 volunteers for the 2016 Rio Games.

Table 6-3: Initial Recruiting Stages for the 2016 Rio Olympics

Phase	Activity	Description
1.	Registration	Online application process requiring passport documentation
2.	Online Dynamics	A virtual assessment of situations volunteers may face at the Games
3.	Language Leveling	An opportunity to demonstrate proficiency in multiple languages
4.	Interviews	An 18-month period to conduct virtual and/or in-person interviews
5.	Test Events	Opportunities to demonstrate competency at sporting events staged by International Federations in selected cities in Brazil
6.	Letter of Invitation	Official letters remitted to accepted volunteers in November of 2015

Data from International Olympic Committee. www.olympic.org

DISCUSSION QUESTIONS

1. How do the functions in talent acquisition and recruiting differ, and how are they similar?
2. What are the differences between a job description and a job announcement?
3. What features of an ATS would appeal to a professional sports franchise?
4. What should intercollegiate athletic administrators consider in determining the type of collection and storage system for candidates applying for a full-time position in the department?
5. What is the purpose and process for initially reviewing a candidate's application?

APPLIED ACTIVITIES

1. Analyze three sport-specific search engines for locating job advertisements, and develop a chart to highlight the advantages and disadvantages of each for the job seeker and for the organization.
2. Select and visit a sports organization in the area, and ask to review job descriptions for several positions. Using the job descriptions, practice preparing a job announcement for each. Next, consider the location best suited to publicize each job announcement, and research the costs and other factors associated with posting (length of time for posting, whether the site has capabilities for job seekers to upload résumés, etc.).

CASE STUDY

Recruiting Talent for the MLB Cleveland Indians Business Operations

For many professional sports franchises, the stadium, field, arena, or coliseum is the business entity responsible for hiring concession workers, cleaning staff, ushers, and other game-day or seasonal workers. The MLB Cleveland Indians, 2016 World Series runner-up, are one of several professional organizations that do not rely on third-party vendors to supply seasonal staff. They recruit and employ their own.

The Cleveland Indians represent a professional baseball franchise in the American League Central Division. Since 1994, the Indians have competed at Progressive Field in downtown Cleveland, Ohio, in the Gateway District adjacent to Quicken Loans Arena, home of the 2016 World Champion Cavaliers. The Indians sold out 455 consecutive games between 1995 and 2001. Their seasonal staff includes approximately 1500 employees and 12 to 15 interns. The human resource office is responsible for securing these temporary workers in addition to approximately 250 full-time employees for business operations (M. Vu, personal communication, March 31, 2016). Business operations is considered a separate entity from baseball operations, which is the department responsible for recruiting players and coaches.

In 2010, Mailynh Vu was hired as assistant director of talent acquisition for the Indians on the tail end of Mark Shapiro's reign as general manager. Her role is to manage all recruitment activities for the Indians' business operations while overseeing the Internship and Executive Development Fellowship program. Essentially, she is directly responsible for ensuring the procurement of over 1700 positions in the organization, including full-time workers, temporary employees, and interns. Prior to her current position with the Indians, Vu resided in Washington, DC, where she worked as a university recruiter for DC Energy. She has experience as a recruiter for companies in manufacturing, strategy consulting, energy trading, and professional sports.

Expanding the Human Resource Department

Recent growth in the human resource (HR) department was tied to the strategic vision for the Indians in investing the effort and resources to secure top talent in the business operations side of the franchise that mirrored the investment in effort and resources to secure top talent on the baseball field. Executives believed the care and diligence that were afforded to recruiting and developing player personnel would pay high dividends if the same attention was given to recruiting and training employees on the operations side.

The original HR specialists reporting to the vice president of human resources included Vu

and her counterpart, the assistant director of talent development and engagement. The two collaborated as a tag team. Vu would seek out and acquire the talent, only to "hand them off" to her cohort for training and development. A staff assistant provided general administrative support. Vu compared the roles to the baseball operations side of the organization, noting that she was essentially the scouting director, and her colleague was in charge of talent management (M. Vu, personal communication, March 31, 2016).

To optimize the best use of time and resources to secure and develop talent in business operations, two full-time employee positions were added in human resources. On the recruitment end, a new full-time manager of "seasonal" hires permitted Vu to focus on full-time procurement. On the training side, a new full-time coordinator of development was added.

An open search was conducted for the position labeled the "Coordinator of Development." Although the initial preference was to source an outside candidate with considerably "fresh" perspectives for the organization, in the end, an internal employee proved to be the best candidate to assume the role. The new coordinator previously worked for 7 to 8 years in "fan services" as a seasonal, then full-time employee. He expressed interest in the new role, and after going through an extensive interview process along with several other candidates, the young man with a reputation for exceptional service was unanimously selected as the favorite applicant.

The new manager of seasonal talent acquisition, Valencia "V" Kimbrough, was also an internal hire, having served full time for over 10 years as the facility maintenance coordinator. Vu was inspired by the work ethic of Kimbrough in addition to her professionalism and aptitude in recruiting, retaining, and effectively managing diverse personalities working in maintenance, custodial services, and housekeeping. The skill set of the coordinator matched the requisites for the new position.

Recruiting Executive- and Senior-Level Employees (No Sports Experience Needed)

The job of talent acquisition is simply to find and secure talent. For the Indians' executive- and senior-level employees, the mandate is to seek and secure the absolute best talent. When scouting professional baseball players, baseball knowledge is absolutely a necessity. For executive positions with professional teams, however, recruiters aren't necessarily searching for candidates with *any* degree of sports knowledge. According to Vu, sports knowledge is unessential because "transferable skills" are key to business operations (M. Vu, personal communication, March 31, 2016).

Vu finds success by sourcing candidates from business organizations with a great reputation for a particular business niche. For example, Proctor and Gamble Corporation (P&G) is noted for exceptional brand management and would be ideal for sourcing candidates in the marketing department. In applying this strategy, the Indians have procured a communications specialist previously employed at Crain's Business Cleveland, a weekly publication from a media conglomerate recognized for exceptional journalism. The Indians also procured a senior finance director from PricewaterhouseCoopers, a Web developer who worked at Apple, Inc., and a director of strategy and analytics who was previously employed as an investment banking analyst for Merrill Lynch. The strategy to source candidates who are doing exceptional work with companies and organizations with exceptional reputations for a particular business acumen has served the Indians well.

For Vu, implementing the strategy for finding top talent for senior and executive positions typically begins by considering the requisite skills for succeeding in the particular position and listing extraordinary companies recognized for attracting and grooming employees with that particular competency. The most labor-intensive step is scouring LinkedIn profiles to find candidates whom she believes she might be able to entice to leave a particular business to join the front office of a professional baseball team. She seeks out candidates from the company "list" with transferable skills and then assesses their likelihood of procurement based on their LinkedIn history of geographic migration, promotions, enhanced roles, certifications, or possibly a previous connection to Ohio. From there, it is a tedious process of being resourceful in the effort to track down good contact data and to decide whether to make a connection through a cold call, e-mail, or message to reach the acclaimed superstar. On occasion, this involves joining a public group or association to make the connection. The goals when making a connection are to establish credibility, inform the individual of an opportunity, and convince the targeted candidate to consider the position. Vu's skill, experience, and personality are the secret ingredients that can entice one of her cold-call clients with zero baseball knowledge to join one of the top MLB organizations in the business.

Recruiting Entry-Level Employees

In contrast to the philosophy in recruiting senior-level office positions, when Vu's office needs to fill entry-level seasonal vacancies for the Indians, sports knowledge is a highly desirable characteristic. That knowledge assists in keeping stadium ushers, ticket clerks, retail sales associates, and grounds crew workers motivated in what many consider conventional and routine jobs.

A more traditional recruiting strategy to source candidates for entry-level positions involves advertising on electronic job boards, attending career fairs, and visiting college campuses. Vu or one of her colleagues will often visit the homes of senior citizens and attend meetings for local community groups to recruit temporary workers. Relationship building with professors, community leaders, and retirement home managers who are a source of leads and recommendations has become an important strategy to source entry-level workers. Additionally, the Indians' HR office conducts 10 to 12 information interviews each month to develop a pipeline of candidates and to disseminate knowledge regarding role requirements, available positions, and expectations of working in professional baseball.

Although Teamworkonline.com has sustained a reputation in professional sports for advertising vacancies, the Indians prefer using their own website for postings in addition to traditional and broader search engines such as Monster.com and Career Builder. On rare occasions, Vu has invested in Indeed.com, which earns revenue through a pay-per-click model. The Indians are one of the few professional teams that do not use Teamworkonline.com.

With the addition of a full-time recruiter focusing specifically on attracting seasonal labor, the Indians' HR department has been able to enhance its efforts in recruiting full-time executive- and senior-level employees who are—or who can easily become—rock stars. The goal to attract and retain exceptional talent throughout all areas in business operations of the major-league club is being sustained as a result of a supportive management team and the intentional efforts of an HR staff empowered to exceed every expectation of the organization.

CASE STUDY QUESTIONS

1. Why is the term *talent acquisition* used rather than *human resource* in the titles of personnel recruiting for the Indians organization?

2. What are the differences in recruiting strategies for attracting entry-level versus senior- or executive-level employees in the Indians organization?

3. Why does the Indians organization annually conduct over 100 informational interviews for students and entry-level job seekers?

4. What ethical considerations are there in sourcing potential candidates from outside organizations who may or may not be seeking a new employment opportunity?

REFERENCES

Allen, J., & Bartle, M. (2014). Sport event volunteers' engagement: Management. *Managing Leisure, 19*(1), 36–50.

Annear, S. (2013, December 9). Registration now open for people that want to volunteer at the 2014 Boston Marathon. *Boston magazine*. Retrieved from http://www.bostonmagazine.com/news/blog/2013/12/09/boston-marathon-volunteers-2014/

Behrend, T., Baker, B., & Thomson, L. (2009). Effects of pro-environmental recruiting messages: The role of organizational reputation. *Journal of Business Psychology, 24*, 341–350.

Blanc, S., & Masami, M. (2016, July 8). *Tokyo Olympics looking for volunteers, may have hard time finding them*. Rocket News 24. Retrieved from http://en.rocketnews24.com/2016/07/08/tokyo-olympics-is-looking-for-volunteers-may-have-a-hard-time-finding-them/

Bowser, Jr., G. (2014, June 30). The sports résumé: Is functional or chronological best? *Black Enterprise*. Retrieved from http://www.blackenterprise.com/career/the-sports-résumé-step-1-format/

Breaugh, J., Greising, L., Taggert, J., & Chen, H. (2003). The relationship of recruiting sources and pre-hire outcomes: Examination of yield ratios and applicant quality. *Journal of Applied Social Psychology, 33*(11), 1559–1816.

Chelladurai, P. (2006). *Human resource management in sport and recreation* (2nd ed.). Champaign, IL: Human Kinetics.

FIFA.com. (2017). *Volunteers.* Retrieved from http://www.fifa.com/worldcup /organisation/volunteers/faq/

Gold Coast 2018 (2017). *Volunteering.* Retrieved from https://www.gc2018.com /take-part/volunteering

Greene, R. (2014, February 14). Sochi 2014: By the numbers. *CNN.* Retrieved from http://www.cnn.com/2014/01/08/world/europe/russia-sochi-numbers/

hrlab.com. (2015). *Ultimate software best fit and competitors.* Retrieved from http:// www.hrlab.com/ultimate-software-competitors.php

International Olympic Committee. (2013). *Final report of the IOC Coordination Committee. Games of the XXX Olympiad, London 2012.* Retrieved from https:// stillmed.olympic.org/Documents/Games_London_2012/Final%20Cocom%20 Report%20London%202012%20EN.pdf

Karl, K., Peluchette, J., & Hall, L. (2008). Give them something to smile about: A marketing strategy for recruiting and retaining volunteers. *Journal of Non-Profit and Public Sector Marketing,* 71–96.

Kjeldal, S., Rindfleish, J., & Sheridan, A. (2005). Deal-making and rule-breaking: Behind the façade of equity in academia. *Gender and Education, 17*(4), 431–447.

Lee, C., Hwang, F., & Yeh, Y. (2013, January 1). The impact of publicity and subsequent intervention in recruitment advertising on job searching freshmen's attraction to an organization and job pursuit intention. *Journal of Applied Social Psychology, 43,* 1–13.

Mahony, C., Mondello, M., Hums, M., & Judd, M. (2006). Recruiting and retaining sport management faculty: Factors affecting job choice. *Journal of Sport Management, 20,* 414–430.

Maurer, S., & Cook, D. (2011). Using company web sites to e-recruit qualified applicants: A job marketing based review of theory-based research. *Computers and Human Behavior, 27,* 106–117.

Miller, J., Whisenant, W., & Persersen, P. (2007). The communication of opportunities and barriers to prospective applicants: An analysis of interscholastic athletic administrative job announcements. *Physical Educator, 62*(2), 73–80.

MLS Press Box. (2014, December 11). *55 college seniors invited to 2015 Adidas MLS player combine.* Retrieved from http://pressbox.mlssoccer.com/content /55-college-seniors-invited-2015-adidas-mls-player-combine

Mlssoccer.com. (2017). *2017 Superdraft.* Retrieved from http://www.mlssoccer.com /superdraft/2017/tracker?utm_source=tracker&utm_campaign=SuperDraft&utm _medium=img

Morgan, J. (2003). Employee recruiting and the Lake Wobegon effect. *Journal of Economic Behavior and Organization, 50,* 165–182.

Nichols, T. (2011, December 12). *Comparative analysis of recruiting and compliance software companies.* Paper written as a member of the Athletic Department Compliance Office at the University of Indiana, Bloomington, IN.

Pedulla, J. (2014, January 28). The price for Super Bowl volunteers. *New York Times,* B10.

Penn State Athletics. (2008, November 25). *Men's soccer assistant coach James Walker leaving Penn State.* Retrieved from http://www.gopsusports.com/sports/m-soccer/spec-rel/112508aaa.html

Phillip, B., Meade, A., & Kroustalis, M. (2008, September). Online recruiting: The effects of organizational familiarity, website usability, and website attractiveness on viewers' impressions of organizations. *Computers in Human Behavior, 24*(6), 2992–3001.

PyeongChang2018.org. (2017). *Organizing committee.* Retrieved from http://www.pyeongchang2018.org/horizon/eng/page/sub02/sub02_07.asp

Reeve, C., & Schultz, L. (2004, December). Job-seeker reactions to selection process information in job ads. *International Journal of Selection and Assessment, 12*(4), 343–355.

Rio2016.com. (2015, November 26). *First 50,000 volunteers for Rio 2016 Olympic and Paralympic Games selected.* Retrieved from http://www.rio2016.com/en/news/first-50000-volunteers-for-rio-2016-olympic-and-paralympic-games-selected

Rio2016.com. (2017). *Volunteer's journal.* Retrieved from http://www.rio2016.com/volunteers/

Rooy, D., Alonso, A., & Fairchild, Z. (2003 June/September). In with the new, out with the old. Has the technological revolution eliminated the traditional search process? *International Journal of Selection and Assessment, 11*(2), 170–174.

SAP. (2017). *SAP for sports and entertainment.* Retrieved from https://assets.cdn.sap.com/sapcom/docs/2015/02/123fa464-157c-0010-82c7-eda71af511fa.pdf

Schlesinger, T., Klenk, C., & Nagle, S. (2015). How do sport clubs recruit volunteers? Analyzing and developing a typology of decision-making processes on recruiting volunteers in sport clubs. *Sport Management Review, 18,* 193–206.

Schmidt, J., Chapman, D., & Jones, D. (2015, March 25). Does emphasizing different types of person–environment fit in online job ads influence application behavior and applicant quality? Evidence from a field experiment. *Journal of Business Psychology, 30,* 267–282.

Super Bowl Host Committee for Houston. (2016, August 17). *Host committee announces volunteer recruitment center/BBVA Compass to support host committee volunteers.* Retrieved from http://www.housuperbowl.com/host-committee-announces-volunteer-recruitment-center

Teamwork Online LLC. (2014). *Current available jobs that match Orlando. Facility operations/security: Event guest relations for Daytona International Speedway.* Retrieved from http://mls.teamworkonline.com/teamwork/jobs/jobskey.cfm?s=orlando#73490

Thielsch, M., Traumer, L., & Pytlik, L. (2012, April 4). E-recruiting and fairness: The applicant's point of view. *Information Technology Management, 13,* 59–67.

Tribevibe.com. (2014, July 28). *Indians facility maintenance coordinator inspires summer of service project, recognized by east Cleveland.* Retrieved from http://tribevibe.mlblogs.com/tag/valencia-kimbrough/

Whisenant, W. (2005). In Texas it's football: How women have been denied access to the AD's office. *International Journal of Sport Management, 6,* 343–350.

Whisenant, W. (2008, February). Sustaining male dominance in interscholastic athletics: A case of homologous reproduction . . . or not? *Sex Roles, 58,* 768–775.

CHAPTER 7

Blue Chippers and Bench Warmers

SCREENING AND SELECTING EMPLOYEES IN SPORTS ORGANIZATIONS

When Gene Smith [vice president and director of athletics] interviews someone, he's not interested in X's and O's. By the time they get to him, we know they can do the job duties. Gene wants to get to know the person, and he wants to know the person's values. Assessing how a candidate will fit into the organizational culture is a huge priority, which is why we include so many individuals in the screening process. We want to have an accurate sense of how a coach or administrator will fit into our culture. We want to know if an individuals' core values align with our core values. We ask a lot of questions about an individuals' past experiences and how they handled each situation, and then we benchmark their responses against how we think they should have handled the situation.

Kim Heaton
Executive Director of Administration
Former Director of Human Resources
The Ohio State University Athletic Department

LEARNING OBJECTIVES

1. Identify two general types of interviews and the considerations for arranging interviews.

2. Identify components and the value of a weighted-criterion-based rating scale in evaluating applicants.

3. Prepare questions for each of the three primary phases of an interview for an entry-level sports position.

4. In addition to interviews, explain the value of each type of screening tool for evaluating applicants for a job in the sports industry.

5. Identify items included in a background check for youth coaches.

KEY TERMS

Applicant criterion chart	Employment interview	Reference checks
Applicant screening	Fair Credit Reporting Act	Situational questions
Assessment tests	Formal interview	Technical questions
Background checks	Open-ended questions	Weighted-criterion chart
Background questions	Predictive index	Wonderlic Test
Behavioral questions	Prescreening interview	
Closed-ended questions	Rating chart	

Lead-Off

Talent acquisition encompasses all the human resource activities to entice and secure a qualified candidate to join the organization. After defining and publicizing a job opening, an organization must thoroughly screen applicants to narrow the field down to select the single best candidate most likely to fit into the organization's culture. Talent acquisition essentially ends when a selected candidate accepts a position and begins the onboarding process.

The sports industry includes many high-pressure positions where employees are expected to work for intense periods of time followed by periods of calm. Working for a sports facility, a collegiate athletic department, a conference office, or for a professional sports franchise requires long hours during peak periods of games and activities. The same is true for employees working in ski resorts, ice rinks, golf courses, outdoor pools, and other seasonal or service-related sports businesses where weather conditions dictate participation. These types of organizations are interested in applicants who can meet the demands of a specific season. It is important to use a systematic **applicant screening** process for determining the best individuals for these types of temporary or seasonal jobs in addition to full-time year-round positions.

The screening phase is used to narrow a field of candidates. After one, two, or more rounds of scanning résumés and further reviewing application materials, preselected applicants begin the interview process. In addition to interviews, the screening process to narrow the field of applicants may incorporate assessment tests, reference checks, and background checks. Taking the time to conduct background reference checks can be the difference in hiring the right candidate. Research demonstrates that the time invested in the screening phase results in more favorable attitudes toward the overall recruitment process (Rafaeli, 1999).

Sports managers and supervisors involved in talent acquisition should be aware of the actual costs for replacing personnel, which is approximately one-fifth of the salary for the position (Boushey & Glynn, 2012). The actual cost per hire can be calculated after all expenses have been incurred and is an accurate depiction of what the organization spends. To calculate the actual cost for recruiting, the event expenses are added to advertising fees and any costs associated with outsourcing services (e.g., search firm or agency). The depreciation for an applicant tracking software (ATS) system may also be considered in calculating recruitment expenses. The event expenses relate specifically to recruiting and include the cost of accommodations, meals, mileage or car rental fees, entertainment, and fees for a facility rental if an interview is conducted off-site. Knowing the cost per hire is valuable information for recruiters to accurately budget for planned vacancies and for being diligent in acquiring the right person for the job.

This chapter overviews screening activities, including interviews, assessment tests, reference checks, and background checks. This chapter also overviews the process of selecting candidates, including the cost factors and notification procedures.

Interviews

Interviews are crucial to the screening process and are considered the most important interaction between employer and applicant (Boucher, Morese, & Chant, 2001; Stier, Schneider, Kampf, Wilding, & Haines, 2006). Screening applicants requires an assessment of the characteristics, personality traits, and qualifications of candidates not readily evidenced on an application or résumé. Interviews provide insight into forecasting how a candidate might or might not perform within an organization. Employment sources vary in their estimations regarding the optimal ratio of interviews to applications in the screening process, which range anywhere from 2% to 25% (Bridgespan Group, 2015, p. 2; Commonwealth of Massachusetts, 2009; Harris, 2014; Smooke, 2013).

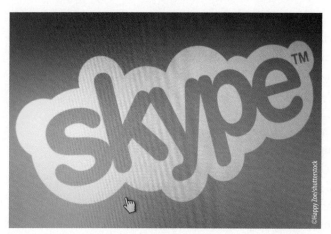

Skype is one virtual tool for interviewing candidates.

TYPES OF EMPLOYMENT INTERVIEWS

An **employment interview** is a meeting whereby one individual questions another to assess suitability for a job. Common modalities to conduct interviews include face to face, over the phone (mobile), and via digital or online platforms such as Skype, the GroupMe app, Google Hangouts, iPhone FaceTime, and Facebook Video Messenger, to name a few. Computer-mediated interviews conducted through video-conferencing and instant-messaging software have been a cost-effective means for employers to reach a broad applicant pool (Behrend, Toaddy, Thomson, & Shareck, 2012). Slowly trending is the prerecorded video, where applicants are sent a series of questions and instructed to video record their responses. One of the advantages for the applicants is the opportunity to record themselves multiple times.

Two distinct categories are **prescreening** interviews for the purpose of eliminating applicants on established criteria and **formal interviews**, which assist in final decisions to select the most likely candidate who should be hired. In a study of hiring practices for campus recreational directors in higher education, 66% of the more than 500 respondents indicated phone interviews were conducted before an in-person interview (Stier et al., 2006). The nature of the position, proximity of candidates, and time parameters have an effect on whether phone or computer-assisted interviews are used for prescreening. The greater the level of the position (e.g., director level vs. entry level), the more likely prescreening interviews will occur. For example, only 6% of student workers in a campus recreation department reported receiving a phone interview prior to an in-person interview (Stier et al., 2006).

Prescreening Interviews

Prescreening interviews are designed to narrow the field of candidates to a short list of the most viable applicants (typically, two to five candidates) who will be interviewed in greater depth. These brief interviews are typically conducted via a phone call or through a virtual electronic Web-based audio/video transmission source. The phone call or computer-aided communication saves time and cuts costs associated with on-site visits.

On occasion, prescreening interviews are conducted in person at job fairs, such as the Baseball Winter Meetings or a similar event hosted by a professional franchise, a university career center, or a municipality. For example, the Major League Baseball (MLB) Seattle Mariners (2015) incorporated prescreening interviews at Safeco Field during a hiring event for game-day parking attendants, guest-services hosts, elevator hosts, ticket collectors, and security personnel. The National Intramural and Recreation Sports Association (NIRSA) provides an informational session on vacancies, which may lead to an informal on-site interview for campus recreation jobs (Stier et al., 2006).

The Seattle Mariners occasionally conduct prescreening interviews at Safeco Field for game-day workers.

Prescreening interviews may conducted be in a group or one-on-one setting, but almost always, they are brief compared to a structured, more formal interview. A typical 10-minute prescreening interview serves to ensure candidates understand the job and salary parameters while allowing the employer to gain valuable information about an applicant's background to help determine if the person is a viable candidate. The prescreening interview additionally assists in assessing verbal communication skills and the ability to establish rapport, especially with many sectors of the sports industry requiring a customer-service skill set.

Although most prescreening interviews are relatively short in duration, there is the opportunity for longer dialogue if time permits. Businesses such as Under Armour may conduct multiple prescreening interview sessions for even entry-level employees (see **Action Shot 7-1**).

In addition to eliminating candidates, the purpose of the prescreening interview is to learn information about candidates' work experience; their knowledge, skills, and abilities; and a bit about their management style and career goals if time permits. To learn more about an applicant, open-ended questions can be asked to probe deeper into whether a candidate should be considered a finalist for the formal interview.

Formal Interviews

Formal interviews are provided to the few qualified candidates considered finalists for a position. The formal interview is for the purpose of the employer deciding whether or not to hire the candidate. The formal interview usually takes place in person; however, virtual interviews are also available

◱ ACTION SHOT 7-1

Under Armour Prescreening Interviews

Sports retailer Under Armour typically interviews candidates for entry-level positions such as sales associates and cashiers two times, whereas managerial candidates may experience three interviews. The company practices a policy of conducting a prescreening phone interview approximately a week following the submission of an application and other required materials. A portion of the candidates receiving a phone interview are selected for an in-person interview, which may or may not result in a job offer for entry-level positions. Managerial candidates selected for the first round of in-person interviews are further narrowed to a select few who meet with Under Armour hiring officials, generally consisting of district managers, store managers, and supervisors. Under Armour has also used group interviews to prescreen for eligible workers in addition to phone interviews.

Data from Job-applications.com (2015).

to the recruiter. Typically, the higher a position is within a company, the longer the interview, the more structured the interview, and the greater the number of personnel involved.

The formal interview provides a wealth of information not easily assessed in reviewing résumés, application files, or through initial prescreening activities. Most importantly, questions in a formal interview allow the employer to directly compare the competency level of the candidate for performing the responsibilities and tasks identified in a job description against a select few individuals also being considered.

In an assessment of the interview process for athletic trainers, it was suggested that two types of questions should be developed for the interview to focus on dispositions and to correctly interpret job answers. Optimal disposition–focused questions are open-ended and ask candidates to describe professionally related experiences that have personal meaning (Morgan & Wasicsko, 2008). Formal interviews are better for assessing disposition and whether an applicant is a likely fit within the company's organizational culture. The "fit" refers to whether an individual possesses a propensity for exhibiting the characteristic traits and behaviors valued in employees of the organization. For example, an arena football team hiring for a production team member searches for candidates who are outgoing, creative, and team-oriented. Formal interviews allow recruiters to appraise these personal characteristics, which are not easily or quickly able to be assessed in a 10-minute prescreening phone interview. Likability is another factor more likely to be gauged in a formal interview through studying whether candidates smile, appear confident, and engage the interviewer.

Considerations in Arranging Interviews

There are numerous factors to consider when arranging an interview, such as the number of individuals involved, the method of communication, the location and format, the number of interviews necessary to determine the final candidate, the time period to conduct meetings, and budgets. A detailed recruitment/talent assessment plan will address each factor.

Number of Individuals

A candidate for a social media director position for a Major League Soccer (MLS) franchise may interview with multiple departments, and a university seeking a head basketball coach may arrange a full day of interviewing with different stakeholder groups. A candidate for a night-shift supervisor at a public batting cage may only interview with the owner. Although one-on-one interviews are most common, especially for entry-level employees, group interviews are also a routine practice in sports organizations. Group interviews may involve a single prospective employee facing a panel of interviewers or a single recruiter meeting with a group of applicants at the same time. The number of individuals refers to the number of candidates being interviewed for a position as well as the number of individuals conducting the interviews.

Method of Communication

The method of communication refers to how the interview will be conducted. The most common method is face-to-face interviewing; however, virtual methods of communication have risen in popularity to reduce the impact on time and travel expenditures. Virtual methods of communication are conducted through the telephone or through Web-based modalities such as Skype, Google Hangout, and FaceTime.

Location

The location for an interview considers where the meeting will take place. Although the frequency of interviews conducted in cyberspace through Web-based virtual tools or the over the telephone have increased over the years, most final interviews are conducted on-site at one of the hiring organization's facilities. Interviews may also be conducted off-site. For example, while serving as the active head football coach at the University of Louisville,

Professional teams and universities have been known to lease space in airport terminals to interview high profile coaches or administrators.

Bobby Petrino interviewed for the Auburn University head job at a small airport in Indiana (Schlabach, 2014). Off-site locations such as a restaurant or airport are commonly used as a convenience to the interviewee or to reduce the potential for information becoming public, especially if a candidate is still bound to a current employment contract. The location for a formal interview on-site or off-site should be in a private, quiet location that is accessible to individuals with a disability.

Format

The format of the interview refers to whether questions and phases of the meeting are structured or unstructured. The unstructured interview is conducted as a free-flowing conversation without a predetermined set of questions that presumably permits the interviewer to observe more significant and relevant behaviors. The unstructured interview allows the interviewer discretion of what questions to ask, and they are usually open-ended.

Structured interviews, on the other hand, include predetermined questions and typically a standard rating or evaluation form. Spontaneity is sacrificed for the consistent treatment of applicants and to prevent raters from making quick judgments. These types of interviews allow the replication of a fixed set of questions that are asked in the same order.

Structured interviews have been identified as the preferred format to more accurately predict job success than informal approaches. In research on the utility of interview types, however, the unstructured interview was found to be more accurate for assessing judgments about a candidate's job-related personality traits (Blackman, 2002). Candidates spent a significantly longer period of time talking in an unstructured interview format than those in structured settings, but there was no significant correlation between the number of personality-relevant questions and self-agreement by the interviewer.

The format of the interview used for screening employees for sports positions will vary based on the nature of the job, the time available, and the preference of the interviewer. Regardless of the type of interview, the ultimate goal is the same—to determine the likelihood that an individual will succeed if hired for the position.

Number of Interviews

The number of interviews considers how many times an individual will meet regarding his or her candidacy for a position. For example, a candidate may participate in several virtual interviews before being invited to participate in a face-to-face interview. Other candidates may interview only once or may interview at an off-site location before being interviewed on-site.

Time Period

The time period includes the amount of time (days, weeks, months) an organization will take to conduct interviews. Ideally, an organization intends to hire an individual within a reasonable amount of time from closing applications (e.g., 2–6 weeks). The time period considers the length of time for each round of interviews and is influenced by the number of candidates and the availability of both the interviewee and the interviewer(s). A 15-month interview window from March 2015 through May 2016 was necessary to screen, interview, and hire the 70,000 volunteers for the 2016 Olympics (Rio2016.com, 2016). The website for the 2020 Olympics in Tokyo, Japan, indicated a 2-year window for recruiting and securing volunteers (Tokyo2020, 2017).

Budgets

An organization's recruiting budget has implications for determining the location and methods of interviews in addition to the number of candidates and the number of interviews that will be conducted. The cost for an in-person interview may include transportation (mileage, air and ground transport, rental car, and/or parking), accommodations, meals, and entertainment expenses. On occasion, facility rental fees are accrued if conducting an interview off-site such as in a hotel meeting room. The recruiter in addition to candidates may incur expenses as well which should be reflected in budgets.

Anatomy of an Interview

Generally, an interview is divided into three sections: the introduction, middle, and closing. The introduction sets the initial stage to clarify the purpose, the middle allows for the interviewer to ascertain the information necessary to narrow a selection, and the closing provides direction in the process.

INTRODUCTION

During the introduction, the interviewer should provide a welcome and engage in small talk to help the candidate feel at ease. The interviewer also typically describes the interview process and outlines the duties and responsibilities of the vacant position. The goal of the introduction phase is to establish a level of comfort while establishing a tone for the interview as either informal and unstructured or professional.

MIDDLE

The middle section of an interview includes the questions that will assess the qualifications and potential fit of the candidate within the organization. Typically, the interviewer asks general background or framework questions to clarify information provided in the application materials. Next, open-ended questions are asked to allow the candidate to distinguish his or herself from the competition.

CLOSING

The closing allows the candidate an opportunity to ask questions or share concerns. The closing also provides direction in the recruiting process by providing information on the tentative timeline and the feedback mechanisms (phone call, letter, or e-mail) for informing candidates of a decision.

Interview Questions

Interview questions may be closed- or open-ended questions. **Closed-ended questions** allow for only a selected response such as yes or no. **Open-ended questions** permit the interviewee to elaborate on a response and explain an answer. Following is a list of basic open-ended questions that may be asked on a prescreening phone interview:

- *Why are you currently searching for a new position?*
- *Is the salary range we have set for this position within your acceptable range?*
- *What are the top three duties in the job you now have or in your most recent job?*
- *What are some typical decisions that you make, and how do you make them?*
- *What do you think you would do for this organization that someone else wouldn't?*
- *What is your ideal working situation?*

Questions during an interview should not make a candidate feel uncomfortable or provide a legal challenge for unlawful questions that may be considered discriminatory (see **Box 7-1**).

BOX 7-1

Topics to Avoid Addressing in an Interview

- Complexion
- Physical characteristics
- Arrest record
- Armed forces discharge
- Owning or renting housing
- Mode of transportation to and from work
- Credit ratings
- Nationality of applicant or family
- Name of next of kin for contact
- Place of birth

- How candidate learned second language
- Religious beliefs or religious holiday observances
- Change of name/maiden name
- Current or previous marital status
- Preferred form of address (*Miss* or *Mrs.*)
- Children
- Participation in sports activities in high school
- Age
- Date of graduation from high school
- Medical conditions

Interview questions can be categorized into four areas: (1) background, (2) technical, (3) behavioral, and (4) situational. Each type of questions serves a distinct purpose for assisting recruiters in screening candidates.

BACKGROUND QUESTIONS

Background questions are general questions designed to elicit information regarding a candidate's employment history or educational attainment. The purpose of background questions is to learn the profile of the applicant. Typically, the background of the applicant can be learned from reviewing a résumé or application, but these basic, historical information–seeking questions are a means to begin an interview and make the candidate feel more comfortable before being asked more thought-provoking questions. For example, someone applying to work for the National Hockey League (NHL) New York Rangers may be asked a background question about his or her hockey experience. Examples of background questions include:

- Tell me about yourself.
- What is the highest degree you have earned?
- Where was your first full-time job?
- What are some of your strengths and weaknesses?

TECHNICAL QUESTIONS

Technical questions are used to assess whether the candidate can perform a particular job. Questions pertaining to technical competence for a ticket executive with a professional National Football League (NFL) or MLB team would include whether the candidate has experience with paperless ticketing (e.g., Flash Seats), evidence of his or her selling skills (e.g., achieving sales quotas), and skills in customer service. For a position as a compliance director for a university athletic department, technical questions would assess competency in understanding of rules, experience submitting reports for secondary or major infractions, experience processing appeals, and knowledge or experience with using compliance software.

BEHAVIORAL QUESTIONS

Behavioral questions require the candidate to recall a story or provide an example to demonstrate a particular behavior. They are based on the premise that past behavior is a good predictor of future behavior. These types of questions can be tailored for specific positions. A candidate applying for a job as a cashier in a retail sporting goods store or as a guest-services desk manager for a health club may be asked to describe a time where he or she provided exceptional customer service or solved a customer complaint. Similarly, a candidate interviewing for a position as a box-office manager for a stadium may be asked to explain how he or she typically greets new clients.

SITUATIONAL QUESTIONS

Situational questions or stress questions are similar to behavioral questions but are staged with a hypothetical or actual workplace scenario to elicit a response that would assess how a candidate would react. When asking a situational question, the interviewer provides a story or scenario and instructs the interviewee to describe how he or she would resolve the issue. For instance, an applicant for a manager position at a health and fitness center may be provided with a scenario of receiving a phone call from a member regarding an aerobics instructor with alcohol on his or her breath and then be asked to role play the follow-up conversation with the member and with the employee. Similarly, the candidate applying for the box-office manager position may be given a situation where a credit card of an arriving spectator doesn't scan properly, followed by a question asking how he or she would handle the guest.

Evaluating Interviews

The key to evaluating interviews is to be as objective as possible. It is relatively easy for a supervisor conducting multiple interviews for a cashier at a sporting goods store to form a subjective appraisal of the candidates he or she believes are best suited for the position or whom he or she simply likes the best or finds the most attractive. However, each interview should be evaluated using an unbiased preconception of a candidate based on how his or her responses align with the job qualifications. In other words, objectivity instead of subjectivity is the preferred method of evaluating interviews to screen applicants.

Administrators evaluating an interview may elect to create an answer key to questions by identifying the likely response that is desired from a top candidate, an average candidate, and a poor candidate. The most common and objective evaluation method for evaluating interviews is to use a rating chart, occasionally referred to as a criterion rating chart. **Action Shot 7-2** provides an example of how a criterion chart and ranking system was created to assess the most desirable characteristics of athletic trainers applying for vacancies.

A second evaluation method that provides validity in accurately evaluating interviews is predictive indexing. Regardless of the method used, it is important to provide an evaluation within a relatively short time period after completing an interview and to use a consistent format for each and every applicant.

It is also recommended that multiple individuals are involved in the interview and the evaluation of the interview to increase the reliability of the results. When multiple individuals are involved in using a rating chart or an **applicant criterion chart** scoring system, there is a greater likelihood for consensus when determining the best candidate to recommend for a position. Scores from multiple reviewers can be averaged or added together to indicate a combined assessed value for a candidate. In addition, discrepancies in rater scores on a particular criterion allows for greater scrutiny of an applicant's qualifications.

Rating Chart

A **rating chart** is an extremely common tool to evaluate an interview. A chart identifies a predefined list of criteria with a system that permits an individual to easily evaluate the item. The rating chart can also be identified as an evaluation chart, a panel consensus form, a ranking form, a criterion chart, or any similar derivative that describes an appraisal of items pertaining to the interview.

▶ ACTION SHOT 7-2

Criteria for Selecting Athletic Trainers

A survey of companies and organizations advertising for a certified trainer in the vacancy postings published by the National Athletic Trainers' Association ranked desirable characteristics in the hiring criteria of employees in high schools, universities, professional sports, clinics, and other industrial areas. The results suggested that regardless of the work setting, the most desirable characteristics were personal qualities such as communication skills, enthusiasm, initiative, maturity, initiative, self-confidence, ambition, and problem-solving skills (Kahanov & Andrews, 2001).

In addition to personal qualities, criteria responses on interviews represented categories related to workplace attributes, education, and professional experience. Subjects scored each criterion on a scale of 1 to 7 representing a range from most important to not important at all. Educational experience was represented by criteria such as grade point average, honors and awards, and college minor. Workplace attributes included entrepreneurialism, membership in a professional association, and willingness to relocate. Professional experience was represented by a master's degree or military experience (Kahanov & Andrews, 2001).

Based on research of desirable traits for success as an athletic trainer, interview questions can be crafted to align with a criterion rating chart that would assess the degree to which candidates possess important attributes. Interview questions and a rating chart would assess the degree to which candidates for an athletic trainer position are effective communicators and demonstrate enthusiasm, initiative, self-confidence, and problem-solving skills deemed important to job success.

A relatively easy tool for creating a rating chart is Microsoft Excel, where columns and rows can represent information important for evaluating a single candidate, as shown in **Table 7-1**. The simple charting method can be used to check off an item (e.g., competency, qualification, or behavior) when the interviewer feels the candidate has met or demonstrated the criteria, such as a minimum education attainment, 2 years of related experience, or a friendly personality. The evaluation system may alternatively include a number ranking to assess the degree of qualifications or desired traits determined by interviewing a candidate (see Table 7-1).

TABLE 7-1: Sample Rating Form for an Entry-Level Interview

Interview Rating Form

Applicant Name: _____   Position: _____

Criteria	Description of High Proficiency	Rating: Low–High
Professional Appearance:	Applicant looks clean and neat and dresses appropriately for interview standards.	1 2 3 4 5
Professional Conduct:	Applicant smiles, makes eye contact, introduces self, shakes hands, sits appropriately, demonstrates confidence, projects enthusiasm and friendliness.	1 2 3 4 5
Communication Skills:	Applicant uses proper grammar, actively listens, avoids filler words *(um, uh, you know)*, and responds with short, appropriate answers.	1 2 3 4 5
Background and Experience:	Applicant is able to describe volunteer, work or personal experiences that relate to the workplace.	1 2 3 4 5
Questioning Skills:	Applicant also asks questions appropriate to interview that demonstrate research of the company/organization.	1 2 3 4 5
Résumé and Application:	Documents are neat, clean, and well prepared.	1 2 3 4 5

Comments

Weighted-Criterion Chart

Microsoft Excel can also be used to create a weighted-criterion chart. **Table 7-2** provides an example of a weighted-criterion chart adapted from a competitive youth hockey organization for girls in Canada (Gloucester-Cumberland Ringette Association, 2005). First of all, a weighted chart is different than a ranking system due to the values placed on criteria. A rating chart considers all criteria to be equal, but a weighted chart distinguishes the value of each criterion by assigning a point value that coincides with the importance of a criterion with respect to the effective performance of the job. For example, a criterion chart for a golf course superintendent vacancy would assign a higher point value for an education degree in the field of turf or

TABLE 7-2: Sample Weighted-Criterion Chart for Selecting Youth Hockey Coaches

Criteria	Weight	Candidate 1		Candidate 2	
		Raw Score	Adjusted	Raw Score	Adjusted
Coaching credentials—general	30%	8	24.0	5	15.0
Coaching credentials—Ringette	10%	8	8.0	7	7.0
Most recent coaching evaluation	10%	8	8.0	6	6.0
Parent/player feedback	5%	10	5.0	8	4.0
Communication skills—verbal	5%	10	5.0	8	4.0
Experience as a Ringette player	5%	0	0.0	10	5.0
Communication skills—written	5%	10	5.0	8	4.0
Performance on interview	20%	8	16.0	9	18.0
Age of coach versus age of players	5%	7	3.5	7	3.5
Experience in team sports	2%	10	2.0	10	2.0
Gloucester-Cumberland resident	2%	0	0.0	10	2.0
Gender	1%	0	0.0	10	2.0
TOTAL	100%	81	77.5	98	72.5

Data from the Gloucester-Cumberland Ringette Association (2005).

golf course management as opposed to other degrees or a higher value to experience as a superintendent as opposed to the candidate's rapport with members. Similarly, an evaluation of a candidate's interview may include a weighted measurement where problem-solving ability constitutes 50% of a score, and assessment of experience and likeability each account for 25% of the overall score.

To design a weighted-criterion chart, a decision matrix can be developed by inputting the candidates to rank (e.g., Candidates 1, 2, and 3), the decision criteria (e.g., age of coach vs. age of players), and the importance of each criterion (a percentage value). Evaluators may assign a raw score for each item (i.e., 0–10) and adjust the score based on the assigned weight by multiplying the two. For example, a raw score of 5 when weighted at 30% as in the example of the general coaching credentials identified in Table 7-2 would yield an adjusted score of 15, whereas a weighted value of 5% would yield an adjusted score of 2.5. Adding the scores at the bottom of each candidate's column allows for a comparative review.

Additional Screening Tools

Although interviews are a valid tool for screening applicants, additional measures to ensure an applicant is the right fit for an organization will decrease the likelihood of hiring the wrong person. These measures include assessment tests, background checks, and reference checks.

ASSESSMENT TESTS

Assessment tests are used to screen job applicants on the basis of specific behavioral, knowledge, or skill areas. There is a growing market for employment aptitude and ability tests, the majority of which are Web based and easy to administer. The cost of administering and scoring an assessment test is typically per instrument, or they can be ordered in bundles. An employer can easily find a test to assess personality, numerical or spatial reasoning, critical thinking, situational judgment, inductive reasoning, error-checking skills, creativity, customer-service orientation, sales motivation, career motivation, management skills, clerical aptitude, or work integrity. The Society of Human Resource Managers (SHRM) offers hundreds of online aptitude tests to measure everything from depression to sales achievement potential.

The purpose of an assessment test is to determine if a candidate has the right skills for the position or if the candidate is a good fit for the corporate culture. The standardization and objectivity of assessment testing can be a valuable supplemental tool in the screening process. The general purpose of the assessment test is to evaluate the potential success of the candidate in the organization. Two assessment tests used in sports organizations are the Wonderlic Test and the predictive index.

Wonderlic Test

Since 1968, the NFL has administered a 12-minute, 50-question **Wonderlic Test** at its annual rookie combine to assess the cognitive ability of draft picks before a contract can be offered. The assessment tool, which is administered to job candidates in over 50,000 organizations around the world, evaluates an individual's cognitive ability to learn, solve problems, and follow instructions. Citing the potential for racial bias and a low correlation with predicting success on the job, the NFL replaced the test in 2013 with a longer-version instrument designed to measure attributes in motivation, competitiveness, passion, and mental toughness (Batista, 2013). The new Player Assessment Tool measures 16 traits considered as predictors of successful performance

Quarterbacks like Tom Brady are among those who typically rank highest among scores on the Wonderlic Assessment Test formerly used throughout the NFL.

in the NFL. Individual franchises have administered similar aptitude tests for players as a supplement to the on-field physical tests, medical assessments, and clinical interviews.

The Wonderlic Test is one of many assessment tools used to pre-screen job seekers and help employers predict how someone will perform in the workplace. The client list includes many mainstream businesses, such as Lehman's, Kramer Beverage Company, North Mississippi Medical Center, Scott Chevrolet, and Subway Restaurants (Wonderlic.com, 2017). Similarly, Sports Aptitude is a behavior-based analytics tool used by over a third of National Basketball Association (NBA) franchises to predict how draft picks may thrive under pressure or fit into a program (Langley, 2011). The co-creator of the test consults with a number of professional franchises to assist in assessing the situational performance of players.

Predictive Index

The **predictive index** is a job analytics tool that allows recruiters to quantify the behavioral requirements of a position and assess an applicant's level of similarities to or differences from the criteria. As an indicator of "job fit" between the applicant and the vacancy, predictive indexing is used by 20% of Fortune 500 companies around the world (Russell, 2015).

The predictive index permits an applicant 10 minutes to check off the adjectives (86 total) that most accurately describe his or her personality. The results are then matched with a system devised by the recruiter to distinguish the characteristics most likely to contribute to effective performance.

Also referred to as personality profiling, predictive indexing has been used in the sports industry by coaches to evaluate potential recruits in the NFL and NBA and in the realm of intercollegiate athletics. One of the earliest collegiate coaches to administer a personality test to potential players was Pat Summitt, the late coach of the Knoxville Tennessee Lady Volunteers basketball program.

As many as 30 university teams reportedly have used an Australian-based athlete assessment firm for predictive indexing (Eisenberg, 2013). In addition, a former NBA coach for the Charlotte Hornets relied on a predictive index to identify how a recruit or an assistant coach might fit into a college basketball program at Marist College (Eisenberg, 2013).

REFERENCE CHECKS

Reference checks that verify personal and professional references are a standard by which a hiring official validates a candidate's credibility and honesty in his or her application and interview. References are typically contacted over the phone once an organization finalizes the selection and before an offer is made to the candidate. The individual conduct-

Former Tennessee Lady Vols Basketball Coach Pat Summit was one of the earliest coaches to administer personality tests to evaluate potential recruits.

ing a reference check for employment verification may seek to learn more about a candidate's professional background and/or his or her character. A basic verification check of employment serves as confirmation of dates worked, title, and salary; however, the correspondence is also an opportunity to obtain more detailed information regarding an appraisal of the applicant's performance, his or her ability to meet demands of the job, and most importantly, the organization's willingness to rehire the individual.

Reference checks may unveil potential problems in applicants, especially when there are conflicting statements between the applicant and the reference. Although rare, the preferred recommendation is to contact a third-party trusted professional known by both the candidate and the individual conducting the reference check. Therefore, a common practice is to contact personnel who may not be identified on a potential employee's list of references.

Due to legal risks, questions relating to a candidate's age, religion, ethnicity, or any other potentially discriminatory characteristic should be avoided. Requesting a recommendation from a reference for an additional contact who might be familiar with an applicant's performance is not uncommon.

BACKGROUND CHECKS

Unlike the reference check, a thorough **background check** is typically an expense to recruiters; however, it is also a valid and reliable tool to screen a candidate

Criminal background checks for volunteer youth sport coaches is mandatory in many states.

before making a final hiring decision. A background check is an investigation of an applicant's financial, criminal, educational, and/or employment history through public or confidential sources.

The NBA Dallas Mavericks (2013) franchise is just one of many sports organizations that note in various job announcements that employment is contingent upon a successful background check. Municipal recreation departments require background checks and fingerprinting for all volunteers for government-sponsored activities. The National Collegiate Athletic Association (NCAA) requires "participant approval," including a criminal background check, for all coaches and operators of NCAA-certified events. Fitness facilities, Young Men's Christian Association (YMCA) facilities, professional sports organizations, sports agencies, and retail sports businesses also routinely conduct background checks on potential employees. The California State Senate passed a bill requiring any organization conducting community recreation programs for youth to provide parents with notification of whether coaches and organizers have undergone criminal background checks (Chorneau, 2014). Baltimore County in Maryland also passed legislation mandating criminal background checks for volunteer coaches.

The following is an example of background-check procedures for the Springfield Department of Parks and Recreation (2017) for individuals applying for a volunteer youth sports coaching position:

> *The third-party contractor conducting the checks will cross-reference the screening results with the disqualifying crimes listed in this policy. A pass/fail grade will then be emailed to the Parks and Recreation Department based on the cross-reference. A passing grade indicates a volunteer/coach has qualified per policy to participate. A failing grade indicates a volunteer/coach has not qualified per policy to participate. All information pertaining to the background check will remain secure, subject to the applicable laws requiring disclosure.*

A background check is not required by law, but the procedure assists in preventing an employer from making a poor hiring decision. The research on a candidate's history may include an identification check (address and date of birth) and a review of public criminal records, sex offenses, motor vehicle violations, credit reports, and social media activity. Verifying these and other types of records is a standard procedure in most organizations, especially in the field of coaching, which has come under heavy scrutiny since a recent scandal involving former Penn State University football assistant coach Jerry Sandusky, who was indicted on 40 counts of sexual abuse involving minors (Mihoces, 2011).

Public opinion has suggested that stricter background checks may have alerted Penn State to detect concerns before hiring Assistant Football Coach, Jerry Sandusky, convicted on dozens of counts of sexual assault and child molestation.

Background checks are part of the process of coaching certification in countries such as Iceland (V. Johannesson, personal communication, October 20, 2016). Restrictions on the eligibility to coach sports in Europe is much stricter than the United States, which relies on parent volunteers. Certification for coaches in European sports is tiered, and even those coaching 4- and 5-year-olds must undergo extensive training and background checks.

In addition to credit history and criminal records, background checks serve to also verify education records, previous employment, achievements, professional licenses, immigration status, and Social Security status. Finally, a drug screening, polygraph lie detector test, and even a physical exam may be part of the procedures to screen candidates before a hiring decision.

According to a survey conducted by the SHRM (2012), 69% of organizations conduct background checks of criminal records. In the event a candidate is not hired based on criminal or other public records, the individual must be notified and provided an opportunity to dispute the accuracy or completeness of the information obtained. Although free background checks of public criminal records via an Internet search engine are available, a preferred method is to contract with a credible outside agency to minimize the potential for the legal challenge of negligent hiring. Most organizations opt to outsource background checks to service providers requiring moderate fees. For example, the NCAA requires all individuals who engage in coaching or operating and managing NCAA-certified events to complete an annual basic verification and criminal background check at their own expense through First Advantage (2017), a third-party employment screening provider (NCAA, 2013).

Although public criminal records and credit reports are part of a typical background check, many sports organizations go the extra mile in scrutinizing applicants as a method to protect their image and minimize the risk of hiring an individual with incongruent values or behavior. For instance, prior to hiring a coach, administrator, or support staff member, the compliance director or an athletics administrator typically consults with the NCAA Department of Infractions for a review of violations. Maintaining integrity in the operations of programs and activities is at the core of university values, and according to a report on college athletics and the law, unethical conduct or impermissible benefits are the most prevalent abuses by coaches (O'Brien & O'Brien, 2013).

Despite the emphasis on hiring individuals who display ethical conduct and integrity, on occasion, misrepresentation has been overlooked in hiring intercollegiate athletics personnel (see **Action Shot 7-3**). Misrepresentation of credentials is not exclusively an issue for intercollegiate athletics. Sports agents who aren't licensed to practice in a particular state are subject to fines. In 2014, a high school football coach in Florida falsified transcripts and information on his résumé pertaining to his athletics participation (Clark & Shipley, 2014). In 2002, the first female serving as president and chair of the U.S. Olympic Committee resigned after it was discovered she had not earned a doctorate degree from Arizona State as her résumé indicated (Litsky, 2002).

Cases of misrepresentation in employment or academic history speak to an individual's character and integrity. Background checks are a means to ensure viable candidates are trustworthy while helping to avoid potential hires of individuals who are not honest about their credentials.

Background checks have been extended to include both random and targeted screening of an individual's presence on social media sites, such as LinkedIn, Facebook, Twitter, and Instagram. An organization should first, however, include a statement on its standard employment application regarding reserving the right to check on the veracity of a potential employee's personal information. Social media sites may provide an indication of a potential candidate's interests, hobbies, and communication skills in addition to a snapshot of his or her personal behavior; however, caution must be given to someone who may rely on unverified information from Internet sources for hiring decisions.

Verifying that a coach or any employee is void of sexual offenses or criminal records demonstrates a prudent managerial approach to screen candidates prior to a final selection. Of great importance is to refrain from violating the federal **Fair Credit Reporting Act**, which regulates third-party agencies that collect and report on an individual's public or personal information. Handled correctly, background checks serve as an effective tool in the screening process. The associated costs of a background check are either absorbed by the organization or passed on to the job seeker as a condition for employment consideration.

▶ ACTION SHOT 7-3

Background Checks and Academic Fraud in Intercollegiate Athletics

Once upon a time, Charles S. Harris claimed to have received a master's degree in journalism from the University of Michigan in Ann Arbor. It wasn't true, but in 2004, Averett University chose to overlook the discrepancy and announced it had hired Harris as the new athletics director. Two years earlier, Harris withdrew his acceptance offer for the position of director of athletics and recreation at Dartmouth College in Hanover, New Hampshire, upon discovery of misrepresentation of his academic records on his résumé (Suggs, 2004). Harris had over 25 years of experience in higher education athletics as the former athletics director at Arizona State University and the University of Pennsylvania and as a former commissioner for the Mid-Eastern Athletic Conference.

A head soccer coach with a 43–17–4 record who guided the UCLA Bruin's men's soccer team to the 2002 NCAA Final Four resigned after university officials discovered his academic degree was from a diploma mill. Todd Saldana had received a bachelor's degree in psychology from Columbia State University in Louisiana. A year later, the school was forced to shut down by law enforcement for issuing fraudulent degrees (Times Wire Services, 2002).

In 2014, the University of South Florida decided not to hire Steve Masiello, who was serving as the Manhattan College's head men's basketball coach. A background check revealed Masiello never graduated from the University of Kentucky as his biography indicated on the Manhattan's basketball athletic website (Johnston, 2014). Masiello was retained as the head coach for Manhattan College.

One of the most infamous cases of employment record fraud in intercollegiate athletics resulted in the resignation of George O'Leary as the head football coach for the University of Notre Dame within 5 days of his appointment. It was discovered that O'Leary had embellished his academic and athletic accomplishments while previously at the University of New Hampshire. Inaccuracies were discovered in O'Leary's biographical information regarding earning varsity letters in football and completing a master's degree from the university (Fountain & Wong, 2001). Soon after his release, O'Leary was hired as head football coach and interim athletic director at the University of Central Florida. He retired in 2015 but was retained by the university through 2020 at an annual salary of $200,000 (Berkowitz, 2015).

Selecting Candidates

The selection stage is where sports managers will most likely have the opportunity to negotiate employment agreements and implement individually designed compensation packages. In selecting a candidate, no particular screening tool is a single predictor of a successful hire. A criterion chart or some type of data-driven decision model, however, provides at least partial validity and objective measures to aid a decision. The composite results of all screening strategies are considered to aid the decision of the best candidate to offer a position. Factoring in a candidate's application materials, his or her interview, personal references, and all additional information available provides a professional profile from which to make a selection that yields the likelihood of a successful hire.

The right hire is the final candidate who is the most qualified and can best achieve performance results while aligning with the corporate culture. In other words, the right hire has the requisite skills for the position and is a "good fit" for the organization. Validating a decision through a committee consensus is ideal when possible; however, care should be given to avoid groupthink for the sake of saving time in the process.

NOTIFICATION OF HIRE

Once a candidate is selected as the finalist, he or she is notified of an official job offer, which includes pertinent information on compensation and benefits, an official title, the starting date, and possibly advancement opportunities. Herein is the stage where compensation, moving expenses, start dates, vacation leave, and other items may be negotiated. For most entry-level, part-time, and seasonal/temporary work, a straight compensation figure is a nonnegotiable item in the form of an hourly wage. When hiring a full-time salaried position such as a regional manager for a sports retail company or an associate director of athletics for an intercollegiate program, the candidate may or may not negotiate the compensation package information.

Typically, a 24- to 48-hour window is advisable for a candidate to consider an offer; however, discretion is provided for maintaining flexibility in the recruiting timeline to ensure the right hire. If a job offer is not accepted, the hiring organization has several options, including making a counteroffer to the top candidate, making an offer to the second candidate, or reopening the search with a stronger commitment to recruiting qualified applicants. In all cases, the recruiting timeline is extended.

Recruiting plans may clarify that prior to any public announcement of a candidate accepting an offer in writing, all discarded applicants who participated in a final interview are notified of the decision.

ONBOARDING

The onboarding process is a function of familiarizing and socializing the employee with his or role in the organization. Gathering required documents to process payroll or certify confidentiality for protected passwords is only the initial step in the process of onboarding. Essentially, the selected candidate

---

BOX 7-2

Sample Forms Included in Employee File when Onboarding

- **Federal** W-4 and state tax forms
- Public school district withholding
- I-9 Form
- Health, life, and disability insurance enrollment forms
- New employee form
- Automatic payroll deduction (direct deposit)
- Emergency contact information
- Equal employment identity form
- Security form for credentials
- Copies of official identification

---

has already agreed to the employment position; therefore, onboarding ends the hiring phase and begins the training regime. The onboarding process is the first step before the orientation familiarizes and socializes the employee with his or her role in the organization. Upon acceptance, the onboarding process begins with a welcome letter and a file created for the new employee that is used to organize human resource documentation (see **Box 7-2**).

The federal I-9 is the standard form all employees complete upon initially being hired to verify information about his or her identity and eligibility status. The W-4 is used to determine an employee's federal tax withholding for the U.S. government to ensure payroll reflects the appropriate tax contributions. This form includes information on marital status, dependents, and any additional withholding that a person may request beyond the regular tax rate. The "personal allowance" designated on the W-4 will determine the amount of federal tax withheld from the employee's wages. New employees are often also required to complete a state tax withholding form with similar information to the W-4.

Depending on the organization's human resource practices, selected candidates may be required to complete a preoffer information release authorization form protecting the company from liability for misrepresentation by the applicant in the recruiting process. The candidate should be required to submit an acceptance in writing as part of an official hiring form. In some cases, a personnel requisition form may need to be completed to identify approvals for budgetary implications and to formalize supervisory reporting lines.

Recap

Talent acquisition culminates in the single best candidate to fill a vacancy and accept a job offer. One of the most important phases of talent acquisition is screening candidates. Tools for screening candidates include interviews, assessment tests, background checks, and reference checks. Criterion rating charts and assessment tools enhance objectivity when screening and evaluating candidates, but subjectivity and judgment will always be a part of the decision process.

Employers have a duty to exercise reasonable care in their hiring decisions. Checking a potential employee's references and conducting background checks to verify criminal records, employment history, and other pertinent information serve as final steps to screen candidates. Background checks on criminal and sexual misconduct have become standard practice in the field of coaching. Employers often scan social media pages as part of a background check but must be careful to comply with the federal Fair Credit Reporting Act.

Once a candidate is selected, communication channels close the recruiting process and begin the onboarding process for the new employee. Knowing the cost of hiring is important to assist recruiters in accurately creating budgets for planned vacancies and in understanding the financial burden of replacing workers.

🌐 GLOBAL SPOTLIGHT 7-1

International Cricket Council Recruitment Management System

For the 2015 Men's Cricket World Cup hosted by Australia and New Zealand, the ICC posted job announcements for the temporary paid employment positions of city transportation manager, overlay and logistics coordinator, and spectator and fan services coordinator (ICC Cricket World Cup, 2015). The following excerpt from the ICC *Recruitment and Management Guide* specifically addresses the process for screening and selecting paid positions.

The International Cricket Council (ICC) has access to a *Recruitment and Management Guide* to assist volunteer board members tasked with hiring paid operational employees (Pepsi ICC Development Team, 2009). With origins dating to 1973 (women) and 1975 (men), the ICC has operated the quadrennial Cricket World Cup. The Pepsi ICC Development Programme was established in 1997 for the purpose of furthering the development of the sport for the 105 member countries belonging to the ICC (Sportanddev.org, 2012).

International Cricket Council Recruiting Process

Short List and Interview

- *Once the application period is closed, the role of selecting a short list of candidates for interview begins.*

- *Work through the applications and CVs looking for candidates with the skills and experiences required in the job description. Depending on the number of applications, this might be a job for one or two people. Two people will also be able to cross reference with each other to develop a more consolidated short list.*

- *Again depending on the number of candidates, you may decide to conduct one or two rounds to interviews. Either way, more than 8 to 10 people would be a lot to interview and therefore anywhere between 4 and 8 would be appropriate.*

- *Interviews may be either face to face or over the phone. To be fair to all candidates, you should ask predominately the same list of questions initially, while more open discussion may take place after that.*

- *Questions should be based around finding out about the candidates' previous work experiences and whether they have the required skills to do the job. Finding out what the candidates' salary expectations are is important, as is understanding when they could begin the role. It is also important to give all candidates an opportunity to ask their own questions about the role and the organisation [sic].*

- *If a second interview takes place—likely with only 2 or 3 candidates—you may also ask the candidates to complete a presentation*

on how they would approach the role if they were successful. Some discussion on the salary for the position may also take place in the second interview.

- *Once the interview process is complete you should be in a position to select the preferred candidate. Before making an offer, however, remember to conduct an independent reference check. This would involve speaking to referees provided by the preferred candidate.*

Offer and Appoint

- *In offering the role to the preferred candidate, formal notification of the salary along with all terms and conditions of the role should be provided. Some negotiation may take place at this point.*

- *Once agreement between both parties is confirmed, an official offer letter and contract of employment should be supplied by the NCB for the new staff member to sign.*

- *It is often good practise [sic] to include a probation period in the contract of three or six months.*

- *Only once the contract has been signed should a public statement announcing the appointment be considered.* (Pepsi ICC Development Team, 2009, pp. 4–5)

DISCUSSION QUESTIONS

1. Why is it important to conduct screening activities after interviewing candidates?
2. What are the advantages of a weighted criterion–based rating scale in evaluating applicants in the sports industry?
3. Why are background checks necessary for youth coaches?
4. What are the advantages and disadvantages of using the aptitude tests that evaluate personality traits of rookie draft picks in the NBA and NFL as a screening tool for entry-level or administrative employees in sports organizations?

APPLIED ACTIVITIES

Research a job opening in the sports industry from the list of popular search engines. Review the qualifications and requirements, and develop a weighted criterion–based rating scale for the position.

CASE STUDY

Screening and Selection in The Ohio State University Intercollegiate Athletic Department

In the Big Ten Conference, all 14 member institutions have a human resource (HR) department dedicated solely to athletics. These units operate as an auxiliary enterprise to the central university HR department, which has become more common for large institutions. In the Big Ten, all athletic HR units have a close relationship with the central office for their institution. The Ohio State University (OSU) athletic staff directory lists three full-time HR personnel.

In 2015, *Forbes* ranked the OSU athletic department as the fourth best organization to work in for sports (Belzer, 2015). The department employs well over 300 full-time employees, and on football game days, there are an estimated 400 volunteers and another 300+ part-time, temporary staffers, according to Kim Heaton, executive director of administration and former director of HR for the athletics department. Among the subunits listed on the department's staff directory are the Schottenstein Center and Levy Restaurant for Ohio State.

As a state institution, the Buckeye's employ workers classified as holding a civil service or a non–civil service position. The U.S. Department of State mandates that candidates for civil service positions are hired on the basis of proven professional merit. According to statistical summary reports for fall 2015, 5003 employees out of 44,023 full-time personnel were classified as civil service workers (OSU, 2016 p. 5). A vast majority of OSU's hourly wage employees in the athletics department fall under this category, including office administrators, facility operations personnel, and technical staff. Coaches, administrators, and many support staff positions (i.e., directors and above) are considered non–civil service workers.

After an initial review of application materials to discard candidates who do not meet minimal criteria for a civil service position, the résumés of all remaining applicants are matched against the job classification, which lists minimum criteria. Each base criterion (i.e., demonstration of customer-service skill, experience with Microsoft

Excel, etc.) is independently graded according to the applicant's qualifications. The university is required by the state of Ohio to provide proof of the grading and rating system and that the yield of candidates selected for an interview is truly representative of the individuals with the highest scores/grades.

Non–civil service workers do not require proof of a merit system to validate top candidates, and no formal criterion chart or rating scale is used in hiring coaches and administrators. Head coaches at OSU are mandated to go through a degree-verification process to validate their educational background.

Regardless of status, all full-time personnel at the university are required to undergo a criminal background check coordinated by the Ohio Attorney General's Bureau of Criminal Investigation. The OSU background-check policy applies to all faculty, staff, appointees, applicants, and third-party staffing vendors (OSU, 2014). Volunteers, graduate associates, and student employees are exempt from the criminal background check when covered by a unit program approved by the Office of Human Resources.

Final candidates considered for a position must sign a Background Check Disclosure, Authorization, and Release form. The text in appointment/offer letters for candidates selected as a finalist for a position includes a provision that employment is contingent upon successful completion of a background check. The OSU's Central Human Resource Office also provides fingerprinting services 4 days per week and employs a full-time background check coordinator.

The director of HR for the athletic department is a direct report to the associate vice president of HR in the central office. Among the two offices as well as the hiring unit, there is a great deal of coordination. For example, the central office typically contacts references on a candidate's official list, and the hiring unit sources mutual networks to check references not on the list. With extensive coordination, communication, and systems of accountability, OSU manages to provide a model for screening and selecting employees for a potential fit within the athletic department or anywhere throughout the entire institution.

CASE STUDY QUESTIONS

1. What different screening processes are required of most hourly wage employees in the OSU Athletic Department, and why are they required?

2. What types of employees are exempt from a full criminal background check in the OSU Athletic Department, and what conditions apply?

3. Why would the Central Human Resource Office refrain from conducting reference checks for potential athletic department employees who are not on an applicant's official list?

4. What type of systems or procedures can be incorporated to avoid duplication of processes and maintain optimum efficiency between the HR department in athletics and the Central Human Resource Office?

REFERENCES

Batista, J. (2013, February 21). N.F.L. tries new method for testing mental agility. *New York Times*. Retrieved from http://www.nytimes.com/2013/02/22/sports/football/nfl-introduces-new-way-to-test-a-players-mental-agility.html?_r=0

Behrend, T., Toaddy, S., Thomson, L., & Shareck, D. (2012). The effects of avatar appearance on interviewer ratings in virtual employment interviews. *Computers in Human Behavior, 28*, 2128–2133.

Belzer, J. (2015, March 2). The best organizations to work for in sports. *Forbes SportsMoney*. Retrieved from http://www.forbes.com/sites/jasonbelzer/2015/03/02/the-best-organizations-to-work-for-in-sports/#74211dc92502

Berkowitz, S. (2015, October 26). UCF will pay George O'Leary $200,000 a year through 2020, school says. *USA Today*. Retrieved from http://www.usatoday.com/story/sports/ncaaf/2015/10/26/george-oleary-central-florida-200k-through-2020/74653906/

Blackman, M. (2002). Personality judgment and the utility of the unstructured employment interview. *Basic and Applied Social Psychology, 24*(3), 241–250.

Boucher, R., Morese, K., & Chant, P. (2001). Employee-selection practices and public relations. *NIRSA Journal, 25*, 57–65.

Boushey, H., & Glynn, S. (2012, November 16). There are significant business costs to replacing employees. *Center for American Progress*. Retrieved from https://www.americanprogress.org/issues/economy/reports/2012/11/16/44464/there-are-significant-business-costs-to-replacing-employees/

Bridgespan Group. (2015). *Processing applications and screening résumés*. Retrieved from https://www.bridgespan.org/insights/library/hiring/nonprofit-hiring-toolkit/processing-applications-and-screening-resumes-(1)

Chorneau, T. (2014, March 7). Law would encourage youth sports background checks. *Cabinet Report*. Retrieved from https://www.cabinetreport.com/politics-education/law-would-encourage-youth-sports-background-checks

Clark, R., & Shipley, A. (2014, November 25). Ex-Miramar coach Strout faked transcript, Ohio State says. *Sun Sentinel*, Sports, A1.

Commonwealth of Massachusetts. (2009, September 5). *Structured interviews. Human Resources Division model hiring plan*. Mass.gov Executive Office of Administration and Finance: Human Resources Division.

Dallas Mavericks. (2013, March 24). *Employment opportunities: Premium sales account executive*. Retrieved from http://www.mavs.com/frequently-asked-questions/employment-opportunities/

Eisenberg, J. (2013, June 3). Personality profiling is latest method coaches are using to evaluate potential recruits. *Yahoo Sports*. Retrieved from http://sports.yahoo.com/blogs/ncaab-the-dagger/personality-profiling-latest-method-coaches-using-evaluate-potential-143500770.html

First Advantage. (2017). *Employment background checks and identify verification*. Retrieved from https://www.fadv.com/products/solutions/employment-solutions.aspx

Fountain, J., & Wong, E. (2001, December 14). Notre Dame coach resigns after a few days and a few lies. *New York Times*, Sports, A1.

Gloucester-Cumberland Ringette Association. (2005, October 13). Factors assessed by the coaching selection committee. *Handbook for selecting coaches for the Gloucester-Cumberland Competitive Ringette Program.*

Harris, P. (2014, January 7). Only 2% of applicants actually get interviews: Here's how to be one of them. *Workoplis.com.* Retrieved from http://www.workopolis.com/content/advice/article/only-2-of-applicants-actually-get-interviews-heres-how-to-be-one-of-them/

ICC Cricket World Cup. (2015). *Careers.* Retrieved from https://xjobs.brassring.com/tgwebhost/searchresults.aspx?PartnerId=25939&SiteId=5127&Function=LinkQuery&LinkId=6

Job-applications.com. (2015). *Under Armour job interview questions and tips.* Retrieved from http://www.job-applications.com/under-armour-job-interview-tips/

Johnston, J. (2014, March 26). USF hire off because Masiello didn't get degree. *Tampa Tribune.* Retrieved from http://tbo.com/sports/colleges/usf-bulls/usf-deal-with-coach-falls-through-20140326/

Kahanov, L., & Andrews, L. (2001, October–December). A survey of athletic training employers' hiring criteria. *Journal of Athletic Training, 36*(4), 408–412.

Langley, T. (2011, June 22). Player-aptitude reports are critical for NBA prospects. *Wired.com.* Retrieved from http://www.wired.com/2011/06/sports-aptitude-nba-draft/

Litsky, F. (2002, May 25). U.S. Olympic chief quits over her lies on college degrees. *New York Times,* Sports, A-1.

Mihoces, G. (2011, November 11). Sandusky's fall from grace takes down a community. *USA Today,* Sports, 5C.

Morgan, T., & Wascisko, M. (2008, November 1). Identifying effective athletic trainer dispositions during the interview process. *Athletic Therapy Today,* 25–29.

National Collegiate Athletic Association. (2013). Participant approval for operators and coaches. Background check approval. Retrieved from http://www.ncaa.org/sites/default/files/Policy_2013_Participant_Approval_Program_11062013.pdf

O'Brien, D., & O'Brien, T. (2013, February 21). Consider attorneys' advice to build successful, ethical sports program. *Campus Legal Advisor.* Retrieved from http://www.campuslegaladvisor.com/article-detail-print/consider-attorneys-advice-to-build-successful-ethical-sports-program.aspx

Pepsi ICC Development Team. (2009). *International Cricket Council Development Programme. Recruitment and management guide.* Pepsi ICC Development Team.

Rafaeli, A. (1999). Pre-employment screening and applicants' attitudes toward an employment opportunity. *Journal of Social Psychology, 139*(6), 700–712.

Rio2016.com. (2016). *Volunteer's journal.* Retrieved from http://www.rio2016.com/volunteers/

Russell, B. (2015). Effective hiring with predictive index [Blog]. *Bullhorn Reach.* Retrieved from http://blog.bullhornreach.com/post/17317213394/effective-hiring-with-predictive-index-pi

Schlabach, M. (2014, January 9). Bobby Petrino fools them again. *ESPN.com.* Retrieved from http://espn.go.com/college-football/story/_/id/10264367/louisville-cardinals-surprise-destination-bobby-petrino

Seattle Mariners. (2015). *Job opportunities. 2015 job fair.* Retrieved from http://seattle.mariners.mlb.com/mlb/help/jobs.jsp?c_id=sea

Smooke, D. (2013, February 13). Marketo says, "80 candidates: 8 interviews: 1 hire" [Blog]. *Smart Recruiters*. Retrieved from http://www.smartrecruiters.com/blog/marketo-says-80-candidates-8-interviews-1-hire/

Society of Human Resource Managers. (2012, July 19). *SHRM finds fewer employers using background checks in hiring*. Retrieved from http://www.shrm.org/about/pressroom/pressreleases/pages/backgroundchecks.aspx

Springfield Department of Parks and Recreation. (2017). *Recreation league coaches background screening policy*. Springfield, TN: Author.

Sportanddev.org. (2012). *Growing participation with the International Cricket Council*. Retrieved from https://www.sportanddev.org/en/article/news/growing-participation-international-cricket-council

Stier, W., Schneider, S., Kampf, S., Wilding, G., and Haines, S. (2006). Current hiring practices of campus recreation directors of NIRSA institutions. *Recreational Sports Journal, 30,* 100–115.

Suggs, W. (2004, May 7). Athletic director caught in 2002 résumé scandal gets a second chance. *Chronicle of Higher Education,* A41.

The Ohio State University. (2014, April 14). *Office of Human Resources background check policy 4.15*. Retrieved from https://hr.osu.edu/public/documents/policy/policy415.pdf

The Ohio State University. (2016, June 30). *Appendix A. Quarterly update*. Retrieved from http://u.osu.edu/treasurer/files/2014/09/June-30-2016-22cb3xt.pdf

Times Wire Services. (2002, February 1). Coach resigns amid diploma problems. *Contra Costa Times,* Sports, C08.

Tokyo2020.com. (2017). *Volunteers. Frequently asked questions*. Retrieved from https://tokyo2020.jp/en/faq/

Wonderlic.com (2017). *Client list*. Retrieved from http://www.wonderlic.com/resources/client-stories

Game Time

EXECUTING A WINNING PERFORMANCE

Preface

Losing Is Not an Option

"Losing is not an option" is a phrase emphasizing a relentless attitude toward winning. Supervisors win when employee performance exceeds expectations. That performance is predicated on numerous factors addressed in Phase III.

Supervision and leadership have a direct impact on employee performance. Interviews with coaches of men's and women's soccer and basketball programs at six National Collegiate Athletic Association (NCAA) III institutions indicated that perceptions of the quality of supervision served as a catalyst for job dissatisfaction and were a potential reason individuals consider leaving their current positions in athletics (Dixon & Warner, 2010, p. 156). The quality of supervision was measured by the level of leadership, management, and support provided by the department's director of athletics.

The research on coaches and the multidimensional factors affecting job satisfaction illustrates the contents of Phase III, which addresses supervision as a driver of productivity and performance. Information intertwines with the foundational components of human resources outlined in Phase I (strategic human resource management, compensation and benefits, negotiations, and employment law) and builds upon the sequence of recruiting and talent acquisition activities contained in Phase II. Once a candidate is hired and assigned to a supervisor, the organization begins the regime of training and performance management activities to elicit the optimal productivity and workplace behaviors.

Chapter 8 addresses the components of orientation and training programs. It distinguishes employee training from employee development and describes the five steps for designing effective training programs. It describes how well-organized orientation detailing company policies and procedures in addition to the unwritten norms addressing the culture of an organization assist in acclimating a new employee and provide the foundation for more meaningful work relationships. The chapter highlights how managers and supervisors must design, administer, and evaluate training activities that serve to meet the needs of the organization. The case study profiles an Adidas national training specialist in Eastern Europe who describes how redefining systems' thinking in store clerks facilitated the turnaround of an underperforming store.

Chapter 9 explores leadership and management in sports organizations. The chapter initially addresses the importance of staff supervision in shaping activities to support the mission of the organization. Leadership theories and styles are addressed in the context of their application to supervising employees in different sectors of the sports industry. The foundational components of managerial functions, skills, and roles are addressed, along with an overview of organizational structures common in sports organizations. Action Shot features describe the new duties of an entry-level employee promoted to a warehouse supervisor for the National Football League (NFL) Browns and how managerial roles apply to the job duties of a commissioner for an intercollegiate athletics conference. The case study examines leadership in a profile of the former Minister of Sport and Youth for the country of Romania.

Chapter 10 addresses motivation and performance management as the crux of influencing productivity. The chapter describes the six steps of performance management and defines the purpose, frequency, contents, and methods of conducting performance appraisals. The case study profiles motivational tools used to improve performance at Holloway Sportswear, a designer, manufacturer, and distributor of primarily outerwear active apparel.

Chapter 11 begins by addressing employee behavior and how to supervise workers with difficult personalities. Conflict is explored from the perspective of what constitutes functional and dysfunctional conflict. The chapter describes how individuals may apply one of five basic resolution techniques to resolve workplace issues ranging from disagreements in athletic budget cuts to an argument between coaches over the color to paint a locker room. The chapter also addresses discipline, termination, and stages of performance counseling using the example of critiquing sports officials.

Sports supervisors and managers who adopt a philosophy that losing is not an option are more likely to invest energy into training and motivation to ensure a winning performance by their employees.

Reference

Dixon, M., & Warner, S. (2010). Employee satisfaction in sport: Development of a multi-dimensional model in coaching. *Journal of Sport Management, 24,* 139–168.

CHAPTER 8

Practice Makes Perfect

TRAINING AND DEVELOPMENT IN SPORTS ORGANIZATIONS

Training is an important activity in sports organizations at all levels. The goal for our staff is to provide the 30 teams in the league with the knowledge, support, resources, and skills to promote the personal, professional, and social development of players. The National Basketball Association [NBA] Office for Player Development coordinates the following routine educational training programs specifically for players:

- *Generation Next Program (for players 20 years old and younger)*
- *Business of Basketball Seminar*
- *Media Training*
- *Pre-Draft Information Training*
- *Draft Participants Player/Family Seminar*
- *Rookie Transition Training Program*
- *Summer League Meetings*
- *Team Awareness Meetings*

Dr. Janice Hilliard
Former Vice President—Player Development
National Basketball Association (NBA)
2001–2016

LEARNING OUTCOMES

1. Distinguish between orientation, standard operating procedure training, and refresher training in the sports industry.

2. Identify the opportunities and challenges of the techniques used to train employees in different sports settings.

3. Distinguish between synchronous and asynchronous training.

4. Apply the five steps of designing a training program to a sports organization.

KEY TERMS

Apprenticeship	Job-specific skill training	Soft-skills training
Asynchronous training	Kirkpatrick model	Standard operating procedures
Best in class	Lecture	
Best practices	Nonroutine training	Synchronous training
Case study	Onboarding	Systems development
Cyclical training	On-the-job training	Systems implementation
Discussion	Organizational analysis	Task analysis
Employee analysis	Orientation	Technical training
Employee development	Refresher training	Training needs assessment
Employee training	Role playing	Virtual training
Hybrid training	Routine training	

Lead-Off

Performance management encompasses numerous activities but essentially begins with orientation, the initial training an employee receives after accepting a job offer or filling a vacancy. In human resource management, the term **employee training** refers to the planning effort by an organization to facilitate the competencies of a particular job (Noe, 2002). Employee training is apparent in every organization, from the National Basketball Association (NBA) headquarters to the local batting cage. **Employee development** is a broader term accentuating an individual's growth and future performance rather than his or her immediate job role. Unlike training, employee development is not apparent in all sports organizations.

The primary outcome of properly administered workforce training is for employees to master the skills, behaviors, and knowledge necessary to perform their roles optimally and thereby contribute to an organizations' efficiency, effectiveness, and productivity. It is an indication of improperly trained personnel if, for instance, the clock operator of a basketball game continuously miscalculates the number of fouls on a player or a public-address announcer consistently mumbles, has long pauses, or has excessive trouble in the pronunciation of names. Properly administered training reduces the likelihood of unintended mistakes and blatant ineffectiveness. In addition, training results in a reduced need for close supervision and possible surges in profitability and retention rates.

Among the general derived benefits of training for an employee are an increase in the quality of communication with superiors and colleagues, mastery of new responsibilities on the job, improved teamwork, general improvements

There are many types of routine and non-routine employee training programs such as a week-long immersion program for sport administrators and coaches in Thailand (pictured).

in the quality of workplace results, an increase in the opportunity for promotion, and the development of new workplace initiatives (Vuta & Farcas, 2015). Research also suggests the outcomes of effective training assist the organization in staff retention and develop greater employee loyalty (Beynon, Jones, Pickernell, & Packham, 2015).

Ranging from a first-day orientation session to an apprenticeship to a week-long immersion conference, sports managers and supervisors appreciate the wide variations in the format, content, and duration of training activities available. The characteristics of the sports industry sector and the organization in addition to the leadership and the knowledge and skill sets of the employees all factor into how programs are designed and implemented. For example, because there is a heavy reliance in many sectors of sports to employ a high volume of seasonal, temporary, and volunteer labor, any training must be tailored to fit the characteristics of these types of workers. Training becomes an ongoing function replicated many times for each new batch of seasonal or temporary workers. A similar scenario occurs in the retail industry when training seasonal workers for the Christmas holidays.

This chapter describes orientation and additional training programs common in the sports industry. The chapter also includes information to include in a policy manual and information to conduct a training needs assessment. Finally, the chapter addresses tools and methods to evaluate training effectiveness.

General Classifications of Training

Training can be categorized into two types: **routine** and **nonroutine**. The basis for categorizing the type of training is the prerogative of individual organizations; hence, training classified as routine in one organization may be considered nonroutine for another. For example, annual training for certification in cardiopulmonary resuscitation (CPR) and first aid is considered routine for a municipal swimming pool complex; however, such training may be nonexistent at a sporting goods manufacturing company.

ROUTINE TRAINING

Routine training typically addresses the needs of all employees; however, it is not to the exclusion of any type of standard training provided to individual employees or groups in an organization. A second general characteristic of routine training is that it takes place on a regular schedule, such as within 1 week of hiring a new employee or at specific intervals (e.g., weekly, monthly, semiannually, or annually). Orientations, skill training, on-the-job training, cyclical training, and refresher training typically fall under the scope of routine or ordinary training.

There are seemingly endless examples of routine training regimes throughout sport sectors. For example, the general Labor Code in Romania includes provisions for vocational training in economic organizations where companies are obligated to provide professional staff development once every 2 to 3 years (Vuta & Farcas, 2015). The NBA conducts annual routine training programs for numerous constituents in the league (see **Action Shot 8-1**). The Kalahari, a resort with an indoor–outdoor water park in Sandusky, Ohio, conducts orientation on a weekly basis for new employees (see **Action Shot 8-2**).

▶ ACTION SHOT 8-1

Training Programs for Players and Player Development in the NBA

The NBA Department for Player Development is a founding member of the Professional Association of Athlete Development Specialists (PAADS), the training organization for all professional sports leagues (paads.org, 2017). In addition to the NBA, PAADS global partners, for example, include the U.S. Olympic Committee, the National Football League (NFL), the Women's Tennis Association (WTA), and the Atlantic Coast Conference (ACC). PAADS strives to assist organizations and individuals in developing "the whole person in an athletic context" (paads.org, 2017). PAADs also conducts an annual Player Development Summit (ADS) and the Executive Athlete Academy.

The director of player development for each NBA team reports to a league director. The league director for player development provides team directors with one-on-one coaching, programming guidance, support, and resources to assist their player programming and individual work with individual players. The league and team player development directors meet annually with team officials (team visits) to provide feedback on programming and player support services. In addition to the league and team player development director, these meetings are attended by the designated NBA vice president, members of the coaching staff, and the team's general manager.

One of the primary roles of the director of player development for a National Basketball Association (NBA) franchise is mentoring and looking after the younger and newer members of the team. These positions are essentially responsible for educating players in areas off the basketball court to better equip them for life in the league and what is in store after their careers are over. Some of the primary areas addressed in training for players include family demands and relationships, financial management, cultural diversity and inclusion, career apprenticeship programming, and personal security (Taylor, 2016).

Although topics may differ slightly, the NBA also provides training programs for players in the NBA, NBA Development League, and the Women's National Basketball Association (WNBA). Mandatory Team Awareness Meetings (TAMs) for NBA and Development League players may address health and antidrug programs, the Player Assistance Program, financial education, and continuing education and the career development programs.

Courtesy of National Basketball Association
The information for action shot 8-1 was obtained from a telephone conversation with Dr. Janice L. Hilliard, NBA Vice President of Player Development, in December 2015 regarding training the NBA Player Development Department provides for league and team player development directors and players.

📹 ACTION SHOT 8-2

Kalahari Water Park—First-Day Orientation

America's largest indoor waterpark located in Sandusky, Ohio, spans over three football fields. Kalahari Resort and Convention Center includes both an indoor and outdoor water park, an adventure park, an animal park, over 200,000 feet of convention space, nine restaurants and lounges, and hundreds of rooms and suites. Orientation occurs regularly every Wednesday evening at 5:30 p.m. beginning with a check-in and a tour through the tunnels and secret passages located underneath the first floor of the resort. Throughout the tunnels are signs noting historical milestones, trivia, and background information such as the Kalahari motto and company values. Regardless of whether an employee serves as a lifeguard, a housekeeping attendant, a restaurant hostess, a program coordinator, or a sales executive, 100% of new hires receive the standard first-day orientation tour.

NONROUTINE TRAINING

Nonroutine training is administered at the discretion of the management or leadership team and is generally considered outside the scope of ordinary operations for an organization. Sports managers and supervisors may administer a one-time special instructional program to facilitate a "brush up" on important skills, introduce new equipment or software, or assist an employee in overcoming a particular skill deficiency. For instance, an individual may be provided the time and resources to attend a conference or workshop to obtain a special coaching certification or to acquire new knowledge about software for editing digital media platforms in sports. These activities in addition to soft-skills workshops such as a cultural sensitivity or a personality assessment seminar may all fall under the umbrella of nonroutine training depending upon the organization's definition.

Types of Training

It is important to distinguish types of training from methods of training. The term *methods of training* refers to how training is administered, whereas the term *types of training* refers to a classification system based on general purpose. There are numerous names to identify types of training common in sports organizations, such as safety training, equipment training, team training, and management training. Some common types of routine training include orientations and standard operating procedure (SOP) training. Several common types of nonroutine training include refresher training, technical training, and soft-skills training.

ORIENTATION

The initial behaviors and work attitude a newcomer exhibits are highly influenced during the early socialization period to a job. Virtually all organizations provide training during this early period in the form of an **orientation** to acclimate a new employee to his or her workplace. The orientation is the most common form of routine training which begins after the **initial onboarding** process.

According to the National Association for Sport and Physical Education (NASPE), areas that should be addressed in a standard orientation for high school sports coaches include the philosophies, policies, and expectations of the school, sports program, and state association; procedures for removing or suspending a player from practice, a meet, a game, or a team; how coaches will be evaluated; liability and insurance coverage; components

Examples of Material to Include in an Employee Policy Manual

a. An introduction that includes an overview of the company, often including company history and mission statement

b. A statement of the normal working hours and information related to the Fair Labor Standards Act and any minimum wage and/or overtime provisions that are relevant

c. A section covering benefits (some may be one general page outlining benefits and other companies may have several sections within the handbook that describe in detail insurance, retirement plan, and paid time off)

d. A section that covers prohibition on drugs/alcohol in the workplace

e. A harassment policy

f. A discrimination policy

g. An explanation of how employee discipline is handled

h. A social media policy

i. The use of employer related electronic devices/computers

j. Workers' compensation policy

Note: The employee policy manual is typically distributed and reviewed during an orientation.

of privacy issues related to personal health information (Health Insurance Portability and Accountability Act [HIPAA]); eligibility guidelines; codes of conduct; and information on safety and emergency medical procedures (NASPE, 2005). Additional topics addressed in an orientation for interscholastic sports coaches include policies on social media, concussion protocol, rule changes, behavior expectations, and budgets (Breithaupt, 2016, p. 3).

Sports managers and supervisors design orientations and onboarding processes to create socialization interactions with organization leaders, coworkers, and workgroups within the company. In the orientation for high school coaches, a welcome or introduction to trainers, teachers, and administrators (i.e., athletic director, principal, and superintendent) typically precedes the more tactical information on ethical conduct or the annual collective fundraiser. A well-defined and executed orientation ensures a newly hired individual is equipped with the policies, rules, and expectations relative to his or her job while introducing the new employee to the organizational culture (refer to **Box 8-1**). Rules or principles of the company as well as the language or jargon unique to the company are all transferred during this period.

Well-designed orientation programs facilitate confidence for understanding roles within the organization while allowing the new employee to acquire the political knowledge of how groups and individuals interact. The process acclimates workers to a new environment and ensures that expectations are set by both the organization and the employee. A new employee's expectations include whether he or she is truly a good fit for the company and whether the organization truly operates in the manner identified during the recruitment and selection stage. The employer's expectations are typically focused on the contributions of the employee to becoming a valued and productive member of the workforce.

Variations in an orientation may be triggered by the experience or geographic mobility of the new hire. Newcomers may include someone who is a veteran of the organization but new to a particular department or role, someone who is experienced in the industry but brand new to the organization, or someone who is brand new to both the industry and the organization. Orientations may therefore be tailored to address a target audience, such as the younger and less experienced workers, transfers from different divisions, or individuals who are brand new to the area. Orientations for new hires who have never lived in the area typically include introductions to community officials and information on education systems in the area, real estate, city services, and general points of interest.

A starting point for developing an orientation program is to create a checklist including all of the items a new employee needs to know, such as new employee paperwork, benefits, and company policies and procedures (see **Box 8-2**). The orientation should address both general company-wide information applying to all employees and job-specific information for a particular position. All employees should be oriented to the physical layout of the company and items such as the organizational structure, chain of command, reward systems, health and safety standards, disciplinary processes, technology systems, and grievance procedures.

Orientation packages typically include a signature page documenting receipt of the employee handbook and verification for understanding each item addressed on the checklist. The underlying goal of the orientation is to ensure that each new hire is clear about his or her role within the organization, understands his or her specific performance expectations, is

BOX 8-2

Checklist for Activities in an Orientation

- Welcome letter
- Assignment of a buddy or mentor
- Facility tour and introductions
- Policy review (employee handbook)
- Administrative procedures review (payroll, benefits, etc.)
- Position information

📽 ACTION SHOT 8-3

Columbus Blue Jackets—Orientation for Interns

Human resource personnel for the National Hockey League (NHL) Blue Jackets in Columbus, Ohio, supervise a 2-week training program for each new group of interns (C. Sparks, personal communication, April 24, 2014). Interns typically start as a group either at the beginning of each hockey season or at the beginning of the summer. Interns are welcomed by a current player and then matched with a mentor from their respective departments. Professional developmental activities are incorporated throughout the training, such as an assignment to prepare a biography for each of the other interns in the program and meetings with executives from both the franchise and from the arena management company. There are other activities that are included in the ongoing training, such as teambuilding activities and professional development opportunities (e.g., résumé building).

comfortable in the new environment, and is able to seek out and obtain the necessary information needed to be proficient in his or her job.

Depending on the type of employee (full or part time, seasonal or permanent), the time of onboarding and orientation training can vary. Some orientations may take 1 hour, whereas some may take weeks to ensure an employee is ready to start the job. **Action Shot 8-3** depicts a standard multiweek orientation program provided for interns working with the National Hockey League (NHL) Columbus Blue Jackets. It is important to know the company, the department, and the type of employees who will be hired in order to determine the appropriate length and contents of an orientation training.

STANDARD OPERATING PROCEDURES (SOP) TRAINING

The manager of a health and fitness center would customize training for a new front-desk supervisor differently than the training of an aquatics coordinator. Some parts of training, however, may be uniform for all employees and are referred to as **standard operating procedures** SOPs for the organization.

Examples of SOPs in the sports industry include how to open and close a facility, the order of notification in the event of an emergency, how to greet members entering a country club, how to seat fans entering a ballpark, and how to conduct mandatory aquatic checks at a recreation facility.

SOP training is the routine follow-up to orientation and ensures employees are knowledgeable of the standard procedures for an organization. For instance, a new assistant ballpark operations manager for an MLB team would initially participate in a generic orientation to become familiarized with the park and the organization. His or her training would then focus on learning the standard operational aspects of the machinery used for field maintenance services, the procedures for equipment inventory and repair requests, and processes for any and all additional duties under his or her scope of responsibilities. Similarly, organizations may require employees to pass a certification demonstrating they can properly operate the company cash register at a ballpark merchandise store or correctly instruct clients on fitness equipment at a health club.

The goal of routine SOP training is to ensure the employee will perform a standard function according to the procedure identified by the organization. The value of the SOP training is that it can be used to ensure consistency and quality within the organization while also guaranteeing, to a certain degree, that the right people are trained correctly for the job. In a front-desk role of a service-oriented sports facility (wellness center, gym, or recreation building), the SOP for greeting customers may include a 20-second window for making verbal contact.

SOPs are often published in a training manual. Considering the audience and the complexity of a procedure, the developer of the procedure may incorporate a stand-alone diagram such as a flowchart to suffice over the writing of technical instructions. In developing written instructions, labels are typically used and organized in an outline format. Instructions are written as a process map that includes action items directing an employee in a step-by-step method of performing a particular function. The steps are often written in concise, short "command" sentences that begin with an action verb, but longer descriptions are also common (refer to **Action Shot 8-4**).

Steps or processes are typically organized chronologically with abbreviations and acronyms used sparingly. When developing an SOP for the first time, pilot testing instructions assists in ensuring instructions are clear and accurate and can facilitate employee buy-in or widespread support. After implementing and practicing SOPs, scheduled reviews should take place periodically to ensure continued accuracy in light of changes. For example, stadiums and arenas acquiring greater accessibility to wireless frequencies

🎬 ACTION SHOT 8-4

U.S. Armed Forces Sports Standard Operating Procedures

Ordering uniforms for any U.S. Navy football or basketball competition is part of the armed forces standard operating procedures.

When David Maurice Robinson played basketball for the U.S. Naval Academy from 1983 to 1987, there were procedures for ordering and issuing the uniforms he and his teammates competed in each season. Following is a segment of the Armed Forces manual on standard operating procedures (SOPs) for sports pertaining to purchasing competition uniforms.

Purchasing Competitive Uniforms

a. Host Service is responsible for purchase of all competitive uniforms. Uniforms for higher-level competition are purchased annually with athletes retaining all uniforms and issued items upon completion of each competition. Basketball is the exception where all competitive men's and women's uniforms will be returned to the designated POC.

b. Armed Forces Sports Council Secretariat AFSCS will issue an authorization letter to the Service Representative and the Host Project Officer 90 days prior to the Armed Forces Championship. The team captain in coordination with the Service Representative and the Host Project Officer will issue the items to the team delegation and will return all unused excess items.

c. Armed Forces Teams advancing onto National Championships will use the Armed Forces Sports emblem on their competitive uniform and "USA" on their bags and warm-ups.

The example provides information for individuals authorized to purchase uniforms for competition as well as for the individual who issues and collects uniforms. SOPs for uniform purchases provides clarity for anyone new who would be in the position to order uniforms. (U.S. Armed Forces, 2013 p. 14).

would alter their procedures for communications between department employees and may even impact procedures for suites attendants in reordering concessions for guests.

To train employees in SOPs, instructors should provide a demonstration and allow the worker to imitate a procedure. Depending on the complexity of a procedure, self-instruction by reviewing a manual may suffice over a hands-on approach.

Refresher training reinforces knowledge, skills, and abilities and may take place as a one-time activity or on a recurring cyclical basis.

REFRESHER TRAINING

Rwanda's Karate Federation (Ferwaka) hosted a 2-day refresher training workshop in the spring of 2014 for 25 coaches from martial arts schools and clubs around the country (Mugarura, 2014). **Refresher training** reinforces the desired knowledge, skills and abilities important to an organization or association. Although this type of training could occur as an isolated, one-time activity, it may also be scheduled routinely.

Routine refresher training may be scheduled on a continuous basis, or it may be scheduled in a cyclical format if attached to a specific time period, such as an annual retreat or a monthly update. **Cyclical training** is widely used in the sports industry. Game-day or ballpark operation crews receive some type of training prior to the start of the season, regardless of whether it is a little league program or a major professional franchise. Procedures before a game, during a game, and after are reviewed to reinforce the performance criteria expected for each position, whether an employee is a freshly hired face or an experienced veteran.

Training a game-day management staff requires that employees fully understand their assignments respective to their area, such as crowd control, pre-game setup, ticket sales, guest suite supervision, media guide distribution, press box services, concessions, or any of the other functional area. The simple operation of the shot clock or procedures for handling a pass gate, for instance, needs to be reviewed or practiced even if the position is occupied by someone considered highly experienced. Outdoor recreation departments, outdoor aquatic centers, municipal parks, professional leagues, collegiate athletic departments, and mega-sports such as the Olympics and World Cup are similar in that they require a cyclical training. Once a season or mega event is essentially over and there is a lull or cooling off period before being repeated, the processes for recruiting, hiring, and training are also repeated.

Sports officials, lifeguards, athletic trainers, sports agents, and sports lawyers are required to participate in refresher courses or training to maintain their active certification to practice their trade. The NCAA hosts an annual convention and numerous regional rules seminars providing new education or refresher training for coaches and administrators.

Virtually all professional associations in the sports field organize some type of conference, convention, symposium, or educational workshop for members to keep abreast of industry trends and issues. These programs are the ideal avenues for refresher training.

When designing refresher training, it is important to identify the specific skills or information to be included. Reflective observation from previous training activities ensures the information being reinforced is aligned with the original objectives while also providing opportunities for administrators to teach an enhanced method or reveal new insights that may not have been available during the previous training period.

The NCAA Regional Rules seminar is an example of refresher training. Seminars are conducted on an annual basis each summer.

JOB-SPECIFIC SKILL TRAINING

In sports, there are a variety of jobs within an organization. A person may be hired who has the ability to do the job but needs some specific training to be successful at that job. **Job-specific skill training** is training that is provided to an employee that focuses on the knowledge and skills needed to be successful in their roles and responsibilities. For example, entry-level ticket sales positions are typically filled by recent college graduates who may have the ability to do the job but need training on the knowledge and skills to execute effectively in a sales role. For one, training ensures employees are armed with foundational knowledge of the organization and the arena/stadium (seat locations) in addition to ticket sales prices and packages available (e.g., preloaded value for concessions). As well, training may include practical information on phone skills, overcoming objections, how to close a sale, upselling, and servicing a client to provide the requisite sales skills to be successful.

As an exercise for job-specific training in the fitness industry, a fitness professional may be provided instructions to design the blueprints for a health-related program (e.g., walking program, educational lecture series, or weight-loss program). Upon completion, the training facilitator reconvenes and asks probing questions about the individual's thought process for creating and executing the program to gain a sense of the employee's knowledge for getting approvals, following protocol, and meeting deadlines (Garrity, 2013).

Job-specific skill training does not apply to all employees. It is specific to each job. A stadium usher does not need to know how to screen guests, and a security guard does not need to know how to seat guests, which is why training is specific to each position. Similarly, a fitness instructor doesn't need to know how to sell memberships, and the membership director doesn't need training on how to design an effective health-related program.

TECHNICAL TRAINING

Occasionally referred to as "hard skills," **technical training** is similar to job-specific training because the purpose is to teach employees the operational aspects to use specific equipment or technology. Technical training can certainly be included in the orientation, SOP training, or refresher programs, but because of the complexity of some technologies, technical training may be considered a stand-alone type of instruction. Technology in the sports field is widespread, ranging from ticketing solution packages to tracking devices, physical fitness machinery, scouting tools, and media devices. Virtually every position in the sports industry may incorporate some degree of technology, and therefore, some degree of operational knowledge in the form of technical training is common for many jobs.

SOFT-SKILLS TRAINING

Soft-skills training is used to teach desired traits, characteristics, or behaviors for employees. Occasionally, soft-skills training is referred to as forums for teaching "people skills." Similar to technical training, soft-skills training may be included in a standard orientation or may be a stand-alone program. Popular soft-skills training topics include leadership, diversity, customer service, conflict resolution, emotional intelligence, personality, decision making, etiquette, time management, and group integration.

Research in soft-skills training for organizations specializing in outdoor adventure, such as wilderness camping, mountaineering, and ropes courses, indicated that leadership competency was a highly desirable trait for employees. The additional competencies deemed important in personnel working in outdoor-adventure jobs included knowledge of group dynamics, judgment and decision making, risk analysis and awareness, and safety skills (Twehous, Groves, & Lengfelder, 1991, p. 118).

The value of soft-skills training may be questioned by those concerned with quantifying the investment of time and resources to the bottom line of increased productivity, profitability, or organizational effectiveness. The context of the sports experience may also factor into subjective assessment of the necessity of soft skill training since it seems logical there is a great need for leadership competency in a field such as outdoor adventure. Measuring the outcomes of soft-skills training investment is typically a subjective appraisal without tangible benefits.

Soft skill training focuses on broad topics such as leadership, conflict resolution, ethics, diversity, and interpersonal communication.

Administering surveys and employing a mystery shopper to review membership options at a fitness center are methods to assess the degree to which identified behaviors or desirable attitudes (e.g., customer service) are apparent in employees. Measuring the return on investment from soft-skills training continues to be a critical component of leveraging support and resources for these programs. Applying metrics to predefined objectives for the training establishes parameters to evaluate effectiveness. In the example of leadership competency training for outdoor-adventure specialists, for example, metrics may include some calculation of accident reports.

Training Methods

The method of training refers to the techniques employed to obtain the desired outcomes in information, behaviors, and skills. Selecting the appropriate method is contingent upon the following factors:

1. Maturity of the audience
2. Goals for training
3. Capabilities and expertise of the training facilitator
4. Amount of time allocated
5. Budgets and resources available

There are numerous training methods available. A trainer may select to use some type of face-to-face interaction through lectures, discussions, role playing, tests, case studies, and demonstrations. Alternatively, a trainer may use methods that rely on technology, such as webinars, virtual simulation, Internet classes, cloud-based platforms, software tutorials, CDs, and digital applications, to disseminate information and enhance skills. In most instances, a combination of methods known as **hybrid training** is used for training purposes. Hybrid training refers to a combination of face-to-face and virtual instruction. An overview of a variety of methods used in administering orientations, SOP training, refresher training, technical training, and soft-skills training assists in defining the strengths and limitations of each as they apply to training workers in the sports industry.

ON-THE-JOB TRAINING

On-the-job training is a method often used for specific job skill training as it relies on the employee's work unit to teach the skills and information required for performance. The speed of processing and retaining information is enhanced while training on the job. Employees may learn in an unsupervised setting or they may assume a role as an understudy or apprentice assigned to a more experienced worker. This type of training is one of the most common after the onboarding process to ensure the new hire practices the competencies in a realistic setting.

On-the-job training is also used to upgrade the expertise of an employee (e.g., management training) and to cross-train workers. One of the values of on-the-job training is a cost and time savings for the organization because performance goals can be achieved without a separate training program.

An **apprenticeship** is one type of on-the-job training method practiced in sports. An apprenticeship is a temporary work assignment for a fixed period of time (e.g., 6 months or a year) using on-the-job training to teach or enhance an individual's skills, knowledge, and abilities (see **Action Shot 8-5**).

It is important that supervisors and managers who use on-the-job training recognize the teaching–learning aspect required instead of assuming the trainee will perform up to standards simply by being "thrown into the fire." The unstructured or self-directed approach to on-the-job training may be seen as an acceptable practice for basic functions such as operating a soda fountain in a concession stand or dry mopping a floor during time-outs of a basketball game; however, it is important to include supervision and expectation requirements to improve the likelihood that inappropriate behaviors and bad habits are not exhibited. For instance, safety may be compromised in the event an inexperienced worker is left unsupervised to teach wrestling maneuvers during a youth camp. To minimize the risks of self-directed training programs, a learning package should be incorporated in addition to an evaluation. The evaluation used in self-directed learning should reference back to a specific criterion of the objectives.

🎬 ACTION SHOT 8-5

Canadian Apprenticeship with National Sports Programs

The Provincial/Territorial Coaching Representatives, the Coaching Alliance of Canada, and the Canada Games Council (CGC) partner for the Women in Coaching Canada Games Apprenticeship Program. Two female coaches are assigned to interact with practitioners during the multisport experience. Canada also offers an apprenticeship for females to work directly with 40 national sports programs up to and during the Olympic Games. A report on the impact of Women in Coaching National Team Apprenticeship Program (WiC NTAP) indicated 64% of the participants earned a salary increase and 60% experienced a promotion in their coaching positions (Whitehead, 2011).

The apprenticeship targeting female coaches exemplifies the benefits of live experience under the supervision of a professional. Ultimately, training leads to improved knowledge and skills, which will increase an individual's marketability for a promotion within an organization or another employment opportunity.

The basic components of effective on-the-job training include demonstration, practice, and feedback (Noe, 2002, p. 219). Ideally, an experienced worker demonstrates a skill while the inexperienced worker observes and then imitates the actions. Feedback reinforces whether the action was completed properly or improperly. Finally, administering an evaluation of performance criterion assists in ensuring the objectives of on-the-job training are adequately met.

Action Shot 8-6 depicts a year apprenticeship trainee program offered by the Major League Baseball's Atlanta Braves organization. Typically, a temporary employee is paid but is not guaranteed a continued position with the organization after the training period (months or a year) concludes.

LECTURES AND DISCUSSIONS

A traditional **lecture** involves the dissemination or transfer of information to an audience in a relatively short time span. A **discussion** includes verbal feedback, an exchange of information, or a dialogue between the facilitator and the learner or between learners. Lectures may be presented in a face-to-face interactive format or prerecorded and embedded in a digital, audio, or video

▶ ACTION SHOT 8-6

Major League Baseball (MLB) Atlanta Braves
Career Initiative Training Program

The Atlanta Braves organization offers a 1-year, paid apprenticeship–type "on the job" trainee program for selected individuals who have earned an undergraduate degree. Trainees may be assigned to one of the following areas:

- Digital Marketing
- Entertainment
- Production
- Promotions
- Publications
- Community Affairs
- Marketing
- Ticket Sales
- Guest Services
- Special Events
- Corporate Partnerships—Sales
- Corporate Partnerships—Service
- Stadium Operations and Security
- Ticket Operations
- Media Relation/Baseball Information
- Public Relations Operations

Participants are paid hourly for approximately 37.5 hours per week; however, benefits are not included (Atlanta Braves, 2015). Tyrone Brooks, hired in 2016 as Major League Baseball's Director of Diversity Pipeline Program, acknowledged his participation in the 1996 Braves Career Initiative Training Program for minorities. The semester-long front-office immersion program provided on-the-job training that launched Brooks's career in professional baseball (Langosch, 2011).

format. A lecture allows the facilitator to control the environment for auditory learning because as the sole source of expertise (e.g., a lecture on pool safety regulations or protocol for a referee during pre-game activities).

A drawback to face-to-face lectures are that the instructional pace is preset and doesn't account for individual differences in learning styles or cognitive recall ability. Prerecorded lectures embedded in a computer-based course or in another type of technological media device, however, do provide for individuals to set their own instructional pace.

Lectures and discussions are easier to design or create than many other methods of training. Simply adding several carefully prepared questions to a lecture provides an impetus for trainee participation through interactive discussions. Often a lecture may be accompanied by supplemental material, such as a PowerPoint slide show, a video, a demonstration, or a visual aid. Cyclical training such as a weekly staff meeting or an annual refresher course may use lecture and discussion techniques to inform workers of the objectives being shared. The lecture method does offer challenges to keep an audience interested and motivated in a topic and to facilitate an environment conducive to the exchange of a discussion.

ROLE PLAYING AND SIMULATIONS

Role playing allows trainees to act out situations or issues that may occur in the workplace by assuming a role and/or responding to a predetermined scenario. Also referred to as simulations, practice sessions, and mock drills, role plays are an extremely effective training tool in sports. One of the most frequent applications in a sports setting is to teach emergency response skills. Athletic directors, camp directors, and sports facility managers who are instrumental in developing a crisis management plan often simulate situations such as a stadium evacuation, an injured fan, a boating accident, or an inclement weather drill.

Referees and umpires use role playing to practice mechanics.

Role playing is common in training sports officials through scrimmages and mock situations simulating real game situations, such as a disruptive fan incident or a double flagrant foul. Athletic trainers and sports broadcasters also employ role-playing techniques to practice their trade.

Simulations and role playing are the most popular form of experiential learning and provide the most realistic means to train the behaviors of individuals in specific situations. Although active learning is more entertaining than the traditional lecture or discussion, there are challenges to ensuring realism is part of a scenario. In addition, there are challenges to assuring the sustainability of a learned behavior in a live setting because it is impossible to predict how an individual would react in a realistic versus a staged setting. Role playing is often used in customer-service training for employees who deal with customers on a regular basis. It is also used in sales training to help prepare sales staff for the variety of situations they will encounter on the phone and in person with prospective season ticket holders or group sales customers.

The key to effective training through the role play or simulation method is linked to the expertise and flexibility of the facilitator. When designing a mock simulation or role-play scenario for training purposes, it is highly desirable to form triads or small groups. Providing explicit instructions and instant constructive feedback facilitates greater learning.

CASE STUDIES

The **case study** training method is similar to simulations in that they are based on a situation or scenario. The difference is that case studies are based on real life experiences and do not depend on active participant engagement. Whether the narrated account is presented in a written or vocal format, the intent of the case study is for the trainee to develop cognitive reasoning from studying past experience and to apply theory to reality. In the sports industry, the case study method is used to train employees in best practices (e.g., customer service focus in renewing personal seat licenses) or operational procedures (e.g., concession venues) by studying what similar organizations have applied.

Often the learner examines and analyzes a case to form his or her own perception of what was right or wrong about how a situation was handled or to practice rational decision making through the identification of alternatives and solutions to solve a problem. Cases are a great means for sports organizations to teach employees problem-solving skills (e.g., how to overcome objections in group ticket sales) or to highlight legal principles (e.g., NCAA compliance). A current trend is an emphasis on best-in-class training versus best practices. Whereas **best practices** emphasize the preferred or prudent methods or means of performance, **best in class** focuses on benchmarking performance with the highest standard in the industry.

The advantage of case studies is that it allows for self-guided learning with an emphasis on realistic information that includes constraints and conditions. When presented for a group, it enhances interpersonal skills and fosters an environment that allows for an appreciation of different opinions. The case study method develops skills in synthesizing multiple pieces of information into a plan or explanation.

A disadvantage can be when facilitator bias occurs or insufficient information leads to faulty conclusions. Case studies typically lend themselves to several alternatives or multiple perceptions, thereby limiting the means to validate one "best" outcome. They are also time-consuming compared with straightforward lectures.

VIRTUAL TRAINING

The NFL considered virtual reality devices to simulate a white male harassing a black female as part of workplace diversity training for employees (Nash, 2016). **Virtual training** provides learning opportunities with the assistance of technology when geographic distance precludes face-to-face interaction. There are numerous names for virtual learning, including but not limited to eLearning, mobile learning, online learning, and virtual classes. The basic modalities used for virtual training include the Internet, online classrooms, webinars, cloud-sharing applications, software tutorials, podcasts, apps, and digital streaming devices. Virtual reality simulators are another tool used for training.

Synchronous training incorporates participant involvement at the same precise time through a medium such as a conference call, a live online chat room, or a video conference. A facilitator may broadcast information to trainees who are linked through a conference website, chat window, or phone line. The National Parks and Recreation Association (2014), for example, provides virtual webinar training on topics such as implementing policies for smoke-free parks, developing sustainability initiatives, and conducting criminal background checks.

Asynchronous training offers greater flexibility because it allows for just-in-time or an on-demand learning experience. Participants do not schedule their participation around a predetermined time. The Internet may simply facilitate a self-study learning environment if the trainee is on the receiving end of an e-mail or downloads a tutorial (Wulf, 1996). An

© pickingpok/Shutterstock

Virtual equipment is increasing in popularity to facilitate realistic simulation training. The NFL considered using virtual training for diversity awareness.

"America's Sports University®"

TAKE A FREE
ONLINE COURSE

Courtesy of United States Sports Academy

The United States Sports Academy offering free online courses is an example of asynchronous training.

example of asynchronous virtual training is one of the many continuing Education Certification Programs (e.g., coaching, fitness, and personal training) that are administered by the U.S. Sports Academy (2017)).

Most virtual training using the asynchronous format is self-paced and doesn't require a facilitator. For example, many online self-directed training courses are available to become certified as a personal fitness trainer, a group fitness training expert, or a nutritionist.

Typically, an individual pays a fee to access online learning modules designed to prepare the participant to take an exam, which may be scored automatically. With the proliferation of online certifications designed for personal fitness trainers, the credibility of a program not associated with a professional organization should be highly scrutinized.

On occasion, an organization will compensate employees for completing online training programs. The City of Vancouver (2017) in the state of Washington, for example, compensates employees for time spent completing online required training programs for the division of parks and recreation. These online training programs range from a six-minute Run-Hide-Fight program for surviving an active shooter scenario to a 70-minute Inclusion, Diversity, and Harassment Prevention workshop.

Although the popularity of virtual training is skyrocketing, opponents to this method target the reliance on and expense of equipment, which may be outdated or insufficient to allow for easy use. There is also a challenge in overcoming time-zone differences in synchronous training or a simple learning curve in understanding and appropriately using technology.

1 • Training needs assessment

2 • Goal identification

3 • Systems development

4 • Systems implementation

5 • Evaluation

Figure 8-1

Five-phase model for designing employee training

Designing Training

The effectiveness of training initiatives to achieve specific learning outcomes is contingent upon multiple factors, such as the design, content, facilitator, and delivery of information. Managers and supervisors tasked with developing and administering training typically undergo a deliberate process that includes the five steps described in **Figure 8-1**.

TRAINING NEEDS ASSESSMENT

The first step in designing training is for the sports manager or supervisor to conduct a **training needs assessment** based on an analysis of the organization, jobs, and employees. The needs assessment determines the necessity or advantages of training. The breadth and depth of an assessment process varies depending on the size and complexity of the organization. Conducting a training needs assessment for a local batting cage employing only three seasonal workers is vastly different from determining the training necessary for the front-office staff of the Florida Marlins with over 200 full-time employees and 1000 seasonal workers. The process may be an informal assumption of what employees need to perform the required job tasks, or it may incorporate a systematic analysis to determine gaps in skill or expertise as well as the necessary activities to overcome deficiencies.

New jobs, new employees, new technology, new equipment, outdated systems, or a lack of basic skills may all prompt an organization to invest time, money, and expertise into a training program. These pressure points are often the impetus triggering a needs assessment to determine who will be trained and whether training will be outsourced or developed and administered by someone internal to the business. Conversely, the needs assessment may also result in decisions to replace an employee or redesign a job as opposed to administering training.

A competency chart is a method for sports managers to assess the proficiency level of employees relative to performance traits deemed important for a particular job. Descriptions for levels of proficiency are ascribed for each trait to create a rating system, and a rater uses observations, documents, or facts to benchmark an individual's performance with the corresponding proficiency level. An assigner for officials may utilize competency charts during a scrimmage or actual live game to rate skills and determine training needs. These types of evaluation instruments assessing actual performance provide metrics and quantifiable data for benchmarking or to note "teachable" areas to close gaps if a deficiency is apparent.

The three components of a needs assessment are the organizational analysis, task analysis, and employee analysis.

Organizational Analysis

A task analysis is also useful for the assessment phase of designing employee training to provide a detailed account of all functional activities filled by paid personnel or volunteers. The **organizational analysis** determines the context in which training will occur and is largely contingent upon the support of the leadership team and the company's business strategy. Decisions for allocating financial resources and determining the amount of company time available to invest in training are an important responsibility that affects the structure, duration, and specificity of educational activities. If the organizational analysis indicates the company intends to devote time and money to training, then the needs assessment process continues with an analysis of the tasks and employees.

Task Analysis

A **task analysis** is a detailed account of all functional activities filled by employees or volunteers. Typically, an organizational chart denoting hierarchal relationships defines authority channels and isolates functional activity areas. The account is a report of routine and nonroutine tasks and the skill requirements or responsibilities expected of the individuals comprising each unit or functional area. The job description used in hiring personnel is often used as the foundational document to develop a detailed task analysis chart.

Employee Analysis

The **employee analysis** assesses the strengths and deficiencies in skills, knowledge, and abilities of the current workforce. The performance of each employee is evaluated as it aligns with the requisite skills and tasks of a specific position. For instance, a performance appraisal of a highly experienced and skilled employee may indicate no training is necessary. Otherwise, a gap between the assessed skill level and knowledge base of an employee and the levels required for optimal performance would indicate the points of emphasis in the design of an appropriate training program to improve effectiveness.

There are numerous techniques used to conduct an employee analysis, including general observation of workers, questionnaires completed by employees or managers, reviews of technical manuals and records, and interviews. Multiple methods are usually used to improve the accuracy and validity of information.

GOAL IDENTIFICATION

In the second phase of the model for designing employee training, identifying the goals naturally follows the needs assessment because the information yielded by the appraisal of the organizational, task, and individual analyses provides baseline data for decision making. Identifying the goals for employee training should naturally follow the needs assessment because the information yielded by the appraisal of the organizational, task, and individual analyses provides baseline data for decision making. Carefully crafted goals serve as the foundation for developing a system of training to enhance and optimize a level of performance that far surpasses minimum standards.

The gap between an actual performance level on a particular competency and the desired performance level is what should drive the creation of training goals. These goals prioritize what sports managers and supervisors should be included in training.

Initially, the individual tasked with designing training should identify broad goals to improve knowledge, skills, and abilities. Broad goals are transformed into measurable learning outcomes or more specific objectives that eventually drive the development of the tools, techniques, and systems to administer

Key performance indicators are important to assess whether minimum standards have been met after a training regime.

training. Ensuring that a goal can be measured provides a foundation for assessment and evaluation of whether the desired learning outcome of training is actually achieved.

A quantifiable goal for each of the 1000-plus sports programs belonging to the NCAA is for 100% of their respective coaching staffs to pass the annual standardized recruiting test. Only coaches who have achieved 80% on the 40 questions within 80 minutes are certified by the NCAA (2016) to permissibly contact student-athletes off-campus. To assist with 100% of coaches earning 80% or higher on the test, athletics departments may arrange training sessions to brief staff members on new or "tricky" rules, or they may allow the open-book format for testing to serve as training.

When designing goals, it is important to consider the ability and willingness of the audience in addition to the parameters of the training program, such as the time allowed and the standards indicating an acceptable level of proficiency. If only general or broad goals are used, then key performance indicators (KPIs) need to be employed to assess whether minimum standards have been met after training is provided. For example, if a general goal for intercollegiate athletics department is rules compliance, KPIs should be listed under a heading such as "Zero recruiting violations" or "100% of coaches earning 80% or higher on the standardized recruiting test within the academic year."

Systems Development

The third phase in the model for designing employee training is Systems Development to actually create the blueprints or instructions for conducting the training. **Systems development** for human resource management involves sports managers and supervisors designing the blueprints or instructions guiding

Systems Development Tasks: Phase III in the Model for Designing Employee Training

1. Write learning outcomes for training.
2. Determine the content of training.
3. Determine the sequence of content.
4. Determine the delivery mode (virtual or face to face; synchronous or asynchronous).
5. Determine the delivery methods.
6. Acquire or create applicable training materials.
7. Create evaluation materials.
8. Create a schedule.

the training of employees to meet performance expectations. The systems are essentially the detailed lesson plans that identify the parameters (e.g., type, method, duration, resources) intended to yield the desired performance results.

Systems consider the strategies to transfer training by teaching employees what needs to be done, how it should be done, and why to do it. In the sport of soccer, research demonstrated that after 6 weeks of studying video-based training modules applied to evaluating whether a tackle was a foul, the lowest-ranking officials significantly improved their decision making (MacMahon et al., 2014, p. 137). The research supported the system that was selected for the purpose intended.

Designing systems for training is a craft that builds opportunities for improving and optimizing organizational efficiency and effectiveness. It should be approached in a process-oriented manner that will create ease for facilitators to effectively implement the planned activities. Pertinent questions must be addressed to ensure that employees become fully knowledgeable of their area and will have the requisite skills to perform their required tasks: What needs to take place for training employees? What format should be used to train employees? What time frame is appropriate?

When designing systems for training, sports managers and supervisors should include the nature of the training content, the needs of the learners, the maturity of the learners, the availability and knowledge of facilitators, sources of funding, availability of times and locations, duration, and the technology available (see **Box 8-3**).

Systems Implementation

The fourth phase of the model for designing employee training is the implementation of training systems which is just as important as the design and development phase. The implementation of training systems is just as important as the design and development phase. There are two basic strategies for **systems implementation**. The first places accountability for knowledge transfer on the learner, and the second places accountability on the facilitator. The initial strategy (learner accountability) assumes an individual is willing and able and that the training systems, resource materials, and atmosphere can all be constructed to facilitate self-directed learning. An example would be requiring youth sports coaches to engage in the National Federation of High Schools (NFHS) online concussion education program.

The second strategy places accountability for the transfer of training on a facilitator who controls the environment, sequencing, and content. The primary advantage to this strategy is that it is extremely effective in providing the instantaneous feedback to improve learner comprehension. The key to optimizing learning is the competency of the facilitator. When implementing facilitated training, instructors have the ability to adapt content or teaching styles to meet the specific needs of the participants.

An emerging trend to ensure facilitator preparedness is train-the-trainer certification programs. The aim of train-the-trainer programs is to ensure competency and to standardize how information and skills are delivered. Prospective facilitators are taught by master or expert trainers to become proficient in the subject matter and the delivery techniques for teaching specific skills and information.

Evaluation

Evaluation is the fifth and final phase of the model for designing employee training to ensure the effectiveness of achieving the desired goals and to drive decisions for potential changes in strategies or content. Evaluation of training is important to ensure the effectiveness of achieving the desired goals and to drive decisions for potential changes in strategies or content. The Kirkpatrick (1998) Four-Level Model of Evaluating Training Effectiveness, or **Kirkpatrick model**, considers how trainees react to training, the content learned, change in behaviors when training is applied, and the impact of training on the organization.

It is important in game-management training, for instance, that employees fully embrace training and understand their assignments, whether it be crowd control, pre setup, ticket sales, guest suite supervision, media guide distribution, press box operations, or any of the other areas related to the game. The training facilitator needs to ask the pertinent questions or administer an assessment (test, quiz) of some type to ensure that the employees are knowledgeable of their area and have the skills to perform the required tasks for effective game management. Often in live training sessions, the facilitator incorporates a "checkpoint" to assess the audience's level of understanding or attention span. Surveys and pretests/posttests are other evaluation tools to assess the anticipated outcomes of training and learner reactions.

Evaluating the reaction to training can be as simple as studying the verbal cues and body language of trainees or asking probing questions to assess comprehension and interest. By observing or surveying participants, the developers or facilitators of the training program can determine what methods or modes of communication work best for ensuring the employees are receiving and being attentive to the information provided.

It is also ideal to assess the impact training has on the organization. Facilitators should ideally pinpoint the relationship between the training program and the targeted outcomes, such as production efficiency, product quality, employee turnover, sales increases, profit margins, market share, or customer satisfaction. For instance, game-management staff members who are aware of safety-first priorities and are trained to be attentive to the needs of the customer may have an impact on attendance. By evaluating the satisfaction level of the spectators specifically in terms of the treatment they received from the game-management personnel and by evaluating the correlated relationship to attendance and return attendance, the designer of the training program can adjust the training content accordingly.

Sports managers and supervisors should be knowledgeable of the cost and time needed to implement training. The evaluation process is important to improve training initiatives or determine if training is no longer necessary.

Recap

In the sports industry, there is a heavy reliance in many sectors on the employment of a high volume of seasonal, temporary, and volunteer labor, which impacts training. Training and education are important functions for organizational effectiveness and efficiency. Routine and nonroutine training are apparent in sports organizations. Examples of different types of workplace training to transfer knowledge and skills to employees include orientations, training on SOPs, and refresher training

There are numerous methods available to train employees, which may be self-directed or facilitated by a trainer or instructor. Asynchronous training that is autonomous and self-paced is vastly different than synchronous programs requiring participants to be engaged at the same time. Virtual training is growing in popularity due to the increased availability, accessibility, ease of use, and lower cost of technology. With all methods of training, advantages and disadvantages must be considered to determine the most appropriate techniques to meet the training objectives.

The effectiveness of training for achieving the desired learning outcomes is contingent upon multiple factors, such as the design of the training program, content, facilitator, and delivery of information. The Kirkpatrick four-level model of evaluating training effectiveness allows for scrutiny of the learning achieved, the impact of training on the organization, the reaction of trainees, and changes in behavior when applying training. The five phase model for designing effective employee training programs includes: (1) needs assessment, (2) goal identification, (3) systems design, (4) systems implementation, and (5) evaluation. A deliberate and process-based approach to designing an effective training program increases the likelihood of organizational efficiency and effectiveness.

🌐 GLOBAL SPOTLIGHT 8–1

International Sport Training Certificate Programs in Thailand

Courtesy of Sompob Janfag

Among the participants in the 2017 International Sport Management Certificate training program was Mr. Sompob Janfag of the Thailand Fencing Federation under the Royal Patronage of his Royal Highness the Crown Prince. Janfag is also the host of a nationally syndicated daily morning sports radio broadcast.

The international certificates in sport management and sport coaching are two training regimens offered through a partnership between the Sports Authority of Thailand (SAT) and the United States Sports Academy (USSA) based in Daphne, Alabama. The six-part series aims to assist sport practitioner and administrators in developing coaching competencies or skillsets for promoting, growing, and organizing sports.

Each series includes an intense week-long residential training session combining case studies, lectures, discussions, focused workshops, and on occasion, live simulations. One segment of a coaching course, for example, may require a field trip to a facility where participants use props and equipment to teach the skills and rules of a sport to the rest of the class (i.e., badminton, Taekwondo, or Muay Thai boxing). Similarly, the administrator's course

focusing on the structure and functions of international sport includes instruction and activities for executing best practices to design a bid proposal for hosting a sport tourism event.

Coaches and administrators are tested at the end of the week to determine their continuation to the next component of their respective program. Each class accommodates 25–35 coaches or administrators authorized and funded by the SAT which operates under the Ministry of Tourism and Sports. For example, among the 32 enrolled in the 2017 administrator certificate class were directors and executives from many of the country's national sport federations and military divisions such as the Royal Thai Air Force. Participants represented sport federations such as the Thailand Golf Association under Royal Patronage of His Majesty the King, the Royal Aeronautic Sports Association of Thailand, the Sports Association for Intellectual Disability of Thailand, and the Woodball Association of Thailand.

A percentage of participants are typically a member of Thailand's entourage at the Olympic Games. Even one of the official interpreters, Pichit Muangnapoe, has attended and worked with athletes during the 2008, 2012, and 2016 Olympic Games. Muangnapoe is a sport psychologist at the Sport Authority of Thailand and part of the faculty at Srinakharinwirot University. He coaches Miss Sutiya Jiewchaloemmit, a world class shotgun athlete, but also works with Olympic weightlifters, boxers, Taekwondo athletes, and other shooters. Having served as an interpreter for the international training certificates for 12 years, Muangnapoe has seen the value of training programs in providing coaches and administrators more practical knowledge to use

Members of the 2017 International Certification in Sport Management Program organized by the Sports Authority of Thailand and the United States Sports Academy.

directly in their work (P. Muangnapoe, personal communication, March 28, 2017).

The training concludes with a selection of 15–20 participants from the Thailand program traveling to America for a sport tour that includes visits to the Olympic facilities in Salt Lake City, Utah and IMG Sports Academy in Bradenton, Florida. The annual financial guarantee from the Royal Thai government demonstrates the commitment to fund training that supports the SATs mission to serve as the principle office to implement policies and regulate sports at all levels.

DISCUSSION QUESTIONS

1. What are the anticipated strengths and limitations of a lecture, a case study, and a role-play demonstration for a manager of a corporate fitness center training employees about new club finances and membership promotions?
2. What are the strengths and limitations of virtual and face-to-face, instructor-led training on the appropriate operating and cleaning procedures for new weight-room equipment in a professional sports team locker room?
3. Discuss the emerging trend of train-the-trainer programs and how it can be applied in the sports industry.
4. When training student-workers assigned to game operations for a collegiate football contest, what is the importance of evaluating the student-worker's reactions to training as well as the impact training has on the athletics department?

APPLIED ACTIVITIES

1. Work with two or three others to visit and observe how activities are carried out at a sports facility or organization. Assuming the role of independent training consultant team, conduct an assessment of the training needs, and design the necessary training to meet those needs.
2. Imagine you are the director of athletics at a NCAA Division III institution. Use the five-phase model for designing employee training to design a system of continuous training on recruiting and eligibility rules for your staff.
3. Create a system to evaluate the effectiveness of a training program provided to entry-level accountant executives at IMG Learfield Ticket Solutions.

CASE STUDY

Training Program Drives Results in a Romanian Adidas Store

Adidas is a German multinational retail company featuring athletic shoes, apparel, and sports equipment. Founded in 1949 by Adolf Dassler, the Adidas group currently owns Reebok, Taylor Made, Ashworth, and Runtastic (Austria).

The first Adidas store in Romania opened in 2003, 13 years after a revolution that ended the communist regime and paved the way for a free-market society. As of 2016, there were 37 stores employing 240 workers in the country bordering Serbia, Bulgaria, Moldova, Hungary, and the Ukraine. Istanbul, Turkey, serves as the hub for Adidas district managers in most of the stores scattered around Eastern Europe. Regional "hubs" in India, the Middle East, and Africa are collectively identified as Adidas Zone Middle for Emerging Markets, which report to headquarters in Dubai, United Arab Emirates.

Shortly after the first Adidas store opened in Romania, a relatively young territory manager by the name of Tibluia (Tibi) Tuluca hired a young man who had previously worked as a stock clerk for a Nike shoe store. Tibi eventually worked as a national sales manager for Puma before leaving the sports retail industry to open Armada Marketing, a local Romanian creative advertising agency.

Marian Achim, the clerk Tibi hired, began his career with Adidas as a sales associate for a store in Bucharest. He quickly rose through the ranks to become a shift manager, a store manager, a visual merchandising manager, and finally, the training specialist for all of Romania's Adidas stores. Throughout his quick ascent, Marian was continuously placed at higher-performing stores that generated greater profits and sales margins. In total, he was an integral part of 20 store openings, accounting for almost two-thirds of all Adidas locations in the country. His product-line knowledge and exceptional people skills were both part of the reason he was selected as the national training specialist.

In addition to designing and implementing annual management workshops and monthly orientation programs for new sales associates, the training specialist occasionally works directly in underperforming stores to effect a turnaround strategy. In 2014, Marian was placed in a store that failed to hit its target sales quota for 4 straight months. Reportedly, there were morale issues among employees, who were generally pessimistic and disengaged. Marian went into the store and took a month to assess and diagnose the situation. He used secret shoppers to provide feedback on the customer experience. He worked in the store for days to learn pressure points and to troubleshoot some of the causes of the insufficient performance.

Next, Marian resorted to personal coaching and mentoring as part of his training regime. He devised a tactic to develop team camaraderie among the staff by encouraging employees to forget about sales margins and, alternatively, identify a new achievable goal. Collectively, the staff identified and incorporated a new goal focusing on increasing the conversion rates of customers who walked into the store and made a purchase. Marian trained the employees to effectively deal with customers who were returning goods. He taught the eight steps of customer service, and he trained the staff to focus on alleviating customer frustrations when entering the store to make a return. One tactic that assisted the conversion goal was to invite customers with returns to browse the store while paperwork was handled. With a fresh outlook on defining productivity, the store not only met the new target conversion rates, but it also managed to exceed the corporate sales goal figures that had eluded the store for almost half a year.

Marian Achim continues in the role as a national training specialist for Romania. He remains connected to the former manager who sensed a tremendous potential in a young clerk who now uses training and education to contribute to the success of Adidas in Eastern Europe.

CASE STUDY QUESTIONS

1. What factors led to Achim being selected as a national training specialist for Adidas?

2. How did Achim succeed in turning around an underachieving store?

3. What learning outcomes from the case seem culturally universal?

REFERENCES

Atlanta Braves. (2015). *2015 Trainee program*. Retrieved from http://atlanta.braves. mlb.com/atl/ticketing/trainee_program.jsp

Beynon, M., Jones, P., Pickernell, D., & Packham, G. (2015, February 1). Investigating the impact of training influence on employee retention in small and medium enterprises: A regression-type classification and ranking believe simplex analysis on sparse data. *Expert Systems,32*(1), 141–154.

Breithaupt, C. (2016, July). *Letter to superintendents and principals addressing orientation of university interscholastic sponsors, advisors, coaches, and directors.* Retrieved from https://www.uiltexas.org/files/policy/2016-17-orientation -packet.pdf

City of Vancouver. (2017). *Parks and recreation employee training*. Retrieved from http:// www.cityofvancouver.us/parksrec/webform/parks-recreation-employee-training

Garrity, B. (2013, September 1). How to onboard a fitness professional. *Journal of Active Aging,* 44–56.

Kirkpatrick, D. L. (1998). *Evaluating training programs: The four levels* (2nd ed.). San Francisco, CA: Berrett-Koehler Publishers.

Langosch, J. (2011). Brooks' steady climb leads to Buc's front office. *Pit News.* Retrieved from http://m.pirates.mlb.com/news/article/16601062/

MacMahon, C., Mascarenhas, D., Plessner, H., Pizzera, A., Oudejans, R., & Raab, M. (2014). *Sports officials and officiating. Science and practice.* London, England: Routledge.

Mugarura, R. (2014, March 20). Rwanda: Twenty-five karate coaches in refresher training. *New Times Global Media.* Retrieved from http://www.newtimes.co.rw /section/article/2014-03-20/73998/

Nash, C. (2016, April 11). *NFL to use virtual reality training where staff is harassed by a white man.* Retrieved from http://www.breitbart.com/tech/2016/04/11 /nfl-to-introduce-virtual-reality-diversity-training/

National Association for Sport and Physical Education. (2005). Coaches Council and the National Council for Secondary School Athletic Directors: Program orientation for high school sport coaches. *Strategies, 18*(6), 21–22.

National Association of Collegiate Directors of Athletics. (2017). *Level I coaching certification.* Retrieved from www.nacda.com/sports/nacda/spec-rel /082504aaa.html

National Collegiate Athletic Association. (2016). *Division III rules test.* Retrieved from http://www.ncaa.org/governance/division-iii-rules-test

National Parks and Recreation Association. (2014). *Recorded and archived public webinars.* Retrieved from http://www.nrpa.org/Professional-Development/E-Learning /Webinars-Archived/

Noe, R. (2002). *Employee training and development* (2nd ed.). New York, NY: McGraw-Hill.

Taylor, M. (2016). Interview with Greg Taylor, senior vice president of player development for the NBA. *Player Personal Development Magazine.* Retrieved from http://ppdlife.com/greg-taylor-senior-vp-of-player-development-for-the-nba/

Twehous, J., Groves, D., & Lengfelder, J. (1991). Leadership training: The key to an effective program. *Social Behavior and Personality, 19*(2), 109–120.

U.S. Armed Forces. (2013). Higher-level competition. In *2013 Armed Forces sports standard operating procedures* (p. 14). Retrieved from http://armedforcessports .defense.gov/Portals/19/Documents/2013%20SOP/2013%20Final%20SOP.pdf

United States Sports Academy. (2017). *Continuing education certification programs.* Retrieved from https://ussa.edu/continuing-education/certification-programs/

Vuta, R., & Farcas A. (2015, September 1). The role of training in organizational development. Management and economics. *Revista Academiei Fortelor Terestre, 2*(79), 367–372.

Whitehead, L. (2011, March). Report on the impact of Women in Coaching National Team Coaching Apprenticeship Program. Coaching Association of Canada.

Wulf, K. (1996, May). Training via the Internet. *Training and Development,* 50–55.

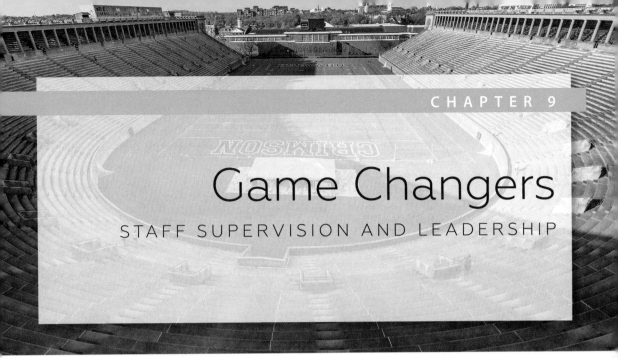

Game Changers

STAFF SUPERVISION AND LEADERSHIP

Among the most important components of effective staff supervision is establishing agreed-upon goals, priorities, and values.

James Delany
Commissioner—Big Ten Conference

LEARNING OUTCOMES

1. Describe how supervision is closely linked to leadership and management.
2. Identify the managerial functions, skills, and roles of sports supervisors.
3. Describe characteristics and behaviors of sports professionals who exhibit authoritative, participative, and laissez-faire leadership styles.
4. Distinguish the characteristics of transactional and transformational sports leaders.
5. Identify the advantages and disadvantages of hierarchical and matrix structures in sports organizations.
6. Distinguish characteristics of effective and ineffective sports supervisors.
7. Design a successful staff meeting.

KEY TERMS

Authoritative leadership

Behavioral leadership theories

Charismatic leadership

Conceptual skills

Contingency leadership theories

Decisional roles

Hierarchical divisional structure

Hierarchical functional structure

Informational roles

Interpersonal roles

Interpersonal skills

Laissez-faire

Leadership

Managerial effectiveness

Managerial roles

Matrix Structure

Multidimensional Leadership Model

Participative leadership

Situational leadership theories

Technical skills

Trait leadership theories

Transactional leadership

Transformational leadership

Lead-Off

It is no secret that the sports industry is extremely diverse in terms of size, scope, growth stage, and geographical reach. How human resource functions and responsibilities are approached within organizations is heavily influenced by the characteristics of those organizations. The type of the sports organization (private, public, nonprofit, commercial, professional, amateur, municipal, or recreational), the size (small, medium, large), the growth stage (start-up, growing, mature, or declining), the geographical reach (local, regional, national, continental, or global), the organizational structure (functional, divisional, or matrix), and the choices made by the organizational leadership to determine how work is to be organized all factor into who and how human resource activities are accomplished.

The essence of supervision is leadership and communication to direct activities supporting the mission of the organization. Supervising a temporary workforce for a mega-sports event (e.g., the U.S. Open or the Super Bowl) or overseeing a permanent staff at a sports facility such as an athletic department or recreation center requires effective leadership, clarity in performance expectations, and accountability. Supervisors are employees whose primary duty is the performance of management or business operations that include exercising "discretion and independent judgment over matters of significance" (U.S. Department of Labor, 2008). Supervisors have the authority to make an independent choice, relatively free from immediate direction or supervision.

In the sports realm, a supervisor could be the chief executive officer (CEO) at a Young Men's Christian Association (YMCA) facility, an aquatic coordinator at a recreation center, or the head, assistant, or associate director of athletics in a college athletic department. A sports supervisor could also be an event manager who oversees hundreds of part-time event staff or a vice president of marketing who supervises a handful of professionals. Supervisors may be designated as an owner, president, department head, manager, crew chief, or director. The title of the central figure accountable for staff supervision, however, is not nearly as important as the scope of responsibilities to impact the performance of his or her employees.

Stadiums and arenas employ numerous supervisors to oversee hundreds of employees working a game day.

Whether specializing in an area of sports business, coaching, health and wellness, or exercise training where turnover may be fairly high, entry-level personnel in sports occupations may have opportunities to assume a supervisory role early in their career. Undoubtedly, one of the unique characteristics of the massive sports industry is the rapid upward mobility of employees to positions with greater responsibilities (see **Action Shot 9-1**).

Management and leadership are among the seven common professional components for the accreditation of sports management academic programs (Commission on Sports Management Accreditation [COSMA], 2016, p. 25). This chapter explores leadership, management, and supervision in the context of sports.

Leadership

Leadership can be described as influence—nothing more, nothing less. While it is generally recognized as the ability to influence others toward a common goal, the sports industry has no shortage of personalities exemplifying extraordinary leadership. There is a reason that some of the most recognizable examples of great leaders in the sports industry are coaches who win championships or team owners who hire the successful coaches who win championships. The leadership qualities exhibited by successful coaches are a core competency often exhibited in supervisors who effectively motivate their employees to the highest performance levels. The same is true for the leadership qualities demonstrated by successful sports commissioners,

🎬 ACTION SHOT 9-1

Climbing the Ranks from Entry Level to Supervisor at First Energy Stadium

Dan Kurta, a sports management graduate from Tiffin University in Ohio, began his career in 2012 as a retail warehouse supervisor for the Cleveland Browns. After 9 months, he was promoted to a warehouse manager responsible for a staff of 10 employees. Less than 2 years later, Dan was promoted to assistant general manager of retail operations for Legends Hospitality, which services the Browns, San Francisco 49ers, Dallas Cowboys, New York Yankees, and other professional franchises. Jointly owned by the Cowboys and Yankees, Legends has expanded globally and employs over 80,000 (D. Kurta, personal communication, March 29, 2017). In 2016, the company acquired International Stadia Group (ISG) based in London, England, a sport hospitality unit servicing venues and events in Europe, Africa, and the Middle East. ISG clients in Europe include Manchester City and FC Barcelona.

Dan manages a staff that services First Energy Stadium and occasionally services major sports events such as the Indianapolis 500 and National Collegiate Athletic Association (NCAA) Final Four. In addition to his responsibilities for warehouse maintenance, inventory control, and managing multiple retail vendor locations, he regularly hires staff, trains employees, and implements incentives to develop a team approach for carrying out daily operations (D. Kurta, personal communication, November 9, 2016). He attends professional development events such as the NFL Consumer Products Summit to learn more about the industry and the impact on retail decisions (D. Kurta, personal communication, March 24, 2017).

presidents of national and international sports organizations, founders or owners of retail sports companies, sports agents, and athletic directors (ADs).

Successful sports coaches have delivered countless speeches and authored best-selling leadership textbooks applying knowledge from the field of coaching to motivating staffs and improving business organizations. Adopting techniques similar to athletic teams offers powerful lessons for management professionals in mainstream business in applying practices to goal setting, staff supervision, teamwork, and performance management performance (Shonk & Shonk, 1988). Business organizations seek advice and leadership lessons from successful coaches with winning records in hopes the advice would improve their organizational goals and staff morale.

Grimes and Chressanthins (1994) indicated the capability to lead a large and diverse staff was one of the most desired traits of Division I ADs in the NCAA. Although the research is dated, the statement is still applicable to describe the importance of leadership skills for today's ADs. Additional research identifies financial management, experience with revenue-producing sports, external relations, decision making, and communication skills as important competencies for ADs (Lumpkin, Achen, & Hyland, 2015; Sagas & Cunningham, 2004). Grimes and Chressanthins (1994) also identified the importance of financial budget management, problem-solving abilities, and strategic planning. Similarly, decision-making skills, effective communication skills, and budget preparation were deemed important competencies for sports facility managers (Case & Branch, 2003).

The role as a leader is imperative to staff supervision; therefore, exploring foundational leadership theories in addition to the application of leadership styles and types is important in the study of supervision. Distinguishing successful and unsuccessful leadership facilitates the inclination for an individual to improve his or skills as an effective staff supervisor.

LEADERSHIP THEORIES

Leadership theories are typically classified into broad categories: (1) trait theories, (2) behavioral theories, and (3) contingency or situational theories. Each of these classifications assists in explaining the complexities of leadership and how it can be applied to staff supervision.

Trait Theories

Trait leadership theories focus on the personal attributes of a leader as opposed to those of a follower. In essence, trait leadership is used as justification for the argument that individuals are born leaders with innate qualities that predispose them to leadership.

Early research suggested one of the characteristics of a leader is possessing a "striking physical personality" in addition to traits of honesty, good faith, a strong sense of justice and sympathy, courage, persistence, good nature, originality, initiative, intellect, forethought, and sound judgment (Bernard, 1926). Among the list of leadership traits purported by John Gardner (1989) are intelligence and action-oriented judgment, eagerness to accept responsibility, understanding of followers and their needs, skill in dealing with people, and capacity to motivate people.

Specifically within the sports industry, researchers have defined desirable traits apparent in successful athletic trainers, female administrators, and coaches. For example, ambition, a willingness to delegate, discipline, open-mindedness, adaptability, resilience to stress or change, and ethical behavior were noted as important traits associated with success in the field of athletic training (Kutz, 2008). Charisma, inspiration, and individual consideration were the traits apparent in successful young female intercollegiate athletics administrators at Canadian universities (Doherty, 1997; Doherty & Danylchuk, 1996). Finally, traits associated with respect, humility, vision, toughness, care, passion, competence, organizational skills, discipline, and effective communication were noted in successful sports coaches (Doherty, 2004).

Charismatic leadership, a term coined by Max Weber (1958) is among the classification of trait theories defined as a type of authority an individual possesses when having a mission or vision to inspire others. A study of charismatic leadership in the Turkish Handball Association indicated a correlation between educational attainment and perceptions of a leader's attitude towards individuals. Specifically, handball players with less education had a significantly greater perception than players with higher levels of education regarding the extent of trust and personalized interest a coach displayed with each team member (Celik & Valcinkaya, 2015, p. 130).

In general, charisma is a construct claimed to be rooted in an individual's personality and a quality that distinguishes ordinary from extraordinary individuals. Charismatic leaders have been described as possessing self-confidence, assertiveness, and a strong conviction in one's own belief (Bass, 1985; Bass & Avolio, 1990). Originally claimed as a characteristic especially exhibited by political leaders, religious statesmen, and leaders of primitive tribes, charismatic leadership has also been attributed to successful sports leaders. For example, Phil Knight, co-founder of Nike, Inc., is credited with demonstrating charisma when inspiring his employees to join the mission to overcome a common foe and maintain its market position ahead of Adidas and other competitors (Slack & Parent, 2006, p. 302).

Phil Knight, CEO of Nike, demonstrates charismatic leadership in addressing the company's market place position over rival Adidas.

© rvlsoft/shutterstock

Behavioral Theories

Behavioral leadership theories focus on a leader's influence due to the ability to effectively accomplish tasks or develop relationships with subordinates. Classic behavioral studies include the Ohio State Studies, the Michigan Studies, and the Blake Mouton Managerial Grid (Blake & Mouton, 1964). All three studies were based on the premise of two distinctive behavioral characteristics: (1) a greater concern for people or, (2) a greater concern for productivity.

Production-oriented or job-related behaviors are those involving planning and organizing tasks. For example, ballpark operation managers are process oriented and obligated to manage logistical activities to ensure the safety and security of patrons, players, and staff. Therefore, individuals in these roles typically have a greater concern for productivity. Leaders with higher scores in this area also usually had more productive work groups (Dubrin, 2007).

Relationship-oriented or people-related behaviors are exemplified by leaders who demonstrate greater trust, mutual respect, and support of employees (Katz, Maccoby, & Mors, 1950). Managers and supervisors with a high concern for people were found to be friendly, approachable, and accessible to their employees, who in turn demonstrated greater work satisfaction and lower turnover rates than individuals working for individuals who were more task focused (Dubrin, 2007).

Successful sports managers and supervisors tend to exhibit both task-centered and people-centered behaviors. A sports facility supervisor must develop a rapport with his or her employees but must also be accountable for effective oversight of daily operational procedures for effective club management. Leadership behaviors may sway from being more focused on relational activities with staff to being more direct in delivering orders with strict deadlines. Being aware of variances in personal behavior can assist a sports manager in effectively supervising a staff.

Contingency/Situational Theories

Fielder's (1964) contingency model, the Hersey-Blanchard (1969) situational model, and the Vroom decision tree (Vroom & Yetton, 1973) are contemporary leadership theories focusing on the interaction between situational variables and leadership characteristics and are referred to as **contingency leadership theories** or **situational leadership theories**. These models suggest leadership behavior is dependent on the relationship of the leader, the subordinates, the task or situation, and the scope of power or authority of the leader. The premise permits a leader to change his or her behavior to be more task centered or people centered based on the situation or the characteristics of the individuals being lead. An athletic trainer may exhibit pure task-centered behaviors when dealing with an on-field injury but would adapt his or her leadership style to become more people centered when teaching a class on concussion prevention.

Leadership effectiveness is partially dependent upon the leader's ability to tailor his or her behavior based on the demands of the situation and the maturity level of subordinates. The model considers the extent followers are willing and able to be led. The combination of leader characteristics, follower characteristics, and the situation impacts the supervisor's preferred leadership style, which, according to the Hershey-Blanchard (1969) model, include telling, selling, participating, and delegating. In applying the model to the sports industry, an example is the supervision of ballpark operation employees at a stadium. The stadium operation's manager may choose to be a hands-on leader and participate in the demonstrating procedures to store tarps or clean dugouts, especially if his or her employees are relatively new and inexperienced. If the workers are volunteer interns, the manager may need to additionally "sell" the idea of how good work ethic can lead to increased responsibilities, recognition, and possibly rewards. The more experienced the stadium employees, the easier it is for the ballpark operations manager to simply explain to the workers what needs to be done or to delegate the responsibility to a trusted assistant.

The Vroom–Yetton (1973) decision model is yet another theory to explain the appropriate leadership that should be exhibited by a supervisor given a particular situation. Depending on the time constraints, the significance of the decision, and the willingness and ability of the followers, a supervisor may alter his or her leadership style. The consequential actions for the leader when faced with a choice are to (1) make decisions alone; (2) consult individually with staff members and make a decision alone; (3) define the problem and boundaries, but allow the group members to make the decision; or (4) delegate the decision to the discretion of the group.

LEADERSHIP STYLES

The study of leadership style, or the way leaders provide direction and motivate others, has resulted in several classifications. Recent research in the realm of sports coaching explores behavioral and interactional models as well as the dichotomy of autocratic and democratic leadership styles (Crust & Lawrence, 2006; Hiroto, Anderson, & Verardi, 2015). Common traditional classifications for leadership styles include the authoritarian, participative, and laissez-faire styles purported by Lewin, Lippit, and White (1939); the transactional and transformational leadership styles proposed by Burns (1978, as cited in Gomes, 2014); and the multidimensional model purported by Chelladurai and Saleh (1978).

Authoritative

Authoritative leadership, also referred to as authoritarian or autocratic leadership, is exhibited by individuals who are direct and make decisions independently, such as coaching legend Bobby Knight, who exhibited strict, vocal, and domineering behaviors during his tenure at Indiana University. This style has also been referred to as an autocratic or dictator style of leadership indicative of many Division I coaches in the Football Bowl Series. A study of leadership style in cross-country coaching indicated an authoritative approach was the predominant style used in designing workouts (Jenny & Hushman, 2014). A study of high school football coaches self-reporting leadership style noted that autocratic was their least preferred style (Weaver, 2016). The autocratic style was more pronounced in coaches with more experience.

Participative

Participative leadership is exhibited by leaders who are considered fair and egalitarian and who involve others in decision making, such as the sports professionals who serve as executives for national and global organizations (e.g., International Olympic Committee [IOC], National Collegiate Athletic Association [NCAA]). The participative leadership style has also been described as a democratic style.

Legendary former Coach Bobby Knight was often identified as an authoritarian leader.

Laissez-Faire

The **laissez-faire** or free-reign leadership style is exhibited by supervisors who have little interaction with subordinates. The coach or advisor for a collegiate club rugby team may be described as laissez-faire if he or she assumes the necessary leadership role to communicate pertinent information for games but is also an active player on the squad.

Transactional and Transformational

Burns (1978, as cited in Gomes, 2014, p. 14) distinguished two mutually exclusive styles of leadership as transactional and transformational. **Transactional leadership** involves the exchange of rewards, such as wages or favors, in return for productive effort from employees. Often, transactional leadership has been viewed as politics of exchange. **Transformational leadership**, on the other hand, relies on emotional appeal and personal influence to inspire productivity in employees, often beyond the workers' normal capacity. Transformational leaders have been described as visionaries who communicate high expectations and empower others. Research suggests that managers and supervisors exhibit both transactional and transformational styles of leadership depending on the situation (Bass, 1985).

Intercollegiate athletics administrators, athletic trainers, and coaches have been described predominantly as transformational in their styles of leadership (Burton & Peachey, 2009; Doherty, 1997; Doherty & Danylchuk, 1996; Manning, 2012; Peachey & Burton, 2011; Zuest, 2003). While findings consistently verified that athletic administrators demonstrate a greater propensity for a transformational as opposed to a transactional leadership style, Doherty (1997) concluded that females and younger administrators typically demonstrated a greater degree of transformational styles than their male or older counter-parts. Similarly Manning (2012) made the same conclusion for NCAA Division I athletic administrators as opposed to those who worked in Division II or III departments. The research of Burton and Peachey (2009; Peachey & Burton, 2011), however, contradicted Manning's research in that it found no significant differences in degrees of transformational styles exhibited by NCAA ADs based on divisional differences.

Intercollegiate athletics is a high-pressure work environment similar to many sectors of the sports industry. The limited research suggests that a transformational leadership style is best suited for leading a staff in the dynamic field of sports. The ability to inspire employees to perform beyond their normal capabilities is a highly desired quality of sports supervisors.

Multidimensional

Chelladurai (1984; Chelladurai & Saleh, 1978, 1980) developed a **multidimensional leadership model** when assessing behaviors of coaches based on Lewin et al.'s (1939) styles of leading and directing others. Chelladurai and Doherty (1998) focused specifically on the authoritative/autocratic and participative/democratic leadership styles in the decision-making habits of coaches and suggested that the most effective leaders can alter their styles based on the context of the situation. The preferred leadership style of coaches based on perceptions of athletes in Canada, Japan, Australia, and the United States noted cultural differences in whether authoritative or participative leadership attributes were favored (Brooks, Ziatz, Johnson, & Hollander, 2000; Chelladurai & Saleh, 1980; Sherman, Fuller, & Speed, 2000).

Chelladurai's multidimensional model blends instructional behaviors (training), motivation tendencies, and two decision-making styles. The convergence intuitively selects an optimal authoritative or participative style based on a congruence between the leader's activities (e.g., organizing practice and providing instruction) and the follower's preferred leadership behavior (e.g., knowing his or her leader is supportive or direct). The result is a behavioral style that is best suited to the context of the situation. The multidimensional model purports that effective sports supervisors are those who are able to modify their leadership style to meet the needs of the situation and audience.

Management

Management is by no means synonymous with leadership, but it is important in the function of supervision. Leadership, as stated previously, refers to a competency or skill set in successfully influencing others. Although effective managers are often considered effective leaders, the two are not always interconnected. Organizations can identify examples of effective managers who are ineffective as a leader and vice versa.

In business terms, management is a descriptive term for the positions within a department or organization with decision-making authority, such as a CEO or aquatics director. Often, organizations identify the management team as all the individuals with the appropriate titles and authority who are designated as belonging the elite group. Organizations create a clear distinction between management and staff by virtue of title and authority. ADs, commissioners, club CEOs, and other sports administrators with responsibility for staff supervision have the appropriate titles and decision-making authority. Important to foundational knowledge of management is an understanding of organizational structure, managerial functions, and managerial roles.

ORGANIZATIONAL STRUCTURE

The size, structure, and complexity of an organization determine the number of supervisors and their scope of responsibilities. For example, staff supervision for a local sporting goods store employing 25 full- and part-time workers is far less complex than the supervision required for the approximately 15,000 volunteers and additional paid staff at the 2018 Gold Coast XXI Commonwealth Games in Queensland, Australia. Supervisor–employee relations exist when a staff member receives a directive from an employee with a higher-ranking position.

The structure of an organization pinpoints the direct relationship and reporting lines of an employee to his or her superior. The structure also clarifies the span of control or the number of subordinates reporting to a particular supervisor. The larger the size of the organization (e.g., a professional NFL stadium vs. a small fitness gym), the greater the number of supervisors employed.

Reporting lines and communication channels within the organizational structure are important when considering the proximity or physical location of the supervisor and employee. On large college campuses with multiple athletic facilities spread over numerous acres of land, it is not practical for the director of athletics to be in close proximity to all of his or her direct reports. In many cases, the top management or administrative team may occupy a particular building or wing of a facility, whereas coaches and support staff are dispersed among other areas on campus (e.g., the office for the swim coach typically is in proximity to the aquatic facility). One of the advantages of this remote reporting relationship in large university athletic departments is that employees value their ability to work independently without a supervisor micromanaging their work.

Most organizations incorporate a type of hierarchical business structure with multiple layers that resembles a pyramid. The "staff" at the bottom of the pyramid report to first-line supervisors, who report to middle managers, who report to top management, which may be represented by a president, owner, or CEO. Another common configuration for organizational staff charts incorporates a matrix model as opposed to the hierarchical structure which is defined typically by either functional or divisional factors.

Functional Hierarchical Structure

Hierarchical functional structures represent the dominant or practical activities of the organization, such as player personnel, marketing, ticketing, and community engagement. Like most professional sports organizations, the Cleveland Browns (2016) franchise segments its staff according to functions of management, coaching, player personnel, football support, football operations, brand and fan development, sales and marketing, finance and accounting, information technology, administration, communications, stadium operations, and its foundation.

The Ohio State University (OSU) Athletic Department is also represented by a functional hierarchical structure. At the top of the organizational chart for OSU's 400+ personnel is the president of the institution followed by the vice president/director of athletics and the deputy director of athletics. The directors and head coaches reporting to middle managers represent the first line of the OSU Athletic Department supervisors who oversee operative employees, such as assistant and volunteer coaches, managers, and many support staff positions (e.g., assistant communication directors or the game-day promotions coordinator). OSU's middle-management layer includes six associate ADs who report to two senior associate ADs, who report to two executive associate ADs, representing the fourth, fifth, and sixth lines on the department's organizational chart.

The advantage of a functional hierarchical structure is the directness in the path of supervision. There is a clear representation of the supervisor–employee relationship. However, hierarchical structures tend to be laden with inefficiencies when too many layers of middle management are represented.

The Ohio State University athletic department includes over 400 employees.

Divisional Hierarchical Structure

The **hierarchical divisional**, or multidivisional, **structure** groups personnel according to what the organization defines as divisions. Divisions are subunits within a parent corporation. One of the most common sets of divisions is geographical (e.g., continents, countries, regions, states, provinces, or cities). For example, Home Team Sports is a division of Fox Sports Media Group, which is a division of 21st Century Fox. The NCAA governance structure is divided into Divisions I, II, and III. The Major League Baseball (MLB) American

Fox Cable Network is segmented by divisions which includes sports, news, and entertainment.

and National Leagues are segmented according to East, West, and Central divisions. *Sports Illustrated* is part of the Entertainment Division of Time, Inc.

Divisions may be segmented according to products (e.g., apparel, footwear, or equipment), projects (e.g., grassroots or global outreach), geographic markets (e.g., North America, Asia, South America, and Europe), or customer types (e.g., wholesale or retail). The multidivisional model has the advantage of facilitating rapid growth initiatives, and it provides a clear representation of supervisor–employee relationships, similar to the functional hierarchical structure. The autonomy of a divisional manager provides accountability for results, but the one disadvantage is the potential for political interference through competing divisions.

Matrix Structure

Large retail sports conglomerates such as Nike, Under Armour, and Adidas are often organized by a **matrix structure** whereby employees report to multiple supervisors. Nike represents one of the most complex matrix structures even though it underwent a major reorganization to become a "flatter, simpler organization aligned around geographies, categories, functions, and retails" (Nike, Inc., 2009, p. 24). Nike's Sustainable Business and Innovation (SBI) division, for example, focuses on sustainable products, manufacturing, and marketplaces, requiring team members to report to three supervisors in the department's matrix structure.

Matrix structures can result in turf wars or lack of accountability, which can erode an organizational culture if not managed properly. Although there is a potential for conflict, employees in a matrix structure typically have the ability to work on multiple short-term projects through a results-driven culture. Workers have broader ranges of responsibilities, but decisions may take longer than necessary. The reality is that the matrix structure is a necessity for many sports organizations, and the key to adaptation is the identification of the supervisory relationships that are aligned with performance evaluations.

MANAGERIAL FUNCTIONS

The principles of management have been classified into four basic functions: (1) planning, (2) organizing, (3) leading, and (4) controlling (Fayol, 1916, as cited in Brodie, 1962, p. 311). All four managerial functions are exercised by a supervisor when directing employees on behalf of an organization; however, leading is most closely aligned with the act of supervision. The four functions basically describe a manager's job. The following job definition for a sports management supervisor in Portland, Oregon, addresses three of the managerial functions:

> *A Sports Management Supervisor is responsible for planning, organizing and directing the activities and operations of the Parks and Recreation Bureau's citywide athletics program. The incumbent has full supervisory responsibilities for subordinate supervisors, full-time, part-time, seasonal staff and volunteers at multiple sites and is responsible for developing, implementing and evaluating a wide variety of athletic programs to meet the needs and interests of City residents.* (City of Portland, 2007)

Planning

Front-office personnel in professional sports franchises are constantly planning how to market special promotions, attract more spectators, or negotiate a sponsorship agreement. A supervisor demonstrates the managerial function of planning when designing goals and determining how to achieve the goals. Planning, whether strategic, operational, or tactical, addresses the requisite knowledge and skills needed in personnel to meet organizational goals. Planning encompasses a process of determining the course of steps to achieve goals and includes activities related to goal-setting, developing a mission, strategizing, and implementing actions.

Organizing

Coaches who develop detailed practice plans exercise the function of organizing. Organizing requires more detailed logistical planning of what tasks are necessary to achieve a goal, how they are to be grouped, and how they should be executed. Organizational plans are based on the premise of designing a blueprint of activities, time tables, responsible personnel, and necessary recourses to achieve measurable goals. Supervisors essentially organize their daily work with consideration for their staff performance expectations to achieve organizational expectations. Organizing is a managerial function addressing the structures and human resources to accomplish tasks.

Leading

The leading function is the essence of supervision because it refers to providing work instructions, communicating expectations, resolving conflicts, and motivating groups or individuals to perform directives. A university club sports director demonstrates the leading function when conducting a staff meeting with referees, scorekeepers, and other employees. The leading function emphasizes a human element of supervision in directing personnel, delegating tasks, communicating, making decisions, facilitating teamwork, and motivating employee. Personality research and studies of job attitudes, motivation, and leadership contribute to effective supervisory practices for particular situations.

Controlling

The control function is demonstrated by managers who monitor organizational performance and assess whether goals and objectives are achieved. Control also assesses performance deviation from set standards, such as when a ticket executive falls short or exceeds sales goals. For example, sports facility managers typically calculate member usage, traffic, rental income, and other areas against predetermined daily, monthly, or quarterly goals. The information is important for managerial decision making to improve organizational performance and can lead to recognition of the need for specialized training, a change in personnel, or a redesign of processes and procedure.

MANAGERIAL SKILLS

Closely linked to managerial functions are the general skills of a manager, which are described as (1) conceptual, (2) technical, and (3) interpersonal.

Conceptual

Conceptual skills are similar to the skills used in the functions of planning and organizing, whereby a supervisor analyzes and diagnoses situations such as a

Umpires demonstrate technical skills of their profession when working game assignments.

drastic profit loss or a change in leadership. Conceptual skills allow a supervisor to determine a course of action. Athletic administrators in college sports are continuously conceptualizing how to achieve success for their departments, institutions, and teams. Conceptual skills are more important for upper-level management (e.g., commissioners, CEO's, owners, athletics directors) as opposed to first-line managers (e.g., coaches and sports coordinators).

Technical Skills

Knowledge of **technical skills** is more important to first-line managers as opposed to upper management. For example, specialized knowledge in how to access statistical software live-game reports for basketball, baseball, softball, or track is a technical skill necessary for a sports communications assistant but not necessarily the director of athletics.

Technical skill merely identifies the specific knowledge or aptitude necessary for a particular job, such as a sports agent requiring proficiency in contract negotiations or a referee requiring a skill set for demonstrating proper officiating mechanics. Often referred to as "hard skills," technical skills are practical applications of specialized knowledge for job performance.

Interpersonal

Interpersonal skills are often referred to as "soft skills" or "people skills" and refer to communicating and interacting with others, whether individually or in a group setting. Sports supervisors demonstrate interpersonal skills when conducting staff meetings, disciplining employees, or negotiating an advertising rate for a radio spot. There are numerous domains of interpersonal skills, including oral communication, nonverbal communication, active listening, and reflecting. Supervisors must be adept in using interpersonal skills in an upward direction when communicating with superiors and downward when interacting with subordinates. Effective lateral communication with employees that share similar levels of authority is also an important interpersonal skill.

Managerial Roles

Managerial roles refer to the general responsibilities of an individual with managerial or supervisory authority. Assistant and associate athletics directors in NCAA Division III intercollegiate athletics departments are often acknowledged for "wearing multiple hats" because many have dual roles as a head coach and/or professor and/or administrator. Although roles are very similar to managerial skills, the roles of a sports manager are more definitive of duties and responsibilities.

General research on managerial roles notes three broad classifications: (1) interpersonal, (2) informational, and (3) decisional (Mintzberg, 1973). Subsets of roles are incorporated into each general category. **Interpersonal roles** include those of figurehead, leader, and liaison in representing the organization as a member of the management team. **Informational roles** include those of monitor, disseminator, and spokesperson in influencing the performance of staff members. Finally, **decisional roles** include those of entrepreneur, disturbance handler, resource allocator, and negotiator in maintaining harmony within the organization. **Action Shot 9-2** provides examples of activities of a Conference Commissioner in intercollegiate athletics which correlate with each of Mintzberg's managerial roles.

🎬 ACTION SHOT 9-2

Mintzberg's Managerial Roles Applied to NCAA Conference Commissioners

Mintzberg's (1973) roles have been applied to the sports industry. The three most frequently practiced roles among NCAA Conference Commissioners were found to be disseminator, liaison, and disturbance handler, and the least practiced roles included figurehead, negotiator, and resource allocator (Quarterman, 1994). Roles have also been researched among athletic directors belonging to the National Association of Intercollegiate Athletics (Quarterman, Allen, & Becker, 2005). **Table 9-1** presents examples of how conference commissioners in intercollegiate athletics perform Mintzberg's managerial roles in overseeing athletic departments at member institutions.

TABLE 9-1: Managerial Roles of Commissioner for Intercollegiate Athletics

Interpersonal		
Figurehead	Performing ceremonial duties on behalf of the conference office	Representing the conference at the NCAA convention or championship events
Leader	Influencing subordinates to work effectively in the office	Conducting performance evaluations, rewarding or disciplining employees, acting as a role model
Liaison	Maintaining a network of outside contacts to benefit the conference	Networking at the National Association of Collegiate Directors of Athletics (NACDA) or National Collegiate Athletic Association (NCAA) annual convention; meeting media personnel or prospective sponsors
Informational		
Monitor	Perpetually scanning information useful to the conference	Reviewing print, radio, televised, and Internet media sources; lobbying for information at an NCAA meeting;

Disseminator	Transmitting information to conference members	Conducting conference calls with athletic directors or institutional presidents; sending informational memos or e-mails regarding rule clarifications or other business
Spokesperson	Transmitting information to individuals or groups outside of the conference	Conducting a press conference for conference business; Sending media releases; Serving as a keynote speaker
Decisional		
Entrepreneurial	Searching for new ideas and implementing changes on behalf of the conference	Developing new revenue streams or introducing new technology
Disturbance Handler	Making decisions to deal with unexpected changes impacting the conference	Resolving conflict among member institutions (e.g., transfer eligibility, game protests, schedules)
Resource Allocator	Making decisions regarding resource utilization (personnel, time, money, space, or the conference)	Distributing enhancement funds to members, permitting usage of the conference office for meetings
Negotiator	Bargaining with individuals, groups, or organizations on behalf of the conference	Negotiating media deals or with outside contractors

Data from Mintzberg's Managerial Roles for Intercollegiate Athletics Conference Commissioners (Quarterman, 1994, p. 121-132).

Supervisors assume different managerial roles as they engage in different activities that influence the performance of their employees. Generally, the responsibilities of a staff supervisor include establishing systems for measuring performance goals, providing the tools (e.g., equipment, computers, and reports) for employees to accomplish their work, providing necessary training, serving as a resource, and holding staff accountable (see **Box 9-1**).

BOX 9-1

Responsibilities of Executive, Administrative, and Professional Employees

- Interviewing, selecting, and training employees
- Setting and adjusting pay and work hours
- Maintaining production or sales records
- Appraising employee productivity
- Handling employee complaints and grievances
- Disciplining employees
- Planning and appropriating work among employees
- Providing for the safety and security of employees
- Monitoring or implementing legal compliance

From U.S. Department of Labor (2015, pp. 35–36).

Management in Practice

Managers may positively or negatively affect whether an organization is able to achieve the intended mission. Sports organizations universally employ both effective and ineffective managers. Best practices ensure managers can readily distinguish the behaviors and actions considered effective and ineffective. Another practical application enhancing the managerial role is the application of planning and executing effective meetings.

MANAGERIAL EFFECTIVENESS

Managerial effectiveness is often described in terms of business results in achieving or exceeding organizational expectations. In a profit-driven organization, managerial effectiveness may be measured according to revenue generation. In a competitive sports environment, managerial effectiveness may be measured in the outcome of a championship. In a recreational sports environment, managerial effectiveness may be measured in terms of the skill and knowledge acquisition of participants.

There are certain qualities and traits that are consistent in effective managers. The United Nations (2015, pp. 2–3) proposes that effective managers hold themselves accountable; operate on the basis of values; are enabled by emotional, technical, and conceptual competence; and manage people, actions, and change to achieve individual, work unit, and organizational results. In general, effective managers are good leaders and good communicators with the ability to build relationships and develop high achievement potential in others. Personal characteristics include trustworthiness, integrity, self-motivation, confidence, a good business acumen, delegation skills, decision-making skills, and relationship qualities. **Action Shot 9-3** identifies desirable traits and behaviors of effective supervisors in the field of intercollegiate athletics.

Effective management has the potential to propel an organization well beyond its anticipated goals. Higher employee retention rates and improved morale are two factors linked to managerial effectiveness, but it is important for organizations to identify the specific indicators to measure effectiveness, such as a threshold score on an employee or client satisfaction survey or the market value of the company stock from quarter to quarter.

MANAGERIAL INEFFECTIVENESS

Coinciding with the day after the regular NFL season ends, Black Monday is a colloquial term to describe the date and fate of unfortunate coaches and/or general managers who are fired immediately after the season for losing records. There is a distinction between failing to achieve the objectives of the organization and failing in duties as a supervisor, but sometimes the two are related.

▶ ACTION SHOT 9-3

Alfreeda Goff's Tips for Effective Staff Supervision

Courtesy of Alfreeda Goff

Alfreeda Goff retired from her role as chief of staff and senior associate commissioner of the Horizon League in 2015 after 40 years of leadership roles in intercollegiate athletics. As a former director of athletics and chief of staff, Goff has mastered the art and science of effectively supervising a staff. She currently serves as a senior associate for the athletics division of Spelman Johnson, an executive search firm serving higher education. Following are Goff's tips for effectively supervising a staff (A. Goff, personal communication, March 24, 2017):

1. Communicate clearly and often with the individuals you supervise to ensure that they understand your expectations.
2. Take time to listen to those you supervise because they may have ideas or suggestions that may enhance the work area/environment/work outcome.
3. Help create an environment that people want to work in on a daily basis—be creative in where people have their workstations and what they look like, and encourage staff to feel like it is their space.
4. Be open to change in processes.
5. Provide professional development opportunities for the staff.
6. Help the staff stay in step with technology through updated equipment and education.
7. Provide the staff with an evaluation based on agreed-upon goals.
8. If a senior-level management team is used, take time to educate team members on their responsibilities and leadership requirements in regard to staff.
9. Acknowledge when you have made an error—you will not always be right.
10. Acknowledge and embrace diversity and inclusion throughout the workplace.
11. Allot time periodically to have staff outings—some with just staff and others with family and significant others—to facilitate social time outside of the office.
12. Have a flexible game plan.
13. Know that a smile will win more people over to your side than a frown.

Although a greater understanding of leadership, motivation, empowerment, and decision-making strategies assists in the development of effective supervisory skills, it is also important to address the characteristics of ineffective supervisors to distinguish desirable and undesirable behaviors. Ineffective supervision is a detriment to an organization and a primary reason for dismissal after an individual has been afforded due process and an opportunity to correct documented behavior determined to be inappropriate or counterproductive. Ineffective supervision was also the most frequently reported cause of low employee morale and a negative impact on the profitability of work groups, and behaviors perceived as ineffective in supervisors accounted for the number one reason why workers voluntarily leave a company (Northstar360, 2014).

The sports industry has its share of ineffective supervisors, ranging from a public high school coach or instructor who engages in reckless conduct outside of his or her scope of employment to a retail sports manager who commits fraud or corruption. Most examples of ineffective supervision, however, are less obvious and relate to a lack of a supervisory skill set in areas such as communication, leadership, organization, or prudent decision making. **Box 9-2** presents a list of commonly cited ineffective supervisory practices, and **Action Shot 9-4** provides some tips for changing ineffective behaviors.

BOX 9-2

Common Ineffective Managerial Practices

- Fails to clarify performance expectations
- Only deals with organizational problems when they mushroom out of control
- Fails to provide performance feedback
- Rushes to fire employees on the spot, neglecting to follow applicable laws of due process
- Lacks perception to recognize when employees are unhappy or dissatisfied
- Micromanages experienced or self-motivated employees
- Does not communicate effectively with staff
- Is reactive instead of proactive
- Fails to mentor, motivate, or develop employees

- Remains inflexible in decision making
- Takes credit for positive work of employees and denies blame
- Chooses favorites and makes excuses for incompetency
- Demonstrates unpredictable and erratic behaviors
- Lacks focus and follow-through
- Uses discipline inappropriately
- Fails to listen to staff
- Criticizes in public
- Delegates too often
- Causes dissension among staff

CHAPTER 9 | Game Changers

▶ ACTION SHOT 9-4

Alfreeda Goff's Tips for Ineffective Leadership

Ineffective supervision can be characterized by numerous actions, ranging from failure to communicate to being deceitful. Goff's analysis of what actions constitute ineffective staff supervision and a few tips for changing behaviors (in italics) are as follows:

1. Addressing your staff as if they are children—*profanity is never an acceptable means of communication.*
2. Setting timelines for tasks/responsibilities that are unreasonable and cannot be attained
3. Pitting staff against each other—*don't take sides.*
4. Providing inadequate equipment and expecting outstanding work results
5. Treating one gender different than the other in an effort to show that you are not biased
6. Allowing the staff to work in silos—*teamwork must always be the norm.*
7. Changing processes without input from others
8. Asking for advice, then when given, telling the individual it was stupid or totally ignoring it
9. Making an error/mistake and blaming it on someone else—*take responsibility.*
10. Using technology as your only means of communication—*be in the office and meet with people face to face.*
11. Being a workaholic and expecting your staff to be the same—*have a life.*
12. Forgetting to be a mentor
13. Fighting all the battles—*choose those you know you can win and will help you; others you may have to walk away from and come back to deal with at another time and in another way.*

MEETING MANAGEMENT

Sports managers responsible for staff supervision often use meetings to keep personnel informed and motivated. Meetings are more than a strategy to inspire employees with emotional appeals or the promise of rewards in exchange for high performance levels. They are the lifeblood of supervision in light of the importance of communication clarity (see **Box 9-3**).

Sports organizations in the business of servicing spectators, fans, or clients routinely hold employee meetings to ensure clarity in job roles before events and activities. Stadium supervisors at the Joker Marchant field in Lakeland, Florida, routinely meet with their staff the morning of every spring training home date to ensure assignments are understood in respect to special game-day promotions or potential challenges with weather conditions.

The frequency, duration, audience, and content of meetings should ideally be planned to avoid counterproductiveness or a waste of valuable time. For example, if the turf manager at a baseball stadium is conducting a meeting brief on tarp operations, the sound technician for the press box should not be included. Similarly, a monthly "state of the organization" meeting may increase information exchange for employees, but a newsletter or e-mail may be able to accomplish the same result without losing valuable productive time.

Supervisors for the Detroit Tigers routinely meet with their staff at Joker Marchant Stadium, site of the team's spring training facility

Meetings are what most employees and supervisors view as a necessary evil. Many employees dread meetings that focus on a topic for too long without a solution or consensus, deviate from the objective purpose, permit one person to dominate discussions, avoid or vaguely address an important topic, or permit infighting and conflict. The supervisor who plans and controls for these potential pitfalls increases the likelihood of changing the mindset of the inherent value of participating in well-organized and executed staff meetings. **Box 9-4** describes a number of considerations in planning and running an effective meeting.

Recap

Staff supervision encompasses many concepts originating in foundational managerial studies. Supervisors in sports organizations benefit from

BOX 9-4

Best Practices: Planning and Running Meetings

Before the Meeting

- Schedule meetings at convenient times during work hours.
- Schedule the room and arrange for any additions (technology or hospitality).
- Communicate the time, location, duration, and agenda of the meeting in advance.
- Consider the amount of time to devote to each agenda item.
- Anticipate questions, concerns, and delays.
- Involve only necessary participants, and make sure the meeting is necessary.
- Distribute all related documents in advance when possible, including any prework assigned.
- Arrive early.

During the Meeting

- Begin on time.
- Provide copies of the agenda.
- Communicate the charge or purpose of the meeting, including the anticipated outcome.

- Appoint someone to maintain minutes or scribe notes.
- Encourage but manage differences of opinions and ideas.
- Encourage balanced participation among attendees.
- Pause and summarize ideas and opinions (stay on task).
- Refrain from meeting for over an hour.
- Provide time at the end for an "open floor" so participants can voice opinions or ask for clarity.
- Create an effective follow-up plan with action items, including the responsible party and deadlines.

After the Meeting

- Debrief after the meeting for continuous improvement (consider processes, constraints, and good points).
- Follow up with individuals who have role assignments after the meeting.
- Send notes or meeting minutes to group members in a timely manner.

foundational knowledge of management functions (plan, lead, organize, and control), management skills (interpersonal, conceptual, and technical), managerial roles (informational, interpersonal, and decisional), and organizational structures (functional, divisional, and matrix).

Especially relevant to management and supervision are the concepts of leadership. Trait, behavioral, and situational theories of leadership provide a context to infer the antecedents, processes, and outcomes that affect styles of leadership. Authoritative, participative, and laissez-faire are three common leadership styles addressed in managerial studies. Chelladurai (1984; Chelladurai & Saleh, 1978, 1980) blended the three styles to develop a multidimensional model exhibited by intercollegiate athletic coaches.

Research in the field of athletics has also noted that although coaches and ADs more frequently exhibit transformational leadership qualities than transactional leadership qualities, success is not exclusively grounded in one particular style.

A study of staff supervision is enhanced by examining the characteristics and behaviors of both effective and ineffective supervisors. All managers and supervisors engage in staff meetings for a variety of purposes, ranging from information exchanges to opportunities to build relationships. Addressing activities before, during, and after a meeting improves the likelihood that participants will remain engaged and reap the intended benefits of a well-planned staff meeting.

 GLOBAL SPOTLIGHT 9–1

Mintzberg's Managerial Roles in Iranian Sports Federations

Among sports federation leaders in Iran, the three most frequently practiced managerial roles purported by Mintzberg (1973) were found to be resource allocator, disseminator of information, and disturbance handler (Ramezani et al., 2011). The most emphasized role of resource allocator was attributed to the responsibilities of sports federation managers to develop and maintain operational budgets.

The least practiced managerial roles of a sports federation manager in Iran were found to be negotiator and figurehead (Ramezani et al., 2011). These findings support the more restrictive and compliant culture of Middle Eastern countries shrouded in strict government and religious control. In 2015, Abdolhamid Ahmad, Iran's Deputy Minister of Sports, proposed a new atmosphere in stadiums by announcing that women and families would be permitted access to sporting venues within the next year for the first time since 1979 (Mullen, 2015). Sports federations managers working in tightly controlled countries may not have the scope of authority to negotiate deals and agreements. The statement from Ahmad was to announce the decision made by Iran's National Security Council, specifically, the Interior Ministry (Erdbrink, 2015). Ahmad exercised the managerial role of disseminator of information—he acted as the messenger. He had little to do with negotiating the outcome for women in his country.

DISCUSSION QUESTIONS

1. How can the decisional roles described by Mintzberg (1973) be applied to a sports facility supervisor?
2. How do the behaviors of participative and authoritative leaders in the sports industry differ?
3. Explain whether hierarchical or matrix structures pose the greatest disadvantage to large sports organizations, noting how proximity factors into the analysis.
4. How do the characteristics of transactional and transformational leaders in the sports industry differ, and are the types mutually exclusive to effective coaching or administration?
5. What traits distinguish effective from ineffective supervisors in sports organizations?
6. Explain the importance of planning the frequency, duration, audience, and content of meetings.

APPLIED ACTIVITIES

1. Complete the assessment in **Exhibit 9-1** to determine your preferred leadership style. Prepare a paragraph to explain the implication of the findings in your current environment, and speculate on whether your preferred leadership style may change over time.
2. Review two of the following classic sports movies from the following list, and prepare a slide show to demonstrate the leadership lessons in each:
   - *Field of Dreams*
   - *Remember the Titans*
   - *We Are Marshall*
   - *Rudy*
   - *Hoosiers*
   - *Invictus*
   - *Jerry Maguire*
   - *Brian's Song*
   - *Miracle*
   - *Chariots of Fire*
   - *Moneyball*
   - *The Glory Road*
   - *Unbroken*

EXHIBIT 9-1: PREFERRED SITUATIONAL LEADERSHIP STYLE FOR ATHLETICS PERSONNEL

Following are 12 situations that involve an intercollegiate athletic department. Consider that you are in the role of athletic director, assistant athletic director, or head coach. In other words, you have authority. Select one alternative that most closely describes what you would do in each situation. Don't be concerned with the right answer; select the alternative you would really use.

Instructions: Review the 12 statements and circle a, b, c, or d for each.

1. Your new rookie coach seems to be developing well. The coach's need for direction and close supervision is diminishing. What do you do?
   a. Stop directing and overseeing performance unless there is a problem.
   b. Spend time getting to know the coach personally, but make sure the coach maintains performance levels.
   c. Make sure things continue to go well; continue to direct and oversee closely.
   d. Begin to discuss new tasks of interest to the coach.

2. You assigned your assistant coach, Jill, the task of registering campers for the first of three weekly overnight sessions, specifying exactly how you wanted it done. Jill deliberately ignored your directions and did it her way. On the evaluations form from week 1, parents complained that the process was not efficient enough. This is not the first problem you've had with Jill. What do you decide to do?
   a. Listen to Jill's side, but be sure the job gets done right in the future.
   b. Tell Jill to do it again the right way, and closely supervise the job.
   c. Tell her the parents are unhappy, and let Jill handle it her way.
   d. Discuss the problem and possible solutions to it.

3. The members of your support staff work well together; the department is a real team. Because of traffic problems, the president approved staggered hours. As a result, you can change your department's hours for support staffers. Several of your workers have suggested changing the hours. You take what action?
   a. Allow the group to decide its hours.
   b. Decide on new hours, explain why you chose them, and invite questions.
   c. Conduct a meeting to get the group members' ideas. Select new hours together, with your final approval.
   d. Send around a memo stating what hours you want.

4. You hired Bill, a new employee in compliance. He is not performing at the level expected after 1 month of training. Bill is trying, but he seems to be a slow learner. What do you decide to do?

a. Clearly explain what needs to be done, and oversee his work. Discuss why the procedures are important; support and encourage him.

b. Tell Bill that his training is over and that it's time to pull his own weight.

c. Review the task procedures, and supervise Bill's work closely.

d. Inform Bill that his training is over, and tell him to feel free to come to you if he has any problems.

5. Helen, your athletics office manager, has had an excellent performance record for the past 5 years. Recently, you have noticed a drop in the quality and quantity of her work. She has been experiencing a family problem at home. What do you do?

a. Tell Helen to get back on track, and closely supervise her.

b. Discuss the problem with Helen. Help her realize that her personal problem is affecting her work. Discuss ways to improve the situation. Be supportive and encouraging.

c. Tell Helen you're aware of her productivity slip and that you're sure she will work it out soon.

d. Discuss the problem and solution with Helen, and supervise her closely.

6. Your organization frowns upon smoking but does allow smoking in certain areas. You just walked by a nonsmoking area and saw Jay smoking. He has been with the organization for 10 years and is a very productive worker. Jay has never been caught smoking before. What do you do?

a. Ask him to put it out, and then leave.

b. Discuss why he is smoking, and ask what he intends to do about it.

c. Give him a lecture about not smoking, and check up on him in the future.

d. Tell him to put it out, watch him do so, and tell him you will check on him in the future.

7. The members of your athletics department usually work well together with little direction. Recently, a conflict between two graduate assistant coaches (Sue and Tom) has caused problems. As a result, you take what action?

a. Call Sue and Tom together, and make them realize how this conflict is affecting the department. Discuss how to resolve it and how you will check to make sure the problem is solved.

b. Let the group resolve the conflict.

c. Have Sue and Tom sit down and discuss their conflict and how to resolve it. Support their efforts to implement a solution.

d. Tell Sue and Tom how to resolve their conflict, and closely supervise them.

8. Your assistant sports communication director, Jim, usually does his share of the work, with some encouragement and direction. However, he has migraine headaches occasionally and doesn't pull his weight when this happens. The others resent doing Jim's work. What do you decide to do?

a. Discuss the problem, and help him come up with ideas for maintaining his work; be supportive.

b. Tell Jim to do his share of the work, and closely watch his output.

c. Inform Jim that he is creating a hardship for the others and should resolve the problem alone.

d. Be supportive, but set minimum performance levels, ensuring compliance with the levels.

9. Barbara, one of your most experienced and productive workers, came to you with a detailed fundraising idea that may be feasible to implement. She can do her present job and this new assignment. You think it is an excellent idea. What do you do?

a. Set some goals together. Encourage and support her efforts.

b. Set up goals for Barbara. Be sure she agrees with them and sees you as being supportive of her efforts.

c. Tell Barbara to keep you informed and to come to you if she needs any help.

d. Have Barbara check in with you frequently so you can direct and supervise her activities.

10. Your senior accountant asked you for a special budget report for sports teams. Frank, a very capable head coach who usually needs no direction or support, has all the necessary skills to do the job. However, Frank is reluctant because he has never done a budget report. What do you do?

a. Tell Frank he has to do it. Give him direction, and supervise him closely.

b. Describe the project to Frank, and let him do it his way.

c. Describe the benefits to Frank. Get his ideas on how to do it, and check his progress.

d. Discuss possible ways of doing the job. Be supportive. Encourage Frank.

11. Jean is a great coach and even won a conference championship last year. However, her monthly recruiting and practice logs are constantly late and contain errors. You are puzzled because she does everything else with no direction or support. What do you decide to do?

a. Go over past reports with Jean, explaining exactly what is expected of her. Schedule a meeting so that you can review the next report with her.

b. Discuss the problem with Jean, and ask her what can be done about it. Be supportive.

c. Explain the importance of the report. Ask her what the problem is. Tell her you expect the next report to be on time and error-free.

d. Remind Jean to get the report in on time and without errors.

12. The members of your support staff are very effective and like to participate in decision making. A consultant was hired to develop a new method for your department using the latest technology in the field. What do you do?

a. Explain the consultant's method, and let the group decide how to implement it.

b. Teach them the new method and closely supervise them.

c. Explain the new method and the reasons it is important. Teach them the method, and make sure the procedure is followed. Answer any questions.

d. Explain the new method, and get the group's input on ways to improve and implement it.

Scoring and Interpretation

Using the following table, circle the letter you selected for each situation in the assessment. Add up the number of circled items per column, and record in the last row. The column with the highest total is your preferred leadership style. There is no correct or best normative leadership style. Following the table is an explanation of the results.

	S1—Decide	S2—Consult	S3—Facilitate	S4—Delegate
1.	c	b	d	a
2.	b	a	d	c
3.	d	b	c	a
4.	c	a	d	b
5.	a	d	b	c
6.	d	c	b	a
7.	d	a	c	b
8.	b	d	a	c
9.	d	b	a	c
10.	a	c	d	b
11.	a	c	b	d
12.	b	c	d	a
Total				

Explanation

S1   **Decide:** You make decisions alone. You autocratically tell people how to implement your decisions and follow up to make sure the performance is maintained, or you tell people what to do and make sure they continue to do it.

S2   **Consult:** You talk to individuals or the group for input in a supportive way before you make the decision. As a consulter, after making the decision, you also tell people how to implement your decision and follow up to make sure performance is maintained, and you support and encourage them as they implement your decision.

S3   **Facilitate:** You have a group meeting to get input from members, and you attempt to support the group to agree on a decision within the boundaries set by you; in other words, you still have the final say on the decision. As a facilitator, you are supportive and encouraging to the group members to both make the decision and implement the decision.

S4   **Delegate:** You let the group make the decision within limits. As a delegator, you don't tell the group what do to or facilitate the group during the decision making and its implementation.

Reproduced from Tiell, B., & Smith, M. (2010). Preferred Situational Leadership Style for Athletics Personnel. Commonwealth Coast Conference Leadership and Gender Equity Workshop for Senior Woman Administrators and Athletic Directors. Modified from a leadership assessment based on the Vroom-Yetton Decision Tree Model as cited in Dubrin, A. 2005. Fundamentals of Organizational Behavior, 3e. Thompson Southwestern Publishers.

CASE STUDY

Gabriela Szabo—A Lesson in Global Sports, Leadership, and Politics

Courtesy of Gabriela Szabo

Former Romanian Olympic gold medalist Gabriela Szabo, recently served as Minister of Youth and Sports, the highest ranking national government position in the sports industry.

The minister of sport is the highest-ranking government position appointed in many countries to oversee all levels of athletic competition, from grassroots to high performance. In Romania, a country ruled by communism for all but the past 25 years, the most recent minister happened to be an extremely dynamic female with a doctoral (PhD) degree who is no stranger to pressure.

Gabriela Szabo, a retired mid-distance runner, won the gold medal at the 2000 Sydney Olympics in the 5000-meter race and earned both a silver and a bronze medal at the 1996 Atlanta Games. She stood among a tier of predominantly male politicians representing Romania's esteemed ministers until the government collapsed in November 2015 following a massive political protest dubbed the "Colectiv Revolution." The resignation of the country's prime minister resulted in a mass turnover of cabinet positions, including Gabriela's role, which was handed to yet another ex-Olympian.

Position and Influence

Szabo, the petite female with a massive influence on sports from the Eastern European country bordering Serbia, Bulgaria, Moldova, Hungary, and the Ukraine, is a mixture of beauty, grace, and authority. In a personal meeting to discuss contributions to a sports textbook, her eyes smiled as she summoned guests to "please, sit closer" at a conference table in an office sparsely adorned with sports memorabilia. Although polite and engaging, Minister Szabo was seemingly preoccupied while acknowledging the need to increase the overall number of female sports leaders around the world. She was open about ambitions to assist Olympians in their transition back to mainstream society following their athletic careers and about her own story in ascending to a demanding political position, balancing a personal life, and delaying professional aspirations while in office. Her body language, however, indicated she was carrying the weight of a nation on her shoulders.

The pressure for Minister Szabo on that particular day stemmed from the gymnastics team's disappointing 13th-place finish at the World Championships a day prior, making it the first time in 40 years that a team from Romania would fail to automatically qualify for the upcoming Olympics. Frustration was driven by the perception of a lack of return on investment compared with the massive funding provided for training elite athletes in a culture where failure is not an option. It is a culture Szabo has perpetuated throughout her life in pursuing a career as an elite runner, scholar, public figure, and sports advocate. In turn, she also demonstrates compassion yet maintains high performance standards and expectations of excellence and accountability in constituents.

Minister Szabo's apologetic gestures were sincere as she explained the necessity to cut short a prearranged meeting to alternatively meet with an impromptu pair of official visitors, possibly from the International Gymnastics Federation or another sector of the Romanian government. In less than 12 minutes, a long-anticipated meeting between a professor and Romania's sports minister was over, but lifelong lessons would be forged in understanding global sports, politics, and leadership.

Personal and Professional Background

Gabriela Szabo was born in 1975 to a mother from Romania and a father from Hungary. At the age of 12 or 13, she met Gyongyossy Zsolt, who became her one and only coach as well as her eventual husband. Zsolt and his protégé married in 1999, just months before Szabo was recognized as the World Athlete of the Year by the International Athletics Foundation and the World Sportswoman of the Year by the World Sport Press Association. Their reception in a small village outside of Bucharest was held at a huge palace once owned by former communist dictator Nicolae Ceausescu. A year after their marriage, Gabriela won her Olympic gold medal, which served as redemption following her second- and third-place medals in the previous Olympic Games. Reportedly, her daily training regimen, primarily in South Africa, included up to 16 hours of sleep and 35 kilometers of running.

She retired from racing in 2005 at the age of 30 and still holds the European record for the 3000-meter race. Since retiring, she has earned a PhD in sport, served as an executive (vice president) of the Romanian Athletics Federation as well as the Romanian Olympic and Sports Committee, and served as a member of the European Athletics Council. Although she is no longer employed in the official capacity of Minister of Youth and Sport, she remains founder and president of the "Sport for Life" campaign and is an official Ambassador of Tourism for Romania.

Views on Sport, Leadership, and Human Resources

Szabo acknowledges that contemporary sports— at its elite end, at least—is complex because the products it delivers to participants and fans are so idiosyncratic. She notes that "professional sports are, in large part, just another form of business with a range of special features that demand a customized set of practices to ensure its effective operation." She is very in-tune with the impact of human resources and staff supervision for managing international competitions such as the Olympics and World Championships:

> Major sports events need a large workforce, often composed primarily of volunteers or casual workers, for a short period prior to the event, during the event, and directly following the event. The rapid increase and decline in staffing within a short period is a complex and significant human resource management problem. It requires systematic recruitment, selection, and orientation programs in order to attract the staff, and simple yet effective evaluation and reward schemes in order to retain them. (G. Szabo, personal communication, October 27, 2015)

Gabriela Szabo prides herself on being a collaborative and effective leader, especially in the role of Minister of Youth and Sports, where she advocated for facilities, funding, and programs to meet the needs of elite athletes while also encouraging mass sports participation for a healthy lifestyle. While being a good team player, she feels it is important to give back to others. She also understands the components of management and the dynamics of situational leadership in sport, politics, business, and life:

> Leadership is a complex composite of commendable personal attributes and ways of acting that results in employees and athletes believing in the leader's judgment and direction and wanting to execute or fulfill the leader's assignments and expectations. When applying generic management principles to the sports and leisure

context, it is necessary to understand the fragmented nature of the industry. Such heterogeneity, in both the internal and external environment, often leads to unique challenges. Through my experience, I discovered that effective leadership is dynamic and is based on a complex series of interactions between leader, group members, and situational constraints. This way, the positive outcomes (performance and satisfaction) will occur when there is congruence between the leader's behavior, the group members' preferred leadership behavior, and the behavior that is required in relation to the situation. (G. Szabo, personal communication, October 27, 2015)

CASE STUDY QUESTIONS

1. What makes Gabriela Szabo one of the top leaders in sports?

2. Do you believe Gabriela's story represents a typical life in Romania?

3. How would you describe her leadership style?

4. What factors in Gabriela's life shaped her leadership style and demeanor in her role as the Minister of Youth and Sports?

5. How should Gabriela handle the criticism regarding a lack of return on investment compared with the massive funds provided for training elite athletes?

REFERENCES

Bass, B. (1985). *Leadership and performance beyond expectations.* New York, NY: Free Press.

Bass, B., & Avolio, B. (1990). *Transformational leadership development: Manual for the Multifactor Leadership Questionnaire.* Palo Alto, CA: Consulting Psychologists Press.

Bernard, L. L. (1926). *An introduction to social psychology.* New York, NY: Holt.

Blake, R., & Mouton, J. (1964). *The managerial grid: Key orientations for achieving production through people.* Houston, TX: Gulf.

Brooks, D. D., Ziatz, D., Johnson, B., & Hollander, D. (2000). Leadership behavior and job responsibilities of NCAA Division 1A strength and conditioning coaches. *Journal of Strength and Conditioning Research, 14*(4), 483–492.

Burns, J. M. (1978). Leadership. New York, NY: Harper & Row. In Gomes, A. (2014). *Transformational leadership: Theory, research, application to sports.* Portugal: University of Minho, School of Psychology.

Burton, L., & Peachey, J. (2009). Transactional or transformational? Leadership preferences of Division III athletic administrators. *Journal of Intercollegiate Sport, 2*, 245–259.

Case, R., & Branch, D. (2003, June 1). A case to study competencies of sport facility managers. *International Sport Journal*, 25–38.

Celik V., & Valcinkaya, K. (2015, January 1). An examination of charismatic leadership characteristics of handball coaches: Perceptions of handball players. *Journal of Physical Education and Sport Science, 9*(1), 118–132.

Chelladurai, P. (1984). Discrepancy between preferences and perceptions of leadership behavior and satisfaction of athletes in varying sports. *Journal of Sport Psychology, 6*, 27–41.

Chelladurai, P., & Doherty, A. (1998). Styles of decision-making in coaching. In J. M. Williams (Ed.), *Applied sport psychology: Personal growth to peak performance* (3rd ed., pp. 115–126). Mountain View, CA: Mayfield.

Chelladurai, P., & Saleh, S. D. (1978). Preferred leadership in sports. *Canadian Journal of Applied Sports Sciences, 3*(2), 85–92.

Chelladurai, P., & Saleh, S. D. (1980). Dimensions of leader behavior in sports: Development of a leadership scale. *Journal of Sport Psychology, 2*, 34–45.

City of Portland. (2007, December 17). *Class specification: Sports management supervisor.* Retrieved from http://www.portlandoregon.gov/bhr/article/254796

Cleveland Browns. (2016). Staff directory. *Cleveland Browns 2016 media guide.* Retrieved from http://prod.static.browns.clubs.nfl.com/assets/docs/pdf/Cleveland-Browns-Media-Guide.pdf

Commission on Sports Management Accreditation. (2016, May). *Common professional components. Accreditation principles manual and guidelines for self-study preparation.* Retrieved from http://www.cosmaweb.org/accreditation-manuals.html

Crust, L., & Lawrence, I. (2006). A review of leadership in sport: Implications for insight. *Online Journal of Sport Psychology, 8*(4), 28–48.

Doherty, A. (1997, July 1). The effect of leader characteristics on the perceived transformational/transactional leadership and impact of interuniversity athletic administrators. *Journal of Sport Management, 11*(3), 275–286.

Doherty, A., & Danylchuk, K. (1996). Transformational and transactional leadership in interuniversity athletics management. *Journal of Sport Management, 10*(3), 292–309.

Doherty, M. (2004, January 19). Defining a leader. *Sporting News, 228*(3), 44.

Dubrin, A. (2007). *Fundamentals of organizational behavior* (4th ed.). New York, NY: Cengage Learning.

Erdbrink, T. (2015, April 4). Iran will allow women in stadiums, reversing a much-criticized rule. *New York Times.* Retrieved from http://www.nytimes.com/2015/04/05/world/middleeast/iran-will-allow-women-in-sports-stadiums-reversing-a-much-criticized-rule.html

Fayol, H. (1916/1949). *Administration Industrielle et Générale.* Paris, France: Dunod. As cited in Brodie, M. (1962, September). Henri Fayol: Administration Industrielle et Générale—A reinterpretation. *Public Administration, 40*(3), 311–317.

Fielder, F. E. (1964). A theory of leadership effectiveness. In L. Berkowitz (Ed.), *Advances in experimental social psychology* (pp. 149–190). New York, NY: Academic Press.

Gardner, J. (1989). *On leadership.* New York, NY: Free Press.

Grimes, P., & Chressanthins, G. (1994). Alumni contributions to academics: The role of intercollegiate sports and NCAA sanctions. *American Journal of Economics and Sociology, 53*(1), 27–40.

Hersey, P., & Blanchard, K. (1969). An introduction to situational leadership. *Training and Development Journal, 23,* 26–34.

Hiroto, V., Anderson, D., & Verardi, C. (2015, December 1). Leadership dimensions preferred amongst Brazilian soccer coaches. *Journal of Physical Education and Health, 4*(6), 31–36.

Jenny, S., & Hushman, G. (2014, July 1). A case study of a successful men's NCAA division I distance running coach: To what extent is decision-making humanistic? *The Sport Journal.* Retrieved from http://thesportjournal.org/article/a-case-study-of-a-successful-mens-ncaa-division-i-distance-running-coach-to-what-extent-is-decision-making-humanistic/

Katz, D., Maccoby, N., & Morse, N. (1950). *Productivity, supervision and morale in an office situation.* Ann Arbor, MI: Institute of Social Research, University of Michigan.

Kutz, M. (2008, July 1). Leadership factors for athletic trainers. *Athletic Therapy Today, 13*(4), 15–20.

Legends. (2016, November 1). *Legends announces acquisition of International Stadia Group.* Retrieved from http://www.legends.net/legends-announces-acquisition-of-international-stadia-group/

Lewin, K., Lippit, R., & White, R. (1939). Patterns of aggressive behavior in experimentally created social climates. *Journal of Social Psychology, 10,* 271–301.

Lumpkin, A., Achen, R., & Hyland, S. (2015). Education, experience, and advancement of athletic directors in NCAA member institutions. *Journal of Contemporary Athletics, 9*(4), 249–265.

Manning, L. (2012, May). *NCAA athletic directors' self-perspective of transformational/transactional leadership.* Doctoral dissertation, Department of Educational Leadership, East Carolina University, Greeneville, NC.

Mintzberg, H. (1973). *The nature of managerial work.* New York, NY: HarperCollins.

Mullen, J. (2015, April 5). Iran to ease ban on women attending sports events involving men. *CNN.* Retrieved from http://www.cnn.com/2015/04/05/middleeast/iran-women-sports-events/

Nike, Inc. (2009). Strategy. *2007–2009 Corporate responsibility report.* Retrieved from http://www.fibre2fashion.com/sustainability/pdf/NikeSustainabilityReport.pdf

Northstar360. (2014, May 29). The high cost of doing nothing. *Lack of supervisor training results in lower productivity, profitability.* Retrieved from http://northstar360.com/tag/ineffective-supervisors

Peachey, J. W., & Burton, L. J. (2011). Male or female athletic director? Exploring perceptions of leader effectiveness and a (potential) female leadership advantage with intercollegiate athletic directors. *Sex Roles, 64,* 416–425.

Quarterman, J. (1994, May). Managerial role profiles of intercollegiate athletic conference commissioners. *Journal of Sports Management, 8*(2), 129–134.

Quarterman, J., Allen, L., & Becker, A. (2005, April). Managerial roles of directors of athletics of the NAIA: The Mintzberg model. *International Journal of Sports Management, 6*(2), 165–182.

Ramezani, Z., Khabiri, M., Alvani, S., & Tondnevis, F. (2011). Use of Mintzberg's model of managerial roles to evaluate sports federations managers of Iran. *Middle-East Journal of Scientific Research, 10*(5), 559–564.

Sagas, M., & Cunningham, G. B. (2004). The impact of supervisor support on perceived career outcomes of the senior woman administrator. *International Journal of Sport Management, 5,* 229–242.

Sherman, C. A., Fuller, R., & Speed, H. D. (2000). Gender comparisons of preferred coaching behaviours in Australian sports. *Journal of Sport Behavior, 23*(4), 389–406.

Shonk, W., & Shonk, J. (1988, June). What business teams can learn from athletic teams. *Personnel, 65,* 76–80.

Slack, T., & Parent, M. (2006). Charismatic and transformational leadership. In *Understanding sport organizations: The application of organizational theories* (pp. 301–303). Lower Mitcham, South Australia: Human Kinetics.

United Nations. (2015). *Model at a glance. Profiles of an effective manager for managerial excellence in the United Nations.* Retrieved from https://hr.un.org /sites/hr.un.org/files/Profile%20of%20an%20Effective%20Manager_0.pdf

U.S. Department of Labor. (2008, July). *Fact sheet 17B. Exemption for executive employees under the Fair Labor Standards Act.* Retrieved from https://www .dol.gov/whd/overtime/fs17b_executive.pdf

United States Department of Labor. (2015). *The Fair Labor Standards Act: Executive, administrative, and professional exemptions [PowerPoint presentation].* Retrieved from https://www.dol.gov/whd/overtime/presentation.ppt

Vroom, V., & Yetton, P. (1973). *Leadership and decision-making.* Pittsburgh, PA: University of Pittsburgh Press.

Weaver, K. (2016). Exploring leadership characteristics of high school football coaches. *Kentucky Alliance of Health, Physical Education, Recreation, and Dance Journal, 52*(2), 24–29.

Weber, M. (1958). The three types of legitimate rule. *Berkeley Publications in Society and Institutions, 4*(1), 1–11.

Zuest, G. (2003). Transformational and transactional leadership by athletic training education program directors. *Dissertation Abstracts International,* UMI 3117391.

CHAPTER 10

Clutch Play

MOTIVATION AND PERFORMANCE
MANAGEMENT IN SPORTS ORGANIZATIONS

*High-performing and satisfied staff is one of, if not the most critical assets of any orga-
nization. It is important to discuss performance with staff when they are doing a good
job and not just when a punitive conversation is warranted. Occasional 'nice jobs' go
a long way to recognize and reinforce successful behaviors and help build confidence.*

David E. Gilbert
President and Chief Executive Officer
Greater Cleveland Sports Commission and Destination Cleveland

Courtesy of David Gilbert

LEARNING OUTCOMES

1. Identify how theories of motivation can be applied to employees working in
   a sports business setting.
2. Distinguish the effects of intrinsic and extrinsic motivation on the performance
   of employees in the sports industry.
3. Distinguish performance management from performance appraisals.
4. Identify and describe the five phases of a performance management system.
5. Identify and describe the purpose of a performance management system.
6. Understand performance appraisal methods.
7. Identify biases in performance appraisals.

KEY TERMS

Behavioral anchored rating scale	Graphic rating scale	Performance appraisals
Central tendency error	Halo effect	Performance management
Contrast error	Hierarchy of needs	Positive reinforcement
Critical incident report	Horn effect	Recency error
Expectancy	Instrumentality	Self-actualization
Expectancy theory	Intrinsic motivation	Theory X
Extinction	Leniency error	Theory Y
Extrinsic motivation	Motivation	Valence
First-impression bias	Negative reinforcement	Weighted checklists

Lead-Off

Leadership and management are cornerstones to effective staff supervision, and motivation is a driver for performance. Leadership, management, staff supervision, and motivation all have a direct influence on managing employee performance.

Expecting superior staff performance is an attitude of successful organizations, whether a professional Major League Baseball (MLB) team or a local gymnasium. It is no accident when the Milwaukee Brewers or a Curves Gym in Snellville, Georgia, boasts record attendance or record profits. Successful businesses with supervisors who effectively motivate their employees to be results-driven incorporate well-planned performance management systems that facilitate continuous improvement in individuals, groups, and the entire organization.

Performance management is a process or set of activities with many parts. The general process includes defining performance objectives, planning motivational strategies, executing performance enhancers, and monitoring the results of the desired outcomes. This chapter addresses the theories and applications of motivation in sports organizations. It also addresses components of an effective performance management system and the design, use, and biases of performance appraisals.

Motivation

Supervisors skilled in the ability to motivate their staff have a greater likelihood of reaping the rewards of high performance. Part of the job of a supervisor involves understanding what drives someone to perform and administering the appropriate motivation strategy to elicit performance that meets or exceeds expectations. Sports coaches are prime examples of master motivators in their ability to influence individual player and team performance. Coaches know what motivates a player to go beyond 100%, whether it is fear of a consequence for failure or the promise of a reward for success.

Sports managers and supervisors primarily know that motivation is what initiates and guides goal-oriented behaviors. It is more than inspiring employees to achieve the organization's mission. It is one of the essential activities in supervising a staff for high performance.

Motivation may be in the form of a reward or a punishment or in providing autonomy and discretion in allowing an employee to make independent decisions. Employees may respond differently to the same motivation tactic. Different individuals and different situations may call for different motivation techniques to increase the likelihood of the best results. Understanding motivation in terms of staff supervision includes understanding theories of motivation and being conscientious in selecting the appropriate strategy most likely to produce the desired performance.

Coach Mike Krzyzewski (Duke University Blue Devils and Team USA) is renowned for his ability to motivate players to peak performance.

THEORIES OF MOTIVATION

Theories of motivation explain why individuals behave in a specific manner. The basic theories of motivation applied to staff supervision in the sports industry includes Maslow's (1943) hierarchy of needs, McGregor's (1960) Theory X and Theory Y, and Vroom's (1964) expectancy theory.

Maslow's Hierarchy of Needs

Maslow (1943) purported that motivation is a result of satisfying needs, which are prioritized in a model resembling a pyramid. The **hierarchy of needs** theory of motivation assists supervisors in understanding that each employee progresses through many levels of needs in fulfilling his or her role within the organization. Whereas the general manager for a professional franchise may view employment as fulfilling a lifelong dream, which satisfies a higher-level need in the pyramid, a beer vendor at the stadium may find his or her motivation to exhibit good work ethics stemming from a lower-level need to simply retain his or her job and avoid being fired.

Maslow's Hierarch of Needs pyramid is considered "outdated" since its inception in 1943 but the basic levels still are used to explain employee's motivation.

At the base of the pyramid are physiological needs, such as the oxygen, sleep, and nutrients needed to stay alive. The second level includes safety needs, such as adequate shelter, personal safety, and employment security, which is a motivator for employees who only aspire to receive a paycheck and have little to no interest in expanding or enhancing their role in the organization. The third level, social needs, is represented by a need for communal interaction, whether with family, friends, or colleagues. LeBron James's decision in 2010 to leave Cleveland for the Miami Heat when courted with lucrative offers from multiple National Basketball Association (NBA) teams was partially fueled by a social motivation to reconnect with Dwayne Wayne and Chris Bosh (Windhorst, 2010). Although other dynamics contributed to the final decision of 2010, James's connection with Bosh and Wayne from their affiliation on Team USA during the 2006 World Championships in Japan and the 2008 Olympics in Beijing factored into the decision that sent the prized free agent to South Beach.

The fourth level of Maslow's pyramid is the need for esteem, exhibited by high levels of confidence, respect, and recognition for achievements. Coaches and administrators are often driven to succeed through this type of motivation, which fulfills a need to be recognized for hard work and dedication. By awarding achievement certificates and expressing formal praise on a regular basis, supervisors facilitate satisfaction of an employee's need for esteem.

At the peak of the pyramid is the need for **self-actualization** by virtue of validation for a high-order cognitive function, such as creativity, professional growth, or problem-solving ability. Personnel in sports organizations motivated by the need for self-actualization inherently find work fulfilling when they feel at least partially responsible for implementing successful programs or reaching milestones (e.g., surpassing a fundraising goal or achieving a win against a ranked opponent). Supervisors facilitate motivation through self-actualization by establishing challenging yet realistic goals and providing personnel the discretion to autonomously make decisions that influence results.

Theory X and Y

McGregor's (1960) Theory X and Theory Y are founded on the premise that managers perceive that the motivation behind effort and performance is largely based on whether their employees like or dislike work. **Theory X** applies to supervisors with an underlying belief that employees innately dislike working, are inherently lazy, avoid responsibility, and have little ambition. These supervisors monitor employees closely and often use direct threats, ultimatums, or other forms of coercion to control and motivate workers to achieve the required levels of productivity. Staff supervisors focus on work rules, policies, and procedures as motivation tactics to inspire employees to meet performance

Supervisors asserting McGregor's Theory X of Motivation believe entry level workers at a front desk of a health club need to be monitored closely.

expectations without a penalty. Typically, entry-level or brand-new employees, such as a fitness assistant or a desk attendant at a health club, are supervised more closely simply because trust hasn't been established, and the supervisor may have a preconception that workers would rather be engaging in activities not associated with the workplace.

Conversely, **Theory Y** applies to supervisors who believe employees are integrated into the organization, seek additional responsibilities, and genuinely find fulfillment or a high degree of satisfaction from their work. Under these conditions, supervisors do not feel a need to monitor their employees as closely. Under the premise of Theory Y, supervisors are more inclined to empower employees and provide opportunities for workers to demonstrate initiative and autonomy for decisions affecting the organization.

A supervisor who operates under the conditions of Theory X may alter his or her motivation strategies to assume greater Theory Y behaviors if, for example, employees demonstrate initiative or a desire for greater responsibility. Providing an IMG-Learfield ticket accountant at a university with autonomy to research data management software or the opportunity to attend a sales combine sponsored by the NBA Minnesota Timberwolves are attributes of a supportive, Theory Y supervisor; however, high levels of productivity are not guaranteed. A Theory X supervisor may deem it appropriate to motivate the IMG-Learfield ticket accountant with daily quotas, which also does not guarantee the highest performance, either. Staff supervision requires managers and directors to understand the needs and motivations of their employees and to be flexible in applying Theory Y and Theory X motivators in hopes of gaining the optimum results.

Expectancy Theory

The **expectancy theory** of motivation purported by Vroom (1964) implies that increased effort to achieve desired results will be demonstrated if there is an outcome associated with meeting or exceeding expectations that has value to the employee. The basic formula for the Vroom expectancy theory is

$$Motivation = Expectancy \times Instrumentality \times Valance$$

The first factor of **motivation** is **expectancy**, or a belief in a successful outcome by virtue of self-efficacy and adequate resources. The second factor is **instrumentality**, the belief that increased effort will produce desired results. The third factor is **valance**, or the value attributed to a possible reward.

Instrumentality is explained as the belief that performance is tied to a reward, such as a ticket sales associate for an MLB team expecting to receive something positive for having the highest performance results. The resulting instrument (e.g., bonus pay or an extra vacation day), as long as it has merit, is the motivational driver for increasing efforts to sell. Valance is represented by the personal merit value placed on an expected reward or benefit (Cunningham & Mahoney, 2004). Bonus or commission pay may be a great motivator for the top salesperson, whereas an extra vacation day or an opportunity to receive an autographed jacket or a free game ticket may not be perceived as being as valuable or motivating as the cash option.

APPLICATION OF MOTIVATION

Sports managers and supervisors are challenged to determine what type of motivation will yield the best results for each individual employee because a one-size-fits-all model is rarely effective. Not all members of a basketball team respond positively when a coach uses in-your-face brash directives and ultimatums as a means to motivate performance. Some players crumble and lose self-esteem, whereas others may be inspired to work harder. Determining the appropriate application of motivation strategies includes understanding differences in what motivates individuals to their highest performance levels. In a work setting, supervisors commonly use positive reinforcement and/or negative reinforcement to elicit the desired behavior.

Positive Reinforcement

Intrinsic (internal) and extrinsic (external) motivation are the two general categories of **positive reinforcement** that are likely to correlate with improved performance. **Intrinsic motivation** is an intangible, internal force that influences an individual's drive to exhibit greater performance efforts. Tapping into what innately drives someone to want to work harder or achieve more requires sports supervisors to build relationships and recognize the internal cues that express or trigger fulfillment in his or her employees.

Selling the benefits of a fun work environment is one means to appeal to a particular audience that thrives on the intrinsic motivation of working in a cool place and being associated with sports every day. Other individuals may thrive on praise, public acknowledgement, or recognition to drive performance. A new job title, increase in the scope of job responsibilities, or connections with valued employees are all forms of intrinsic motivation. Research concluded that simply reaping the benefits of professional training was the positive reinforcement viewed as highly motivating to a Division I National Collegiate Athletic Association (NCAA) event management staff regardless of whether the workers were full-time or part-time employees (Cunningham & Mahoney, 2004). Similarly, volunteers working in sports were more motivated in their jobs when they believed they had an emotional connection to a sport, to an activity, or to the organization (Green & Chalip, 1998, p. 17). Money is a stronger motivator of performance than a thank-you note, but money is not always available for the purpose of positive reinforcement, which is why creativity is necessary to provide intrinsic motivators that will yield high-performance results.

Extrinsic motivators such as bonus pay, raises, stock options, trophies, extra vacation time, or a promotion (with a pay increase), are the tangible rewards tied to performance achievement. These types of motivators are controlled or granted by an individual (typically the supervisor) and considered external to the work itself. Commission-based pay is often used in professional sports to motivate a sales employee to achieve greater performance levels. Coaching contracts for Division I NCAA football and basketball customarily include incentive clauses for bonus pay tied to variables such as conference standings, postseason qualifications, win–loss record, and even graduation or academic progress rate (APR).

Examples of the use of extrinsic motivators is plentiful in the field of sports. Volunteers working as stadium or parking attendants at a collegiate or professional game are often provided with a concessions voucher, a parking voucher, a logo T-shirt, or an invitation to a staff appreciation party in exchange for their donated services. Many of the unpaid interns working for minor-league and major-league sports are often provided with benefits or perks such as lunch with the owner, a training workshop featuring a player, an incentive stipend, or even free housing opportunities.

Extrinsic rewards don't have to be expensive. Ideas for low-cost extrinsic motivational rewards include a reserved parking place, a personal service such as a car wash or house cleaning, a comp or flex day, or a certificate for a local restaurant. As with the example of the basketball players who each respond differently to the motivation and leadership style displayed by a coach, employees also behave differently in their responses to extrinsic motivators based on the perceived value.

It has been suggested that intrinsic motivators are more powerful in eliciting desired performance over time but that an extrinsic motivator can supersede or replace intrinsic motivation. For example, a martial arts trainer who is intrinsically motivated by teaching karate to advanced students may find that he or she is expending greater time and effort in selling studio memberships rather than instructing classes because a commission-based pay structure (an extrinsic motivator) supersedes the passion for teaching. Regardless of the ability to provide intrinsic or extrinsic motivators, supportive supervisors must recognize which incentives truly work or don't work with their direct reports to improve performance or develop stronger commitment.

Negative Reinforcement

Negative reinforcement and punishment are used to discourage inappropriate or nonproductive behavior. Negative reinforcement is not always a punishment, however. The motivation to avoid undesirable behaviors such as tardiness or absenteeism stems from the sanctions or consequences outlined in the employee policy and procedure manual. To discourage rule violations, the NCAA's committee on infractions has the authority to assess monetary fines and sanctions (i.e., scholarship and postseason limits, vacated records, or the death penalty) for violations. Similarly, a recreation supervisor may dock a lifeguard's hours or submit a letter of reprimand if an individual violated a fraternization policy or failed to file an accident report.

One form of negative reinforcement is **extinction**, which involves withdrawing or failing to provide a reinforcing consequence in order to modify behavior. For example, the media director for a sports franchise may ignore the employee who has a habit of rudely interrupting colleagues during department meetings but alternatively acknowledge his or her contributions when appropriately delivered. Failing to acknowledge the employee is a method to facilitate the employee recognizing a connection between appropriate and inappropriate comments.

The advantage of using negative reinforcement and punishment as a motivation tool for staff for performance management is because of the

🎬 ACTION SHOT 10-1

Motivation Through Negative Reinforcement in Youth Sports

In youth sports, negative reinforcement is highly frowned upon despite an unequivocal number of examples where coaches seem overzealous in punishing the mistakes of their players. A volleyball coach in northwest Ohio emphasizes that he expects nothing but mistake-free performance from his youngest group of players, aged 10 to 12. He tolerates little in terms of ineffectiveness and has zero qualms about yelling directly in the face of a 10-year-old who shanks a pass or mishandles a set. He expects a 10-year-old to perform the same as a high school athlete in terms of knowing where to move on the floor, having the emotional discipline necessary to handle pressure situations, and demonstrating the physicality to execute the most basic skills inherent in the game.

The underlying belief is that by establishing the correct physical mechanics and performance expectations at an early age, the player never learns inappropriate behavior or becomes susceptible to emotional distractions. Therefore, the athlete becomes conditioned to meet or exceed coaches' expectations through the use of negative reinforcement. After winning six state high school volleyball championships and numerous national championships with his 12-under and 15-under teams, the coach is well respected despite his use of negative reinforcement as the primary motivational tool to improve performance.

likelihood of eliciting an immediate behavioral change despite the expected consequences of lowering morale. In sports organizations, supervisors should carefully consider the use of negative reinforcement and punishment as motivation tools to influence performance (see **Action Shot 10-1**).

Performance Management

Performance management refers to the system that ensures that organizational processes exist to maximize the productivity of employees, teams, and, ultimately, the organization (Mondy, 2008, p. 224). There is much more to performance management than just providing a prize to motivate a staff to design the most creative fan engagement campaign or sell a minimum number of game tickets.

A high-performing staff is likely apparent in organizations that view performance management as a set of systems and processes that permeates all levels of the business and fosters an environment of open and continuous communication between supervisors and subordinates. Supervisors who understand and effectively manage all parts of a performance management system reap the benefits of achieving desired outcomes, especially when striving for continuous improvement and valuing employees as an important asset.

STEPS IN PERFORMANCE MANAGEMENT SYSTEMS

Effective performance management systems are process oriented and include an appraisal cycle that sets standards, assesses employee performance relative to the standards, and provides feedback. Communicating the performance expectations to employees is vitally important. Whether the information is disseminated in the initial orientation, in a weekly informational meeting, in the employee handbook, or through e-mail correspondence, workers in a business need to know, understand, and accept the measurable standards by which their performance is evaluated. Best practices for performance management systems suggest a process approach (see **Figure 10-1**).

The steps in a performance management system involve (1) defining performance standards, (2) conducting a gap analysis, (3) planning improvement activities, (4) executing, (5) monitoring, and (6) reporting.

1 • Define performance standards

2 • Conduct gap analysis

3 • Determine improvement strategies

4 • Implement improvement strategies

5 • Monitor performance

6 • Make adjustments as necessary

Figure 10-1

Six-steps to a performance management system

Define Performance Standards

Defining performance standards refers to identifying current standards of performance in addition to the desired standards or goals for an employee, department, or organization. For example, the vice president of retail sales and service for the NBA Brooklyn Nets Team Shop identifies individual and store sales in a given day, week, month, and season and establishes the baseline standards for acceptable performance in the same period. Additional activities in the initial stage of performance management involve defining data definitions, critical success factors, assumptions, and the scope of performance in terms of deliverables by individuals or groups. Often strategic planning is incorporated to analyze job information for accuracy and relevancy before developing performance goals that correlate to the organization's mission.

Conduct a Gap Analysis

A gap analysis involves measuring an employee's or group's actual performance and comparing it to the predefined baseline standards. Identifying whether the individual or group has a performance deficiency or if he, she, or they are exceeding minimal expectations is integral to determining if intervention is necessary. The appraisal process assists in selecting appropriate strategies to elicit the desired results. If a comparison of the average game-day sales revenue for the Brooklyn Nets Team Shop for a specified period falls well below the defined standards, the prudent approach is to diagnose the antecedents and continue performance management steps.

The Brooklyn Nets team shop has daily, weekly, monthly and seasonal sales performance standards.

Determine Improvement Strategies

Once employee or group performance has been compared to baseline or optimal performance standards and a deficiency is exposed, an assessment of potential causes for lower performance assists in determining the appropriate motivation strategies that will likely elicit the desired results. The Brooklyn Nets vice president of retail sales may plan individual and group training sessions to address customer service or strategies for overcoming objections when closing deals. Rewards may be designated for individuals or the department for exceeding target sales projections. During this stage, supervisors determine deadlines, acquire the necessary resources, and determine accountability for implementing strategies to improve performance.

Implement Strategies

The implementation stage naturally follows the selection of the appropriate strategies for the desired results. For example, the in-depth training workshop and bonus compensation plan to incentivize the NBA Brooklyn Nets retail sales team is put into motion with the intention to assist individuals in reaching their quotas according to the performance standards.

Monitor Performance

Monitoring includes the activities, information, and metrics to evaluate the performance of individuals, teams, and the organization. If the Nets retail sales department staff falls short of projected quotas, employee appraisals, reviews of customer satisfaction surveys, and observations of general office behaviors or interactions with clients will likely provide the diagnostics for identifying probable causes of deficiencies. Herein is where performance appraisals are important in the process. There are many techniques available to monitor performance.

Make Adjustments as Necessary

If performance is meeting or exceeding standards, no adjustments may be necessary. When performance sustains levels below minimum standards, supervisors must determine the next course of action. Adjustments may include lowering the baseline minimum for performance standards, adjusting the strategies to elicit desired outcomes, or changing personnel.

Sports supervisors use data from performance appraisals and other reports to determine the consequential actions or activities that are likely to change misaligned behaviors or attitudes. Reports validate decisions for salary adjustments, counseling and coaching sessions, additional training, layoffs, dismissals, promotions, or recognition opportunities. Because human judgment is infallible and performance management is characteristic of open communication, it is important to include a grievance and appeals process to ensure distributive justice in fair and equitable treatment of employees, especially in the event of a dismissal.

Performance Appraisals

Performance appraisals, also referred to as employee evaluations, are integral to the performance management system. Differences exist in the style, content, frequency, duration, and structure of employee evaluations, but regardless of the variations, the task of appraising performance is still a primary responsibility of sports managers to ensure effective supervision. **Action Shot 10-2** provides examples of informal and formal means to administer a performance appraisal in an intercollegiate athletic setting. **Action Shot 10-3** and **Exhibits 10-1** and **10-2** provide realistic examples of appraisal forms used to assess performance.

PURPOSE

The performance appraisal serves many functions and is an integral tool in effective performance management systems. Some performance appraisals facilitate a comparison of actual behaviors to pre-established baseline standards. For the purpose of growth and development, managers and supervisors

▶ ACTION SHOT 10-2

Examples of Formal and Informal Staff Performance Appraisals

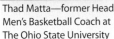

Thad Matta—former Head
Men's Basketball Coach at
The Ohio State University

Sometime during the last half of the academic calendar, the former commissioner for the Division II National Collegiate Athletic Association (NCAA) Great Lakes Intercollegiate Athletic Conference (GLIAC) in Midland, Michigan, carved out time to write an evaluation report on the performance of each of his four full-time staff members. The Ohio State University (OSU) Division I NCAA Athletic Department, with over 400 full-time employees, has a more formal review process.

In June of 2014, Gene Smith, vice president and director of athletics for OSU, signed a Coaching Staff Performance Review for former Head Basketball Men's Coach Thad Matta. The standard evaluation form acknowledges that *Full-time employees of the Department of Athletics must submit their parts of the evaluation to their manager by a date in May and the manager must meet to discuss the review before submitting the final evaluation to the Human Resource Office* (Smith, 2014).

generally use data from appraisals to determine what actions would assist in improving performance for the individual, the department, or the organization. Evaluating an employee's productivity and effectiveness is, therefore, the primary reason to conduct performance appraisals.

Information from an appraisal can be used to design strategies and training protocols to improve gaps in performance by focusing on deficient skills and/or behavioral areas. Comparing a series of evaluations for one employee can provide the worker and his or her supervisor with a gauge of the areas of growth and development over time. In addition to serving as a tool for improving communication, performance appraisals provide documentation to support reasons for dismissing an underperforming employee.

▶ ACTION SHOT 10-3

Performance Evaluations of High School Officials—State of Missouri

Registered officials seeking to work at a high school athletics contest must go through an appraisal process prior to being sanctioned by the state. The following excerpt presents a section of the Missouri State High School Activities Association (2017, p. 16) standards for official ratings based on the—2016-17 official handbook.

Standards for Officials Ratings

Scope: Baseball, basketball, football, soccer, softball, swimming, volleyball, and wrestling officials are rated by member schools for each senior high school regular season varsity game or match they officiate. Officials are not rated in the postseason. Officials are not rated in track, gymnastics, field hockey, and water polo.

Phases of Officiating Rankings

1. **Verbal Communication Skills:** Did the official show respect when communicating with coaches, players, scorers, etc.? Was the official able to get the message across without raising his/her voice?
2. **Appearance:** Physical appearance. Was uniform proper and neat? Was the official agile and athletic?
3. **Effort:** Ability to follow the play or match (hustle or effort exerted). When the tempo of play increased did the official exert extra effort to stay in position to observe the action?
4. **Control:** Ability to manage players and coaches. Did the official maintain control of the game or match? When the contest heated up was the official able to restore calm?
5. **Consistency:** Strictness and consistency in the official's decisions and rule interpretations. Were decisions influenced by spectators, players, or coaches or the game situation?
6. **Professionalism:** Manner in which decisions were made. Did the official demonstrate confidence in his/her decisions? Were the decisions made promptly and without undue emotion?

Rating Schemes

1. **State Caliber Official:** Capable of working postseason contests (Sectionals thru Finals).
2. **District Caliber Official:** Capable of working district contests but not beyond.

3. **Varsity Caliber Official:** Capable of working varsity contests but not ready for districts or beyond.
4. **Sub-Varsity Caliber Official:** Capable of working nonvarsity contests but not ready for varsity contests.
5. **Unsatisfactory Official:** Coach must include the reason for a 5 rating when submitting the ratings online on the Missouri High School Athletic Association (MSHSAA) website.

Quarterlies

The ratings are first calculated for individual officials. The upper quartile, median and lower quartile are calculated from the ratings for all officials for the particular sport involved. The upper quartile (the best ratings are the lowest ratings as 1 is the best rating and 5 is the worst rating) is the rating above which one-fourth of the officials and below which three-fourths of the officials rank; the median is the point above which one-half of the officials rank and below which one-half of the officials rank; the lower quartile is the rating below which one-fourth of the officials rank and above which three-fourths of the officials rank.

EXHIBIT 10-1: EMPLOYEE PERFORMANCE APPRAISAL—EXAMPLE 1

Performance Appraisal Form

This form is used to evaluate the performance of employees at COMPANY.
Period covered (month/day/year): from _____ to _____

_____	_____
Employee Name	Employee Number
_____	_____
Title	Department
_____	_____
Working title	Length of time in position
_____	_____
Supervisor	Date of evaluation

Performance Rating Scale

The overall performance rating is assigned to indicate the level at which the employee has performed during the appraisal period. Assign an overall performance rating, and then provide comments in support of the rating.

Rating	Performance Definitions
5	Exceptional—Performance at this level is in excess of established expectations. The employee consistently exceeds expectations in the outcomes achieved in work quality, quantity, and timeliness. The employee exhibits leadership among peers in all dimensions of the work performed.
4	Exceeds Expectations—Performance at this level often exceeds established expectations and standards of work quality, quantity, and timeliness. The employee exhibits mastery of most dimensions of the field of work performed.
3	Meets Expectations—Performance at this level meets established expectations and standards for work quality, quantity, and timeliness. The employee competently achieves the requirements of the position.
2	Needs Improvement—Performance at this level is below the level expected of an employee in the position. Improvement is required in significant dimensions of the job in order to meet the expectations and standards for work quality, quantity, and timeliness.
1	Unsatisfactory—Performance at this level is unacceptable. The employee often fails to achieve basic requirements of the position and has exhibited little or no improvement in job performance. The employee performing at this level should not be continued in this position; or where extenuating circumstances exist, the employee should be retained only upon significant improvements within a fixed period of time.

Indicate the rating next to the category of evaluation. Provide specific comments related to the category in the Comments section.

Rating	Category
	Job Knowledge—Understands the information and responsibilities pertinent to the job and demonstrates necessary expertise and knowledge of technology. Continues to learn, expand knowledge, and apply creativity to seek solutions. Comments: _____ _____ _____ _____
	Organizational Skills and Productivity—Plans and prioritizes work effectively. Coordinates, prepares, and presents projects well and follows through with assignments. Produces quality work and a satisfactory quantity of work. Delivers on time and within budget. Meets deadlines. Comments: _____ _____ _____ _____

	Communication Skills—Effective in communicating with others, including coworkers, superiors, and customers, using both verbal and written skills necessary for the job. Listens well. Articulates well. Comprehends and understands information and explanations. Keeps others informed. Shares information. Comments: _____ _____ _____ _____
	Interpersonal skills and professionalism—Cooperates with coworkers, team leader, and supervisor. Is a productive team member. Shows a high degree of professionalism in person, in e-mail, and on the telephone. Exhibits initiative and self-direction. Maintains a positive and respectful attitude. Shows enthusiasm about work. Accepts feedback well. Demonstrates loyalty and commitment. Comments: _____ _____ _____ _____
	Problem Solving and Decision Making—Anticipates and identifies problems. Uses logic and sound judgment to solve problems and make decisions. Comments: _____ _____ _____ _____
	Management and Leadership Skills—Employee's work and behavior exhibit commitment to the COMPANY's mission, vision, and goals. Comments: _____ _____ _____ _____

Employee Signature _____   Date _____

*Employee signature indicates that employee has read and discussed this performance appraisal with employee's supervisor. It does not necessarily indicate agreement with any rating or statements contained herein.

Supervisor Signature _____   Date _____

EXHIBIT 10-2: EMPLOYEE PERFORMANCE APPRAISAL—EXAMPLE 2

This form is used to evaluate the performance of employees at COMPANY.

Period covered (month/day/year): from _____ to _____

_____   _____

Employee Name   Employee Number

_____   _____

Title   Department

_____   _____

Working title (optional)   Length of time in position

_____   _____

Supervisor   Date of evaluation

Supervisor   Date of Evaluation

_____

Performance Appraisal

- Use a current job description.
- Rate the person's level of performance, using the definitions that follow.
- Review with employee each performance factor used to evaluate his or her work performance.
- Give an overall rating in the space provided, using the definitions that follow as a guide.

Performance Rating Definitions

The following ratings must be used to ensure commonality of language and consistency on overall ratings:

Outstanding	Performance is consistently superior
Exceeds Expectations	Performance is routinely above job requirements
Meets Expectations	Performance is regularly competent and dependable
Below Expectations	Performance fails to meet job requirements on a frequent basis
Unsatisfactory	Performance is consistently unacceptable

Performance Factors/Rating:

Communication—Measures effectiveness in listening to others; expressing ideas, both orally and in writing; and providing relevant and timely information to management, coworkers, subordinates, and customers.	Outstanding	
	Exceeds Expectations	
	Meets Expectations	
	Below Expectations	
	Unsatisfactory	
	NA	
Decision Making/Problem Solving—Measures effectiveness in understanding problems and making timely, practical decisions.	Outstanding	
	Exceeds Expectations	
	Meets Expectations	
	Below Expectations	
	Unsatisfactory	
	NA	
Job Knowledge—Measures effectiveness in keeping knowledgeable of methods, techniques, and skills required in own job and related functions; remaining current on new developments affecting COMPANY and its work activities.	Outstanding	
	Exceeds Expectations	
	Meets Expectations	
	Below Expectations	
	Unsatisfactory	
	NA	
Customer Responsiveness—Measures responsiveness and courtesy in dealing with internal staff, external customers, and vendors; employee projects a courteous manner.	Outstanding	
	Exceeds Expectations	
	Meets Expectations	
	Below Expectations	
	Unsatisfactory	
	NA	

Employee strengths/accomplishments:

Performance areas needing improvement:

Employee comments:

Information from appraisals may be used to assist administrators in decisions on restructuring or reorganizing workflow among departments. Administrators commonly use information to facilitate decisions on salaries, promotions, demotions, transfers, or changes in job assignments. For example, all full-time personnel at New York University (NYU), including coaches and athletics staff, are hired on a probationary status. Depending on their status as an administrator or professional, a clerical or technical employee, or a service staff member, the probationary period ranges from 3 to 6 months (NYU Office of Human Resources, 2000). At the conclusion of the probationary period, a review of attendance, punctuality, work quality, and other areas is conducted by the supervisor to determine whether the hire qualifies to become a NYU regular employee.

Employee evaluations can also serve as a tool to protect an organization from unfounded charges of discrimination. Evaluations serve as evidence of providing an underperforming employee written notification regarding his or her deficiencies and the opportunity to make improvements. These actions associated with employee notification are known as due process. Having documented notes lessens the chance that a lawsuit will be filed for an illegal dismissal or lack of due process.

FREQUENCY

Part of the determination of the frequency of performance reviews is based on the purpose of employee evaluations. Formal appraisals may be tied to a fiscal cycle for facilitating promotion decisions and budget implications for employee compensation (although supervisors should be cautioned against tying performance appraisals to compensation due to legal concerns surrounding inconsistencies that may exist in administering appraisals). Most formal employee performance appraisals are administered on an annual basis; however, quarterly or 6-month intervals may be preferred, especially if for the purpose of employee development. Account executives for an MLB franchise, for example, may receive weekly or monthly feedback on whether they hit target goals for ticket sales but are also evaluated more thoroughly on their overall performance on a 90-day, 6-month, or annual basis.

CONTENTS

The contents of a performance appraisal should include specific criteria that align with the behaviors, skills, and competencies identified in a job description

(Cunningham & Dixon, 2003, p. 180). For example, assessing the employee's familiarity with effective exercise recommendations for toning the shoulders and biceps would be appropriate for a strength and conditioning coach but not for assessing the skills of the compliance coordinator. Measurable components or key performance indicators (KPIs) for specific criteria should also be included in a standard evaluation. Finally, performance appraisals should include a location to record comments by an evaluator and a signature (and date) line for the evaluator and the employee to acknowledge receipt and review actions.

In terms of behavioral characteristics that may be included in a performance appraisal, some may be universal for all employees in the organization (e.g., dependability or initiative), whereas others may be more specific to a department or division (e.g., familiarity with concussion protocol). Exhibits 10-1 and 10-2 provide examples of generic employee evaluation or appraisal forms. **Table 10-1** provides a competency list that could be included in a performance appraisal that assesses the effectiveness of sports coaches.

TABLE 10-1: Process- and Outcome-Related Behaviors of Coaches	
Dimension	**Example**
1. Team Product	Win–loss record; playoff opportunities
2. Personal Product	Winning an award; requested for a speaking engagement
3. Direct Task Behavior	Motivating others toward higher performance; recruiting quality athletes
4. Indirect Task Behavior	Scouting opponents; Community Service
5. Administrative Maintenance Behavior	Monitoring eligibility, budget management; adhering to rules
6. Public Relations Behavior	Conducting summer camps; involvement with professional associations

TABLE 10-2: Comparison of Competencies for The Ohio State University Coaches and Competencies Identified in Selected Research

Ohio State University Athletics	Cunningham and Dixon (2003)
1. Academic success of the program	Academic outcomes
2. Competitive success of the program	Athletic outcomes; recruit quality athletes
3. Commitment to compliance	Ethical behavior
4. Student-athlete welfare	Athlete satisfaction
5. Leadership	Ethical Behavior
6. Communication	Athletic outcomes
7. Budget management	Fiscal responsibility
8. Public Relations/donor relations	N/A

Based on previous research by MacLean and Chelladurai (1995) and MacLean and Zakrajsek (1996), Cunningham and Dixon (2003) developed a performance appraisal model for intercollegiate athletic coaches that identifies areas of performance outcomes and behaviors. **Table 10-2** compares the domains of the model by Cunningham and Dixon (2003) with current competencies identified on coach evaluation forms administered by The Ohio State University. The one omission in the Cunningham and Dixon (2003) model is in the area of public relations, which was rated the least important performance factor among coaches and administrators as reported by MacLean and Zakrajsek (1996).

METHODS

There is a wide variation of methods used to evaluate performance, just as there are many variances in contents. On one end of the spectrum, the owner of a local sporting goods store may use recall of general observations or critical incidents to informally evaluate the performance of his staff. A large sports manufacturing and distribution plant, on the other hand, may implement a more formal performance appraisal system that includes a standard company rating form completed by the employee, a supervisor, a peer, and a subordinate in addition to a review of customer satisfaction reports.

Some organizations may use 360-degree performance feedback to assess performance because it provides multiple data sets, but the time investment does not always make this approach feasible. 360-degree feedback includes multiple perspectives from the employer, the employee, and others knowledgeable about the employee's performance (e.g., peers and subordinates). In assessing the performance of a head sports coach, for example, the intercollegiate athletic director (AD) may interview student-athletes, require the head coach to complete a self-evaluation, and administer appraisal forms to assistant coaches.

Observation and Critical Incident Reports

Supervisors are trained to observe the performance of their staff on a continuous basis. When incidents occur outside what is perceived as a normal range of performance, the supervisor may choose to write a report to place in the employee file. For example, a fitness center manager may submit a **critical incident report** after learning that an aerobics instructor failed to report that a member participating in the class sustained an injury that required medical attention. Critical incident reports can also include examples of exemplary performance, such as a sports retail store clerk organizing a company team to participate in a walkathon fundraiser benefitting multiple sclerosis research.

Weighted Checklist

Weighted checklists, such as the example in **Table 10-3**, include a list of descriptive statements based on job performance (e.g., "works well with other departments"), each of which is marked by a score (e.g. 1–5) by the evaluator in terms of its application to the employee. Statements may have different weights assigned to distinguish the importance of a statement. For example, a higher weighted value would be given to an item assessing whether the employee routinely makes mistakes in calculating chemical levels for an aquatics facility, whereas a lower weight would be given to an item assessing whether the employee keeps a tidy workplace.

TABLE 10-3: Sample Weighted Checklist

Trait	Weight	Performance Scale Rating (1–5)
Emphasizes academic priorities to student-athletes.	2	____
Appears in postseason competition.	1.5	____
Demonstrates ethical conduct and compliance.	1.5	____
Works well with other coaches and office personnel.	0.5	____

Rating Scale: 1 = poor / 5= excellent

Graphic Rating Scale

A **graphic rating scale** lists specific traits of the employee relative to the job (e.g., dependability, achieving results, communication, and likability) followed by a range of performance standards represented by either a number and/or a qualitative appraisal term. Two examples of appraisal terms include whether the employee falls below, meets, or exceeds expectations (a 3-point scale) or whether performance is perceived as excellent, above average, average, below average, or poor (a 5-point rating scale). A description is occasionally provided to demonstrate conditions or standards for the employee to fall into a particular range for a trait. The description can be qualitative or quantitative. **Table 10-4** presents an example of a section of an item on a graphic rating scale for a qualitative assessment.

Behavioral Anchored Rating Scale

A **behavioral anchored rating scale** (BARS) is similar to a graphic rating scale in that it uses a quantitative rating assigned to narrative examples of good and poor performance. For each behavioral item, characteristic descriptions correlate with a rating scale (e.g., 1 = poor and 10 = exceptional). Evaluators identify a number that best represents the appraisal of the trait criteria exhibited by the employee. **Table 10-5** provides an example of a BARS that assesses the behaviors involved in maintaining recruiting logs.

TABLE 10-4: Graphic Rating Scale with Qualitative Performance Measures

	Excellent	Above Average	Average	Below Average	Poor
Maintaining Recruiting Logs	☐	☐	☐	☐	☐

TABLE 10-5: Sample Behavioral Anchored Rating Scale (BARS)

Trait	1	2	3	4
Maintaining recruiting logs	Employee doesn't maintain accurate records of dates and details for reporting monthly contacts with prospective student-athletes.	Employee maintains accurate dates and details and for reporting monthly contacts with prospective student-athletes, but reports are sloppy or unorganized.	Employee maintains accurate dates and details and for reporting monthly contacts with prospective student-athletes. Reports are relatively neat and organized.	Employee is highly organized in maintaining accurate dates and details for reporting monthly contacts with prospective student-athletes. Reports are extremely neat and organized.

Score _____

Administering Performance Appraisals

After a racetrack manager at a motorsports park reviews the employee evaluations for the safety crew, he or she follows up by either praising individuals on a job well done or providing constructive criticism for areas needing improvement. Sports supervisors, managers, and executives know the appraisal must be fair and impartial.

SUGGESTIONS FOR BEST PRACTICES

Best practices to ensure that the performance appraisal is properly completed include the following:

- Set aside time to thoroughly evaluate the employee. Avoid interruptions and distractions. This is an important tool, so make the appropriate time for it.
- Be consistent within the performance appraisal and between employees.
- Be honest. Don't gloss over problem areas, and don't understate excellent work.
- Focus feedback on behavior and performance.
- Provide specific examples of observed behavior that support your comments.
- Focus on the entire year of behaviors, not just recent events.

After completing a review of the performance appraisal, the supervisor should meet face to face with the employee to engage in dialogue regarding his or her assessment and any intended follow-up actions. Written comments should be documented on the appraisal form or in the employee file. Following the meeting, the employee and employer should both sign and date materials, which should be stored appropriately.

It is ideal for supervisors to provide feedback directly to employees on an ongoing basis rather than saving up to share information only during an official performance review. In other words, the performance appraisal should not have any surprises but should be a review of performance over a specified period of time.

PREVENTING ERRORS IN RATING

Regardless of the type of appraisal system used, supervisors involved in evaluating the requisite skills and behaviors of employees should be aware of potential rating errors. Although performance appraisals should be objective, there is a potential for intentional or unintentional subjective bias. Untrained supervisors may inadvertently distort information.

To minimize the chance of rating errors, it is important to train supervisors in the performance appraisal process and to have some type of checks-and-balance system to ensure evaluations are consistent across departments. For example, if the youth activities director for a municipal recreation department generally rates employees in his or her department low, whereas the membership director is especially lenient and gives staff high ratings, the result is inaccurate data that give an unfair advantage to staff members who were appraised by the lenient manager. Following are examples of common biases in appraisal systems:

- **Leniency Error:** Leniency is a common error in performance evaluations if a supervisor rates all employees generally high in each performance area. The director of community engagement for a pro team who consistently scores each staff member as a 9 or 10 on a 10-point rating scale is likely guilty of leniency error.
- **Central Tendency Error:** A common error in performance evaluations is to avoid rating anyone extremely low or extremely high in any category. The director of an indoor soccer facility evaluating club coaches demonstrates the central tendency rating error when he or she marks employees as average or slightly above average and excludes superior or poor performance rankings.
- **Halo Effect:** The halo effect occurs when the evaluator has a cognitive bias shaping his or her overall impression of an employee based on one particular positive characteristic that overshadows negative traits. A summer camp director who admires a counselor because he or she is the first to report to duty each morning demonstrates the halo effect if the director rates the counselor high in all evaluation categories, regardless of actual performance.
- **Horn Effect:** The horn effect is the opposite of the halo effect and occurs when a single negative characteristic overshadows an abundance of positive traits. The horn effect leads to an overall negative appraisal that may not necessarily be accurate. Similar to the example illustrating the halo effect, a summer camp director critical of a counselor who is the last to report to duty each day demonstrates the horn effect if he or she rates the counselor low on all or most performance criteria, regardless of actual behaviors.

- **Recency Error:** Recency error occurs when a supervisor evaluates someone based on the merits of his or her most recent performance without considering a complete profile. A lacrosse coach who just signed a blue-chip recruit from an out-of-state team a couple of weeks prior to his or her annual performance review may receive undeserved favorable evaluations due to the recent success.
- **First-Impression Bias:** First-impression bias occurs when an individual is judged favorably or unfavorably based on an initial impression only. A collegiate sports communication director demonstrate first-impression bias if his or her evaluation of a newly hired assistant marketing coordinator who interviewed extremely well focuses on the initial interaction at the expense of considering a complete performance profile.
- **Contrast Error:** Contrast error occurs when the evaluator bases an appraisal on a comparison of the employee's performance with the performance of an individual who has a similar position within the company rather than basing it on preset standards. A health club owner demonstrates contrast error if the criteria on the performance evaluation measuring whether employees exceed new-member sales goals are based on a direct comparison with the average sales of the club's veteran top performer as opposed to a set of pre-identified standards.

Recap

Motivational theories assist in understanding the intrinsic and extrinsic incentives that may influence performance and commitment levels in volunteers, part-time or temporary staff, and full-time employees in the sports industry. Maslow's hierarchy of needs theory addresses lower-order and higher-order needs that motivate an individual. McGregor's Theory X and Theory Y purport that managers adjust their leadership style based on the inherently lethargic and unhappy (Theory X) or self-motivated and determined (Theory Y) characteristics of employees. Finally, the expectancy theory of motivation emphasizes that successful performance is the result of a belief that increased effort with the correct incentives that have value to the worker will lead to desired results.

Although part of effective supervision is understanding the motivation, attitudes, and actions of subordinates, performance appraisals serve to assess and document the behavior, conduct, and requisite skills of an employee. Performance appraisals are the most significant aspect of a performance management system because employee evaluations provide data and information to measure outcomes. Effective staff supervision requires an appraisal of employee performance to assist in decisions for the betterment of the organization. There are numerous modes of evaluative worker assessments that provide supervisors with valuable information.

Performance management encompasses much more than simply administering and providing feedback on an annual employee evaluation. Performance management is viewed as a continual process of monitoring employee activities, providing feedback, and devising improvement programs if necessary. The primary ingredients in an effective performance management system include defining performance objectives, planning motivational strategies, executing performance enhancers, and monitoring and reporting results of the desired outcomes from workers and an organization. Organizations with effective performance management systems operate under a philosophy of open communication and continuous improvement for achieving the organizational goals.

🌐 GLOBAL SPOTLIGHT 10-1

Motivation of Professional Team Owners in North America and Europe

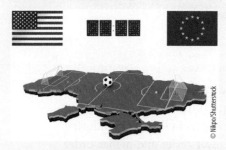
© Nikpo/Shutterstock

One of the functions and decisions of a team owner or manager is the hiring of on-field talent. Talent typically increases expenses for a club while also improving opportunities to win a greater number of games and potentially increasing season revenue. Owners motivated primarily by money sign players who will most likely maximize the difference between season revenues and season costs.

Professional sports team owners are among the richest individuals in the world. A popular debate in professional sports is whether maximizing profits or winning provides a greater motivation for the behavior and decisions of a team owner.

An economic-based theory suggests that an owner's primary objective is money and that North American professional sports owners behave as profit maximizers (Noll, 1974; Rottenberg, 1956; Vrooman, 1995). Conversely, it has been suggested that professional sports franchise owners in Europe are utility maximizers who focus on winning rather than monetary gains (Fort, 2000; Kesenne, 2008; Sloane, 1971).

When motivated primarily by winning, the behaviors of the owner focus on the recruiting efforts of their staff to acquire top coaches and talent, with little concern for the cost or length of an available contract. Conversely, owners motivated more so by profit margins supervise their staff in a manner that gives greater emphasis to business planning and short-term promotional activities to drive attendance and increase revenue streams. Actions, decisions, and behavior toward the staff are all influenced by the motivational priorities of the organization because motivation fuels effort, and performance is largely influenced by motivation.

DISCUSSION QUESTIONS

1. What types of motivational incentives would likely be most effective for improving the performance of entry-level staff versus managerial executives in a professional sports franchise?
2. Provide examples of types of intrinsic and extrinsic rewards to motivate volunteers working at a World Championship in track and field.
3. Discuss the difference in objective criteria and subjective performance measures in a rating scale for assessing the competencies of a summer camp sports counselor.
4. What are important considerations for and elements of designing an effective performance appraisal system?

APPLIED ACTIVITIES

1. Design a performance management system for a residential summer sports camp, and include an employee appraisal form.
2. Read the Global Spotlight on the motivation of professional team owners in North America and Europe. Next, research the *Forbes* lists of the world's most valuable soccer teams and National Football League (NFL) teams. Finally, conduct additional research on the differences between professional sports in North America and Europe, and prepare a response to whether you agree with the statement that team owners are motivated by different objectives in the two continents.

CASE STUDY

Employee Motivation and Performance Management at Holloway Sportswear

Self-motivated individuals typically exhibit intrinsic characteristics such as ambition, initiative, and determination, but motivation from a supervisor can produce even higher levels of performance, regardless of whether an individual possesses these desired traits. Organizational success is partially fueled by supervisors who keep their employees engaged and motivated. Holloway Sportswear, Inc., is an example of a company that invests time, money, and energy into performance management techniques designed to provide substantial dividends in terms of increased employee productivity and overall business profitability.

Background

Founded in 1946, Holloway Sportswear, Inc., has approximately 220 employees who design and sell high-quality active wear. Headquartered in

Shelby County, Ohio, near Dayton, the company is most renowned for pioneering the varsity letterman jacket, which has sustained a domestic market position in the United States as one of the most profitable product lines.

Holloway apparel items are primarily sold to sporting goods and team uniform dealers, promotional products distributors, and college bookstores. In addition, the company has a direct-to-consumer online e-commerce website. The overarching goal for Holloway Sportswear is to provide premium apparel at a reasonable value. Strategies to accomplish this goal include a commitment to investing in people, processes, and innovation; abstaining from commercial and celebrity athlete endorsements that would increase prices; and a relentless focus on reaching the company's full potential (Holloway Sportswear, 2016).

At the helm of Holloway Sportswear is President Mark Vonderhuevel, hired in 1994 as controller before being promoted to treasurer and executive vice president. In 2006, Vonderhuevel facilitated acquisition by Augusta Sportswear, a corporation also owning sports brands High Five and Jones & Mitchell. The director of human resources for Holloway Sportswear indicates employees genuinely adore Vonderhuevel as a down-to-earth leader who speaks from the heart (J. Manning, personal communication, February 4, 2016).

A Culture of Customer Service

Holloway Sportswear professes the importance of maintaining a reputation as an industry leader in customer service. Among the company's core values are excellent products, top quality and consistency, professional customer service, and reliability. In advertising vacancies for the company, Holloway Sportswear (2016) publicizes a statement describing the people, products, and culture of the company as "accessible, resourceful, informative, and vibrant." Addressing the necessity of ensuring employees perform to their role expectations for following the core values relative to exceptional customer service, Holloway's president explains,

> Our success is built on executing each transaction with our customers/consumers in a way that allows their experience to exceed their expectations every time. Breakdowns in any function of an organization, whether dealing directly with our customer/consumers or not, can result in a poor experience. Therefore, it is critical that each person understand their role and objectives and how their performance is measured against those standards. (M. Vonderhuevel, personal communication, January 18, 2016)

Performance Management at Holloway Sports

Holloway Sportswear's performance management system includes multiple components designed to assess and shape employee behaviors to align with the company's objectives. Approximately 1 months after an employee is initially hired, supervisors conduct one-on-one counseling sessions to informally review performance and discuss improvement and strengths. Employees are more formally evaluated on an annual basis, and a standardized reporting system using an Excel spreadsheet permits multiple supervisors to grade workers on a series of skills and behavioral attributes. The report card is used to facilitate compensation decisions. In terms of performance management, Vonderhuevel explains,

> When our managers conduct performance counseling for one of their employees, the goal is to provide specific feedback to the employee on both positive behavior

as well as areas that need improvement to meet the personal/professional objectives for that employee. The objectives are built around an alignment with the overall objectives of the organization and part of the process is to reinforce the role each person plays in the overall success of the company. We try to simplify our corporate mission to an easy to understand/remember concept of service with the standard that we are all here to make good things happen for other people. This fosters a sense of responsibility not just to our customers/consumers but to each other and the broader community in general. We encourage service and participation in charitable organizations/efforts within the community. We solicit feedback from our customers and share that across the organization. We provide monthly feedback on company results and conduct annual state of the company meetings to foster open communication about overall performance. (M. Vonderhuevel, personal communication, January 18, 2016)

In addition to informal initial counseling sessions, formal employee evaluations, and the annual report card system, Holloway incorporates motivational programs and tools to keep employees engaged and to build on the company's corporate culture that emphasizes a crucial link between service and performance. Several years ago, the company began administering the Emotional Intelligence (EI) Inventory to all employees, and the results are now used for both personal and professional development. Booklets, presentations, videos, posters, signs, cards, and other tools are incorporated from InspireYourPeople.com, a company in Richmond, Virginia, specializing in employee motivational training for corporations and schools. Common

InspireYourPeople.com (2016) programs used for employee training at Holloway include the following:

- 212—The Extra Degree: This is based on the premise that the 1-degree-difference between 211 and 212 is enough to change hot water to producing steam powerful enough to run a locomotive. Similarly, employees can be taught to embrace the value of how even the smallest amount of extra effort, care, and attention can produce enormous results.
- SMOVE (Smile and Move): This emphasizes strategies that inspire the self and others to exhibit service-oriented behaviors by embracing a positive attitude at all times and taking action.
- Crossing the Line: This addresses an organizational and individual commitment to making deliberate choices that go beyond mediocrity in actions and activities.
- Love Your People: This encourages employees to exhibit kindness and accountability toward each other and the people they serve on behalf of the organization.

After becoming inspired by one of the SMOVE motivational programs, Vonderhuevel trademarked the Holloway SMUNCH. Once a month, the president hosts a nonworking luncheon by invitation only for 10 to 12 hourly employees who are provided with an informal opportunity to engage with members of the senior management team. It's a relatively inexpensive way to facilitate an open-door policy at all levels while fostering socialization and communication. Quantitative assessment metrics, an entrepreneurial spirit, and a compassionate leader all factor into the image of Holloway Sportswear as a frontrunner in the industry for model employee behavior and performance.

CASE STUDY QUESTIONS

1. How is the performance management system at Holloway Sportswear linked to compensation?

2. What type of items likely appear on an employee's grade report?

3. According to Mark Vonderhuevel, what is the goal of the performance counseling sessions?

4. Of the InspireYourPeople.com programs identified, which would be favored as potentially having the biggest impact on employee performance? Why?

5. Why is it important for Holloway Sportswear to be considered a frontrunner in the industry for model employee behavior and performance?

REFERENCES

Cunningham, G. B., & Dixon, M. (2003). New perspectives concerning performance appraisals of intercollegiate coaches. *National Association for Physical Education in Higher Education: Quest, 55,* 177–192.

Cunningham, G. B., & Mahoney, K. (2004). Self-efficacy of part-time employees in university athletics: The influence of organizational commitment, valence of training, and training motivation. *Journal of Sport Management, 18*(1), 59–73.

Fort, R. (2000, September). European and North American sport differences. *Scottish Journal of Political Economy, 47*(4), 431–455.

Green, B., & Chalip, L. (1998). Sport volunteers: Research agenda and application. *Sport Marketing Quarterly,* 7(2), 14–23.

Holloway Sportswear. (2016). *Jobs.* Retrieved from https://holloway.recruiterbox.com/

InspireYourPeople.com. (2016). *Inspiring presentations.* Retrieved from http://www.inspireyourpeople.com/category/presentations/

Kesenne, S. (2008). *The economic theory of professional team sports: An Analytical treatment.* Cheltenham, United Kingdom: Edward Elgar Publishers.

MacLean, J. C., & Chelladurai, P. (1995). Dimensions of coaching performance: Development of a scale. *Journal of Sport Management, 9,* 194–207.

MacLean, J., & Zakrajsek, D. (1996). Factors considered important for evaluating Canadian university athletic coaches. *Journal of Sport Management, 10*(4), 446–462.

Maslow, A. (1943). A theory of human motivation. *Psychological Review, 50,* 370–396.

McGregor, D. (1960). *The human side of enterprise.* New York, NY: McGraw-Hill.

Missouri State High School Activities Association. (2017). —*2016-17 Official handbook of the Missouri State High School Activities Association.* Retrieved from https://www.mshsaa.org/resources/pdf/1617OfficialsManual.pdf

Mondy, R. (2008). *Human resource management* (10th ed.). Upper Saddle River, NJ: Pearson/Prentice Hall.

New York University Office of Human Resources. (2000, April 1). *Policy: Probationary period.* Retrieved from http://www.nyu.edu/about/policies-guidelines-compliance /policies-and-guidelines/probationary-period.html

Noll, R. (1974). *Government and the sport business.* Washington, DC: Brookings Institution.

Rottenberg, S. (1956). The baseball players' labor market. *Journal of Political Economy, 64*(3), 242–258.

Sloane, P. (1971, June). The economics of professional football: The football club as a utility maximizer. *Scottish Journal of Political Economy, 17,* 121–145.

Smith, E. (2014, June 3). The Ohio State University Department of Athletics Coaching Staff Performance Review. Retrieved from https://www.scribd.com /document/243276463/Thad-Matta-job-review

Sochi 2014 Organizing Committee. (2013, December 5). *Sochi 2014 volunteer team is prepared for the games.* Retrieved from http://vol.sochi2014.com/en /news/11/11201/

Vroom, V. (1964). *Work and motivation.* New York, NY: Wiley.

Vrooman, J. (1995). A general theory of professional sports leagues. *Southern Economic Journal, 61*(4), 971–990.

Windhorst, B. (2010, July 10). Inside "the decision": Miami's coup was a "surprise" built on long-coveted goal of James, Wade and Bosh. *The Plain Dealer.* Retrieved from http://www.cleveland.com/cavs/index.ssf/2010/07/inside_the _decision_miamis_cou.html

Time Out

PERFORMANCE COUNSELING AND CONFLICT RESOLUTION IN SPORTS ORGANIZATIONS

Each case of performance counseling is different and unique. If a coach, player, or regular office employee in the National Football League (NFL) needs assistance working through personal or professional challenges, we want to ensure everyone has the opportunity to receive independent assistance without being judged.

Troy Vincent
Executive Vice President of Football Operations
National Football League

LEARNING OUTCOMES

1. Provide an example of counterproductive behavior in a sports setting for each of the four workplace deviance classifications.

2. Apply conflict resolution techniques for scenarios in a sports setting.

3. Identify the purpose of the beginning, middle, and end phases of a performance counseling session.

4. Understand the concept of progressive discipline and apply characteristics of the red-hot stove principle.

5. Identify tips for terminating an employee.

KEY TERMS

Accommodation

Aggressive personality

Avoidance

Collaboration

Competition

Compromise

Conflict

Counterproductive behavior

Discipline

Due process

Dysfunctional conflict

Employment at will

Functional conflict

Indecisive personality

Inverted U theory of performance

Narcissistic personality

Passive personality

Performance counseling

Performance-improvement plan

Personal aggression

Phases of performance counseling meeting

Political deviance

Production deviance

Progressive discipline

Property deviance

Red-hot stove principles

Termination

Thomas–Kilmann model

Workplace deviance

Lead-Off

The sports industry includes organizations generally described as "fun" places to work, which has the potential of positively influencing the attitudes and behaviors of personnel employed by fitness centers, health clubs, sailing and yacht clubs, workout gyms, stadiums, arenas, ball fields, golf courses, aquatic centers, university athletic departments, or other sports companies, associations, and agencies. Despite the overabundance of employees with positive attitudes in the workplace, there are plenty who demonstrate differing degrees of counterproductive behavior. Performance management can be a challenge for staff supervisors dealing with difficult personalities or deviant behavior.

During his active period as a pitcher for the Major League Baseball (MLB) Atlanta Braves, John Rocker was suspended for 73 days and fined $20,000 by then-commissioner Bud Selig for making disparaging public comments about a teammate during a *Sports Illustrated* interview (Kurlantzik, 2001). Although Rocker appealed the commissioner's decision based on his

Turner Field was the home of former Atlanta Braves pitcher John Rocker whose outspoken nature caused numerous public controversies.

© claudio zaccherini/Shutterstock

constitutional rights of guaranteed free speech, the former reliever was still disciplined and required to participate in sensitivity training.

There are countless examples throughout all sectors of sports businesses where someone in a supervisory role must address behavior issues. Understanding general information about employee behavior and strategies to deal with counterproductive behavior is an expectation of supervisors in their role as disturbance handlers. **Action Shot 11-1**, however, addresses the challenges in disciplinary actions for behaviors that are unpopular or undesirable, but not necessarily in violation of organizational policy.

▶ ACTION SHOT 11-1

National Anthem Protests Challenge Athletics Administrators

In 2016, Colin Kaepernick, a back-up quarterback with the National Football League (NFL) San Francisco 49ers, set off a wave of silent protests coinciding with the playing of the U.S. national anthem before sport contests. Athletic administrators at all levels have been put in positions to decide how to address similar behavior in consideration of individual rights afforded by the U.S. Constitution and violations of organizational rules and regulations for appropriate conduct expectations.

Fans raise fists in a silent protest during the national anthem while wearing San Francisco 49er no. 7 jerseys representing Colin Kaepernick.

© Henryk Sadura/Shutterstock

Kaepernick's intention to sit, then kneel during the national anthem was to protest police brutality and racial injustice in similar fashion to the raised "black-gloved" fists of American's Tommy Green and John Carlos during the gold medal ceremony at the 1968 Olympics in Mexico City (Kane & Tiell, 2017, p. 7). Several teammates joined Kaepernick's 2016 season of silent protesting in addition to players from NFL teams around the league (Cacciola, 2017). Within several months, similar protests were reported at 52 high schools, 39 colleges, 1 middle school, and 2 youth teams in 35 states and 3 countries overseas (Gibbs and Khan, 2016). Players from at least three teams in the WNBA, a gold medal swimmer competing in Brazil, and USA soccer player Megan Rapinoe all followed suit with a form of silent protest during the national anthem.

Kaepernick's actions ignited a national debate over constitutional rights and the power of sports as a public forum while challenging athletic administrators who decide the fate of copy-cat behavior. Although there are special rules as to when someone is protected by the Constitutional 1st amendment, the employer, in this case, the NFL, would have needed regulations in place stipulating what an athlete could and could not do if there was a decision to punish players for kneeling, locking arms, raising fists, sitting, or turning their back during the national anthem. The Collective Bargaining Agreement for the NFL (2011, p. 204) addresses "conduct detrimental to the integrity of, or public confidence in, the game of professional football," but does not include any specific language prohibiting non-violent protests such as those exhibited by players during the 2016 season.

The National Basketball Association (NBA), however, is a different story. The *Official Rules of the National Basketball Association 2015–2016* (2015, p. 61) includes a clause stipulating "Players, coaches and trainers are to stand and line up in a dignified posture along the sidelines or on the foul line during the playing of the National Anthem." In 1996, the NBA exercised this clause when they suspended former Denver Nugget's player Mahmoud Abdul-Rauf for not standing in a dignified fashion during the national anthem (Koenig, 1998). Thus, while NBA players can be vocal in their agreement with the actions of Kaepernick and others who express themselves in a gesture of silent protest (e.g., locked arms or raised fists), it would be a violation of the league's policies to engage in similar behavior during the anthem.

With knowledge that administrators in public institutions cannot withhold privileges afforded by the U.S. Constitution, high school and college athletic directors may be subject to legal repercussions for punishing an athlete who sits or kneels during the pledge of allegiance or national anthem. Private institutions may invoke more stringent conduct requirements, but administrators at all levels must remain cognizant of individual rights and apply a prudent managerial approach to addressing behavior without a knee jerk reaction.

In the aftermath of the 2016 NFL season, Kaepernick, a free agent, pledged $1 million from his foundation to support services for the underprivileged. He also expressed his intentions to stand for the national anthem before future NFL games since he had satisfactorily raised awareness toward issues of oppression and injustices affecting minorities (Schefter, 2017).

Sports supervisors who are effective in their jobs are skilled in conflict resolution, performance counseling, and discipline administration. Effective supervisors use the results of employee evaluations to substantiate information that is helpful in determining strategies to address performance deficiencies. They also effectively deal with behaviors and actions that are not contributing to the mission of the organization.

This chapter addresses employee behavior, with an emphasis on counterproductive behaviors. This chapter also addresses conflict resolution and discipline in addition to performance counseling.

Employee Behavior
The behavior of an employee on the job and off the job can positively or negatively affect performance. Applying corrective action when a staff member

demonstrates negative attitudes or deviant/poor behavior on the job is the supervisor's duty; therefore, managers, head coaches, and directors are at an advantage if they understanding the types of positive and negative behaviors that can be encountered on the job.

Employee behavior is a function of how a worker interacts directly on the job with colleagues, supervisors, management, board members, customers, and/or clients. Attitude plays an important role in the behaviors demonstrated on the job, which can be segmented into those that either benefit or potentially harm an organization (Sharma & Thakur, 2016). For example, a recreation desk attendant satisfied in his or her role is likely to be outwardly friendly to clients, whereas a second employee who is seemingly dissatisfied with his or her role may avoid eye contact with members. It is important for a supervisor to pay attention to subtle cues to determine if there is a minor problem that needs to be addressed or whether these actions are actually signs of a bigger problem.

Positive attitudes toward the job and the workplace are more likely to occur in an organization that strives to create a supportive work environment, fosters open communication, and builds on a culture of mutual respect and teamwork. Examples of positive work-related behaviors include dependability, diplomacy, cooperativeness, professionalism, maturity, initiative, empathy, and respect. Acknowledging positive attitudes and creating a positive culture leads to an increase in employee satisfaction, which results in increased productivity (Susanty & Miradipta, 2013; Williams & Shiaw, 1999).

On the other hand, negative or counterproductive work-related behaviors such as aggressiveness, favoritism, indecisiveness, arrogance, and rudeness typically lead to deficiencies in productivity. The antecedents of job dissatisfaction (e.g., personality conflicts, work–life integration issues, demands of the job) affect the level of satisfaction in the workplace (Baker, 2011). Changes in an organization, for example, can be a huge factor in explaining a negative attitude and consequential counterproductive behavior such as absenteeism. Supervisors who understand that a change in processes or procedures can possibly influence the attitudes of their staff will benefit from early detection. **Action Shot 11-2** illustrates how department supervisors for the National Basketball Association (NBA) Cleveland Cavaliers anticipated negative reactions to potential job eliminations in the ticket office when LeBron James was re-signed to the franchise. The example demonstrates how sports managers and supervisors perceptive to cues associated with undesirable attitudes have a greater likelihood of pinpointing and correcting behaviors potentially leading to dissatisfaction and loss of productivity.

🎬 ACTION SHOT 11-2

The LeBron Effect on Employees

When LeBron James was re-signed by the National Basketball Association (NBA) Cleveland Cavaliers before the 2014–2015 season, the organization took time to consider the impact on the season-ticket sales staff, who underwent drastic changes in their role assignments in a very short time. Employees were immediately apprehensive about their job security given the instant surge in season-ticket sales and the fact that all 41 home games were sell-outs long before the season kicked off. With less inventory to sell, there was less of a need for the large ticket sales staff employed by the Cavaliers.

The Cavaliers' response was to involve the staff in determining new role assignments to service other occupants of the Quicken Loans Arena, which include the Gladiators Arena Football team and the Lake Erie Monsters hockey team. By involving the staff in decisions regarding their future, management was able to influence the attitudes and behaviors of the former Cavaliers season-ticket sellers. The Cavaliers' management team assisted the staff in overcoming natural resistance to change by involving employees in decisions, keeping everyone well informed, and providing the time to adjust to and plan for change. Many of the former sales associates for the Cavaliers' organization were retained and given new roles in the organization. Thus, the *LeBron effect* refers to adjustments within the organization due to a major change.

COUNTERPRODUCTIVE BEHAVIOR

Organizations with supportive work environments and supportive supervisors who thoroughly screen candidates and validate behavioral traits through references are still at risk for employing workers who demonstrate disruptive or deviant work behaviors. The reality is that some individuals can easily conceal toxic or counterproductive personality traits from a superior or an interviewer. Regardless of the extensive efforts an organization may use to screen candidates, organizations remain susceptible to employing workers with undesirable behavioral tendencies. It has been suggested that when sports organizations enter the for-profit, entertainment industry, characterized by "assimilation of hypercompetitive values," there is a higher predisposition or inclination for employees to demonstrate unethical behavior (Kjeldsen, 1992; Malloy & Zakus, 1995). Sports managers and supervisors employed in sectors of the industry considered high-pressured jobs must be prepared to encounter subordinates exhibiting behaviors that deviate from the norm of ethical or moral conduct.

Counterproductive behaviors are activities that intentionally or unintentionally hinder the achievement of organizational goals. Examples include avoidance of responsibility, verbal aggression (rudeness), and violence toward others (Yanling, Erhua, Lirong, & Yang, 2014, p. 882). Common antecedents to counterproductive behavior include organizational constraints, organizational injustice, incivility, and interpersonal conflict (Chen & Spector, 1992; Hunter & Penney, 2014; Spector & Fox, 2002). Being aware of circumstances and the environmental conditions that potentially contribute to counterproductive behaviors may assist supervisors in determining the appropriate corrective actions.

TYPOLOGY OF WORKPLACE DEVIANCE

Deviant behavior cannot be attributed to personality alone. Organizational climate and culture play a role in employee behaviors. For example, if a fitness club director doesn't discipline a worker who routinely arrives late for his or her shifts, other employees may also begin arriving late or engaging in other deviant behaviors, such as stealing petty cash. Classifications of counterproductive behaviors can be attributed to difficult personalities, or they can be grounded in behavioral research, as in Robinson and Bennett's (1995) categorization of four types of **workplace deviance**: (1) production deviance, (2) property deviance, (3) political deviance, and (4) personal aggression.

Production Deviance
Production deviance includes activities that intentionally reduce the productivity or efficiency of an organization, such as leaving early, taking excessive breaks, wasting resources, or intentionally working slowly. It is relatively easy to imagine how a head coach would physically punish a student-athlete who demonstrates this type of behavior; however, if it were an assistant coach who demonstrated a lack of discipline, the employment relationship would dictate a different type of disciplinary action.

Political Deviance
Occasionally referred to as office politics, **political deviance** in the workplace involves the use of favoritism, inner circles, gossip, and fabrications of the truth to gain access and opportunity to influence decisions, with negative intentions. Office politics, if used for the right intentions, can lead to positive behaviors, as in the case of garnering financial support

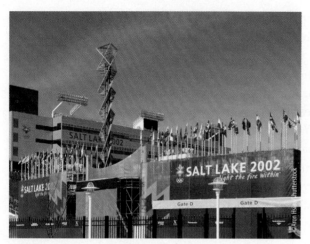

The Salt Lake City Olympics served as a backdrop for property deviance by overzealous executives of the Organizing Committee who committed bribery and fraud in an attempt to persuade IOC officials to select the site for the 2002 Winter Games.

for a new fan engagement project by forming a friendly coalition to influence management. If behavioral intentions are damaging, as exemplified by sabotaging a coworker's opportunity for a promotion for personal gain, such behavior is classified as deviant.

Property Deviance

Property deviance is demonstrated by employees who intentionally mislead others or damage the organization. An example of blatant property deviance includes the indictments against key executives of the Salt Lake City Olympic Organizing Committee for conspiracy to commit bribery, fraud, and racketeering in persuading members of the International Olympic Committee (IOC) to select the 1994 host city for the Winter Games (Longman, 2000).

Property deviance also can occur in less clear-cut situations. Debating why an executive for a national Olympic Committee would accept a bribe or why a person would act in a way that would damage the organization seems counterproductive to most. Sports supervisors must look beyond their own perspective and motivations and stay observant for behaviors that would be indicators of property deviance. For example, box office employees have access to cash and credit card information. It is important to conduct background checks for all employees, especially those who will have access to money and financial information. A background check still might not weed out someone who has yet to exhibit this type of behavior. A person who is struggling to make rent or is just too tempted by the large amount of cash available may breach the moral code of ethics by removing cash for personal gain.

Personal Aggression

Personal aggression includes verbal or physical acts against another person. The NFL suspended a Miami Dolphins player for harassing a teammate, which prompted an investigation into pervasive bullying (O'Mahoney, 2014). Antoine Vermette of the National Hockey League (NHL) Anaheim Ducks received an automatic 10-game suspension for attacking an official with his stick a month following a similar transgression by a player with the Arizona Coyotes (Traikos, 2017). In December 2012, Mike Rice, former men's basketball coach at Rutgers University, was fined $50,000 and suspended for three games after a video showed him "shoving and kicking players and pegging basketballs at players' heads" (Kussoy, 2013). Julie Hermann, the athletic director hired to "clean up" the image of the Rutger's program following the Rice incident, had been accused of calling her players "whores, alcoholics, and learning disabled" when serving as the head volleyball coach at the University of Tennessee (Red, 2013).

Personal aggression is often a motivational tactic used in the coaching profession.

There is a gray area in considering what constitutes a supervisor's assessment of acceptable and unacceptable aggression in the workplace (Farh & Chen, 2014; Ogunfowora, 2013). In the case of Hermann, Rice, Vermette, and the former Miami Dolphins player, behavior would be categorized as unacceptable. Similarly, a university athletic director who uses negative reinforcement (yelling, screaming, taunting, and threatening) to motivate his or her coaching staff to work harder in acquiring donations for the department's fundraising golf outing is also displaying a form of personal aggression considered unacceptable in the eyes of most administrators. Personal aggression toward a subordinate, peer, or supervisor is detrimental to achieving organizational goals and should be dealt with swiftly and decisively.

DIFFICULT PERSONALITIES

Sports supervisors are in a role where they must distinguish between whether an individual truly manifests a difficult personality that need to be contained or whether the employee simply does not get along well with others. Employees who exhibit negative behaviors are different from employees who don't mesh well with the department or group. Negative behaviors are apparent in employees who fail to act respectfully, work productively, or conform to socio-vocational expectations (Lee & Rosen, 1984).

To avoid potentially raising the level of conflict when dealing with a difficult employee, it is important for supervisors to refrain from an immediate response if strong emotion is present. It is also important for supervisors to use effective managerial skills to assess, document, and correct counterproductive behaviors to minimize dysfunctional conflict and remain on course for achieving performance expectations.

Four types of difficult personalities that can lead to counterproductive behavior in the workplace are narcissistic, passive, indecisive, and aggressive.

Narcissistic

Someone with a **narcissistic personality** displays excessive self-interest at the expense of others, lacks empathy, monopolizes conversation, requires excessive admiration, takes credit for all or most of the work, and is often described as egocentric (Mansi, 2009). An example of a narcissistic personality is an athletic director who, when meeting with the university president, takes credit for all aspects of the latest successful marketing initiative that generated a budget surplus of $15,000, when in reality, the associate athletic director of marketing created and led the implementation of the marketing initiative. LeBron James was labeled a narcissist by the NBA Cleveland Cavaliers' majority owner Dan Gilbert (2010) when the superstar left the organization to sign with the Miami Heat in 2010.

Supervisors should manage personal expectations directly and often privately. It is important to have established trust, authority, and respect for the individual. Narcissistic individuals can be difficult to manage, given their self-interest and large egos, but not impossible. Having direct conversations will improve the chances for changed behavior if the presence of authority exists, but it becomes more difficult if the narcissistic personality is in a leadership role as opposed to a subordinate role. If the supervisor is the narcissist, employees have to weigh the concerns over voicing displeasure with the narcissist's actions and inaction, which will likely lead to dissatisfaction in their job. It is important for the productivity of an entire staff or the organization to document the outcomes and behaviors of a narcissist and to be selective in addressing counterproductive issues with the support of or in the presence of a superior.

After beating cancer and raising awareness as well as millions of dollars to fight the disease, Lance Armstrong was stripped of seven Tour de France victories due to PED violations. Armstrong is noted for his arrogance and narcissism having blatantly and repeatedly lied about his involvement with doping.

Passive

The **passive personality** is exemplified by an employee who is not assertive, exhibits introverted behavior, doesn't speak up or contribute in group settings, won't defend his or her ideas, and typically takes things personally. Supervisors should be cognizant of staff members with introverted and passive tendencies. Engaging these individuals by directly calling on them to solicit feedback in a group setting or meeting personally behind closed doors to make the employee more comfortable are two techniques to potentially modify behavior. Supervisors should find ways to reward passive individuals when they share ideas to encourage future active involvement.

Indecisive

Individuals with an **indecisive personality** have difficulty making decisions. Indecisive employees can be the procrastinators who lack innovation or individuals considered too analytical. Although former MLB commissioner Bud Selig left a positive legacy following his reign, an arguably poor demonstration of indecisiveness led to declaring the 2002 All-Star Game a tie after 11 innings (Bodley, 2002). The following year, the collective bargaining agreement (CBA) established a rule declaring that the league winner of the All-Star Game would be granted home-field advantage during the World Series. That rule remained in effect until the 2016–2020 CBA reverted home-field advantage back to the pennant team with the best record (Stephen, 2016).

Indecisiveness can be a product of managers trying to please too many people in their decision making (staff, supervisors, clients). Indecisiveness may also be problematic in employees hired for their superior intellect or analytical expertise when problem solving becomes a seemingly never-ending quest to explore possibilities and alternatives as opposed to a conclusive solution. Employees who are afraid of the consequences of poor decisions are likely to be indecisive.

Supervisors should encourage indecisive employees to rationalize decisions by developing a chart of pros

An indecisive decision to declare the 2002 MLB All-Star Game a tie led to the ruling that home-field advantage for the World Series would be determined by the winner of the All-Star Game. The rule remained in effect for 14 years until a new MLB commissioner and new CBA in 2016 overturned the mandate.

©Eric Broder Van Dyke/Shutterstock

Coaches may demonstrate an aggressive personality, often as a result of being over-passionate about their role.

and cons or to rationalize objections to a decision with facts and justification. Allowing employees to make decisions and fail can promote an environment of innovation and engagement, but mistakes have consequences that may be detrimental to an organization. A sports marketing executive who makes a decision simply to overcome indecisiveness runs the risk of a costly mistake for a failed campaign. Sports supervisors with an indecisive staff member can rely on their own managerial effectiveness to create checks and balances for decisions.

Aggressive

Employees with an **aggressive personality** thrive on confrontation, blame others, use offensive body language, and can be described as argumentative, demanding, opinionated, defensive, critical, and/or condescending. This behavioral style is often apparent in coaches or referees who are overly passionate about their roles, such as Bobby Knight, Indiana University's former basketball coach, who had a lengthy history of physically and verbally abusing players, officials, and administrators (Kriegel, 2000).

Supervisors need to quickly step in and contain the situation, often moving the angry or confrontational employee into a private area and asking open-ended questions to learn the underlying catalyst for an outburst. Aggressive behavior is actually sought after in some positions. For example, executives and managers often look for team associates to be somewhat aggressive in the pursuit of ticket sales or in securing corporate partnership deals. Research has noted competencies deemed important for sales positions in sports include an adaptive approach and the ability to "close" (Pierce & Irwin, 2016). A passive approach is typically not conducive to closing a sale. This acceptable aggression is much different from behavior that needs adjustment.

Conflict

Sports organizations in every sector of the industry are susceptible to **conflict**, whether it is manifested as a dispute with a supplier, a disagreement between two executives deciding which department budget to use for expensing a recruiting trip, contentious infighting during collective bargaining negotiations, of a difference in opinion for the final candidate to assume a coaching vacancy. Effective staff supervision requires managers to recognize and address conflict when it is counterproductive for an organization.

FUNCTIONAL CONFLICT

Because some conflict may be considered beneficial for an organization, not all conflict needs to be resolved. A little conflict is welcomed to potentially improve performance when it serves as a catalyst for the scrutiny of important decisions; this is referred to as **functional conflict**. Playing the devil's advocate when evaluating an idea for a new halftime promotion at an NFL game may result in a respectful debate that considers the true feasibility and value or return on investment if implementing the new promotion. Positive conflict can minimize stagnation or groupthink or can strengthen the relationships of members who practice respect and tolerance. Collaborative conflict in an organization such as discussions regarding renovations to a weight-room facility or over draft picks is positively correlated with employee satisfaction (Choi, 2013). The positive side of conflict encourages open-mindedness, especially when engaging in a debate.

The inverted U theory of performance (see **Figure 11-1**) purported by Thomas (1979) explains the relationship of conflict and performance and suggests that a certain degree of conflict can improve performance, but as conflict intensifies, the more likely it is that performance will decrease. An example of the inverted U theory is illustrated in the case of a sports marketing firm in which associates politely disagree while brainstorming on the contents for a direct-mail campaign. Such disagreement may be highly productive in distinguishing the feasibility of implementing an idea until conflict escalates to the point of individuals disassociating or disengaging from the project. The conflict can potentially result in a lack of uniform consensus, delays in the process, and an overall decline in productivity.

CONFLICT RESOLUTION TECHNIQUES

Most conflict in organizations is considered **dysfunctional conflict**, especially when it interferes with the performance of an individual or impedes the organization in achieving goals and objectives. When dysfunctional behavioral conflict is apparent, supervisors must consider a resolution strategy

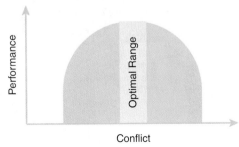

Figure 11-1 Inverted U Theory

that is best for the organization in minimizing a performance deficiency. Regardless of whether conflict is a result of personal differences, structural differences, or communication differences, the supervisor must manage the conflict by confronting employees when appropriate and resolving issues constructively. The dysfunctional or negative side of conflict is tension and poor performance.

The Thomas–Kilmann (1974) model for resolving conflict is a widely accepted managerial tool that advocates resolution though one of five techniques focusing on (1) competition, (2) collaboration, (3) avoidance, (4) accommodation, or (5) compromise. Each style provides a unique opportunity to effectively resolve conflict given the individuals involved and the context of the situation.

Competition

The use of **competition** for resolving conflict is applicable to situations where unpopular decisions need to be implemented, such as budget cuts in a university athletic department. A competitive style is also necessary to take immediate and decisive control of a situation, such as a fight that breaks out on a basketball court. The more severe the behavior of a subordinate, the more likely competitive techniques will be necessary.

Collaboration

Collaboration to resolve conflict works best when multiple perspectives are too important to be compromised, such as in the case of a task force comprised of National Collegiate Athletic Association (NCAA) conference commissioners and athletic trainers discussing concussion litigation and prevention protocol. Similarly, collaboration is a positive tool to build relationships by merging insights and is useful for developing staff cohesiveness.

Avoidance

Avoidance techniques treat conflict as a trivial issue and allow the individuals involved in a behavioral conflict time to rethink their viewpoints and possibly alter their perceptions. For example, an athletic director may walk away from two basketball coaches arguing over the color preferences for new lockers to purposefully institute a cooling-off period for the coaches to regain perspective.

A fight breaking out on a basketball court may necessitate officials or coaches using a competitive conflict resolution style to settle the dispute.

Accommodation

Accommodation techniques are useful when issues are more important to the other party and when allowing others to seemingly have their "way" is possible without damaging reputations. For instance, a ski instructor at a mountain resort may opt out of a special assignment to permit a fellow instructor the opportunity to take the assignment. This gesture is also a means to build social credits or to maintain harmony in a group. Accommodation may also be the only option in the face of being outmatched or in a losing battle, such as a case of the director of a municipal sports commission conceding a bid to host a championship event when a competitor is seemingly the front-runner.

Compromise

Compromise is used to settle conflict when goals are important but not worth the effort and time of further disruption. It is also used when the opposing side has a degree of power and is committed to mutually exclusive goals. Often, a neutral playing site for a championship contest is the compromise resolution when two team owners or coaches are otherwise arguing over being awarded home-field advantage. Compromise is often used when competition and collaboration are unsuccessful.

Performance Counseling

Following a review of an employee's evaluation or appraisal, supervisors can validate or justify a choice in rewarding positive behavior or punishing poor performance (Fitch, 2011). Punishment may extend to a dismissal or disciplinary measures. The alternative is an intercession or performance-enhancement initiative through counseling. Ideally, counseling is the best alternative in addressing a performance deficiency in lieu of disciplining or firing an employee (Lee & Rosen, 1984).

Performance counseling refers to the supportive activities by a manager or supervisor intended to improve an employee's productivity and effectiveness in the workplace. Counseling assists the employee in defining and working through barriers impacting the employee's job performance. In conducting performance-counseling sessions, supervisors must ensure confidentiality to minimize the risk of legal implications due to a breach of privacy (Lee & Rosen, 1984). In fact, the organization should create legitimate, enforceable expectations of confidentiality.

Whether detected in an annual evaluation or through simple, daily observation, lags in performance can usually be diagnosed and corrected. For example, a professional stadium employing a will-call ticket account agent who receives poor scores on sections of a performance evaluation related to technical knowledge or customer service skills may benefit from performance counseling as opposed to the company investing time and money to replace the worker. Effective performance counseling can be a more cost-effective and long-term solution for overcoming deficiencies.

Although performance evaluations may provide evidence that intermediary action is necessary, most supervisors initiate performance counseling on an ongoing basis as an opportunity or need arises. Effective supervisors in a continuous-improvement organization are trained to recognize and address deficiencies at the onset before they become more serious in nature and require more drastic measures.

PREPARING FOR A COUNSELING SESSION

Before conducting a performance-counseling session, the supervisor should adequately prepare for the meeting and consider the objectives for the opening, middle, and end phases. Obtaining information from performance appraisals is especially important to articulate specific behaviors and validate the reason why counseling is necessary. The supervisor should be versed on the employee's position description and responsibilities as well as the company's policies and procedures. He or she should collect and review evaluation forms, performance plans or instructional documents, e-mails, and any notes or reports pertaining to actual performance.

The recreation industry includes a fair number of young and inexperienced supervisors who may lack the confidence to effectively conduct a meeting on performance issues with their employees. Managers who are not comfortable may make mistakes and undermine the intentions of the session (Atwater, Waldman, Carey, & Cartier, 2001). Training and education are important in overcoming a reluctance to provide feedback and in developing the competencies to effectively navigate through the stages of a performance-counseling session. Counseling requires skill in diplomacy and interpersonal relations to elicit productive participation from the employee. There is a level of assuredness, empathy, and sensitivity necessary to adequately address the catalysts for productivity issues and the potential solutions.

Training can assist supervisors in developing the skills necessary to effectively provide performance feedback and to reinforce the need to establish a professional, nonjudgmental tone during the meeting. Feedback comments should focus on performance, not the individual. Feedback should also be descriptive, not judgmental. Softening the tone but not the message is a useful tactic to emphasize a distinction in what is said and how it is said. Remaining in control of emotions while also being prepared to diffuse any emotional flare-ups from the employee are important assets when conducting a counseling meeting. Engaging in role-play exercises, observing professionals engaged in performance-counseling or discipline sessions, and practicing scripted commentary in front of a mirror can assist supervisors in gaining the confidence to effectively provide feedback.

Logistically, the supervisor should schedule the date and time for the meeting in a private location and ensure the employee is provided adequate advanced notice. The employee should also be notified that the purpose of the session is for discussing performance.

Adequate preparation increases the likelihood that a performance-counseling meeting will end with the desired results. Success is largely contingent on a deliberate approach to progressing through each phase of a performance-counseling session. Strategically, the supervisor should consider the intentions and activities in the opening, middle, and summary phases of a privately scheduled meeting.

PHASES OF A PERFORMANCE COUNSELING MEETING

There are three **phases of a performance counseling session**, each having a distinct purpose. The first phase is the opening to set the tone and clarify the primary purpose; the middle phase addresses deficiencies and solution; and the summary phase ends the meeting, ideally with a mutual understanding of the follow-up actions necessary to improve performance. The underlying philosophy is that the session will elicit an improvement in employee performance as opposed to creating an irreconcilable situation that could lead to termination.

Opening Phase

The opening phase of a counseling session should specifically clarify that the purpose of the meeting is to improve performance in a particular deficiency area. At the onset, the supervisor should express a level of confidence in the employee and a sincere desire to work together for the purpose of improvement. Making the employee feel that he or she is an active participant sets a collaborative tone early and assists to de-escalate any possible confrontational behavior. Supervisors should direct employees who want to vent or address issues outside of the specific performance area to schedule a follow-up meeting with the appropriate supervisor.

Accompanying an explanation of the purpose of the meeting should be examples of deficient performance exemplified in either work samples, an annual review, customer-satisfaction reports, critical incident reports, e-mails, or other documentation. The opening phase should also articulate the impact of the problem on other employees or on the department and organization. For example, a team shop clerk at an NBA sports arena who routinely fails to digitally enter inventory logs before closing can simply be directed to start inputting handwritten data into a software program before leaving the building. However, convincing the clerk to be more diligent in his or her operational duties may be easier if an explanation is provided on the impact to the administrator who has to arrive early each morning to enter data so that daily reports for a tight-ship upper-management team won't arrive late.

Middle Phase

After setting the tone, clarifying the performance deficiency, and identifying the impact on coworkers or the organization in the beginning of the meeting, the middle phase of the counseling session should include greater dialogue between the supervisor and employee to identify potential causes and suggestions for solutions. The middle of the meeting should also articulate the organization's expectations for satisfying performance criteria in addition to the necessary changes needed to overcome a performance gap.

A great deal of active listening is beneficial during this middle stage. Poor performance may be a result of an employee not knowing what is expected, not knowing how to do a particular job, being unaware of how he or she is performing, having a poor working relationship with a coworker, or perceiving a lack of organizational support and assistance from the supervisor. A successful counseling session will pinpoint underlying reasons for poor performance and facilitate problem-solving efforts.

Open dialogue allows the meeting to become a problem-solving session and enables the supervisor to demonstrate a sense of judicial fairness in the process. For example, a meeting with a night clerk at an NBA team shop who consistently fails to meet the early morning deadline for inventory reports may generate several viable solutions, such as permission for the clerk to input data from home after hours or restructuring of the closing duties to allow a second employee to manually input data while the clerk concentrates on routine closing operations. Directing the clerk to initially provide his or her own suggestions for improving performance creates a feeling that the clerk is an active participant in the process, which also increases the likelihood of the employee's acceptance of the final decision in how the problem will be resolved.

The role of the supervisor is to act as an advisor, steers the conversation towards the best solution, and provides the support necessary for changes. Additional training or upper-management support may be necessary for implementing changes. The role of the supervisor is to assist in removing the barriers inhibiting performance so that work can be accomplished according to the prescribed standards.

Occasionally, a counseling session may reveal that substandard performance, such as excessive tardiness or evidence of a lack of customer-friendly behaviors, may stem from a personal issue, such as a relationship issue or substance-abuse problem. If health, psychological, or social issues are affecting work performance, employees should be referred to the organization's employee assistance program (EAP), which is the entity providing support services to assist employees in dealing with personal issues.

Summary Phase

The most important factor in a successful counseling session is for the subordinate to agree to the activities or actions determined to improve performance. The summary phase focuses on a **performance-improvement plan** (PIP) outlining the solutions to address the deficiencies as well as the next steps for reviewing and monitoring performance.

Once there is concurrence or agreement on the solution that will yield the necessary improvements, there should be two copies of written confirmation of the counseling session, with one copy provided to the employee and the second placed in his or her file (see **Box 11-1**).

BOX 11-1

Information to Include in Documentation to Confirm Performance-Counseling Session

- Identification of the performance area to be improved
- An explanation of and metrics for satisfactory performance standards
- A list of actions or activities to improve the performance
- Support and resources that will be provided to assist the employee in making improvements

- The consequences for failure to abide by the conditions of the PIP
- A plan for reviewing the employee's progress
- The date and the signatures of both the supervisor and employee

The meeting should end on a positive note, with the supervisor expressing confidence that the employee can make the necessary changes and highlighting the employee's areas of strengths. The summary phase should also include a scheduled follow-up meeting as a progress check for accountability.

When counseling employees, the sandwich approach is occasionally used. The sandwich approach provides positive feedback before and after identifying the specific performance deficiency. Advocates of the sandwich approach claim that an individual's self-esteem remains intact and that anxiety or discomfort is diminished if the accompanying praise is genuine and relevant. Ending on a "high" note can be perceived as instilling confidence in future performance. The criticism of the sandwich approach, however, is that it does little to increase the negative consequences of the performance deficiency which is "buried" between praise (Bergen, Bressler, & Campbell, 2014, p. 4). Positive comments can devalue the negative feedback and may send a conflicting message as to the primary purpose of the supervisor's communication efforts. Athletic administrators and managers who use the sandwich approach must ensure the summary phase includes the other aforementioned criteria to ensure the counseling session will be effective.

Technology may be incorporated during employee counseling sessions. An athletic director, for example, may use video monitoring as evidence based support of disruptive coaching behaviors (e.g., throwing clipboards or kicking chairs). **Action Shot 11-3** depicts the use of a sophisticated video system in MLB used during routine performance counseling sessions between supervisors and umpires.

Discipline

Discipline may be a consequence of performance counseling, or it may be administered in lieu of counseling. Discipline refers to the actions intended to enforce compliance or obedience and as a measure to modify behavior or manage performance. Willful violations of NCAA, conference, or institutional rules by a collegiate coach or athletics staff, for example, typically results in immediate disciplinary action or termination, depending on the severity.

Discipline procedures vary from organization to organization. Some organizations use a **progressive discipline** system where, depending on the type of disciplinary action, employees go through a progression of discipline before termination is considered. Often, the first instance of employee discipline results in a verbal warning, the second instance results in a written warning, a third instance results in a suspension from work, and a fourth instance results

▶ ACTION SHOT 11-3

Performance Counseling for Sports Officials

Sports officials may seem immune to criticism, but the reality is that performance counseling incorporating negative feedback is essential for improving their style, mechanics, judgment, and knowledge of the game. Conferences and associations impose rules and regulations requiring evaluations of officials to continue in their profession. Establishing degrees of standards and continual performance monitoring assists in improving the quality of officials and referees

Sports officials must be consistent, fair, honest, decisive, and approachable. They must display good game-management skills, work well with their partners or crew members, present a favorable appearance, react appropriately under pressure, and interact appropriately with coaches and players. Counseling is necessary when officials experience difficulty in their behaviors or actions that impede desired performance. However, due to the nature of officiating, counseling is routinely administered not only as a means to improve mechanics or knowledge of the game but also to address how to advance in the ranks of officiating.

One technique in performance counseling of Major League Baseball (MLB) umpires is the use of a video tool invented by Fox TV that incorporates five cameras to show where pitches were relative to the strike zone within four-tenths of an inch (Sabini, 2002). The QuesTec video system provides documentation of consistency in calling strikes and can be used in a counseling session as evidence of a particular deficiency area (e.g., inconsistency may be pinpointed to primarily high or inside pitches).

Ralph Nelson, a former vice president of umpiring who resigned in 2013, signed a multiyear deal with QuesTec for the use of the system in a majority of MLB ballparks. Nelson incorporated an independent team of 12 evaluators to collect and assess data on umpire performance via in-person sessions or using video. A separate team of six evaluators collecting the same information was assigned to counsel umpires on their performance. Crew chiefs were directed to address issues relative to demeanor and behaviors, but the two-tier evaluator system was used to counsel umpires on primary performance areas such as strike-zone consistency (Sabini, 2002).

in termination. Other organizations simply have a disciplinary action process that is dependent on the type of corrective action needed. The underlying premise is to impose a disciplinary system that is impartial, with sanctions based on "commonly accepted standards of justice and fair play" (Kravit, 1986).

It is important for organizations to have clearly written employee handbooks that outline guidelines, expectations, and potential consequences. Federal laws, state laws, contract law, the doctrine of employment at will, and the company philosophy all come into play with how an organization handles employee discipline, including due process. Regardless of the type of discipline, it is very important to document the disciplinary action in the employee's personnel file.

There are several key elements to include in a disciplinary action form, including contact information, a detailed description of the employee action or behavior and (if applicable) the reference to a policy code, the type of discipline imposed, and appropriate signatures (see **Exhibit 11-1**). A disclaimer statement should note that the employee's signature attests to him or her receiving the information and does not definitively indicate agreement with the disciplinary action.

It is a prudent managerial practice to instill a progressive discipline system whereby penalties become more severe for repeat offenses. Employee manuals provide the guidelines for defining the areas of behavioral expectations and resulting progressive disciplinary actions for failing to comply with rules and regulations. These guidelines extend to professional players in sports leagues as well. The MLB and NFL, for example, are grappling with establishing fair and consistent disciplinary sanctions for off-field behavior, such as sexual misconduct and abuse. Progressive discipline is also a customary practice throughout the sports world in addressing doping violations. Sanctions may range from short-term suspensions to lifetime bans, as was the case in the decision handed down in 2016 to Valentin Balakhnichev, former president of the All-Russia Athletic Association, for involvement in doping violations of track and field athletes (Strout, 2016).

The seriousness of the offense as a major or minor infraction, the duration, and the frequency of the problem all affect the type of discipline sanctions imposed. For example, the Manitoba Ringette Association (2016, p. 41-42) in Canada, which governs the city's youth hockey leagues, identifies disciplinary measures for minor and major infractions, which are distinguished by whether failing to achieve expected standards of conduct brings harm to others or to the organization. The sanctions range from a verbal or written apology to expulsion and suspension of funding. Other considerations for selecting the appropriate disciplinary sanction for differing situations in the sports industry include the work history of the employee, the degree or disregard of warnings for possible action against a violation, the implications for other employees, and any extenuating circumstances.

EXHIBIT 11-1: DISCIPLINARY ACTION FORM

Employee Name:
Department:
Supervisor:

Disciplinary Action

Date of Incident:

Description of Violation:

Disciplinary Action Taken

_____ Verbal Warning   _____ Suspension

_____ Written Warning   _____ Termination

_____ Other (please describe): _____

Details of Incident:

_____

_____

_____

_____

_____

Action Taken by: _____   Title: _____

Supervisor Signature: _____   Date: _____

Other Signature: _____   Date: _____

The COMPANY is an at-will employer. This disciplinary action is *not* part of a progressive discipline system, and warnings and discipline are not required prior to termination.

Employee Signature: _____   Date: _____

Typically, the first-case or less severe disciplinary violations result in an informal conversation or an oral or written warning documented and placed in a personnel file for a short duration. Written reprimands placed in a permanent file, suspension, and termination are more severe discipline measures used by supervisors.

CHARACTERISTICS OF EFFECTIVE DISCIPLINE

When disciplining employees, supervisors and organizations may consider applying McGregor's (1960) **red-hot stove principles**, which emphasizes impartiality, immediacy, advanced warning, and consistency.

Impartiality

In terms of impartiality, supervisors should treat everyone the same when disciplining someone for a rule violation, just as a hot stove doesn't discriminate who will be burned. Impartiality requires supervisors to focus on the act or behavior and not the individual. For example, whether providing a verbal warning or levying a small fine, the director of athletics should be impartial in the discipline measures for the first time or repeated time a coach fails to submit recruiting logs by the deadline.

Immediacy

Immediacy suggests that discipline should be administered within a reasonable time frame after a violation, just as a hot stove imparts an immediate sensation when touched. The discipline for failure to submit recruiting logs on time, for example, should be within 48 hours of the deadline and not delayed.

Advanced Warning

Advanced warning implies that employees should have an indication of what constitutes disciplinary action, just as a hot stove provides advanced warning of a hot sensation as a hand moves closer to the actual surface. Employee handbooks, guides, or manuals are the blueprints or the "advanced-warning" documents that address discipline procedures for employees who violate a policy or procedure. Ideally, employees sign a form documenting the review and receipt of company policies or the employee handbook. Coaches should be provided with written confirmation of the deadline to submit recruiting logs each month (e.g., by the 15th of the month, the first Friday, etc.).

Consistency

Consistency refers to the replication of discipline for each and every violation, just as a hot stove is consistent in burning someone every time it is touched. Similar to the characteristic of impartiality, the first violation of each coach who fails to submit a recruiting log by the deadline should be disciplined.

Terminating Employees

The most severe discipline measure is **termination**, which is one of the most unpleasant activities of a supervisor. Even more unpleasant is an allegation of wrongful termination, as in the case of a former San Diego State University basketball coach awarded over $3 million in a whistleblower lawsuit (Ziegler, 2016).

Former Penn State University football coach Joe Paterno was a beloved figure in the sports world, but was ultimately fired during a painstaking sex scandal involving former assistant coach Jerry Sandusky. Paterno died a few months following his dismissal.

Termination is the final step in progressive discipline actions whereby the employee–employer relationship is ended. In order to refrain from violating organizational policy or state and federal laws when terminating an employee for disciplinary reasons, supervisors should be sensitive in handling situations, seek advisement, and consider whether legal statutes such as employment at will and due process will apply.

Supervisors must be also be aware of disgruntled employees who may retaliate with violence after being terminated. A former gym instructor dismissed from the Equinox Fitness Center in Coral Gables, Florida opened fire in the facility killing the club manager and wounding another employee before committing suicide with a self-inflicted gunshot (Reynolds, 2017). While not all circumstances can be predicted or prevented, managers must remain alert to the possibility of workplace violence. Understanding employment at will and due process while adhering to a protocol when terminating an employee are logical managerial practices that may minimize erratic behavior by a disgruntled worker.

Employment at will means that the employee can be terminated by the organization for any reason (other than an illegal reason), without cause (National Conference of State Legislators, 2015). Regardless of whether an employment agreement (employment contract) is in place, employees are employed "at will" in most states. Documentation is important to verify the

Former legendary basketball coach Jerry "the Shark" Tarkanian was allegedly denied due process upon being dismissed by UNLV.

reasons for termination in the event the employee decides to pursue grievance procedures through a union, court of law, or governing body.

Due process is the legal obligation of a government organization to inform contracted employees of impending termination and to provide the opportunity for corrective action. One of the most prolific due process legal cases in the sports industry involved the violation of constitutional rights in the suspension and forced resignation of Jerry "the Shark" Tarkanian. The late Tarkanian, former head basketball coach, initially sued the University of Nevada Las Vegas (UNLV) and then the NCAA when, due to multiple rule violations, he was suspended in the mid-seventies (Otto & Stippich, 2008). Multiple lawsuits at the state and Supreme Court level ensued whereby challenges for failure to provide due process was the central theme, especially after Tarkanian was forced to eventually resign from UNLV. It was determined that no dissatisfaction with his performance had prompted the termination (*NCAA v. Tarkanian,* 1988). Tarkanian eventually dropped two law suits against UNLV after agreeing to a settlement. Tarkanian also settled with the NCAA who conceded $2.5 million in lieu of a trial after 25 years of litigation (Sandomir, 1998).

It is advisable for supervisors to provide documentation of following organizational policies for disciplinary action or for engaging in alternate dispute resolution (mediation and counseling). Documentation of this nature is a means to demonstrate due process is afforded to employees prior to termination. The case for terminating an employee for poor performance should clearly reflect due process was provided in communicating the standards applied to determine the level of performance improvement. Supervisors should follow general protocol when terminating an employee to assist in ensuring legal compliance and to remain fair and judicial in handling termination cases (see **Box 11-2**).

Terminations are never easy. According to a review of the legal ramifications when terminating an at-will employee, any given termination is likely to be challenging because "each side presents its own potentially unique permutations of conclusions and positions" (Zins, 2012, p. 296).

BOX 11-2

General Protocol for Termination of an Employee

1. Have a documented, legal reason to terminate an employee.
2. Consult with an attorney or someone with employment law knowledge prior to addressing the employee.
3. Terminate in person.
4. Provide evidence of the reason for the termination.
5. Treat the employee with dignity and respect.
6. Anticipate reactions to the termination.
7. Ensure the employee returns keys or other company property.
8. Communicate with other employees accordingly.

From the case of the disgruntled fitness center employee in Coral Springs who murdered his former manager to the case of the former UNLV coach who claimed a lack of due process when he was forced to resign, the litany of ramifications after a termination can challenge organizations. A prudent managerial approach when dealing with terminations assists supervisors to anticipate and minimize acts of retaliation but does not keep an organization entirely immune from potential vengeance.

The employment relationship often starts off with high expectations from both sides that the employment relationship will work well. Unfortunately, that isn't always the case. Poor behavior, negative attitudes, underperforming employees, violation of employee handbook guidelines, and various other reasons can lead to the employment relationship needing to be terminated.

Regardless of the reason for termination, it is important that supervisors treat the employee with respect and courtesy, which lessens the possibility of violent outbursts. Anticipating negative emotions toward the supervisor and organization is common; however, it is not appropriate to make the employee feel good or positive about the situation (Zins, 2012).

If an employer has engaged with the employee in a supportive manner, provided clear rules for employment, and provided performance counseling, the termination should not be a surprise situation and should be able to be handled in a mature, professional, respectful manner.

Recap

Effective supervisors understand the impact difficult personalities and counterproductive behaviors can have on an organization. A typology of workplace deviance includes production deviance, property deviance, political deviance, and personal aggression. Several common types of difficult personalities in the workplace includes narcissistic, passive, indecisive, and aggressive. There are numerous examples of these types of personalities in sports settings.

Effective supervisors also understand the impact of both the functional and dysfunctional sides of conflict as well as different methods to resolve conflict. When resolving conflict, knowledge of the individuals involved and the context or history of the situation facilitates a decision regarding whether to settle disputes through competition, compromise, collaboration, avoidance, or accommodation.

Performance counseling to address deficiencies is an alternative to discipline and is often used throughout the sports industry, especially for umpires, referees, and officials. It is essential to carefully plan the conversation before conducting a counseling session and to collect artifacts for evidence of performance. The opening phase of the counseling meeting sets the tone and identifies specific deficiencies. The middle phase is a two-way dialogue addressing antecedents and possible solutions. The summary phase indicates the conditions of a PIP as well as the next steps in monitoring production and behaviors.

Finally, discipline is common in organizations and is addressed in employee manuals or guides. Effective discipline adheres to the red-hot stove principles of providing advanced warning and remaining impartial, consistent, and immediate in delivering punitive action. The severest form of discipline is termination.

GLOBAL SPOTLIGHT 11-1

Personality of English Soccer Coach Leads to Dismissal

Italian-born soccer player Paolo Di Canio played in over 500 professional games and scored over 100 goals before starting his career as a manager in 2011 for Swindon Town Football Club in England. He grew up in a working-class district of Rome during World War II and used soccer to fuel aggression at an early age. Di Canio was appointed to coach the Premier League Sunderland Association Football Club (AFC) in the United Kingdom, but he was dismissed after 13 games for behavioral issues involving harsh treatment of players (Hardy, 2013).

Di Canio, a self-proclaimed fascist with a portrait of Mussolini tattooed on his back, was described by his former squad as exhibiting irrational behavior, and he had no qualms about making disparaging remarks about his players in public or levying fines for misconduct. A former teammate shared that Di Canio, "can't handle people, and he can't handle different personalities, and in the world of football, you're doomed if you can't do that" (Yourke, 2014). The disgraced manager admits he prefers confrontation and has been cited for his use of a campaign of fear to motivate performance.

Prior to the dismissal, the club's chief executive officer (CEO) intervened to address the coach's confrontational style of management.

The Sunderland CEO's attempt at performance counseling failed, and the manager was released.

Di Canio has yet to manage another club since being fired by Sunderland in 2013. In January 2017, it was reported that the media company Sky Sports Italia had hired Di Canio back as an analyst after parting ways in September of 2016 amidst viewer complaints of arm tattoos "seemingly" representing tributes to Adolf Hitler and Benito Mussolini (Tuckey, 2017).

DISCUSSION QUESTIONS

1. Identify two counterproductive behaviors of employees, and explain the strategies to effectively manage each type of behavior.
2. What is the most important step in a performance-counseling session? Why?
3. Assuming you are the direct supervisor for the individuals described in the following scenarios, identify which conflict resolution techniques you would select and why.
   a. Two employees in the marketing department of a Minor League Hockey front office disagree on the target market and timing for a direct-mail campaign.
   b. Two employees in a small-town fitness facility are debating on who should clean the bathrooms at the end of the following shift.
   c. A maintenance attendant at the stadium where you are employed explains that he overheard another employee mention that your newly hired merchandise inventory clerk has a registered weapon in her locker.

APPLIED ACTIVITIES

DEAL WITH IT: For each of the following scenarios, prepare a script of what you would say to your employee and the actions you believe are necessary to modify his or her behavior.
   a. The digital communications coordinator at the arena is angry because he was excluded from a department meeting held to evaluate

new vendor proposals. This employee was invited to the meeting, but he could not attend due to a personal scheduling conflict. He is very angry, and in front of everyone, he says the following to you, the supervisor: "The purpose of the meeting was to make a decision as a team. How can we do that when all of us were not present? The meeting should have been rescheduled for a later time when the entire department could attend."

b. You are a new parks and recreation manager for a medium-size market community who inherited an entire team of 12 individuals whom you did not hire. There is one person who won't speak up at your weekly staff meetings, and when you ask him for ideas, he consistently says, "I will get back to you on that. I need time to process." The problem is, he never gets back to you! You are becoming increasingly frustrated with his inability to communicate and feel it is time to respond differently to his "processing" statement.

c. Kris, the quality control director in your department, supplies you with information on a monthly basis so that you can prepare a product development status report. Kris is very pleasant and extremely helpful. Over the last few months, you have had to remind her to e-mail the report information, which she typically sends at the 11th hour. This peer apologizes profusely for consistently being late and blames the tardiness on having too much on her plate. Kris's last email said, "I am running behind with your report. Please bear with me another day or two because I am totally slammed at work. I've been here almost every night until 9:00 p.m." Her e-mail is aggravating because it means you will be unable to meet the deadline for submitting the report.

CASE STUDY

Alcoholism as a Disability Challenges Supervisory Discipline in Sports Arena

Nick Saban, head football coach of the University of Alabama, hired Steve Sarkisian as an assistant for the 2016 season. Sarkisian, was fresh off of being terminated from his position as head football coach at the University of Southern California (USC) due to a series of alcohol-related incidents. In February 2017, after one game as the Offensive Coordinator for the University of Alabama, Sarkisian left to become a coordinator for the National Football League (NFL) Atlanta Falcons, who just finished their season as the Super Bowl runner up to the New England Patriots (Moriarty, Kirk, and Godfrey, 2017).

When terminated by USC, the institution had followed protocol for progressive discipline and

©bleakstar/shutterstock

University of Alabama Coach Nick Saban was questioned for hiring an assistant coach who was terminated from a previous post after a series of alcohol related incidents.

While newly employed as the Offensive Co-ordinator with the NFL Falcons in 2017, Sarkisian reportedly remains in treatment to battle alcoholism (McClure, 2017).

According to the state of California's Fair Employment and Housing Act (FEHA), alcoholism can be defined as a disability if it limits an individual's major life activities, such as work (Wilson, 2016). The penalties for alcohol and substance abuse are inconsistent because sanctions are the privy of an organization (i.e., workplace policies), and circumstances widely vary as to the context of violations while on work time or personal time.

Larry Eustachy, men's basketball coach at Colorado State University as of 2017, admitted he was a functioning alcoholic when he was fired from Iowa State University (Hochman, 2016). Pictures had surfaced of Eustachy partying with underclassmen. Former Oklahoma basketball coach Eddie Sutton resigned as head coach of Oklahoma State following a car crash in which he was cited for driving under the influence of alcohol (Weiss, 2006). The former coach admitted to treatment for alcoholism at the Betty Ford Center several years before his initial hire. After his resignation and a second treatment program for alcoholism, the university provided him a contract to engage in fundraising and speaking engagements on substance abuse (Baldwin, 2006).

adhered to principles of due process. Sarkisian received an initial verbal reprimand from his immediate supervisor after appearing intoxicated at a booster event. He was also provided a written disciplinary notice that he would be terminated if there were a repeat incident and was afforded assistance by the university to modify his behavior. After two more alleged incidents with alcohol while on the job, the coach was placed on a leave of absence and then terminated (Heaton, 2015). Shortly thereafter, Sarkisian retaliated by filing a multibillion-dollar wrongful-termination lawsuit against USC for failure to accommodate a disability described as "alcohol dependency" (Wolf, 2015). The case went to binding arbitration in early 2016, without further disclosure.

CASE STUDY QUESTIONS

1. What progressive disciplinary procedures were afforded to Sarkisian after he violated alcohol policies while at USC?

2. Who should prevail in the arbitration case? Why?

3. Can an employee be terminated for alcoholism if alcoholism is classified as a disability? Why or why not?

4. Are there ethical ramifications for Coach Saban at the University of Alabama in hiring Sarkisian?

REFERENCES

Atwater, L., Waldman, D., Carey, J., & Cartier, P. (2001). Recipient and observer reactions to discipline: Are managers experiencing wishful thinking? *Journal of Organizational Behavior, 22*(3), 249–270.

Baker, K. (2011). Antecedents and consequences of job satisfaction: Testing a comprehensive model using integrated methodology. *Journal of Applied Business Research, 20*(3), 31–43.

Bergen, C., Bressler, M., & Campbell, K. (2014, September). The sandwich feedback method: Not very tasty. *Journal of Behavioral Studies in Business, 7,* 1–13.

Bodley, H. (2002, July 11). No tying in baseball. *USA Today,* 1C.

Cacciola, S. (2016, September 27). To kneel or not to kneel. Team protocol comes into play. The New York Times. B-11.

Chen, P. Y., & Spector, P. E. (1992). Relationships of work stressors with aggression, withdrawal, theft and substance use: An exploratory study. *Journal of Occupational and Organizational Psychology, 65,* 177–184.

Choi, Y. (2013, April 1). The influence of conflict management culture on job satisfaction. *Social Behavior and Personality, 41*(4), 687–692.

Farh, C. I. C., & Chen, Z. (2014). Beyond the individual victim: Multilevel consequences of abusive supervision in teams. *Journal of Applied Psychology, 99,* 1074–1095.

Fitch, B. (2011, March 1). The two roles of supervision in performance counseling. *FBI Law Enforcement Bulletin,* 10–15.

Gibbs and Khan (2017, November 3). Tracking the Kaepernick Effect: The anthem protests are spreading. Think Progress. Retrieved from https://thinkprogress .org/national-anthem-sports-protest-tracker-kaepernick-284ff1d1ab3e

Gilbert, D. (2010, July 9). Cavaliers owner mad as hell. *The New York Post*, Late City Final, 103.

Hardy, M. (2013, September 24). *Paolo Di Canio was fired by Sunderland for 'systematic destruction' of his players.* Independent. Retrieved from http://www.independent .co.uk/sport/football/premier-league/paolo-di-canio-was-fired-by-sunderland -for-systematic-destruction-of-his-players-8835606.html

Heaton, S. (2015, August 25). USC's Steve Sarkisian not the first coach to be disgraced by the bottle. *Claremore Daily Progress Oklahoma*, Sports.

Hochman, B. (2016, October 20). Larry Eustachy, CSU Rams basketball coach, past addiction, problems. *Denver Post*. Retrieved from http://www.denverpost .com/2012/11/10/larry-eustachy-csu-rams-basketball-coach-past-addiction-problems/

Hunter, E., & Penney, L. (2014, May 1). The waiter spit in my soup! Antecedents of customer directed counterproductive behaviors. *Human Performance, 27,* 262–281.

Kane, D., & Tiell, B. (2017). Application of normative and virtue ethics to explain Colin Kaepernick's silent protest in the NFL. Manuscript submitted for publication.

Kjeldsen, E. (1992, May 1). The manager's role in the development and maintenance of ethical behavior in sport organizations. *Journal of Sport Management, 6,* 99–113.

Koenig, K. B. (1998). Mahmoud Abdul-Rauf's suspension for refusing to stand for the national anthem: A "free throw" for the NBA and Denver Nuggets, or a "slam dunk" violation of Abdul-Rauf's Title VII rights? *Washington University Law Quarterly*, 377–405.

Kussoy, H. (2013, April 3). WILD RICE video reveals crazed Rutgers coach abusing players. New York Post Late City Final, p. 72.

Kravit, S. (1986, December 1). The role of counseling in the discipline process. *The Arbitration Journal, 41*(4), 60–62.

Kriegel, M. (2000, March 17). The choke's on Knight, NCAA. *New York Daily News,* 94.

Kurlantzik (2001, April 1). John Rocker and employee discipline for speech. *Marquette Sports Law Review,* 185.

Lee, S., & Rosen, E. (1984, January 1). Employee counseling sessions. Ethical dilemmas. *Personnel and Guidance Journal,* 276–279.

Longman, J. (2000, July 21). Leaders of Salt Lake Olympic bid are indicted in bribery scandal. *New York Times.* Retrieved from http://www.nytimes.com/2000/07/21/sports/olympics-leaders-of-salt-lake-olympic-bid-are-indicted-in-bribery-scandal.html

Malloy, D., & Zakus, D. (1995). Ethical decision making in sport administration: A theoretical inquiry into substance and form. *Journal of Sport Management, 9,* 36–48.

Manitoba Ringette Association. (2016). *Section 10: Discipline and complaints policy. Constitution and Bylaws and Operating Policy, 2015–2016.* Retrieved from http://ringettemanitoba.ca/wp-content/uploads/2016/08/224131-846565.manual.pdf

Mansi, A. (2009, December). Coaching the narcissist. How difficult can it be? Challenges for coaching psychologists. Paper presented at the first European Coaching Psychology Conference. *The Coaching Psychologist, 5*(1), 22–25.

McClure, C. (2017, February 9). *Steve Sarkisian grateful for opportunity with Falcons.* ESPN. Retrieved from http://www.espn.com/nfl/story/_/id/18654561/new-atlanta-falcons-oc-steve-sarkisian-treatment-alcoholism-thankful-opportunity

McGregor, D. (1960). The Human Side of Enterprise. McGraw Hill.

Moriarty, M., Kirk, JU., and Godfrey, S. (2017, February 17). *Sarkisian leaving Alabama for Falcons amid disagreement with Nick Saban.* SBNation. Retrieved from http://www.sbnation.com/nfl/2017/2/7/14533830/steve-sarkisian-atlanta-falcons-alabama-offensive-coordinator

National Conference of State Legislators. (2015). *The at-will presumptions and exceptions to the rule.* Retrieved from http://www.ncsl.org/research/labor-and-employment/at-will-employment-overview.aspx

The National Basketball Association. (2015). Player/team conduct and dress. Official rules of the National Basketball Association 2015-2016. Retrieved from https://turnernbahangtime.files.wordpress.com/2015/11/official-nba-rule-book-2015-16.pdf

National Football League. (2011, August 4). League Discipline. Collective Bargaining Agreement (2011-2020). Retrieved from https://nfllabor.files.wordpress.com/2010/01/collective-bargaining-agreement-2011-2020.pdf

NCAA v. Tarkanian, 499 U.S. 179 (1988).

Ogunfowora, B. (2013). When the abuse is unevenly distributed: The effects of abusive supervision variability on work attitudes and behaviors. *Journal of Organizational Behavior, 34,* 1105–1123.

O'Mahoney, C. (2014, September 1). Calling an audible: Time to change the NFL locker room policy. *Texas Review of Entertainment and Sport Law, 16*(1), 71–86.

Otto, K., & Stippich, K. (2008, June 1). Revisiting Tarkanian: The entwinement and Interdependence of the NCAA and state universities and colleges 20 years later. Journal of Legal Aspects in Sport, 18, 2. 243–308,

Pierce, D., & Irwin, R. (2016, June 1). Competency assessment for entry level sport ticket-sales professionals. *Journal of Applied Sport Management, 8*(2), 54–75.

Red, C. (2013, May 29). Wrong Knight move AD's woes no surprise to courtroom foe. *New York Daily News.* p. 58.

Reynolds, S. (2017, April 8). *Official: Ex-gym employee shoots 2 in Florida, kills self.* ABC News. Retrieved from http://abcnews.go.com/US/wireStory/person-dead-shooting-mall-south-florida-46675698

Robinson, S., & Bennett, R. (1995). A typology of deviant workplace behaviors: A multidimensional scaling study. *Academy of Management Journal, 38*(2), 555–572.

Sabini, D. (2002). Special report: Evaluating officiating performance. *National Association of Sports Officials.* Retrieved from http://www.ofoa.ca/SpecReptEval.pdf

Sandomir, R. (1998, April 3). Maverick coach wins battle and collects from NCAA. *The New York Times.* A-1.

Schefter, (2017). Colin Kaepernick to stand during national anthem next year. ESPN. Retrieved from http://www.espn.com/nfl/story/_/id/18805744/colin-kaepernick-stand-national-anthem-next-season

Sharma, A., & Thakur, K. (2016, January 1). Counterproductive work behaviour: The role of psychological contract violation. *International Journal of Interdisciplinary Approach and Studies, 3*(1), 13–27.

Spector, P. E., & Fox, S. (2002). An emotion centered model of voluntary work behavior: Some parallels between counterproductive work behavior and organizational citizenship behavior. *Human Resource Management Review, 12,* 269–292.

Stephen, E. (2016, December 2). World Series home-field advantage no longer determined by All-Star Game. *MLB News.* Retrieved from http://www.sbnation.com/2016/12/1/13804504/mlb-all-star-game-world-series-home-field-advantage-cba

Strout, E. (2016, January 7). IAAF hands lifetime bans to officials involved in Russian doping scandal. *Runners World.* Retrieved from http://www.runnersworld.com/performance-enhancing-drugs/iaaf-hands-lifetime-bans-to-officials-involved-in-russian-doping-scandal

Susanty, A., & Miradipta, R. (2013, June 1). Employee's job performance: The effect of attitude toward works, organizational commitment, and job satisfaction. *Journal Teznik Industry, 15*(1), 13–24.

Thomas, K. (1979). Organizational conflict. In S. Kerr (Ed.), *Organizational behavior* (pp. 151–181). Columbus, OH: Grid Publications.

Thomas, K., & Kilmann, R. (1974). *The Thomas–Kilmann conflict mode instrument.* Mountain View, CA: CPP, Inc.

Traikos, M. (2017, February 16). Just out of line; Vermette slashing official comes at 'crazy' time: Fraser. Toronto Sun. S10.

Tuckey, I. (2017, January 16). *Can I do better this time? Paolo Di Canio: West Ham legend returns to Sky Sport Italia after controversy over 'fascist' tattoo*. Retrieved from https://www.thesun.co.uk/sport/football/2620628/paolo-di-canio-west -ham-legend-returns-to-sky-sport-italia-after-controversy-over-fascist-tattoo/

Weiss, D (2006, February 18). Sutton charged, then snubbed. New York Daily Post. Sports. 68.

Williams, S., & Shiaw, W. (1999). Mood and organizational citizenship behavior. The effect of positive affect on employee organizational citizenship behavior intentions. *Journal of Psychology, 133*(6), 656–669.

Wilson, T. (2016, January). Alcoholism and disability discrimination: Lessons from the USC coach. *Employment Law Commentary, 28,* 1.

Wolf, S. (2015, December 14). Sarkisian sues USC over termination; former coach blames Haden for wrongful firing as he sought rehab. *Redlands Daily Facts*, B9.

Yanling, Y., Erhua, Z., Lirong, L., & Yang, J. (2014, July 1). The influence of work-place ostracism on counterproductive work behavior: The mediating effect of self-control. *Social Behavior and Personality: International Journal, 42*(6), 881–890.

Yourke, D. (2014, January 28). *Not in a million years! Hutchison says Di Canio will never manage again after blasting 'rotten' Sunderland players*. Retrieved from http://www.dailymail.co.uk/sport/football/article-2547547/Not-million-years -Don-Hutchison-says-Paolo-Di-Canio-never-manage-again.html

Ziegler, M. (2016, September 28). Beth Burns wins wrongful termination lawsuit vs. SDSU. *San-Diego Union Tribune*, Sports. Retrieved from http://www .sandiegouniontribune.com/sports/aztecs/sd-sp-burnsverdict-20160928-story.html

Zins, D. (2012, March 1). Managing the exit: Negotiating an employment termination. *Harvard Negotiation Law Review, 17*, 289–310.

Post-Game Extras
PREPARATION NEVER CEASES

Preface
Never Stop Learning

The mantra "Never Stop Learning" encourages managers and supervisors to continuously search for and review data and information on employment issues and trends affecting the sports industry and their organizations. For example, labor statistics may assist professionals to anticipate growing or shrinking employment markets. According to the U.S. Department of Labor (2015a), an estimated 14,800 new vacancies are anticipated through 2024 for sports coaches and scouts. Similarly, 23,400 openings for aerobics instructors or fitness trainers and 38,900 vacancies for recreation workers are anticipated throughout the same period to meet industry demands (U.S. Department of Labor, 2015b). These positions represent only a fraction of sports-related occupations that the Bureau of Labor Statistics projects will require additional workers in the future. The projected increase is attributed primarily to increases in high school enrollment, expansion of sports programs as a recruitment tool in colleges, and a general growing interest in collegiate and professional sports.

An analysis of trends in the sports marketplace provides insight for managers and supervisors regarding potential implications for talent sourcing in light of socio-environmental changes in the industry. Noting that revenues from media rights are increasing annually at a much faster rate than gate receipts, for example, provides cautionary signs to consider the changing nature of workforce competencies in sports sectors devoted to the production and delivery of games and entertainment. The compound annual growth of media rights in the sports industry at 8.1% in 2012 outpaced gate receipts, which declined by 1.8%, even though more revenue ($15,825 billion vs. $11,619 billion) was derived through ticket sales (PricewaterhouseCoopers, 2016, p. 3). Revenues from media rights are projected to rise above ticket sales for the first time in 2019 and will continue to outpace and outearn gate receipts.

These changing economic drivers in the sports marketplace will affect talent divisions and the way human resource professionals in certain sports organizations decide to allocate resources for recruiting and training personnel. Trends in tech-savvy audiences choosing to experience sports in nontraditional ways will continue to shift labor priorities for sports organizations. There is a greater demand for procuring tech-savvy sports management professionals who can deliver content through a vast array of emerging technologies in order to satisfy consumer needs.

Managers in the sports industry must continually assess market and industry trends as well as their strategic human resource priorities to sustain operational effectiveness. Staying abreast of employment trends and issues and potential implications for their organizations assists sports managers and supervisors in effectively executing their roles.

Phase IV delivers in providing information on the trends and issues that shape managerial practices and decisions related to human resource functions in sports organizations. The final section addresses an array of workplace topics that illustrate the somewhat unique nature of the industry as a fast-paced, demanding field.

Chapter 12 addresses diversity and inclusion in sports organizations, as well as strategic initiatives to increase diversity and to facilitate a climate and culture considered accepting of inclusivity. The chapter also offers a unique view of the challenges of a transgender strength and conditioning coach in a National Collegiate Athletic Association (NCAA) Division II athletic department and the fall-out from the North Carolina "Bathroom Bill" which resulted in the National Basketball Association (NBA) moving the location of the 2017 All-Star Game and the NCAA changing locations for seven championship events.

Chapter 13 addresses a hodgepodge of workplace issues in sports organizations, from work–life balance and burnout, to ethical conduct. The chapter overviews bullying and sexual harassment, both of which have drawn considerable attention in sports occupations. The case study highlights an example of ideal ethical behavior exemplified by the executive director of the National Association of Collegiate Directors of Athletics (NACDA) as well as examples of questionable ethical conduct demonstrated in the Penn State University football sexual abuse scandal and corruption associated with the International Federation of Association Football (FIFA).

Chapter 14 addresses occupational trends in the industry, with a focus on emerging themes for higher education in preparing future practitioners for positions in sports fields. The value of a career coach, mentor, and sponsor is emphasized, and professional development needs and opportunities for employees in sports occupations are explored as they relate to career stages.

The foundational components of strategic human resource planning, employment law, negotiations, and compensation and benefits administration continue to span through Phase IV. Strategic human resource planning, for example, is addressed in a section devoted to developing strategies to increase gender and/or ethnic diversity and handling sensitive issues resulting from hiring an employee with a disability or one who expresses a nontraditional sexual or gender orientation. Legal areas of employment are interwoven into a synopsis of harassment in sports organizations. Compensation and benefit packages are addressed as opportunities to assist employees in achieving effective work–life integration. Finally, the value of effective negotiations is mentioned as a tool to create optimal schedules for avoiding burnout.

Readers who make an effort to never stop learning will find enrichment through every phase of a textbook that reminds practitioners that a managerial approach to human resources in sports has the potential to lead to the greatest success.

REFERENCES

PricewaterhouseCoopers. (2016). *PwC sports outlook: At the game and beyond—outlook for the sports market in North America through 2020*. Retrieved from http://www.pwc.com/us/en/industry/entertainment-media/publications/sports-outlook-north-america.html

U.S. Department of Labor. (2015a, December 17). *Occupational outlook handbook: Coaches and scouts*. Retrieved from http://www.bls.gov/ooh/entertainment-and-sports/coaches-and-scouts.htm

U.S. Department of Labor. (2015b, December 17). *Occupational outlook handbook: Aerobics instructor and fitness trainers*. Retrieved from http://www.bls.gov/ooh/personal-care-and-service/fitness-trainers-and-instructors.htm

CHAPTER 12

A Must-Win Ballgame

DIVERSITY AND INCLUSION
IN SPORTS ORGANIZATIONS

While working for 14 years at the National Collegiate Athletic Association (NCAA) headquarters and now at the headquarters for the USA Track and Field, I've always had the privilege of working with leaders who placed a high value on diversity and inclusion. Leadership drives it all. In the NCAA, former president Dr. Myles Brand was more visible and verbal on the issue, but current President Mark Emmert always spoke up when asked. They had different approaches to working on issues, but they both supported diversity and inclusion in separate capacities, and we never lost financial support or employee resources. In the USA Track and Field office, we see diversity in hiring practices, access to professional development, and leading the charge on key issues on the international front. Both organizations require accountability. The United States Olympic Committee (USOC), for instance, requires data tracking on diversity recruitment efforts and to account for gender and ethnicity in the hiring of both staff and athlete support.

Kim Ford Morgan
Director of Business Development
USA Track and Field (USATF)
Former Director of Minority Inclusion
National Collegiate Athletic Association (NCAA)

LEARNING OUTCOMES

1. Identify trends and resources for tracking gender diversity in sports organizations.
2. Identify trends and resources for tracking ethnic diversity in sports organizations.
3. Describe strategies and initiatives to increase gender and ethnic diversity in sports organizations.
4. Distinguish diversity from inclusion in employment.
5. Describe strategies and initiatives to improve the organizational climate for LGBT employees working in sports.

KEY TERMS

Cultural diversity

Diversity

Equal Employment Opportunity Commission

Gender identity

Inclusion

Lesbian, gay, bisexual, and transgender (LGBT)

Lesbian, bisexual, gay, transgender, and questioning (LGBTQ)

Organizational climate

Rooney rule

Sexual identity

Sexual orientation

Transgender

Workforce diversity

Lead-Off

Sports has always been a profession dominated by white males, especially in positions of leadership. Despite efforts to diversify athletic departments and sports agencies at all levels, women and ethnic minorities remain the two categories of underrepresented populations in the industry.

In 2016, the Buffalo Bills made history in the National Football League (NFL) by hiring Kathryn Smith as the first female assistant coach in the league, a year after the league hired Sarah Thomas as the first full-time female official. In the National Basketball Association (NBA), the San Antonio Spurs made history in 2014 by hiring Becky Hammon as the league's first female full-time assistant coach, and the NBA players association (NBAPA) elected Michelle Roberts as the first woman to lead a union representing male athletes. Commissioner Adam Silver prophesized that before long, he believes a woman will be named head coach

Kathryn Smith was hired by the Buffalo Bills as the first female assistant coach in the NFL.

of a NBA franchise and as soon as 2018, more women would be officiating in the league (Youngmisuk, 2017).

Jessica Mendoza made history in 2015 when the Olympic softball star became the first female broadcast analyst for a nationally televised postseason Major League baseball (MLB) game. Mendoza became part of the regular line-up for ESPN's Sunday Night Baseball in 2016. Manon Rheaume from Canada made history back in 1992 as the first female in the National Hockey League (NHL) when she was a goal keeper in three exhibition games for the Tampa Bay Lightning (Wakiji, 2011). No woman has been signed to an NHL contract sense.

Throughout the sports field, there is evidence of females who make headlines for tremendous strides in the male-dominated business as coaches, administrators, referees, and even owners. Data for 2015 indicated that almost 400 men's collegiate teams had a female as their head coach (Lapchick, 2016, p. 41). However, the percentage of women working in sports, especially in leadership positions, is marginal, at best. The scenario is similar for ethnic minorities.

Rapper Jay-Z part owner of the Brooklyn Nets, is one of few minorities with ownership stakes in professional sports.

Although a majority of players in the NBA and NFL are African Americans, ethnic minorities are underrepresented in leadership positions throughout professional sports leagues. Michael Jordan was the only African American in the role of majority owner of any professional sports franchise for a number of years after purchasing the Charlotte Hornets. Twenty-three ethnic minorities had a minor stake in NBA franchises in 2015, including Will and Jada-Pinkett Smith for the Philadelphia Sixers and Jay-Z for the Brooklyn Nets (Hoenig, 2014). Doc Rivers of the Los Angeles Clippers was the only African-American President in the NBA in the 2015–2016 season (Spears, 2016).

Diversity in hiring is an important issue for sports supervisors and managers to understand and practice. Diversity extends well beyond the scope of ethnicity and gender to include

For many years, NBA legend Michael Jordan was the only person of color to have controlling interest as a majority owner of any professional franchise.

demographic and psychographic constructs. Workforce Diversity is based on specific characteristics, such as attitudes and beliefs, position rank, age, experience, education, disability status, socioeconomic status, generational differences, sexual orientation, gender identification, and relationship status. Diversity celebrates uniqueness, individuality, and differences.

Equally important is the topic of inclusion, which is celebrated in organizations where diverse populations interact respectfully and differences are valued. The focus on inclusion in sports has generated attention for issues involving sexual orientation and gender identification, such as those affecting members of the lesbian, gay, bisexual, and transgender (LGBT) community. **Action Shot 12-1** describes the leverage the NBA and National Collegiate Athletic Association (NCAA) used to impart changes in North Carolina legislative actions involving transgender individuals.

▶ ACTION SHOT 12-1

North Carolina Bathroom Bill Flushed by National Collegiate Athletic Association (NCAA) and National Basketball Association (NBA) Boycotts

The 2017 NBA All-Star game was moved from Charlotte, NC to New Orleans LA in protest of the North Carolina Bathroom Bill requiring individuals to use public restrooms according to the biological sex on their birth certificate.

The University of North Carolina (UNC) Tar Heels from Chapel Hill won the 2016–17 NCAA Division I men's basketball tournament championship. The previous September, the NCAA made the decision to move seven championships out of the Tar Heel state to protest the Public Facilities Privacy and Security Act that required individuals to use public restrooms matching the biological sex on their birth certificate (General Assembly of North Carolina, 2016). NBA Commissioner David Silver also made the decision to move the 2017 All-Star Game from Charlotte, North Carolina to the Smoothie King Center in New Orleans, Louisiana to protest the controversial and discriminatory legislation against transgender individuals (Berman & Phillips, 2017).

The NCAA's Board of Governors was the entity that moved 2016 and 2017 championships for Division I women's soccer, lacrosse, and golf; Division III men's and women's soccer and tennis; and Division II baseball to protest house bill (H.B.) 2 which limited legal protection for lesbian, gay, bisexual, and transgender (LGBT) individuals. The short window between the NCAA announcement and the 2016 women's soccer championship tournament resulted in the cancellation of thousands of hotel rooms, refunding over 7500 presold tickets, locating and contracting with new broadcast partners, redesigning logos to reflect the new championship city, and replacing balls and signage to reflect the updated logos (Burnsed, 2017).

The first and second round NCAA Division I men's tournament basketball games featuring number 1 regionally seeded UNC and number two seeded Duke University were also moved from North Carolina to nearby Greenville, South Carolina in protest of the "bathroom bill" (Tracy, 2017).

During UNC's championship run, the North Carolina state governor signed a bill that repealed and replaced H.B. 2 (Berman & Phillips, 2017). Thereafter, the NCAA agreed to permit North Carolina to host championship events and the NBA announced the state would host the All-Star game in 2019.

In the short aftermath of the NCAA and NBA agreeing to resume events in North Carolina, the state's General Assembly proposed new legislation (H.B. 738) prohibiting public institutions receiving state funds from extending media rights to their conferences and association (Minnick, 2017). Essentially, the new legislation would permit the General Assembly to approve the withdrawal of University of North Carolina and N.C. State from the Atlantic Coast Conference (ACC) in the event of another boycott. Duke and Wake Forest, however, are private institutions and would not be affected in the event of a conference or association-wide boycott in the state.

If H.B. 2 were to have remain in effect, an Associated Press analysis estimated a $3.7 billion revenue deficit over 12 years from lost revenues in the state of North Carolina (Berman & Phillips, 2017). The retribution over gender-based bathroom laws would also have extended to the entertainment industry with significant income lost from canceled concerts.

The North Carolina state bathroom law distinguished biological gender from gender identification which has been purported to diminish the constitutional rights of transgender and gay individuals. Protection against sex or gender-based discrimination is provided through federal employment laws, however, state legislation determining bathroom privileges demoralizes the judicial rights of the LGBT community. An opinion that may surface from the facts in the North Carolina Bathroom Bill case is that politics and sports remain closely entwined and the role of organizations with cash lined pockets to serve as moral arbitrators will continue to play a role in society.

Initiatives to promote diversity and inclusion in sports organizations and governing bodies attempt to change ideologies related to prejudice, inequity, hegemony, and homophobia. Sports managers and supervisors operate in an industry where these societal ideologies can hinder the effectiveness of organizations if allowed to permeate the climate and culture. Those organizations that fail to create a supportive, respectful, and inclusive environment that values diversity are more susceptible to harassment and legal issues.

This chapter overviews gender, ethnicity, and sexual diversity, as well as strategies to increase workforce diversity, such as affirmative action (AA) programs. This chapter also addresses LGBT workers employed in the sports industry and strategies for sustaining an inclusive work environment.

Diversity

Diversity refers to constructs or dimensions used to explain individual differences. **Workforce diversity** identifies differences in employees based on dimensions of demographic or psychographic criteria. Examples of demographic criteria include gender, ethnicity, sexual orientation, age, marital status, parental status, educational attainment, socioeconomic status, and physical abilities. Examples of psychographic variables include religious beliefs, political views, and other ideologies.

Sports organizations are historically lacking in both gender and ethnic diversity.

GENDER DIVERSITY

Two reports have been tracking decades of gender-related statistics, including a longitudinal study of women in intercollegiate sports and a diversity report card spanning college and professional sports. In college coaching,

The percentage of female collegiate coaches of women's teams has decreased despite an overall increase in the number of teams.

Acosta and Carpenter (2014) reported that the percentage of females serving as a head coach of a women's team decreased over the decades (from over 90% in 1972 down to 43% in 2014), and of the 2080 women's teams added between 2000 and 2014, only 35% had a female head coach. Less than 25% of women's track and field, swimming and diving, and ski teams employed a female at the helm in 2014 compared with over 85% of women's collegiate field hockey, lacrosse, synchronized swimming, and equestrian programs.

TABLE 12-1: 2014 Report: Females Employed in NCAA Intercollegiate Athletics Programs

Position	All	I	II	III
Female head coach of women's team	4154 (43%)	43%	36%	47%
Female paid assistant coach of women's team	7503 (57%)	3077 (54%)	1529 (58%)	2897 (60%)
Female unpaid assistant coach of women's team	1142 (52%)	438 (51%)	302 (52%)	402 (53%)
Female director of athletics	239 (22%)	37 (11%)	69 (23%)	133 (30%)
Female athletic administrators	1642 (36%)	734 (32%)	387 (38%)	523 (42%)
Athletic departments lacking a female administrator	**11%**	**1%**	**12%**	**18%**

Data from Acosta and Carpenter (2014).

Table 12-1 presents a profile of administrative and coaching positions in the NCAA by division. In terms of administration, whereas Division III includes the most females serving as directors of athletics, it also includes the most universities without a woman in any type of administrative role. Acosta and Carpenter (2014, p. 51) note that institutions in the southern region of the United States have the highest percentage of males serving as directors of athletics and the highest percentage of departments without a female in an administrative role. Most women in administrative support staff positions in intercollegiate athletics work as skills coordinators, business managers, and compliance coordinators. Over 90% of positions as sports information directors across all three divisions were occupied by males in 2014–2015 (Lapchick, 2016).

The NCAA headquarters employed Judy Sweet as the first female president in 1991. In 2015, the headquarters employed almost 500 personnel (493 total) which has steadily increased each year (Lapchick, 2016, p. 35). The Institute for Diversity in Sport began recording gender statistics for college athletics in 1998. **Table 12-2** presents a comparison of data between 1998 and 2015. Gender data for Division I conference commissioners were originally recorded in 2007 when three women (11%) occupied positions. In 2015, 27% of Division I conferences had a female commissioner (Lapchick, 2016, p. 36).

TABLE 12-2: Report of Female Representation in the NCAA Office

Position	2015	1998
NCAA executive senior vice president	4 (24%)	4 (25%)
NCAA managing director	38 (45%)	N/A
NCAA administrator	161 (53%)	53 (49%)
Total of NCAA staff (full time)	**283 (57%)**	**N/A**

Data from Lapchick (2016).

With the exception of the league office in the Women's National Basketball Association (WNBA), women continue to be underrepresented in positions of leadership throughout professional sports leagues in the United States (see **Table 12-3**).

TABLE 12-3: 2016 Report: Females in Professional Sports (Not Including Players)

	NBA	WNBA	NFL	MLB	MLS
Number of franchises in each league	30	12	32	30	20
League office	335 (40%)	16 (70%)	363 (33%)	76 (29%)	57 (37%)
Majority owner	3 (7%)	14 (40%)	13 (N/A)	8 (16%)	1 (2.6%)
President/chief executive officer	4 (7%)	5 (33%)	0 (0%)	0 (0%)	2 (5.9%)
General manager	0 (0%)	5 (50%)	0 (0%)	0 (0%)	0 (0%)
Vice president	93 (22%)	29 (27%)	59 (21%)	74 (18%)	15 (15%)
Team senior administration	196 (24%)	29 (24%)	169 (21%)	500 (28%)	51 (25%)
Professional team administration	937 (36%)	218 (44%)	1218 (33%)	416 (27%)	152 (29%)
Head coach/manager (MLB)	0 (0%)	5 (42%)	0 (0%)	0 (0%)	0 (0%)
Assistant coach/coach (MLB)	1 (.5%)	13 (57%)	1 (.1%)	2 (.7%)	0 (0%)

Note: Percentages represent the percentage of females in a particular position and exclude support staff positions, such as administrative assistants, office managers, and staff assistants. Team senior administration includes senior directors, assistant general managers, chief legal counsels, and various director positions. Team professional administration includes employees with the titles representing a coordinator, supervisor, or administrator of a functional area.

Data from Lapchick (2016).

RACIAL AND ETHNIC DIVERSITY

America has been metaphorically referred to as a melting pot in terms of the varied racial and ethnic groups that live and work in the United States. *Race* refers to an individual's physical features, whereas *ethnicity* describes an individual's heritage or background. Ethnicity does not indicate where someone was born; hence, many U.S. citizens belong to a specific ethnic group due to the birthplace of one or more of their ancestors.

When a non–U.S. citizen or immigrant is employed by an American business, diversity is added to an organization. Immigration is especially prevalent in sports as the number and percentages of foreign-born athletes and coaches in American professional leagues and university teams have increased.

In addition to the legal framework for employing individuals from different ethnic groups and cultures, sports managers and supervisors need to consider assimilation issues. Language barriers, time-zone adjustment, food, and medicine are just several items that could prove challenging when an employee from a country outside of the United States joins an organization. Cultural assimilation is a crucial component that must be addressed with personal consideration. For example, foreign employees must be able to read and comprehend a contract, and they must comply with taxation rules. These distinctions factor into **cultural diversity**, a concept related to but genuinely distinct from racial and ethnic diversity. Cultural diversity expresses the extent to which psychographic variables (attitudes, values, and beliefs) are shared by an identifiable group (Doherty & Chelladurai, 1999; Kamphoff, Gill, Araki, & Hammond, 2009).

Ethnicity, and not necessarily country of origin or cultural background, is tracked by scholars and professionals in the sports industry. For example, during the 2016 season, the NBA, NFL, and Major League Soccer (MLS) employed at least 35% ethnic minorities (Lapchick, 2016). During the same year, over 35% of assistant coaches in all major leagues (NBA, NFL, MLB, NHL, MLS, and WNBA) were "non-white" (Lapchick, 2016).

Reports demonstrate that the higher the position in professional sports, the more likely it is that a white male is in the role (see **Table 12-4**). Among ethnic minorities, African Americans hold the most positions in professional sports leagues, followed by Latinos and Asians. The NBA is considered the leader among men's professional sports for diversity in hiring, and the MLS employed the highest percentage of ethnic minorities in the league office in 2015 (Lapchick, 2016).

TABLE 12-4: 2016 Report: Ethnic Minorities in Leadership Roles in Professional Sports

	NBA	WNBA	NFL	MLB	MLS
Number of franchises in each league	**30**	**12**	**32**	**30**	**20**
League office	299 (35%)	6 (16%)	280 (26%)	76 (29%)	56 (36%)
Majority owner	2 (5%)	7 (20%)	1 (.03%)	1 (2%)	4 (11%)
President/chief executive officer	3 (5.3%)	2 (20%)	1 (3%)	0 (0%)	1 (6%)
General manager/director of player personnel	4 (13%)	2 (20%)	5 (16%)	4 (13%)	4 (19%)
Vice president	79 (18%)	11 (10%)	30 (11%)	58 (14%)	4 (4%)
Team senior administration	195 (24%)	20 (21%)	150 (21%)	352 (19%)	30 (15%)
Team professional administration	832 (32%)	166 (34%)	808 (24%)	346 (23%)	93 (18%)
Head coach/manager (MLB)	9 (30%)	3 (25%)	6 (19%)	3 (10%)	4 (20%)
Assistant coach/coach (MLB)	66 (44%)	11 (48%)	236 (31%)	108 (38%)	12 (14%)

Note: Percentages represent the percentage of people of color employed in a particular position. The report excludes support staff positions, such as administrative assistants, office managers, and staff assistants. Senior administration includes directors, assistant general managers, managers, and various director positions. Professional administration includes equipment managers and employees with such titles as coordinator, supervisor, or administrator of a functional area.

Data from Lapchick (2016).

African Americans are rare in the professional coaching ranks and especially in MLB.

In college athletics during 2014–2015, people of color represented approximately 13% of all head coaches in NCAA Division I, 13% in Division II, and 9% in Division III (Lapchick, 2016). There was also a higher percentage (5.2% vs. 5.0%) of female coaches of men's teams in Division III programs in 2014–2015 than African American coaches in men's programs (Lapchick, 2016). Only 12.5% of athletic directors in NCAA Division I institutions were members of an ethnic minority group in 2014–2015.

Strategies to Increase Diversity in Sports Organizations

Whether through a resolution, policy, mandate, or a new initiative, efforts to diversify the racial and gender makeup in sports organizations can yield great benefits toward achieving performance objectives. A diverse workforce has the potential to help organizations gain a competitive edge by developing new attitudes and outlooks for problem solving and tapping into new markets for engaging a wider fan base. Franchises, stadiums, athletic departments, recreation centers, sports manufacturing firms, and retail stores that are proactive in hiring underrepresented populations (i.e., women and ethnic minorities) can reap the benefits of attracting new customers, extending the range of brand awareness, and making a positive contribution to social responsibility by operating as a business that values diversity. Common strategies to diversify sports organizations described herein includes tailoring the verbiage used in job announcements, targeted channels for advertising vacancies, implementing AA plans, taking advantage of grant programs, and leveraging multilevel homologous relationships.

JOB ANNOUNCEMENTS AND TARGETED ADVERTISING CHANNELS

The job announcement may be the single most effective tool in recruiting anyone, including the quality diverse applicants organizations wish to attract. The U.S. **Equal Employment Opportunity Commission** (2017) mandates that all qualified individuals have fair access and equal consideration when competing for job opportunities, irrespective of race, color, ethnicity, religion, gender, sexual orientation, age, or disability. Therefore, including a statement on the job announcement identifying the Equal Employment Opportunity Commission (EEOC) is a small but fundamentally important detail to encourage diverse hiring practices. Similarly, job announcements in the sports industry that encourage women and minorities to apply specifically addresses a focus to attract the underrepresented populations.

The job announcement seeking qualified, diverse candidates does little if it is not seen by the populations that the company or organization seeks to attract. Targeted outreach strategies include advertising vacancies in publications, media outlets, job fairs, and other events that serve minorities and women in sports. Such strategies also include networking or utilizing search firms connected with organizations specifically for minorities and women in the sports industry. For example, the Women's Sports Foundation, Women Leaders in College Sports, Black Sports Agents Association, and the Minorities Opportunities Athletic Association are associations with the opportunity to post advertisements and to network at their respective conferences or social events. Additionally, posting vacancies or interviewing applicants at an all-women's institution or a historically black college or university are additional target outreach strategies for conducting diverse candidate searches.

AFFIRMATIVE ACTION PLANS

AA refers to policies, programs, and procedures favoring members of a disadvantaged group (e.g., minorities and women in sports). The concept was addressed in respect to the dearth of minorities in managerial positions in professional MLB by Friend and Leuns (1989) a decade prior to the league initiating the Selig rule (see **Action Shot 12-2**). AA has been addressed in the context of professional sports, intercollegiate and scholastic sports, and national governing agencies.

AA may range from the passive support of nondiscrimination policies to mandatory inclusion of all categories of the underrepresented populations in a candidate pool. A soft quota system may be promoted to set expectations that some women and minorities will be among those considered for a position (i.e., the Selig rule). Other programs may require a hard quota, often a result of a class-action lawsuit, which specifies the minimum standard for actual interviews or hires from the underrepresented population (Friend & Leuns, 1989, p. 152). Action Shot 12-2 addresses what is considered a hard quota system for the NFL and a soft quota for the MLB.

AA policies and plans are voluntary unless the employer is a federal contractor or subcontractor (with over 50 employees and a contract of $50,000 or more) or if a court has mandated that an employer must take AA to remedy past discriminatory practices. The Metropolitan Sports Facility Authority (2016), for example, circulates a detailed AA plan while the Philadelphia Phillies reportedly published AA plans in the mid-80s just prior to MLB being challenged by minority leaders to adopt a plausible solution to overcome institutionalized racism in the hiring of general managers (Boswell, 1987).

In 1990, USA Today featured a column by Phil Knight, co-founder and chairman emeritus for Nike, Inc., addressing AA information he shared with managers over a 4-year period. Knight (1990) projected Nike would have a minority member on the board of directors within a year, a minority vice president within 2 years, and would maintain a minimum threshold of 21% minority representation for the next 1000 new employees hired. Seventeen years later amidst allegations that black employees were segregated into lower paying jobs, Nike agreed to pay $7.6 billion to settle a class-action discrimination lawsuit to over 500 current and past employees in its Niketown Chicago store (Wall Street Journal, 2007).

Many job advertisements in the field of intercollegiate athletic coaching and administration publish the disclaimer that they are "EEO/AA"

▶ ACTION SHOT 12-2

NFL Rooney Rule Expands to Cover Women—MLB Selig Rule Exemplifies "Soft" Quota

Often mistakenly cited as affirmative action, the **Rooney rule** in the National Football League (NFL) was legislated as a means to diversify the representation of minority head coaches among the professional football league. Established in 2003 and named after Pittsburgh Steelers' owner Dan Rooney (a leader in NFL owners in providing opportunities for minority coaches), the rule requires teams to interview minorities for head coaching and senior director of football operations jobs. The rule was crafted partially in response to the study "Black Coaches in the N.F.L.: Superior Performance, Inferior Opportunities," which demonstrated that black coaches, despite higher winning percentages, were more likely to be fired and less likely to be hired than their white counterparts. The report indicated that black coaches reached the playoffs 67% of the time compared with 39% for white coaches and that black coaches won an average of 1.1 more games per year than white coaches (Proxmire, 2008, p. 2).

Although many people consider this a form of affirmative action, in reality, there are no official quotas or expectations for filling positions with a certain number of minority candidates; however, fines may be imposed at the discretion of the commissioner for tampering with or deviating from the requirement.

In 2015, the NFL ruled against a complaint from an outside alliance claiming the Washington Redskins violated the Rooney rule in conducting a search to fill a general manager position (Maske, 2015). As of 2017, only the 2003 Detroit Lions had been found guilty of violating the rule; the franchise was subject to a $200,000 fine after hiring Steve Mariucci as head coach without interviewing a minority candidate despite extending offers to five minority applicants (Detroit Free Press, 2014; Proxmire, 2008, p. 5).

The Rooney rule is one step that a major sports league has taken to ensure that minorities are getting opportunities at the highest levels in sports. Many will argue the effectiveness or lack thereof, but it is one example of a professional sports league making an effort to remedy past discrimination and ensure that minority applicants are considered for high-level positions.

In 2009, the Rooney rule was expanded to require franchises to interview a minority for any senior football operations positions within the NFL. In 2016, the NFL commissioner announced that the rule would be extended once again to require franchises to interview a female for every executive-level vacancy (Patra, 2016).

Created in 1999, the Selig rule in Major League Baseball (MLB) also promotes inclusive hiring practices in professional sports for higher-level positions in a franchise. However, the difference between the Rooney rule and the Selig rule is that the latter only requires a woman and minority to be "considered" for an opening (Glanville, 2016). No one has to actually interview a minority candidate. The soft quota only requires the MLB to track individuals internally considered for a vacancy.

In the decade preceding the Rooney rule, there were 92 open head coach positions, for which seven minorities were selected (7.6% of all hires); in the decade following, there were 87 vacancies, 17 of which were filled by minorities, increasing the percentage of minority hires to 19.5% (Fox, 2015). The percentages of minorities and women in senior positions in the MLB remain relatively low.

🎬 ACTION SHOT 12-3

Executive Search Firms' Commitment to Affirmative Action
and Diversity in Recruiting Athletics Personnel

Many university athletic departments (e.g., University of Indiana–Bloomingdale, University of Oregon, Illinois State University, and Duke University) publicly acknowledge affirmative action plans for women and minorities to ensure all aspects of personnel programs are administered without regard to race, religion, sexual orientation, and so forth. Search firms contracted to identify candidates for university athletic departments must comply with the affirmative action policies and programs mandated by clients to ensure a diverse candidate pool of qualified applicants is available.

It is an underlying presumption that search firms exert great effort to follow best practices in human resources to ensure diversification of qualified applicants. Elizabeth "Betsy" A. Alden, PhD, serves as president emeritus for Alden & Associates, Inc., a division of Spelman Johnson Executive Search and Consulting Firm focusing on intercollegiate athletics and higher education. According to Alden, affirmative action policies are necessary, but they are only one of many compliance issues to consider with respect to recruitment and hiring processes in human resources (E. Alden, personal communication, April 25, 2016).

Alden notes that although search firms are expected to present clients with a diverse pool of candidates, it can be both disappointing and frustrating when minority applicants fail to be considered by hiring authorities. Athletic departments, Alden believes, seem to be protected by a "bulletproof shield," with too many instances of someone being hired as a result of a connection to the hiring official, without consideration of diversity.

Alden suggests that "diversity is too often ignored in the hiring of many intercollegiate athletics positions, while vacancies in academics seem to fall under greater scrutiny to ensure female and minority consideration and representation" (E. Alden., personal communication, April 25, 2016).

employers meaning they adhere to principles of equal employment opportunities and AA. Higher education, which has tremendous ties to federal funding, is generally an active participant in AA programs. Executive search firms servicing higher education institutions are familiar with the mandates that guide recruitment of personnel (see **Action Shot 12-3**).

There is no one specific way to create an AA program or plan. These types of plans and programs are tailored to the employer. The general goal of an AA plan is to ensure that the organization's workforce reflects the utilization of the underrepresented populations (i.e., women and/or minorities) compared with the qualified pool available for the types of open positions

BOX 12-1

Information Supporting AA Efforts

- Job postings (examples and data on where posted)
- Copies of equal opportunity/affirmative action policies
- Details of where equal opportunity/affirmative action policies are posted

- Examples of how equal opportunity/affirmative action policies are shared with employees
- Tracking information addressing applicant demographics (separate from employment applications)
- Tracking information of employment demographics

in the company. Best practices suggest sports supervisors and managers should maintain records of any and all pertinent information that supports affirmative action efforts (see **Box 12-1**).

An equal or greater number of minorities or women in a particular job group is the desirable outcome of an effective affirmative action program, however the ambitious goal is challenging to attain if confined to the current system of leadership and operations in sectors of sports such as professional leagues. Tracking where job postings are placed as well as the number of minority and women applicants assists in authenticating diversity efforts.

An affirmative action program will typically include a detailed organizational chart, a workforce analysis, and administrative forms. A detailed organizational chart should clearly illustrate the organizational structure of the company or agency, and it should include a hierarchy of personnel and the department structure(s). Workforce analysis worksheets represent employee data for the entire company, for each division/department, and for each level of worker (executive, administrative, etc.). The workforce analysis worksheet example in **Table 12-5** is similar to the EEO-1 report that all employers (even private employers) with over 100 employees are required to file.

SPONSORED PROGRAMS

Grant programs, mentorship programs, internships, and fellowships targeting specific ethnic or gender categories provide a means to develop a pipeline of diverse candidates for sports vacancies. The NCAA and other sports associations provide numerous opportunities for women and/or minorities to attract diverse candidates into the industry (see **Box 12-2**).

TABLE 12-5: Workforce Analysis Worksheet

Job Classification	Job Title	EEO-1 Category	Job Group	Total Employees	Male	Female	White	Black/ African American	Asian/ Pacific Islander	American Indian/ Alaska Native	Hispanic
Associate	Inside Sales Rep	3	1	14	10	4	12	2	0	0	0

BOX 12-2

Examples of Grants and Programs Targeting Women and/or Ethnic Minorities

- NCAA: Strategic Alliance Matching grant for Division II and III conference offices or institutional athletic departments; includes sharing 3 years of the cost of hiring a female for a newly created or enhanced position in mid- to senior-level administrative positions
- NCAA: Division III minority and female internship program and a Division II Coaching Enhancement Grant

- NFL: Bill Walsh Ethnic Minority Coaching Fellowship and Ethnic Minority Scholarship
- NBA: Ethnic Minority Scholarship; also supports the National Black MBA Association and the National Society for Hispanic MBAs
- MLS: Recruiting Female Athletes Committee

Many of these initiatives are shared and discussed among members of the Diversity and Inclusion Sports Consortium, which includes industry specialists from collegiate sports, the U.S. Olympic Committee, and professional associations such as National Association for Stock Car Auto Racing (NASCAR), the Professional Golf Association (PGA), the Ladies Professional Golf Association (LPGA), the MLS, U.S. Tennis Association (USTA), NFL, MLB, NHL, and NBA. The PGA, for example, was inspired to create a Diversity & Inclusion Council, and within several years, 51% of the national staff was comprised of females (PGA of America, 2016). Similarly, the initiatives of the MLS helped to fill two-thirds of its internship opportunities with women and minorities in 2015.

Sports organizations truly seeking to broaden their talent pool must initially make a commitment to embracing diversity before instituting programs and tools designed to attract, secure, and retain employees from the underrepresented populations. A supportive organizational culture stemming from a leadership team that values diversity and supports initiatives and programs to expand talent pools and recruit qualified women and minorities is vital to achieving diversity initiatives. Otherwise, policies such as the Rooney rule are necessary to address discriminatory hiring practices.

The LPGA provides part time and full-time internship opportunities for females in efforts to develop a pipeline of female candidates qualified for full-time positions.

Additional measures to diversify a workforce include establishing diversity expectations, ensuring search/selection committees include minority and female members and reopening searches if a candidate pool isn't suitably representative of diversity by the closing dates for applications. Conducting a search for a candidate over a period of days rather than weeks may compromise the goal of a diversified candidate pool. A rush to hire with a quick replacement scheme rarely honors diversity and inclusion.

Competitive salaries, targeted mentoring programs, overt communication of diversity initiatives, and established support systems for minorities in the community are additional means to increase the likelihood that sports organizations will be able to recruit and retain a diverse workforce with minority representation. University presidents, boards, and campus officials must understand that athletics has unique needs, and athletics must understand that it can't just "abandon the traditional hiring process" to fill posts quickly. In the grand scheme, it is a combination of initiatives and efforts and a supportive administration that will likely yield a greater number or percentage of diversity hires.

HOMOLOGOUS REPRODUCTION

A unique employment phenomenon that potentially affects diversity is homologous reproduction. The theory of homologous reproduction contends that a male supervisor is more likely to hire a male employee, whereas a female supervisor is more likely to hire a female candidate, thereby preserving the dominant gender. The phenomenon is cited throughout the literature as a primary reason for the decline of female head coaches and administrators in intercollegiate athletics because, essentially, the abundance of men in leadership positions perpetuates a bias toward hiring male candidates

(Sagas, Cunningham, & Teed, 2006; Stahura & Greenwood, 2001; Stangl & Kane, 1991; Whisenant, 2008).

On the other hand, homologous reproduction can also serve as a strategy or tool for diversification whereby a minority job seeker targets organizations led by minorities. In cases where women have decision-making authority in the selection of employees (i.e., female athletic directors), homologous reproduction suggests that these institutions will likely experience an increase in the number of females. Similarly, minority athletic directors may experience homologous reproduction and exhibit a preference for hiring minorities as coaches and support staff.

Homologous reproduction in the field of sports projects a practice of controlling employment pools through a predetermination of desired characteristics in potential candidates. Whether managers consciously or unconsciously hire individuals based on judgments of social characteristics, as suggested in the theoretical framework for homologous reproduction, the fact remains that women are disproportionately represented within leadership roles throughout the sports industry.

In recruiting for positions within the field of sports, the use of objective criteria-based ranking systems and a group process for selecting candidates assists in minimizing the threat of homologous reproduction. In fact, conscious efforts to ensure diversification in a field of candidates through strategic initiatives, such as prolonging the process or making concerted efforts to reach an underrepresented group, are effective managerial practices for hiring personnel.

Inclusion

Sports has been described as an exclusive space that privileges some over others (Kamphoff, Armentrout, & Driska, 2010; Krane, 2001; Krane & Barber, 2005). An inclusive space, on the other hand, embraces the opposite ideology by emphasizing overt acceptance of all diversity categories. **Inclusion** encompasses every demographic and psychographic or lifestyle dimension of the workforce. In addition to gender and ethnic differences, inclusion accounts for disabled employees and members of the **LGBT** community. Beyond the categories of race, ethnicity, gender, disability, sexual orientation, and gender identification, inclusion also emphasizes acceptance of differences in ideas, opinions, (religious) beliefs, and attitudes. Organizations that value inclusion assimilate all cultures, ethnicities, genders, classes, social backgrounds, sexual preferences, and divergent personalities into the lifeblood of the business, without prejudice.

Diversity and inclusion are intertwined. Over time, human resource management has evolved to place greater emphasis on "inclusion" as a new way to address diversity. Inclusive organizations are noted for celebrating diversity as an effective management practice in social responsibility (Doherty & Chelladurai, 1999). Highlighting inclusion has permitted organizations to reframe diversity initiatives that have been marginalized. A new focus framing diversity in terms of its inventiveness, imagination, and competitiveness is permitting organizations to continue to adapt to changing times. **Action Shot 12-4** describes the evolution of the NCAA headquarters in making inclusion a greater priority in policy and programming over the years.

Anti-gay propaganda laws passed by Russian President Vladimir Putin caused dissent during the 2014 Sochi Winter Olympics.

LGBT WORKERS

In 2015, Curt Miller became the first openly gay coach of a professional team when he signed a contract to lead the Connecticut Sun in the WNBA (Maloney, 2016). Three years earlier, when he was initially introduced as the new head coach of the Indiana Hoosiers women's basketball program, Miller acknowledged his male partner and twin sons at a press conference. The Connecticut Sun and University of Indiana demonstrated an organizational commitment to inclusiveness by, first, hiring Miller and, second, by supporting his decision to publicly acknowledge a lifestyle choice.

Sexual orientation and gender identification are two categories that many organizations emphasize when addressing programs and policies for inclusion. By demonstrating acceptance of all individuals in an organization, no one category is singled out. **Sexual orientation** refers to the emotional, physical, and sexual attraction toward a particular gender (e.g., the same gender, the opposite gender, or both) and aligns with the colloquial terms for lesbian, gay, and bisexual individuals. **Gender identity** refers to whether an individual identifies more so as a male or female, regardless of biological sex. **Transgender** individuals have a gender identity that differs from their biological sex. Research has suggested that a majority of employees in sports organizations prefer not to reveal their sexual orientation at work and that parents express varying degrees of support for LGBT individuals coaching

📽 ACTION SHOT 12-4

Inclusion and the National Collegiate Athletic Association (NCAA) Headquarters

In college athletics, the NCAA underwent a transformation from what was once a fragmented structure of supporting gender and ethnic diversity to one that is inclusive of lesbian, gay, bisexual, transgender, and questioning (**LGBTQ**) individuals and individuals with disabilities. The NCAA is a member of the Diversity and Inclusion Sport Consortium established in 2012. Among the other organizations belonging to the consortium are the National Football League (NFL), Major League Baseball (MLB), National Hockey league (NHL), National Basketball Association (NBA), Women's National Basketball Association (WNBA), U.S. Olympic Committee (USOC), Professional Golf Association (PGA), and U.S. Tennis Association (USTA).

For many years, Kim Ford served as director of minority inclusion at the NCAA. She began working as an NCAA intern in 2000. During Ford's initial years, gender and diversity issues were addressed through an office of Education Outreach, which provided the professional development funding and programming for ethnic minority interests. At the time, the Office for Gender Equity was a department that focused on Title IX, the Committee for Women's Athletics, awards, and the annual Gender Equity Forum (K. Ford, personal communication, April 19, 2016).

Dramatic restructuring occurred in 2010 which resulted in the Office of Diversity and Inclusion replacing the Office for Gender Equity. A new statement of inclusion was drafted, and the name and scope of the annual Gender Equity Forum changed to the NCAA Diversity and Inclusion Forum. Charlotte Westerhaus, Rosie Stallman, and Karen Morrison are three former NCAA office staff responsible for the department's efforts to promote gender equity, diversity, and inclusion.

A synthesis of ideology toward the stand-alone significance of "inclusion" occurred in 2012, resulting in another reorganization whereby the Office of Diversity and Inclusion was renamed the Office of Inclusion, and the annual NCAA Diversity and Inclusion Forum was renamed the Inclusion Forum (K. Ford, personal communication, April 19, 2016).

In 2016, the NCAA Office of Inclusion Staff directory included Senior Vice President Bernard Franklin (chief inclusion officer) and two directors of inclusion, one assigned roles for gender equity and LGBTQ issues, and the second assigned to race, ethnicity, and disabilities (which includes pregnancy as a temporary disability). According to the NCAA Office of Inclusion (2016), the primary mission is to:

> Enable programming and education that sustains foundations of a diverse and inclusive culture across dimensions of diversity including, but not limited to age, race, sex, class, creed educational background, disability, gender expression, geographical location, income, marital status, parental status, sexual orientation and work experiences.

their children (Cunningham & Melton, 2014; Ragins, Singh, & Cornwell, 2007; Sartore & Cunningham, 2009). **Action Shot 12-5** profiles an NBA executive who is a role model for the LGBT community.

In 2014, protests and threats of boycotting the Sochi Olympics were rampant due to laws passed by Russia's President Vladimir Putin prohibiting propaganda of nontraditional sexual attitudes or relations distributed to minors. Russia's federation government has been besieged by complaints over widespread restrictions of civil liberties and discrimination against racial, ethnic, religious, political, and sexual minorities (United States Department of State, 2013). The International Olympic Committee (2014) revised its anti-discrimination policy prohibiting discrimination on the basis of sexual orientation in response to a Russian mandate that prohibited minors from receiving propaganda of homosexulism. Most organizations include similar anti-discrimination language when drafting diversity and inclusion policies.

▶ ACTION SHOT 12-5

National Basketball Association (NBA) Executive Rick Welts Is a Role Model for the Lesbian, Gay, Bisexual, and Transgender (LGBT) Community

Rick Welt, the first openly gay high ranking executive in an American professional sport league is credited with creating the NBA All-Star Game, the 1992 Dream Team, and the WNBA.

Rick Welts, 2016 president and chief operating officer of the Golden State Warriors, previously served as executive vice president and chief marketing officer for the NBA. He is credited with establishing the NBA All-Star Weekend in 1984, promoting the 1992 "Dream Team," and his role in creating the Women's National Basketball Association (WNBA) in 1997.

Welts publically revealed his sexual orientation when serving as president and chief executive of the Seattle Sonics in 2011. He is noted as the first prominent executive in American sports leagues to confirm he is gay. In 2016, Welts's story was featured on HBO's *Real Sports*.

When initially discussing his public disclosure concerning his sexuality, Welts said, "This is one of the last industries where the subject is off limits. Nobody's comfortable in engaging in a conversation" (Barry, 2011). Referred to as a modern-day civil rights pioneer, Welts has since indicated that societal acceptance has changed toward the LGBT community working in sports since his 2011 disclosure and suggested that an announcement in 2016 "might not make the paper at all" (Killion, 2016).

Coaches, managers, and office executives in professional sports are taking steps to educate themselves on means to create a more welcoming environment for LGBT athletes and employees. Role models such as Rick Welts pave the way for LGBT employees to succeed in professional sports organizations.

In professional sports, leagues are enforcing anti-discrimination and anti-harassment policies, and they are also promoting education of LGBT issues. Billy Bean, a former MLB player who is openly gay, was appointed as the MLB Ambassador for Inclusion in 2014, with responsibilities to lead efforts in creating greater inclusion of LGBT athletes in professional sports. In 2013, the NFL and NHL addressed LGBT issues at their annual rookie symposium, which included former players serving as ambassadors to educate athletes on best practices in engaging with colleagues who are not heterosexual. The *Best Practices for Inclusion of LGBTQ Student-Athletes and Staff in NCAA Programs* manual includes a "Coming Out" guide and checklist for LBGTQ coaches. The manual expresses that,

> The benefits of coaching as an openly LGBTQ coach need to be considered and balanced with concerns about discrimination. Coaching as an openly LGBTQ person also helps to dispel stereotypes and fears that others have about LGBTQ people and provides role models for other LGBTQ athletes and coaches. (Griffin & Taylor, 2017, p. 29)

More states are adding gender identity and expression to their nondiscrimination policies (Franklin, Ford, & Morrison, 2011, p. 5). The decision for a LGBTQ coach to reveal his or her sexual orientation or gender identity, however, is a personal judgment call. An assistant softball coach at the University of California, Los Angeles, featured in the information addressing "Coming Out" guidelines notes that as a "closet" coach, he diminished his potential as a leader, whereas revealing his sexual orientation allowed him to serve as a role model (Griffin & Taylor, 2017, p. 28).

Although the passage of time may affect societal attitudes toward homophobia and prejudice in sports, as Rick Welts alluded to in Action Shot 12-5, human resource personnel in the industry are challenged in their roles to address LGBT issues. Compliance with legal protections and an intentional approach to fostering an inclusive environment promoting respect and tolerance for all employees remain crucial responsibilities for managers and supervisors of sports organizations.

The complexities of sports culture and homophobia open up a breeding ground for workplace issues involving LGBT employees. Human resource implications for sports organizations employing LGBT workers center on legal compliance with protections from employment discrimination and creating a welcoming, supportive environment facilitating inclusion.

In 2011 in the United States, there were no federal laws preventing managers from basing personnel decisions on an individual's sexual orientation, and fewer than half of all states had such policies (Cunningham & Melton, 2011). In general, LGBT employees frequently do not receive legal protections from discrimination related to hiring, training, promotions, and termination. The Employment Non-Discrimination Act (ENDA) of 2013 is a bill that would make it illegal to fire, refuse to hire, or fail to promote an employee based on real or perceived sexual orientation or gender identity (Congress. gov, 2013). Although it passed in the Senate, the bill has since stalled in efforts to become enacted as federal law.

STRATEGIES TO PROMOTE INCLUSION

An inclusive workplace is one that recruits, hires, promotes, and trains individuals from diverse backgrounds. In sports organizations, measures of **organizational climate** can extend to evidence of team camaraderie and observable signs and symbols in offices and locker rooms that display company values (Scott, 2014, p. 65). Employees who perceive the organizational climate of their respective business or company to be inclusive would generally agree to being employed at a progressive organization that is accepting and respectful of differences in all individuals.

Sports managers have a role in shaping the perception of employees regarding whether their organization is one that does or doesn't celebrate diversity and practices inclusion. Inclusiveness is referenced in describing the climate of an organization and generally refers to the conditions of the work environment, such as policies, practices, and procedures that influence the behaviors and performance of employees. Organizational climate is manifested in individual attitudes toward variables such as trust and support in working relationships, the perceived value of work quality, and attitudes toward tolerance (Huseinagić & Hodz', 2011).

Sports supervisors, coaches, and administrators are effective in working with diverse classifications of employees if strategies, policies, and educational programs are implemented that promote a climate and culture of workplace inclusion and abolish discrimination and/or harassment. Examples of strategies to support or facilitate inclusion include establishing a task force or committee to assess the climate of an organization toward inclusion or to align with associations and allies that champion LGBT equality or minority and gender issues. Strategies may also include targeted recruitment of diverse classifications of employees and research on best practices by organizations noted for fostering an inclusive work environment.

Designating a restroom or locker room as single use and/or gender neutral is a means to demonstrate consideration for LGBT employees in addition to including language for welcoming spouses and partners to social functions. Policies for improving organizational climate may include establishing a workplace code of conduct, developing anti-harassment rules and penalties, and addressing benefits for partners. Individuals developing or enforcing policies and procedures for personnel must address provisions for same-sex relationships or domestic partners under the Family Medical Leave Act (FMLA).

The language of employee policy manuals is important if serving to promote an inclusive workplace culture, such as the identification of "partner" in addition to "spouse." Finally, policies should address confidentiality of disclosure of sexuality, whether for purposes of filing for same-sex benefits or for other reasons where discretion is expected as a professional courtesy.

Workshops and education programs addressing inclusion are evolving rapidly. Ideally, employers and supervisors should participate in sessions addressing how to foster inclusive workplace environments, what to include in anti-discrimination employment policies, and how to handle domestic partner benefits. Sessions for employees, on the other hand, should address tolerance and homophobia as well as diversity awareness. Employee orientations should include resources for LGBT workers, international employees, and minorities while also addressing confidentiality as a right and professional expectation.

Recap

One of the common employment issues throughout sectors of the sports industry is the lack of diversity in gender and ethnicity that has permeated the field, especially in leadership positions. The investment of financial resources and time in proven strategies to recruit and retain more women and ethnic minorities demonstrates support for diversity. Fundamental to any action designed to increase the number or percentage of minority or female candidates for employment positions in entry or executive levels is a commitment to the value of diversity by the leadership team.

Related to diversity is the concept of inclusion. Whereas diversity addresses differences in the demographic or psychographic attributes of employees, inclusion is the practice of acknowledging, accepting, and respecting dissimilarities. Inclusion encompasses all categorical references for employees (e.g., gender and ethnicity) and often is used in addressing sexual orientation, sexual identification, and disabilities. Many organizations in the sports industry either knowingly or unknowingly employ one or more workers belonging to the LGBT community. The most common human resource implications for LGBT workers include same-sex benefits and maintaining a workplace that is supportive of inclusion.

GLOBAL SPOTLIGHT 12-1

Perspectives on Sports and Diversity in Selected Countries

A team of Australian researchers noted that "sport organizations can attempt to differentiate themselves from others in a competitive marketplace by 'specializing' in an area of diversity in which there is a particular need or gap in provision" (Spaaij et al., 2014). The importance of diversity cannot be understated as a global phenomenon in sports; however, achieving diversity is a challenge shared around the world.

The United States has Title IX, which promotes gender equity in federally funded sports, and the United Kingdom addresses disability and gender along with race and ethnicity through federally mandated Equality Standards. Government funds for sports are only available to organizations meeting minimum standards. In Australia, however, there are no national laws

that provide either incentives for diversity or disincentives for lack of diversity (Spaaij et al., 2014). There are concerns as to whether policies translate into practice for sports organizations when considering the dearth of women and minorities in leadership positions in sports organizations throughout the United States, England, Australia, and the rest of the world.

The Australian Football League and Cricket Australia publicize diversity policies within their organizations and are considered atypical by virtue of being relatively proactive in valuing and promoting diversity. The diversity statements, however, focus on participation opportunities. The majority of the cricket and association football clubs do not consider managing diversity as part of their core business, according to surveys of professional and county clubs (Spaaij et al., 2014).

The Football Association, which governs the Premier League and other football clubs throughout Europe, focuses on diversity initiatives, especially intentions to hire coaches and managers of black, Asian, and ethnic minority (BAME) backgrounds. According to the British Broadcasting Corporation (2014), 12 years after the NFL adopted the Rooney rule, only 19 of 552 (3%) of the elite coaching positions in the English Football League were occupied by blacks or ethnic minorities.

The 2014–2015 English Football League's third Inclusion and Anti-Discrimination Action-Plan continued to address measures to "widen" the diversity of the workforce beyond just the coaching ranks. The plan addressed promoting open and transparent recruitment processes and working with black players and their representatives to identify their educational and career progression needs while supporting and implementing programs to build experienced coaches with higher levels of qualifications from BAME communities. The 2013–2014 English Football League (2014) Action-Plan addressing the goal to "Widen Football's Talent Pool" includes the following priorities:

- The Football Associations' equality monitoring tool is to be implemented across football and targets set to increase the number of people choosing to provide this data.

- 50% of County Football Associations are to establish Inclusion Advisory Groups.

- The Football Associations and Professional Football Association (PFA) are to support the "On Board" governance training for a further cohort of predominantly BAME candidates.

- The Football Association is to deliver a Women's Leadership Programme, for women aiming for senior management or board roles.

- The Football Associations is to continue to deliver positive action programs to recruit more BAME, female and disabled coaches, referees, tutors and adjudicators.

- The Football Associations, with the assistance of counties and clubs, to publicize and further deliver actions to increase participation and develop talent amongst Asian boys and girls.

- The Football Associations is to deliver two workshops with clubs, leagues and County Associations to gain active support for lesbian, gay, bisexual, and transgender (LGBT) inclusion messaging and projects.

The Chair of the Football Association's Inclusion Advisory Board noted the scope of the original 2013–2014 action plan, remarking, "In addition to looking at racial equality, homophobia and LGB&T inclusion, the plan also addresses gender equality and sexism, disability access, mental wellbeing and the abuse of disabled people, as well as engagement with Asian and faith-based communities" (Rabbats, 2014).

The 2015–2016 action plan published achievements to date noting equity standards mandated for all clubs, greater inclusion of advisory groups, and the celebration of black history month, international woman day, and LGBT history month (English Football League, 2016, p. 10–11). In promoting diversity, there is an underlying rationale that attracting talent of diverse backgrounds is beneficial for team and club performance. Whether programs, practices, or policy-level initiatives at the federal or organizational level have actually been effective in promoting diversity in sports organizations around the world remains questionable.

DISCUSSION QUESTIONS

1. Explain diversity in sports employment and the correlation with inclusion.
2. What strategies can be implemented to increase the numbers or percentages of minorities and women working in sports organizations?

3. How can homologous reproduction actually become an advantage for minorities and females in the sports industry?
4. What strategies can sports organizations implement to ensure a supportive environment for LGBT workers?

APPLIED ACTIVITIES

1. Design a poster that addresses inclusion to be displayed in a workout facility on a large campus.
2. Perform a cursory review of the staff directory for a professional team in the NBA, WNBA, NFL, MLS, or MLB. To the extent possible, report on the gender diversity in executive positions and throughout the franchise. Compare the results with information published in the most recent Racial and Gender Report Cards published by Richard Lapchick available at http://www.tidesport.org/reports.html.

CASE STUDY

The Transgender/Intersex Strength and Conditioning Coach

Information for this case was based on multiple interviews. To maintain anonymity, "Terry" and "ABC University" are pseudonyms.

In 2011, a small, private Midwestern university took advantage of a NCAA Strategic Alliance Matching Grant to hire "Terry" as the athletic department's newest strength and conditioning coach. Terry was a double-sport athlete and alumni of the university who excelled as an All-American goalie on the women's soccer team. Three years after being hired, colleagues were instructed to refer to "Terry" as a male after revealing to the athletics staff that he had filed a legal name change and had gone through treatments that had alter his physical appearance. It was a classic admission of a transgender whereby an individual identifies their gender classification as being opposite of his or her biological birth sex.

Fast forward to 2017. Terry recently parted from ABC University upon accepting a job out of intercollegiate athletics. In the interim, Terry revealed that he is actually biologically classified as "intersex" because a medical team determined the presence of "androgen insensitivity syndrome (AIS)," which essentially meant that he had the physical makeup of a female but the genetic makeup of a male when born. Also referred to as testicular feminization, approximately 1 in 20,000 births are known to have the male XY chromosomes but are identified physically as a female (Edens-Hurst, 2017). In essence, Terry's biological traits were never truly male or female.

There are numerous educational resources addressing inclusion for LGBTQ athletes and students, but very little detailing human resource implications for a LGBTQ faculty of staff, let alone an intersex employee. The case herein only scratches the surface of the emotional, psychological, physiological, and legal implications of a transgender or intersex individual. The primary objective is to reinforce the need for organizations to facilitate an inclusive environment, allowing all employees to thrive in their work experience.

Formative Years

In Terry's earliest memories, around 7 years old, he knew that he wasn't supposed to be a girl. He just knew. His upbringing, however, otherwise determined that societal expectations toward gender identity would prevail. Terry grew up in the small farming town, the youngest of nine children in a conservative Roman-Catholic family. He attended Catholic grade school until the fourth grade. His mom dressed him in skirts, gave him dolls to play with, and primped his hair every day. Terry always packed a pair of pants and changed in the bathroom before the school bell rang.

Terry played basketball and football with the boys, but his teachers told him that he needed to stop. He hung out with his dad in the garage every day after school, tinkering on cars, and could change a gear shift at age 10, but his mom told him to stop. Instead, Terry spent more time shooting hoops and eventually earned a scholarship to play on the women's basketball and soccer teams at ABC University. He described never wanting to be in the locker room with his high school or college female teammates for very long because he felt uncomfortable, similar to how a woman would feel if she had to enter the men's locker room to change in front of a bunch of naked guys.

Physiological Transformation

Terry described the constant charade of trying to conform to societal expectations for a female despite his preferred gender identity as a male, not realizing that he was actually an intersex. The physical transition included testosterone therapy in the form of biweekly injections for the rest of his life to maintain hormonal levels that are slightly lower than those of an average male in puberty. Terry also had what he referred to as "top surgery" (a mastectomy) to remove his breast tissue and to prevent breast cancer, which is prevalent in his family history. One side of Terry's female reproductive anatomy was not fully developed, and reoccurrences of cysts assisted in a decision to have a full hysterectomy in his mid-20s. The decision to have a mastectomy and hysterectomy was more of a medical health benefit than a cosmetic alteration.

After years of enduring surgeries accompanying the medically necessary transformation, a team of doctors discovered Terry was one of few individuals in the world born with the physical makeup of a female, but the genetic makeup of a male, which actually classified him as intersex as opposed to just a transgender. An intersex individual is described as anatomically and genetically ambiguous. One of the most publicized cases of an intersex is Caster Semenya of South Africa, a prominent track star who won a gold medal in the women's 800-meter race at the 2016 Rio Olympics. Semenya, who has been at the center of gender-verification testing controversy, identifies as a female despite possessing "both male and female sex characteristics, as well as testosterone levels in a range higher than average for women" (Wells & Darnell, 2014, p. 46).

In terms of physical changes, the biggest misconception expressed by Terry is that people think someone gets stronger with testosterone therapy, but that isn't always the case. As a certified strength and conditioning coach, Terry suggested that although genetic makeup plays a significant role, if trained correctly, a female body can do almost as much as a male's body (e.g., lifting weights or working out).

Legal Name Change

A legal name change for Terry (his first name was legally changed) was important in the process of self-identifying as a male. However, the process was long and arduous. Before legally changing his name in 2013, Terry signed up for Kohl's credit card using the new name, which didn't match any personal forms of identification (i.e., birth certificate and driver's license). Confusion and misunderstanding were common in ordinary business dealings. He was mistakenly accused of fraudulent activities on more than one occasion.

The official/legal name change required the assistance of a lawyer to petition the court, which further mandated a published notice of the hearing. The court also required Terry to complete a declaration of gender change form complete with certified signatures from a physician/psychologist. Thereafter, an official name change was a matter of submitting applications and paying the required processing fee.

Thereafter, Terry had the necessary court documentation to legally change his name on his house title, vehicle title, credit cards, bank accounts, and utility bills. The court documentation had also permitted Terry to change the first name on his official college transcripts, diploma, and all of his employment identification forms required to process payroll, insurance benefits, and federal/state taxes.

Workplace Experiences

Upon graduating college, Terry earned a personal trainer certification from the National Academy of Sports Medicine and worked at a local fitness center. On one occasion before starting testosterone treatments, a client complained that a female was changing in the men's locker room. Thereafter, Terry primarily used a private bathroom.

In addition to working at the fitness center, Terry assisted the women's basketball team at his alma mater (ABC University) by designing and supervising off-season workouts. Eventually, he was hired full time by the university's athletic department as one of a few institutions in the country to employ a full-time female strength and conditioning coach. Terry's nickname in college had always been a derivative of his last name, which is how student-athletes and coaches most often referred to him as on a daily basis.

Even with the legal name change, there were no changes in the daily routines and workplace experiences in training collegiate student-athletes. While researching the processes to change his name on his academic records, Terry met with ABC University's assistant vice president for diversity and equity (also the Title IX Coordinator) who suggested disclosing his legal name and gender identity to his supervisor (the director of athletics [AD]). With permission, the assistant vice president briefed the AD on the employee's gender and name change.

Terry's initial conversation with his AD took place 2 years after the legal name change, and it was mutually decided that he should personally address the athletic staff. At the first department meeting of the academic year, Terry announced that he had changed his name and emphasized his desire for just wanting everyone to feel comfortable around him, whether on or off campus.

For whatever reason, Terry suspected half of the staff "already knew" his story, and although everyone was provided an opportunity to ask questions publically or privately, only one close colleague actually did ask a question in private. It was apparent that Terry's declaration of changing his name and identifying as a male was a foregone conclusion to the athletic staff. Otherwise, Terry described the reaction as positive; coaches and athletic administrators didn't treat him any differently following the staff meeting. Terry also described a feeling of relief and closure after notifying the staff of his name change, especially considering it took less than 5 minutes to publicly disclose his news. At the time, he had no idea he was diagnosed with AIS, which partially explained why he identified as a male his entire life. No one questioned his sexual identity, his role in the department, or anything that was said in the athletic staff meeting. It was as if everything in the athletic department was back to status quo without ever skipping a beat, and in no time, the strength and conditioning coach was right back in the weight room, training his student-athletes. In hindsight, it may have been less of a reaction if it were known at the time that he was actually classified as an intersex. The AD confirmed the positive reaction to Terry's disclosure at the staff meeting and indicated that absolutely nothing had changed following his announcement. Far more important than acceptance of his gender identification was the mutual respect of his colleagues in accepting Terry as just another employee of the university. For the AD, Terry was still a university employee expected to fulfill his role in the athletic department. Gender identification did not change any of those expectations.

There were only minimal administrative as a result of Terry's name change and identification as a male when he had been known as a female his entire life. In addition to updating personnel files and forms with the legal name, the communications director had to determine the appropriate language for addressing gender when preparing Terry's biography for the athletics staff directory website. Following is a summary of what appeared as Terry's biography when employed by the university:

> Terry is beginning his seventh season as the strength and conditioning coach at ABC University. A 2007 graduate of ABC

University, Terry was an accomplished athlete in both soccer and basketball. A goalie for the women's soccer team from 2003–2006, Terry set the school standard for 19 career shutouts including a single-season record 14 shout-outs in 2006 while earning All-American honors. He received his certification from the National Academy of Sports Medicine (ABC University, 2015).

Terry concedes that professors, colleagues, family, and friends who knew him by his original female name will, over time, get used to referring to him as a male. Although mistakenly using the wrong pronoun (*she* vs. *he*) is common, Terry acknowledges that it isn't easy to recondition the brain to a new frame of reference. On the bright side, new student-athletes on campus only knew him as a male strength and conditioning coach and not a former female star athlete because in his mind, and hopefully in the minds of his colleagues, "that person doesn't exist anymore."

Afterthoughts

Perhaps, much of Terry's experiences may have been different throughout his entire life if it were known from the beginning that he was an intersex, or perhaps, nothing would have been different. Information on transgender and intersex employees is extremely rare. In sports and athletics, information and research focus primarily on participation opportunities for student-athletes. For universities and athletic departments to create a supportive environment, the most important ingredient is an open mind. There are resources on college campuses, in conference offices, and at the national level addressing transgender and intersex issues that can assist in sensitive employment areas. There is much more to maintaining an inclusive work environment for transgender and intersex employees than designating gender-neutral bathrooms.

CASE STUDY QUESTIONS

1. What is the difference between a transgender employee and an intersex employee?

2. Speculate on the different outcomes for Terry and/or ABC University if it were known he was an intersex individual when being considered for the position as the Head Strength and Conditioning Coach for the athletic department.

3. After reviewing the case, what appear to be the biggest challenges for intersex employees?

4. How surprising was the reaction of the athletic staff to Terry's announcement?

REFERENCES

Acosta, V., and Carpenter, L. (2014). *Women in intercollegiate sport. A longitudinal national study. Thirty-seven-year update.* Retrieved from http://www.acostacarpenter .org/

Barry, R. (2011, May 16). Going public. NBA figure sheds shadow life. *New York Times,* A-1.

Berman, M., & Phillips, A. (2017, March 1). North Carolina governor signs bill repealing and replacing transgender bathroom law amid criticism. The Washington Post. A02.

Boswell, T. (1987, June 16). *Affirmative action in baseball should go from the bottom up.* The Los Angeles Times. Retrieved from http://articles.latimes.com/1987-06-16 /sports/sp-7529_1_affirmative-action-plan

British Broadcasting Corporation. (2014, November 14). *Premier League clubs to develop ethnic minority coaches.* Retrieved from http://www.bbc.com/sport /football/30049688

Congress.gov. (2013). *S.815: Employment Non-Discrimination Act of 2013.* Retrieved from https://www.congress.gov/bill/113th-congress/senate-bill/815

Cunningham, G., & Melton, N. (2011, May, 1). The benefits of sexual orientation diversity in sport organizations. *Journal of Homosexuality, 58,* 647–663.

Cunningham, G., & Melton, N. (2014). Varying degrees of support: Understanding parents' positive attitudes toward LGBT coaches. *Journal of Sport Management, 28,* 387–396

Detroit Free Press. (2014, January 2). *As Detroit Lions look for coach, NFL diversity committee believes process "going the right way."* Retrieved from http://archive.freep .com/article/20140101/SPORTS01/301010061/detroit-lions-nfl-diversity-committee

Doherty, A., & Chelladurai, P. (1999). Managing cultural diversity in sports organizations: A theoretical perspective. *Journal of Sport Management, 13,* 280–297.

Edens-Hurst, A. (2017). Androgyn insensitivity syndrome. U.S. National Library of Medicine. Retrieved from https://medlineplus.gov/ency/article/001180.htm

English Football League. (2014). *English football's inclusion and anti-discrimination action plan. Season 2013–14 update and focus for the future.* Retrieved from file:///C:/Users/btiell/Downloads/english-footballs-inclusion-and-anti -discrimination-action-plan%20(1).pdf

English Football League. (2016). *English football's inclusion and anti-discrimination action plan. 2015–16 report and future priorities.* Retrieved from file:///C: /Users/btiell/Downloads/11267-english-footballs-inclusion-and-anti -discrimination-action-plan.pdf

Fox, A. (2015, May 19). How the Rooney rule succeeds. . .and falls short. *ESPN.* Retrieved from http://espn.go.com/nfl/story/_/id/12867233/rooney-rule-opened -doors-minority-head-coaching-candidates-do-more

Franklin, B., Ford, K., and Morrison, K. (2011, August). *NCAA inclusion of Trans-gender student-athletes.* National Collegiate Athletic Association Office of Inclusion.

Friend, J., & Leuns, A. (1989). Overcoming discrimination in sports management: A systematic approach to affirmative action. *Journal of Sport Management, 3,* 151–157.

General Assembly of North Carolina. (2016, March 23). Session Law 2016-3. House Bill 2.

Glanville, D. (2016, June 3). Now is not the time to give up on the Selig rule. *ESPN.* Retrieved from http://www.espn.com/mlb/story/_/id/15915660 /do-not-give-selig-rule

Griffin, P. & Taylor, H. (2017). *Champions of respect: Best practices for inclusion of LGBTQ student-athletes and staff in NCAA programs.* National Collegiate Athletic Association. Retrieved from https://www.ncaapublications.com /p-4305-champions-of-respect-inclusion-of-lgbtq-student-athletes-and-staff -in-ncaa-programs.aspx

Hoenig, C. (2014, April 30). Major league white: How pro sports aren't what they seem. *Diversity Inc.* Retrieved from http://www.diversityinc.com/news /major-league-white-pro-sports-arent-seem/

Huseinagić, E., & Hodz̆, A. (2011, September). Importance of emotional intelli- gence to sport actors and its influence in creating organizational climate. *Sport Scientific and Practical Aspects, 8*(1), 43–48.

International Olympic Committee. (2014, December 9). *Olympic Agenda 2020 Recom- mendations* Retrieved from https://stillmed.olympic.org/media/Document%20 Library/OlympicOrg/Documents/Olympic-Agenda-2020/Olympic-Agenda -2020-20-20-Recommendations.pdf#_ga=1.58721965.1200660115.1490906670

Kamphoff, C., Gill, D., Araki, K., & Hammond, C. (2010, April 1). A content analysis of cultural diversity in the association for applied sport psychology's conference. *Journal of Applied Psychology, 22,* 231–245.

Kamphoff, C. S., Armentrout, S.M., & Driska, A. (2010). The token female: Wom- en's experiences as Division I collegiate head coaches of men's teams. *Journal of Intercollegiate Sport, 3,* 297–315

Killion, K. (2016). Rick Welts, Warriors exec, strives to be example for gay youth. *San Francisco Chronicle.* Retrieved from http://www.sfchronicle.com/warriors /article/Rick-Welts-Warriors-exec-strives-to-be-example-7182265.php

Knight, P. (1990, August 21). Nike is pushing progress for minorities. USA Today. 8A.

Krane, V. (2001). We can be athletic and feminine, but do we want to? Challenging hegemonic femininity in women's sport. *Quest, 53*, 115–133.

Krane, V., & Barber, H. (2005). Identity tensions in lesbian intercollegiate coaches. *Research Quarterly for Exercise and Sport, 76*, 67–81.

Lapchick, R. (2016). *The racial and gender report card.* Institute for Diversity and Ethics in Sport. University of Central Florida. Retrieved from http://www.tidesport.org/reports.html

Maloney, J. (2016, January 22). Curt Miller seeks to "establish a culture" with young Connecticut Sun. *WNBA.com.* Retrieved from http://www.wnba.com/news/curt-miller-connecticut-sun-new-head-coach/

Maske, M. (2015, January 7). Diversity group files complaint over Redskins GM search; NFL finds no violation. *Washington Post.* Retrieved from http://www.washingtonpost.com/news/football-insider/wp/2015/01/07/diversity-group-files-complaint-over-redskins-gm-search/

Metropolitan Sports Facility Authority. (2016). 2015-16 Affirmative Action Plan. Published by the State of Minnesota. Retrieved from http://www.msfa.com/content/AGENDAS/Affirmative%20Action%20Plan%202015%20-%202016.pdf

Minnick, B. (2017, April 12). Bill would pull NC colleges out of ACC if state is boycotted again. *CBS North Carolina.* Retrieved from http://wncn.com/2017/04/11/bill-would-pull-nc-colleges-out-of-acc-if-state-is-boycotted-again/

National Collegiate Athletic Association Office of Inclusion (2016). *Office of Inclusion mission.* Retrieved from http://www.ncaa.org/ncaa-organizational-structure/membership-and-student-athlete-affairs/office-inclusion

Patra, K. (2016, February 4). Roger Goodell: NFL creating a Rooney rule for women. *NFL.com.* Retrieved from http://www.nfl.com/news/story/0ap3000000632320/article/roger-goodell-nfl-creating-a-rooney-rule-for-women

PGA of America. (2016, February 26). *PGA of America milestones in diversity.* Retrieved from https://www.pga.org/articles/pga-america-milestones-diversity

Proxmire, D. (2008, December). Coaching diversity: The Rooney rule, its application and ideas for expansion. *American Constitution Society for Law and Policy.*

Rabbats, H. (2014). Introductory letter. In English Football League, *English football's inclusion and anti-discrimination action plan. Season 2013–14 update and focus for the future.* Retrieved from file:///C:/Users/btiell/Downloads/english-footballs-inclusion-and-anti-discrimination-action-plan%20(1).pdf

Ragins, B., Singh, R., & Cornwell, J. (2007). Making the invisible visible: Fear and disclosure of sexual orientation at work. *Journal of Applied Psychology, 4*, 1103–1118.

Sagas, M., Cunningham, G. B., & Teed, K. (2006). An examination of homologous reproduction in the representation of assistant coaches of women's teams. *Sex Roles, 55*, 503–510.

Sartore, M., & Cunningham, G. (2009). Sexual prejudice, participatory decisions, and panoptic control: Implications for sexual minorities in sport. *Sex Roles, 60*, 100–113.

Scott, D. (2014). *Contemporary leadership in sport organizations.* Champaign, IL: Human Kinetics.

Spaaij, R., Farquharson, K., McGee, J., Jeanes, R., Lusher, D., & Gorman. S. (2014). A fair game for all? How community sports clubs in Australia deal with diversity. *Journal of Sport & Social Issues, 38*(4), 346–365.

Spears, M. (2016, June 1) *The distressing lack of black leadership in the NBA.* Retrieved from http://theundefeated.com/features/the-distressing-lack-of-black-leadership-in-the-nba/

Stahura, K., & Greenwood, M. (2001). Occupational employment patterns within women's intercollegiate athletics. Revisiting homologous reproduction. *Research Quarterly for Exercise and Sport, 71*, A-110.

Stangl, J. M., & Kane, M. J. (1991). Structural variables that offer explanatory power for the underrepresentation of women coaches since Title IX: The case for homologous reproduction. *Sociology of Sport Journal, 8*, 47–60.

Tracy, M. (2017, March 31). Basketball outsize role in repeal of bathroom bill. *The New York Times*, B-9.

U.S. Equal Employment Opportunity Commission. (2017). *Overview.* Retrieved from https://www.eeoc.gov/eeoc/index.cfm

United States Department of State. (2013). Russia 2013 Human Rights Report. Executive summary. United States department of Department of State Bureau of Democracy, Human Rights, and Labor. Retrieved from https://www.state.gov/documents/organization/220536.pdf

Wakiji, D. (2011, May 13). Women in the NHL: An idea on ice. ESPN-W. Retrieved from http://www.espn.com/espnw/news/article/6529908/idea-ice

Wall Street Journal. (2007). Nike settles discrimination lawsuit for $7.6 million. Wall Street Journal. B1, 9.

Wells, C., & Darnell, S. (2014). Caster Semenya, gender verification and the politics of fairness in an online track & field community. *Sociology of Sport Journal, 31*, 44–65.

Whisenant, W. (2008, February). Sustaining male dominance in interscholastic athletics: A case of homologous reproduction. . .or not? *Sex Roles, 58*, 768–775.

Youngmisuk, O. (2017, March 28). *Adam Silver wants NBA head coach sooner than later.* ESPN. Retrieved from http://www.espn.com/nba/story/_/id/19021351/nba-commissioner-adam-silver-wants-woman-head-coach-sooner-later

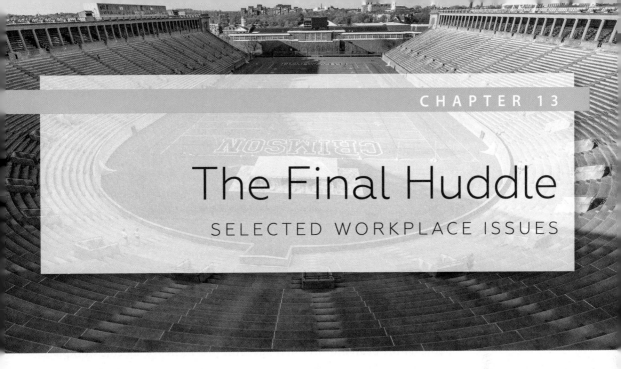

CHAPTER 13

The Final Huddle

SELECTED WORKPLACE ISSUES

Ethics are based on common sense, doing the right things, and having the right core values. Perhaps what drives unethical behavior in collegiate coaches is that they get to a point where they become bulletproof. They feel pressure from supervisors or the institution and may decide to take shortcuts in order to satisfy or exceed expectations. Unfortunately, victories may become more important than the good of the game or the welfare of the student-athlete. A coach's focus may get out of order. It's human nature. It happens. It shouldn't, but it does. We are all fallible.

Bob Vecchione
Executive Director
National Association of Collegiate Directors of Athletics

LEARNING OUTCOMES

1. Identify workplace issues prevalent in sports organizations.

2. Identify antecedents and consequences for work–life conflict.

3. Identify strategies at the personal and the organizational level to improve work–life conflict in sports organizations.

4. Describe remedies to minimize burnout, especially among coaches in sports organizations.

5. Describe individual and organizational strategies to improve ethical conduct in sports organizations.

KEY TERMS

Bullying	Hazing	Quid pro quo
Burnout	Hostile work environment	Sexual harassment
Compressed workweek	Job sharing	Telecommuting
Ethical conduct	Life and Work Balance Inventory	Work–life balance
Flex time		Work–life conflict
Flexible work arrangements	Maslach Burnout Inventory (MBI)	Work–life integration
Harassment		

Lead-Off

Every organization has workplace issues, whether a member of the corporate world, educational institution, small business, nonprofit, or government agency. Ethical conduct is one subject permeating all business institutions, but the nature of an industry may affect the prevalence of specific workplace issues and the degree to which individuals tasked with human resources must address them. For instance, the prison/correctional industry is likely to be more susceptible to workplace violence, whereas manufacturing and mining industries generally have a higher rate of occupational safety violations.

The sports industry is not without its unique characteristics and influences that affect the types of workplace issues generally apparent in athletic departments, professional franchises, health clubs, gymnasiums, and retail stores. The fragmented segments of the sports industry mean that the type and prevalence of workplace issues vary widely throughout organizations. Retail sporting goods stores will typically experience a greater frequency of workplace issues related to employee theft, whereas professional sports may be prone to greater instances of burnout.

© Dusit/shutterstock

This chapter provides an overview of a small segment of workplace issues that are generally apparent in the sports industry; however, there are exceptions to what employees in organizations experience. Selected workplace issues addressed in this chapter include work–life balance, burnout, ethical conduct, and harassment.

Work–Life Balance

Work–life balance is an issue for all types of employees in the sports industry, regardless of gender, marital status, or family status. When the sports organization becomes a demanding work environment and the perceived role expectations on the job supersede an individual's personal/family obligations to adhere to the needs of the department and/or organization, **work–life balance**, also known as work–life integration, is interrupted, and conflict is inevitable. **Work–life conflict** also works in reverse when personal demands supersede work obligations. Research has indicated personal sacrifices in time and energy for the sake of the business contribute to high levels of work–life conflict and that the type of business (i.e., a dynamic, pressure-induced environment) is a contributing factor (Kossek, Colquitt, & Noe, 2001).

Conflicts in demands between roles at work and life are unavoidable but can often be managed (Boles, Howard, & Donofrio, 2001; Greenhaus & Beutell, 1985; Greeenhaus & Powell, 2003). A sports facility director may face conflicts arising from a family illness that coincides with the timing of hosting a tournament. A coach who wants to start a family yet still move up the career ladder may be hesitant due to a lack of working in a family-friendly environment, and an athletic trainer who wants to be devoted to both his or her athletes and his or her own children may find there aren't enough hours in the day to satisfy both constituents.

Work–life balance issues, are prevalent in the sports industry. Managing human resources in sports organizations necessitates understanding the nature of the industry (or industry sector), understanding the antecedents affecting conflict as well as the consequences, and applying strategies to improve work–life balance.

ANTECEDENTS TO WORK–LIFE CONFLICT

In 2006, the National Collegiate Athletic Association (NCAA) implemented the **Life and Work Balance Inventory**, which was completed by over 4000 athletics personnel. Of the responses received, 42% of the sample agreed that they were able to adequately balance their current life and athletics commitments effectively, whereas 40% of the sample disagreed (NCAA Digest, 2006). The phenomenon is apparent in all sectors of the sports industry when work and personal demands overlap.

When the demands of an individual's professional life and his or her personal responsibilities compete, work–life balance is adversely impacted due to role incongruity. The fact that work–life conflict is bidirectional (work interferes with personal obligations and vice versa) suggests that antecedents can be categorized as either job-related or life-related factors. Research more frequently suggests that antecedents to work–life conflict can be categorized as sociocultural, organizational, or personal (Dixon & Bruening, 2005; Dixon et al., 2008; Mazerolle, Goodman, & Pitney, 2015). Categorizing stressors according to these three domains also assists when formulating the strategies to potentially improve work–life balance.

Sociocultural factors include the general nature of the industry. The sports field generally attracts people who are competitive and passionate about their work. This leads to a dynamic and productive environment but one in which work–life balance can be a low priority. The very nature of intercollegiate and professional sports demands nontraditional work hours on nights and weekends, thus further adding to work–life conflict. The same is true for other sectors of the field. Also considered an antecedent to work–life balance are societal perceptions, such as the role of the female generally as the primary caretaker.

At an organizational level, stressors relate to workplace characteristics, including job pressures, workplace policies, work hours, organizational structure, and workplace roles. Antecedents typical in the sports industry may include long hours, required travel, lack of control over work schedules, inadequate staffing, and unsupportive supervisors. These demands interfere with personal responsibilities and time. Concern for a sick parent, spouse, child, or pet potentially causes a strain on job roles as an individual's attention is diverted from work responsibilities.

Finally, on a personal level, an individual's personality, temperament, and emotional maturity may contribute to work–life balance issues in terms of how stress is perceived and handled. Personal factors may be a hindrance or a benefit for individuals faced with work–life balance issues.

CONSEQUENCES OF WORK–LIFE CONFLICT

In the face of work–life conflict or any stressor, the consequences may affect an individual physically, emotionally, and/or psychologically. Anxiety, depression, irritability, exhaustion, and a weakened immune system are all potential concerns for individuals experiencing problems with work–life balance. In general, individuals experiencing work–life conflict are at risk for adverse impacts to their health and well-being.

Poor work–life balance generally has negative consequences for an organization. If work–life conflict results in low levels of job satisfaction, increases in absenteeism, or a higher frequency of the use of employee assistance programs (EAPs), an organization may experience adverse financial consequences, low morale, and the loss of productivity.

One of the consequences of an industry perceived to be laden with work–life balance issues is the loss of potential talent. As younger generations fill the higher-level positions in sports organizations, including coaches, referees, trainers, support staff, and managers, a greater emphasis on work–life balance is likely to be needed. Gen X, Gen Y, and the millennial generation have all been described as unique from previous generations in their increased interest in balancing their lives with their work. These attitudes may negatively affect an individual's desire to work in the sports industry if it is perceived as a deterrent to effective work–life balance.

Research in intercollegiate athletics supports the notion that the dilemma is driving talented young coaches and administrators, especially women, out of the profession (Bruening et al., 2008; Dixon et al., 2008; Lough, Tiell, & Osborne, 2008). To prevent further decline of the number of women in many sectors of the sports industry, the promotion of a climate or culture of work–life balance should be undertaken (Tiell et al., 2006). When recruiting young coaches and administrators in any sector of the sports industry, this approach may allow an organization to secure a top talent while a competitor struggles to understand how it failed to secure the employee (Lough et al., 2008). Therefore, the consequence of an industry that is considered unconducive to work–life balance is a difficulty in recruiting and retaining talent. Job seekers may shun employment in a sector of the sports organization for fear of an inability to effectively manage work–life balance.

STRATEGIES FOR EFFECTIVE WORK–LIFE INTEGRATION

Strategies to improve **work–life integration** are most effective at the organizational and personal level. Because sports is a hyper-competitive industry, it is difficult to impart strategies on a sociocultural level that would likely impact the industry as a whole. There have been strides to assist intercollegiate athletics in minimizing time demands for coaches and personnel by instituting national policies for seasons of competition, permissible

Pat Summitt, former women's basketball coach at the University of Tennessee, was a strong advocate for family-friendly programs. Her son, Tyler, often traveled with the team.

recruiting periods, and the length of out-of-season workouts, for example. Overall, however, grandiose efforts to change the culture of the sports industry in order to achieve better work–life balance for employees are not predicted for the near future.

Work–life balance may be enhanced at the organizational level through leadership that embraces the inherent value of creating a supportive climate for employees to effectively minimize conflicting role demands. Although research suggests that such benefits as flexible scheduling and onsite child care can reduce the stress associated with work–family conflict, there is evidence indicating that such policies are not utilized in both corporate and university settings (Dixon et al., 2008) (see **Table 13-1**).

TABLE 13-1: Division I Athletic Administrators' Perceptions of Programs Available and Used to Enhance Work–Life Balance

	Program Exists	Program Used
Compensatory time off for working required overtime	63.3 %	39.4 %
Flexible work arrangements through job sharing	75.9 %	34.3 %
Compressed work week options	49.5 %	15.5 %
Telecommuting options	50.5 %	17.9 %
Child-care arrangements or resource finder/referral service	53.5 %	25.8 %
Family travel options for athletic events/activities	68.5 %	43.5 %
Wellness programs for employees	79.6 %	57.9 %
Family access to fitness and exercise opportunities	80.2 %	59.5 %
Referrals to resource providers for family-related problems	81.5 %	55.2 %
Programs for family problems (EAPs)	79.3 %	53.0 %
Government-mandated time off for dependent care (child/elder)	84.5 %	63.9 %
Paid paternity leave	80.4 %	55.5 %
Family emergency care leave	92.1 %	76.6 %
Phased or partial retirement plans	79.9 %	59.5 %
Tuition reimbursement	86.7 %	76.9 %
Sabbaticals	47.6 %	08.3 %
Work–life task force or committee	51.6 %	18.5 %

Note: The second column reports the percentage of the sample indicating that the program exists; the third column reports the percentage agreeing or strongly agreeing that the program is used by coaches, administrators, and support staff.

TABLE 13-2: Divisional Results: Availability of Programs for Work–Life Balance Reported by Athletic Administrators

	Division I		Division II		Division III	
	AD	**SWA**	**AD**	**SWA**	**AD**	**SWA**
Compensatory time off for required overtime	63.7%	62.8%	26.9%	30.7%	27.8%	23.9%
Flexible work arrangements— job sharing	62.5%	54.3%	16.7%	14.8%	17.8%	24.5%
Compressed work week options	51.2%	47.7%	38.0%	39.8%	37.8%	33.5%
Telecommuting options	50.0%	50.8%	15.7%	17.0%	22.2%	20.6%
Child-care arrangements or resource finder/referral service	57.1%	50.3%	15.7%	12.5%	21.7%	19.4%
Family travel options for athletic events/activities	70.8%	66.8%	35.2%	37.5%	34.4%	38.7%
Wellness programs for employees	83.9%	75.9%	25.0%	30.7%	27.8%	29.7%
Family access to fitness and exercise opportunities	84.5%	76.4%	9.3%	14.8%	7.2%	9.0%
Referrals to resource providers for family-related problems	85.1%	78.4%	13.0%	13.6%	11.7%	9.0%
Programs for family problems (EAPs)	79.8%	76.9%	37.0%	42.0%	40.0%	47.1%
Government-mandated time off for dependent care	80.4%	87.9%	25.0%	29.5%	31.1%	29.7%
Paid paternity leave	82.1%	79.9%	4.6%	3.4%	10.0%	6.5%
Family emergency care leave	89.9%	94.0%	11.1%	10.2%	7.5%	7.7%
Phased or partial retirement plans	81.0%	78.9%	37.0%	50.0%	41.1%	45.8%
Tuition reimbursement	83.9%	88.9%	25.0%	21.6%	31.1%	27.7%
Sabbaticals	47.0%	47.7%	3.7%	5.7%	4.4%	6.5%
Work–life task force or committee	56.0%	47.7%	13.0%	18.2%	19.4%	16.8%

Note: AD, athletic director; SWA, senior woman administrator. Over 900 administrators responded to the survey developed and administered by Dr. Bonnie Tiell.

There are also differences in the availability of programs according to divisions in the NCAA (see **Table 13-2**). Research has found that programs directed toward improving work–life balance are available more often in Division I athletic departments than in Division II or III institutions (Lough et al., 2008).

Although Tables 13-1 and 13-2 focus on the perception of administrators in intercollegiate athletics, the results can be generalized throughout the sports industry. With the exception of sabbaticals, the programs listed may be applicable to professional sports, high school athletics, recreational sports, sports agencies, or locations specializing in manufacturing or sales.

One major key to managing the work–life struggle is to examine and redefine workloads. Some of the best solutions highlight a derivative of job sharing or "creative task coordination," whereby staff members perform duties based on what is the most efficient use of time instead of what is in someone's traditional job description. For example, if one staff member is in charge of game management for men's basketball and another for women's basketball, the two managers would benefit from dividing the dates of doubleheaders. They might also be encouraged to trade event-supervision duties throughout the season—if an important family event comes up for one, the other can cover the game that night in exchange for a night off the following game date.

Creative task sharing has also been formalized when individuals share titles and divvy up responsibilities according to what works best for the organization. For example, the 2016–2017 Kentucky Wesleyan University (2017) women's basketball program lists Caleb and Nicole Nieman as cohead coaches. Similarly, Ruben Volta and Ed Jackson are listed as cohead coaches of women's beach volleyball at Sacramento State University (2017).

Another way to ease the workload is to add staff members who are not seeking a great deal of compensation. The field of sports management is unique in the sense that securing interns, graduate assistants, or community volunteers willing to videotape a practice, announce a game, supervise a recreation program, or serve as a stadium usher is not difficult. Many colleges are formalizing internship positions and utilizing graduate assistants for the business side of athletics in addition to the traditional coaching ranks. Work–study programs are also utilized to help coaches and staff delegate tasks, such as laundry detail, van cleanup, video exchanges, and camp registrations. Interns and community volunteers are prevalent in all sectors of the industry, including professional sports, agencies, retail sales, sports tourism, and recreation. Although many community members will volunteer purely out of altruism, they can be thanked for their efforts with nonmonetary gifts, such as game tickets, team apparel, and social opportunities at university-sponsored events.

On a personal level, individuals can enhance their own work–life balance by setting boundaries. Although a willingness to go the extra mile for the organization is generally applauded, administrators and managers need to know that if an employee chooses to say no to a request or opportunity, it should not be instinctively viewed as a lack of dedication to the job. Along the same lines, administrators and coaches should take a hard look at all the "extras" they and their subordinates do in their jobs, ranging from organizing the department's holiday social, to

Interns or volunteers can alleviate work overloads for coaches and staff.

implementing the student-athlete-of-the-month honor, to lining up a guest speaker on nutrition for a team. Sometimes these tasks can be delegated to others, and if not, they should at least be acknowledged and, as deemed appropriate, evaluated as part of the staff member's job.

To avoid losing good staff members in the sports industry, administrators need to discover ways to accommodate individuals who want to step out of a role to address work–life conflicts, such as elder care or starting a family. Some sports organizations have added daily child care (on- or off-site) to benefit packages to help retain talented employees. Essentially, organizations may value the cost of the benefit as being less than the cost of a national search for a replacement hire. Intercollegiate athletic departments have been known to permit employees' entire families to travel to playoff games. This practice allows coaches, athletic trainers, and other athletic personnel to maintain a sense of balance during periods of intense workload. Benefit packages may be available to pay for a child-care provider to accompany a team when it travels.

When an assistant volleyball coach at the University of South Alabama requested fewer responsibilities so she could devote additional time to her newborn, the administration supported her move to a part-time position by adding a half-time position to supplement the program (Tiell et al., 2006). In some cases, making these accommodations means fitting the pieces of the personnel puzzle together in a different way, which may require a new level of strategic planning. The potential reward is that employees may feel more energized because they are doing exactly what they want to do without fear of losing their proverbial place on the career ladder.

Finally, technology should be addressed as both a potential hindrance and benefit for improving work–life balance for employees in the sports industry. Personnel must not only be well versed in how to use the technology but also disciplined in turning it off. Additionally, there should be realistic expectations of employee availability. Personnel working four evening games in a row should not be expected to answer an e-mail from home at 6 a.m. the following morning. Nor should they be expected to check cell phone messages every hour. The technology is there so they can use it at home to make their job easier, not so that they can be on call at all hours of the day and night.

Flexible Work Arrangements

Flexible work arrangements alter the traditional 8-hour, 5-day-per-week work schedule to any format acceptable to the employer. Compressed workweeks, flex time, telecommuting, and job sharing are examples of alternative arrangements for scheduling work. Throughout the sports industry, which is plagued by long and nontraditional hours, all forms of flexible work arrangements have the potential to facilitate greater productivity; however, caution must be given to minimize or eliminate potential negative consequences.

An example of a **compressed workweek** is permitting an employee to work 10-hour shifts over a 4-day period as opposed to 8-hour shifts over 5 days. Although possible benefits include saving on transportation costs or improving mental health due to having a longer stretch of time off, not all jobs are conducive to this type of arrangement. For example, a training room for an intercollegiate athletic department needs to have coverage throughout the week, and a compressed workweek schedule that leaves even one day uncovered would not be acceptable.

Flex time permits employees to select the part of the day or week on which they will report. Organizations, such as YMCAs and fitness facilities, may mandate that their employees must be on the payroll (or clock) during heavy-traffic periods but may also permit staff members to select whether to schedule their remaining hours before or after the peak period. The caution would be to ensure employees do not take advantage of the flexibility and to ensure proper staffing levels for special occasions outside of the traditional peak period.

Telecommuting permits employees to work from home or a remote location and increases the geographic reach for a talent pool. The practice requires discipline as well as access to the necessary technology, equipment, software, services, bandwidth, or infrastructure, depending on responsibilities. Telecommuting has arguably questioned the value of face-to-face interaction, true performance results, and the interface between personal and professional activities. The primary role of an intercollegiate athletics head coach requires face-to-face interaction with his or her staff and players, but auxiliary duties, such as scouting game film, placing recruiting calls, and completing practice logs, may be able to be performed outside the office setting.

True **job sharing** (not creative task coordination) is an arrangement utilizing two individuals to perform the duties of one. For example, two part-time office managers for the inside sales department of a Major League Soccer (MLS) team may be permitted to share the hours ordinarily worked by one full-time employee. In any job-sharing arrangement, it is important to assess role divisions and to consider overlaps that have budget implications.

Not all organizations or jobs in the sports industry are conducive to flexible work arrangements. In intercollegiate athletic departments, for example, the highest-ranking female administrators in the office (the senior woman administrators) generally noted that compressed work weeks and telecommuting are not utilized in their departments (Dixon et al., 2008, p. 149). When alternate work arrangements are used, administrators must continuously assess the usage and outcomes for the organization, department units, and employees.

Burnout

Burnout is a topic in human resources that sports managers and supervisors need to be aware of in order to effectively monitor their own performance and the performance of their staff. The lack of adequate work–life integration

The coaching industry is prone to burnout.

can contribute to burnout, which manifests as emotional exhaustion, fatigue, and diminished efficiency, primarily caused by prolonged stress.

Although a great deal of literature on burnout in the sports industry focuses on the athlete, a fair amount focuses on the occupation of coaching. Coaching is especially prone to burnout due to the nature of the profession as being highly demanding and requiring a great deal of commitment. In general, the long hours expected by employees working in many sectors of the sports industry—whether coaching, officiating, athletic training, or otherwise—contribute to work–life conflict, emotional exhaustion, and the potential for burnout. A research study in Europe indicated that one in four elite coaches of national sports teams in Norway and Sweden were reported to have experienced characteristics of burnout near the end of the season (Bentzen, Lemyre, & Kenttä, 2016).

STRESS AND BURNOUT

The primary antecedent to burnout is stress. Individuals experiencing burnout are typically conflicted by disillusionment with their role when they perceive inadequacy in meeting personal performance standards. Situational factors contributing to stress and occupational burnout may include a lack of social support (at home or work), dysfunctional workplace dynamics, and the demands of a particular role assignment. Personal factors that may have a significant effect on the occurrence of burnout include an individual's coping skills, emotional maturity, and tolerance for ambiguity or dysfunction. Feeling overwhelmed or experiencing a diminished sense of motivation and interest in work obligations are two manifestations of burnout.

A tool to measure occupational burnout is the **Maslach Burnout Inventory (MBI)**, which assesses an individual's perception of emotional exhaustion, depersonalization, and personal accomplishment. One study using the MBI involving 345 NCAA Division I intercollegiate athletic coaches indicated that a collaborative leadership style resulted in lower levels of occupational burnout (Ryska, 2009, p. 484). It has also been suggested that female coaches experience burnout more frequently than their male counterparts (Durand-Bush, Collins, & McNeill, 2012; Kelley, Eklund, & Ritter-Taylor, 1999; Kelley & Gill, 1993).

STRATEGIES TO MINIMIZE BURNOUT

Open dialogue and a supportive work climate are necessary to assist supervisors in monitoring employees who may be susceptible to burnout. Understanding

BOX 13-1

Suggested Techniques for Supervisors to Minimize or Prevent Burnout of Coaches and Athletic Personnel

1. Provide realistic expectations of role assignments.
2. Be sensitive to time and situational demands.
3. Define successful performance beyond winning percentages and championships.
4. Provide adequate resources (time, personnel, finances).
5. Provide adequate support systems.
6. Maintain open communication and an open-door policy.
7. Conduct "check" points to gauge reaction to stressors.
8. Create a supportive culture by fostering teamwork, respect, collaboration, and empathy.
9. Encourage employees to make a habit of self-reflection.
10. Encourage employees to take personal time.
11. Provide or acknowledge recognition and rewards.
12. Educate employees annually by addressing symptoms, coping skills, and available resources for dealing with potential burnout.
13. Provide education on the art and science of delegation.
14. Encourage a retreat before a season and a refresher after a season.
15. Be flexible to accommodate requests that may alleviate stress.
16. Mandate that coaches follow dead periods and encourage time away from work.
17. Get to know employees on a personal basis and learn interests and personality traits.
18. Make all staff members responsible for preventing burnout by knowing and reporting signs.

the nature of the work and the pressures accompanying the ebbs and flows of a good or poor season assists general managers and athletic directors to predict periods of potential emotional exhaustion in coaches and their staff. Knowing the general nature or personality of employees is important to detect possible changes in moods (irritability) or behavior (excessive tardiness or any substance abuse).

Addressing an individual who has experienced burnout requires managerial skill in either reversing the emotional effects, providing an opportunity for reassignment, or deciding to terminate an underachieving coach or employee. Arranging counseling through an EAP or redefining goals and personally coaching an employee experiencing burnout may contribute to lengthening his or her appointment and reinvigorating enthusiasm. Best practices suggest that supervisors are proactive in actions and activities that prevent or minimize the occurrence of burnout (see **Box 13-1**).

Ethical Conduct

Ethical conduct is another topic in the area of human resources driving the performance of sports managers in their own behavior and in manifesting the desired behavior of their staff. Ethical conduct or principled behavior is an

Former NFL player Ray Rice was released by the Baltimore Raven's and suspended indefinitely by the NFL in 2014 for a domestic violence case. His appeal was granted but he remained a free agent entering the 2017 season.

expectation in any work environment, but athletics and sports programs appear prone to violations. In intercollegiate athletics, the NCAA's reporting and enforcement structure for minor and major rule violations by coaches and staff is intended to make the institution culpable for the actions of employees. However, between 2001 and 2010, 53 athletic departments out of 102 in the Football Bowl Subdivision (FBS) had committed a major rule violation, according to the Division I Committee on Infractions (Lederman, 2011). The previous decade was marked by 52 major rule violations. Research indicates that both the number and severity of rule violations have been continually increasing (Mahony, Fink, & Pastore, 1999).

In 2014, the National Football League (NFL) adopted a new code of personal conduct policy that applied to all personnel (owners, coaches, players, front-office staff, etc.). The revisions, which included specific language about sexual assault and abuse in addition to outlining disciplinary action and due process, were adopted 2 months after former running back Ray Rice was released by the Baltimore Ravens and indefinitely suspended by the NFL for domestic abuse. The premise of the policy is that, "everyone who is part of the league must refrain from conduct detrimental to the integrity of and public confidence in the NFL" (NFL, 2014). Rice's suspension was eventually lifted after a lengthy appeal, but the running back remained a free agent entering the 2017 NFL season.

SCOPE OF UNETHICAL BEHAVIOR

The scope of unethical behavior in sports includes a wide range of conduct issues, ranging from minor levels of unsportsmanlike behavior to major degrees of criminal activity. Additional topics related to unethical conduct for employees considers issues of fairness, integrity, substance abuse, gambling and wagering, confidentiality, proper use of funds, disclosure of outside activities, inappropriate relations, nepotism, and criminal behavior. **Action Shot 13-1**, for example, profiles the range of unethical behavior prohibited in college athletics, but all levels of sports require employees and professionals to conduct themselves ethically in the name of the law and the general expectations of their industry as well as the organization.

Ethical conduct is an expectation in coaching or administering youth sports, but the expectation becomes diluted at many levels of competition

▶ ACTION SHOT 13-1

NCAA Rule 10.1 Ethical Conduct

The National Collegiate Athletic Association (NCAA) rule manual includes an article on ethical conduct that includes definitions and sanctions for a variety of issues ranging from knowledge of banned substances to illegal wagering to sportsmanship. The following is derived in part from the NCAA Division I Manual of Bylaws pertaining specifically to Rule 10.1, Un-Ethical Conduct (NCAA, 2015, p. 45).

Unethical conduct by a prospective or enrolled student-athlete or a current or former institutional staff member (e.g., coach, professor, tutor, teaching assistant, student manager, or student trainer) may include, but is not limited to, the following:

a. Refusal to furnish information relevant to an investigation of a possible violation of an NCAA regulation when requested to do so by the NCAA or the individual's institution;

b. Knowing involvement in arranging for fraudulent academic credit or false transcripts for a prospective or an enrolled student-athlete;

c. Knowing involvement in offering or providing a prospective or an enrolled student-athlete an improper inducement or extra benefit or improper financial aid;

d. Knowingly furnishing the NCAA or the individual's institution false or misleading information concerning the individual's involvement in or knowledge of matters relevant to a possible violation of an NCAA regulation;

e. Receipt of benefits by an institutional staff member for facilitating or arranging a meeting between a student-athlete and an agent, financial advisor, or a representative of an agent or advisor;

f. Knowing involvement in providing a banned substance or impermissible supplement to student-athletes or knowingly providing medications to student-athletes contrary to medical licensure, commonly accepted standards of care in sports medicine practice, or state and federal law;

g. Failure to provide complete and accurate information to the NCAA or institution's admissions office regarding an individual's academic record (e.g., schools attended, completion of coursework, grades, and test scores);

h. Fraudulence or misconduct in connection with entrance or placement examinations; or

i. Engaging in any athletics competition under an assumed name or with intent to otherwise deceive.

The NCAA Committee of Infractions declared that the former head football coach at West Texas A&M University engaged in unethical conduct when providing false information during an NCAA investigation (NCAA, 2016a). The list of perpetrators of Bylaw 10.1 is exhaustive. Several notorious cases have included the sex abuse scandal involving former football coach Jerry Sandusky of Penn State University, academic fraud at the University of North Carolina in 2015, and the 1986 Southern Methodist University (SMU) football scandal resulting in what is referred to as the "death penalty."

Four pairs of female Chinese badminton players were disqualified for throwing matches at the 2012 London Olympics.

primarily due to temptations associated with financial gains or prestige. Responsibilities in coaching and administration are primarily geared toward the safety, health, and well-being of athletes, whether it is in a Pop Warner youth football game, a YMCA league, a college gymnastics competition, a professional baseball game, or an Olympic trial event. Ethical conduct involves following rules and regulations. Breaches in standards of ethical conduct are rampant in sports as individuals, coaches, administrators attempt to gain a competitive edge.

Lying (e.g., Lance Armstrong's doping scandal), cheating (e.g., NFL New England Patriots' "deflate-gate"), withholding information (e.g., NFL "concussion-gate"), and stealing (e.g., NFL New England Patriots' "spy-gate") are general examples of ethical conduct violations that permeate sports. At the elite level of Olympic sports, attempts to cheat the system are marked in history (1988—Ben Johnson stripped of gold medal for doping; 2002—Canadian skating team is awarded gold following judging scandal; 2012—Chinese badminton players expelled for deliberately losing). College athletic programs are besieged with recruiting violations and academic fraud cases, and high school and youth sports share a wealth of ethical misconduct by overzealous coaches and parents.

CODES OF CONDUCT

The nature of competitive sports and the human condition ensure that sports will continue to struggle with questions of ethics. It is customary for leagues, franchises, tournaments, and conferences to maintain a standard code of conduct for employees. Developing ethical conduct expectations is an initial step, but investigating, disciplining, and publicizing violations of ethical conduct has a role in creating awareness.

Sports managers and supervisors should periodically review the codes or standards of ethical and professional conduct for employees in addition to penalties for violating behavioral expectations. Involving employees when developing a code of conduct assists in widespread acceptance. Employees should also be required to sign a code or statement of ethical conduct as a means to demonstrate that they have reviewed and understand what is expected in terms of behavior.

Statements or codes of ethical conduct defining behavioral expectations for employees are personalized to an organization or industry. Many community or municipal recreation departments issue a code of conduct to guide coaches, parents, and participants in addition to league commissioners and department personnel.

In general, the code or statement should define expected behaviors in language that is simple, concise, and easily understood by the intended audience. Individuals tasked with preparation of the initial draft should constitute representation of a cross-section of employees. The code should also be revised and updated periodically to reflect regulatory or compliance changes. Finally, punitive actions for violating ethical conduct should be explicit and should fit the circumstances.

Harassment in the form of cyber bullying has escalated through inappropriate text messages or comments on social media devices.

Harassment

Harassment is a difficult topic that supervisors, managers, and human resource personnel must address in sports organizations. Harassment is a form of employment discrimination that, depending on the circumstances, violates Title VII of the Civil Rights Act of 1964, the Age Discrimination in Employment Act of 1967 (ADEA), or the Americans with Disabilities Act of 1990 (ADA). A safe working environment free from physical, psychological, or emotional harassment is an expectation of employees in all organizations. Harassment covers a wide range of unacceptable behavior, ranging from repeated physical intimidation to unwelcome jokes. Psychological harassment through social media has escalated in recent years.

Bullying is a form of harassment that is prevalent in interscholastic, intercollegiate, and professional sports. In addition to bullying, there are many types of harassment situations (i.e., religious or racial harassment, stalking) that might arise in sports organizations whether in an office, locker room, bathroom, parking lot, playing field, or gym. The most litigated harassment situation in the workplace is sexual harassment.

SEXUAL HARASSMENT

The U.S. Equal Employment Opportunity Commission (EEOC) has provided guidelines as to what type of behavior constitutes **sexual harassment** in the workplace, including the following:

Unwelcome sexual advances, requests for sexual favors, and other verbal or physical conduct of a sexual nature constitute sexual harassment when this conduct explicitly or implicitly affects an individual's employment, unreasonably interferes with an individual's work performance, or creates an intimidating, hostile, or offensive work environment (EEOC, 2016a).

There are two forms of sexual harassment: (1) quid pro quo and (2) hostile work environment. **Quid pro quo**, or "this for that," is when an employer explicitly or implicitly puts conditions on employment based on the employee's submission to unwelcome sexual advances. A **hostile work environment**, on the other hand, occurs when unwelcome sexual advances or other verbal/physical conduct of a sexual nature affects an individual's employment, unreasonably interferes with an individual's work performance, or creates an intimidating, hostile, or offensive work environment.

Sexual harassment can come in many forms. It can be as straightforward as a recreation supervisor telling a youth program counselor that he or she will only get promoted if he or she consents to sexual activity with the authority figure. It also may not be straightforward and may alternatively include offensive jokes and/or kidding with another employee. Examples of sexual harassment include verbal kidding, continued verbal commentary about a person's body, displaying sexually suggestive photos in the workplace, any unwelcome physical contact, and statements to an employee that sexual favors must be granted for continued employment.

Research suggests sexual harassment is a widespread issue in athletics and sports (Brackenridge, 1997; Claringbould, Knoppers, & Elling, 2004; Fasting, 2015; Hogshead-Maker & Steinbach, 2003; Masteralexis, 1995; Moorman & Masteralexis, 2008). Unequal power relationships (i.e., coach and player), the inherent culture of sports as a supercharged competitive environment, and the unwelcomed intrusion of women in historically male-dominated institutions have been cited as conditions making the industry susceptible to sexual harassment. A comprehensive study in Canada noted that one-fifth of female athletes had been sexually harassed by their coach (Hogshead-Maker & Steinbach, 2003).

With or without managerial forethought into education and accountability, all organizations are susceptible to sexual harassment. Forms of sexual harassment involve sexually oriented comments, taunts about dress or appearance, condescending behavior, offensive phone calls or pictures, fondling, and any unwanted physical conduct. According to longitudinal statistics reported by the EEOC (2016b), approximately 87% of sexual harassment charges are filed by a female.

The National Basketball Association (NBA), NFL, National hockey League (NHL), Major League Baseball (MLB), and MLS all have dealt with sexual harassment allegations. In 1992, an undisclosed amount was awarded to a *Boston Herald* reporter who sued the NFL New England Patriots for sexual harassment that occurred in the team locker room. In 2007, Anucha Browne (Sanders), a former executive for the NBA New York Knicks, won over $11 million in a highly publicized sexual harassment and retaliation case (see **Action Shot 13-2**). In 2010, a female

Two athletic administrators at the University of Minnesota resigned in 2015 after sexual harassment allegations surfaced. The university was cleared of creating a climate of inappropriate sexual conduct.

reporter was allegedly sexually harassed by members of the NFL New York Jets in a locker-room incident (Farrar, 2010). Alleged incidences of sexual harassment have also occurred in NASCAR, ESPN, and the U.S. Olympic Committee (Braziller, 2015; Fish, 1991; Jensen, 2008; Michaelis, 2003; Zambito, 2008). In a survey of female sports print media professionals, slightly over 50% reported experiencing sexually harassing behavior in a 12-month period (Pedersen, Lim, Osborne, & Wisenant, 2009).

College athletic departments are among sports organizations considered highly susceptible to sexual harassment incidents. Athletics employees at the University of Minnesota, University of Notre Dame, Bowling Green State University, California State University at Berkley, Ohio State University, and the University of Alabama represent only a handful involved in some type of sexual harassment allegations in the past few years. In 2015, the athletic director and an associate athletic director at the University of Minnesota resigned after allegations of sexual harassment surfaced; however, the institution was cleared of creating a "climate" of inappropriate sexual conduct (Shipley, 2015). In the wake of the scandal, the university's president instituted an institution-wide policy that requires mandatory reporting and, if warranted, team-related sanctions in the wake of any form of harassment.

According to the U.S. Department of Education, sexual harassment of students by a coach or university employee is considered a form of discrimination (Office of Civil Rights, 1997). As indicated, sexual harassment is prohibited under Title IX and is also covered under Title VII of the Civil Rights Act of 1964. The U.S. Department of Education requires schools receiving federal funds to designate a Title IX coordinator, which enhances the

▶ ACTION SHOT 13-2

Sexual Harassment Case: Anucha Browne (Sanders) and Isiah Thomas

One of the most prolific sexual harassment cases in an athletic setting is the federal court decision involving Isiah Thomas, then coach for the National Basketball Association (NBA) New York Knicks. The Hall of Famer who played 13 seasons with the Detroit Pistons was accused of sexually harassing Anucha Browne (Sanders), former senior vice president of marketing for Madison Square Garden. James Dolan, owner of the New York Knicks and Madison Square Garden, was ordered to pay $11.6 million in punitive damages to Browne, who claimed she was fired in retaliation for reporting the sexual harassment and conditions of a hostile work environment (McKissic, 2007; Sandomir, 2007).

The Aftermath

After the multimillion-dollar judgment, former NBA Commissioner David Stern commented that the Knicks demonstrated that they're "not a model of intelligent management" and that checkpoints and decisive action would have eliminated the issue (Sandomir, 2007). Testimony in the case suggested the Knicks demonstrated a "frat boy mentality" which Dolan denied (Zambito, 2007). Stern's statement and attitude reinforce the need for a managerial approach by sports leagues to prevent sexual harassment and inappropriate behavior.

Since the charges, the NBA has ramped up educational efforts for players and employees on the topic of sexual harassment. In-person training on diversity and "Respect in the Workplace" is mandatory for all league employees every 2 years. A separate track is designed for executives focusing on manager accountability for sexual harassment. All new hires must complete the Respect in the Workplace training during their new-hire orientation (Lapchick, 2016).

In 2015, HBO's *Real Sports* interviewed Jim Dolan, who claimed that Browne made up the allegations and that a not-guilty verdict should have been rendered. Thomas, too, disputed Browne's claims and maintained his innocence in the case (HBO, 2015).

Where Are They Now?

- *Anucha Browne (Sanders)*: Before working at Madison Square Garden for the New York Knicks, Browne leveraged sponsorship and marketing for IBM in conjunction with several Olympic Games for over a decade. Following the settlement, Browne was hired as senior associate athletic director of the University at Buffalo. In 2012, Browne was named senior vice president of women's basketball championships for the NCAA and was serving in the same capacity in 2017.

- *Isiah Thomas*: Before being named general manager and eventually coaching the Knicks, Thomas coached the Indiana Pacers after his playing career finished. Following the settlement, Thomas was hired as the head men's basketball coach at Florida International University. In 2015, Dolan named Thomas president and alternate governor of the New York Liberty Women's National Basketball Association (WNBA) team, which received extensive criticism. The New York Liberty's home court is Madison Square Garden.

opportunity for complaints to be handled judiciously and confidentially.

BULLYING

In 2013, Prince Amukamara of the NFL New York Giants was dumped in a cold tub of water. Soon after, a Miami Dolphins player quit the team and entered a hospital to receive treatment for emotional distress due to excessive bullying, which prompted a 144-page report commissioned by the NFL. The report indicated that bullying extended to other Miami

Former Miami Dolphins player Richie Incognito was one of several who engaged in a bullying episode that led to a 144 page report commissioned by the NFL.

Dolphins staff, and the main perpetrator, Richie Incognito, was suspended indefinitely; however, the suspension was lifted in 2015 (Hill, 2015). There are reports in the NFL of rookies being "required" to pay over $10,000 for a meal or to drive to a Denny's once a week to bring back breakfast. Players have been forced to run through a gauntlet in which they are kicked or punched by teammates or have endured having their heads shaved for refusal to engage in a ritual (Hochman, 2013).

Football is not the only arena to find alleged cases of bullying. In 2015, the varsity female softball coach at Brown University was accused of bullying her players (Ruffin, 2015). In the past few years, former female basketball players at Oakland University, Boston University, and Indiana University–Purdue University Indianapolis have accused their female head coaches of varying degrees of bullying (Fraser, 2015; Hohler, 2014; McCabe & Snyder, 2013). It is important to note, however, that different laws offer different protections for employees compared to students. Title IX may apply in employee and in student harassment situations, but Title VII of the Civil Rights Act of 1964 applies only to employees.

Bullying is a form of forced intimidation or **hazing** that may be interpreted as a rite of passage common in team sports. In the MLB, for example, the New York Yankees, Tampa Bay Rays, and New York Mets have required rookies to dress in themed costumes, which may be regarded as simply a form initiation or a case of hazing or a demonstration of bullying, depending on someone's viewpoint. Bullying may be physical, verbal, or virtual (cyberbullying), considering texting and social media avenues. The culture of sport, and especially football, raises a concern for the proliferation of bullying.

Workplace bullying in the sports industry is also a concern in athletic training rooms. Of 723 trainers working in college athletic departments, 106 (14%) reported having experienced some form of bullying (Weuve, Pitney, Martin, & Mazerolle, 2014). Most bullying incidents are considered dispositional, meaning that cases are isolated to an individual. There is concern, however, that the culture of competitive sports (e.g., football and basketball) and locker-room insularity create a systemic problem for sectors of the industry that are likely to breed harassment and bullying.

PREVENTING AND ADDRESSING HARASSMENT

Prevention of harassment is crucial to ensuring that any form of sexual harassment, bullying, taunting, and violence does not occur in the workplace. It is also important for an employer to prevent harassment by communicating the harassment policy, explaining what can be considered harassment, explaining that harassment will not be tolerated, and then by following its own policies and taking action when a claim of harassment occurs. Human resource professionals or individuals in the role have an obligation to educate employees on workplace bullying and sexual harassment.

An example of a harassment policy is included in **Exhibit 13-1**. The EEOC (2016c) recommends that policies provide a clear explanation and examples of prohibited conduct and assurances of confidentiality and protection against retaliation for individuals filing a complaint. In addition, the EEOC (2016c) recommends providing instructions for the complaint process; assurance of prompt, thorough, and impartial investigation; and assurance of appropriate corrective action pending the assessment of a violation.

Human resource personnel, supervisors, athletic directors, and managers across the sports industry use training opportunities to educate employees on harassment issues and policies. Policy manuals typically address anti-harassment conduct, the repercussions for violations, and instructions to report complaints. Training and education emphasize the cognition of scenarios that represent a fine line between appropriate and inappropriate conduct. Human resource personnel also play a role in defining a grievance process for reporting harassment, such as the flowchart identified in **Figure 13-1**.

EXHIBIT 13-1: SAMPLE POLICY: HARASSMENT

Note: This is a sample policy provided for educational purposes and should not be construed as legal advice. This sample policy should not be used without being reviewed by appropriate legal counsel to ensure accuracy with local, state, and federal laws and company policy.

EMPLOYER is committed to providing an environment that is free of discrimination on account of race, color, sex/gender, religion, age, national origin or ancestry, physical or mental disability, or any other consideration made unlawful by federal, state, or local laws.

One form of such discrimination is harassment. EMPLOYER will not tolerate any action by any person that constitutes harassment of an employee. Harassment is defined as slurs or other verbal or physical conduct relating to an individual's race, color, national origin, veteran status, ancestry, religion, disability, age, or sex/gender by an employee, including a coworker or supervisor, where such conduct either: (a) is made an explicit or implicit term or condition of employment; (b) is used as the basis for employment decisions affecting an employee; (c) has the purpose or effect of substantially interfering with an employee's work performance; or (d) creates an intimidating, hostile, or offensive work environment.

Acts of harassment can take a variety of forms, ranging from subtle pressure for sexual activity to physical assault to racial or ethnic slurs. Some examples of the kind of conduct that may be defined as harassment include the following:

- Verbal kidding
- Continued or repeated verbal abuse, sexually suggestive objects or pictures placed in the work area, sexually degrading words to describe the person, or propositions of a sexual nature
- Unwelcome physical contact
- Threats or insinuations that the person's employment status or conditions may be adversely affected by not submitting to sexual advances

Any employee who experiences or observes conduct believed to constitute harassment, report such conduct to NAME PERSON & TITLE & CONTACT INFORMATION so that the incident may be investigated and any prompt remedial action needed may be taken.

Any supervisor who is aware of a harassment situation is obligated to report the matter to NAME PERSON & TITLE & CONTACT INFORMATION.

This policy has been established to ensure employees that the issue of harassment will be dealt with in a prompt and confidential manner. Employees will not be penalized for reporting an incident of harassment or participating in an investigation.

Note: This is a sample policy and should not be construed as legal advice. Employers should have an attorney familiar with all federal, state, and local laws review policies before enacting.

Civil Rights Equity Resolution Policies & Procedures

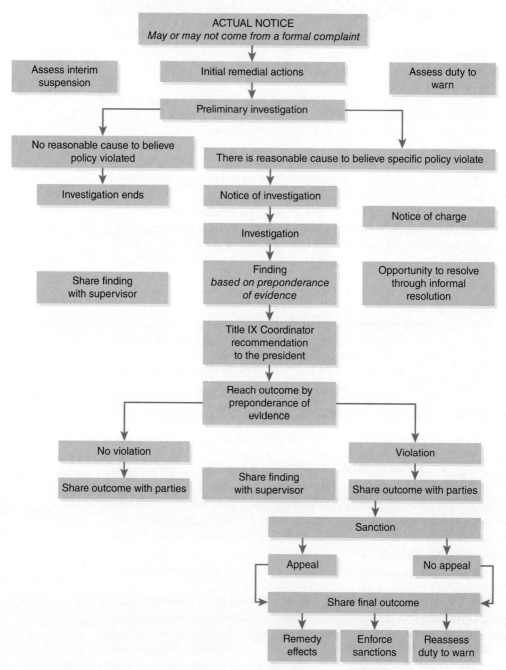

Figure 13-1 Tiffin University Office of equity, access, and opportunity civil rights equity resolution procedures chart

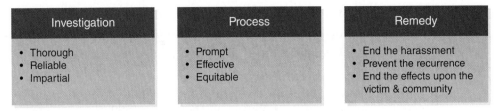

Figure 13-2 Desired objectives for three important components of harassment claims: the investigation, the process, and the remedy.

FLOWCHART FOR HARASSMENT GRIEVANCE

It is also important for human resources to practice prudent managerial practices in investigating reports of harassment by being thorough, reliable, and impartial (see **Figure 13-2**). The procedure should be effective and equitable while emphasizing a sense of time sensitivity. The objectives for remedying cases should strive to end harassment, prevent recurrence, and remedy the effects to the victim and community (S. Perry-Fantini, personal communication, May 3, 2016).

HARASSMENT GRIEVANCE CONSIDERATIONS

The NFL was the first professional sports league to pilot a virtual reality training demo addressing harassment. During the training, virtual scenarios were created, such as an African American female avatar being harassed by a white avatar (della Cava, 2016). The perceived value of virtual training is to potentially create a longer-lasting impact for trainees, who can better "feel" what it is like to be in specific situations. The NFL also conducts sessions focusing on respect in the workplace at its annual Career Development Symposium. Individual teams and players in the NFL as well as other professional leagues have adopted anti-bullying campaigns.

Although specific sexual harassment training or education is not mandated by federal law, it is mandated by some state laws as a measure to help prevent occurrences. Following are suggestions for guidelines to minimize or prevent sexual harassment that can be applied to sports organizations (Pedersen et al., 2009, p. 346):

1. Develop and publicize a sexual harassment policy.
2. Develop and publicize a grievance procedure to resolve sexual harassment complaints.
3. Conduct periodic sexual harassment sensitivity training sessions.
4. Establish discussion groups where employees can discuss the issues involving sexual harassment within the organizational culture.
5. Survey employees to determine if sexual harassment is occurring.

Recap

The scope of workplace issues in the context of managing human resources for sports organizations is broad. The sports industry is prone to work–life conflict and burnout, especially in the coaching profession. In addition to educating employees on the antecedents and consequences of work–life conflict, human resource professionals should also emphasize strategies at an individual and organizational level to assist workers in effectively integrating personal and professional responsibilities.

Ethical conduct is a concern in all levels of sports. Sports organizations should stress the standards of ethical behavior for their employees. Statements of professional conduct or codes of conduct are often included in employee manuals. Important to sustaining an organization that adheres to high standards of ethical conduct is to investigate, punish, and publicize breaches of ethical conduct.

Inclusive workplaces promote equality. Harassment has been linked to locker rooms, team buses, sidelines, and the offices of numerous sports organizations. Common forms of harassment include sexual harassment and bullying. An infamous sexual harassment case in sports involving NBA Hall of Famer Isiah Thomas resulted in a disputed $11.6 million judgment to a former executive of the New York Knicks who claimed she was fired in retaliation for reporting harassment. Policies for anti-harassment are prevalent in all levels of sports. The ultimate objective is to provide a safe working environment for employees.

🌐 GLOBAL SPOTLIGHT 13-1

Sexual Harassment and Olympic Governance Oversight

In October 2015, the president of the Canadian Olympic Committee (COC) resigned amidst sexual harassment complaints by three female employees. A third-party workplace review indicated a majority of COC members had witnessed or experienced years of harassment (Hall, 2016).

Four members of the South Korean women's curling team who competed in the 2014 Sochi Olympics resigned from their club amidst a pervasive culture of sexual harassment and abuse by an assistant coach (Hyun-woo, 2014). The Olympic Council of Asia banned an Iranian football team equipment manager for sexually harassing a female games volunteer at the Asian Games, and similar allegations surfaced against a gymnastics coach from India (Around the Rings, 2014).

According to a survey by the U.S. Equal Employment Opportunity Commission (EEOC) in cooperation with the Sports Federations and Olympic Committee of Hong Kong, approximately 90% of national sports organizations did not have an anti-sexual harassment policy and did not report a sense of urgency in the need to craft one (Hong Kong Government, 2015). The EEOC organized a seminar in cooperation with the Leisure and Cultural Services Department of Hong Kong to assist national sports organizations with formulating sexual harassment policies.

Over 100 coaches involved in the USA swimming Olympic development programs have received lifetime bans for inappropriate sexual conduct.

In 2017, a federal judge unsealed complaint files from USA Gymnastics involving sexual abuse and misconduct by 57 coaches in the system (Kwiatkowski, Evans, and Alesia, 2017). Over 360 complaints by U.S. gymnasts were filed in a 20-year period asserting inappropriate sexual conduct by coaches and trainers. Labeled the worst sexual abuse scandal in U.S. history, Dr. Larry Nassar, a former sports medicine doctor at Michigan State University and former team doctor for USA Gymnastics, allegedly sexually abused over 100 athletes in his tenure including gold medal gymnasts (Reid, 2017). Terminated by USA Gymnastics in 2015, Nassar was being held without bail in a Michigan on counts of first degree sexual misconduct with a girl under the age of 13 and several federal charges of child pornography (Armour & Axon, 2017; Mather, 2017; Reid, 2017). The President and CEO of USA Gymnastics resigned in 2017 amidst the mounting pressure of the federation's inappropriate handling of sexual abuse complaints over the years and Michigan State was facing lawsuits from over 40 women treated by Dr. Nassar (Armour & Axon, 2017).

Over 100 former coaches of USA Swimming, the Olympic developmental program for the United States, have received lifetime bans for sexual abuse allegations (Hannigan, 2015). A recent case involved a 62-year-old coach who received a 40-year prison sentence for sexually abusing over a dozen girls, one of whom became pregnant.

Only in the past decade has the International Olympic Committee (IOC) been truly earnest in efforts to eliminate human rights violations of sexual harassment and sexual abuse in sports. Sexual harassment was addressed at the 2006 IOC Medical Commission's consensus meeting on Sexual Harassment and Abuse in Sport and at the 2009 IOC Congress in Copenhagen. In 2007, the IOC published a consensus statement on sexual harassment noting that the prevalence appeared to be higher in elite sports and that members of an athlete's entourage who are in positions of power and authority appear to be the primary perpetrators. The consensus statement addresses a request by the IOC for every National Olympic Committee to develop an athlete protection and anti-harassment infrastructure. The 2016 Rio Olympic Games were the first to actually provide a framework to protect and safeguard athletes from harassment and abuse by establishing guidelines for reporting (IOC, 2016).

At the 2013 African-Asian Women Sports Forum in Kuwait, the IOC unveiled a toolkit for preventing sexual harassment. The target audience comprised athletes, coaches, National Olympic Committees, International and National Federations, athlete entourages (e.g., trainers, personal assistants, sports psychologists), and "chefs de missions" (IOC, 2013). The toolkit includes videos portraying scenarios of sexual abuse and information for preventing or remedying the occurrence. Instructional materials focus on coach-specific actions to prevent or remedy gender harassment, hazing, sexual abuse, and homophobia.

DISCUSSION QUESTIONS

1. What strategies can assist in minimizing work–life conflict for employees in the sports industry at the personal, organizational, and societal levels?
2. How is burnout related to work–life conflict, and why is the phenomenon widespread in the coaching profession?
3. With all three governing bodies for intercollegiate athletics in the United States in addition to almost every athletic department publishing definitions of ethical behavior and sanctions for violating codes of conduct, why are there so many infractions reported each year?
4. What is the difference between bullying and hazing?
5. What is the legal recourse for someone who believes he or she is a victim of sexual harassment?

APPLIED ACTIVITIES

1. Using the Internet, locate and review an employee code of conduct for a professional league, a franchise, a university, and a national governing body for sports (e.g., IOC, Association of American Universities). Identify the similarities and differences in the codes and whether punitive action is provided for conduct violations.
2. Visit the IOC sexual harassment website at www.olympic.org/sha and view several of the videos. Prepare a PowerPoint presentation to address categories of sexual harassment and coach-specific actions to address each type.
3. In the role of a residential sports camp director, develop a code of conduct for counselors.

CASE STUDY

Ethical Conduct in Sports Organizations: The Good, the Bad, and the Ugly

Unethical conduct is manifested predominantly in situations of an abuse of power and influence. It is apparent in politics (e.g., Watergate and Benghazi), boardrooms (e.g., Enron), and in plenty of sports scandals. Many U.S. professional leagues and top global sports entities would likely rank poorly if ever there were a sports corruption index (SCI) evaluating the ethical conduct of leagues, associations, and federations. Transparency International's corruption perception index touts the virtues of Denmark and Finland while condemning the likes of North Korea and Somalia. Similarly, the sports world is filled with clean, virtuous, competitive programs, but unethical conduct rears its ugly head in the form of unjust, immoral, or illegal activities at every level, from Pop Warner little league football to professional global organizations.

Examples of recent ethical violations in sports are prevalent. International Olympic Committee (IOC) President Thomas Bach called for lifetime bans of thousands of Russians involved in the statewide doping scandal that spanned every Olympics from Turin 2006 to Rio 2016 (Butler, 2016). Kuwait authorities filed a $1 billion lawsuit against the IOC for barring Kuwait from the 2016 games due to government influence (Toumi, 2016). A total of 36 boxing referees from the 2016 Rio Olympics were suspended indefinitely pending an investigation into a judging scandal (James, 2016). In the United States, the California State University Northridge basketball program earned a 3-year probation and a 1-year postseason ban and was forced to vacate wins over a 5-year period as a result of academic misconduct by a former director of operations (NCAA, 2016b, p. 17).

Sports has become a prime vestibule for corruption due to an increase in political and private interests shrouded by a multibillion-dollar industry where decisions, governance, deals, and negotiations typically take place behind elitist closed doors. The following three cases exemplify ethical behavior of sports organizations that can be placed in the categories of the good, the bad, and the ugly and highlight the need for sports supervisors to remain cognizant of ethical behavior in personal and business matters.

The Good

The National Association of Collegiate Directors of Athletics (NACDA) headquarters is a model organization for ethical conduct. Based in Westlake, Ohio, it is the professional organization for intercollegiate athletic administrators and services over 1600 member institutions. Executive Director Bob Vecchione has been at the home office for 23 years and cannot recall a single serious infraction of misconduct or unethical behavior within the headquarters. Most of the credit, he explains, can be attributed to former executive director Mike Cleary, who was "a phenomenal judge of character" (M. Vecchione, personal communication, May 5, 2016). Cleary died on New Year's Eve, 2015. He had a 50-year tenure with the NACDA, having worked with five National Collegiate Athletic Association (NCAA) presidents.

Although it is considered a small business, with fewer than 20 on staff, the NACDA employed over 200 interns and numerous full-time workers in Vecchione's tenure. Only one individual had ever been dismissed, and that was due to breaching a handshake deal over the expected length of employment. "To me, your word is your bond," according to Vecchione (personal communication, May 5, 2016). That experience has been the closest example of unethical behavior in the NACDA headquarters. It may be considered a minor conduct infraction, but the executive director knows it's important to teach interns the value of trust and to serve as a role model.

Vecchione believes assessing an applicant's moral character is as simple as devising a standard set of questions that includes an ethical scenario and benchmarking responses against other candidates and what NACDA values as compatible with the organization's mission and guiding principles. There is value in assessing an individual's fit within the organization to determine if he or she can be trusted and will become a positive influence on staff.

The Bad

The late Joe Paterno was never brought up on criminal charges in the 2011 Penn State University scandal.

Penn State University's athletic department has had a long tradition of excellence and integrity. Its athletic motto is "Success with Honor." Joe Paterno served as head football coach for over 40 years and was lauded as a father figure, with teams consistently achieving one of the highest grade point averages in Division I. During his lengthy tenure as the winningest coach in NCAA Football Bowl Series history, his program was never sanctioned for a major rule violation until 2011, when his defensive coordinator was found guilty of 45 counts of sexually abusing boys and the university was charged with a cover-up scheme.

Penn State's board of trustees dismissed Paterno as well as the university's president. The athletic director and a senior vice president who resigned were charged with felony perjury, and the former president was charged with obstruction of justice. All charges were eventually reversed by a Pennsylvania Superior Court (Snyder & McCoy, 2016).

The NCAA levied tremendous fines against the institution ($60 million), stripped scholarships and postseason eligibility, and vacated 111 of Paterno's 409 victories. In 2014, the postseason and scholarship ban were lifted, as was the

monetary fine, and Paterno's victories were restored. Paterno had died of a heart attack 2 years earlier—just 2 months after he was fired. Penn State has paid over $60 million to victims, and allegations have surfaced that Coach Paterno was informed of sexual abuse by his former assistant as early as 1976 (Court of Common Pleas of Philadelphia County, 2016, p. 2).

Vecchione's suggestion that a coach's focus may get out of order and that victories may become more important than the good of the game is all too true for Penn State. The university placed success above honor and deemed loyalty more important than what was morally and ethically prudent.

The Ugly

FIFA, scheduled to host the World Cup in Russia in 2018, has been marred by unethical conduct including kickbacks and bribes to executive in exchange for votes for host cities.

Vecchione contends that money doesn't force unethical behavior, but it is a negative factor in the entire equation that contributes to the misalignment of priorities and values. The Federation International Football Association (FIFA) is clearly a model of unethical behavior in sports, exemplifying the abuse of power that can lead to widespread corruption. FIFA's ethics committee banned former president Sepp Blatter from all football (soccer) activities for 8 years. The committee was formed in 2012, well after many allegations of unethical behavior took place. Dozens of the organization's executives as well as high-ranking sports marketing and broadcast officials have faced indictment by the U.S. Department of Justice and the Swiss Attorney General's office.

There are allegations of Qatar buying the bid to host the 2022 World Cup and executives receiving monetary bribes for votes to award the 2010 and 2018 Cup to South Africa and Russia, respectively. Sports marketing firms have been accused of bribing FIFA officials in exchange for exclusive television contracts. There is a long history of kickbacks, racketeering, wire fraud, and match-fixing in the sport and among FIFA executives.

Established in 1904, the international governing body for soccer has demonstrated a systemic problem of corruption in sports. In this case of global injustice, INTERPOL is just one entity that has assisted in bringing justice to the world of soccer. In 2016, Switzerland's Gianni Infantino, general secretary of Europe's Football Federation, was elected to succeed Blatter as FIFA's president. The global association faces an uphill battle in convincing the world of its reform policies coinciding with the presidential election. Among FIFA's (2016) reform resolutions is a "clear separation between political and management functions" and "Universal Good Governance Systems."

Summary

One act committed by one individual does not automatically classify an organization as corrupt, but failing to address a culture of improprieties or permitting unethical practices to persist without recourse creates vulnerability for corruption. Transparency, accountability, integrity, and ethical leadership are cornerstones in establishing boundaries and guiding appropriate behavioral expectations for sports organizations of all sizes.

NACDA's executive director Bob Vecchione has a commonsense approach to ethical behavior in noting the simplicity of doing what is right and encouraging others to do the same. His suggestion that everyone is fallible is a lesson that rings true for those involved in the scandals uncovered at Penn State University and FIFA.

CASE STUDY QUESTIONS

1. Does the size of the NACDA office staff have any influence on the organization being considered a model of ethical conduct?

2. Under what conditions would Coach Joe Paterno have been indicted on perjury charges in the Penn State University scandal?

3. Why wasn't FIFA's Ethics Committee enough to ensure good governance and prevent the corrupt behavioral practices of many of its executives?

4. Is there a possibility that the Penn State University athletics department or FIFA can restore their images to become a model sports organizations for ethical conduct?

5. What in this case exemplifies a relationship between legal wrongdoing and unethical behavior?

6. Which of Bob Vecchione's insights addressed in the case makes the strongest point for enforcing and maintaining ethical conduct in sports organizations?

REFERENCES

Armour, N. & Axon, R. (2017, March 17). *USA gymnastics CEO steps down.* USA Today. 1C.

Around the Rings. (2014, September 17). *Olympic Council of Asia issues warning after sexual harassment cases.* Retrieved from http://aroundtherings.com/site/A__48376 /Title__Olympic-Council-of-Asia-Issues-Warning-After-Sexual-Harassment-Cases/292 /Articles

Bentzen, M., Lemyre, P. N., & Kenttä, G. (2016). Development of exhaustion for high performance coaches in association with workload and motivation: A person-centered approach. *Psychology of Sport and Exercise, 22,* 10–16.

Boles, J., Howard, W., & Donofrio, H. (2001). An investigation into the inter-relationships of work-family conflict, family-work conflict, and work satisfaction. *Journal of Managerial Issues, 13,* 376–391.

Brackenridge, C. (1997). He owned me basically. Women's experiences of sexual abuse in sport. *International Review for the Sociology of Sport, 32,* 115–130.

Braziller, Z. (2015, November 11). Berman in sex-harass suit. *New York Post,* p. 48.

Bruening, J., Dixon, M., Tiell, B., Osborne, B., Lough, N., & Sweeney, K. (2008). Work–life culture of collegiate athletics: Perceptions of supervisors. *International Journal of Sport Management, 9*(3), 250–272.

Butler, N. (2016, December 8). Bach calls for lifetime Olympic bans for Russians involved in manipulating doping samples on eve of McLaren Report findings. *Inside the Games.* Retrieved from http://www.insidethegames.biz/articles/1044600 /bach-calls-for-lifetime-olympic-bans-for-russians-involved-in-manipulating -doping-samples-on-eve-of-mclaren-report-findings

Claringbould, I., Knoppers, A., & Elling, A. (2004). Exclusionary practices in sport journalism. *Sex Roles, 51,* 709–718.

Court of Common Pleas of Philadelphia County. (2016, May 4). *The Pennsylvania University v. Pennsylvania Manufacturers' Association Insurance Co.* Retrieved from http://www.courts.phila.gov/pdf/opinions/131103195_6152016124713 726.pdf

della Cava, M. (2016, April 10). Virtual reality tested by NFL as tool to confront racism, sexism. *USA Today.* Retrieved from http://www.usatoday.com/story/tech /news/2016/04/08/virtual-reality-tested-tool-confront-racism-sexism/82674406/

Dixon, M., & Bruening, J. (2005). Perspectives on work–family conflict in sport: An integrated approach. *Sport Management Review, 8*(3), 227–253.

Dixon, M., Tiell, B., Lough, N., Osborne, B., Sweeney, K., & Bruening, J. (2008). Work–life interface in intercollegiate athletics: An examination of policies, programs, and institutional climate. *Journal for the Study of Sports and Athletes in Education, 2*(2), 137–160.

Durand-Bush, N., Collins, J., & McNeill, K. (2012). Women coaches' experiences of stress and self-regulation: A multiple case study. *International Journal of Coaching Science, 6*(2), 22–43.

Farrar, D. (2010, September 10). Jets addressing alleged harassment of female reporter. *Yahoo Sports.* Retrieved from http://sports.yahoo.com/nfl/blog/shutdown_corner /post/Jets-addressing-alleged-harassment-of-female-rep?urn=nfl-269361

Fasting, K. (2015, June-August). Assessing the sociology of sport: On sexual harassment research and policy. *International Review for the Sociology of Sport, 50,* 437–441.

Federation International Football Association. (2016). Governance. The reform process. Retrieved from http://www.fifa.com/governance/how-fifa-works/the-reform-process.html

Fish, M. (1991, December 14). Settlement with former employee linked to alleged sexual harassment. *The Atlanta Journal Constitution,* A8.

Fraser, J. (2015). *Athletes speak up over female coaches who bully.* Retrieved from http://www.healingwalls.org/athletes-speak-up-about-female-coaches-who-bully/

Greenhaus, J. H., & Beutell, N. (1985). Sources of conflict between work and family roles. *Academy of Management Review, 10,* 76–88.

Greenhaus, J. H., & Powell, G.N. (2003). When work and family collide: Deciding between competing role demands. *Organizational Behavior and Human Decision Processes, 90,* 291–303.

Hall, V. (2016, April 14). Olympic committee boss vows action after Aubut fiasco. *Vancouver Sun,* Sports, C11.

Hannigan, D. (2015, January 10). US Swimming's appalling history of abuse continues to seep out, with the number of banned coaches now at 106. *The Irish Times,* Sports, 7.

HBO. (2015, October 20). *Real Sports with Bryant Gumbel. Episode 223: Another shot.* Retrieved from http://www.hbo.com/real-sports-with-bryant-gumbel/episodes/0/223-episode/index.html

Hill, T. (2015, August 26). Former NFL player Jonathan Martin: I considered suicide multiple times. *The Guardian.* Retrieved from https://www.theguardian.com/sport/2015/aug/26/nfl-player-jonathan-martin-miami-dolphins-bullying

Hochman, B. (2013, November 17). Locker room culture a strange place behind closed doors of Denver's pro sports teams. *Denver Post.* Retrieved from http://www.denverpost.com/broncos/ci_24539739/take-peek-behind-closed-doors-denver-s-four-major-professional-sports-franchises

Hogshead-Maker, N., & Steinbach, S. (2003, spring). Intercollegiate athletics unique environments for sexual harassment claims: Balancing the realities of athletics with preventing potential claims. *Marquette Sports Law Review.* Retrieved from http://scholarship.law.marquette.edu/sportslaw/vol13/iss2/2

Hohler, B. (2014, March 8). Bullying accusations continue against BU coach. *Boston Globe.* Retrieved from http://www.bostonglobe.com/sports/2014/03/08/women-basketball-coach-accused-bullying/TtKz57Gs9qXbvk1SBtIpuM/story.html

Hong Kong Government. (2015, September 25). EOC holds seminar on formulation of anti-sexual harassment policy in sports sector. Newswire report. *Hong Kong Government News.*

Hyun-woo, N. (2014, March 29). "Curls Generation" members quit over coach's alleged abuse. *Korea Times.* Retrieved from http://www.koreatimesus.com/curls-generation-members-quits-over-coachs-abuse/

International Olympic Committee. (2007, February 8). *IOC adopts consensus statement on sexual harassment and abuse in sport. IOC press release.* Retrieved from https://www.olympic.org/news/ioc-adopts-consensus-statement-on-sexual-harassment-and-abuse-in-sport

International Olympic Committee. (2013, November 19). *Women and sport forum for Asia and Africa. Association of National Olympic Committees.* Retrieved from http://www.acnolympic.org/anoc-news/olympic-movement-news/2013/11/women-and-sport-forum-for-africa-and-asia/#

International Olympic Committee. (2016, July 21). *IOC implements measures to safeguard athletes from harassment and abuse in sport.* Retrieved from https://www.olympic.org/news/ioc-implements-measures-to-safeguard-athletes-from-harassment-and-abuse-in-sport

James, C. (2016, October 7). KO blow as Rio 36 benched. *The Sun* (England), Sports, 56.

Jensen, D. (2008, December 19). NASCAR, ex-official settle $225 million suit. *St. Petersburg Times,* 11-C.

Kelley, B., Eklund, R., & Ritter-Taylor, M. (1999). Stress burnout among collegiate tennis coaches. *Journal of Sport and Exercise Psychology, 21,* 113–130.

Kelley, B., & Gill, D. (1993). An examination of personal/situational variables, stress appraisal, and burnout in collegiate teacher-coaches. *Research Quarterly for Exercise and Sport, 64*(1), 94–102.

Kentucky Wesleyan University. (2017). *Women's basketball coaches.* Retrieved from http://www.kwcpanthers.com/coaches.aspx?rc=153&path=wbball

Kossek, E. E., Colquitt, J. A., & Noe, R. A. (2001). Caregiving decisions, well-being, and performance: The effects of place and provider as a function of dependent type and work-family climates. *Academy of Management Journal, 44,* 29–44.

Kwiatkowski, M., Evans, T., and Alesia, M. (2017, March 5). Judge releases USA court files. Even some convicted coaches avoided bans for years, court documents say. Dayton Daily News. Z-4.

Lapchick, R. (2016). The racial and gender report card. Reports. *Institute for Diversity and Ethics in Sport, University of Central Florida.* Retrieved from http://www.tidesport.org/reports.html

Lederman, D. (2011, February 7). Half of big time programs had major violations. *USA Today.* Retrieved from http://usatoday30.usatoday.com/sports/college/2011-02-07-ncaa-infractions_N.htm

Lough, N., Tiell, B., & Osborne, B. (2008). Athletic administrators' perceptions of work–life balance policies: A divisional comparison. *Journal of Contemporary Athletics, 3*(4), 327–347.

McCabe, M., & Snyder, M. (2013, July). Players' shocking allegations against former NCAA women's basketball coach. *USA Today.* Retrieved from http://www.usatoday.com/story/sports/ncaaw/2013/07/21/oakland-university-fired-coach-beckie-francis-special-report/2573613/

Mahony, D. F., Fink, J., & Pastore, D. (1999). Ethics in intercollegiate athletics: An examination of NCAA violations and penalties—1952–1997. *Professional Ethics, 7*(2), 53–74.

Masteralexis, L. (1995) Sexual harassment and athletics: Legal and policy implications for athletic departments. *Journal of Sport and Social Issues, 19,* 141–156.

Mather, V. (2017, February 23). Gymnast ex-doctor faces new charges. The New York Times. B-11.

Mazerolle, S., Goodman, A., & Pitney, W. (2015, January). Achieving work–life balance in the National Collegiate Athletic Association Division I setting, part I: The role of the head athletic trainer. *Journal of Athletic Training, 50*(1), 82–88.

McKissic, R. (2007, October 3). UB staffer wins $11.6 million suit; Former executive of Knicks sues team for sex harassment. *Buffalo News*, 1A.

Michaelis, V. (2003, February 14). USOC woes multiply with sexual harassment charge. *USA Today*, 1C.

Moorman, A. M., & Masteralexis, L. P. (2008, February). An examination of the legal framework between Title VII and Title IX sexual harassment claims in athletics and sport settings: Emerging challenges for athletics personnel and sport managers. *Sport and Recreation Law Association Journal of Legal Aspects of Sport.* Retrieved from http://journals.humankinetics.com/doi/abs/10.1123/jlas.18.1.1

National Collegiate Athletic Association. (2015). *Bylaw article 10.10.1 Unethical conduct. NCAA Division I rules manual.* Retrieved from https://www.ncaa publications.com/p-4388-2015-2016-ncaa-division-i-manual-august-version -available-august-2015.aspx

National Collegiate Athletic Association. (2016a). *West Texas A&M public infractions decision.* Retrieved from https://www.ncaa.org/sites/default/files/INF _West-Texas-Public-Infractions-Decision_20160323.pdf

National Collegiate Athletic Association. (2016b). *California State University Northridge public infraction decision.* Retrieved from https://www.ncaa.org/sites /default/files/2016INF_CSUNPublicInfractionsDecision_20161207.pdf

NCAA Digest. (2006, August 28). Life–work balance. *NCAA News Archives.* Retrieved from http://fs.ncaa.org/Docs/NCAANewsArchive/2006/News+Digest /ncaa%2Bdigest%2B-%2B8-28-06%2Bncaa%2Bnews.html

National Football League. (2014, December 10). *NFL owners endorse new personal conduct policy.* Retrieved from http://www.nfl.com/news/story/0ap3000000441 758/article/nfl-owners-endorse-new-personal-conduct-policy

Office of Civil Rights. (1997). *Sexual harassment guidance 1997.* U.S. Department of Education Retrieved from https://www2.ed.gov/about/offices/list/ocr/docs /sexhar01.html

Pedersen, P., Lim, C., Osborne, B., & Wisenant, W. (2009). An examination of the perceptions of sexual harassment by sport print media professionals. *Journal of Sport Management, 23,* 335–360.

Reid, S. (2017, March 29). Gymnasts at Senate testify on sex abuse; Sport's governing body draws lawmakers' fire for failing to take action. The Daily News of Los Angeles. A1

Ruffin, T. (2015, April 23). Softball coach Flynn accused of bullying players. *The Brown Daily Herald.* Retrieved from http://www.browndailyherald.com/2015/04/23 /softball-coach-flynn-accused-of-bullying-players/

Ryska, T. (2009, December 1). Multivariate analysis of program goals, leadership style, and occupational burnout among intercollegiate sport coaches. *Journal of Sport Behavior, 32*(4), 476–488.

Sacramento State University. (2017). *Roster. Women's beach volleyball.* Retrieved from http://www.hornetsports.com/sports/sandvball/2015-16/roster

Sandomir, R. (2007, December 11). Garden settles sexual harassment case. *New York Times*, D1.

Shipley, J. (2015, December 1). UMN athletics cleared of most sexual "climate" issues. *St. Paul Pioneer Press.* Retrieved from http://www.twincities.com/2015/12/07/umn-athletics-cleared-of-most-sexual-climate-issues/

Snyder, S., & McCoy, C. (2016, January 23). Ruling reverses charges against Spanier, others in Sandusky case. *Philadelphia Inquirer,* A-01.

Tiell, B., Dixon, M., Sweeney, K., Lough, N., Osborne, B., & Bruening, J. (2006). Progressive programs: Stopping the pull. *Athletic Management, 18, 63–67.*

Toumi, H. (2016, June 23). Kuwait sues International Olympic Committee for $1b. Gulf News (Kuwait). Retrieved from http://gulfnews.com/news/gulf/kuwait/kuwait-sues-international-olympic-committee-for-1b-1.1851237

U.S. Equal Employment Opportunity Commission. (2016a). *Overview.* Retrieved from http://www.eeoc.gov/eeoc/index.cfm

U.S. Equal Employment Opportunity Commission. (2016b). *Charges alleging sexual harassment FY 2010–FY 2015.* Retrieved from http://www.eeoc.gov/eeoc/statistics/enforcement/sexual_harassment_new.cfm

U.S. Equal Employment Opportunity Commission. (2016c). *Model EEO programs must have an effective anti-harassment program.* Retrieved from http://www.eeoc.gov/federal/model_eeo_programs.cfm

Weuve, C., Pitney, W., Martin, M., & Mazerolle, S. (2014, September). Experiences with workplace bullying among athletic trainers in collegiate settings. *Journal of Athletic Training, 49*(5), 696–705.

Zambito, T. (2007, December 11). *Anucha Browne Sanders settles suits.* New York Daily News. Retrieved from http://www.nydailynews.com/news/anucha-browne-sanders-settles-suit-article-1.274361

Zambito, T. (2008, August 30). ESPN stars off the hook in sex-harass suit. *New York Daily News,* 24.

CHAPTER 14

Eying the Future

PROFESSIONAL DEVELOPMENT AND CAREER TRENDS IN SPORTS

Anytime you can marry technology and sport, you will find a spot. People thought Twitter would eventually go away, but it didn't. The immediate future will see apps that can help fans upgrade their seats in real time, and there will be an uptick in analytics by both teams and athletes. If a son or daughter wanted to major in or go into sports, I would suggest finding a way to merge sports with anything in the technology field.

Molly Fletcher
The Molly Fletcher Company

Courtesy of Molly Fletcher

LEARNING OUTCOMES

1. Assign professional development activities in the sports industry that best align with each of the four career stages.

2. Distinguish the advantages and challenges for sports organizations that internally design and administer professional development programs.

3. Identify examples of external opportunities for employees in sports organizations to engage in professional development.

4. Distinguish the roles of career coaches, mentors, and sponsors.

5. Identify trends affecting employment in sports careers.

6. Identify trends in sports management career preparation.

KEY TERMS

Bridge employment	Forum	Sponsor
Career stages	Mentoring	Symposium
Certificate program	Oversaturated market	Trainee program
Coaching	Panel	
Encore career	Professional development	

Lead-Off

Sports managers and supervisors who keep abreast of career trends and industry developments are more likely to adapt to changes and leverage opportunities for advancement. Sustaining a lengthy career in the sports industry requires a personal investment in developing professional knowledge and skills on a continuous basis while leveraging relationships across a wide spectrum of business and educational settings.

Throughout organizations and at every career stage, professional development becomes an important tool to adapt to rapidly changing environmental conditions, such as market fluctuations, technology advancements, or labor supplies. Sports businesses with human resource specialists or managers who address the personal and professional needs of employees during each stage reap the benefits of investing in activities that can pay high dividends in terms of overall performance for the organization.

The varied nature of the sports industry dictates the vast array of professional development opportunities. Whether employees seek specialized certifications or attend seminars and conferences tailored to their job are choices dependent on available time and financial resources as well and the general practices of their profession.

Career trends are affected by changes in demographics, economic conditions, technology, and other elements. These factors also influence trends in career preparation for specific occupations. In terms of career preparation in the sports industry, there is an increase in specializations relative to academic programs, an increase in affiliations and partnerships with sports organizations, and a gradual influx of specialized certifications.

This chapter addresses professional development in the sports industry from the standpoint of internal programs, external programs, and interpersonal relationships. The chapter also addresses the changing needs for professional development through various career stages. Finally, the chapter explores factors affecting trends in sports occupations and preparation strategies for careers in sport.

Professional Development

Professional development is a form of training with a focus on long-term growth in a career. The varied nature of the sports industry adds to the need to capitalize on professional development that is specialized and proven as effective for advancement in the field. Organizations embracing professional development in addition to other types of short-term training are likely to reap the benefits of employees who are more satisfied and productive in their field. Intended outcomes of development initiatives include increased proficiency in leveraging and nurturing networks, mentoring advantages, and the acquisition of specific knowledge, skills, and abilities relevant to jobs in the field.

Many positions in sports are part of a service-oriented profession characterized by a workforce comprised of an abundance of seasonal and voluntary labor. However, the market is also filled with numerous stable, full-time positions. The variations in the sectors of the industry and the types of employees require professional development initiatives that are tailored to meet individual needs for advancement within sectors of the industry.

Professional development, however it is designed and for whatever audience, can be divided into three areas. The first area includes internally administered education programs, the second includes programs administered through external organizations or agencies, and the third area includes interpersonal relationships in the form of coaches, mentors, and sponsors.

INTERNAL PROGRAMS

Most organizations incorporate some type of internal professional development. The incentive for management and human resources to incorporate time and programming for professional development is to improve the skills and competencies of employees. Professional development controlled by the organization becomes the best tool for succession planning through the development of an internal talent pool.

Professional development administered internally may be a one-time event to address a specific topic, as exemplified by a fitness center that provides a workshop on effective customer service skills or a racetrack that hires a consultant to address the power of teamwork with employees. Internally administered programs may also be part of a lockstep or continuous learning environment where employees are expected to participate in a series of professional development sessions, such as a sports theme restaurant requiring workers to pass a monthly online achievement test on a variety of areas integral to the organization's operation (i.e., special promotions, food safety, customer service, etc.). Sports organizations may hold professional development meetings to comply

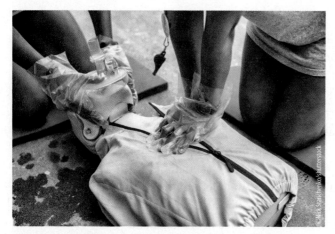

Lifeguards complete continuing education courses to maintain certification.

The Atlanta Braves offer a Trainee Program which provides front-office experience.

with professional regulatory requirements, such as National Collegiate Athletic Association (NCAA) rules or continuing education to remain certified as a lifeguard or athletic trainer.

The popularity of **trainee programs** used for professional development is increasing in professional sports. Management trainee programs are already considered mainstream development tools in business. These are relatively lengthy assignments that include specialized instruction and training for employees of an organization who are being groomed for specific positions. A post-graduate sales trainee program may span the course of 10 to 15 months, without the guarantee of full-time long-term employment. Trainees typically rotate through different departments of a professional team over the course of months to learn the roles and responsibilities of positions while also receiving education on general professional development areas ranging from organizational culture to navigating through career stages.

In addition to the Atlanta Braves (2017), the Major League Baseball (MLB) Pittsburgh Pirates (2017) also operates a trainee program identified as the Building Ultimate Careers in Sports (BUCS) Academy. The BUCS Academy is a year-long professional development program only for college graduates. Approximately 18 candidates selected for the academy participate in specialized training provided by the Pirate's Ticket Sales and Services Management team. The temporary employees receive training for cold-call strategies and increasing client satisfaction while also attending workshops and seminars focusing on sales techniques and the culture of selling for a professional sports franchise (Pittsburgh Pirates, 2017).

The benefit of creating and investing in internal professional development opportunities is the ability to tailor programs to meet a specific organizational need and to aid in succession planning. Internal programs may also offer

The Pittsburgh Pirates who play at PNC Park also offer a Trainee Program titled BUCS, which represents "Building Ultimate Careers in Sports."

a more economical means to service employees by leveraging in-house expertise or securing a consultant as a less expensive alternative to financing travel, lodging, and fees for workers to attend professional development offered by outside entities. A disadvantage of internally designed and administered programs, however, is the loss of professional communities and networks that are core to externally promoted programs.

EXTERNAL PROGRAMS

Opportunities for individuals to participate in externally offered professional development are almost endless, whether education is offered through an institution, a national governing body convening an annual convention, an online self-development course, or an independent agency. External programs are offered in many varieties, including conventions, conferences, seminars, panels, workshops, symposiums, and classes. Virtual programs tailored for professional development are also on the rise.

There are an extraordinary variety and number of external professional development opportunities in sports. The NCAA and the Women Leaders in College Sports (formerly the National Association of Collegiate Women Athletic Administrators [NACWAA]) co-sponsor the Women's Leadership Symposium in Intercollegiate Athletics, which promotes the recruitment and retention of females in the industry. The World Olympians Association (WOA) hosts an educational forum each year preceding the summer Olympics to address how sports can contribute to global peace, humanitarianism, and social welfare. The annual National Sports Forum is the largest gathering of executives and practitioners representing sports sales, promotions, and entertainment entities throughout a broad spectrum of teams and leagues. Numerous coaches associations meet annually for conventions, forums, or workshops.

Professional development, tailored to an audience, may be tiered in order to distinguish levels of authority or baseline competency. The NCAA's Leadership Development Unit established eight categories for offering professional development programming to students and professionals employed at member institutions and conference offices. (NCAA, 2014, see **Box 14-1**).

Common formats for professional development include forums, symposiums, and panels. Forums and symposiums use variations of the traditional lecture or discussion packaged as educational programs, primarily for professional development and soft-skills training. A **forum** is a discussion-based series of presentations on a similar topic, such as diversity or labor relations in sports. The **symposium** is closely related because it incorporates a series of lectures or discussions but is differentiated by the inclusion of an ever-present moderator throughout the program. The **panel**, often used in forums and symposiums, is a single discussion-based session featuring a moderator addressing a topic with multiple experts.

Some forums and symposiums are one-time programs, whereas others are repeated annually, biannually, or on a quadrennial cycle. These educational training programs are ideal for engaging large groups but may be expensive for participants if the location is at a great distance from the employer. Remote access through a video-conference or digital streaming device to virtually participate in a session has become more common, but challenges exist in terms of accessible, affordable, and reliable equipment. Typically, symposiums and forums are not ideal to teach hands-on skills that lend themselves to more individualized demonstration methods.

BOX 14-1

NCAA Professional Development Program Categories Defined by Student-Athlete Affairs

1. Category one (student-athletes)
2. Entry level (interns and graduate assistants)
3. No supervisor experience (coordinators, position coaches)
4. Department managers (directors, position coaches, assistant or associate athletic directors or commissioners)
5. Senior staff: senior, executive, or deputy athletic directors, coaches, commissioners
6. Athletic leadership: athletic directors and head coaches
7. Conference leadership: commissioners
8. Campus leadership: college and university presidents

Beyond the scope, professional development is a component of many local, state, national, and international governing bodies throughout the sports and recreation industry. Some target underrepresented populations in the industry, such as women and minorities (see **Action Shot 14-1**). Sports management scholars, for example, are afforded professional development through conferences and programs offered by the North American Society for Sport Management (NASSM), the World Association of Sport Management (WASM), and from any of a number of niche associations ranging from the Sport Lawyers Association (SLA) to the International Council of Sport Science and Physical Education (ICSSPE). There is an association or society for coaching every sport imaginable in addition to general coaching associations offering certifications and advice for best practices.

▶ ACTION SHOT 14-1

Professional Development Programs Tailored for Women and Minorities in Intercollegiate Athletics

© 2017 National Collegiate Athletic Association. Women Leaders in College Sports

The NCAA and Women's Leadership Symposium is an example of professional development programming focusing on the recruitment, retention, and advancement of females in intercollegiate athletics.

The National Association of Collegiate Women Athletics Administrators (NACWAA), which changed its name to Women Leaders in College Sports in 2017, originally partnered with Higher Education Resource Services (HERS-Mid America) in 1995 to create the NACWAA/HERS Institute for Administrative Advancement (West, 1999; White, 2012). The premier "level one" development program for women in intercollegiate athletics administration continues through a partnership with the National Collegiate Athletic Association (NCAA) and Women Leaders in College Sports (2017). The success of the week-long residential program targeting entry-level administrators prompted organizers to offer the seminar on both the East and West Coasts for the first time in 2002 and has continued to grow to accommodate approximately 90 participants annually (Women Leaders in College Sports, 2017). Segments of the training include policy implementation, leadership skills, financial planning, management skills, work and communication styles, team building, negotiations, and a history of Title IX and women's athletics.

Women Leaders in College Sports also designed and implemented the first Executive Institute (EI) in 2002 to train and enhance opportunities for women with significant experience to move into positions as athletics directors, conference commissioners, or chief executive officers (CEOs). Partnering with the NCAA, Women Leaders in College Sports continues to administer both the EI and the Leadership Enhancement Institute (LEI), which is composed of graduates of the Institutes for Administrative Advancement. The EI and LEI have included workshops on such areas as contract negotiations, television packaging, capital campaign funding, facility development, leadership, working relations with university CEOs, and the process for an athletics director search.

Similarly, the NCAA has developed and administers several initiatives to provide leadership training for women and minorities in intercollegiate athletics. For example, the NCAA Pathway Program (formerly the Fellows Program) identifies and provides a year-long intense training regimen for senior-level minorities and women who aspire to positions as athletics directors and conference commissioners (NCAA, 2017a). The impetus for the program, which began in 1997, is partially attributed to the Minority Opportunities and Interests Committee (MOIC) and the Committee on Women's Athletics (CWA), which jointly advocated for a training ground modeled after the American Council on Education's Fellows Program that focused on preparing females and minorities for advancing in administrative positions.

Each NCAA fellow is assigned an NCAA executive mentor and focuses throughout the training on gaining an overall understanding of intercollegiate athletics and the impact of intercollegiate athletics within the organization. The fellows attend the annual NCAA convention and participate in a retreat led by national leaders who address current issues and practices in athletics administration. Programming includes emphases on marketing, public relations, budgeting, booster relations, leadership, strategic planning, compliance, fundraising, diversity training, and management training.

The NCAA (2017b) operates a 2-year Leadership Institute focusing on professional development and career enhancement for a select group of ethnic minorities. The program represents the NCAA's commitment to addressing the critical shortage of senior-level ethnic minorities involved with athletics programs at member institutions and conference offices. The Leadership Institute focuses on enhancing job-related competencies in selected areas through practical work experiences and several week-long intensive workshops. Programming is led by a diverse group of recognized leaders in business, higher education, and intercollegiate athletics.

In 1999, as a means to help encourage women to enter and stay in the field of intercollegiate athletics, a group of female administrators in the Midwest organized a seminar similar to the educational initiatives of the Women Leaders in College Sports and the NCAA but with an emphasis on making the programs accessible and highly affordable to a larger audience. This initiative was called the Women's Leadership Symposium in Intercollegiate Athletics (WLS). In 2013, the NCAA and Women Leaders in College Sports collectively took ownership of the WLS and now administer the annual 3-day seminar to provide resources and education for females looking to enter or advance in the industry. Approximately 100 female students and aspiring administrators within their first 5 years of employment in any area of intercollegiate athletics benefit from the professional development program each year.

Officials, athletic trainers, physical fitness trainers, lifeguards, scouts, sports agents, facility managers, and many other practitioners in the industry are certified or licensed through a recognized a governing agency. Sports executives, commissioners, athletic directors, camp directors, sports marketers, and all professional positions in the industry are afforded opportunities to belong to a member association or governing agency providing professional development. Regardless of the provider, the goals of professional development remain relatively similar in facilitating education for the purpose of advancing skills, knowledge, and competencies; creating networks; and enhancing opportunities for growth and career advancement.

COACHES, MENTORS, AND SPONSORS

A third category describing methods of professional development is through interpersonal relationships with a coach, mentor, or sponsor. All three relationship-oriented professional development initiatives provide individualized attention to enhancing skills, competencies, and knowledge for job performance or attainment.

Coaching involves one-on-one support as an experienced individual oversees and provides feedback on a specific activity or function performed by an individual with less experience. The "coach" ensures the trainee understands the training objectives and oversees progress as the learner performs tasks and makes decisions on his or her own. Some coaches interact by asking a lot of probing questions, whereas others take a more hands-on approach and observe and intervene throughout. Academic advisors traditionally assume a coaching role when working with students and discussing career initiatives.

Mentoring focuses on the relationship of a more experienced individual who imparts his or her expertise and knowledge on someone else. The two aspects of mentoring are career functions and psychosocial functions (Kram, 1985). Research has suggested that mentored individuals report higher rates of promotions than non-mentored individuals and that mentoring assists younger persons in advancing more quickly to higher levels of administration (Dreher & Ash, 1990; Roche, 1979; Weaver & Chelladurai, 2002; Whitley, Dougherty, & Dreher, 1991).

In cases where a mentor is used specifically for training purposes, the relationship may be formal, as in the example of a mentor being assigned to acclimate a new hire to the office environment during the orientation. In other cases, the relationship may be informal, without an obligation by

Legends, such as the late Pat Summit and Mike Krzyzewski, have mentored or sponsored numerous coaching basketball protégés in their careers.

a mentor, who may not even be aware that he or she is assuming the role of the experienced professional. Mentors are quite often associated with professional development for their ability to influence career directions. The trainee is typically labeled as a protégé or a mentee.

Whereas a mentor may or may not be aware of his or her role, a sponsor, on the other hand, has a definite invested interest in his or her protégé. **Sponsors** are individuals in positions of authority or influence who intentionally advocate for the development and advancement of another individual. Sponsors are more essential as individuals advance higher in their careers and competition for promotions is intensified (Kram, 1985). In the sports industry, referrals within the context of the "old boys" and "old girls" networks are an influential source of persuasion. Sponsors are especially prevalent in intercollegiate and professional sports communities as commissioners, general managers, athletic directors, and individuals who have climbed the ranks in authority and welcome opportunities to promote aspiring young talent they have been associated with in their circles.

Greater attention has been given to the role of a mentor and sponsor in training athletics personnel. Between 2012 and 2017, athletes, coaches, and sport administrators from 63 counties participated in a global sport mentoring program operated by the U.S. Department of State (2017). A formal mentoring programs for sport coaches are available throughout many countries around the world. New Zealand, for example, organizes mentoring programs to train coaches in their national sport organizations with assistance of regional and cross-sport training activities (Sport and Recreation New Zealand, 2010).

Associations such as Women Leaders in College Sports (2017) and Women in Sports and Events (2017) also conduct formal mentoring programs focusing on professional development and resource building. Over time, many of these mentoring relationships evolve into a sponsorship role.

One of the positive outcomes of mentoring, especially in the coaching domain, is when protégés' emulate desired behaviors of an experienced professional while integrating their own philosophy and coaching style (Bloom,

Bush, Schinke, and Salmela, 1998, p. 278.) Important to formalizing a mentoring program is the inclusion of an orientation overviewing expectations as well as the frequency and modes of communication. In several instances, a mentoring triad has been formed to include three individuals at varying stage of their careers who interact over a specific period. Workshops and professional associations are more often addressing the role of sponsors in addition to mentors in career advancement and professional development.

Career Stages in the Sports Industry

Careers generally gravitate through early, middle, and late stages during an individual's job progression throughout the life span when he or she is considered "employable." Throughout each **career stage**, the motive for professional development differs. The four stages addressed herein are as follows:

1. Exploration
2. Entry and establishment
3. Middle and maintenance
4. Late and disengagement

Advancement or job-related migration through each stage may or may not be within a single industry or industry sector. For example, the traditional career stages for a collegiate athletic director begin as a student enters the workforce as a graduate assistant coach. Next, the individual may advance in the ranks to an assistant, associate, and/or head coach while assigned duties as an administrator along the way. Finally, the individual may advance through the ranks of higher levels of authority to an eventual position as director of athletics (see **Figure 14-1**). Before disengagement from a career, the individual may or may not assume a position as a consultant.

Each stage is still within the scope of intercollegiate athletics and may or may not occur at the same institution. On the other hand, a collegiate athletic director may have once worked outside of higher education. For example, the athletic directors at Long Beach State University (2017) and at the University of North Dakota (2016) respectively worked for Gaylord Sports Management and as an executive at the National Children's Cancer Society before assuming their administrative roles in college sports. Similar scenarios occur in different positions in sports where career stages may seem more like a rock-climbing wall with varied routes to the top as opposed to a one-directional stepladder.

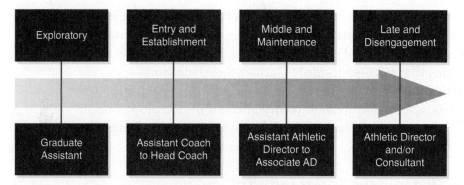

Figure 14-1 Example of the traditional path of an intercollegiate athletic director or consultant advancing through each of the four career stages

EXPLORATION

In the exploration stage, generally spanning an individual's formal education while in college, professional development focuses on understanding the depth and breadth of jobs in the field and the realities of employment. Individuals begin to make industry contacts and participate in field experiences while also developing interpersonal and communication skills.

Sports organizations need all types of business-minded professionals; hence, there is no definitive educational path leading to a career in sports. Depending on the type of sports organization or facility, there are needs for educated and experienced employees in everything from security studies and information technologies to mechanical engineering and horticulture. Stadiums, teams, university athletic departments, and corporate business enterprises, such as Nike, Gatorade, ESPN, and International Management Group (IMG), all hire professionals experienced in law, finance, media, and public relations. In terms of the exploration stage for the sports management industry, pursuing a specialized degree in sports is the most common avenue, but it is not the exclusive route.

The appeal of a specialized degree in sports management was slow to catch fire until sports were accepted and promoted as a multibillion-dollar global industry in the 1980s and 1990s. The need for specialized preparation

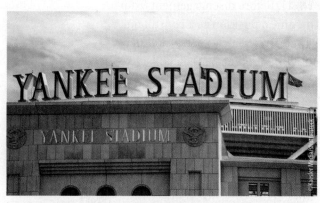

Yankee Stadium is just one example of sport enterprises that searches and hires business professionals on a regular basis.

for individuals working in the sports industry is largely credited to Walter O'Malley, former owner of the Brooklyn/Los Angeles Dodgers, who advocated for greater skill sets needed to manage ballparks, stadiums, arenas, marinas, and racetracks. O'Malley advocated that specialized training was necessary to fill executive positions for teams and leagues at all levels (Brown and Kreutzer, 2001; Ohio University, 2017; Tiell, 2012).

Before 1980, there were fewer than 20 schools listing a graduate or undergraduate major related to the management of sports (Parkhouse, 1978). In 1988, 109 universities offered a related degree (Brassie, 1989, p. 158), and in 2003, approximately 166 institutions offered a specialized sports degree (Jones, Brooks, & Mak, 2008). According to listings published by the NASSM (2017), the number of institutions entering or sustaining a foothold in the marketplace to train sports industry professionals has grown to over 411 colleges and universities, which represents almost a third of the number of colleges in America (1,281 total) that are sanctioned by the NCAA to compete in varsity sports,. **Action Shot 14-2** profiles the evolution in the standard academic components suggested as ideal for a sports management curriculum.

▶ ACTION SHOT 14-2

Accreditation and Components of a Sports Management Curriculum

When sports management degree programs exploded in the early 1980s, the need for quality control prompted the development of academic associations to monitor and advise institutions on specialized curriculum in the field. Founded in 2007, the Commission for Sports Management Accreditation is the entity that is most widely recognized for broadly monitoring sports curriculum. The early rule of thumb was that sports management programs needed to include three academic areas:

- Foundational courses (management, accounting, history, etc.),
- Applied courses (sports finance, sports business, sports facility management), and
- Practical field experience (Brassie, 1989).

These areas have expanded to the following seven domains (Commission on Sports Management Accreditation [COSMA], 2016, p. 13):

1. Social/psychological
2. Management
   a. Sports management principles
   b. Sports organization management/event and venue management
   c. Sports leadership
   d. Sports governance
3. Sports ethics
4. Sports marketing and communication
5. Sports finance, accounting, and economics
6. Legal aspects of sports
7. Integrated experiences (e.g., internships and capstone experiences)

Managers and supervisors typically assess the access to internships, field experience, and interaction with industry professionals to assist in predicting whether an entry-level candidate will be proficient in planning and supervising sports (Tiell, 2012). Generally, students majoring in sports management or a related degree have intentions to work in the sports industry; therefore, professional development in the career exploration stage focuses on introducing the myriad of job opportunities and the realities of employment in the field while emphasizing an experiential component.

Whether an institution offers a business- or education-based sports management major, practical experience is the one common component vital to sustaining programs that prepare students for positions in sports organizations. Sports management academic programs are notorious for facilitating experiential learning. These relatively short-term field experiences or internships, however, may only provide short-term exposure to elements of supervision. Sports management preparation should include theoretical and applied learning in the area of human resources to prepare students expecting to work in sports organizations (Tiell, 2015).

During the exploration stage for college students, professional development activities typically include internships and informational interviews, speaker series, shadowships, apprenticeships, conferences or workshops, and career fairs as stepping-stones to begin networking with specialists in the industry (Tiell, 2011). In terms of speakers, certified sports agents, sports media personalities, league executives, or sports marketing executives are more accessible than ever before. Technology allows for speakers from anywhere in the world to visit classrooms through teleconferencing, GoToMeeting, Skype, podcasts, FaceTime, or virtual dialogue rooms embedded in online learning platforms, such as eCollege, Moodle, Canyon, and Blackboard.

Access to and information from sports professionals still can't replace the hands-on learning through field experiences designed to develop important supervisory or technical skill sets. Students need to engage in opportunities that allow them to pitch a discounted ticket package, organize and conduct a pre- or postevent

Internships and practicum experience in sports are a necessary component for formal education of sport management students.

meeting, manage a game-day crisis, fulfill a sponsorship request, or execute a fan-friendly promotional campaign.

Although institutions create the means to make their programs attractive through unique degree titles, the bottom line is that the career exploration stage requires institutions to provide a strong professional development component. Institutions deliver on the promise of professional development in the exploratory stage by promoting their established connections, meaningful field experiences, and a strong curriculum that facilitates employment success in the sports industry (Tiell, 2012).

ENTRY AND ESTABLISHMENT

The entry and establishment career stage is earmarked as the period when individuals break into an industry and gain practical experience over the first several years of gainful employment. This stage is characterized by a psychological assessment of a job meeting or matching expectations, a need to attain the foundational baseline skills required for successful job performance, and a level of knowledge of an organization's structure, function, and culture (Rennekamp & Nall, 1994).

Professional development during the entry and establishment stage of a career may include membership in professional organizations; participation in workshops, symposiums, and other training programs; and connections with a mentor. The Adidas apprentice program highlighted in the end-of-chapter Global Spotlight is an example of a trainee program for the purpose of cultivating talent. In a training program, entry-level employees are hired temporarily and trained by an organization to learn specific knowledge and technical skills over the course of months or years. Apprenticeships, occasionally referred to as dual-training programs, may or may not have an academic component. Trainee programs (i.e., management trainee programs) are typically designed for individuals who have already earned a college degree.

Entry into a career in sports is often a difficult task primarily because of an **oversaturated market** in many industry sectors, which implies there are more qualified individuals than there are positions available. The abundance of qualified candidates applying for a relatively small pool of available jobs is staggering in some sectors of the industry, such as professional sports. The number of universities offering a sports management undergraduate major has also skyrocketed over the past decade, whereas the entry-level job pool in the sports world has expanded only minimally. Any increase in the number of new jobs created in the sports industry isn't even close to the rise in the number

Not all entry-level jobs in the sports industry (e.g., ticket takers, sales associates, front desk greeters, merchandise cashiers, warehouse workers, concession vendors, or ushers) require a specialized degree in sports management.

of students with sports management degrees graduating each year, which affects the entry-level market.

Many entry-level positions in sports organizations are available to applicants regardless of their major. The scope of individuals applying for entry-level positions ranges from thousands of recent college graduates with sports-specific degrees and certifications to individuals transitioning into a new field for the sake of greater flexibility or an opportunity to work in a field with a different culture. Employers hiring for entry-level jobs in a wide spectrum of industries (sports included) seek individuals who demonstrate basic competencies in effective communication and responsibility, with little regard for an individual's actual major. A ticket-taker at an MLB field or a front-desk greeter at a health club doesn't necessarily need to be someone who has a degree in sports management. Adding pressure to the typical job seeker who just earned his or her baccalaureate diploma in sports management is a sea of graduate students with master degrees who are seeking the same entry-level positions (Tiell & Walton, 2014).

Research on career avenues for sports management graduates noted that the most likely entry-level position is through intercollegiate athletics. A study exploring job attainment after graduate school reported males more frequently secured employment as an assistant coach at the Division II or III level, and most women secured positions as an assistant coach in a Division I institution (Kjeldsen, 1990). For those students securing jobs in the professional arena, entry-level positions were most frequently reported within sales or advertising, with more males finding employment in a team sports setting (e.g., baseball, football) and more females gaining employment in individual sports, such as the Ladies Professional Golf Association (LPGA) and the Association of Tennis Professionals (ATP). Among the jobs most frequently reported as an individual's first position in professional sports and intercollegiate athletics was assistant or administrative assistant. For an individual's second job in the field, the most frequently reported job was manager or director if working in professional sports or head coach if working in intercollegiate athletics (Kjeldsen, 1990).

Although the data from Kjeldsen's 1990 study were restricted to one institution, the results are fairly representative of the nature of careers in sports management at the entry and establishment stage. The best opportunities for gainful employment in sports at an entry-level position are in coaching and sales or in trending jobs with high growth potential, such as a production assistant for a sports network or social media coordinator for a sports team (Clapp, 2013).

MIDDLE AND MAINTENANCE

The middle and maintenance stage of a career refers to the period of employment after the entry and establishment stage. The time period when an individual is in the middle and maintenance stage of his or her career is open to interpretation. It is a period between an individual's first job and the years when he or she considers leaving the profession. It has been suggested that the mid stage of a career begins approximately 10 years after the initial entry into the market and lasts approximately 15 to 20 years (Kokemuller, 2015; Super, 1987). Professionals note wide variances in what is considered a middle stage due to career transitions or temporarily opting out of employment for reasons, such as the decision to be a stay-at-home parent.

Although the business of sports is an oversaturated market at the entry level, the occupational employment growth data otherwise indicate an industry that is healthy and vibrant for employees during the middle and maintenance stages. Overall, there has been a fairly significant increase in the number of new jobs available in the sports industry over the past few decades, primarily to professionals in the middle stages of their career (see **Tables 14-1** and **14-2**).

TABLE 14-1: Occupational Growth in Jobs Across Sports Industry Categories, 2010–2014

Sports Industry Category	2010 Jobs	2014 Jobs	%Change
Sports teams and clubs	76,411	82,698	8.6%
Promoters of sports and similar events with facilities	76,269	99,445	30.4%
Promoters of sports and similar events without facilities	31,481	41,091	30.5%
Other spectator sports	54,545	53,548	(-1.8%)
Racetracks	44,672	40,712	(-8%)
Agents and managers—athletes, entertainers, artists	30,748	35,899	16.8%
Total	314,125	353,654	12.6%

Data from Auerbach (2014).

TABLE 14-2: Occupational Growth by Position Categories in the Sports Industry, 2010–2014

Position Category in a Sports-Related Industry	2010 Jobs	2014 Jobs	% Change
Meeting and event planners	3,136	5,136	39%
Audio and video equipment technicians	6,491	8,268	29%
Market research analysts—marketing specialists	1,818	2,308	27%
Public address and announcers	2,040	2,530	24%
Administrative assistants, except legal, medical, executive	5,193	6,417	24%
Agents/business managers—athletes and performers	9,493	11,641	23%
Radio and television sports announcers	1,174	1,428	22%
Accountants and auditors	1,952	2,314	19%
Producers and directors	2,881	3,490	21%
Public relations specialists	3,301	3,875	17%
Ushers, attendants, ticket takers	25,441	30,388	19%
Security guards	13,975	16,253	16%
Office clerks	6,068	7,054	16%
General or operations managers	5,611	6,476	15%
Amusement and recreation attendants	5,336	6,110	15%
Coaches and scouts	7,769	8,349	7%
Athletes and sports competitors	9,535	9,775	3%

Data from Auerbach (2014).

Growth has occurred as a result of expansion teams in the National Football League (NFL), National Basketball Association (NBA), MLB, Major League Hockey (MLH), and Major League Soccer (MLS), among others; an increase in the number of collegiate football bowl games (up to 40 in 2015–2016); more sanctioned tournaments in golf and tennis; global expansion of tournaments and league offices; new recreation facilities and health clubs being built; and new sports added in college athletic departments (Tiell & Walton, 2014). In addition, the U.S. Department of Labor (2015) projects 6% growth in entertainment and sports occupations, which would add approximately 46,000 jobs over the 10-year period from 2014 to 2024.

Employment in the middle and maintenance stage is typically accompanied by increased responsibility and titles demonstrating a scope of authority. Throughout the sports industry, directors, coordinators, vice presidents, and managers are generally considered to be in the middle stage of their careers and are overseeing organizations and departments. These individuals are considered to be in their prime in terms of potential for productivity and performance. Professional development is a means to remain current with industry trends and remain highly effective in directing personnel and projects.

When employment is indicative of a ladder approach with significant advancement within a single industry, the motivation for professional development may be to enhance an area of expertise, become more adept as an independent contributor to a profession, increase engagement with a professional community, or create a more distinctive professional identity (Rennekamp & Nall, 1994). For individuals who have switched industries over time, the motivation for professional development may focus more on reinvention to gain expertise in a particular skill.

Throughout the middle and maintenance stage and regardless of whether employment has been within a single industry, professional development may include an element focusing on analysis of organizational roles to make selective lifestyle decisions, such as strategies to improve financial stability or work–life integration. Traditionally, professional development in the middle segment of an individual's career involves continuous learning to avoid obsolescence and remain marketable.

LATE AND DISENGAGEMENT

Most individuals in the late and disengagement stage of a career have achieved some type of respect from colleagues and have been employed in one or more positions of influence. After 30 to 40+ years as a head coach or an athletic director or in almost any vocation, professional development focuses more on how to transition out of a current role as opposed to how to continue enhancing skills and abilities.

Motivation for professional development during the later stages of an individual's career may be triggered by a desire to stimulate thought in others or to develop coaching and mentoring relationships. The motivation may also be inspired by a desire to attain leadership roles within professional circles or to develop additional networks with other organizations. Strategies to avoid burnout and transition effectively into retirement (e.g., understanding elder-care benefits) are familiar topics for the late-stage worker.

Older generations may seek "bridge" jobs, such as a golf course attendant before disengaging from the workforce.

Officials, front-office executives, scouts, coaches, general managers, exercise specialists, and directors with significant experience often strive to develop opportunities and strategies to maintain connections with professional circles when entering retirement. These and other individuals may seek some type of **bridge employment** opportunity during the late and disengagement stage to transition out of a demanding full-time position and into a less stressful part-time job before leaving the workforce entirely. Similar to bridge employment is an **encore career** often started late the career stage or upon retirement and often devoted to a social cause or higher purpose (Burke, Cooper, and Antoniou, 2015, p. 385). It has been surmised that encore careers are a means to re-enter the workforce while bridge jobs serve as a means to phase "out" of the labor force (Boveda and Metz, 2016, p. 157).

A study on aging workers supported by the Alfred P. Sloan Foundation estimated that 60% of full-time employees over the age of 50 seek a bridge or encore job before retirement (Cahill, Giandrea, & Quinn, 2007, p. 9). Six years later, an Associated Press survey indicated 80% of full-time employees over the age of 50 planned to work past retirement age (Bentz, Sedensky, Tompson, and Agiesta, 2013).

Someone who has worked in a high-pressure role in sports for his or her entire career may seek employment as a pro-shop attendant at a golf and country club or, the individual heading toward retirement may assume a position as a senior advisor or consultant. Gayle Bibby-Crème of the NBA Cleveland Cavaliers, for example, transitioned into the role of vice president of special projects in the late stages of her career. Similarly, after retiring from a 40-year career in intercollegiate athletics, Alfreeda Goff, former senior associate commissioner and chief of staff for the Horizon League, joined the advisory team at Spelman Johnson, an executive search firm in higher education.

In the athletics industry, consulting is a relatively common encore career for individuals with specific expertise and a vast professional network. For example, College Sports Solutions (2015), which conducted a feasibility study for the NCAA Division I University of Alabama at Birmingham's decision to cut or reinstate football, has seven former Division I athletic directors on staff (Solomon, 2015). Former professional athletes and managers also have a propensity to gravitate toward bridge jobs to stay connected to the game. At age 69, Jim Leyland became a special assistant to his replacement with the Detroit Tigers after retiring as their general manager (Manzullo, 2014). Retired professional baseball player Barry Bonds eventu-

Since retiring after the 2014 season, former MLB Detroit Tigers Coach Jim Leyland serves as a "special assistant" for the organization.

ally became a hitting coach for several MLB franchises, including the San Francisco Giants and the Florida Marlins (Snyder, 2015).

In Israel, military officers have gravitated toward encore careers in the sports management industry. Both the military and sport federations in Israel are supported by government funding and there are no academic programs in the country supporting sport management (Galily and Shimon, 2012). Individuals finishing their military careers have been identified as likely candidates for leadership roles in sport federations due to similarities in occupations, such as staff management, budget management, and project management (Galily and Shimon, 2012).

Bridge jobs and encore careers serve not only as a source of income, but they also facilitate quality of life by becoming an outlet for socialization as well as physical and mental fitness. Professional development for the worker in the late or disengagement stage should focus not only on post-retirement benefits but also on maintaining opportunities to stay engaged in the workforce if an individual chooses.

Trends in Sports Occupations

Trends are situations or characteristics that persist in a general direction over time, thereby distinguishing them from an anomaly or incongruity. Career trends describe what is generally occurring in terms of employment. Trends in sports employment have been greatly influenced by the rise in the popularity of analytics, technological advancements easing penetration into global markets, the proliferation of sophisticated "smart" sports arenas, and the increasing emphasis on fan engagement (Mooney, 2014). These influences, spurred by advancements in technology and communication, influence career trends in all industries. Two additional factors affecting career trends across industries include economic volatility and societal or demographic changes. Sports managers and professionals need to remain cognizant of these and other changes or fluctuations that may have a long-term impact on employment.

ECONOMIC VOLATILITY

Although the sports industry has been seemingly impervious to economic down-cycles, as evidenced by the continuous development of new tournaments and arenas as well as expanding audience markets, there is fierce competition for positions in the field. Many sectors of sports continue to increase employment opportunities, especially those for the mid-range stages of a career, but there still has been evidence of downsizing and declining jobs throughout the industry.

In March 2016, the retail chain Sports Authority filed for Chapter 11 bankruptcy and closed 463 stores and distribution centers, affecting thousands of employees throughout the United States (Salamone, 2017). Almost a year later, MC Sports, originating in Grand Rapids Michigan in 1946, closed 66 stores in the Midwest after also filing for bankruptcy protection (Kokomo Tribune, 2017). ESPN is scaling back their on-air talent division in 2017, only months after cutting 300 employee positions which represented approximately 4% of the network's global workforce (Garcia, 2017),

Sports Authority closed 140 stores in North America in 2016.

Professional sport leagues have trimmed staffs over recent years for a variety of reasons. The 2012 NHL lockout resulted in layoffs for teams, including the Florida Panthers and Ottawa Senators (Reynolds, 2012). The 2008 economic recession in the United States triggered the NFL headquarters to cut 150 jobs out of approximately 1000, primarily in the headquarters and film division (Battista, 2008). The recession also resulted in the NBA headquarters cutting its staff by 80 employees; the NHL cutting staff by 50%; the MLB's Internet division cutting 20 jobs; the U.S. Olympic Committee cutting 50 jobs; and Gillette Stadium, home of the New England Patriots, cutting its workforce by 5% (Battista, 2008; Belson, 2009; Johnston, 2012). Although not related directly to the recession, ESPN laid off 100 media personnel the spring of 2017 in an effort to "reposition" itself for the future (Bonesteel, 2017)

Despite layoffs and downsizing, the sports industry as a whole experienced occupational growth between 2010 and 2014 (see Tables 14-1 and 14-2). Growth is expected to trend upward, however, and jobs in the industry are requiring greater specialization (e.g., social media director or e-marketing coordinator).

SOCIETAL AND DEMOGRAPHIC CHANGES

Shifts in demographics suggests that career trends in all organizations will likely include an older and more diverse workforce. At the time of publication, a large number of Baby Boomers will be leaving the workforce; however, staying on the job longer than previous generations has been a trend, resulting in an aging workforce. This trend is evidenced by an increase in the number of millennial and Generation Y workers available to enter the labor market who are unable to secure a job in a tightened marketplace where retirement is being postponed by older employees. The sports industry is already identified as one that is oversaturated at the entry level, and demographic trends indicate that it will remain difficult to secure employment if fewer vacancies are available.

Similarly, as America has been dubbed a "melting pot" due to the proliferation of greater cultural diversity, the workforce has also experienced an increase in ethnic and racial diversity. The population of available workers in America may represent greater diversity, but industry segments may not be hugely affected if a predominant culture of excluding minorities persists. The sports industry is one that generally is dominated by white male employees in front offices, administrative positions, and coaching ranks (Lapchick, 2016).

TECHNOLOGY AND COMMUNICATION IMPROVEMENTS

Improvements in technology and communication have permitted more employees to work from home and to work more efficiently, regardless of whether they are in the office or a remote location. In the sports industry, organizations are employing more specialists to cater to fans or clients who are accustomed to smart technology. Professional sports teams are employing analytic experts with technical, economic, and math degrees to decipher

Sport teams are increasingly hiring social media coordinators, digital content specialists, analytic researchers, and web designers to keep up with the rapid pace of improvements in technology and communication tools.

As fans become accustomed to expecting the interface of sports with digital and mobile technology to improve the live game experience, career preparation in the industry is evolving to meet the needs of consumers.

data, statistics, and information. Teams and university athletic departments are increasingly employing social media coordinators to engage fans and clients.

In general, the emphasis on knowledge-based workers has increased due to improvements in technology and communication. An important human resource implication is recognizing the need for teaching employees how to use new or updated technologies. Analytics is becoming a cross-discipline program with sports management degrees in higher education, whereas social media is an integrated sub-discipline in communication and marketing.

Technology has created ease and affordability in accessing digital messaging and engaging in synchronous global communications, which has generally changed how employees integrate work and personal time. The sports industry is already noted as a culture with long, nontraditional hours and poor work–life balance. Enhancements in technology and communications have influenced the trend for employees to work more frequently from remote locations.

Trends in Career Preparation for Sports Occupations

Technology has also affected the changing professional needs of workers in the industry. In the Industry Voice feature, Molly Fletcher suggests that morphing sports and technology provides greater marketability for a job in sports. Professionals in the industry note that the changing landscape of fan engagement will require a "fresh" approach to interactive game experiences in stadiums and arenas, with video boards and mobile apps as opposed to outdated exhibits (e.g., Hall of Fame) targeting older generations. In addition, the "wild west" of marrying sports with data analytics, which relies on technology to cleanse, analyze, and present information, requires a highly tech-savvy and trained workforce. The rapidly evolving needs of the industry are shaping trends in career preparation for sports occupations.

The influx of specialized curriculum, the popularity of affiliations and partnerships with sports organizations, and certificate programs are examples of how career preparation is evolving to meet industry needs. These trends ideally improve the acquisition of knowledge, skills, and abilities in the industry to improve the likelihood of job attainment.

SPECIALIZED CURRICULUM

A trend in career preparation for the sports industry is for educational institutions to diversify curriculum and provide greater technical and applied knowledge. Instead of a generic sports management degree, educational institutions are offering degrees that focus on niches in the industry. Potential employers may seek to capitalize on talent that has been exposed to a focused and specialized curriculum that matches their particular area or sector of sports (see **Box 14-2**).

BOX 14-2

Specialized Sports-Related Degrees or Certificates Available in Higher Education

- Motor Sports Management (Belmont Abbey, North Carolina)
- Sport Media (Ithaca College, New York)
- Golf Course Management (Ferris State, Michigan)
- Professional Tennis Management (Methodist University, North Carolina, and Ferris State, Michigan)
- Martial Arts Management (Horizons University, France)
- Sport Communication (Ashland University, Ohio)
- Sports Marketing (Tiffin University)
- Sport and Tourism Management (Troy University)
- Sports Announcing (Centralia University, Washington)
- Extreme Sports Management (Southampton Solent University, England)
- Sport Business (Saint Leo University, Florida)
- Sports Analytics Specialization (Northwestern University, Illinois)
- Turf Management (Delaware Valley University, Pennsylvania)
- Sports Field Management Certificate (The Ohio State University, Ohio)
- Rodeo Production Management (Laramie County Community College, Wyoming)

Belmont Abbey College offers a specialization in Motorsports Management, demonstrating an increased specialization in academic curriculum.

The purpose of specialty degrees is to potentially increase the marketability of students while also differentiating from competitor institutions offering "generic" sports management programs. Professional development therefore becomes completely focused on the niche market.

Greater specialization in the curriculum is expected in a master or doctoral program, which is why individuals focused on landing a satisfying first job in the sports industry and making sports their life career are seeing high value in earning a graduate diploma. The extra year or two invested into advanced studies serves to delay student-loan payback and buys extra time to perform formidable job prospecting, knowing the tendency for employers to consider the maturity level of their applicants in addition to their résumé experience and qualifications. Appreciating the fact that sports is an oversaturated market is a significant reason students take the plunge and enter graduate school. In 2017, NASSM lists 32 doctoral programs, 241 master programs, and 411 undergraduate programs in the field of sport management. Three years prior, only 241 institutions offered a master degree in sports management which represented 44% of the institutions offering a bachelors in the content area (Tiell & Walton, 2014).

Sport management degrees are available from numerous institutions outside the United States, however, most are only in a bachelor program. NASSM (2017) lists 32 sport management programs available in Europe, 16 in Canada, 17 in Australia and New Zealand, 19 in Asia, 2 in Africa, and 1 in India.

AFFILIATIONS AND PARTNERSHIPS

A second trend in sports management career preparation includes an increase in affiliations and partnerships between educational entities and sports organizations. Agencies, associations, leagues, franchises, and facilities operating as sports enterprises have increasingly leveraged affiliations and partnerships with academic entities. Whether to create opportunities for continuing education and professional development or grow future talent or enhance a positive image relative to social responsibility and civic engagement, there are numerous benefits for a sports business to form a relationship with an educational entity beyond just serving as a hub for credit-based field experience. Conversely, the benefit for an educational institution is to take advantage of a living classroom or learning laboratory with access to industry professionals, facilities, and special projects.

The U.S. Sports Academy (USSA) in Daphne, Alabama, partnered with the National Association of Collegiate Directors of Athletics (NACDA) for several years in offering a certification in intercollegiate athletic administration. The University of Idaho's sports management program partners with the Professional Golf Association (PGA). Tiffin University in Tiffin, Ohio, has leveraged an affiliation with the WOA to run a humanitarian project for underprivileged youth in host cities for the 2012 (London) and 2016 (Rio) Olympic Games. Similarly, the International Academy of Sports Science and Technology in Lausanne, Switzerland, has close ties with the International Olympic Committee (IOC). Georgetown University's Sports Industry Management Program and the NHL Washington Capitals partnered for a season to create a fellowship for graduate students to immerse themselves in game-day activities with front-office personnel (Georgetown University, 2008). The University of Colorado (Colorado Springs) and the MLS Colorado Rapids established a partnership whereby tailored practicums are part of the first college business degree with a soccer concentration.

Additional examples of partnerships between sports organizations and academic entities are prevalent, especially relative to the concept of the mutual benefits associated with experiential learning through ticket sales. Students from Belmont Abbey College work with the National Association for Stock Car Auto Racing (NASCAR) Hall of Fame to develop a business plan for selling a race experience that includes interactive exhibits, a viewing party, and a tour. The University of Central Florida sells tickets for the NBA Orlando Magic; Robert Morris University works with the MLB Pittsburgh Pirates; the University of Memphis partners with the NBA Grizzlies; and Baylor University uses a call center to sell tickets for FC Dallas, Houston Astros, Texas Rangers, San Antonio Spurs, and the Houston Rockets. The Astros, in fact, actually provide sales leads for students in addition to 30 hours of training, which includes hands-on experience tracking clients using a Microsoft Dynamics cloud-based customer relationship management (CRM) program. These academic and business partnerships may include financial incentives, exchanges in intellectual property, or contractual service agreements combined with the benefit of increased market recognition (Tiell, 2012).

▶ ACTION SHOT 14-3

MLB Cleveland Indians Collegiate Ticket Sales Competition

The MLB Cleveland Indians host a collegiate ticket-sales competition with area universities. Training is provided onsite.

Courtesy of Bonnie Tiell

Sports organizations typically choose to partner with sports management programs to enhance hands-on professional development for individuals in the exploration stage while benefitting from the advantage of training future employees with little monetary investment. For example, the Major League Baseball (MLB) Cleveland Indians, 2016 World Series runner-up, partnered with select sports management and sports marketing programs to create a collegiate ticket sales competition as a means to prepare students for potential jobs in professional sports. The program requires students to sell game tickets, but in addition to "perks" and "incentives" for their efforts, participants have the opportunity to interact with staff and executives from the Indians during a training workshop on campus and a half-day workshop at the ballpark. Annually, student representatives from participating colleges have presented case studies, promotion ideas, and marketing plans to a team of executives. At one point, 11 universities participated in the collegiate competition, demonstrating how friendly rivalries can promote collaboration among professors for the benefit of student learning. Upon graduating, the first "student" commissioner from the original institution was hired to a trainee program, promoted to a full-time sales position after one season, and promoted to oversee the collegiate competition in her second year (A. Madison via personal communication, December 2, 2015).

CERTIFICATE PROGRAMS

A third trend in career preparation for sports management fields is the surge in certifications. **Certificate programs** are becoming more popular as short-range, intense study programs resulting in documentation of a specialized skill or competency. There is a rise in the popularity of nondegree training certificates, which increase the marketability of those looking to break into sports right out of college, advance within a career, or transition into the industry from a completely different occupation.

Numerous accredited universities offer certificate programs related to sports management, primarily in the form of continuing education or a master degree. A cursory search on the Internet for "sports management certificate program" will produce pages of options. For example, the U.S. Sports Academy (2017) offers online certificate programs with continuing education units (CEUs) in areas, such as collegiate compliance, sports security management, personal training, and sports injury management. Universities are recognizing the financial and marketing advantage in providing certifications. Two novel programs include George Washington University's (2017) Sport Philanthropist Executive Certificate and Nova Southeastern University's (2017) Sport Revenue Generation Certificate.

Independent sports agencies and governing bodies have continued to benefit from the business of sports certificate programs. In certain practitioner positions throughout the industry (e.g., officials, scouts, lifeguards, fitness specialists, agents), a certificate is required to work within the occupation. Certification for lifeguarding is available through the Red Cross, the YMCA, or the American Lifeguarding Association. Personal fitness professionals may obtain certification through the American Council on Exercise, the American College of Sports Medicine, the Aerobic and Fitness Association of America, the National Academy of Sports Medicine, the National Strength and Conditioning Association, or any of a dozen or more related professional organizations.

Most certificate programs offered through independent sports agencies, however, are for the sole purpose of developing proficiency or mastery in a sector of the industry and not tied to compliance or regulatory requirements. For example, the National Association of Sports Commissions (2017) offers certification and professional development tailored to individuals working in the sports travel industry. Sports Management Worldwide (2017) offers a certificate in Motorsports Management, and the Union of European Football Associations (2017) offers a certificate in Professional Football Management in cooperation with Lausanne University in Switzerland.

Almost every professional association for every niche of the sports industry has the opportunity to create certificates. Many associations have taken advantage of a membership belonging to a professional community where certification can bolster career advancement. Of great importance for human resource personnel and managers with authority to provide resources and time for employees to participate in a certificate program is to research the credibility of the organization providing the program and to measure the perceived benefits in terms of a return on investment.

Recap

Individuals working in human resources acknowledge the linkage between training and professional development. Development of an employee is an ongoing process that extends well beyond training. Effective human resource practices use training to focus on specific short-term organizational needs and embrace development as a long-term growth initiative focusing on the professional needs of the individual. Professional development is administered either internally by the organization where an individual is employed, externally through professional associations or independent agencies, or through personal relationships in the form of a coach, mentor, or sponsor.

The motivation for professional development varies with each career stage of an individual, but the underlying purpose remains as a means for continuous education to enhance adaptation in the face of environmental changes in the industry. The four general career stages are (1) exploratory, (2) entry and establishment, (3) middle and maintenance, and (4) late and disengagement.

Professional development during the exploration stage focuses on understanding the depth and the breadth of the field, with a focus on experiential learning (e.g., internships and shadowships). The entry and establishment stage is characterized by an oversaturated market in the sports industry, and the motivation for professional development extends to understanding an organization's structure, function, and culture. During the middle and maintenance stage, employees typically have increased responsibilities and may assume positions as board members for professional organizations or community associations while transitioning to the role of a mentor. The sports industry is a healthy market for job seekers in their middle and maintenance stage. Finally, the motive for professional development during the late and disengagement stage typically involves a focus on the changing financial and social aspects associated with retirement and opportunities to stay engaged through lifelong learning. Individuals in the late career stage are often seeking a bridge job or an encore career to remain engaged in the labor force past retirement age.

Several factors that have had an effect on career trends in the sports industry include fluctuations in economic conditions, societal and demographic changes, and improvements in technology and communications. Trends in sports career preparation include an increase in specialized curriculum, an increase in affiliations and partnerships with sports organizations, and the proliferation of certificates.

🌐 GLOBAL SPOTLIGHT 14–1

Professional Development Opportunities—Adidas Group

The Adidas Group (2017) offers several types of professional development opportunities in countries around the world considered strategic business ports. Development programs are tailored to different audiences in different markets in an effort to create a global talent pipeline.

In China, a management trainee program is offered. Applicants must be a Chinese citizen residing in the country. In addition, the candidate must have graduated with a master degree within 12 months or be within 12 months of finishing the graduate-degree requirements. The areas of focus include human resources, sales, marketing, finance, operations, and retail. Participants engage in three rotations concentrated in training and action learning activities for the selected area. Each rotation spans 6 months before a successful candidate is placed in a starting managerial position.

In the Herzogenaurach, Germany, home office for the Adidas Group (2017) which includes Adidas, Reebok, TaylorMade Golf, and CCM Hockey brands, area residents can participate in an apprenticeship program spanning 2 to 3 years. During the apprenticeship, participants rotate every 3 to 6 months through the following six positions: (1) information technology specialist, (2) warehouse logistics specialist, (3) industrial management assistant, (4) retail management assistant, (5) sales associate, and (6) shoemaker. The vocational-style development program creates opportunities for technical immersion in jobs within the Adidas group that are highly specialized. Candidates must be fluent in both English and German. Positions pay higher than the minimum wage for Germany, with annual raises (Adidas Group, 2017).

For college graduates anywhere in the world who are fluent in English, the Adidas Group (2017) also offers a functional training program (FTP) in the areas of product marketing, global sales, finance, human resource, corporate communication, and product creation. Candidates in the program are matched with a senior-management mentor and progress through three stages of development, each spanning approximately 6 months. The first assignment is in Germany, and the second includes two international assignments as an expat in locations, such as Sao Paulo, Brazil; Tokyo, Japan; and Lo, Vietnam. Finally, candidates are dispersed to several task groups where members collaborate virtually to complete assignments.

Throughout the program, participants engage in numerous development conversations and receive part of their training at a state-of-the-art Adidas Group Learning Campus. The program pays the market rate and focuses on multinational team building, network connections, and the development of detailed specialist knowledge (Adidas Group, 2017). Although a full-time position is not guaranteed, the goal of the FTP is to place successful candidates in an Adidas store if they have performed well.

DISCUSSION QUESTIONS

1. What is the motivation for engaging in professional development activities within the sports industry for each of the four career stages?
2. What are the advantages and disadvantages for sports organizations in designing and administering professional development programs for their employees?
3. What must managers and human resource personnel in the sports industry consider when deciding to invest time and resources in professional development opportunities for employees that are offered through a professional organization or independent agency?
4. What sociocultural influences have affected the availability and types of mentors and sponsors in the sports industry?
5. What are the advantages and disadvantages of a triad mentoring relationship?
6. The trends in sports career preparation described in this chapter emphasize increased specialization in curriculum, affiliations, and certificate programs. In the next ten years, will the rate of growth in each of the trends identified increase dramatically, moderately, or not at all? Why or why not?
7. Why do the Adidas Group and other sports organizations invest in functional trainee or apprenticeship programs, and what measures of evaluation of such programs are appropriate?

APPLIED ACTIVITIES

1. Assume the role of an executive for an MLS franchise in a mid-size metropolitan city. Within 10 miles is a private college offering an undergraduate degree in sports management with an enrollment of 200 students. Consider the benefits of an affiliation with the local university, and design a comprehensive program to engage sports management students throughout their 4 years of study.
2. Select a segment of the sports industry in which you are interested in potentially being employed. Create a database of four individuals you believe would be extraordinary mentors and who could become part of your professional network once you have reached the middle and maintenance stage. Include as much contact information as possible, and prepare a statement identifying the means to make an initial connection as well as to nurture the relationship over a 10- to 15-year period.
3. Compare and contrast sports certificate programs offered through educational entities (e.g., a university or college) and those offered by independent agencies or governing bodies.

CASE STUDY

Agents and Agencies Focus on Servicing Niche Markets in Adapting to Trends Impacting Sports

Changes in global economics, technology, and human capital have influenced sports businesses to continually assess and adapt in order to capitalize on trends and influences in the marketplace. One of the most predominant developments in the industry over time has been a reliance on increased specialization. Agents and agencies, such as Molly Fletcher and International Management Group (IMG), Worldwide have leveraged their expertise to locate, create, or simply service niche markets, such as collegiate licensing, digital sports, personalized business training, Olympic sponsorships, golf course management, and ticketing solutions.

Molly Fletcher

Molly Fletcher was lauded by CNN as the female Jerry McGuire, responsible for securing over $500 million in deals as a sports agent and president of client representation for CSE in Atlanta, Georgia. She has been featured in segments by ESPN, Forbes, and *Sports Illustrated*, and she represented sports personalities, such as Tom Izzo, Bobby Cox John Smoltz, Erin Andrews, Matt Kuchar, Joe Theismann, and Doc Rivers.

In 2010, Fletcher parted with CSE to create her own company, MWF Holdings. Today, she is CEO of the Molly Fletcher Company and delivers professional development programs for hundreds of Fortune 500 companies, sports teams, colleges, and tech start-ups. Her 30-second "Fearless Friday" clips on social media keep her message relevant as she delivers countless coaching sessions and keynote speeches focusing on professional development and personalized business advice.

The transition was "organic," according to Molly (M. Fletcher, personal communication, April 26, 2016). While she continued to represent clients after departing CSE, she was primarily speaking

at colleges and collecting royalties from her first book, *Your Dream Job Game Plan*. As her popularity quickly ascended, she disengaged as an agent and shifted her career focus to promoting her personal brand as an author, speaker, and business consultant/coach.

In the midst of her transition, she noticed a gap for athletes and coaches in managing their social media presence in cyberspace. Thus, she launched "Fletcher Digital," a strategic social branding tool designed to monetize and maximize connectivity among followers on Twitter, Facebook, Instagram, YouTube, and LinkedIn. She continues leveraging her experience and style to sustain her own game-changing presence in the industry. Fletcher has published additional sports-business books, offers online and personalized training, and remains in high demand as a keynote speaker.

Mark McCormack and IMG Worldwide

IMG Worldwide has over 3000 employees in over 30 countries. Founded in the early 1960s in Cleveland, Ohio, by Mark McCormack, the company has adapted to over 50 years of changes in politics, technology, and economics. Tabbed as the inventor of sports business, McCormack essentially launched the first sports agency business, with Arnold Palmer and Jack Nicklaus as early clients. For several decades, IMG garnered 25% of an athlete's total earnings, including prize money (Anderson, 1981).

During the early years, IMG focused primarily on the golf and tennis markets before branching into other niche segments. Over time, the agency has represented the likes of Tiger Woods, Annika Sorenstam, Peyton Manning, Maria Sharapova, Serena Williams, Pele, Venus Williams, Novak Djokovic, Kristi Yamaguchi, John McEnroe, Cam Newton, Andre Agassi, Martina

Navratilova, John Maddon, Matt Stanford, Nadia Comaneci, Wayne Gretzky, Derek Jeter, Bob Costas, Jeff Gordon, Scott Hamilton, and Joe Montana, to name a few.

In 1993, the company included over 1000 employees in 75 offices throughout 21 countries (Hosking, 1993). A decade later when McCormack passed away, the company had grown to include over 2500 employees in 100 offices throughout 32 countries (Dabkowski, 2003). IMG had already represented modeling agencies, produced sports television programs, owned a basketball team in China, acquired European soccer stadiums, created sports academies, built golf courses, and handled special projects for Mother Theresa and the pope.

Shortly after McCormack's death, IMG was purchased for $750 million by Ted Forstmann, who expanded the company further into a global sports, fashion, and media business. Forstmann passed away in 2011, and the company was eventually purchased for 2.4 billion by William Morris Endeavor (WME) and Silver Lake Partners (Smith, 2014). One of the biggest coups in recent years includes securing a deal with Visa to handle the company's marketing activities with the International Federation of Association Football (FIFA) World Cup, the NFL, and the 2016 Olympic TOP Sponsor program (Lefton, 2015).

One of IMG's growth strategies includes acquisitions of sports entities. IMG College was launched in 2010 to handle ticketing solutions, sponsorships, multimedia rights, intellectual property, promotional assets, and merchandising and licensing deals for athletic departments, tournaments, and bowls. The division was possible only after acquiring Host Communications, International Sports Properties (ISP), and the Collegiate Licensing Company. According to Kate Grant, vice president of human resources, no one predicted that IMG College would become a significant revenue driver and the centerpiece of its business model (K. Grant, personal communication, February 27,

2015). Financial documents from IMG Lending (Mickle, 2014) indicated IMG College revenues in 2013 totaled $487 million, whereas the Media division totaled $448 million and the Sports & Entertainment division totaled $626 million.

The year IMG college was launched was the same year the Worldwide Headquarters moved from Cleveland to New York. IMG maintains an office in Cleveland with around 95 employees, but the company trimmed 3% of the global workforce (approximately 100 employees) in 2015 (Smith, 2014). The layoffs coincided with a massive restructuring effort to eliminate redundancies and trim millions in expenses.

Assisting in the restructuring efforts was Grant, who was hired in 1992. Grant remains in Cleveland, which is home to the finance, human resources, legal, and information technology departments. She views her role as a human resource business partner for IMG's global entities. She works in three-person teams to develop multiyear strategies for staffing, succession planning, and training needs. Her partners typically include an in-house finance director and a business unit leader, such as the head of the Honda Classic or IMG Golf in London.

IMG Worldwide is constantly adapting, constantly mining new talent, and constantly strategizing to facilitate intentional growth. The internship program, according to Grant, can be considered an 8-week interview, with 10% to 11% of the workforce in the United States having come out of the program (K. Grant, personal communication, February 27, 2015).

A subsidiary of WME Entertainment, LLC, IMG offers "consulting, event management, hospitality, league development, licensing, media distribution, media production, performance, speaker, sponsorship, strategic initiative, talent representation, ticketing, venue, and video archive services, as well as integrated academic, athletic, and personal development programs (Bloomberg, 2017). The range of services demonstrates the broad spectrum of sport agencies.

CASE STUDY QUESTIONS

1. Why did Molly Fletcher leave the sports agency business?

2. How does Fletcher Digital exemplify trends in sports that affect human resources?

3. What are the human resource implications when IMG acquires smaller sports entities or branches into niche markets?

4. Speculate on how IMG Worldwide has managed employee growth over five decades.

REFERENCES

Adidas Group. (2017). *Functional training programs.* Retrieved from http://careers .adidas-group.com/functional-trainee-program.aspx

Anderson, D. (1981, July 13). Palmer to the pope. *New York Times,* C-4.

Atlanta Braves. (2017). *Trainee program.* Retrieved from http://atlanta.braves.mlb .com/atl/ticketing/trainee_program.jsp

Auerbach, D. (2014). Advice and resources: Job trends. 22 of the fastest growing sports jobs. *Careerbuilder.com.* Retrieved from http://advice.careerbuilder.com /posts/twenty-two-of-the-fastest-growing-sports-jobs

Battista, J. (2008, December 9). Feeling pinch: NFL will cut about 150 jobs. *New York Times.* Retrieved from http://www.nytimes.com/2008/12/10/sports /football/10nfl.html

Belson, K. (2009, October 26). In sports business, too many hopefuls for too few positions. *New York Times.* Retrieved from http://www.nytimes.com/2009/05/27 /sports/27class.html?_r=0

Bentz, J., Sedensky, M., Tompson, T., & Agiesta, J. (2013, October). *Research Highlights: Working longer - Older Americans attitudes towards work and retirement.* The Associated Press. NORC Center for Public Affairs Research.

Bloom, G., Bush, N., Schinke, R., and Salmela, J. (1998). The importance of mentoring in the development of coaches and athletes. *International Journal of Sport Psychology*, 29. 267–281.

Bloomberg. (2017). *Media. Company overview of IMG Worldwide, Inc.* S&P Global Market Intelligence. Bloomberg. Retrieved from https://www.bloomberg.com /research/stocks/private/snapshot.asp?privcapId=167997

Bonesteel, M. (2017, April 27). ESPN cuts big names in latest layoffs. The Washington Post. D02.

Boveda & Metz. (2016, June 1). Predicting end of career transitions for baby-boomers nearing retirement age. *Career Development Quarterly, 64.* 153–168.

Brassie, P. (1989). Guidelines for programs preparing undergraduate and graduate students for careers in sport management. *Journal of Sport Management, 3,* 158–164.

Brown, M., & Kreutzer, A.(2001, December 24). Mason led the way in training sports executives. Sports Business Journal. Retrieved from http://m.sports-businessdaily.com/Journal/Issues/2001/12/20011224/Opinion/Mason-Led-The-Way-In-Training-Sports-Execs.aspx

Burke, R., Cooper, C., and Antoniou, A. (2015). *The Multi-generational and Aging Workforce*. Cheltenham, UK: Edward Elgar Publishers.

Cahill, K., Giandrea, M., & Quinn, J. (2007, April). *Downshifting: The role of bridge jobs after career employment* (Center on Aging Worker at Boston College Brief 06.1-11). Retrieved from http://www.bc.edu/content/dam/files/research_sites /agingandwork/pdf/publications/IB06_DownShifting.pdf

Clapp, B. (2013, June 29). Entry level jobs with real growth potential. *Workinsports. com*. Retrieved from http://www.workinsports.com/blog/entry-level-sports -j.bs-with-real-growth-potential/

College Sports Solutions. (2015). *The CSS team*. Retrieved from http://www .collegesportssolutions.com/the-css-team

Commission on Sports Management Accreditation. (2016, June). Common professional component. *COSMA accreditation principles and self-study preparation* (p. 13). Arlington, VA: Author.

Dabkowski, S. (2003, May 10). IMG says it's business as usual while its driving force remains in a coma; the money game. *The Age* (Australia), Sports, 5.

Dreher, G., & Ash, R. (1990). A comparative study of mentoring among men and women in managerial, professional, and technical positions. *Journal of Applied Psychology, 75*, 539–546.

Galily, Y., & Shimon, P. (2012). The transition of retired military officers to a second career in sport management: The Israeli case. *Journal of Multidisciplinary Research, 4*(2), 5–17.

Garcia, A. (2017, March 6). *ESPN lay-offs to hit on camera personalities. CNN Money Sport*. Retrieved from http://money.cnn.com/2017/03/06/news/companies /espn-layoffs-talent/

George Washington University. (2017). *Sports philanthropy executive certificate*. Retrieved from http://business.gwu.edu/programs/professional-certificates /sports-philanthropy/

Georgetown University. (2008). Sports industry management program and Washington Capitals partner to create fellowship for students. *Sports Industry Management*. Retrieved from https://www.facebook.com/notes/georgetown -university-masters-program-in-sports-industry-management/gu-sim-washington -capitals-partner-on-new-fellowship-program/35109321606

Hosking, P. (1993, July 18). Profile: Business guru to a tee; Agent Mark McCormack got the big money into sport, but has also written management books on watching people. Patrick Hosking tests the tips on the author. *The Independent* (London), Business on Sunday, 11.

Johnston, C. (2012, September 20). Lockout means cuts at NHL offices. *The Record* (Waterloo-Ontario), Sports, C2.

Jones, D., Brooks, D., & Mak, J. (2008). Examining sport management programs in the United States. *Sports Management Review, 11*(1), 77–91.

Kjeldsen, E. (1990). Sport management careers: A descriptive analysis. *Journal of Sports Management, 4,* 121–132.

Kokomo Tribune. (2017, February 20). MC Sports closing following liquidation sale. *Kokomo Tribune,* Indiana.

Kokemuller, N. (2015). What does mid-career professional mean? *Houston Chronicle.* Retrieved from http://work.chron.com/midcareer-professional-mean-29000.html

Kram, K. (1985). *Mentoring at work.* Glenview, IL.

Lapchick, R. (2016). 2015-16 racial and gender report card. *University of Central Florida, Institute of Diversity and Ethics in Sport.* Retrieved from http://www.tidesport.org/reports.html

Lefton, T. (2015, January 15). IMG wins shootout for biggest Visa properties. *Street & Smith's Sports Business Journal,* 10.

Long Beach State University. (2017). *Athletic news. Vic Cegels. Position: Athletic director.* Retrieved from http://www.longbeachstate.com/genrel/cegles_vic00.html

Manzullo, B. (2014, January 8). Jim Leyland says he will be "special assistant" to Dave Dombrowski, Detroit Tigers. *Detroit Free Press.* Retrieved from http://www.freep.com/article/20140108/SPORTS02/301080147/1050/rss15

Mickle, T. (2014). WME outlines plans for IMG. *Street & Smith Sports Business Journal,* 1

Mooney, L. (2014, April 28). Five key trends that are driving the business of sports. *Stanford Business.* Retrieved from https://www.gsb.stanford.edu/insights /five-key-trends-are-driving-business-sports

National Association of Sports Commissions. (2017). *CSEE certification.* Retrieved from http://www.sportscommissions.org/certification

National Collegiate Athletic Association. (2014). Mission, goals, and program measures: NCAA Student-Athlete Affairs, Leadership Development Unit.

National Collegiate Athletic Association. (2017a). *NCAA Pathway Program.* Retrieved from http://www.ncaa.org/about/resources/leadership-development /ncaa-pathway-program

National Collegiate Athletic Association. (2017b). *NCAA Leadership Institute.* Retrieved from http://www.ncaa.org/about/resources/leadership-development /ncaa-leadership-institute. Morgantown, WV: Author.

North American Society for Sport Management. (2017). *Academic programs:.* Retrieved from https://www.nassm.com/Programs/AcademicPrograms

Nova Southeastern University. (2017). *Master's programs: Sport revenue generation certificate.* Retrieved from http://www.business.nova.edu/certificates /sport-revenue-generation/

Ohio University. (2017). Walter O'Malley. History of the founder. Retrieved from https://business.ohio.edu/4812.aspx

Parkhouse, B. L. (1978). Professional preparation in athletic administration and sport management. *Journal of Physical Education and Recreation, 49,* 22–27.

Pittsburgh Pirates. (2017). *B.U.C.S. Academy.* Retrieved from http://pittsburgh.pirates .mlb.com/pit/ticketing/inside_sales_mission.jsp

Rennekamp, R., & Nall, M. (1994, June). Growing through the stages: A new look at professional growth. *Journal of Extension, 2,* 1.

Reynolds, T. (2012). Lockout already taking toll: Panthers, Senators are already laying off after three days. *The Daily News,* A10.

Roche, G. (1979). Much ado about mentoring. *Harvard Business Review, 57,* 17–28.

Salamone, A., (2017, January 6). Burlington to move into old sports authority. *The Morning Call.* A4.

Snyder, M. (2015, December 4). Marlins announce Barry Bonds as hitting coach. *CBS Sports.* Retrieved from http://www.cbssports.com/mlb/eye-on-baseball/25400805/marlins-announce-barry-bonds-as-hitting-coach

Solomon, J. (2015, April 6). UAB hires new sports consultant to study cutting football. *CBS Sports.* Retrieved from http://www.cbssports.com/collegefootball/writer/jon-solomon/25137763/uab-hires-new-sports-consultant-to-study-cutting-football

Smith, M. (2014, December 8). IMG will cut workforce by 3% in coming weeks. *Street & Smith Sports Business Journal,* 8.

Sport and Recreation New Zealand (SPARC) (2010) *Coach Mentor programme (sic),* Wellington NZ: SPARC.

Sports Management Worldwide. (2017). *Motorsports management course.* Retrieved from https://www.sportsmanagementworldwide.com/courses/motor-sports-management

Super, D. (1987). Life career roles: Self-realization in work and leisure. In D. T. Hall (Ed.), *Career development in organizations* (pp. 95–119). San Francisco, CA: Jossey-Bass.

Tiell, B. (2011, September–October). Going online to get ahead in sport management curriculum. *Sports Destination Management Magazine,* 24–29.

Tiell, B. (2012, May–June). An evolving education in sport management curriculum. *Sports Destination Management Magazine,* 28–35.

Tiell, B. (2015, May/June). Teaching responsibility and due diligence: Preparing sports management students for roles as a sports supervisor. *Sports Destination Management Magazine,* 28–35.

Tiell, B., & Walton, K. (2014, May 23). The sports management graduate education advantage. *Sports Destination Management Magazine,* 24–39.

UNDsports.com. (2016). *Athletics. Brian Faison: Athletic director. University of North Dakota.* Retrieved from http://www.undsports.com/ViewArticle.dbml?ATCLID=3744273

Union of European Football Associations. (2017). *Certificate in professional football management.* Retrieved from http://www.uefa.org/football-development/academic/national-edition-cmf/

U.S. Department of Labor. (2015, December 17). *Occupational outlook handbook: Entertainment and sport occupations.* Retrieved from http://www.bls.gov/ooh/entertainment-and-sports/home.htm

U.S. Department of State. (2017). The global sports mentoring program. Retrieved from https://globalsportsmentoring.org/

U.S. Sports Academy. (2017). *Continuing education: Certificate and certification programs.* Retrieved from https://ussa.edu/continuing-education/

Weaver, M., & Chelladurai, P. (2002). Mentoring in intercollegiate athletic administration. *Journal of Sport Management, 16,* 96–116.

West, C. (1999, June). *Notes on the history of women in intercollegiate athletics.* Presentation at the National Association of Intercollegiate Athletic Administrators and Higher Education Resource Center Midwest (NACWAA/HERS) Institute for Administrative Advancement, Bryn Mawr, PA.

White, J. (2012). HERS Institute: Curriculum for advancing women leaders in higher education. *Advances in Developing Human Resources, 14*(1), 1–17.

Whitley, W., Dougherty, T., & Dreher, G. (1991). Relationship of career mentoring and socioeconomic origin to managers' and professionals' early career progress. *Academy of Management Journal, 24,* 331–351.

Women in Sports and Events. (2017). *Program information: Mentoring.* Retrieved from http://wiseworks.org/resources/within/information/

Women Leaders in College Sports. (2017). *Women's leadership symposium.* Retrieved from http://www.womenleadersincollegesports.org/WL/events/womens-leadership-symposium/WL/Events/womens-leadership-symposium.aspx?hkey=3f59e4aa-df8d-4468-969a-2ae860035b27

Accommodation A conflict resolution technique where one party neglects his or her own concern to satisfy the concerns of the other party.

Affinity chart A diagram organizing a large number of ideas into groups based on natural relationships.

Aggressive personality Behavior exhibited by an individual who takes charge, is overly assertive, and is overly dominant and controlling.

Agreement The arrangement or settlement of a negotiated outcome.

Alternative dispute resolution The methods and techniques used to settle a disagreement or opposing views without seeking legal recourse.

Analytics A process to systematically examine data to determine patterns, trends, or relationships.

Applicant An individual who has fulfilled the initial requirement of applying for a position.

Applicant criterion chart A chart depicting a list of characteristics and information deemed important for an employment position.

Applicant screening A preliminary assessment of characteristics or qualifying attributes of a prospective employee for a job opening.

Applicant tracking system (ATS) The system used to manage recruiting documents and materials, typically through sophisticated software applications.

Apprenticeship A temporary work assignment for a fixed period of time (e.g., 6 months or a year) using on-the-job training to teach or enhance an individual's skills, knowledge, and aptitude.

Arbitration A form of alternative dispute resolution whereby an independent and neutral party evaluates evidence from each side of a case and is empowered to make a binding decision or award.

Assessment Activities to measure progress or achievement of an activity or action.

Assessment test   A test that uses results to screen job applicants on the basis of some specific behavioral, knowledge, or skill areas.

Asynchronous training   Training that can be administered on demand permitting learners to study at their own pace.

At-will employee   A worker who can be terminated without warning or without the organization having to provide just cause.

Authoritative leadership   A style of leadership exhibited by individuals who are direct and make decisions independently.

Avoidance   A conflict resolution technique where one party is unassertive or uncooperative by not pursuing personal concerns or concerns of the other individual.

Background checks   An investigation of an individual's financial, criminal, educational, employment, and/or other historical information through public or confidential sources.

Background questions   Questions designed to elicit information regarding a candidate's employment history or educational attainment.

Balanced scorecard   A comprehensive business tool that tracks key elements of an organization's activities aligned with its vision and strategic initiatives to measure how management is achieving the desired outcomes related to finances, internal business operations, customers, and innovation.

Bargaining range   The distance between the reservation points of each party.

Behaviorally anchored rating scale   An assessment tool that uses a quantitative rating assigned to narrative examples representing ranges of good and poor performance.

Behavioral leadership theories   A set of leadership theories based on the premise of whether a leader's influence is based more on a concern for directing tasks or for developing relationships.

Behavioral questions   Questions requiring the candidate to recall a story or provide an example to demonstrate a particular behavior.

Benchmarking   The process of comparing measurable information about different aspects of an organization with a prescribed standard.

Benefit   An indirect reward given to an employee as part of their employment.

Best practices   Benchmarking performance according to a preferred or prudent standard in the industry that may or may not also be considered "best in class."

Best in class   Benchmarking performance according to the highest standard in the industry.

Boiled frog phenomenon   A metaphor to describe consequences related to reactions to incremental changes in the environment that go unnoticed.

Bonus   A type of compensation that is a one-time payment and is not part of an employee's base pay.

Brainstorming   A process to spontaneously generate ideas without interpretation or evaluation.

Breach of contract   A legal condition for terminating a relationship when one party fails to fulfill or honor his or her part of an agreement.

Bridge employment   A job that fills the gap between a full-time position and leaving the workforce completely.

Bullying   Forced intimidation or hazing, which may be physical, verbal, or virtual.

Burnout   A manifestation of emotional exhaustion, fatigue, and diminished efficiency primarily caused by prolonged stress.

Buyout clause   A contract provision noting a payout to the other party for terminating a contract without cause.

Career stages   An individual's job progression throughout the time span when he or she is considered "employable."

Case study   Information based on real-life experiences to explain, clarify, or develop interest in an aspect of an organization, system, industry, individual, or situation.

Central tendency error   Avoiding rating anyone extremely low or extremely high in any performance category in an employee evaluation.

Certificate program   A short-range, intense study program resulting in documentation of a specialized skill or competency upon satisfactory completion or mastery of program components.

Charismatic leadership   Displayed by an individual with the ability to motivate and inspire others primarily through his or her personality.

Closed-ended questions   Questions that only have a single answer and can be answered with a one-word response (yes or no) or a short phrase.

Coaching   One-on-one support from an experienced individual who oversees and provides feedback on a specific activity or function performed by an individual with less experience.

Collaboration   A conflict resolution technique considered "value-added" where both parties work together to satisfy their own and each other's concerns.

Collective bargaining   The process of negotiating conditions of employment, which leads to a collective bargaining agreement (CBA).

Collective bargaining agreement   The document representing an agreement of labor conditions that was collectively agreed upon by an organization's workers and management entities.

Communication strategy chart   A graphic representation segmented by audience defining the message content, time period, method of transmission, and messenger.

Compensation   The monetary and nonmonetary rewards provided by a company to an employee in exchange for work.

Competition   A conflict resolution technique where both parties seek to satisfy their own concerns at the other individual's expense.

Compressed workweek   Extending the hours worked in a day to reduce the days worked in the week (e.g., working 10-hour shifts over a 4-day period as opposed to 8-hour shifts over 5 days).

Compromise   A conflict resolution technique where both parties forego part of their concerns to mutually reach an agreement.

Conceptual skills   Skills of a manager or employee related to the processes of thinking, analyzing, and decision making.

Conflict   A disagreement or a sense of opposition or disharmony.

Constitution   A document that provides the foundation for the operating principles of a government or organization.

Contingency leadership theories   A set of leadership theories focusing on the interaction between situational variables and leadership characteristics (synonymous with *situational leadership*).

Contract   A legally binding agreement between and accepted by two entities enforceable by a judicial court system.

Contrast error   An appraisal that compares an employee's performance to that of an individual with a similar position within the organization without regarding preset standards.

Counterproductive behavior   Behavior that intentionally hinders the achievement of organizational goals (also referred to as *deviant behavior*).

Critical incident report   A report of an incident that occurs outside of what is perceived to be a normal range of performance.

Cultural diversity   Values, attitudes, beliefs, actions, opinions, and expectations shared by an identifiable group.

Cyclical training   Regularly scheduled training sessions, such as annual risk assessment training or monthly compliance training sessions.

Dashboard   A visual diagram of business elements used to measure performance.

Decisional roles   Roles of a manager or supervisor related to activities as an entrepreneur, disturbance handler, resource allocator, and negotiator for the purpose of maintaining harmony within the organization.

Delphi technique   A collaborative decision-making technique including expert information deciphered and addressed by a facilitator in a process to reach a consensus.

Disability insurance   Covers a qualifying individual due to becoming mentally or physically disabled.

Discipline   Actions intended to enforce compliance or obedience and as a measure to modify behavior or manage performance.

Discriminate   To unfairly treat a person or group of people differently from other people or groups of people.

Discussion   A verbal or written exchange of information and/or a dialogue between two or more individuals.

Disparate impact   Theory of liability in discrimination cases in which an employer has a practice or policy that has an unintentional discriminatory effect on a protected class.

Disparate treatment   Theory of liability in discrimination cases in which an employer has intentionally discriminated against an individual.

Dispute   A disagreement or opposing views.

Distribution channels   The locations for dispensing and publicizing employer information, such as application materials and documents (e.g., job descriptions).

Distributive negotiations   A negotiations strategy focusing on dividing or allocating a fixed sum between two parties.

Diversity   Explaining individual differences according to a specific dimension.

Document and/or material collection   The method in which materials are submitted to the hiring organization as either an electronic or hard copy.

Due process   The legal obligation of an organization to inform contracted employees of impending termination and to provide the opportunity for corrective action.

Dysfunctional conflict   Conflict that is considered negative and detrimental to performance.

Electronic storage system   The technology systems used to organize information and data in electronic or digital format.

Employee   Generally, a person employed by an organization, although the legal definition of *employee* varies by law.

Employee analysis   An analysis of the strengths and deficiencies in the knowledge, skills, and abilities of the current workforce.

Employee development   A broad term describing activities by an organization to facilitate an individual's growth and future performance rather than his or her immediate job role.

Employee inventory   A comprehensive list of employees in an organization accompanied by selected data (e.g., date of hire, part-time or full-time status, certification, etc.).

Employee training   The activities of an organization that help the employee achieve the competencies of a particular job role.

Employment at will   A condition whereby an employee can be terminated by an organization for any reason (other than illegal), without cause.

Employment interview   A meeting where one individual questions another to determine suitability for a job opening.

Employment law   Body of law that governs the employer–employee relationship.

Equal Employment Opportunity Commission   The federal agency assigned by the U.S. government that enforces employment discrimination laws.

Equity in Athletics Disclosure Act   A requirement of the U.S. Department of Education for reporting of gender-equity information by any and all schools receiving federal funding.

Essential functions   Tasks or responsibilities of a particular position that are fundamental to the job.

Ethical conduct   Principled behavior.

Executive order   A rule issued by the president of the United States to the executive branch of the government.

Expectancy theory   A motivation theory by Victor Vroom suggesting that an employee's increased efforts will result in the desired performance outcome if attached to some type of meaningful reward.

External candidate   An applicant for a position who is not associated with the organization.

Extinction   Withdrawing or failing to provide a reinforcing consequence in order to modify behavior.

Extrinsic motivation   Motivation from tangible rewards or factors that influence an individual's drive to exhibit greater performance efforts.

Failure to reasonably accommodate   A category of discrimination in an employment context relevant for specific types of cases, such as religion or disability.

Fair Credit Reporting Act   A federal law that regulates third-party agencies that collect and report on an individual's public or personal information.

First-impression bias   Judging an individual favorably or unfavorably based on an initial impression only.

Flex time   A condition whereby employees are able to select what part of the day or week they may report to begin and end work responsibilities as long as overall hour requirements are maintained (e.g., selecting to work from 7 a.m. to 4 p.m. instead of 8 a.m. to 5 p.m.).

Flexible work arrangements   Altering the traditional 8-hour, 5-day-per-week work schedule to any format acceptable to the employer and employee. The arrangement could include telecommuting, compressed work week, or job-sharing arrangements.

Formal interview   An interview with a prospective employee in which the employer makes a decision regarding whether or not to hire the individual.

Forum   A discussion-based series of presentations on a similar topic.

Full-time equivalent (FTE)   The number of full-time employees who work over 30 hours per week plus the number of hours worked by part-time employees, divided by 120.

Functional conflict   Conflict that is considered positive, improves performance, and facilitates goal achievement.

Gender identity   Pertaining to identification as male or female, regardless of biological traits.

Graphic rating scale   A list of specific traits of an employee relative to the job (e.g., dependability, achieving results, communication, and likability), followed by a range of performance standards represented by either a number and/or a qualitative appraisal term.

Halo effect   The outcome when an evaluator has a cognitive bias shaping his or her overall impression of an employee based on one particular positive characteristic that overshadows negative traits.

Harassment   Systematic or repeated unwanted aggression toward or annoyance of an individual or group.

Hard-copy storage system   A system for storing information and documents in a printed or physical form.

Hazing   A form of harassment common in sports that signifies a rite of passage or initiation into a group.

Hegemonic masculinity   Processes and practices that promote men in a dominant social superiority role over women.

Hierarchical divisional structure   A type of structural chart for employment positions that is designed according to what the organization defines as divisions or subunits within a parent corporation.

Hierarchical functional structure   A type of structural chart for employment positions that is designed according to the dominant activities of the organization.

Hierarchy of needs   A motivation theory by Abraham Maslow suggesting that motivation is a result of satisfying a successive order of needs, which are prioritized in a model resembling a pyramid.

Homologous reproduction   Hiring practices that increase the proportion of the positions held by the dominant group, typically ascribed to the prevailing gender and ethnicity.

Horn effect   The outcome when an evaluator has a cognitive bias shaping his or her overall impression of an employee based on one particular negative characteristic that overshadows positive traits.

Hostile work environment   When unwelcome sexual advances or other verbal/physical conduct affects an individual's employment, unreasonably interferes with an individual's work performance, or creates an intimidating, hostile, or offensive work environment.

Human resources generalist   An individual who has responsibilities and knowledge in more than one human resources specialty area.

Human resources specialist   An individual who has responsibility and knowledge in one specific area of human resources management.

Hybrid training   Training that uses a combination of face-to-face and virtual instruction.

Impasse   A dispute between both sides of the labor force that cannot be settled in a reasonable manner.

Incentive pay   Part of a compensation package that is dependent on the employee meeting certain benchmark criteria.

Inclusion   A philosophy that is accepting and respectful of differences in all individuals.

Indecisive personality   Behavior exhibited by an individual who cannot easily make clear decisions.

Informational roles   Roles of a manager or supervisor related to monitoring and disseminating information or acting as a spokesperson to influence the performance of staff members.

Instrumentality   One of three factors in the expectancy theory relying on a belief that increased efforts produce desired results.

Integrative negotiations   A form of negotiations that seeks to mutually satisfy the needs and interests of both parties.

Internal candidate   An applicant for a position who is currently employed by the organization.

Internal equity   Perceived fairness within an organization for factors such as pay differentials among different jobs or workload.

Interpersonal roles   Roles of a manager or supervisor related to assuming the actions of a figurehead, leader, and liaison in representing the organization as a member of the management team.

Interpersonal skills   Skills of a manager or employee related to communication and interaction with others individually or in a group setting.

Intrinsic motivation   Motivation from a self-desire and internal force that influences an individual's drive to exhibit greater performance efforts.

Inverted U theory of performance   A theory purporting that a certain degree of conflict can improve performance, but as conflict intensifies, the more likely it is that performance will decrease.

Job analysis   A process to determine the duties, functions, skills, and requirements necessary to perform a specific job (sometimes referred to as a *skills inventory*).

Job announcement   An accurate and concise description of a vacant position, including the application procedure.

Job description   A description profile listing the essential duties, responsibilities, skills, and abilities fundamental to the job.

Job sharing   An arrangement utilizing two individuals to perform the duties of one (two individuals working 20 hours each instead of one individual working 40 hours).

Job-specific skill training   Training provided to an employee that focuses on the knowledge and skills necessary to be successful on the job.

Key performance indicators (KPIs)   The information designed to measure and evaluate achievement or progress of business-related activities for an organization.

Kirkpatrick model   A model to evaluate the effectiveness of training according to trainees' reaction to training, the content learned, changes in behavior when training is applied, and the impact of training on the organization.

Labor demand   The types and number of workers necessary to accomplish the organization's goals for a specified market in a specific time period.

Labor relations   The relationship and interactions between management and employees.

Labor supply   The availability of the present workforce in terms numbers and skill sets or competencies to meet demands in a specified market.

Laissez-faire   A style of leadership referred to as "free reign" and exhibited by supervisors who have little direct interaction with subordinates.

Law   Rule or order that is obligatory to observe.

Leadership   The ability to influence and direct others.

Lecture   The dissemination or transfer of information to an audience in a relatively short time span.

Legislative body   An entity having authority to create, amend, or appeal a law.

Leniency error   Rating all employees generally high in each performance area.

LGBT   Acronym for lesbian, gay, bisexual, and transgender.

LGBTQ   Acronym for lesbian, gay, bisexual, transgender, and questioning.

Life and Work Balance Inventory   A survey to assess work–life conflict that was administered by the National Collegiate Athletic Association (NCAA) and completed by over 4000 athletics employees.

Lockout   A tactic used by management to force accommodation or resolution of a labor dispute by temporarily closing a business as a means to prevent and deny employees the opportunity to work and collect wages.

Managerial effectiveness   Related to the ability to achieve business results that meet or exceed organizational expectations.

Managerial roles   The general responsibilities of an individual with managerial or supervisory authority.

Managing applicants   Designating and implementing the system or method to collect and store documents, track candidate information, and communicate throughout the process.

Market analysis   The process to assess the conditions and characteristics of a market.

Market rate   The amount of compensation employers pay employees for a job.

Maslach Burnout Inventory (MBI)   A tool to measure occupational burnout through an assessment of an individual's perception of emotional exhaustion, depersonalization, and personal accomplishment.

Matrix structure   A type of structural chart for employment positions that is designed in a manner that expresses the relationship of each entity to two or more variables.

Mediation   A form of alternative dispute resolution whereby a neutral third party assists both sides in reaching a settlement that is amenable to, and voluntarily accepted by, both parties.

Memorandum of understanding   A nonbinding document establishing a formal agreement between two parties.

Mentoring   A form of professional development where a more experienced individual imparts his or her expertise and knowledge to someone else, whether in a formal or informal arrangement.

Mission statement   A succinct statement or declaration by an organization that defines the core purpose.

Monitoring   The act of observing and checking the progress or status of actions and activities to assess whether they are providing the desired outcomes.

Moral turpitude   Provisions in an employment contract stipulating behavior and conduct expectations considered detrimental to the organization.

Motivation   Actions or activities that initiate goal-oriented behaviors.

Multidimensional leadership model   A theory purporting that a leadership style is based on a congruence between the leader's actual behaviors, the follower's preferred leadership behavior, and the behavior best suited to the context of the situation.

Narcissistic personality   Behavior exhibited by an individual with excessive self-interest at the expense of others.

Negative reinforcement   Removing an unpleasant condition in exchange for meeting or exceeding performance expectations.

Negotiation strategy   The methods or tactics, either integrative or distributive, used to arrange an agreement or transaction.

Negotiation style   The behavioral approach used to arrange an agreement or transaction based on the five modes of conflict resolution: compromise, avoidance, collaboration, competition, or accommodation.

Negotiations   The action or dialogue between two or more parties for the purpose of arranging a transaction or agreement.

Nominal group technique   A decision-making process soliciting input from each member of a group in a structured format that allows for generation of multiple viewpoints evaluated on merit and quality.

Noncompete clause   Part of "other" provisions in a contract specifying a time period precluding an employee from accepting a position with a program that competes with the original organization.

Nonroutine training   Training that is administered at the discretion of the management and is generally considered outside the scope of ordinary operations for an organization.

Onboarding   The process of integrating new employees into an organization through formal documentation, orientation, training, and access to privileges.

On-the-job training   Training that uses the employee's work unit to teach the skills and knowledge required for performance.

Open-ended questions   Questions that permit an individual to provide a lengthier response and the opportunity to revise or expand his or her answer.

Organizational analysis   The process to determine the context in which training will occur, contingent on the support of the leadership team and the company's business strategy.

Organizational climate   The conditions of the work environment, such as policies, practices, and procedures that influence the behaviors and performance of employees.

Organizational flowchart   A diagram or graphic representation identifying the status and relationships of employees within an organization.

Organizational structure analysis   The process of identifying the status and relationships of employees within an organization.

Orientation   The process of familiarizing new employees with information about the organization and/or position.

Outsourcing   Utilizing an outside supplier as opposed to internal labor resources.

Oversaturated market   A condition where there are more qualified individuals than there are positions available within a specific market.

Panel   A single discussion-based session featuring a moderator addressing multiple facilitators.

Participative leadership   A style of leadership referred to as democratic and exhibited by leaders who are considered fair and egalitarian and who involve others in decision making.

Passive personality   Behavior exhibited by an individual who lacks initiative and rarely speaks up or contributes in group settings.

Pay compression   When a long-term employee is paid less or equal to new employees with less experience, education, and skill.

Pension   A program permitting a retired individual to collect wages from an investment fund that the worker or the employer has contributed to during his or her working life.

Performance appraisal   A tool to evaluate, measure, or assess the performance of employees.

Performance counseling   Supportive activities by a manager or supervisor intended to improve an employee's productivity and effectiveness in the workplace.

Performance-improvement plan   A guide or document specifying actions or behaviors for an employee to improve his or her performance.

Performance management   A system or process to ensure organizational practices exist to maximize individual productivity.

Personal aggression   Verbal, emotional, or physical acts against another person.

PEST analysis   A technique to analyze the market or an organization based on political, environmental, sociocultural, and technological factors.

Phases of performance counseling meeting   The three distinct parts of the meeting identified as the opening (to set the tone and clarify the primary purpose), the middle (to address deficiencies and solutions), and the summary (to obtain a mutual understanding of the follow-up necessary to improve performance).

Plaintiff   Party who brings a legal action against an organization and/or person.

Planned vacancies   Open positions resulting from a deliberate, calculated, and intentional action to create availability.

Political deviance   Counterproductive behavior demonstrated by employees who show favoritism or use gossip circles intended for disruptive or negative consequences within the workplace (also referred to as *office politics*).

Portable document format (PDF)   A document that is accessible and able to be viewed regardless of application hardware, software, or operating system.

Positive reinforcement   The stimulus that increases the likelihood that an action or behavior will occur.

Precedent   Previous court decision.

Predictive index   A job analytics tool that allows recruiters to quantify the behavioral requirements of a position and assess an applicant's level of similarity to or differences from the criteria.

Prescreening interview   An interview with the purpose of narrowing a field of individuals into a smaller group.

Prima facie   Set of elements that must be proven by a plaintiff in order to move forward on a claim.

Production deviance   Counterproductive behavior that intentionally reduces the productivity or efficiency of an organization.

Professional development   A form of training addressing long-term growth initiatives and preparation for career advancement.

Progressive discipline   A method of discipline whereby penalties become more severe for repeat offenses.

Property deviance   Counterproductive behavior demonstrated by employees who intentionally mislead others or damage the organization.

Protected class   Groups of persons designated as protected from discrimination by certain laws.

Quid pro quo   Meaning "this for that," occurs when an employer explicitly or implicitly puts conditions on employment based on the employee's submission to unwelcome sexual demands.

Rating chart   A chart that identifies a predefined list of criteria with a system that permits an individual to easily evaluate each item listed.

Reassignment clause   A provision in an employment contract stipulating the conditions of removing an employee from his or her current position followed by a reassignment of duties within the organization.

Recency error   Evaluating someone based on the merits of his or her most recent performance without considering a complete profile.

Recruitment   The first stage of talent acquisition in publicizing job openings and soliciting candidates to apply.

Recruitment flowchart   A planning document that sequences process and identifies necessary resources and accountability for executing activities for advertising and soliciting qualified candidates to express interest in a vacancy.

Recruitment plan   Process to develop guidelines for advertising open positions and soliciting qualified candidates to express interest in a vacancy.

Red-hot stove principles   Principles based on a metaphor to describe the similarities of appropriate discipline measures and the action of touching a red-hot stove in that each ensures impartiality, immediacy, and consistency and provides advanced warning.

Reengineering   Starting over to restructure or reconfigure an organization's personnel reporting relationships or an organization's processes.

Reference checks   Contacting previous employers or individuals who know a candidate personally or professionally to obtain information that validates an applicant's credibility.

Refresher training   Training that reinforces the desired behaviors, skills, and knowledge important to an organization or association.

Reservation point   The point where the best alternative to a negotiated agreement (BATNA) is preferred over continuing negotiations.

Retaliation   Punishment of an employee who suffered an adverse employment action after engaging in some type of protected conduct.

Role incongruity   Roles (responsibilities and tasks) that do not adhere to the usual or expected norms.

Role playing   A form of training whereby individuals act out situations or issues that may occur in the workplace by assuming a role or responding to a predetermined scenario; also referred to as a *simulation, practice session,* or *mock drill.*

Rollover clause   A provision in an employment contract specifying automatic renewal or reappointment.

Rooney rule   A rule requiring National Football League (NFL) teams to interview one or more minority candidates for any head coach or general manager vacancy and at least one female for any executive vacancy.

Routine training   Training designed and conducted to meet the needs of employees as part of a regular schedule.

Salary   Payment for work calculated on a predetermined amount.

Search firm   An independent agency acquired to conduct part or all of the activities for talent acquisition.

Self-actualization   Validation for a high-order cognitive function, such as creativity, professional growth, or problem-solving ability (highest level of needs in Maslow's hierarchy of needs theory).

Severance pay   Voluntary compensation afforded to the employee in the event of a specific type of layoff.

Sexual harassment   Unwelcome sexual advances, requests for sexual favors, and other verbal or physical conduct of a sexual nature.

Sexual orientation   Pertaining to attraction for someone of the same or opposite gender (or for both genders) in romantic or sexual relations.

Signaling theory   A condition whereby job seekers use peripheral cues from a website to draw conclusions about employment opportunities.

Situational leadership theories   A set of leadership theories focusing on the interaction between situational variables and leadership characteristics (synonymous with *contingency leadership*).

Situational questions   Questions where the interviewer provides a story or scenario and instructs the interviewee to describe how he or she would resolve the issue.

Skills inventory   Data on job classifications and the requisite skills, knowledge, or competencies deemed integral for a position (sometimes referred to as a *job analysis*).

SMART goal setting   A technique to identify goals that are specific, measurable, attainable, realistic, and timely.

Soft-skills training   Training designed to teach employees the desired traits, characteristics, or behaviors deemed important to the organization.

Sponsor   An individual in a position of authority or influence who intentionally advocates for the development and advancement of another individual.

Stakeholders   Constituencies with a vested interest in an organization, a project, or a cause.

Standard operating procedures   Procedures considered routine protocol for the organization.

Stare decisis   Latin term meaning "to stand by that which is decided"; the doctrine that a court will rely upon previous court decisions.

Statute   Written law passed by a legislative body.

Stock options   Benefits afforded to an employee whereby the individual is provided the option to buy stock at a discounted or fixed rate.

Strategies   Action-oriented activities to assist the organization in achieving a stated outcome.

Strategy implementation plan   A list of step-by-step activities accompanied by timelines, responsible entities, and resources that expresses how to achieve a strategic goal or stated outcome.

Strategy map   A complex graphic representation of the entire strategic plan to demonstrate the integration, relationships, and interdependencies of each element.

Strike   A tactic used by employees to force accommodation or resolution of a labor dispute by staging a collective, organized, and intentional refusal to work for an organization.

Succession planning   A process for identifying replacements for key positions often from a concerted effort to develop individuals from within the organization.

SWOT analysis   A technique to analyze the environment of an organization by focusing on internal strengths and weaknesses and external opportunities and threats.

Symposium   A discussion-based series of presentations on a similar topic with the inclusion of a moderator throughout the program.

Synchronous training   Training that incorporates participant involvement at the same precise time.

Systems development   Designing the instructions to train employees to meet performance expectations.

Systems implementation   Executing the strategies to transfer knowledge and train employees to meet performance expectations.

Tactical vendor   A company or supplier offering the best service for the lowest price.

Talent acquisition   An encompassing term that describes the recruitment, screening, and selection of candidates.

Task analysis   A detailed account of all functional activities undertaken by employees or volunteers.

Technical questions   Questions designed to assess whether the candidate can perform a particular job by having the requisite knowledge, experience, skills, and/or certification.

Technical skills   Skills of a manager or employee related to the specific knowledge or aptitude necessary for a particular job.

Technical training   Training to teach employees the technical or methodological aspects of the job.

Telecommuting   A condition permitting employees to work from home or a remote location.

Termination   Ending the relationship between the employer and employee regardless of who initiated the departure.

Theory X   A motivation theory of Douglas McGregor purporting that supervisors have an underlying belief that employees innately dislike working, are inherently lazy, avoid responsibility, and have little ambition.

Theory Y   A motivation theory of Douglas McGregor purporting that supervisors believe that employees genuinely find fulfillment or a high degree of satisfaction in their work.

Thomas–Kilmann model   A widely accepted managerial tool that advocates resolution of conflict through one of five techniques focusing on (1) competition, (2) collaboration, (3) avoidance, (4) accommodation, or (5) compromise.

360-degree feedback   A performance assessment based on multiple perspectives from the employer, the employee, and others knowledgeable about his or her performance (e.g., peers and subordinates).

Total rewards   Compensation philosophy that includes monetary and nonmonetary rewards for employees.

Trainee program   Relatively lengthy assignments including specialized instruction and training for official employees of an organization who are being groomed for specific positions.

Training needs assessment   An evaluative process to determine the necessity of training and to identify the parameters (e.g., type, method, duration, resources) that will yield the desired performance results.

Trait leadership theories   Theories that focus on the personal attributes and characteristics of the individual to differentiate leaders from nonleaders.

Transactional leadership   A type of leadership behavior emphasizing exchanging rewards in return for productive effort from employees.

Transformational leadership   A type of leadership behavior of individuals who rely on emotional appeal and personal influence to inspire productivity in employees.

Transgender   An individual whose gender identity does not conform to the assigned biological sex.

Trend analysis   The average of turnover rates over a given time period.

Turnover rate   The rate at which employees or workers are replaced in a given time period.

Unemployment compensation   Wages paid by the state to a qualifying individual who is out of work and actively seeking for employment.

Union   A labor organization comprised of employees of the same trade (e.g., professional baseball players) formed for the purpose of advancing member interests related to working conditions.

Unplanned vacancies   Unexpected openings resulting from an unforeseen situation, such as a resignation, death, or an abrupt on-the-spot termination.

U.S. Department of Labor   An organization of interconnected agencies and offices overseeing federal employment regulations.

Vacancies   Positions that are available within an organization; also called *job openings*.

Valence   One of three factors in the expectancy theory whereby an individual assesses the value attributed to a possible reward.

Vendor management   Activities for researching, procuring, monitoring, and evaluating all aspects of a third-party arrangement.

Virtual training   Training administered with the assistance of computer technology.

Wages   Payments for work calculated from the amount of time worked by an employee.

Web-based applications   Programs or services that are available through a network connection from an Internet provider.

Weighted checklist   A list of behaviors, characteristics, or skills in which each item is assigned a significance value related to performance (typically part of an employee performance appraisal system).

Weighted–criterion chart   A type of rating chart that distinguishes the value of each criterion through a point value that coincides with the importance of the criterion in relation to the effective performance of the job.

Wonderlic Test   An assessment test that evaluates an individual's cognitive ability to learn, solve problems, and follow instructions.

Work–life balance   A balanced integration of personal (life) and professional (work) obligations.

Work–life conflict   When perceived role expectations on the job supersede an individual's personal/family obligations or vice versa.

Work–life integration   The fusion or synergy of work-related and personal obligations into a conglomerate fulfilling purpose.

Workers' compensation   A federal program that ensures an employee will receive replacement wages if injured or disabled while on the job.

Workforce analysis   A data-driven approach to tracking employee information and organizational practices related to labor and staffing.

Workforce diversity   Differences in employees based on specific demographic or psychographic criteria.

Workplace deviance   Deliberate, intentional attempts to cause harm to an organization.

Note: Page numbers followed by *b*, *e*, *f*, or *t* indicate material in boxes, exhibits, figures, or tables, respectively.